The George Beckford Papers

A SMALL HOLDING.

This little article was sent to us on the 7th March, 1918, but somehow it was omitted to be published in the Journal. The local Instructor Mr. Banks, says that it still applies. We have therefore pleasure in publishing it:—

I beg to submit the following report on one of the "Small Holdings" in my district, which might be of some interest.

The owner is Horatio Gordon of Clonmel, who is an old cultivator but who for some reason or other never saw the necessity of becoming a member of the Agricultural Society. I am glad to state that he is now converted and is proud to become a member.

His Holding consists of only one acre, but it would please any one interested in Agriculture to visit it —not so much from the scientific methods adopted, but from the variety of crops packed into this small area, and the results obtainable therefrom. This is another proof of how "the plot around the house" can be utilized in these war days.

The following are what he grows thereon: —Yams, yellow 66 hills, St. Vincent, 32 hills, Negro, 8, white, different varieties, 9 hills; sweet potato, 316 hills, coco 382 roots, toyo, 200 roots, sweet cassava 80 roots, bitter cassava, 100 roots, arrowroot 105 roots, young cocoa trees 348, coffee trees 597, custard apple trees, 3, soursop trees 12, granadilla vines 4, sweet cup 2, kola 12, pomegranate 2, almond 3, cotton 12, annatto 5, mango 4, peppers 12, garden egg, 15, breadfruit 7, broad beans 13, small white beans 60, banana beans 18, chocho 20 vines; mint, different varieties, 22 roots, bitter tobacco 10 roots, smoking tobacco 380 roots, garden balsam 12, sweet Barzel 1, thyme 18, sweet marjoram 12, French thyme 6, parsley 30, okra 100, tomatoes 74, pumpkins 12, cucumber 47, ginger 4, palm trees 1, logwood 2, cedar 5, tambric 20, lime 1, oilnut 1, grapefruit 4, sour lemon 1, star apple 1, damsel 2, cow peas 100 roots, cabbage 80 roots, mustard 100 roots, corn 180 roots, rational 20 roots, naseberry 1, cinnamon 1, mahogany, 1, calabash trees 4, tangerine trees 1, squash 1, sweet gourd 2, pine apples 5, plantain 82, bananas 160, China plantain 4, China Banana 8, sweet orange 5, pinda 12, canes 200, akee 4, jackfruit 4, crotons 74, and other minor plants.

The first point on which I have suggested improvement is the order and regularity in which these should be laid out in the holding. The proper pruning of the crotons to form a good hedge, the proper system of pruning the young cocoa trees, and the attention to the roots to keep off insects, etc., the systematic suckering and pruning of trees so as to prevent over-crowding, proper and systematic trenching, and the regulating of shade trees, and lastly the sanitary condition of the holding. Gooden promises to be a good example of what a small settler can do and has promised to go in for the next cocoa competition.

J.A. BANKS.

Agricultural Instructor.

Reproduced from the *Journal of the Jamaica Agricultural Society*, 1920.

The George Beckford Papers

Selected and Introduced by

Kari Levitt

Canoe Press
Barbados • Jamaica • Trinidad and Tobago

Canoe Press, University of the West Indies
1A Aqueduct Flats   Mona
Kingston 7   Jamaica

09   08   07   06   05   5   4   3   2

CATALOGUING IN PUBLICATION DATA

Beckford, George
The Beckford papers / selected and introduced by Kari Levitt.

p. cm.

ISBN 13: 978-976-8125-40-8

1. Beckford, George. 2. Caribbean Area – Economic
conditions. 3. Black nationalism – Caribbean Area.
4. Agriculture – Economic aspects – Caribbean Area.
I. Levitt, Kari. II. Title

HC151. B425 2000   338.9729 dc-20

Book and cover design by ProDesign Ltd, Red Gal Ring,
Kingston, Jamaica.

Printed in the United States of America.

To the Small Farmers of the Caribbean

Contents

Foreword

According to the sociology of knowledge, we should expect economists in developing countries to bring to the subject of development economics much more than Anglo-American economics. Historical legacies, political forces, institutions, issues of race and class – all these should be of more concern than only formal economic analysis. No one fulfils this expectation better than George Beckford, the author of these Collected Papers.

Although formally educated in neoclassical economics, Beckford questioned its limiting assumptions and sought a more relevant social science. His vision synthesized economics with sociocultural and political factors. This allowed him to explain how the plantation system results in a legacy of perpetual poverty for the majority of people in the plantation economies of the Caribbean, Northeast Brazil, the American South, and Southeast Asia.

The four parts of this volume present the fundamental themes that underlie Beckford's vision: Part 1, Economic Planning, Agricultural Development and Caribbean Regional Integration; Part 2, Towards an Appropriate Paradigm for Caribbean Development; Part 3, Beyond Economics: Issues of Race, Class and Black Dispossession; Part 4, Black Affirmation, Cultural Sovereignty and Caribbean Self-reliance.

In her perceptive introduction, Kari Levitt summarizes the papers in each of these parts (and some other unpublished papers) and places them in their historical context. Her comprehensive essay demonstrates the contributions made by Beckford's unique blend of theoretical formulations, empirical research, policy advice and popular education.

It is now valuable to have the Beckford Papers combined as a set and to be able to read them from both a retrospective and a prospective viewpoint. Indeed, they can be appreciated on at least three levels. First, there is the thought of Beckford from the early days of development economics in the 1950s to the 1980s. Throughout, he demonstrates his deep concern for the causes of underdevelopment in order to answer "why we are poor and what we can do about it". The evolution of his thought is significant in itself – from his early study of the West Indian banana industry to his affirmation of cultural sovereignty and a new political ideology. For him, people were the wealth of the nation. And the proper use of their land was the key to their economic advancement. Especially significant in his thinking was the need to recognize the institutionalization of race in the system of production.

On a second level, there is application to the development problems of the Caribbean. Special attention is given to various development programmes and plans in the Caribbean islands, proposals for comprehensive land reform, and the path to regional integration. Noteworthy is the empirical work on agricultural development in the Caribbean, the implications of peasant and plantation dualism, issues of race, class, and black dispossession, and the interpretation of the Caribbean as one nation.

On the third level, there is a surprising anticipation of issues that will still concern development economists in the future. These papers are not dated. To the contrary, they raise some unsettled questions that the next generation of economists should consider. For example, the non-economic goals of development still have to be emphasized. To Beckford, the overriding objective should be improvement in the "quality of life" of all peoples in the society. This is akin to Amartya Sen's emphasis on entitlements and capabilities. In his attention to the physical environment, Beckford is also modern in stressing what is now termed "sustainable development". Development practitioners will still have to promote rural development in the future, as Beckford always advocated. More broadly, the development of institutions – as the social capital of a nation – will require more attention. Beckford anticipated this by concentrating on the "institutional environment – the nature of economic, social, and political organization". He anticipated the significance of culturally imbedded institutions, as do the economists, historians, and political scientists who now represent the "new institutionalism". And as others in the twenty-first century will have to continue to do, Beckford considered the proper balance between state and market, the relationship of ideology to planning, the contribution of human capital to total factor productivity, and – above all – the way to lessen inequality.

Although the subject matter of development economics became narrower and arguably less relevant during the three decades of Beckford's writing life, this did not affect the range of his multidisciplinary perspective. Nor did it narrow his central concerns. In the future, the subject is likely to become again more visionary and courageous, as it was in the 1960s when Beckford began writing.

This volume will then be all the more instructive and influential in the continuing struggle to eradicate poverty.

Gerald M. Meier
Stanford University

List of Figures

List of Tables

Abbreviations

ACE	Association of Caribbean Economists
AIBGA	All-Island Banana Growers' Association
AMC	Agricultural Marketing Corporation
ANAP	National Association of Small Farmers (Cuba)
ASA	African Studies Association
BAT	Bauxite Alumina Transnational
BITU	Bustamante Industrial Trade Union
BMC	Barbados Marketing Corporation
CACM	Central American Common Market
CAP	Clarendon Alumina Plant
CARICOM	Caribbean Community
CARIFTA	Caribbean Free Trade Association
CBI	Caribbean Basin Initiative
CCP	Cuban Communist Party
CD&W	Colonial Development and Welfare
CDCC	Caribbean Development and Cooperation Committee
CMEA (COMECON)	Council for Mutual Economic Assisitance
CYMMIT	International Institute for Research in Wheat and Corn (Mexico)
DGI	Cuban Intelligence Agency
FAO	Food and Agriculture Organization
GATT	General Agreement on Tariffs and Trade
GNP	Gross National Product
IBA	International Bauxite Association
IBRD	International Bank for Reconstruction and Development (The World Bank)
IITA	International Institute for Tropical Agriculture (Nigeria)
ILPES	Institute for Economic and Social Planning in Latin America
IMF	International Monetary Fund

INRA	National Institute on Agrarian Reform (Cuba)
IRRI	International Rice Research Institute (Phillippines)
JAS	Jamaica Agricultural Society
JBI	Jamaica Bauxite Institute
JLP	Jamaica Labour Party
JTA	Jamaica Teachers' Association
JUCEPLAN	Central Planning Board (Cuba)
KMA	Kingston Metropolitan Area
KSAC	Kingston and St Andrew Corporation
LAFTA	Latin American Free Trade Association
LASA	Latin American Studies Association
MDL	Minimum Desirable Level
MNB	Multinational Bank
MNC	Multinational Corporation
MPL	Minimum Physiologic Level
NJM	New Jewel Movement (Grenada)
NPA	National Planning Agency (Jamaica)
NWU	National Workers' Union
OPEC	Organization of Petroleum Exporting Countries
PNP	People's National Party
PRG	People's Revolutionary Government (Grenada)
PSOJ	Private Sector Organization of Jamaica
SMA	Sugar Manufacturers Association
TNC	Transnational Corporation
UNECLA	United Nations Economic Commission for Latin America
WINBAN	Windward Islands Banana Growers' Association
WISCO	West Indies Sugar Company
WPJ	Workers' Party of Jamaica

Introduction

The well-spring of the Jamaican people lies in the land. It is the land which brought us here. It is on the land that we were transformed from free Africans into slaves for plantation work. It is through the land that we were subsequently to free ourselves from plantation slavery and develop as an independent peasantry. And it is this last achievement which continues to sustain us, however tentatively, through food production and the spirit of independence.

The distinctions between industry and agriculture, town and country, and mental and manual labour must be eroded. Such erosion can only occur by understanding particular peoples: where we are coming from; and what makes us who we are.

The West Indian person is both town and country. The majority can do both mental and manual work. And agriculture is an industry. There are many kinds of industries – industry of the factory; industry of the field; industry of the mind. Human society must aim to integrate all these industries. So that mankind can tailor environment to needs.

Ultimately, PEOPLE will decide everything.

— George Beckford [1975b]

Background

This volume of selected writings by George Beckford traces the unfolding of his work from agricultural economics, to political economy, to the social economy of 'man-space', to the cultural roots of Caribbean creativity and a vision of one independent, sovereign and self-reliant Caribbean nation. His purpose was to reveal the legacy of dispossession originating in the slave plantation experience of African people in the New World; to 'free the mind' from the internalization of attitudes of inferiority and 'Afro-Saxon' mimicry. His vision was the affirmation of the culture of 'overcoming' rooted in the Caribbean 'peasantry' and the land.

The view of the 'plantation' as the original institution of Caribbean economy was an analysis shared with Lloyd Best and other scholars of the New World movement. The originality of Beckford's contribution was in his insistence on the Caribbean peasantry as the repository of the popular culture of self-reliance and independence. The Caribbean peasantry was unique, because it was not traditional in the European, Asian or African sense, but was a product of 500 years of revolt and struggle of slaves and ex-slaves against the plantation system. He saw the hope for Caribbean sovereignty and self reliance in the common culture of a Caribbean nation of English-, Spanish-, French- and Dutch-speaking peoples.

Beckford's vision of development was in advance of mainstream economic doctrine of his time which conflated economic development with economic growth. The quality of life required more than the increasing availability of material goods; it required a society of equity, dignity, and independence. He was also in advance of his time, in his insistence on physical planning of land use for the benefit of present and future generations. Above all, Beckford believed in the resourcefulness and creativity of *people* as the most important economic resource of a society. The Caribbean people, freed from the economic, social and political legacies of the plantation, could, as he wrote "transform what is physically the most beautiful part of the planet Earth into a human paradise" [1984a].

His scholarly writings were enriched by familiarity with the problems of the plantation/peasant societies of the Caribbean, and by the intellectual ferment of decolonization in the English-speaking Caribbean of the 1960s and 1970s. Empirical research, policy advice, popular education and theoretical formulation were complementary aspects of Beckford's approach to his vocation as scholar and teacher. He was uncompromising in his insistence on the importance of training young scholars in independent and critical thought. On the foundation of an education in agricultural and development economics acquired at first class North American institutions, he set an example in relevant economic analysis, carefully researched and infused with the affirmation of the capacity of ordinary people to turn adversity into self reliant economic and cultural achievement.

Beckford graduated from McGill University in 1958 with a BSc in agricultural economics. He proceeded to Stanford University, where he obtained an MA in international economics in 1960, and a PhD in agricultural economics in 1962. He returned to the West Indies in 1963 as lecturer in agricultural economics on the St Augustine campus of the University of the West Indies (UWI) and moved to the Mona campus as lecturer in economics in 1964. The university was then in transition from staffing by ex-patriates to West Indianization. Beckford remained at the lowest rank in the academic hierarchy throughout the period of his most important and seminal work, culminating in *Persistent Poverty: Underdevelopment in Plantation Economies of the Third World* [1972a], written at Stanford where he was invited as visiting professor in 1970. Promotion to senior lecturer came in 1971; reader in economics in 1974; and a personal chair as professor of economics in 1975. From 1969 to 1973 he served as head of the Economics Department, when he resigned over differences with the university administration.

Persistent Poverty brought international acclaim and a stream of invitations to participate in conferences and to address academic audiences in North America, Asia and Africa. By the end of the 1970s, he had established an international reputation, and several of his papers were reprinted in widely read anthologies on development and underdevelopment [Bernstein 1973; Wilber 1979; Livingstone 1980]. Under the influence of the radical political climate of the 1970s, and his personal encounter with the systemic racism of mainstream America, Beckford extended his plantation/peasant analysis to embrace mainland black America from Bahia to North Carolina. Following the completion of *Persistent Poverty*, he outlined a book length, popular study entitled "The Foundations of Black Dispossession". The draft of this manuscript drew criticism from Marxist colleagues who charged him with insufficient appreciation of the role of class. Race and class in Caribbean plantation society were later addressed in a number of papers and in *Small Garden — Bitter Weed: the Political Economy of Struggle and Change in Jamaica*, co-authored with Michael Witter [1980a; 1982b].

In addition to teaching, writing and responding to local, regional and international invitations, Beckford undertook research assignments for the United Nations Economic Commission for Latin America and the Caribbean (UNECLAC), consultancies for preparing development plans for Jamaica, Panama and Belize, and the chairmanship of a Land Reform Commission for St Lucia. In the 1980s, he directed a team of researchers on the impact of the bauxite/alumina industry on rural Jamaica, co-founded the Association of Caribbean Economists (ACE) and co-edited the proceedings of the first ACE Conference, *Development in Suspense* [1988]. In 1984 he visited Malaysia, a South East Asian country with a colonial plantation experience. In 1986 and again in 1987 he was invited to participate in the Afro-American Studies Program at the Third World Centre of the Woodrow Wilson School of Public and International Affairs at Princeton University. In September 1989 the Social Science faculty of the UWI celebrated 25 years of distinguished service by Professor Beckford with a Symposium on "Black Dispossession in the Caribbean and the Diaspora" [Levitt and Witter 1996].

The articles and papers reproduced in this volume have been selected from over 100 published and unpublished writings. They represent three decades of George Beckford's work, from his early days as the first West Indian to be appointed lecturer in agricultural economics by the UWI, to the late 1980s when serious illness and death intervened to cut short his desire to complete his work on black dispossession and affirmation in the Americas. The works are presented in four parts, combining chronological with thematic treatment.

Part I comprises a selection of Beckford's empirical work on agricultural development in the Caribbean, including his impressions of the achievements of the Cuban revolution. In Part II, seminal theoretical and analytical papers on peasant and plantation agriculture are reproduced. From the mid 1970s, Beckford's concerns moved beyond economic analysis to address issues of race, class and black dispossession, presented in Part III. Part IV is structured around themes of black affirmation, cultural sovereignty and Beckford's vision of the entire Caribbean as one nation.

The introduction follows the plan of the book. Emphasis (indicated by italics) is Beckford's, unless otherwise indicated. The selections are briefly summarized and set into historical context. For reasons of space, some of the papers or reports mentioned in the introduction were not included in the volume. References are listed in the bibliography.

Economic Planning, Agricultural Development, and Caribbean Regional Integration

In the 1960s and 1970s governments played the key role in the economic transformation of countries emerging from colonialism. National priorities were set, and contributions of donor countries and agencies were solicited by means of five- or ten-year development plans. Beckford contributed to agricultural development plans in St Lucia, St Vincent, Guyana, Jamaica, Panama and Belize. In all these countries, he advocated measures of comprehensive land reform to provide the peasant smallholder with the necessary resources of land, capital and infrastructure to expand food production for domestic and regional markets.

Following the demise of the Federation of the West Indies (1958-62), Trinidad and Jamaica declared independence. Barbados and Guyana followed in 1966. Starting in the mid 1960s, Beckford and other West Indian university economists worked on a series of regional integration studies, which contributed to the formation of the Caribbean Free Trade Association (CARIFTA) in 1967 and the Caribbean Community (CARICOM) in 1970. It was hoped that regional economic integration would unite the countries of the Commonwealth Caribbean in a concerted effort to escape from underdevelopment. For Beckford, Cuba was an integral part of the region. He was the first West Indian economist to visit that country, where he was profoundly impressed by the participation of the population in the economic and political transformation of a country with problems of underdevelopment, basically similar to those of the rest of the region.

While undertaking empirical and policy research, Beckford was also teaching courses on agricultural and development economics, editing the *New World Quarterly*[1] and lecturing to rural audiences all over Jamaica. The combination of teaching, research and writing theoretical articles and reviews gave Beckford's work qualities of simplicity of exposition combined with the authority of profound and scientific knowledge, born of his own life experience of growing up in rural Jamaica. The ultimate source of Beckford's strength was his respect for the common sense and wisdom of ordinary people, and his commitment to use his education for their economic and social advancement.

Trinidad Draft Five-Year Plan

In 1963, the Economic Planning Division of the Office of the Prime Minister of Trinidad and Tobago published a Five-Year Plan produced under the direction of William Demas. Shortly after arriving on the St Augustine campus in 1963, Beckford co-authored a memorandum of "Comments on the Draft Second Five-Year Plan, 1964-1968" [1963] for submission to the National Planning Commission of Trinidad and Tobago. An abbreviated version appeared in *Social and Economic Studies* [1965a]. Beckford found the projections for agricultural production excessively conservative, and inconsistent with the objectives of increased agricultural employment, improvement in productivity and increased food self-sufficiency.

Beckford's familiarity with export agriculture in other countries, acquired in the course of his doctoral research, provided the basis for his disagreement with the authors of this plan that coconut growing is best done on a large scale. Beckford and his co-author maintained that coconut production had always been predominantly a peasant crop, and that the industry in major coconut producing countries such as Indonesia, Ceylon (now Sri Lanka), India and Malaysia remained in the hands of smallholders.

Ten-Year Development Plan For St Lucia

In 1963 Beckford was commissioned by the government of St Lucia to undertake a study of *Prospects and Proposals for Agricultural Development in St Lucia* [1963], in connection with a Ten-Year Development Programme 1964-73. St Lucia was then the poorest of all the English-speaking Caribbean territories, excepting Montserrat, with GNP per capita less than one half that of Jamaica.

Beckford and co-author L.G. Campbell were Caribbean regionalists who believed that St Lucia could not alone, in the foreseeable future, hope to achieve the levels of development of Trinidad and Tobago or Jamaica. To brighten the prospect, the government and people must project themselves as part of a larger economic unit.

In the early 1950s St Lucia experienced very strong economic growth of 15% per annum; slowing to an average of 7 to 8% in the late 1950s, and 5% in the early 1960s. The banana industry was driving the economy. It was anticipated that the growth dynamic would, in the future, shift from bananas to tourism. The main theme of the development plan was the diversification of agriculture. The plan envisaged expansion of domestic agriculture to meet incremental demand, and the replacement of some of the imported foodstuffs. Recommendations included bringing into production underutilized land on large estates, and the purchase by the government of family lands under multiple ownership and its resettlement by enterprising farmers. To this end, it was recommended that a land commission be set up to take "prompt action" in respect of this proposal. In 1980, Beckford chaired the Land Reform Commission of the Government of St Lucia.

Other recommendations included the establishment of an agricultural development credit bank, "divorced as much as possible from government", with compulsory subscriptions obtained from borrowers each time a loan was granted, and a marketing corporation to contract supplies from farmers, sell to hotels, supermarkets and vendors, regulate the importation of foodstuffs, and develop export markets for surplus commodities. The rest of the report dealt with proposals for soil and water conservation to control soil erosion by the indiscriminate cultivation by small farmers on the steeper slopes where food gardens were generally located. With the development of the banana industry, these problems became more severe. The report proposed a capability classification for land use planning and zoning, so that tourist, housing and industrial development would not adversely affect patterns of agricultural land use.

The West Indian Banana Industry

The subject of Beckford's doctoral thesis was "Secular trends in the growth of major export crop industries". The export crop which attracted his special attention was bananas. In 1964-65 he was engaged as a research consultant at the research division of Harvard University Graduate School of Business Administration, where he co-authored *Tropical Agribusiness Structures and Adjustments: Bananas* [1968], with Henry B. Arthur of Harvard and James P. Houck of the University of Minnesota.

Beckford was the obvious choice to contribute a monograph on the West Indian banana industry to the Regional Economic Integration Studies undertaken on the joint initiative of members of staff of the UWI and the governments of the region. The Institute of Social and Economic Research (ISER) at the UWI was given a grant to conduct these studies. When the Government of Jamaica seized Beckford's passport following his visit to Cuba, the members of the university rejected government support in protest against what they considered a breach of academic freedom. They refused to use any more government funds, and undertook to complete the studies with their own resources.

We reproduce an abbreviated version of "The West Indian banana industry: the scope for rationalization and regional collaboration" [1967a] (chapter 1). An earlier version was presented to the First West Indian Agricultural Economics Conference in St Augustine [Proceedings 1966]. Tables and source footnotes have been eliminated, together with dated information which detracts from the readability of the text. The study examined

the scope for regional cooperation in the production and external marketing of bananas in the light of two main considerations: (a) the uncertainty surrounding the continuation of protected markets and (b) the competition among different countries in the region in the over-supplied United Kingdom (UK) market . . . The study is therefore primarily concerned with the scope for improving the competitive position of the regional industry (p. 1).

West Indian bananas were sold exclusively in the highly protected UK market, where Jamaica and the Windward Islands were engaged in a competition which was over-supplying the market and driving down prices. Beckford explained that the competition between Jamaica and the Windward banana growers was essentially driven by competition between two large multinational concerns – Elders and Fyffes Ltd, a subsidiary of the United Fruit Company, and Geest Industries Ltd. This aspect of the "Windwards-Jamaica banana war" was elaborated in a popular exposition in the *New World Quarterly* [1965d] included in this volume, as "Issues in the Windward-Jamaica banana war" together with an earlier article on "Crisis in the West Indian banana industry" in *Caribbean Quarterly* [1964a].

Projections of the capacity of the UK market to absorb West Indian bananas without further decline in prices underlined the need to rationalize supply and develop new external markets. At the national level, Beckford pointed to the high cost of transporting fruit from the southern parishes of Jamaica to the point of shipping. He suggested that Jamaican banana production be confined to an eastern zone consisting of St Mary, Portland and St Thomas, and a western zone including parts of St James, Westmoreland and Hanover.

At the regional level, he proposed a market sharing agreement based on the fact that Jamaican costs per ton at the point of shipment were higher than costs in the Windwards. In this scheme of "regional export substitution", expansion in banana production and exports would be confined to the Windwards, with matching simultaneous reduction in production in Jamaica to limit the supply of West Indian bananas and support prices in the UK market. Compensation by means of a regional policy could give Jamaican farmers easier access to the Eastern Caribbean market in foodstuffs, and encourage the substitution of food crops for banana. But given the dependence of 35,000 growers in Jamaica on banana cultivation, Beckford thought it unlikely that such a scheme would be acceptable to Jamaican growers.

Other proposals included a regional banana shipping service; the development of markets for West Indian bananas in eastern Canada by direct shipment to Halifax and Montreal, and initiatives to penetrate East European markets where banana consumption was very low).[2] In the 30 years which have passed since Beckford's banana study was written, tourist development has lifted living standards in the Leeward and Windward Islands far above those of Jamaica. But high dependence on the banana trade remains a burning issue, especially in the Windward Islands where, in some countries, banana exports to protected markets in Europe account for over half of all commodity exports.

A Caribbean View of Cuba

For Beckford, Cuba was an integral part of the Caribbean, not in essence different from any other Caribbean territory. In that regard, as in many others, he was in advance of his time, as is evident now that the historically anomalous links of Cuba with the former Soviet Union have been severed, and Cuba looks to the Caribbean region for strengthened economic and cultural ties. Beckford believed that important lessons could be derived from whatever transformation had taken place since the revolution. He visited Cuba in 1965 at a time when Caribbean opinion about Cuba was "simply a reflection of opinions uttered somewhere in the North Atlantic and picked up as gospel by local agencies of information" [1965c: 43] and reported his findings in "A note on agricultural organization and planning in Cuba" for *Caribbean Studies* [1966b] and in "A Caribbean view of Cuba", *New World Quarterly* [1965c].

Both of these papers are included in this volume (chapters 4 and 5). The first described Cuban efforts to diversify an agricultural economy dominated by plantation production of sugar. Initially, agricultural diversification was ruthlessly implemented; sugar lands were ploughed under, making room for food crops. Limited technical knowledge about crops other than sugar resulted in declining output, food shortages, and rationing. After the Soviet Union contracted the purchase of large quantities of sugar, there was a reversal of policy. Increasing acreage was planted with cane, at the expense of crops such as rice and corn. While the livestock and poultry industries experienced substantial expansion, it was decided to depend on imported rice, vegetable oils and potatoes from countries willing to buy Cuban sugar.

Beckford suggested that Cuban economists should examine the extent to which integration of the Cuban economy with that of the Soviet, based on "a *static* neoclassical concept of international trade and specialization" would permit diversification of the Cuban economy and allow for structural transformation in the long run. "In spite of current political realities, the merits of association with the Soviet Union should be assessed in the light of alternative potential associations with other countries of Central America and the Caribbean" [1966b: 7]. He concluded that progress in Cuban agriculture was likely to compare well with that of other Caribbean countries such as Jamaica and Trinidad, where it has been painfully slow, because, as had been noted by Lloyd Braithwaite, "plans are developed from above without midway collaboration from below".[3]

In the *New World Quarterly* [1965c], Beckford compared Cuba with Puerto Rico as "active" and "passive" models of economic and social change, with relevance for Caribbean territories which share a history of colonization, slavery, sugar, foreign-owned plantations and domination by a metropolitan power. The active/passive dichotomy was credited to Lloyd Best. The (passive) Puerto Rican development model, copied in succession by nearly all the other territories,

involves the creation of the 'right' environment in order to attract foreign capital and management and to maintain traditional foreign markets. ('Industrialization by Invitation' is the main feature of the development policy.) The dynamic for change therefore remains in the metropolis. Per capita income grows, but there is little or no change in its distribution [1965c: 44].

The "active" model, by contrast, involved a radical transformation of the economy, with a complete transfer of the dynamic for change from outside the society to within, and the erosion of the plantation system which inhibited the development of an internal cultural and technological dynamic within the region. "Cuba has emerged from the cocoon of the plantation system which still . . . envelopes the rest of the Caribbean . . . Cuba is on this account relevant to the Caribbean" (p. 44). Beckford cited Dudley Seers' observation that Cuba was the only major exporter of primary products in the world to have attempted a very rapid rate of social and economic growth by using techniques of highly centralized planning. For all of these reasons, Beckford considered the Cuban experience to be of special relevance to the Caribbean.[4]

He was struck by three contrasts between Cuba and the rest of the region: the absence of unemployment, prostitution or begging; the omnipresence of education on radio, television and newspapers; and the high level of popular involvement, national cohesion, public order and self-confidence. The chief motive in promoting structural change was to satisfy the expectations of the rural population among whom the commitment for change had been established in the course of the struggle against the old order. Widespread material benefits would strengthen the internal commitment within Cuba, but far reaching structural change would be likely to disrupt (external) traditional metropolitan connections. "If internal commitment were sufficiently strong, and other sources of external support could be secured, then the society would be well placed to make a clean break with the plantation system" (p. 47).

Interestingly, Beckford identified the economic organization of *agriculture* and the system and content of *education* as the key to transferring the dynamic of Cuban development from outside the society to within.[5] "The reforms in agriculture and education (and housing) have had profound effects. They have bestowed considerable material benefits on the bulk of the population; reduced economic and social inequalities; and have given a new sense of purpose to the population" (p. 49). Beckford reported that the revolutionary government began with rather limited programmes for change. The first agrarian reform law provided only for expropriation of excessively large holdings. The state did not engage in production, and titles to land were distributed to the landless peasantry.

A dispute about the refining of Soviet oil in American-owned facilities resulted in the nationalization of United States (US) oil refineries and retaliation by the abolition of the Cuban-US sugar quota. This in turn led to Cuban expropriation of American-owned estates and factories, and a state of siege imposed by the US. The blockade and the promotion of mercenary invasions served to consolidate internal support for the government: "Cubans today take great pride in the fact that they have managed to withstand the economic and military pressure of 'Yankee imperialism'" (p. 50).

The difficulties of making a rapid transition in a country with the structure of pre-revolutionary Cuba forced the government to seek new external alliances. Increasing material assistance from the Soviet Union, Eastern Europe and China carried with it influences which affected the political ideology of the Cuban government: "The 'Marxist-Leninist' posture of the government and its economic and military policies are suggestive of too strong a dependence on the Soviet Union" (p. 52). Since the rest of the region was content to operate within the framework of the passive model, as was clear after the capitulation on Chaguaramas,[6] Cuba stood alone without any regional support.

In view of this, the uncritical adoption of an alien doctrine which could roughly conform with the perspective of the active model can be understood. Cuba was not able to draw on relevant planning models since the social scientists of the region have yet to formulate models relevant to the plantation economy. Cuba had no choice in borrowing uncritically planning techniques from the Soviet Union and Eastern Europe (pp. 52-53).

Beckford acknowledged that, *in the absence of regional support* [emphasis added] structural dependence was inevitable. The legacy of the past dictated that Cuba must sell large quantities of sugar to acquire the capital goods needed for economic transformation: "Cuba's dependence on the Soviet Union can therefore be reasonably attributed partly to the failure of the rest of the Caribbean to provide the kind of support which was necessary to bring about some meaningful regional independence" (p. 53).

He maintained an active interest in Cuba and participated in the first meeting of Caribbean Planning Officials held in Havana in January 1979 under the auspices of the Caribbean Development and Planning Committee (CDCC), the Latin American Institute for Social and Economic Planning (ILPES) and the UNECLA. A report of his visit to Cuba in 1979 was published as "Planning in the Caribbean under Capitalism and Socialism" [1988a], and is included in this volume. In 1981, Beckford led a large Caribbean group of participants to the Conference of Third World Economists in Havana, where the formation of a Caribbean Association of Political Economists was first proposed.[7] In 1987, he addressed the third conference of Latin American and Caribbean economists in Cuba.

British Honduras: Caribbean/Central American Economic Integration

We reproduce Beckford's contribution to a debate on British Honduras (now Belize) concerning the choice between association with the Central America Common Market (CACM) or a Commonwealth Caribbean regional grouping. In "British Honduras and regional economic integration" [1967c] he urged British Honduras, with cultural and historic roots in both these regions, to "quickly put an end to British colonial rule" and join the movement toward Commonwealth Caribbean economic integration taking shape at that time. He suggested further: "Subsequently, British Honduras, drawing strength from its Spanish oriented cultural element could assume the initiative within this narrow Antillean grouping to create a wider Antillean economic union

These were not, however, the only obstacles to increased intra-Caribbean agricultural trade. Marketing infrastructure in terms of collection, storage, standards (sorting and grading), processing, packaging, advertising, financing, risk bearing, buying and selling at various levels (farm, factory, wholesaler, retailer) and market information was underdeveloped everywhere. Surpluses in some territories and shortages in others offered market opportunities, requiring systematic regional market information on prices of agricultural produce. It is noted that shortages in some, and surpluses in other CARICOM countries continue to hold out prospects for increased intra-regional trade.

The study set out an agenda of non-tariff mechanisms for expanding intra-regional trade in food, including formal trading arrangements between government marketing agencies, and the establishment of adequate shipping and air cargo facilities. In reading this report thirty years later, it is interesting to note that Caribbean governments of the day, whether politically independent, as in Jamaica and Trinidad and Tobago, or formally still colonies of Britain, were prepared to assume responsibility for the development and protection of domestic agriculture, including guaranteed prices to farmers, protection from external competition, and the provision of auxiliary services such as a marketing corporation and subsidized fertilizer and other inputs.

Land Reform for the Betterment of Caribbean Peoples

"Land reform for the betterment of Caribbean peoples" [1972c], presented to the Seventh West Indian Agricultural Economics Conference held in Grenada in 1972, proposed an agenda of "institutional" land reform and issues of land use and the quality of life in small, land-scarce, island economies. The article identified three approaches to land reform: the "simple", the "integral" and the "institutional". The first referred to land redistribution with little or no support from other measures; the second comprised institutional changes, principally in credit and extension services, to increase agricultural productivity; the third and most comprehensive kind of land reform was "concerned with the social and economic welfare of rural people. The point is that increased productivity can be achieved without any significant change in the welfare of people involved. In other words, productivity improvements are necessary but not sufficient to guarantee an increase in welfare for society as a whole" (p. 26). Beckford presented a people-oriented definition of agricultural development:

In my view, development is a process by which improvements in the economic and social welfare of people are consistently achieved over time. In this connection, raising the level of farm incomes and reducing inequalities in the distribution of that income among groups involved in farming is important. But we need to go further: (i) to reduce the inequalities in the distribution of income among all groups in the society (including farmers); (ii) to ensure that the society's resources (natural and human) are conserved and their quality improved, to generate welfare improvements for future generations; (iii) to secure a systematic improvement in the 'quality of life' of all people in the society (p. 26).

Ecological and environmental concerns were explicitly addressed:

Land reform, as we conceive the term must encompass all uses of land. Not just farm land, but *all land* [emphasis added] – land for farming, for forestry, for mining, for recreation including tourism, for urban development, etc. This is a rather tall order. But it seems to me that this is the only useful approach to the land reform question for islands in which land is already a scarce resource, and in which population growth coupled with economic diversification are likely to intensify the competition for use of land in the future (pp. 26-27).

Beckford reviewed Caribbean agriculture, characterized by 'dualism', with a plantation/estate sector controlling the best land, and a peasant (small farm) sector with generally poor land. The distribution of land between the plantation and peasant sectors was grossly unequal. In terms of land use, however, Jamaican data showed that the yields per acre of farms under five acres were more than twice as great as yields on the plantations. Small farmers, Beckford argued, displayed a far greater flexibility in the deployment of resource use, and were responsible for the diversification of West Indian agriculture following emancipation.

Because peasant agriculture was more labour intensive than estate cultivation, and had a lower import content, Beckford maintained that redistribution of land from plantations to the peasantry would increase employment and farm incomes, expand foreign exchange earnings, widen the market for domestically produced industrial goods, and contain rural-urban drift. Plantation lands were underutilized for a variety of reasons. Where land was scarce, land was a portfolio asset which could yield high capital gains. Additionally, the planter class viewed land as a social asset, enhancing the owner's social status. Noting the dramatic inflation of land prices and the high propensity to speculate in land by foreigners and by nationals in a position to buy land, Beckford concluded that: "in societies which are short of land and in which there is gross under-consumption by the bulk of the population, holding land as a portfolio asset is nothing short of a moral crime!" (p. 35).

Beckford argued that governments have a responsibility to the people as a whole to correct glaring social injustices by the adoption of a *"comprehensive institutional approach to land reform"*. In his view, the ownership of land by foreigners should be forbidden by law, and the freehold system of tenure should be abolished, because high income élites get a disproportionate share, while unemployment, underutilization and speculation persist. With reference to the African model of communal patterns of land ownership "as a part of our heritage", Beckford proposed that all rural land should revert to state ownership, to be held in trust for society as a whole. Land could then be leased on a long term basis for farming, forestry, or tourism. "Since land is in short supply, it must be used wisely for the benefit of socety as a whole . . . Zoning and countryside planning are necessary to achieve this" (p. 36).

He proposed that public recreation parks with organized mountain sports should be a part of the state's forest development programme (ecotourism), that beaches should be public property; and that companies leasing lands for mining should pay a charge for disturbing the natural quality of the land. In addition to royalty payments for minerals extracted, they should be required to restore the land as best possible. Urban growth should be limited to cities of about 300,000, after which new cities and townships should be established in the countryside: "In this manner the traditional rural-urban dichotomy loses the significance it now has and cities could be planned to better fit into the natural environment" (p. 36). As a move in that direction, he suggested that Jamaica's government offices should be moved out of Kingston.

Beckford's radical approach to land use might appear idealistic. This writer suggests it was both farsighted and realistic. Anybody who has observed the rate of environmental and social degradation of the quality of life in small island countries should consider Beckford's agenda as a serious contribution to a conservationist programme of economic, social and environmental renewal for fragile island ecologies with limited land resources. Most importantly, for Beckford, the land was more than a "factor of production". It was an integral part of the cultural matrix which sustained the livelihood of people.

Agro 21: an Inappropriate Development Model

Agro 21 was a Jamaican government programme of the mid 1980s based on the application of modern technology to large scale agricultural projects with foreign capital and technical advice. We reproduce a revised version of Beckford's presentation to the seminar on Agriculture: Problems and Prospects hosted by the Economics Department at Mona in 1985 (chapter 10). Beckford confronted the approach – and the American consultant – with an alternative programme based on providing the peasant class of Jamaican producers with land and capital to combine with their labour and their entrepreneurial skills. He questioned the need for foreign technical advisors, recalling Jamaica's inventions and innovations in agriculture, including the ortanique, commercially developed by Cuba; the pineapple variety that built the Hawaiian industry; the pioneering livestock breeding of Dr T.P. Lecky and Jamaican pasture management, applied by the Cubans to develop their dairy industry.

"Why is it" he asked, "that Jamaica has developed all this agricultural technology . . . and yet is not able to translate it into production to achieve food self-sufficiency? Where are the entrepreneurs?" He charged that Jamaica's private sector was risk averse, and preferred to invest in commerce, housing and land speculation while Jamaica's small peasant producers were entrapped in a lifetime of poverty and underdevelopment. He predicted that Agro 21 was bound to fail, because it was informed by theories and models that were not applicable to the Jamaican reality. The prediction proved correct. Agro 21 failed, leaving a legacy of increased official external debt of unknown magnitude.

Towards An Appropriate Paradigm For Caribbean Development

Growth and Fluctuations in Tropical Agricultural Exports

In 1964 and 1967, Beckford published two articles in *Economic Development and Cultural Change*, a leading journal of development studies. In "Secular fluctuations in the growth of tropical agricultural trade" [1964b], 21 time series of export volumes of six of the most valuable tropical agricultural commodities were examined and analysed to determine whether long fluctuations ('Kuznets cycles') were characteristic of tropical agricultural trade. The evidence conformed to the view that the observed fluctuations were characteristic of most of the series examined, and were transmitted from the importing countries.

In "Long term trends in banana exports: further evidence of secular fluctuations in tropical agricultural trade" [1967b], Beckford returned to the study of fluctuations in tropical exports, this time dealing exclusively with bananas. Export volumes for eleven tropical American countries, accounting for 80% of world banana trade, were analysed. For most of these countries, bananas alone provided for the bulk of export earnings. Although time series data were not available prior to 1930, and patterns of fluctuations were affected by World War II, and by the diversity of markets served, evidence indicated that demand conditions and capital exports from importing countries were among important factors explaining fluctuations in banana exports. He concluded that so long as the export trades of these countries remain dependent on a few commodities and concentrated market outlets, their economies would remain vulnerable to long swings, as a result of fluctuations occurring elsewhere. "Economic planners in the primary exporting countries need to be aware of this possible association, in order to develop mechanisms to insulate their economies from these imported long term disturbances" [1967b: 330].

"The growth of major tropical export-crop industries" [1964] reproduced in this volume, addressed long term trends for exporters of seven of the most valuable tropical crops in world trade – coffee, rubber, sugar, tea, cocoa, coconut products, and oil palm products. Growth curves were fitted to historic data for 17 major commodity exporting countries. The incidence of poor fits was low. These export crop industries experienced a variety of growth patterns, from spectacular rapid development of the rubber industries to the crawling pace of Brazilian coffee. The common pattern that emerged was the now well-known retardation of growth as industries mature.

Observed differences in growth rates did not appear to derive from crop characteristics or from the nature of the demand for a particular commodity: "The only factor which appears to be of some significance in explaining observed differences in growth propensities is the organization of production" (p. 417). When the 17 industries were grouped into four categories, he found that average growth rates in each category were highest for *small holders* (7.04%); declining progressively for peasant production co-existing independently with plantation (*mixed independent*: 6.60%); small holders dependent on plantations for processing and other facilities (*mixed integrated*: 6.05%); with lowest average growth for *plantations* (5.95%). Deviations from this pattern, such as Colombian coffee and Nigerian oil palm industries, were explained by diversities within the smallholder crop sector.

Beckford suggested that problems of availability of hired labour, necessitating the import of fresh supplies of immigrant workers, might have accounted for the slower response of plantations to market opportunities. Small holders, by contrast, controlled a flexible supply of family labour, and could respond to higher prices by the investment of small amounts of liquid capital required to bring new lands into cultivation. Moreover, financial capital at the disposal of the plantations had a wide range of alternative investment opportunities, compared with the limited range of uses of family labour in smallholder production. For these reasons, with some exceptions, there was a pattern of more rapid growth among smallholder than among plantation industries.

Critique of the Schultz 'High Pay-Off Input' Model

In the mid 1960s, Beckford reviewed a number of studies on the role of agriculture in economic development. The most important of these reviews was published as "Agricultural development in 'traditional' and 'peasant' economies" [1966c]. The two books reviewed were *Agrarian Development in Peasant*

Societies [1964] by Eric S. Clayton and *Economic Crisis in World Agriculture* [1965] by Theodore W. Schultz – a critic of the work of W. Arthur Lewis, who later 'shared' a Nobel prize with him.[9] The review is reproduced in this volume, together with a similar critique of the work of Professor Schultz published in the *Journal of Farm Economics* [1966a] as "Transforming traditional agriculture: a comment" (see chapters 12 and 13).

Beckford argued that a reason for the failure of most governments in low income countries to implement effective programmes of agricultural development was the lack of an adequate theoretical framework by means of which appropriate policies could be devised. Economists used overgeneralized approaches or relied excessively on the special experience of commercial agriculture as practised in North America, Western Europe or Australia. What was needed, according to Beckford, was a typology of world agriculture, such as he later attempted in 1974.

Schultz' oversimplified approach was based on "two simple (economic) models" representing "modern" and "traditional" agriculture. In this model, modern agriculture made a significant contribution to economic growth; traditional agriculture, on the other hand, was characterized by a (low productivity) equilibrium and contributed little to economic growth. But, Beckford argued, the agricultural sector of most underdeveloped countries comprised both "modern" and "traditional" elements and must be viewed in the light of the economic constraints created by their juxtaposition. Moreover, Schultz' world included neither the plantation economies of the Caribbean nor Southeast Asia, nor the semi-feudal regions of Latin America, nor parts of Europe. "Traditional" agriculture would seem to exist only in communal and tribal pockets of Asia, Africa and Latin America, before the introduction of cash crop cultivation for export. This model of traditional agriculture "does not fit the *total* farming sector of most (if any) of the low income countries" [1966a: 1014].

Because traditional agriculture was assumed to use resources "efficiently", underemployment and "surplus labour" were definitionally impossible in the Schultz model. This was the burden of Schultz' critique of the Lewis model of economic development with unlimited supplies of labour [1954]. But the use of labour up to the point where its marginal product was zero, was perfectly rational in peasant economies where land was limited and surplus labour could not be employed profitably outside agriculture. Beckford charged that Schultz' proposition is really linked with an (implicit) assumption that land is abundant: "For the countries of Asia and the Caribbean, it would seem more reasonable to assume that land is relatively scarce . . . redundant agricultural labour cannot be assumed to reflect inefficient resource allocation especially when non-agricultural employment opportunities are limited" (1966c: 157).

The Ruttan-Hayami Induced Development Model

The 'high pay-off input model' served as the theoretical rationalization for the 'green revolution' of the 1960s. High yield varieties of corn, rice and wheat were developed in research institutes and applied in Mexico, the Philippines, the Punjab in India, and elsewhere. These techniques, combined with 'diffusion' of technical advice by extension services, were successful in increasing yields where conditions permitted large expenditures on irrigation, fertilizer and new varieties of seed. The down side of the 'green revolution' was that the concentration of land ownership and the displacement of rural populations aggravated problems of rural poverty and landlessness. In 1971, Professors Ruttan and Hayami, working out of the University of Minnesota, published their "induced development model" in *Agricultural Development: An International Perspective* [1971]. At a seminar at the Stanford Food Institute, they explained that it "attempts to make more explicit the process by which technical and institutional changes are induced through the responses of farmers, agribusiness entrepreneurs, scientists, and public administrators to resource endowments and to changes in the supply and demand of factors and products" [1972: 145–46].

Beckford was visiting Stanford at the time, and was invited to comment. His comments were published together with the Ruttan-Hayami paper by the Food Research Institute [1972b] and reprinted as "The induced innovation model" [1984c]. An extended version of Beckford's comments, prepared in 1973, is included here (chapter 14). Although an improvement on the Schultz model, Beckford was not satisfied that Ruttan and Hayami were really concerned with agricultural *development*, but rather with the growth of agricultural output and improvements in agricultural productivity.

Agricultural development is essentially the study of the process by which the material welfare of the rural population of a country is improved consistently over time . . . there are numerous instances (in the past as well as at present) in which substantial growth of agricultural output is accompanied by no change in the material welfare of the majority of people involved in the process of that growth (pp. 8-9).

In plantation export agriculture this was the norm, rather than the exception, as illustrated by Arthur Lewis in a passage Beckford loved to cite:

Cane sugar is an industry in which productivity is extremely high by any biological standard. It is also an industry in which output per acre has about trebled over the past seventy years, a rate of growth unparalleled by any other major agricultural industry in the world – certainly not by the wheat industry. Nevertheless, workers in the cane sugar industry continue to walk barefooted, and to live in shacks, while workers in the wheat industry enjoy among the highest living standards in the world. However vastly productive the sugar industry may become, the benefit accrues chiefly to the consumer [Lewis 1955: 281].

Beckford concluded that the induced development model of Hayami and Ruttan exposed the fundamental limitations of contemporary theorizing on the nature of the process of agricultural development: "If we are concerned, as I am, with the material welfare of rural people, then the problem must be approached differently from the manner in which the authors have attempted ... this means developing models appropriate to the contemporary situation in Third World countries" (pp. 17-18). This was what Beckford attempted to do in *Persistent Poverty*, his best known and most important work.

Comparative Rural Systems: Development and Underdevelopment

In this article published in *World Development* [1974] and reprinted in a widely used book of readings by Wilber [1979], Beckford adopted the eclectic approach of social philosophers such as Weber and Polanyi who emphasized the importance of value systems or preference hierarchies of different places and times. Polanyi distinguished between *formal* (mainstream) economic rationality with its value bias toward abstractions such as "efficiency" and "productivity" as end goals, and *substantive* (emphasis added) economic rationality whereby people seek to get the most from their resources in terms of their particular value system and preferences. The substantive approach pointed to the need for a typology of peasant producers. The peasant was here defined in terms of a decision maker who uses his own labour and that of his family to transform resources into output. He might or might not utilize hired labour, and was interlocked in some higher order social framework, whether capitalist or socialist. Decisions were thus made within a complex systems of economic and social variables.

A chart illustrated Beckford's world view of agricultural and rural systems, in which the commercial "farm-firm" of the American Midwest appeared as a "special case". Other categories were subsistence: various types of peasantry; feudal, as in Latin America; various types of plantations; integrated corporate agribusiness; bureaucratic socialism as in (the former) Soviet Union; and socialist communalism, as in China (at that time). The paper addresses the economics of resource use and allocation under institutional constraints. It warned against imported (transferred) technology which displaced labour, aggravated the mal-distribution of wealth, transferred the value biases of the exporting countries, and locked the colonial economy tighter into the international capitalist system. Ultimately, the Third World would have to develop indigenous technologies to suit their resource endowments and the value aspirations of their peoples.

A Theoretical Framework for Agricultural Development Planning and Policy

"Towards an appropriate theoretical framework for agricultural development planning and policy" [1968a] was presented to the Third West Indian Agricultural Economics Conference, held on the Mona campus of the University of the West Indies in 1968, organized by George Beckford and chaired by Dr David Edwards. It elaborated on an earlier paper, "Rationalization of West Indian agriculture" [1968c] delivered to a regional conference on devaluation. The Agricultural Economics Conference of 1968 marked a high point in the development of a distinctive West Indian analysis of Caribbean economy. Among invited participants was Lloyd Best who presented his "Model of a pure plantation economy" prepared with the assistance of Kari Levitt in Montreal, at the McGill Centre for Developing Areas Studies. In the editorial preface to the publication of a selection of conference papers in a special issue of *Social and Economic Studies* [1968a], Beckford noted that the governments had invested heavily in the promotion of agricultural development, but the results were disappointing, particularly in domestic agriculture: ". . . there is a feeling among some of our economists that one of the chief reasons for the general failure to 'get agriculture moving' in the West Indies, is that our planners are caught in an unenviable position of having to plan without theory and without facts" [p. 231].

Beckford's point of departure was the hypothesis that underdevelopment in the Caribbean emanated directly from the particular social and institutional character of the plantation system of resource organization, and that development required changes in that structure. Caribbean economy had two main component systems of resource organization: plantation and peasant. The latter, distinguished by small scale units of production with heavy reliance on family labour was poorly endowed with flat, fertile land and other necessary resource inputs; its capacity for development was poor compared with the plantation sector. Marketing arrangements and infrastructure were more highly developed for plantations which, moreover, enjoyed artificially high prices and lower risks, by virtue of metropolitan preferences.

In highly open export oriented plantation economies, market relationships were more important in trade with the rest of the world than within the economy. Food and raw materials were supplied to other countries, not to the domestic non-agricultural sector. Such economies depended on imported supplies of manufactures and even basic foods. The factors governing the terms of trade with the rest of the world did not coincide with those determining internal terms of trade. In closed economies, domestic terms of trade tended to favour agriculture, whereas in open economies, international terms of trade tended to move against plantation economies. Foreign ownership of agricultural sectors of countries in which these enterprises operated. He quoted an authority on plantations to the effect that "[plantations] differ from other kinds of farms in the way in which the factors of production, primarily management and labour, are combined" (p. 322). Production on plantations was specifically for sale in overseas markets. What distinguished plantation production from other kinds of farms was "the substitution of supervision – supervisory and administrative skills – for skilled adaptive labour, combining the supervision with labour whose principal skill was to follow orders" (p. 323).[12] Foreign ownership by a corporate entity was the norm. The plantation was vertically integrated, supplying inputs for its operations and marketing facilities for its output.

Most plantations were originally established in sparsely populated tropical areas, and depended on large scale (involuntary or voluntary) movement of labour from other tropical regions. The plantation system was fundamentally international in character, dependent on external stimulus and enterprise, external markets, and external finance: *"plantations are in practice only a special part of a much wider economic system with a financial and industrial centre usually in a region remote from the plantations"* (p. 324). Beckford suggested that: "The term 'plantation economy' can be used cautiously to describe situations where the dominant pattern of agricultural resource organization is the plantation system" (p. 325). This did not mean that the agricultural sector consisted only of plantations, but that plantations provided the main dynamic for development, affecting sociological and political as well as economic decision making. Peasant producers might be more numerous, as was the case in the West Indies, but because the peasantry was a creation of the plantations, their behaviour reflected the plantation influence. On the basis of such a definition, plantation economies were found in tropical America and tropical Asia, but not significantly in tropical Africa. According to the well known definition of Charles Wagley, the boundaries of Plantation America extended outward from the Caribbean to embrace the northeast of Brazil and the south of the US.

The paper illustrated foreign-owned plantation enterprises in the Americas with case studies of the operations of three multinational companies: Bookers and Tate and Lyle in the West Indies, and the United Fruit Company in Central America. In all of these cases, the locus of decision making was outside the countries in which production activities were carried out. Foreign investors preferred investments which were directly linked with foreign exchange earnings. Surpluses from investment tended to flow back into established export activities – creating rigidities in the adjustment process of the agricultural sectors of the countries involved. Alternately, they were invested in other, more profitable geographic locations. The relevant unit for analysis was therefore the plantation enterprise, and not the nation state in which only a part of the firm's operations were located. Because multinational firms were vertically integrated and operated in many locations, the maximization of profit for the firm as a whole was not dependent on the maximization of profit from its production activities in any one location.

Other characteristics of plantation production treated in the paper were rigidities deriving from capital specificity; alienation of land in excess of expected requirements at the time of the establishment of operations; and geographical dispersion of production to minimize risk of losses. The contribution of plantation agriculture to national economic development was minimal. Beckford quoted from Arthur Lewis' foreword to Gisela Eisner's *Jamaica: 1830-1930*:[13] "So long as productivity is constant in subsistence production, practically all the benefit of increases in productivity in commercial crops accrues to the consumer and not the producer . . . greater productivity is offset by adverse terms of trade" (p. 344). He added that this phenomenon was characteristic not so much of all export agriculture, but of plantation agriculture, in particular.

Despite productivity increases and trade union activities, wages in plantation agriculture remained low. These low wages stood in dramatic contrast to the earnings of skilled supervisory and management staffs, setting the stage for a highly unequal pattern of income distribution among all households in plantation economies. This limited the size of the domestic market and potential scale economies for domestic agricultural producers. Low incomes of the bulk of the population restricted household savings, while the high income classes engaged in conspicuous consumption of luxury imports and invested heavily in non-productive assets. Rigid class lines and weak community cohesion of plantation societies restricted social mobility and adversely affected individual incentives for economic advancement and labour adaptability (p. 346).

Persistent Poverty: Underdevelopment in Plantation Economies

In the preface to *Persistent Poverty* [1972a], Beckford reiterated his fundamental thesis that underdevelopment derived from the institutional environment – economic, social and political organization which was a legacy of historical forces. Persistent underdevelopment in the plantation economies of the world "requires a virtual revolution to bring about significant improvements in the welfare of all Third World people" [1972a: iii]. It was a plea to pursue more rigorously our own independent analysis of the problems facing our societies: "Too often we view our problems through the eyes of metropolitan man; and our analyses of these problems depend too inordinately on analytical constructs developed for, and appropriate to, North Atlantic society, but which may be inappropriate for the Third World" (p. iv).

For Beckford the welfare of Third World peoples did not mean just material welfare, as measured by higher incomes, but all dimensions of social welfare:

An important and often neglected aspect of social welfare is, in my view, *genuine independence* – that is, full freedom of a people to control the environment in which they live, and to manipulate that environment in any way they desire . . . *material advancement can be satisfactory only if it preserves the quality of life that people regard as important* (p. V).

My whole view of plantation economy and society has been profoundly influenced by Lloyd Best. We have been discussing continuously the problems considered in this study for many years . . . Several of the ideas relating to the possibility of change are perhaps as much his as they are mine (p. vi).

Other colleagues including Norman Girvan, Al Francis, Clive Thomas, Havelock Brewster and Owen Jefferson were mentioned as having substantially influenced his thinking. "More indirectly, the work of Celso Furtado, William Demas, and the whole school of Latin American and Caribbean structuralists has left an indelible imprint on my intellectual development" (p. vi).

In a draft text of the introduction to *Persistent Poverty*, Beckford testified that:

The most important influence, however, has been that of the New World Group – an informal association of people from various disciplines who are concerned with developing a genuinely Caribbean view of Caribbean society. The weekly discussion meetings of the group at Mona over the past seven years and the work of editing the *New World Quarterly* have taught me more than I learnt in all my days as student and teacher in different classrooms.[14]

This reference to the New World Group was dropped from the published version of the preface, as was Beckford's acknowledgment of useful comments received from scholars and students at Stanford, University of California at Berkeley, University of Minnesota, University of Wisconsin and Yale University each of which he visited in late April 1970 for a series of seminars. Beckford's exposure to radical intellectual currents on American campuses in 1969 and 1970, and his encounter with Latin American and black American students motivated him to extend his work on Third World plantation economy and society to embrace dispossession among all black people in the New World.

There is no attempt to summarize *Persistent Poverty*. The study evolved over a period of several years, and the principal ideas were contained in the two seminal papers [1968a, 1969] reproduced in this volume (see chapters 16 and 17). A chapter of *Persistent Poverty* was reproduced in a special edition of *Social and Economic Studies* on multinational corporations as "The dynamics of growth and the nature of metropolitan plantation enterprise" [1970b]. A select and annotated *Bibliography of the Political and Social Economy of Plantations* [1970a] with some 300 entries, was prepared by Beckford as a byproduct of research for the book, and circulated for the use of individuals interested in the subject of plantations, two years prior to the publication of the book. It testified to the thoroughness of his research, and to the collegial intellectual environment prevailing at the university at that time.

Reproduced here is the penultimate chapter of the book, entitled "Possibilities for Change and Transformation", where Beckford summarized the obstacles to development attributable to plantation influence, and discussed policy measures to address the problem in Cuba, Ceylon (Sri Lanka), Jamaica and Guyana. The process of economic transformation and development was of necessity painful, and would require a new social ethos and a considerable degree of government intervention.

But economic change alone was not enough. The social reorganization required by the kind of economic change outlined must heal permanently the fractures inherent in the plantation system. Among such measures, the most important were equality between the races and equality of educational opportunities. To mobilize the society for change would require a "new style of politics". This, he suggested, was emerging from two developments: the increasing consciousness among people of the state of chronic dispossession, and Third World analysts who had produced fresh insights into the persistence of material and cultural dispossession. Citing Fanon, Furtado, Césaire, Garvey, Carmichael and James, Beckford believed it was no coincidence that these analysts of plantation society had contributed a disproportionately high share of Third World scholarship.

Regarding the 'brand' of political ideology needed to mobilize action for change, Beckford insisted that capitalism, socialism, communism, and all other known "isms" whether developed in feudal-capitalist Europe, settler-homestead-capitalist North America, feudal-semicapitalism of Asia or elsewhere, were not adequate for the social and political realities of plantation society. With a very high level of material advancement, the US had not solved its own plantation problem: "The persistent state of black dispossession, material and social, in that country is a stark manifestation of this fact" he wrote (p. 232).

We conclude therefore that a new political ideology will be necessary to stimulate social change and action in plantation society. Exactly what that ideology will be like we do not know. What is certain is that it will develop out of the process of change that has already begun; on that account it will be the appropriate ideology for servicing the needs of the new society eventually conceived out of the process (p. 232).

Caribbean Economy

Caribbean Economy: Dependence and Backwardness (1975b), a volume of essays edited by Beckford, was intended as an introduction to Caribbean economy for sixth formers in high schools and first year university students. As the subtitle suggests, the central theme of this volume was that underdevelopment in the Caribbean was associated with dependence. After four years of planning and preparation, the book contained only one-third of the originally commissioned papers. Beckford commented that this reflected a stalemate in the development of Caribbean economic science after its early spurt in the late 1960s. The contributors were George Beckford, Jack Harewood, Kari Levitt, Lloyd Best, William Demas, Norman Girvan, Maurice Odle and Owen Jefferson who prepared a "Reading List in Caribbean Economic Problems". The book was dedicated to the people of the Caribbean, especially to the young people on whose shoulders the burden of transformation must fall (p. vii). Tribute was paid to the inspirational influence of William Demas whose dedication to regional affairs and capacity for hard work and excellence had set the pace for many. Beckford's own contribution, "Caribbean rural economy" [1975b], contains a schematic presentation of previous work by Best and Levitt. His concerns now shifted from economics to the cultural roots of black dispossession and black affirmation in Plantation America from Brazil to the Carolinas. His epilogue to this book signalled a widening of his vision to embrace the cultural and ecological dimensions of economic development:

The distinction between industry and agriculture, town and country, and mental and manual labour must be eroded. Such erosion can only occur by understanding particular peoples: where we are coming from; and what makes us who we are. The West Indian person is both town and country. The majority can do both mental and manual work. And agriculture is an industry. There are many kinds of industries – industry of the factory; industry of the field; industry of the mind. Human society must aim to integrate all these industries, so that mankind can tailor environment to needs. Ultimately, *people* will decide everything (p. 172).

Beyond Economics: Issues of Race, Class and Black Dispossession

The international success of *Persistent Poverty* brought a flood of invitations to address university audiences and attend scholarly conferences in the United States, Canada, Mexico, Cuba, Nigeria, Ghana, and Malaysia. Among the universities visited – some several times – were Stanford, UCLA, Atlanta, Yale, Howard, Pittsburgh, Texas and Minnesota in the US, and McGill, Windsor and Concordia in Canada. His services and advice were sought by international agencies, and regional governments including Guyana, Jamaica, Belize, Grenada, St Vincent and St Lucia. At home, he continued to teach, and to engage in political struggles both within the university and on the larger scene of Jamaican politics.

The Reception of *Persistent Poverty*

By the time *Persistent Poverty* appeared in 1972, the intellectual climate at the university was significantly more radical than in the 1960s. The riots following the banning of Walter Rodney from Jamaica in 1968, the Black Power revolution in Trinidad in 1970, *Abeng* in Jamaica, the appearance of small Marxist groups, the sweeping nationalizations in Burnham's Guyana, and the election of Michael Manley's PNP in 1972, transformed intellectual discourse. Beckford was caught in the ideological cross currents of the Third World nationalism of the "plantation school", Marxist class analysis, and Black Power as a mobilizing force for the cultural and political affirmation of black people in the New World.

A review by Carl Stone [1972][15] greeted *Persistent Poverty* as the most ambitious and exciting presentation of the so-called plantation school:

More synthetic than innovative, it crystallizes, summarizes and applies much of the analytic and theoretical perspectives of the first generation of West Indian economic thought articulated primarily through the New World Group and Journal. The work consequently draws heavily on the ideas of the main theorist of this school of thought, Lloyd Best (p. 481).

Stone raised important criticisms of Beckford's analytical focus. The socialist critique of capitalism, Stone argued, was dismissed too easily and Beckford failed to detect obvious similarities between developed capitalist and plantation societies. The argument that plantation systems were basically different from other less developed, exploited and neocolonial economies was not convincing. Beckford's preoccupation with the conflict between plantations and peasants ignored the growth of a rural wage labouring agroproletariat, which had provided fuel for political resistance and militant mass politics in the plantation system. Finally, Stone critiqued Beckford's "super-ficial analysis of the revolutionary changes in Cuba which fails to recognize the massive transformation of resource allocation, social organization, mass welfare, participatory politics, income redistribution, human resource devel-opment and productivity goals and organization achieved by that socialist revolution" (p. 482).

The major strength of the work, according to Stone, was its lucid, well documented and theoretically insightful analysis of the institutional and economic forces that stood as obstacles in the path of economic and social development in plantation societies, and its in-depth treatment of the histori-cal forces which had shaped the production process and the related social and political features of such societies. Stone concluded that *Persistent Poverty* stood alongside the writings of the Latin American structuralist school and those socialist scholars who had discussed the mechanics of international imperialism. It complemented and filled the gaps in the Marxist literature which discussed imperialism from the global and international perspective.

From the Marxist corner came an attack on "Foundations of black dispos-session", an incomplete draft of a planned companion book to *Persistent Poverty*. An unpublished text of comments by Trevor Munroe [1970], with notes in the margins of the manuscript by Beckford, is instructive. Munroe charged that Beckford's purpose was to strengthen the Black Power move-ment and that his "main argument is that the plantation has given black people in the New World a common experience of 'dispossession' and a common framework for affirmation" (p. 2). Beckford's comment in a marginal note, was "Right!". Against Munroe's complaint that "the plantation is like the Holy Ghost – it is always with us and 'fundamentally' it never changes even though we might realize neither of these things" (p. 7), Beckford wrote: "Hear! Hear!".[16] Beside Munroe's criticism that Beckford included the "Afro-Saxon" in the dispossessed black masses, Beckford wrote "because the masses aspire to Afro-Saxonism!". Where Munroe wrote: "we are left to believe that in Jamaica the 46,000 factory workers are basically the same as the 50,000 peas-ants, and both are basically the same as the 120,000 unemployed. Similarly, that the 73% of Afro-American population in cities is basically the same as the rest [of the population]", Beckford wrote "Correct!". Beckford was accused of "innocence of history or the motion of historical forces" as in "the phenome-non of emancipation without change". In short, Beckford was accused of a "well-intentioned disservice to the movement for black liberation" and effec-tively dismissed as favouring "cultural-nationalist-separatist" views over "reformist-revolutionary-integrationist" positions: "In this sense the work is clearly detached from struggle" (p. 18). Ultimately, the critique was targeted at Beckford's preoccupation with dispossession from the land, whereas agricultural labour, whether wage employed or smallholder was rapidly diminishing in significance. Beckford's analysis was thus dismissed as "a-historical" because it emphasized continuities from slavery to emancipation to the present.

In a number of papers presented in the years following the publication of *Persistent Poverty*, Beckford elaborated his position, taking account of criticisms concerning the capitalist nature of plantation systems, continuity and change, the relevance of the plantation economy model to non-agricultural industries, and issues of race and class. The selected writings include papers identified by Beckford as his more important work. What emerges is Beckford's firmly held belief that consciousness of the common experience of black dispossession was critical to all the struggles of all black people – whether in the Caribbean or in North America. Dispossession from the land, starting with the eradication of native Amerindian populations and the forced migrations of African labour to the New World, continued to the present. It had made migration, whether voluntary or involuntary, a shared experience of the black people of the New World diaspora. Beckford was concerned, above all, with consciousness – with the need to "free the mind" from Afro-Saxon socialization and mimicry of metropolitan values and lifestyles, with all its insecurities concerning the inferiority of black people.

Social Knowledge and Social Change

In "Social knowledge and social change" [1978a], a paper contributed to a project on methodology and social change in the Caribbean, Beckford stressed the importance of the ways in which ideas are generated in society, with special attention to sociology of education. He identified 'colonialism' and 'socialism' as the two main types of social organization which are currently dominant – with the caveat that there were essential differences between the Soviet and the Chinese experiments with socialism – and that he was attracted to the Chinese system which was less bureaucratic and more concerned with people.

He re-stated his differences with Marxist critics. Caribbean social scientists, he charged, had failed to understand the nature and character of "colonialist organization" which had served as the primary mechanism by which the people had been exploited. Social scientists in the Caribbean "still have not isolated and grasped . . . the mechanism by which it continues to keep our people poor and dispossessed" (p. 184). He insisted that the plantation system was the core institution which had led the Caribbean people into a particular form of integration into the international capitalist system, and unless this was understood "we won't understand anything about the process by which we can be liberated from this system" (p. 185).

At the heart of colonialism is capitalism and at the heart of capitalism one finds the plantation system . . . the first capitalist institution which separated labour from the means of production, while at the same time integrating factory-type discipline into the processes of production. Secondly and to my cetain knowlege, the plantation system represented the first successful attempt to institutionalize race as a factor of production. Thirdly, it was the plantation system which planted the seed which gave birth to a whole range of Euro-American economic institutions which have successfully penetrated the social systems of Third World countries in Asia, Africa and Latin America. [The] almost total alienation of our peoples has largely been a consequence of the tightness of our integration into the international capitalist order, which cannot be separated from the ways in which race and class have kept us divided (p. 186).

Alienation among Caribbean social groups, Beckford claimed, was greatest among the majority group of black people, and its intensity diminished the further one moved up the socioeconomic hierarchy through intermediate groups such as the Chinese, toward European elements in our society. This "generates a certain pattern of social dynamics which (to put it very crudely) resembles a kind of volcano where a large mass of black people are trapped into a social system which allows them very few outlets" (p. 186).

Issues of Race and Class

In a sequel to the same project on methodology and social change, Beckford wrote a brief memorandum called "The plantation system and the penetration of international capitalism" in which he critiqued a Marxist analysis which "evades the race question" [1978b]. His comments were specifically addressed to Don Harris who was a participant in the seminar. Starting with the "obvious observation" that, apart from Cuba, the whole Caribbean was fundamentally a part of the international capitalist system, Beckford's concern was to locate our particular place within that system of social and economic organization, and "to look at the social realities of what we call the Caribbean" which he identified as "simply the plantation system" (p. 24):

When I say the 'plantation system' I am not talking about agriculture and planting food, I am talking about the planting of labour, as the critical element. That the labour of the Caribbean is planted here in a specific way in relation to capital . . . is an obvious fact. What is also obvious is that this labour regime is based on race. Race is the specific element in the Caribbean reality. Labour was organized within the Caribbean environment from the very outset, as an interlocking part of an international racist system. This labour is not homogeneous in the classical sense of homogeneous, and therefore not deriving classes in the classical system of Marxist analysis. What I am trying to suggest is that race is *instituted* in *both* the mode of production *and* the mode of exchange (p. 24) [emphasis added].

The institutionalization of race in the system of production created social dynamics which were unique to this type of society. The political framework must therefore embrace the social economy: "It makes no sense whatsoever to try to analyse Caribbean society in terms of labour without race . . ." because different types of labour have different access to the means of production. "It is race which determines whether or not a poor labourer will eventually emerge into a capitalist or whatever in the Caribbean." Beckford charged: "All that was said before my comments could have been said about any society in the world. As social scientists we have neglected the whole element of race in our theoretical frameworks. And this neglect weakens all – including planta- tion work" (p. 25). He insisted that: "We can't get very far in using Marxist theory of analysing Caribbean society until we introduce and integrate race and class in that theoretical apparatus" (p. 26). He added that failure to cope with the racial question was also obvious in Cuba, and suggested that the racial problem would not be solved even after socialism had been achieved, unless we understood the ways in which race had been institutionalized in the social process.

In a plea for the development of a theoretical framework that recognized Caribbean society as a unique part of the international capitalist system, he remarked that "we don't even recognize in our own work the extent to which racism is instituted in the minds of our people. Most of the studies I have looked at evade the race question. Very few of the macro studies which I have seen look at race in any kind of analytical way" (p. 26). A notable exception was Norman Girvan's study "Aspects of Political Economy of Race and Class in the Caribbean and the Americas",[17] presented at a conference on Caribbean social problems organized by Latin American scholars in Mexico City in 1974, and attended by Beckford. In the introduction to the published version of Girvan's paper [1976], Beckford reported that it was received with great inter- est, and "provided a weave that gave design to the fabric of the discussion". The hemispheric view of the capitalist exploitation of non-white labour high- lighted the similarities in the experiences of native American and black people throughout the hemisphere.

Institutional Foundations of Resource Underdevelopment

In "Institutional foundations of resource underdevelopment in the Caribbean", presented at McGill University in 1970, published in the *Review of Black Economy* [1971b] and reprinted by McGill's Centre for Developing Areas Studies [1972d] Beckford stated that "the development of any society's resources depend ultimately on the human resource – people (p. 199). Since the slave era, right up to the present time, the black experience in the New and to forge the larger Central American and Caribbean integration" (p. 52). This article illustrates Beckford's vision of a Caribbean regionalism reaching out from a consolidated Commonwealth Caribbean to embrace Cuba and other Spanish-speaking Caribbean countries of the Antilles, and eventually also Central America.

Regionalizing Agricultural Import Substitution

A shortened version of Beckford's regional integration study, "Intra-Caribbean agricultural trade" [1967], co-authored with M.H. Guscott, is included in this volume (chapter 8). The authors noted that in the postwar period, several territorial governments introduced policies designed to stimulate domestic food production, and suggested policy measures to upgrade and regionalize import substitution in agricultural produce and food products.

The study begins with a description of the institutional arrangements and policies relating to the *internal* [emphasis added] marketing of foodstuffs in the Commonwealth Caribbean.[8] In addition to private informal traders, known variously as higglers, hucksters or peddlers, public marketing entities played an important role in the collection and distribution of domestic agricultural goods in all the territories of the region. With minor variations, agricultural marketing corporations in Jamaica, Barbados, Trinidad and Guyana were empowered to buy at guaranteed prices and sell, collect, transport, store, grade, package, process, import and export agricultural produce. In the smaller territories, still under colonial administration, government marketing departments performed similar functions. It was proposed that trading arrangements between territorial marketing agencies could be formalized to provide an institutional mechanism for the expansion of intra-regional trade.

Recommendations were focused on the regional coordination of guaranteed agricultural prices, and the opening of territorial borders to food imports to encourage increased specialization of production within the region. With the exception of special agreements on rice, and oils and fats, imports from all Caribbean territories were subject to import restrictions in the form of prohibitions (negative lists), licenses and quotas, intended to encourage the production of domestic agriculture. The list of such restrictions was long, numbering 18 products in Jamaica; 29 in Trinidad and Tobago, and 53 in Guyana. A programme of regional import substitution was to be started as part of a coordinated regional agricultural production programme, with the immediate relaxation of territorial restrictions on food imports originating within the region.

plantations depleted the supply of capital for non-agricultural expansion, by repatriation of dividend and interest payments, while agriculture's capacity to earn foreign exchange was reduced by the characteristic high import content of both production and consumption. Spread effects of development spurts in such economies were weak.

Central to Beckford's argument was the co-existence of micro-economic efficiency with overall inefficiency in the allocation of resources within the agricultural sector. Peasant operators seemed to allocate resources *at their command* quite efficiently, and plantation owners allocated resources efficiently *from the point of view of their private accounting.* But peasant owners had insufficient resources at their command because institutional factors limited the supply of land, capital and technical knowledge available to them, and the ruling classes used their political power to maintain the status quo. At the same time, land was seriously underutilized in the plantation sector. This might be rational and efficient from the point of view of plantation owners, but it was inefficient for the agricultural sector and the country as a whole. Redistribution of land was likely to raise output because input costs of small farmers were lower than those of the plantations. A further cause of inefficient resource use was due to the specificity of ancillary services for plantations, with attendant excess capacity, while interior rural areas were without the basic facilities of water and electricity.

Beckford noted that very few economists in the metropolitan countries seemed to appreciate the approach taken in his paper. He cited one of the few agricultural economists who dissented from the majority view: "The real danger with a traditional agricultural model is that it may provide decision makers in developing countries . . . [with] a pseudo sophisticated justification for overlooking possible structural changes in the agricultural sector and . . . [they] may end up placing major emphasis on politically palatable programmes for bringing in new inputs from outside the sector."[10] In his critique of Agro 21, Beckford charged the governments with setting up a proliferation of official agencies, generally funded by external resources, as a substitute for serious institutional land reform.[11]

Agricultural Resource Use and Development in Plantation Economies

"The economics of agricultural resource use and development in plantation Economies" [1969], reprinted in Bernstein [1973] and Livingstone [1980], contained the basic argument of *Persistent Poverty* [1972a]. In this paper, Beckford explored the economic relations, organization and institutions that characterized the plantation system. The concern was not with the efficiency of this type of "firm-farm" but with the efficiency of resource use in the

World has been a continuous process of acculturation and socialization to the norms of the plantation system" (p. 201). This system, based on caste, race and colour, inhibited social mobility and dehumanized the bulk of the population to such an extent that it diminished the level of motivation. Beckford spelt out the consequences of the plantation system in the following passage:

On the whole, the plantation has a demoralizing influence on plantation community. It destroys or discourages the institution of the family, and so undermines the whole social fabric. It engenders an ethos of dependence and patronage, and so deprives people of dignity, security and self respect. It impedes the material, social and spiritual advance of the majority of people . . . we could hardly expect to find a highly motivated population displaying the kinds of characteristics that development demands. The energies of most people in plantation society are spent in trying to beat the system in one way or the other (p. 8).

Among traditions, values, beliefs and attitudes established as a result of long periods of plantation influence, Beckford identified paternalism, anti-technologism, and general attitudes to life and work as contributing to persistent underdevelopment. One of the few areas in which Caribbean people could gain social mobility in the system was through education. Beckford found it

absolutely scandalous that we economists in the Caribbean have never tried to study the level of investment that peasants have made in the education of their children. I suspect that if and when we carry out this exercise we will discover that the level of savings and investment among the peasant sector of black people in the Caribbean has been several times greater than the financial capital mobilized by the foreign commercial banks (p. 203).

The content of education, however, was technologically backward and heavily weighted to the supply of administrative and clerical skills, with little or no emphasis on technical and managerial skills. Because of the importance of export crops and the "plantation psychology" of government officials, little government research expenditure had been channelled into crops grown principally by peasants.

In this paper Beckford answered critics who failed to understand the relevance of the plantation system to economies dominated by non-agricultural activities of mineral resource extraction, manufacturing and tourism. Following Best and Levitt's analysis of "Plantation economy further modified", Beckford explained that the characteristics of the plantation system were reproduced in areas of resource development outside of agriculture. These characteristics included integral connections with the North Atlantic economy; weak internal linkages and "incalculability" of prices, as illustrated by the vertically integrated bauxite industry or package tourism.

Plantations, Peasants and Proletariat in the West Indies

This essay, subtitled "Agrarian Capitalism and Alienation", first appeared in a book published by Cambridge University Press [1977b], and was twice reprinted [1979d; 1979e]. Beckford reiterated his thesis that the chief cause of poverty in the West Indies was the monopoly of land and capital by the plantations. Alienation of land was most severe in those island economies where it was in short supply. "Emancipation came in 1838 and changed things a bit – but only a bit" (p. 322). The peasantry that emerged was a product of, and was dependent on, the plantation system of capitalist organization. Their fortunes, and those of the rural proletariat who continued to work on the plantations, were affected by booms and depressions in the plantation sector.

Booms produced great profits for the plantations, and bonus payments for wage workers; more lands were engrossed and the peasantry was squeezed. Contrarily, depressions produced the opposite effects: workers suffered from unemployment, while peasants benefited as some plantations were forced out of business, and more land became available: "This general pattern has persisted right up to the present time" (p. 323). The concentration of ownership of land and sugar factories resulted in the dominance of plantation agriculture by multinational corporations. Data on the size distribution of farms and of areas farmed for all West Indian countries showed that everywhere the small peasants (those having fewer than five acres) dominated in numbers, but had only a small portion of the farmland.

The number of plantations declined drastically, acreage declined, but total area farmed and employment of wage labour increased, as did the average size of large farms. Output per man on plantations rose by 64% over the period, due to mechanical and biochemical technological improvements, but the plantation workers gained little from these improvements because real wages remained virtually static. Non-agrarian capitalism came on the (rural) scene with mining and tourism during this period. The decline in total farmland was chiefly the result of bauxite mining, while the increase in the number of very small holdings was the result of population increase and official "land settlement" schemes instituted after the revolt of 1938.

Alienation induced resistance on the part of those pushed to the margins of subsistence, in the form of trade union organization, political mobilization, formation of peasant associations, and at the extreme, social revolt or revolution. At one time or another peasants and proletariat in the West Indies had engaged in all these different patterns of resistance – as happened in 1865 in Jamaica and throughout the region from 1935 to 1938. Post[18] identified Tate and Lyle estate workers, dockers, public works employees, ex-servicemen settled on government lands, sugar cane and banana workers as active in the

Jamaican protest movements of 1938. The most militant of these groups were banana workers who were, for the most part, peasant farmers as well. Beckford quoted Post: "It is not primarily as wage workers that the banana plantation workers must be seen, but as peasant farmers . . . I would argue that it was this hunger for land – either to add to an existing plot or turn a landless labourer into a proprietor "which was the main force of the strikers in the banana areas" [Post 1969: 379].

Both peasants and proletariat were involved in the 1938 rebellion. Their joint resistance created a social crisis. The revolts of the 1930s led to less violent patterns of resistance including trade union mobilization of the rural proletariat, political (constitutional) change and the ascendancy of peasant organizations – agricultural societies, cane farmers' associations, banana and citrus growers' associations, whose leadership was however concentrated among larger farmers. Trade unions developed into powerful bargaining agents for the rural proletariat, and in association with political parties, they spearheaded the movement to constitutional independence. Meanwhile, emigration served as one of the main avenues through which the rural population of the West Indies managed to escape alienation by agrarian capitalism.

Emigration and Demographic Change

Emigration was an aspect of alienation not treated in *Persistent Poverty*. During his stay at Atlanta University in 1974, Beckford worked on a major study of "Social structural change and continuity in the English-speaking Caribbean" for the Economic Commission for Latin America [1975d]. A paper presented to the Sixth Annual Meeting of the (US) National Conference of Black Political Scientists in Washington [1975a] summarized the basic argument of that study. The discussion of agriculture in this paper made an important distinction between the *margin of subsistence* barely tolerable by civilized human standards but achieved by the individual with the resources at his command, and the *margin of survival* representing levels of existence which are intolerable, *ie*, where the individual must rely on the goodwill of others or scuffle in order to survive. For the West Indies as a whole, the 'small peasant' was on the margin of subsistence. The rural proletariat was, for the most part, on the margin of survival. Survival in the West Indies was assisted by a high propensity to share by those who could afford to subsidize others. This operated at the level of family and friends as well as on a broader social scale. The degree of alienation was significantly greater for plantation labour than for the small peasantry.

We reproduce the chapter on "Demographic change and its consequences" (chapter 23), from the above mentioned report which presented data on the large waves of migration of the 1950s and 1960s compiled by Caribbean demographers. Notwithstanding overall net migration rates of 20% of natural increase in the 1950s, and 52% in the 1960s, the population of the English-speaking Caribbean increased from 2.7 million in 1943 to 4.3 million in 1970. The estimated loss by the entire region of 1.2 million during the ten years following 1960 was equivalent to nearly one-third of its population in 1960. Emigration was found to be age-selective, with high incidence among young males aged 20 to 34 and gender-selective with high incidence among females of child bearing age. The scale of West Indian migration in the 1960s resulted in a decline in the labour force in almost all countries and territories in the 1970s.

While remittances – approximating in value the large private capital flows into Jamaica of the mid 1960s – contributed to the survival capacity of the major dispossessed populations, the loss by emigration of a disproportionate number of skilled workers, including professional, technical and clerical grades, craftsmen and production process workers, amounted to an estimated 1% of GNP in income foregone. To this must be added the cost to the country of training these emigrants. Beckford remarked that the exposure of Caribbean migrants to metropolitan culture had a distinct demonstration effect on ideas for change and on tastes, facilitating the transmission of Black Power ideology from North America to the Caribbean in the 1960s, and influencing consumption aspirations of the population. The rest of the paper addressed dispossession from the land by internal migration, with data for Jamaica and Trinidad. The data in this article featured in a paper entitled "Race, class and the plantations" presented to the joint meetings of the Latin American (LASA) and African Studies Associations (ASA) held in Texas in 1977, and again at Michigan State University in 1978.

The Social Economy of Bauxite in Jamaican Man-Space

The entry of the bauxite-alumina transnationals after World War II aggravated the displacement of peasant farmers from the hilly interior lands. Unlike most parts of the world where mines are located in remote outlying areas, bauxite mining in Jamaica is imposed on settled rural communities. "It was the independent peasantry and their food producing base-lands which bore the burden of bauxite-mining incursions" (p. 2). This was the central thesis of the findings of a major research project directed by Beckford in the mid 1980s, and published as "Social Economy of Bauxite in Jamaican Man-Space" [1987a].

Previous studies of the bauxite industry in Jamaica researched its impact on the economy and the polity. But for Beckford the economy and the polity were abstractions of the social scientist, disconnected from the daily lives of people. This explains, Beckford's concentration on the peasantry and his use of the concept of the 'social economy', which examined economic factors in terms of their social (people) dimension, and the concept of 'man-space'. The paper elaborated on the dislocation of the manscape through an examination of peasant displacement and relocation, and analysed the implications for the development and underdevelopment of the economy as a whole, concluding with a tentative assessment of the social costs and benefits for rural communities.

A historical overview of 'man and the land' was followed by a detailed description of 'bauxite-alumina in Jamaican man-space' with maps depicting the direction and magnitude of the pattern of internal migration towards the urban conglomeration of Kingston, and the adjoining parish of St Catherine. The study found that there were no 'bauxite towns' in the conventional sense of the term, although the influx of skilled and semi-skilled labour to work on the construction of alumina plants and allied activities increased the population of established towns such as Mandeville and May Pen. Bauxite mining and refining were capital and skill intensive, and had never employed more than 1% of the labour force. There was little or no room for the displaced peasantry to find employment in the industry (p. 20).

Managerial and technical personnel initially brought down from North America, required infrastructural facilities such as special housing, schools for their children, clinics and recreational facilities. Beckford noted that this influx of white people reinforced the old white/black race/class cleavage in Jamaica: "In this sense we can speak of a 'ratooning'[19] of plantation society". In Mandeville, one of the main bauxite towns, there was an area popularly called 'Johannesburg' because of apartheid housing and social practices, as recently as the early 1970s. Over time, the white expatriates were replaced by brown and black Jamaicans: "The Jamaicanization of technical and managerial ranks served to expand and consolidate the 'brown' component within the country's plural society" (p. 21). Regarding the ascendancy of the 'brown' Jamaican through education, and their acculturalization away from their African roots, Beckford explained that these Afro-Saxon people had, from the time of plantation society, acted as brokers between the dispossessed masses of black workers and peasants and the white planter and merchant capitalist class. Their mobility within the bauxite industry depended on the degree to which they proved to be good 'company men'.

The skilled and semi-skilled labour force in the bauxite industry were highly paid and became a unionized 'labour aristocracy' in a society with over one-quarter of its labour force unemployed, and another quarter perhaps, only seasonally employed. The demonstration effect of the high wages in the industry raised the reserve price of labour, and served to aggravate the pre-existing unequal distribution of incomes in the bauxite parishes. With limited job opportunities in bauxite, manufacturing and tourism, unemployment grew, and subsistence wages prevailed in the non-unionized segment of the labour market. The one-city pattern of development of Caribbean plantation society remained unchanged. The peasantry pushed off the land exceeded the capacity of the Kingston region to provide enough jobs. Urban unemployment grew, slums developed apace, and problems of violence, crime, prostitution, drugs and so on escalated. Thousands of people, including the displaced peasantry, migrated. A survey found that migration was the fourth largest type of investment among farmers – an investment in the anticipated back-flow of remittances for survival consumption and to buy house plot and house.

As land available for farming diminished, and farmers' resistance to selling their land increased, the companies introduced resettlement programmes by which farmers were relocated to new communities, to "carve out a whole new man-space out of the new landscape". Detailed research findings on the results of the restructuring of the rural bauxite economy were presented, including its environmental impact. The latter fell into two categories: disturbance of the integrity of the land by removal of top soil and the scooping out of the ore just below the surface of the land; and air and water pollution from bauxite mining, drying plants and alumina processing. Restored mined-out lands could not maintain production of anything other than surface feeding crops, with high risks of erosion. In the early days of bauxite mining, its environmental impact on air and water pollution was not an important consideration. Beginning in the early 1970s, with rising political consciousness, the state became more responsive to complaints concerning pollution, and tentative environmental standards were established.

Bauxite mining and alumina processing fuelled economic growth for two decades, but it dispossessed and dislocated tens of thousands of small producers who left rural areas in search of employment in the city, or migrated to Britain or North America. By the end of the 1960s, unemployment had reached unprecedented levels, and the country was on the brink of revolution. For Beckford, economic development was not about rates of economic growth. It was about the welfare of the people, and the wellspring of the Jamaican people was the land. The peasantry were the main source of the country's food supplies, producing vegetables, roots and tubers, legumes and fruits. Together with imported wheat and wheat flour, rice, cornmeal, dairy products, salt and pickled fish, and chicken necks and backs, this was the basic food basket that made up the diet of the majority of poor people. Organizationally, the Jamaica Agricultural Society (JAS) was described as the forum of the peasantry, and the only organization with the capability and capacity for mobilizing peasants as a class, although leadership was provided by middle and big peasants.

The Roots of Black Poverty

"Plantation capitalism and black dispossession" [1979b] was a review of *The Roots of Black Poverty* [1978], written by Jay Mandle, described by Beckford as a "US Marxist student of plantation society . . . better equipped than the run-of-the-mill lumpen bourgeois 'Marxist' writers of recent vintage, products of the hot-house type of scholarship characteristic of revolutionary times (never in revolutionary places)" [1979b: 132]. Beckford noted that the study of underdevelopment on a world scale had developed very rapidly since the 1960s, and that he himself had developed, and now favoured an integration of Marxian with (Latin American and Caribbean) structuralist formulations. The works of Samir Amin, Thomas Szentes, Arghiri Emmanuel, Clive Thomas and Paul Sweezy were mentioned as instructive in understanding Third World backwardness.

Beckford situated himself ideologically as an intellectual worker in and of the Third World, adding that they are few and far between, and dispersed on the three corners of the globe (pp. 132-33). In extending a qualified welcome to Mandle's book, Beckford underlined his Third World position: "That it really does matter 'where you are coming from' is more obvious to me now than it was in the past" (p. 133). The qualification pertained to what Beckford perceived to be a racialist bias in Mandle's thesis that the struggles of Afro-Americans, prior to the overthrow of slavery, achieved limited success due to their acceptance of the ideology of the dominant class of white planter/owners. Beckford protested.

Nothing could be further from the truth. African slaves never accepted the world view of the white capitalist landlord class. They struggled by violent revolt and revolution. And they samied the white man with *guerilla strategy* called 'Sambo' in some places. Sambo samve boss!! 'Yes massa, yes massa' to get an easier job in the shade of the Great House, to get access to a piece of land for his own provision ground . . . That is not acceptance that massa is god. Black people know that well, as only we can (p. 135).

In a debate with Marxist scholarship concerning the relationship of slavery to capitalism, Beckford maintained that New World slave production was a capitalist social formation, pre-dating industrial capitalism, just as slave guerilla strategy pre-dated the modern guerilla warfare of liberation struggles.

Moreover, he maintained that the agrarian industrialism of the slave planta-tion introduced elements of industrial capitalism before that system spread on a world scale:

plantation agriculture was a militarized production process that put disciplined specialization of work functions into crop production. Furthermore, all plantation commodities underwent some crude product transformation in 'factories in the field' – sugar mills and cotton gins, for example. Accordingly, the slave plantation is at one and the same time, involved in agriculture and agro-industry which *proletarianizes* labour by land monopoly and by factory technology. And it is the particular racist character of this proletarianization that gives plantation capitalism its specific character and dynamics. Mandle entirely misses this point (p. 136).

The future of plantation society in comparative perspective [1979c], pre-sented to a UCLA Symposium on the Political Economy of the Black World held in Los Angeles, May 1979, signalled a shift toward a more explicit treat-ment of class:

My earlier analysis of plantation society has several weaknesses which I attempt to correct (or elaborate) in what follows. Specifically, its handling of the class ques-tion was overshadowed by the emphasis on race; whereas what is needed is a synthesis of how race and class make plantation society a sort of 'special case' in the history of social formations (fn 4, p. 6).

Beckford contends: "'Half slave-half free' is an appropriate description of the economic condition of black people in all plantation societies after Eman-cipation" [1979c: 8].

Emancipation led to the transformation of slave plantation society to subsistence wage plantation society, and share cropping tenancy. The gover-nors of these societies systematically created a 'reserve army of labour' by imported Asian labour – mainly from India. Where the African ex-slaves were able to access land of whatever quality they managed to establish a semi-independent peasantry. Where all available land was engrossed, they had to continue working on plantations for subsistence wages, or they had to migrate. Beckford noted that the mobility of labour into plantation society during the foundation period, and out of it during maturity and decline, was a feature of these societies that gave them "a certain uniqueness" among the general class of capitalist societies. Wages remained at subsistence because plantation production for export was marked by "what is now called 'unequal exchange' ", which kept plantation society backward relative to the industrial capitalist societies. Beckford noted that W. A. Lewis was the first to articulate 'unequal exchange' in "Economic development with unlimited supplies of labour" [1954] and in the *Theory of Economic Growth* [1955].

The economic substructure of society thus remained virtually unaltered in the period after emancipation. While new non-agricultural activities of mining, tourism and light manufacturing diversified the commodity mix of production and made the class structure somewhat more complex, "the institutionalization of race and class remained within the mode of production" (p. 11), and was reflected also in the superstructure of society. In the independent countries colour assumed importance as a proxy for race, and an "ideology of dependence pervades the upper reaches of society . . . possibilities for national advancement were viewed in terms of external assistance for markets, capital, technology and management (p. 12). A plantation society was therefore in constant crisis. Capital-labour conflict was central to all capitalist economies, but in plantation society, antagonism was heightened by the element of race.

There were two patterns of adjustment: "reformism", accompanied by massive out-migration of labour, and "revolution". Regarding the US South, Beckford's assessment of the civil rights movement was that positive achievements in the political realm were not matched by significant improvement of the welfare of black people relative to the white population. In the Caribbean, reformism under the rubric of "cooperative socialism" in Guyana, and "democratic socialism" in Jamaica had done little to change the economic substructure. "Cuba is the only plantation society that has transformed from underdeveloped capitalism to rapidly *developing* socialism . . . the economic, social and political achievements of socialist Cuba are now legend" (p. 17). Beckford noted that the transition to socialism in Cuba was formalized in 1965, and within a decade the internal changes resulted in popular participation, with the introduction of the organs of 'People's Power': "Race was eliminated from the productive and social order, and class receded in importance" (p. 18).

Small Garden – Bitter Weed: Struggle and Change in Jamaica

This book, co-authored with Michael Witter [1980] was written in the late 1970s, when imperialism appeared to be in retreat and popular forces in the ascendancy throughout the Third World. It was the most explicitly Marxist of Beckford's writings, reflecting the growing influence of Marxism within the Jamaican political left in the last four years of the Manley administration. Following re-election in 1976, the government vacillated between a non-IMF "self-reliant democratic socialist path" and an accommodation with the IMF mediated by the newly installed Carter administration in the US. Eventually Manley opted for the IMF, and Beckford was bitterly disappointed with what he perceived to have been a lost opportunity to rally the working people of the country behind the non-IMF alternative. Reproduced in this volume (chapter 27) is a postscript to the book, over George Beckford's signature. This is a historic document in which he expressed his profound disappointment with Mr Manley (pp. 149-51).

Neither Beckford nor Witter was affiliated with Jamaica's communist party, the WPJ.[20] They were positioned adjacent to the PNP 'left' led by D. K. Duncan, General Secretary of the PNP and Minister of National Mobilization, until he was forced to resign in mid 1977. In January 1977, following the decisive electoral victory of Michael Manley in December 1976, Beckford, Norman Girvan, Louis Lindsay and Michael Witter were asked to draw up an "Emergency Production Plan, 1977-78". Suggestions were solicited from the public and over 10,000 responses were received in the space of two weeks. The plan was presented to the Cabinet in March 1977, and effectively rejected when the government capitulated to the IMF in April of that year. A chapter in *Small Garden*, entitled "Scenario transition to socialism" summarizes the approach in this plan. The formalization of community enterprise organizations (CEOs) in Jamaica in 1978 was perhaps the most lasting contribution of the aborted Emergency Production Plan. For Beckford, the community enterprise organization was a promising model for the socialist reorganization of society on participatory principles. A report prepared for a meeting of Caribbbean planning agencies in Havana [1979a] and the appendix to "Caribbean man and the land" [1986b] elaborated a socialist economic and political model based on CEOs.

Following the defeat of the PNP in the election of 1980, which claimed the lives of hundreds of Jamaicans in political violence, and the self-destruction of Grenada's "popular revolutionary" government in 1983, Marxism waned, and the WPJ dissolved itself even before the collapse of communism in Europe in 1989. In the 1980s, the PNP went into prolonged retreat, licking wounds and reassessing policy. Interviewed in 1983 on the failure of the Manley regime by *Frontline: A Review of Black Arts and Culture*, Beckford expressed the view that the weakness of the Manley regime was that it tried to please everybody. It "tried at various times, to please the various contending classes in Jamaica . . . My assessment of the regime was that it went too far to woo the support of the capitalist class" [1983]. But the capitalist class was not induced by all the incentives offered. Instead, the capitalists rejected the regime and its socialist oriented development strategy by crippling the economy. "Economic ruin was one of the two main factors . . . The other was the political violence induced by the then opposition – the Jamaica Labour Party – which created a social condition of insecurity in the population because the government was unable to maintain law and order and guarantee social peace and security" (p. 108).

Black Affirmation, Cultural Sovereignty and Caribbean Self-Reliance

Beckford hoped to complete a book on black dispossession and black affirmation. A draft outline has guided the selection of material for Part IV of this volume. In his draft, the final four chapters were to treat:

- *Affirmation on the land*: the Caribbean peasant economy, with "the Banana Episode" as a case study;

- *Black investment* in skills, physical capital and education;

- *Black political struggle* in the US and in the constitutionally independent countries of the Caribbean; and

- *Black cultural affirmation* in language and literature; music and religion.

Peasant Investment in Agriculture and Education

The year 1968 marked the centennial of Jamaica's banana export industry. With the exception, of a meeting organized by the Oracabessa Citizens' Association and the St Mary Parish Library Association, the event passed unnoticed. The invited guest speaker was George Beckford. His address to the banana farmers and citizens of St Mary was published in the *New World Quarterly* as "Origins, development and future of the Jamaican banana industry: a century of revolutionary struggle of the peasantry" [1971a] and is reprinted here (chapter 28).

Jamaica's banana industry was established in the face of the resolute opposition of the planter class, who feared that the independence of the peasantry would detract from access to the supply of (cheap) labour for their sugar estates. The Morant Bay rebellion of 1865 resulted directly from a dispute about the rights of peasants to lands adjoining an estate. Beckford related the struggles of Jamaica's banana producers to organize the Jamaica Banana Producers' Association in the 1920s to combat the monopoly power of the United Fruit Company. Drawing on his study of the Jamaican banana industry, he noted that the growers' share of gross realization from sales of bananas was declining, due to the monopolistic control of overseas markets by transnational corporations.

Education was another means by which the peasantry had achieved upward mobility for their children. "Education as an instrument of development" [1968b] was the text of a lecture delivered by George Beckford to the annual meeting of the Jamaica Teachers Association (JTA) in 1968. He noted that "investment in human capital" had gained considerable currency in writings in economic development, and he concurred in the "new emphasis" on education as an instrument for development.[21] Education could not, however, be an "active agent" for the transformation of existing economic structures, as long as manpower planning was "passively" responding to the need for skilled manpower to fit into the established order of things:

At the individual level education is viewed as a means of social mobility. Colonial society offered few other avenues of mobility. Now, however I am suggesting that we view education as a means of creating a new society as a means of transforming the economic and social order from that of a colonial plantation society (which it still largely is) into a modern independent society (p. 5).

Beckford described "the kind of society and the kind of development to which I feel we ought to aspire" as a society of "equal opportunity for all", starting with the creation of full employment and full social equality; the development of a confident and truly independent population; an internal cultural and technological dynamic to spread equality and benefit and sustain economic growth and development; and the promotion of the "type of economic development which involves the participation of the total population in the economic and political life of the nation" (p. 3).

But the present system of education was moving in the opposite direction. Textbooks and teaching materials were remote from the real experience of students; students who could not cope with the irrelevancies were condemned to the category of dunce; and the system tended to select the wrong material: "people who only memorize and regurgitate and who have little or no capacity for independent thought and innovation" (p. 4).

Beckford suggested that Jamaica's teachers should exert their influence both in and outside the classroom to stimulate a truly independent style of life, values and culture; to instil in students and adults a profound belief in themselves, and in their ability to help themselves; to encourage selection on the basis of true ability; to bring technical and vocational education on par with grammar school type education; and to produce their own relevant teaching and textbook material. The JTA was exhorted to see itself as an independent force working for the public good, with much to contribute to national life by participating in debates on national issues outside education, and divorced from party politics.

Cultural Affirmation: "We are What we Think Ourselves to be"

"Black man and society"[1970c] was the text of Beckford's comments on papers delivered in a session on West Indian literature at a conference held at the University of Southern California in 1970. Beckford stressed unity in the common cause of all New World black people: "Every black man and woman in the New World is a product of both Africa and Europe . . . Regardless of our individual pigmentation we are both black and white in a profoundly social and cultural sense". He added that some are more black than others, and some more white in terms of mental and psychological make up: "But we are all fundamentally both black and white" (fn p. 2). This was the common experience of black people brought to the New World by white Europeans under the most brutal conditions imaginable, to labour on the slave plantations of Brazil, the Caribbean and the US South: "The black experience throughout the New World has been clearly identical . . . For man is society, and society is man" (p. 2).

"We have to start" he said "with the mind because any human being is what he thinks he is. And, in the present order of things . . . the black man sees himself through the eyes of white European man . . . our standards, which are the basis of such definition of self, are those of the white European. We are what we think ourselves to be." He challenged the designation of New World black language as "dialect" or "creole", and New World black culture as a "sub-culture". He invited his audience to appreciate the oral tradition, the spoken word, the rap, in New World black literature: "The facts of the matter are that people in the West Indies know Louise Bennett and Sparrow better than all the black writers. Same thing in Brazil and the United States" (p. 5). He called for the establishment of black publishing houses, black recording studios, and black organized conferences to facilitate rap instead of debate "as a precondition for the flowering of black consciousness, black literature, black scholarship, etc; and of the institutions to service that whole revolution is, first and foremost, a restructuring of thought and of the whole mental undercarriage of all of us as black people"(p. 5). In Jamaica, Beckford greeted Rasta and the "Culture of Dread", embraced by many working class and middle class youths and some professionals, as the "most positive and dynamic factor within [the] Jamaican body politic and body social at this time, precisely because it provides hope for revolutionary change" [1977a: 46].

Philosophical and Rural Roots of Rastafari

"The sounds and pressures of black survival" was a review article of Ken Pryce's book *Endless Pressure*,[22] in which Pryce presented his research on the "life-orientations" of Jamaicans displaced by emigration from the rural parish of St Thomas, and living in England in a decaying section of Bristol called "Shanty Town". Life was brutal. They lived under constant "pressure". Interpersonal violence and the dance were mechanisms for letting off steam, and "easing the pressure". Pryce identified two major life orientations – the "stable, law abiding" orientation of proletarian respectables, saints and mainliners; and the "expressive disruptable" life style of hustlers and teeny-boppers. The latter, Pryce noted, take their cue from Rasta, Black Power militants and the Rasta message in reggae.

In this lengthy review article [1980a], which contained a detailed account of Pryce's research, Beckford took issue with the author's description of the West Indian as "tribeless, defenceless and without roots of his own" (p. 14). Beckford traced the roots of Rastafari philosophically and politically to Garvey and Bedward[23], and geographically to *rural* Jamaica (emphasis added), and especially to the parish of St Thomas, where Bogle[24] led the struggle for land in the latter half of the nineteenth century. Pryce, he said, might be correct that the Rastas are only "superficially religious" but "he is grossly incorrect in saying that their religious dogmas are solidly buttressed by a conscious and clearly enunciated ideological racism". Beckford protested that "to describe Rasta ideology as racist is to deny the humanity that characterizes the Rasta creed and to debase its very essence" (p. 16).

Pryce was also criticized for his statement that reggae erupted from the shanty towns of Kingston primarily from the need of rude boys, Rastafarians and others to earn a living through music and dance. Beckford exclaimed: "This is totally incorrect!". He located the origins of reggae in a synthesis of Jamaican folk music (mento) and the jazz idiom of black people in the United States, each in turn rooted in the rhythms of Africa, with its highest expression in the Jamaican jazz compositions of trombonist, Don Drummond.

"Lionizing" the Jamaican Male

Beckford's "Introduction" [1980b] to Erna Brodber's "Portrait of the Jamaican male" is unknown because Brodber's multi-volume manuscript of oral testimonies of the life experiences of older Jamaicans – which pre-dated the now fashionable area of 'cultural studies' – remains unpublished. Beckford's reading of the life stories and reminiscences collected by Brodber in interviews conducted all over Jamaica concentrated on "what new information is revealed concerning the Jamaican male". The "portrait of the Jamaican male" which emerged was very different from the conventional perception that the Jamaican male "is irresponsible as a father; is lazy, shiftless and generally backward". It seemed to Beckford that

what emerges is that the Jamaican male has been a lion – an economic warrior – from early youth, in the fight for overcoming economic obstacles in the path of his development. In the process they managed somehow to create social and physical space for themselves, both within Jamaica and outside Jamaica; wherever they were forced to move (pp. 8-9).

Beckford identified three aspects of "the mode of life – of space manipulation by our people; that is to say the way in which they adjusted and expanded economic, social and physical space for themselves". The first aspect was the spirit of the people, their internal strength, their internal resistance, their internal capacity to struggle. "This manifests itself basically in the culture of the people: *defining culture as a way of being of a people*" (p. 10). The second dimension identified by Beckford was in the area of resource use, where people used whatever resources that became available to them within Jamaica's physical space, for their economic advancement. Thirdly, Beckford proposed to examine the area of technological innovation and change. The spirit which emerged from the testimonies collected by Brodber was

the spirit of an African people, a spirit of resistance, of struggle, of overcoming, of lionizing . . . This spirit manifests itself in a lot of ways through all aspects of the culture of our people: in language, religion, music and so on. The being of Jamaican black people is one that is clearly an adaptation to a situation, but an adaptation that is gloriously overcoming (p. 11).

The evidence was in "the music of our Jamaican folk religions: the claphand, the joyousness, the participatory spirit of rejoicing/revival in Pocomania, Church of God, Pentecostal, etc; and in the popular music of people like Don Drummond and Bob Marley" (p. 11).

The lionizing concept was important "because of the symbolism of the lion in African culture, in the African way of being and seeing, and it is emphasized today in the culture of Rastafari". Beckford noted that the testimonies of all of the older Jamaicans who had spent years in foreign countries as immigant workers – most of them in Cuba – were living manifestations of the "capacity of our people to 'lionize' themselves in order to create that space for advancing their situation". In religion, "the Africanness of folk religious ritual is evident. It is religion that springs out of oppression, but the resistance it embodies is not just for survival. It is for overcoming. The Afro-European folk church in Jamaica is the most important religious institution of the majority of our people" (p. 13).

According to Beckford, "Another aspect of the culture is the language. The Jamaican patois is clearly a much more beautiful, rhythmical and poetic language than standard English". It brought out from within people a natural poetry of expression, reflecting the spirit of overcoming. Beckford suggested that a part of the reason for the capacity of Anglo-Caribbean people to adjust to new language environments in Cuba, Panama and other Spanish-speaking countries was an "inherent historical capacity for language appreciation and language development". His account of the way in which human and natural resources were utilized and technological innovations developed by Jamaican people, as revealed in the rich interviews collected by Erna Brodber, testified to his intimate knowledge of the country and its people, and his overriding belief in the capacity of the Jamaican people to overcome apparently insurmountable odds with strength, character and dignity.

Beckford noted that the oral testimony collected by Brodber contradicted the established view of Jamaican men as having weak commitment to family. In looking at different communities, what emerged was more stability in the mountainous peasant communities than in the agrarian capitalist communities of sugar cane barracks where life was dehumanizing. The social cohesiveness of community had been eroded by the "modernization" that came with capitalist development. Nevertheless, Beckford concluded that "The Afro-Jamaican man, the Afro-Jamaican family and the Afro-Jamaican people, are as solid as 'the Rock' from which we come" (p. 32). It is regrettable that this research by one of Jamaica's outstanding creative writers, with its rich introduction by one of Jamaica's outstanding intellectuals remains unpublished.

Cultural Sovereignty and Economic Development

"Cultural sovereignty and economic development"[1982] was the text of Beckford's contribution to the First Conference of Intellectual Workers coordinated by George Lamming and held in Grenada in November 1982, a year before the self-destruction of the Grenada Revolution. This text, which flows with the ease of total conviction of the importance of its message to the people of Grenada, stressed psychological independence as important in conditioning the will of a people to exercise their control over [their] resources, and their power to mobilize them for their own benefit. Beckford emphasized

A culture of independence is the motive force behind the drive for an independent economic and social existence . . . Independence [is] a situation in which the people of a particular nation state (or country) have full control over their resources and total power to utilize these resources . . . to produce whatever mix of goods and services they desire to consume; to distribute such consumption among all the people in some socially acceptable way; and to determine their own pattern of allocating this consumption over time (p. 2).

Economic development was defined as "a process whereby the material welfare of the people of a nation state (or country) is improved consistently and substantially over long periods of time" (p. 2). In presenting an agenda of policy proposals, Beckford read from a long extract of a radio address he made in Jamaica in 1972, shortly after the PNP was elected to office. He believed that the policy proposals made at that time were "eminently feasible over a very short period of time" (p. 28). In his opinion, what was "required to achieve these short term objectives does not necessarily imply an immediate shift to socialism . . . A mixture of different forms of productive organization seems appropriate to achieve these short term targets once there arrives a government ready and willing to try bold new policies" (p. 29). The approach differed significantly from the Leninist orientation which predominated in the councils of the Grenada Revolution, with such tragic consequences.

Elements of the policy approach outlined by Beckford included a national agricultural plan based on small and medium sized farms with individual proprietorship or cooperatives producing food to meet all nutritional deficiencies; manufacturing activities based on an own-account and cooperative approach to provide the most basic and elementary needs of the people; and a state sector for large scale activities such as bauxite mining, electricity and telecommunication. Beckford wrote: "What is being suggested here is that conventional semi-capitalist forms of economic organization are sufficient to provide the productive base needed to eradicate poverty in the short term" (p. 30).

Sovereignty, Self-reliance and the Caribbean Nation State

"Sovereignty and self-reliance: economic implications"[1984a], was the title of Beckford's contribution to the Regional Seminar on Caribbean Sovereignty: Mobilization for Development and Self-reliance, held under the auspices of the PNP of Jamaica in December 1984. His most important and urgent message was that the whole Caribbean was really one nation. Other invited speakers included Michael Manley, P. J. Patterson, Gordon Lewis and George Lamming. Beckford repeated definitions of independence, sovereignty and self-reliance (not autarchy); developed a critique of dysfunctional consumer tastes; inappropriate technologies and underutilized resources; and reviewed the achievements of revolutions in Cuba and in Grenada (1979-83), and the approach of change by negotiation in Jamaica under Manley (1974-80).

The Cuban revolution had succeeded in establishing an independent socialist state in the Caribbean, capable of providing basic material needs for the whole of its population, and the highest standards of education and health services (and the lowest infant mortality rates) found anywhere in Latin America. This was not however achieved without great difficulty. Beckford concluded that no society in the Western Hemisphere could achieve sovereignty and self-reliance without having to confront the imperialist might of the US.

Beckford paid tribute to the remarkable achievements of the Grenada Revolution in terms of the reduction of unemployment, a high rate of economic growth, substantial improvements in health and education services, literacy, school feeding programme, etc. The Grenada experience was one of great hope for the region:

an experience which is of critical importance to us and requires our serious analysis and examination. That split within the NJM (New Jewel Movement) which was engineered by Coard and the subsequent murder of Maurice Bishop and other leaders of the PRG (People's Revolutionary Government) set the stage for the US invasion of Grenada. This reversal has put this region back at least 25 years (p. 70).

In Jamaica, comprehensive social legislation introduced in the early years of the Manley administration brought little or no opposition from any section of Jamaican society, but Manley began to "go a little bit too far" in the eyes of the imperial US when he imposed the bauxite levy, brought together the bauxite producing countries in the International Bauxite Association, negotiated 51% ownership in bauxite producing activities and repatriated bauxite lands to the state. When Manley went to Cuba and saw the achievements of the socialist revolution and came back in a state of euphoria to tell local capitalists that Jamaica had no place for millionaires and there were five flights a day to Miami, "that really set the cat among the pigeons". For Beckford, the lesson to be learned from the Manley experience was "when a movement or a party begins to confront the imperialists where it hurts them, and which therefore brings forth a response from imperialist interests, that movement or party must be prepared to mobilize the population behind this activity or else it is lost" (p. 72).

The lesson Beckford drew from Grenada and Jamaica was "that when you examine the political scenario of transition, we come to the same conclusion as we did in the economic analysis: that no island Caribbean state can go it alone" (p. 73). This, according to Beckford, was the tragedy of Grenada –

because the Bishop regime in Grenada had reached a stage of penetration in the region, where the pluralistic tradition was beginning to be accepted by all the political leaders in the (CARICOM) region. We have regressed from that and today there is marked intolerance of pluralism . . . There is need for the acceptance of a pluralist framework in order to forge regional linkage mechanisms to create a Caribbean nation state (p. 73).

Beckford noted the historical homogeneity that made the Caribbean one nation: "In fact, the Caribbean is one nation; move anywhere you like in the region, and you are at home. It is the same food, same music, the same everything; it is one nation" (p. 73). He warned that there are limits to the extent to which each and every Caribbean country could achieve sovereignty and self-reliance, because we are small societies which are really like sardines in this world of super power politics and imperial sharks. We need to recognize that size is a constraint on our capacities of achieving independent economic development. So we need to think in terms of regional strategies for development at the economic and technical level.

Illustrating the capacity of 25 million people of the Caribbean archipelago to achieve greatness, he listed a "galaxy" of political philosophers including Martí, Garvey, James and Padmore; a "tidal wave" of writers from the English-speaking Caribbean such as Naipaul, Lamming, Walcott and Brathwaite, plus non-English writers such as Carpentier, Guillén, Despestre, Césaire and many others: "the record of the Caribbean cannot be matched by any other country of similar population size (for example, Canada)". Caribbean creativity in the field of music is unsurpassed – steel drum, calypso, mambo, meringue, reggae music (which is the most important popular music in the world today) – "combining poetry, rhythm and social comment (protest) in one musical idiom" (p. 75). Beckford suggests:

This cultural explosion needs to find expression in the realm of politics and philosophy. I am suggesting that for the full realization of this great potential we need to come together as one Caribbean nation. Then, and only then, will we be in a position to be fully independent, sovereign and free to transform what is physically the most beautiful part of the planet Earth into a human paradise (p. 75).

Epilogue

Much has been Achieved; Much Remains to be Done

George Beckford taught in the Economics Department at the Mona campus of the UWI from 1964 until his death in 1990. He believed in the importance of economics as a discipline, and never wavered in his loyalty to the Department of Economics as the most – perhaps the only – important institution in his life, after his family. Beckford was first and always, a teacher and an educator. He was a supremely humane person, as all who knew him can testify, ready at any time to drop whatever he was doing, to give advice or help of whatever kind was needed to students, friends or strangers. He was a professional social scientist, but also a deeply spiritual person, who drew strength from the beauty of the Caribbean natural environment, and the creative expressions of its people in their speech, music, art, and forms of religious worship.

It is appropriate to end this collection of Beckford's work with his plea for a relevant social science. "The struggle for a relevant economics", published in *Social and Economic Studies* [1984b] recorded the history of the Economics

Department which "has systematically provided leadership in the struggle for a relevant social science in the Caribbean. Much has been achieved, yet much remains to be done".

Notes

1 The *New World Quarterly* was produced by New World Groups in Guyana, Jamaica, Trinidad and Montreal. New World described itself as a "movement which aims to transform the mode of living and thinking in the region". The New World Quarterly was initiated by Lloyd Best, and the first issue was produced in Guyana in 1962. Best and Beckford were the principal editors. Contributors included Lloyd Best, George Beckford, James Millette, Norman Girvan, Owen Jefferson, Havelock Brewster, Steve de Castro, Kari Levitt and many others. George Lamming was guest editor of the special issues produced for Guyana and Barbados Independence in 1966.

2 The proposal for West Indies-Canada trade in bananas arose from a study by Beckford and Headley Brown [1967].

3 Beckford quoted from Lloyd Braithwaite: "Rural development in the West Indies". Presented at the UNESCO Seminar on Problems of Rural Life in Central America, Mexico and the Caribbean Region, Mexico City, 1962. Mimeo.

4 "Preface" to D. Seers (ed), *Cuba: the Economic and Social Revolution* (Chapel Hill, NC: University of North Carolina Press, 1964).

5 We draw attention to Beckford's emphasis on *agriculture* and *education* as outstanding achievements of the Cuban revolution. The relative neglect of these two dimensions of economic development has been held responsible for the failure to emancipate the potential inherent in the 'peasant' sector of the Jamaican population from the economic and social legacy of the plantation system.

6 The Chaguaramas peninsula in Trinidad was leased by the British government to the United States in World War II, to serve as a US naval base in the South Atlantic. The lease was for 99 years and the Legislative Council of Trinidad and Tobago was not even consulted. In 1960, Dr Eric Williams, chief minister of Trinidad and Tobago, led a march on Chaguaramas demanding the immediate return of the base, as a site for the capital of the country. The dispute was settled by monetary compensation, and the Americans left a few years later.

7 Beckford convened a caucus of 30 economists from various Caribbean countries attending the Congress of Third World Economists, to set up an Association of Caribbean Political Economists. A steering committee representing the four principal language areas of the region was set up, with Norman Girvan as interim chairman. Eventually funding was obtained from the Friedrich Ebert Stiftung and the ACE was launched in Kingston in 1987.

8 Beckford and Guscott concentrated on internal (country) marketing because a companion study by Brewster and Thomas on the "Dynamics of Regional Economic Integration" focused on inter-regional trade.

9 In 1979, two Nobel prizes in economics were awarded: one to W. A. Lewis, and one to T. W. Shultz.

10 Dale Adams, "Resource allocation in traditional agriculture: comment", *Journal of Farm Economics* (November 1967).

11 In his critical comments on Agro 21, reprinted in the first part of this book, Beckford quoted a fellow economist who pointed out that "when governments cannot plan for development, they have to make like they are planning. Hence they set up ADCs, IDCs, AMCs, LDUCs, FPPs, SSFDPs, JNIPs, Agro 21s, etc. These are nothing more than symbols to the population that development is taking place where manifestly it is not".

12 The quotations are from W. O. Jones, "Plantations" in David L. Sills (ed.), *International Encyclopaedia of the Social Sciences*, Vol. 12.

13 W. A. Lewis, "Foreword" to Gisela Eisner, *Jamaica 1830-1930: A Study in Economic Growth* (Manchester University Press, 1961), pp. xvii-xix.

14 For a brief description of New World, see footnote 1. Beckford was the key person of the Mona New World Group. Lloyd Best was the principal editor of the *New World Quarterly*.

15 Carl Stone, *Social and Economic Studies*, (1972).

16 On several occasions Beckford cited the following description of the plantation by Edgar Thompson: "The plantation is a social institution in just as real a sense as the Catholic Church. It arises to deal with certain eternal problems of an ordered society . . . It is made up of people but, like the church, it is an impersonal and implacable automatism having a set of norms which control all the people who constitute it, planter and labourer alike, who 'belong' to the estate, as though the estate were something existing apart from its people: the plantation demands and dictates" (Edgar Thompson, "The plantation as a social system" in *Plantation Systems in the New World* (Washington DC: Pan American Union, Social Science Monographs VII, 1959) p. 27.

17 Norman Girvan, *Aspects of the Political Economy of Race and Class in the Caribbean* (Atlanta: Institute of the Black World, 1976).

18 K. W. J. Post, "The politics of protest in Jamaica, 1938", *Social and Economic Studies*, 18:4 (1969).

19 The 'ratooning' of the plantation system in the bauxite industry refers to the replication of economic and social structures typical of the plantation's sugar industry. 'Ratooning' refers to a second or third crop of canes, growing from the roots of canes already reaped.

20 Actually, there were two communist paries, the Worker's Party of Jamaica (WPJ), and the much less important Communist Party of Jamaica (CPJ). The WPJ was formally launched in 1978, and dissolved in 1988.

21 It is noteworthy that 30 years ago "investment in human capital" was recognized as essential for economic development. One may ask why it took the economists of the World Bank 30 years to rediscover the critical contribution of education to economic development.

22 Ken Pryce, *Endless Pressure, a Study of the West Indian Lifestyles in Bristol* (Harmondsworth: Penguin Books, 1979).

23 Alexander Bedward was a millenarian revivalist preacher of black redemption who was prosecuted for sedition and "lunacy", and died in a mental hospital.

24 Paul Bogle was a baptist deacon from Stony Gut in the parish of St Thomas. He established an alternative system of justice in the community, and preached against the oppressive post-slavery Jamaican regime. In October 1865, he led an attack on the courthouse in Morant Bay, and was hanged together with George William Gordon. The Morant Bay Rebellion was a landmark in Jamaican history, and Bogle and Gordon were officially declared National Heroes in 1968, joining Jamaica's first National Hero, Marcus Garvey.

Part I

Economic Planning, Agricultural Development, and Caribbean Regional Integration

1

The West Indian Banana Industry*

The Scope for Rationalization and Regional Collaboration

The present study was designed to examine the scope for regional cooperation in the production and external marketing of bananas in the light of two main considerations: (a) the uncertainty surrounding the continuation of protected markets and (b) the competition among different countries of the region in the over-supplied UK market. The first consideration points to the need for improving the overall competitive position of the industry as much as possible; while the second suggests some need for regulating the flow of supplies to the traditional market and for exploring new market outlets. New market opportunities, of course, depend partly on the competitive strength of the industry.

The study, therefore, is primarily concerned with the scope for improving the competitive position of the regional industry. It is also concerned directly with the scope for increasing the returns from the industry to the regional economies; and, indirectly, with the rationalization of agriculture as a whole.

The paper is divided into four main sections. The present state of the industry is examined in the first and this provides the background for considering the scope for rationalization of production and marketing and the scope for regional collaboration in the second and third sections, respectively. The final section considers some policy implications and proposals.

The Present State of the Industry

Export production of bananas in the Commonwealth West Indies is located chiefly in Jamaica and in the four Windward Islands (Dominica, St Lucia, St Vincent and Grenada). To date, Trinidad has exported relatively insignificant quantities; and Guyana has also only recently started to produce for export. The four Windward Islands already cooperate to a significant degree in respect of both production and marketing; and only recently they have come to an agreement with Jamaica in respect of regulation of the flow of supplies to the UK market.

Competitive Position in World Trade

Available evidence suggests that the West Indies stand in a rather unfavourable competitive position in relation to most of the other banana exporting countries of the world.

Average yields in South America are *double* those of the West Indies; in the French West Indies *three times* and in Central America *four times* as high. Average yields do not, however, really reflect relative costs of production. A better indication of competitive positions can be gained from a comparison of estimates of the f.o.b. cost per ton of exported fruit.

Among exporters of stem fruit, only East Cameroon has a higher f.o.b. cost per ton than Jamaica while only Martinique shows a higher cost among exporters of boxed fruit. It should be noted at this point that in comparison with the countries listed above, Jamaica does not have any distinct locational advantage in relation to markets in the UK and Europe. It seems therefore to stand in a relatively weak competitive position, at least in those markets.

From the data above, Latin American countries seem to be the low cost producers of export bananas. The f.o.b. cost per ton for boxed fruit from Ecuador, Central America and the Dominican Republic is not significantly different from that for stem fruit from most other countries.

Jamaica and East Cameroon are notable exceptions. The costs for stem fruit from these countries exceed those for boxed fruit from Latin America by a significant margin. In terms of both Europe and North America, the locational advantage of Jamaica is clearly not sufficient to offset the cost advantage which is indicated for Central America. The estimated f.o.b. cost of boxed fruit from Jamaica is over twice the estimated cost for that from the Dominican Republic and somewhere around 60% higher than that from Ecuador and Central America.

Because world trade in bananas consists of "a number of distinct, almost mutually exclusive trade flows", the West Indies are insulated from competition from the low-cost Latin American producers. Commonwealth bananas are now assured of the British market by virtue of a duty on fruit from outside sources and, more importantly, by an annual limit of 4,000 tons on imports from the dollar area. It is appropriate, therefore, to turn to an examination of the state of that market.

The UK Market and Intraregional Competition

Table 1.1 provides data on the source of banana imports into the UK over the past ten years. It shows that the West Indies are the most important suppliers, and that their share of the market has increased significantly over the period. Imports from the Windward Islands have expanded more than four-fold and, as from 1964, have come within striking distance of annual imports from Jamaica. As a result, a period of intense competition between these regional suppliers has developed. This competition has affected other suppliers adversely; their share of the market has fallen from about 30% in the late fifties to 14% in 1964 and to 6% in 1965. But it has adversely affected the West Indian suppliers as well.

Table 1.1 *Source of banana imports into the UK 1956-65 ('000 long tons)*

Year	Jamaica	Windward Islands	Trinidad	Cameroon	Others	Total
1956	145.7	34.3	3.2	67.1	64.7	315.0
1957	145.6	47.5	7.2	68.8	44.7	313.8
1958	121.4	58.4	4.6	73.6	50.4	308.4
1959	133.2	88.5	5.1	57.0	50.5	334.0
1960	137.8	88.6	3.3	70.3	44.1	344.1
1961	135.9	101.9	2.7	78.4	45.8	364.7
1962	145.0	110.0	1.8	74.2	36.7	367.7
1963	148.9	124.1	0.3	63.8	22.2	359.3
1964	159.7	139.4	-	22.3	27.8	349.2
1965	182.3	170.1	-	8.6	11.2	372.2

Source: Commonwealth Economic Committee, *Fruit,* annual issues and *Fruit Intelligence Monthly.*

Prices have fallen to levels lower than at any other time in the postwar period and have fluctuated considerably. Prices in 1965 and 1966 have been the lowest in the postwar period and the trade has described the market as 'over-supplied'.

Efforts are now being made to redress the situation. A conference of government officials from Jamaica, the Windwards and Britain was convened in July 1966 and agreement was reached on the rationalization of supplies by means of market sharing. According to the agreement, Jamaica is limited to 52% and the Windwards to 48% of the market. From the available information, it is not clear how this arrangement will affect supplies from other Commonwealth countries, such as Guyana and Trinidad.

A further discomforting aspect of the present situation is that a general oversupply in the market is expected to obtain for a number of years to come. According to Food and Agriculture Organization (FAO) projections, export availabilities for supplies to the UK market are expected to be about 650,000 metric tons around 1970, while import requirements are projected to be 456,000 tons at constant prices, 496,000 tons with a 10% fall in price and 544,000 tons with a 20% fall in prices. A similar excess supply situation has been projected for total world trade in bananas.

In the light of these considerations, it would appear that rationalization of the industry and regional collaboration in both production and marketing are matters of importance not only in the short run but in the longer run as well.

Nature, structure and organization of production and marketing

Bananas for export are produced more or less indiscriminately in various parts of Jamaica and the four Windward Islands. Production in many areas not suited to banana production involves extra costs to adjust the ecological environment; for example, heavy fertilization and drainage works to improve soil fertility and structure where soils are deficient in terms of banana requirements; and irrigation where rainfall is inadequate. In Jamaica, production is scattered over the entire island even though the southern parishes are generally regarded as ecologically unsuited to bananas.

It is of some interest to note at this point that banana production in Central and South America (the international low-cost suppliers) is, on the whole, restricted to the most suitable ecological areas and is serviced by an infrastructure of railways, roads and ports which were developed specifically for bananas. This is a result of the fact that the industries there were developed by private foreign-owned fruit companies which were given an option on the most suitable areas. By contrast, West Indian banana production was grafted on to an infrastructure designed for sugar production and was developed by numerous smallholders who had limited access to the more suitable areas. It would, therefore, not be surprising to find locational diseconomies in the West Indian industry.

Bananas are a very demanding crop in respect of management, particularly when the natural environment is unsuitable. Planting densities, cropping patterns, fertilization, irrigation and disease control depend on management decisions that influence yields and costs. In the West Indies much emphasis has been placed on technological improvements in production as a means of improving yields and reducing costs. But these have not had the kind of effect necessary to place the industry in a strong competitive position. This is not to say that expenditures on research and extension have been misplaced. Far from it. What is implied is that rationalization of the industry seems to demand much more than improvements in the general technology of production.

The export banana industry in Jamaica consists of about 35,000 growers cultivating some 85,000 acres and is serviced by the All-Island Banana Growers Association (and an insurance board)in respect of production and by a statutory body – the Banana Board – in respect of marketing. In the Windwards there were about 29,000 growers in 1958, occupying a total of some 31,000 acres with grower associations servicing the industry in respect of both production and marketing. Table 1.2 shows the distribution of growers, acreage and production according to size of farm and the accompanying tabulation summarizes the size distribution of growers:

Table 1.2 *Distribution of banana growers by acreage under production.*

	Jamaica	Dominica	St Lucia	St Vincent	Grenada
Under 10 acres	34,066	7,460	8,050	6,000	5,810
Over 10 acres	484	170	940	310	500
Total	34,550	7,630	8,990	6,310	6,310

By and large, the number of growers in the West Indian industry exceed by a considerable margin the number of growers in other banana exporting countries.

The predominance of small growers in the industry is to be noted. The greatest concentration of growers is on farms of less than five acres. In Jamaica, percentages of growers in this category were 96, 77, 75, 85 and 83. The shares of acreage and output which are accounted for by small growers are, however, disproportionately less. For example, in Jamaica the 96% of growers on farms of less than 5 acres occupy only 58% of total acreage and produce roughly one-third of total output; while the 0.2% of all growers that operate farms over 100 acres in size occupy 23% of total acreage and produce roughly 30% of output.

The inference is usually made that because average yields are lower on small farms than on the large estates, the former represent the high cost element in the industry and that rationalization should be in terms of a transformation which eliminates or reduces the participation of small growers. This conclusion is very misleading since it does not fully recognize the factors accounting for the observed differences in average yields. Small growers, on the whole, occupy lands which are less suited to bananas than the large growers; the former are usually located on steep hillslopes with shallow soils while the latter are generally located in fertile, alluvial valleys and plains. Furthermore, small growers generally follow a mixed cropping patter and consequently have lower planting densities than the large growers who produce bananas as a main enterprise. Thus although the data indicate that yields per acre are lower on small farms, this may be purely a reflection of the use of inappropriate acreage data.

A better indication of the relative performance of small growers is provided by data on the distribution of roots (plant population) and production, by size of farm, for Jamaica: These data suggest that stem output per root is higher on small farms than on the larger farms where the share of total production is disproportionately less than the share of plant population.[1] Furthermore, it cannot be assumed that relatively low yields necessarily reflect relatively high costs of production. For one thing, large farms rely heavily on hired labour for which they must pay competitive wages whereas small growers rely more heavily on family labour which may have a low opportunity cost.[2] Besides, large specialized farms may have heavy overheads directly chargeable to bananas while the low overheads on small farms are spread over a range of crops with only a portion chargeable to banana production.

A recent survey of banana production in St Lucia suggests that there are no significant differences in the performance of small as compared with large growers. The lower stem weights for small farms are, in this case, more or less offset by the higher stem yield per acre. And the somewhat higher cost of production indicated for small farms is more than likely attributable to the methodological bias noted above. All of this implies that the traditional argument that rationalization of the industry can be achieved simply by eliminating the small grower may well be misplaced.

The complex nature of banana production resulting mainly from the problem of disease control has, not unnaturally, led to the development of grower associations in the industry. These associations coordinate disease control, organize fertilizer issue and administer production schemes of one sort or another. Any grower with a minimum of 50 roots in Jamaica and 30 roots in the Windwards can register as a member; financial resources of these associations are derived from a cess on exported fruit. The associations serve a very useful purpose in an industry where coordination would otherwise be difficult because of the large number of scattered smallholders.

Marketing arrangements in the Windward Islands are also supervised and administered by the grower associations, each of which has a contractual agreement with Geest Industries Ltd, for the shipside purchase of total available export supply. Under the terms of the existing agreement, the price paid by Geest Industries to the associations consists of a 'basic payment', a shipping discount, and a share of ripening profits. The basic payment is determined by the 'green market price' – the price at which bananas are sold to green ripeners in the UK (which is determined by consultation between Windward Island Banana Growers' Association (WINBAN) and the company) – and is calculated by deducting company allowances and expenses. The shipping discount is based on utilization of available capacity and is calculated annually for loadings above 80% of capacity. The four associations share, according to the ratio of sales, one-half of the net profit realized by Geest from the sale of Windward Island bananas ripened by the company at its own centres in the UK.

In Jamaica, the Banana Board purchases fruit from growers at buying stations located all over the country; and it retains ownership of the fruit until delivered to wholesalers in the UK. The equalization principle also obtains here since the Board bears all expenses involved in transporting the fruit (by road and rail)from buying stations to ports and in loading on to boats. The Board arranges shipping and overseas distribution by means of shipping and marketing agreements with two agents: Elders and Fyffes Ltd (a subsidiary of United Fruit Co Ltd) which handles about three-quarters of the trade; and the Jamaica Banana Producers Association Ltd, contracted to handle about one-quarter.

The marketing agents, in addition to providing shipping space, are responsible for the discharge of fruit in the UK and subsequent distribution to ripening centres where the fruit is sold at the 'greenboat' price. It is important to note that the two marketing agents operate their own ripening rooms and account for a substantial share of the quantities ripened in the UK. The greenboat price which is realized by the Board must cover a number of payments: growers receipts, transportation to ports of shipment, selection and loading, freight and insurance, unloading and discharge at UK ports, transportation to distribution points in the UK and a commission (2.5%) for the agents. The price is determined and adjusted on the basis of assessment of market conditions by the agents (in consultation with the Banana Board).

On the whole, the Jamaican industry has a heavy administrative superstructure which creates substantial organizational diseconomies.

The Scope for Rationalization of Production and Marketing

Production and Internal Transport

Agricultural policy in the West Indies should generally be guided by the principle that in economies with low land/labour ratios (a land-scarce/labour-abundant factor endowment) land should be carefully economized. It was intimated earlier that there is a strong possibility that locational diseconomies may exist in the West Indian banana industry. This consideration is explored more fully in what follows.

The existing pattern of land use in the West Indies has been influenced to a large extent by the fact that the prices of export crops have more often than not been artificially high in relation to alternative production for the home market.[3]

Another and somewhat related factor is that the organized marketing of export crops has assured farmers of outlets for these products. Bananas have a further inherent advantage deriving from continuous cash receipts which the crop provides throughout the year. Banana production is therefore relatively attractive as a steady source of cash income, especially where alternative land use involves seasonal variations in receipts (as is the case with melons, sugar cane, etc.). These factors help to explain the widespread cultivation of this crop throughout the islands concerned.

In Jamaica, it seems that substantial economies could be derived from shifts in the location of production of most crops. In the case of bananas, a committee of experts from the Ministry of Agriculture have recommended that export production should be restricted to two regions – an eastern zone consisting of the parishes of St Mary, Portland and St Thomas, and a western zone including parts of St James, Hanover and Westmoreland. Such locational adjustments would have several major effects. First, the elimination of marginal-producing areas may lower the overall average cost of banana production. Second, the concentration of production would facilitate disease control and improvements in the technology of production. Third, the costs of purchasing and transporting fruit to ports would be considerably reduced. Fourth, administration of the industry would be less unwieldy and economies in this sphere would thus be secured. Fifth, production of foodstuffs for the home market could be increased if, as it appears, land withdrawn from bananas is suitable for this purpose.

It would be partly a matter of policy as to whether the shifts in location serve to increase or reduce the volume of exportable supply. One proposal that has been made is that there should be little or no change in total banana acreage; that acreage expansion should take place in the selected zones suffi-cient to offset the withdrawal of acreage elsewhere. This would no doubt have the effect of increasing total supply since average yields in the selected zones are probably higher than that in the marginal areas. Alternatively, if no expan-sion were to take place in the selected regions, total acreage would be reduced by some 15,000 acres and export supply would fall by about 30,000 tons. Clearly, the appropriate choice can only be determined after a decision is taken on what are desirable levels of output in terms of market availability and the relationship between output and revenue. If the market-sharing agreement with the Windwards becomes established then this will facilitate decision-making as regards desirable levels of acreage and output.

Some indication of the economies that would be derived from this kind of rationalization can be gained from an analysis of the implied savings in transportation costs alone. Average transportation costs in the selected zones are one-third to one-fifth of those in areas from which it is recommended that acreages should be withdrawn. It means that if the 30,000 tons now being produced in the marginal areas were instead produced in the selected areas, the cost of moving this volume of fruit to ports of shipment would be reduced from about £150,000 to approximately £38,000 (based on assumed average rates of £5 and £1.5.0. for marginal and selected areas, respectively.)

It has been pointed out by McFarlane that

the Jamaican industry is run at a higher overall cost [than that of the Windward Islands] . . . that whereas at the point of purchase from the grower the value per ton of export banana is lowest in Jamaica, at the point of shipping the cost per ton is the highest in the West Indies.[4]

Transportation, buying operations, hurricane insurance, leaf spot cess, shipping and loading and administrative expenses ('consisting largely of grants to the AIBGA and payments for company services') are all relatively high-cost elements in comparison to the Windwards Islands. And the cost of almost all of these items would tend to be reduced as a result of the proposed shifts in the location of production. Some indication of possible production cost economies which could be secured from shifts in the location of production in the Windward Islands can be gained from available cost of production data for farms of similar size groups in different ecological divisions.

These data suggest that there may not be significant production economies to be secured from locational shifts within St Lucia. And that such economies may be offset by transportation diseconomies; for example, it is likely that the cost of transporting fruit from the elevated central area would materially inflate the relatively low production cost indicated for the 5–25 acres farms in that region. Date with which to assess for the 5–25 acres farms in that region. Data with which to assess possible advantages to be gained from locational shifts between the four Windward Islands are not available.

The scope for rationalization of production in the Windward Islands will need to be examined in more detail if and when it becomes possible to travel in order to complete the research. At this point, it is sufficient to say that rationalization there must also be considered in the light of the desirability for diversification of production to reduce the dependence of these economies on bananas. Clearly, some new dynamic is required to sustain the economic development of these territories as the growth rate of banana output declines. And the island economies are now very vulnerable to market fluctuations and the vicissitudes of nature. This introduces new dimensions beyond that of security cost economies and may necessitate shifts in the location of production, and policies designed either to reduce acreages in bananas or to discourage further expansion of capacity.

It would be useful to consider briefly what scope exists for other kinds of production adjustments which may help to improve the competitive position of the industry. These need not be regarded as being alternatives to the proposed national locational adjustments; they could in fact be supplementary. Such cost of production data as are available suggest that labour is an important component of cost. Labour seems to account for over one-half of total production costs. Consequently, any reduction of labour costs would materially reduce total costs. However, banana production will only accommodate a limited amount of mechanization even if this were desirable.[5] In addition, it must be recognized that the banana industry is an important source of employment in these territories. In Jamaica, for example, it is estimated that about 50,000 people are employed in the production of bananas; that represents about one-sixth of the total agricultural labour force. Any mention of mechanization would need to be reconciled with the more pressing need of an expansion of employment opportunities.

Materials are also a major item of cost in producing bananas. One estimate indicates that materials may represent as much as 40% of the cost of establishing an acre of bananas. Though it seems that the share may be considerably lower than this (see McFarlane, footnote) it is reasonable to conclude that any possible reduction of cost of materials (fertilizers, wadding wrap, boxes etc.) would secure significant cost of economies. Fertilizer, in particular, seems to be an important element of production costs. It may be profitable, therefore, to explore the possibilities of lowering the cost of fertilizer and of securing economies in its application.

What all of the foregoing discussion suggests is that there is considerable scope for securing economies of production at the national level, particularly in respect of shifts in the location of production within Jamaica. The possible benefits to be derived from locational shifts within the region as a whole (*ie* between territories) is considered in the section on regional collaboration since the latter would be a *sine qua non* for such adjustments.

Some discussion of the kinds of policy mechanisms which could be introduced to promote the proposed rationalization of production is provided in the last section. It is sufficient at this stage to recognize that such shifts in the location of production as are conceived here would result in considerable dislocation in the rural sector. But since they will secure considerable economies for the industry and *at the same time set the stage for rationalization of agriculture as a whole*, the proposal deserves serious consideration. It seems almost unnecessary to mention that careful planning and appropriate policy mechanisms hold the key to the process of reconstruction.

It is useful to begin by examining present shipping and marketing expenses in order to detect the high cost elements through which the most significant economies can be secured. Data indicate that freight charges are most important, accounting for roughly two-thirds of the total marketing expenses involved in moving bananas from Jamaican ports to wholesalers in the UK. Distribution expenses and discharge at UK ports rank much lower, but are next in importance.

It appears that there is not much room for manoeuvre in respect of discharge and distribution costs. The former involves unloading of fruit at UK docks, reloading on to trucks and railroad cars, cargo dues or wharfage, and wages to riggers. These costs are strongly influenced by prevailing wage rates on British docks; but it is likely that the current shift over to boxed bananas will alter the techniques of unloading in such a way as to lower the labour input and this may well result in reduced costs. Distribution expenses are the actual railway charges for the movement of fruit from UK docks to wholesale points of sale; and payments by the Banana Board are made on the basis of railway and trucking vouchers submitted by the two marketing agents.

From all accounts, it seems most profitable to concentrate attention on the possibilities of securing shipping economies. Studies undertaken by the Secretariat of the General Agreement on Tariffs and Trade (GATT) indicate that for a banana boat with a refrigerated hold capacity of 250,000 cubic feet, an average speed of 17 knots, a load of 95% capacity, a 4% allowance for shrinkage, and no return cargo, the cost per ton of transporting bananas from Jamaica to the UK can be as low as £14.5.8. The actual freight charges on Jamaican fruit over the past few years have been substantially higher than the GATT estimate which is based on no return cargo. Over the period 1962–64, for example, the average freight charge was actually £19.17.2. The disparity seems to be related to the age and ownership of ships in operation and, unquestionably, on the underutilization of available capacity.

The majority of boats operated by the two shipping agents have been at sea for anywhere from 18 to 42 years. These are normally slower boats and operational costs therefore tend to be high. Ownership is of some importance since it appears that freight costs are lower in the case of chartered vessels. The cost per ton for fruit carried in chartered boats on the Jamaica–UK run in 1964 was less than £15 as compared with an overall freight cost of over £20.

It is also necessary to analyse the effect of the escalator provision in the shipping agreement which ties freight rates to the greenboat price. This arrangement seems to give the marketing agents a distinct advantage since they are engaged in ripening activities in addition to shipping.[6] The greenboat price is a cost price to the ripener. A 'unit' increase of £3.10 in the greenboat price raises the shipper-ripener's cost by only £2.9 as the Banana Board loses £1.1 of the increase with extra freight charges. And although a fall in the greenboat price reduces the freight, the shipper-ripener stands to gain on the ripening end through lower input costs. On balance, it seems that only the Board stands to lose since the agents are in a position to hedge profits on shipping transactions against that on their ripening operations. Windward Island producers seem to be better placed in this respect because Geest Industries shares its ripening profits with the growers' associations.

The gross realization of the Banana Board consists of returns from UK sales at the greenboat price, a premium paid by the marketing agents for stems wrapped in Diothene and a quality bonus for boxed fruit, and sales of rejected fruit at Jamaican ports. Net realization is derived after deducting overseas marketing expenses; and from this the Board meets domestic expenses and payments to the grower. The table shows some relevant data for a few years. It indicates that the growers' share of gross realization has been declining steadily and suggests an upward trend in marketing expenses.

Table 1.3 *Sales realization per ton of fruit discharged and payments to growers, Jamaica 1958 and 1962–64*

United Kingdom Sales							
	Gross Realization						
Year	Total £	Fruit £	Premium £	Jamaican Sales £	Net Realization £	Payment to Growers £	Grower Share of Gross Realization %
1958	74.19.2	72.1.8	1.13.0	0.3.8	40.17.9	23.16.0	31.7
1962	61.1.2	59.6.3	1.13.7	0.1.4	31.10.10	16.13.3	27.2
1963	61.16.8	60.1.6	1.13.8	0.1.6	31.9.2	14.12.6	23.6
1964	68.7.2	63.13.8	4.12.9	0.0.9	36.1.2	15.1.9	22.0

Source: Jamaica Banana Board

The foregoing discussion leads to the general conclusion that substantial economies could be secured from a reform of shipping arrangements and that returns to the industry could be increased if an appropriate pricing policy is introduced within the framework of existing marketing arrangements. The difficulties encountered in negotiating new shipping and marketing agreements in Jamaica in recent years suggests that no substantial improvement in the terms, in favour of the Jamaican industry, are likely to be achieved. Industry officials there may, however, try to secure some profit-sharing agreement similar to the Windward-Geest arrangement.

In order to secure the shipping economies that appear to exist, it would be necessary for West Indian banana exporters to establish an independent shipping service for the trade, beginning perhaps with chartered vessels. But since the difficulties involved are greater for any single territory,[7] it seems that such a move would almost certainly be facilitated by regional collaboration. The matter is, therefore, considered further in the following section. For the moment, it is sufficient to note that in addition to the lowering of shipping costs, the establishment of a national or regional service would place West Indian growers in a position to determine and adjust the greenboat price and, thereby, to have a better influence on grower returns. And, furthermore, an increased share of the value added to bananas leaving the West Indies would accrue to the regional economies.

The Scope for Regional Collaboration

In this section, the scope for regional collaboration in production and marketing is considered in the light of the extent to which collaboration per se can promote one or other (or all) of the following: (a) better and more stable market prices and returns to the growers; (b) an improvement in the competitive position of the industry; (c) the development of new market outlets; (d) an increase in the contribution of the industry to the regional economies. insofar as collaboration can achieve these, a strong case can be made in its favour.

Production

Within the existing framework of the industry,it is not unlikely that if all the territories were to combine in the purchasing of material inputs, growers may well be able to secure lower input prices. By and large, grower associations are confronted with monopolistic sellers of materials such as fertiliser. Regional cooperation would place growers in a monopolistic position. It has already been demonstrated (in the foregoing section) that materials are an important item of production costs.

Regional shifts in the location of production deserve to be considered as a means of improving the competitive position of the industry. Studies of the cost of producing bananas in different areas of Jamaica and of the Windward Islands should be undertaken in order to determine locational advantages within the region as a whole. Production is, of course, only one aspect of costs; consideration must also be given to the costs of internal transportation.

As indicated earlier, present costs for moving bananas from farms on to boats are considerably higher in Jamaica than in the Windwards. McFarlane has calculated that the costs involved in 1959 in Jamaica were two to three times in the Windwards. These data suggest that substantial economies could be secured for the regional industry by an expansion of capacity and production in the Windward Islands and a simultaneous contraction in Jamaica.[8] However, it is unlikely that Jamaica would contemplate such a step unless it could secure tangible benefits in return. And the Windward Islands may, for other reasons, wish to diversify their economies from the present almost monocultural situation. A regional policy of 'export substitution' may provide Jamaica with *quid pro quo* for the suggested regional locational adjustments.

McIntyre spells out the possibilities in his discussion of the potential for regional economic cooperation as follows:[9]

. . . a participating country may be willing to trade quicker access to its internal market . . . for greater access to markets in the rest of the world, where it is competing with another participating country. In this case, the latter country will increase its exports to the regional market, at the expense of foregoing *increases* in exports to the rest of the world. This may lead over time, to an increase in exports for both countries, if they are giving up market opportunities for producing goods with low-growth potential for opportunities to export goods with a higher growth potential [emphasis added].

He then goes on to consider the particular case of Jamaica and the Windward Islands in banana exports by hypothesizing that

if Jamaica's *incremental* comparative advantage is in light manufactures, while that of the Windwards is in bananas, it may be to their mutual advantage for the Windwards to encourage their residents to consume Jamaican manufactures, if Jamaica agrees in turn to hold off some of her bananas from the world market. This may not necessarily involve a reduction in Jamaican exports of bananas; all it may mean is that Jamaica will aim at a much slower *rate of increase* in her banana exports [emphasis added].

The argument which is here advanced is that such a policy could be used to secure a market in the Windward Islands for foodstuffs which can be grown in the areas of Jamaica from which bananas are withdrawn.[10] In this manner, regional collaboration would facilitate the internal locational shifts proposed for Jamaica in the previous section and at the same time further improve the regional industry's competitive position. It would also have the overall effect of increasing import substitution of food for the region as a whole and is, therefore, not entirely out of line with existing policies at the national level.

In the light of these considerations, it would appear that the recent agreement on rationalization of supplies to the UK market, based as it is on fixed shares of the market, will tend to impede the rationalization of production which could improve the industry's competitive position. A more appropriate arrangement in this connection would have been to allow for all the *incremental* demand in the UK market to be supplied by the Windwards in exchange for a guaranteed market in the Windwards for Jamaican foodstuffs. Jamaica could then proceed with the internal adjustments proposed above, since the combined home and Windward market for foodstuffs would be sufficiently wide to allow for sizeable areas to be withdrawn from bananas and allocated to production of the required foodstuffs. A contractual arrangement with the Windwards would enable the Jamaican government to establish guaranteed prices and other incentives for farmers in the areas concerned to transfer from bananas to other crops and/or livestock.

Shipping and Overseas Marketing

The need for opening a West Indian shipping line for transporting banana overseas was established earlier. And it was intimated there that regional collaboration would facilitate this. The nucleus for a service of this kind does in fact already exist. A Jamaican enterprise, the Jamaican Banana Producers' Association Ltd, already participates in the trade. This company which began as a cooperative venture is now based on share capital subscribed by growers and it operates 5 of the 15 banana boats serving Jamaica, in addition to ripening centres in the UK. Only 25% of the Jamaican trade is now handled by the company. And it is alleged that one important factor limiting further expansion is the complete dependence on this single source of supplies, with attendant high risks. If the company had access to supplies from all the West Indian territories, this would reduce risks and facilitate its expansion. The company could be extended with share capital subscribed by Windward Island growers to make it a West Indian Banana Producers' Association and a share of the Windward trade could then be reserved for its expanded operation. In the short run at least, heavy reliance could be placed on chartered vessels.

In addition to the favorable effects it would have on shipping and marketing costs a regional banana shipping service would contribute further by reducing current out-payments for shipping services (a balance of payment effect); by increasing government revenues through the payment of company taxes in the West Indies;[11] and by creating additional incomes and employment for West Indians.

It must be recognized, however, that there are a number of problems involved in order to establish the service. At least two of these need to be mentioned here. The first is that it may be difficult to secure sanction for a regional line from the International Shipping Conference. But this may not be necessary for the type of service proposed. The second is that both Jamaica and the Windwards now have contractual agreements with the respective marketing agencies which may not allow for such changes as are proposed during the lifetime of these agreements. In the case of the Windwards, for example, the contract binds grower associations to provide the agent *with all available export fruit*. However, if a new market were to develop this would obviate the present contractual difficulties in the case of Jamaica at least.

The importance of new markets is further emphasized by the current and projected oversupply situation on the UK market (see the first section above). And in this connection, a start has already been made towards regional collaboration. First, the islands were all engaged jointly in a small trade with Italy during the past year; and, second, they have opened up the question of a market in Canada at the official level.[12] The prospects for a trade with Canada seem to be relatively good. Although it was demonstrated earlier that f.o.b. values of Jamaican fruit are higher than those for the Latin American countries now supplying Canada, it is also true that bananas from Jamaica could now enter Canada at a c.i.f. (Montreal) value not significantly different from the values for current Canadian imports. The explanation for this seems to be that because Canada is an extension of the United States market bananas are transported over expensive overland routes from cargoes discharged at various ports in the United States.

The problem still remains, however, that entry into the market may be difficult because of the imperfect nature of the Canadian trade. Government intervention may be necessary and in that event the trade would most likely be offered to all the regional exporters. Regional collaboration in supplying such a market would be highly desirable for a number of reasons: first, to ensure a regular flow of supplies; second, to allow for development of the regional shipping service; and, third, to secure certain economies of ocean transport. The last reason advanced is based on the consideration that Jamaica is somewhat close to the Canadian market and that, consequently, freight costs would be lower on Jamaican than on Windward Island fruit.

Collaboration could be along the following lines. The Canadian trade should be given exclusively to the proposed expanded regional Banana Producers' Association. The Association could charter vessels for the trade and sell directly to ripeners in Halifax and Montreal. Supplies should normally be drawn from Jamaica but the company would have to be provided with an option on Windward Island fruit in the case of a hurricane affecting Jamaica or other shortfalls in Jamaican supplies. Returns from the trade would, of course, be shared equally between Jamaica and the Windwards even though *physical* supplies are normally drawn from the former.

The prospects of securing new markets, other than Canada, for West Indian bananas are not at all bright – chiefly because of the weak competitive position of the industry and the general oversupply situation in world trade.

The Soviet Union is perhaps the only undersupplied importing country at present. But the politics of the situation seems to rule out the possibility of exploring this market both at the national and regional levels.[13] In the present setting that would seem to demand extraregional collaboration with other banana-exporting countries.

Cooperation with Other Countries

The West Indies could benefit materially from cooperation with other banana-exporting countries in several respects. Within the Caribbean there are further possibilities for export substitution with the French West Indies, the Dominican Republic, Central America and Colombia. If the full potential here were to be explored, it may be that a country like Jamaica could eventually and profitably move completely out of export banana production.

The FAO of the United Nations convened the first session of its Banana Study Group early in 1966. Jamaica is a member of the Group while the Windwards are represented by the UK. At present, the Group is concerned mainly with a continuous review of world banana trade and outlook. But as in the case of some other commodities, it could be the nucleus of a future international banana agreement. The West Indies now benefit from participation in the Group since the industry does not have the resources of its own with which to assess long-term market situation and outlook.

Finally, association with other countries provides an opportunity for trying to get Eastern European countries to expand their banana imports. This is a potentially large banana-consuming region. These centrally planned economies with moderately high incomes have "the capacity to import substantial quantities of bananas if controls were relaxed". Some indication of this is given by the fact that "if consumption in these countries rose from its present negligible level of 0.05 kilograms to, say, 3.0 kilograms per head, which was about half the current West European average, imports would be of the order of 1 million tons per annum, the equivalent of one-quarter of total world imports in 1963".[14] The banana-exporting countries as a group should try to influence the Soviet Union to relax its controls on banana imports. Perhaps as a start that country would be persuaded to participate in the FAO Banana Study Group.

Policy Implications and Proposals

The present study has indicated that there is considerable scope for improving the competitive position of the regional banana industry by means of locational shifts within individual territories (Jamaica) as well as between different territories. The proposed shifts would result in economies of both production and internal transportation of bananas. The study has also suggested that the establishment of a regional banana shipping service would serve to reduce present costs of overseas marketing and increase returns from the industry to the regional economies. Implementation of the proposals made would require a significant degree of regional cooperation. It would also require certain policy measures at both national and regional levels.

The locational adjustments proposed for Jamaica should be part of an overall policy to rationalize the pattern of land use. A system of zoning should be applied to all agricultural activity and measures should be introduced to induce farmers to make the required adjustments. Since farmers on the whole tend to be guided by the relative profitability of alternative enterprises, price policies are of major importance. An appropriate structure of output prices is an important initial step; but supplementary measures relating to marketing and other services would be required as well. So far as bananas are concerned, a number of points can be made here in this connection.

Initially, the present practice of buying export bananas throughout Jamaica should be discarded. Instead, the Banana Board should operate buying stations only in the two selected banana zones. In order to continue in export production, then, growers outside of these zones would have to transport their fruit to some point in the selected areas. This would tend to increase their cost of production reduce current profits on bananas and improve the competitive position of alternative enterprises. But it would be further necessary for government actively to encourage the transfer of land to particular uses by offering guaranteed prices and markets and technical assistance for the particular crops into which the land should be transferred.[15]

The savings in banana transportation costs could justifiably be used to subsidize these farmers in making the transfer. It will also be necessary to recognize that bananas provide a steady income flow so that some provision must be made to adjust whatever seasonal income flows alternative crops may involve.

The prices received by growers for export bananas would need to be adjusted in accordance with the desirable total banana acreage and output. This, in turn, will depend on market requirements. If, for example, an expansion of acreage is required part of the economies secured from the rationalization should be passed on to growers in the selected banana areas in terms of higher grower prices. But to maintain current acreage (as was proposed in the second section) no change in grower prices would be necessary. If the adjustments are effected simultaneously with a programme of export substitution with the Windwards, the Jamaica Agricultural Marketing Corporation could make contractual arrangements with farmers in areas from which bananas are to be withdrawn for the purchase of certain foodstuffs in order to satisfy

Windward requirements as well as those of the home market. Such intraregional trade in food products as would arise would, of course, necessitate proper intraregional shipping facilities.[16]

Regional collaboration in the production and external marketing of bananas as envisaged in this study could hardly proceed purely on the initiative of growers themselves. It would be greatly facilitated by an overall policy for regional economic integration. The various studies in this series will provide some basic information with which to assess the benefits to be derived from such a policy. The present study has indicated that the regional banana industry could profit materially thereby. West Indian governments need to anticipate a drastic change in the market for export agriculture as a result of possible loss of preferential markets. Any policy proposals which will serve to strengthen the competitive position of these export industries need to be seriously considered – especially if, as in the present case, the proposals are complementary to existing policies for food-import substitution.

Notes

*An abbreviated version of "The West Indian banana industry: the scope for rationalization and regional collaboration". *Studies in Regional Economic Integration* 2:3 (1967a).

1   This conclusion may not, however, apply to weight yields in terms of exportable supply since average stem weight may be higher on large farms and since the rate of reject may also be lower for production on these farms.

2   As Clayton has suggested, "The peasant cultivator is, in certain circumstances, a low-cost producer of cash-crop products. At least three conditions need to be present for this to apply. That only food crops are production alternatives to a cash crop. That little or no hired labour is used – implying small cash outlay. That production and processing of cash crops on a small scale are relatively simple". See Eric Clayton, *Agrarian Development in Peasant Economies* (Oxford: Pergammon Press, 1964), pp. 74-75.

3   This is the result of preferential arrangements for export crops and a generally open market situation for food consumed at home.

4   Dennis McFarlane, "The future of the banana industry in the West Indies", *Social and Economic Studies* (March 1964), p.73.

5   Regardless of technical possibilities, consideration would have to be given to the cost of machine inputs in terms of scarce foreign exchange and the employment effect of such mechanization in labour surplus economies like the West Indies.

6   The advantage applies *a fortiori* in the case of Elders and Fyffes which ripens the bulk of the fruit transported by that firm.

7   For example, a geographical spread in sources of supply is necessary for banana shipping since wind and hurricane damage in any one territory would materially affect utilization of available shipping space.

8   It is possible that increased production in the Windwards would raise costs above the levels indicated in the tabulation above, particularly if more remote areas have to be brought into production. But it is unlikely that such an increase would raise costs to the level indicated for Jamaica. Some account should also be taken of the possibility that the organizational reforms now taking place in Jamaica may materially reduce the cost indicated above.

9   Alister McIntyre, "Some issues of trade policy in the West Indies", *New World Quarterly* (Croptime 1966), pp. 18-19. This article is also published in somewhat more detail under the title "Decolonisation and trade policy in the West Indies", in *The Caribbean in Transition*, eds. Fust Andio and Thomas Matthews. Proceedings of the Second Caribbean Scholars Conference (Puerto Rico: Institute of Caribbean Studies, University of Puerto Rico, 1965).

10 Consideration would have to be given to the terms-of-trade effect of such export substitution. Prices of bananas will not necessarily move in line with those of the foodstuffs concerned; and either Jamaica or the Windwards may suffer an adverse terms-of-trade effect over time in the particular arrangement here proposed. It may also be argued that Jamaica may be in a position to expand both banana and foodstuff production and will not therefore benefit materially from such an arrangement. But that is a matter which can be better appraised in the light of the companion study by Brewster and Thomas, *The Dynamics of West Indian Economic Integration* (Mona, Jamaica: ISER, University of the West Indies).

11 A firm like Elders and Fyffes which is incorporated in the UK pays company taxes in that country and not in the West Indies.

12 At the Canada-West Indies Conference held in Ottawa, July 1966.

13 A recent appeal by the Chairman of the Jamaica All-Island Banana Growers' Association that efforts be made to establish a banana trade with "Socialist bloc" nations (see *Daily Gleaner*, 11 August 1966) drew no response from government. Months later, the Minister of Trade and Industry stated that his government did not view trade with the Soviet Union as a possibility because the barter arrangement would prove unprofitable for Jamaica and because political factors are involved (see *Daily Gleaner*, 17 December 1966).

14 FAO Committee on Commodity Problems, *Report of the ad hoc Meeting on Banana (Economic Aspects)*, CCP 65/4 (December 1964), p. 3.

15 Guaranteed prices, marketing facilities, etc. for particular crops should only apply in those regions selected for production of those crops. Some knowledge of relevant supply elasticities in all cases would, of course, be essential.

16. Consideration of ways and means of promoting a general intraregional trade in agricultural products is the subject of a seperate paper. See G.L. Beckford and M.H. Guscott, "Non-Tariff Mechanisms for Increasing Intra-Caribbean Trade in Agricultural Products". *Studies in Regional Economic Integration* 2:2 (1967).

2

Issues in the Windward–Jamaica Banana War*

The movement from colonialism to independence in the West Indies in recent years has been associated with internal conflict over one issue or another. There has hardly been a dull moment. The debate on the siting of the Federal capital, the Jamaican oil refinery issue, to federate or not to federate, and during the past year, the Windward-Jamaica banana conflict, are but a few outstanding examples. A clear exposition of the real issues involved in these conflicts is necessary in order to understand the dilemma of West Indian society at this critical state. The present paper attempts to analyse the most recent conflict in these terms.

Ever since the banana became a commodity of international trade in the late nineteenth century, Jamaica has been the chief West Indian exporter. Today, the situation has changed with the four Windward Islands of Dominica, St Lucia, St Vincent and Grenada together rivalling Jamaica for the top berth. All the islands depend almost exclusively on the British market for their banana exports. Export production in the Windwards expanded at a dramatic rate over the past ten years from about 3 million stems a year in 1956 to over 10 million stems in 1964. And by the end of last year Windward supplies to the UK were slightly greater than those from Jamaica. Unfortunately, the combined total of Jamaica and the Windwards exceeded the amount the market could absorb at price levels obtaining in recent years and the bottom fell out of the market. Though prices have rallied since, they have generally remained below seasonal levels of recent years.

These developments have stimulated stormy debates between interested parties as well as between governments. The debates have provided some insight into the factors which create an impasse between West Indian territories over this and other issues. First, the banana war clearly exposes the vulnerability of the territories to manipulation by outside interests when operating as separate units. Second, public discussions arising from the conflict reveal the consistent failure of the West Indian Press (insofar as the *Daily Gleaner* is typical) to analyse regional (and other) issues from the point of view of popular West Indian interests. Third, the conflict reveals the ambivalence of the 'better-off' units like Jamaica in their relations with the 'less advanced' territories on the one hand, and the rest of the world on the other.

In the first place, it will be established that these recent developments in the banana trade have resulted mainly from a conflict between two private firms and that no real conflict of interests existed between banana growers in Jamaica and the Windwards. West Indian growers were caught as pawns in a game between the agents they selected to market their fruit.

The banana industry in the West Indies as a whole consists of numerous small independent growers and a few relatively large producers. Administratively, the industry in the Windward Islands is serviced by grower cooperative-type associations which contract with Geest Industries Ltd, for marketing all export fruit. Decision making is simple, straightforward and relatively well representative of grower interests. And the associations have been able to secure good marketing arrangements from the agent.

The Jamaican industry, on the other hand, is serviced by an inefficient administrative superstructure consisting of the AIBGA, a growers' association, a statutory insurance scheme and the Banana Board, a statutory body which is the sole exporting agent. Recently, the inefficiencies were exposed by a team of foreign marketing consultants though they have been recognized by local observers for several years. The consultants, in fact, merely extended points made by the local Sharp Commission of 1958-59, as they themselves admitted in their report. For exporting fruit, the Banana Board contracts with Elders and Fyffes, a subsidiary of United Fruit Company, and Jamaica Banana Producers Association, a Jamaican grower enterprise; but the latter is allotted only a minor share of total exports. Consequently, it is not considered in the rest of the discussion in this section.

All West Indian growers have the same basic interest: to obtain the best possible prices for all the fruit they supply to the market. This no one will deny. A struggle between growers for market shares is out of line with this basic interest since it is clear that higher prices could be obtained through cooperation, not only in regulating market supplies but also in realizing shipping economics if cooperation were extended to joint shipment by West Indian growers themselves. The marketing agents, on the other hand, are each primarily concerned with earning the highest possible rate of profit. Each agent would be better able to achieve this if it had a monopoly on the market. Elders and Fyffes were, indeed, in such a position before the emergence of Geest Industries; and have therefore, been seriously concerned with the rapid erosion of their controlling and dominant position. There is no question that they would be in a happier position with Van Geest entirely out of the market, but, at worst, they would be prepared to make an accommodation if only they could control the larger share of the market. The rapid growth of Van Geest, on the other hand, must surely have demonstrated to that firm the possibility that one day it might capture the whole market or at worst acquire control of the major share. There has as yet been no evidence that the two are prepared for a compromise market-share agreement. In the normal course of events, some form of market agreement would tend to emerge when competitive tactics (price-cutting, etc.), have resulted in sustained losses by either or both firms.

The point at issue here, however, is that the basic interests of the two groups of West Indian growers are more in line with each other than they are with the private interests of the respective marketing agents. Yet it appears that each agent was able to manipulate the representatives of each group of growers to align with the individual agent and, thus, create an artificial conflict between Windwards and Jamaican grower representatives.

Even before the first big price decline of mid October, grower representatives from Jamaica and the Windwards had decided to meet and discuss "the orderly marketing of fruit in the UK". The meeting had been scheduled for late October 1964. The *Daily Gleaner* of 17 October, 1964 made the following statement in reporting on the forthcoming parley. "The Windwards have always accepted it (agreement on the regulation of supplies) in principle. But they make it clear that they wanted their share of supplies to the market to be on percentage. This the Banana Board (Jamaica) was never willing to concede."

The talks began in Kingston on 22 October, and from the outset it was clear that the issue of market-sharing would be the focus of attention. The *Daily Gleaner* of 23 October, reporting on the opening of the conference stated that: "One of the principal bases for arriving at agreement on not overflooding the market . . . in the future will be the percentage of British demand which each territory is supplying at the time of agreement, informed sources at the Banana Building report."

The grower representatives met by themselves for the first two days. Prior to the conference they had invited their respective marketing agents to join the talks in the closing stages, ostensibly to inform them of whatever decisions the representatives themselves made earlier. But after two days, the representatives could reach no agreement. Time posed no immediate problem. They had a weekend ahead during which time they could have a chance to consult with their government, with others and with themselves informally in order to pave the way for a mutually satisfactory compromise. Instead, they took the traditional, easy, but disastrous, alternative of asking 'outside' interests to solve the problem for them. According to a *Gleaner* report of 24 October:

No formula was agreed . . . Instead it was agreed that the 14 Windward Islands representatives . . . will consult with Mr. N. Van Geest on Monday morning next for evolution of a satisfactory formula. At the same time, the Jamaican representatives . . . will consult with Elders and Fyffes and the Jamaica Banana Producers Association . . . [After that] the two sides will meet again to see if a mutually satisfactory arrangement can be made.

This time the 'outside' arbitrators were the two private firms with vested interests in the final outcome – interests which, as indicated above, are somewhat out of line with those of the growers themselves and which remained irreconcilable in the particular situation. The nature of the case is undoubtedly clearer in retrospect but even at the time it should have been obvious to any serious observer that the difference could not be resolved by reference to the two agents involved in a private struggle for market control. Indeed, this was the surest way to consolidate the impasse. Since there is no evidence that the representatives deliberately wanted the talks to fail, their course of action must be interpreted as reflecting complete ignorance of the real issues involved in the situation.

The same *Gleaner* report of 24 October stated that the reasons why no agreement had yet been reached were (i) that the Windward Islands would not bind themselves without prior Geest approval and (ii) the problem of supply quota (*ie* the quantities of fruit to be marketed in future by Jamaica and the Windwards respectively). Jamaica wanted these to be based on 1963 shipments or on an average of the past three years while the Windwards wanted the quotas to be based on shipments in the last quarter prior to the talks, July–September 1964. Jamaica's proposal was basically preposterous. It would ensure that Jamaica, and Elders and Fyffes, would be continually assured of the major market share. And it made no concession to the fact that the Windwards' production was still expanding while that of Jamaica had been stable for some time.

The Windwards' proposal, on the other hand, involved concession on their part since in any realistic projection of supplies their share of the market in the July-September quarter would be smaller than would normally obtain in subsequent years. In fact, by December 1964 weekly arrivals in the UK from the Windwards exceeded Jamaica's supplies by 25%. In refusing the Windwards' proposal the Jamaica representatives revealed a characteristic shortsightedness and poor judgement. Past experience should have guided them to accept the proposal. For they had once before had the chance to secure a more favourable share if only they had conceded the principle of market-sharing on the occasion when the Windwards had first suggested this as the basis for regulating supplies to the UK. They should, by now, have realized that postponement would always favour the Windwards.

Jamaica's proposal would no doubt have been satisfactory for Elders and Fyffes since it assured them of a major market share which they would otherwise fail to achieve. And they would never accept the Windwards' proposal so long as the one put forward by Jamaica remained a possibility. On the other hand, neither proposal could reasonably have been expected to satisfy Van Geest whose position would improve over time without any agreement. It should have surprised no one when the talks broke down after each delegation consulted with its marketing agent on the question of appropriate market shares.

After the breakdown of the talks, the banana bureaucracy in Jamaica launched a hostile campaign against the Windward Islands. The policy of the Board in fact, seemed to have been dictated more by the private interests of Elders and Fyffes than by the true interests of Jamaican growers, as the following considerations suggest. The *Daily Gleaner* of 4 November, carried the headlines: "Parley fails; Jamaica moves to counter Windwards' drive for 200,000 tons next year." The news item reported on a decision of the Banana Board to launch a "crash programme for bananas" aiming at "250,000 tons (from present 175,000) in 1965". In announcing this, a spokesman for the Board was reported to have said: "it would be just plainly stupid for us, in such circumstances to stand by and allow the market in which we have always held sway to be dominated by those whom we must now regard, regretfully, as our direct competitors."

The *Gleaner* of 21 November further stated that the industry leaders in Jamaica were convinced that "the only way to avoid being pushed around was to have superior production to the Windwards."

As already suggested above, the primary interest of Jamaican and all West Indian growers must be to secure the best possible prices for the fruit they produce for export. It is clear, therefore, that a forced expansion programme would be detrimental to their interest since this would result in oversupply and lower prices for all growers. To the growers themselves, dominance in the market must be a minor consideration, especially if this can only be achieved through a loss in revenue.

More direct evidence that the Banana Board was being used by Elders and Fyffes to help solve the latter's market control problem – at the expense of West Indian growers – is provided by the following news item in the *Gleaner* of 28 November, after prices had fallen to £49.15 a ton with an oversupply of fruit:

Two top executives of Elders and Fyffes . . . flew into Kingston . . . to advise the Banana Board of the marketing position and to arrive at a policy line . . . It is understood that decision was taken to exercise none of the curbs on shipment of bananas which are usually done when colder conditions set in and only best quality fruit is sent forward. The reasoning behind this decision was that any such measure would only cause the Windward Islands to expand their position in the market. It is now official banana industry policy to surrender no ground in the UK banana market.

It is clear from this that the Banana Board had passed the initiative for decision making and policy formulation over to Elders and Fyffes. A Statutory Authority is supposed to be responsible for policy formulation within the framework of overall Government policy. If it cannot perform this function it should be dissolved. In this case, the Board, it seems, was merely acting as an agent for implementing the policy decisions of its marketing agent instead of the reverse! Ironically, these policy decisions were to the detriment of all West Indian growers. For as I indicated in *Caribbean Quarterly* (June 1964):

. . . it is clear that if the proposed expansion (in Jamaica) were to materialize, the only losers will be the growers themselves. The market will absorb the proposed increase in supply only at lower prices than would otherwise obtain; thus the British consumer will pay less for bananas, the marketing companies will earn more from the increased volume handled, the only the West Indian grower stands to lose.

By and large, the way in which industry leaders in the West Indies were exploited by private foreign interests (to the detriment of the growers they represent) is perhaps a reflection of the general bankruptcy of the whole leadership class in the West Indies. But of equal significance is the fact that the West Indies make themselves more vulnerable to this kind of self-destructive manipulation by outsiders when operating as separate units. For it is clear that if we were together as one unit, the scope for artificial conflicts of this type would be reduced.

More interesting days still lie ahead because Fyffes and United Fruit are aware of the limitations to expansion of production in Jamaica and are currently seeking another Commonwealth source of supplies to solve their market control problem. It now seems that British Guiana will be the choice for dupe since negotiations with British Honduras were terminated following Dr Jagan's defeat in Guyana. Earlier plans for production in Guyana had been suspended because the company was uncertain of Jagan's political posture. In a few years, then, Jamaica and Guyana will be at each others throats and the present honeymoon between the Banana Board and Fyffes will be over. The handwriting is on the wall for those who care to see.

———

One of the main functions of a responsible press is to help clarify public issues by exposing the real issues involved in particular situations. When this function is properly performed, the society as a whole is in a better position to evaluate and to demand rational decisions. The scope for arbitrary decisions is thereby reduced.

Throughout the 'banana war' and subsequently, the *Daily Gleaner* editorials provided no enlightenment and its reporting of events has been, on the whole, loose. Its editorials generally supported the Board's (or rather Elders and Fyffes') policy even though it reproduced some enlightened statements from the British press. Two examples will illustrate. In an editorial prior to the October conference, the *Gleaner* of 7 October stated that:

The Windward Islands have already expanded production and reduced costs while Jamaica has not. And any agreement to control production and maintain prices would benefit that country (sic) more than it would Jamaica. Under the present situation . . . we would not be able to dictate terms but would be dictated to.

And after talks broke down and a crisis loomed, a *Gleaner* editorial of 17 November had this to say: "This [Windward Island] expansion has already affected Jamaica's market . . . Since autumn this year, the green-boat price has been decided largely by the Windward Islands agents in the UK Jamaica has been placed in the humiliating position of merely holding on."

The *Gleaner*, it would seem, regarded dominance of Jamaica in the market as a primary objective. For what purpose, it is difficult to say. From an objective point of view, this line of reasoning would suggest that we return to the horse and buggy because this was the dominant form of transportation before the coming of motor cars!

Not once did the *Gleaner* itself suggest that so far as West Indian growers are concerned the conflict was an artificial one created by a struggle for market control by two private firms. Not even after it published the following excerpts from a *Times* (London) editorial in its 4 January issue. The *Times*, commenting on the oversupply situation which resulted in a late December price decline to £39.5 a ton, had this to say: "The glut has now produced an all-in-fight with Fyffes and Jamaica against Geest's and the Windwards . . . While the Jamaican producer faces ruin, Jamaica itself would suffer only a minor cut in its exports if the Windwards won! Is the fight necessary?"

This quotation clearly reveals that most of the points made in retrospect in the present article were obvious to any careful observer at the time. And that the British press showed greater awareness of the issues involved than the *Gleaner*, a West Indian paper! The *Times* editorial was precise in putting the marketing firms in the forefront of the battle while the *Gleaner* continued to interpret the conflict as one between the two groups of growers. The *Times* foresaw 'ruin' for the producer if the fight continued while the *Gleaner* was promoting further oversupply so long as there was more Jamaican fruit than Windward fruit on the market. "Is the fight necessary?" asked the *Times*. Not once was this question posed by the *Gleaner*.

The contrasting postures of the British and West Indian press in the discussion of the crisis is further indicated by the following enlightened excerpts from Lynceus of the *Economist* as reproduced by the *Daily Gleaner* of 20 January , 1965:

Since the beginning of November banana prices have slumped sharply and recently British housewives have been able to buy them at 8d a pound, the cheapest for more than 20 years. The facts behind this seemingly insignificant event have shown how consumers come out strikingly on top when newcomers burst into fields where there is near monopolistic control and when this leads to a period of cut-throat competition. In many sectors of industry and commerce there is ample scope for greater competition, but in the food industry some regard should be paid to the primary producer.

This statement is adequate insofar as it goes. However, it does not take cognizance of the fact that in this case the primary producers in the West Indies have some formal control of their destinies since the competing firms are contracted by the West Indian industry to market the fruit. And that, therefore, the West Indians have themselves to blame for allowing the market situation to get out of their own hands.

The same report continued to give a much more factual picture of the market struggle than the *Gleaner* or any other West Indian publication, except for

New World Fortnightly. It stated that the banana battle involved "two [sic] West Indian islands, the British Elders and Fyffes subsidiary of the mighty American-based United Fruit Company and the Dutch-born Geest brothers . . ." The report continued:

Before the last war and in the immediate postwar the Elders and Fyffes' subsidiary of United Fruit shipped in about 80% of all banana eaten in the UK. The bulk of this crop came from hundreds of small plantations in Jamaica . . . This was a virtual monopoly and so it stayed until 1952 when the Dutch-born brothers, Leonard and Jan Van Geest decided to play David to Fyffes Goliath . . . and signed a contract to buy and market every exportable banana grown on the Windward Islands.

Such a statement of the real market conflict would have set the stage for making the appropriate inferences, had the *Gleaner* been at all responsible to the public.

In the West Indies, only one publication (so far as I know) gave a true picture of what was happening. With its small circulation and limited resources and long before the *Times* and the *Economist*, *New World Fortnightly* (no. 4, 15 December 1964, p. 20) reported on the crisis and concluded as follows:

The real tragedy of this all is that what is essentially a struggle for control of the British market between the two private interests that are contracted to market fruit – Van Geest for the Windwards, and Elders and Fyffes for Jamaica – has been transformed into a struggle between Windwards' and Jamaica's growers . . . The case is clear but the Jamaica banana bureaucracy can only see through the eyes of United Fruit. Come Mr Tallyman! Day deh light!

This was a most significant statement at the time. But it perhaps went unseen, given the limited circulation of *New World Fortnightly*. It does, however, indicate that there are possibilities for incisive and enlightened reporting here in the West Indies if we develop such publications as are committed to uncovering the truth and exposing the real issues confronting West Indian society.

———

Most of us are now well aware of the functional limitations of the conventional West Indian press. The manner in which the *Daily Gleaner* participated in the banana debate is only one example of an everyday phenomenon. It was also bad enough that the representatives of the West Indian industry, particularly those in Jamaica, allowed themselves to be manoeuvred by the private marketing firms. But perhaps the most disconcerting aspect of the entire debate is the fact that when the Jamaican Government formally entered the picture, its spokesman – the Minister of Trade and Industry – endorsed the Banana Board's policy which, as pointed out above, was really handed down by Elders and Fyffes and which was hardly in the true interest of Jamaican growers.

The following excerpt is taken from a policy statement by Mr Lightbourne, Jamaica's Trade Minister, "on his return from Britain where he had talks with Jamaica's agents on the island's banana trade there" (*Daily Gleaner*, 6 February 1965): ". . . it is essential at this time that we continue to sell all we can to Britain, because if we do not the Windwards will flood the market with their surplus production . . . we must not allow the Windwards to take over from us in a market that is traditionally ours."

It appears that Mr Lightbourne, like the Board, allowed himself to be bamboozled by Elders and Fyffes who no doubt seduced him with the argument of traditional Jamaican dominance, as if this could in anyway increase export earnings and bring more incomes to Jamaican banana growers. On the contrary, since dominance would mean oversupply on the market it could only be secured through lower prices to growers. All along, Fyffes was playing on Jamaica's characteristic insularity and petty nationalism which blinded not only the Banana Board and the *Gleaner* but the Jamaican Government as well. None of these could see the real issues involved even though they were obvious enough, as *New World Fortnightly*, the *Times* and the *Economist* were able to demonstrate.

The constitutional independence of Jamaica appears farcical in the particular context. For the Government had the appearance of a puppet for the ventriloquist, Elders and Fyffes. Whereas the chain of policy formulation and decision-making should normally be from the Government to the Statutory Authority then to the Authority's marketing agent for implementation, the actual linkage in this case was backward. A private firm called the tune and all Jamaica jumped.

The minister's policy statement, detrimental as it was to the growers themselves, also shows an extremely unsympathetic approach to a problem crucial to the Windwards' economies and at the same time peripheral to the economy of Jamaica. If an opportunity ever presented itself for Jamaica to restore the confidence of the smaller West Indian territories after its decision to withdraw from the Federation, this was it. Bananas account for less than 7% of Jamaica's total exports. But over 70% of Windwards' exports are derived from bananas. (In St Lucia alone, the share is now about 85%.) Concession to the Windwards would hardly affect Jamaica's export earnings and would perhaps increase revenue to the grower, through higher prices. It would be a demonstration of regional awareness on the part of Jamaica and a show of concern for the less developed smaller territories – all at no monetary cost. Instead, the totally irrelevant argument of a traditional place in the market was the main policy consideration.

It really should not be surprising that the Jamaica Government has shown no concern with the development problems of the 'less advanced' West Indian islands, with which it was once constitutionally associated. After all, even inside Jamaica itself successive administrations have shown little real concern with closing the income and status gaps existing within the country. And, as the saying does, charity begins at home! Yet the same governments have consistently exhorted the more advanced countries to help close the gap between rich and poor countries, classifying themselves conveniently in the latter group in order to obtain concessions and handouts. Jamaica makes the case to the US, for example, that the latter should diversify away from light manufacturing, such as textiles, in favour of countries like Jamaica. What then of Jamaica's position in bananas vis-à-vis the Windward Islands?

Notes

* "Issues in the Windward-Jamaica banana war". *New World Quarterly* 2:1 (1965d); reprinted (1971). N. Girvan and O. Jefferson (eds), *Readings on the Political Economy of the Caribbean.*

1   Consideration of ways and means of promoting a general intraregional trade in agricultural products is the subject of a separate paper. See Beckford and Guscott, *Non-tariff Mechanisms.*

3

Crisis in the West Indian Banana Industry*

Jamaica and the Windward Islands are virtually the only banana exporters in the Commonwealth Caribbean. Both depend exclusively on the British market in which they are protected from non-Commonwealth competition. While Commonwealth bananas enter the UK free of duty, other fruit are subject to a duty of £7.10/- per ton. But more important is the current restriction on imports of fruit from dollar sources which limits imports from the low-cost producing countries of Central and South America to 4,000 tons per annum.

The industry in the Windwards is organized by grower cooperatives which contract with Geest Industries Ltd for marketing the fruit. The administrative superstructure of the Jamaican industry consists of the All-Island Banana Growers Association, the Banana Industry Insurance Scheme and the Banana Board – the last being a statutory body which is the sole exporting agent. The Board contracts with Elders and Fyffes Ltd (a subsidiary of UFC) and the Jamaica Banana Producers Association (a Jamaican enterprise) for marketing fruit in the UK. Both companies act as agents of the Board but Elders and Fyffes handles the bulk of the total.

Historically, Jamaica has been the major source of fruit for the British market. But a rapid expansion of production in the Windward Islands in the postwar period has brought them on par with Jamaica. During the latter part of 1964 Windward supplies to the market exceeded those of Jamaica.

In Jamaica, the change of positions has been interpreted as a crisis, leading the Banana Board to summon a conference with WINBAN to discuss marketing matters. It is significant to note that the marketing firms involved were invited to take part in the discussions.

Despite press releases to the contrary, it is apparent from the aftermath that the talks broke down. Soon after the Windwards' representatives had gone, the Banana Board announced that a crisis faced the Jamaican industry as a result of intense competition from the Windward Islands. And to counteract this Jamaica will aim for a sharp increase in production from the current annual level of just over 150,000 tons in 1965. (This figure was later revised to 250,000 tons.)

Several statements and editorials in the daily press have suggested that every effort should be made to keep Jamaica in its traditional place. Some have even implicitly deplored the independence of Jamaica by arguing that colonial status accords to the growers in the Windward Islands the advantage of a price guarantee financed by the British Treasury. (This argument is not really valid since in point of fact the Windwards price assistance scheme is financed jointly by the growers themselves and the British Treasury.)

The declaration of a crisis and the suggested solution point to Jamaica's ambivalence and the bankruptcy of its banana bureaucracy. But more important, these developments clearly expose the vulnerability of the West Indian territories when operating as separate units. It is no secret that the struggle for control of the British market is really a struggle between two private foreign concerns – Elders and Fyffes and Geest Industries. Thus, by inviting them to participate in the discussions what the representatives of the Jamaica and Windward growers did was to convert a private struggle into a matter of public concern. Needless to say, the presence of these private interests at the conference table made it inevitable that the talks would fail.

What is perhaps most ironical about Jamaica's stand in these developments is that the banana growers in that island are now unwittingly carrying the banner of the UFC – a complete reversal of their historical position. It is well known that the history of Jamaican banana production is marked by the struggle of a banana peasantry to break the stranglehold of United Fruit. Thus it was that they formed the Jamaica Banana Producers Association in the 1920s and got Government to organize statutory control of the industry after World War II. Today the statutory authority seems to be reversing the course of history to the detriment of, not only Jamaican, but all West Indian banana growers. For it is clear that if the proposed expansion were to materialize, the only losers will be growers themselves. The market will absorb the proposed increase in supply only at lower prices than would otherwise obtain; thus the British consumer will pay less for bananas, the marketing companies will earn more from the increased volume handled, and only the West Indian grower stands to lose.

What will be the net effect of expanded volume and lower prices on growers' incomes? In terms of net revenue, two times three is not necessarily the same as three times two! Space does not permit elaboration of the economic consequences of the expansion plan. But it is sufficient to point out that unless the expansion lowers unit costs of production more than the resulting fall in price, growers may in fact be worse off.

The course of action being proposed by the Jamaican banana bureaucracy is not only a historical contradiction but also a reflection of a general ambivalence in the policy of present day Jamaica. Today, in international forums Jamaica's representatives constantly exhort the more advanced countries to help close the gap between rich and poor countries, yet little is done to close the gap either within the West Indies or even inside Jamaica itself. More specifically, they demand concessions from more advanced countries which compete with Jamaica, in certain lines, such as textiles and citrus; and at the same time, they plan to stifle the less advanced West Indian banana economies. The argument must be consistently applied. The case is made, for example, that as a highly developed country the United States should diversify away from light manufacturing such as textiles in favour of countries like Jamaica. Should it not then be that the more advanced Jamaica ought to diversify away from primary banana production in favour of the Windwards?

What these recent developments in the banana industry demonstrate most clearly, however, are the benefits to be gained from regional cooperation. In the first place, if Federation had survived, all West Indian fruit would have been handled by the same marketing agent, thereby eliminating private market struggles. The present 'crisis' would, therefore, never have been created. Second, and more important, West Indians could market their own fruit. Jamaica Banana Producers Association could broaden its share capital base to include Windward growers and be given the full contract for all West Indian fruit. With their established market outlets and increased chartered shipping, it would be relatively easy. In fact, this company, in seeking to expand, has been forced to explore (at some cost) such distant places as Sierra Leone and Cameroon in recent years. In banana marketing a geographical spread of supply areas is needed since wind damage is endemic. But Jamaica and the Windwards could provide them with sufficient spread for the desired expansion.

Such integration as is suggested here need not wait on political federation. But it does need a completely new perspective by West Indians in general, and not least the bureaucrats who administer their affairs. The historical tradition of accepting alien definitions of our problems and the almost complete dependence on outside solutions are again reflected in these recent developments in the banana industry. For what has been suggested in this commentary is that there was in fact no crisis facing Jamaican growers on account of expansion in the Windwards. A crisis will, in fact, come if Jamaica's expansion plans materialize since prices will then fall to unremunerative levels in order to accommodate the increment in supply. What we will then have is a crisis in the West Indies created by West Indians (in this case, Jamaicans) themselves. It has been further suggested that Jamaica's expansion decision appears to be more a solution for United Fruit's market control problem than anything else.

Notes

* "Crisis in the West Indian banana industry" *Caribbean Quarterly* 10:2 (1964a).

4

Agricultural Organization and Planning in Cuba*

Cuba is in an interesting stage of change and transition. As Dudley Seers has indicated, this former plantation economy has been transformed into a centrally planned economy and is, in fact, the only primary producing country to have chosen this path.[1] As such, it is a very fertile area for research, particularly for Caribbean social scientists interested in the economic and social development of the region. But information on Cuba is hard to come by on account of the embargo imposed on that country from outside. The result is that regional social scientists are deprived of the opportunity to analyse the process of transition there. Whenever the opportunity arises for travel to Cuba, members of the profession should feel obliged to contribute to the limited regional store of knowledge about postrevolutionary Cuba. It is in this spirit that the present paper is conceived.

The discussion here is not intended to be exhaustive or very analytical. It is more of a descriptive account based on notes compiled from a number of interviews; and attention is focussed on the planning framework and background policy considerations.

The importance of agriculture in the Cuban economy is sufficiently well known and does not require elaboration here. The economic history of Cuba has largely been a history of agriculture, and of sugar in particular. Prior to 1959, the economy was dominated by plantation production of sugar. And, in spite of recent efforts to diversify the economy, sugar and agriculture are still of paramount importance.

The basic structure of Cuban agriculture has been radically transformed in the period since 1959. Agrarian reform laws were the basic instruments for the break up of the plantation system of production. The first law placed a ceiling of 400 hectares on privately-owned estates and areas in excess of this were expropriated by the State. Land thus acquired was partly distributed to small farmers and partly held as state farms. Soon there were three types of producing units in agriculture: sugar cooperatives, state farms and private farms.

Cuba was at the time divided into 28 agricultural zones and each zone had the responsibility for its own agricultural development, administrative responsibility resting with the army chief in charge. Initially there was no planning as such. By 1960, the authorities saw the need for central coordination and control. With the conversion of the sugar cooperatives into state farms, some form of central control was established. But by the end of 1962, control became unwieldy and planning authorities were advocating decentralization.

In 1963, the Second Agrarian Reform Law reduced the maximum size of private holdings from 400 to 65 hectares and this brought considerable additional areas under state control. At the same time, all state-owned lands were placed under provincial control, as a first step toward decentralization. It seems that this arrangement was intended to be transitory until more appropriate organizational forms were developed. This was achieved in early 1965 when 58 regional 'enterprises' were established as the administrative units of state agricultural production (and planning). This represents a further step toward greater decentralization since the enterprise replaced the province as the basic unit of control.

There are a number of enterprises in each province and a delegate of the National Institute for Agrarian Reform (INRA) is assigned to each province to coordinate the activities of provincial enterprises with national plans and policy. Each enterprise is based on a major commodity and is managed by a state-employed director who is responsible for the development of the enterprise in line with the overall development plan. Incentives for the achievement of planning targets are directed at the workers, with wage differentials corresponding to work actually done. The enterprise obtains credit from the National Bank and uses proceeds from sales of produce to meet expenses. Profits earned by the enterprise go to the state.

Since 1964, the balance of public and private ownership of agricultural land has remained basically unaltered. State farms occupy roughly 65% of all farm land while the remaining 35% is occupied by some 200,000 private 'small' farmers.[2] The latter are all members of the National Association of Small Farmers (ANAP) which channels government services to the private sector and which therefore provides the basis for central control of production in that sector (see Section III below). The private sector of Cuban agriculture is most important in the production of vegetables, coffee, tobacco and livestock.

Agricultural policy in Cuba has always been strongly influenced by international events, and the period since 1959 is no exception. Initially the basic policy was to diversify rapidly, partly because sugar was subjectively associated with a bitter history and partly because this seemed to be an appropriate strategy for a country with vast land resources and a large food import bill. The objective was to meet incremental demand for farm products from domestic sources and to replace imports of certain commodities completely.[3] The policy of diversification was first ruthlessly implemented as areas of sugar cane were actually ploughed under to make way for other crops. But this cannot be attributed simply to 'subjective planning' as has been suggested.[4] It was also no doubt associated with the suspension of the Cuban sugar quota by the United States and the embargo on imports of food from that country.

Curtailment of food imports and the uncertainty of sugar markets must have encouraged a switch of resources from sugar to foodstuffs for home consumption. But there is a limit to the rate of diversification which can be achieved in any economy in the short run. In this particular case, the legacy of limited technical knowledge relating to the production of commodities other than sugar was an important constraint. But there was also an acute shortage of managerial skill which resulted in "the inefficient operation of the state farms" and "considerable disorganization . . . in the cooperatives".[5] These factors were compounded by physical shortages of new supplies such as seed and by the inadequacy of agricultural planning in a country with no past experience with planning of any kind. With these practical difficulties and the prolonged drought of 1961, agricultural output declined while demand had expanded as a result of more equal distribution of income. Food shortages and rationing were the result.

It was clear that some revision of policy was necessary in order to cope with the difficulties. A return to sugar seemed inevitable in the light of the practical obstacles that had been encountered in the attempt at rapid diversification. This proved feasible because new guaranteed markets for sugar had been secured in the Soviet Union and other 'socialist-bloc' countries. The "1962 Reappraisal", as Bianchi describes it, seems to have envisaged the return to sugar cane simply as a short-term operation.[6] But subsequent developments served to enhance the strategic importance of sugar for the long-term development of the economy. In 1963-64, a contract for sales of substantial quantities of sugar was arranged with the Soviet Union for the period up to 1970; and, as a result, expansion of sugar output was given priority in the programme for agricultural development.

This expansion was to be facilitated, in the first instance, by an increase in cane acreage – at the expense of some crops, such as rice and corn, for which the rate of profit was lower than sugar and which Cuba could continue to import. At the same time, it was planned to increase production of vegetables and fruit enough to provide for a surplus for export; and to depend on imported supplies of rice, corn, beans, vegetable oils and some potatoes.

A programme for the development of livestock and poultry was also devised. First, the payment received for the damage done by mercenary invaders at the Bay of Pigs was used to develop the poultry industry. By 1965, egg production exceeded domestic requirements and quantities were available for export and it is anticipated that a similar situation will apply to poultry meat by 1967. A start had been made to develop the pig industry but this programme was suspended because of the high (feed) import content. An elaborate programme for increasing milk production is in process of implementation, while plans for beef production are being drafted.

The milk expansion programme is based on planned improvement in the quality of dairy cattle and pasture improvement. The existing stock of cattle is predominantly Zebu and the output per animal is low. A breeding programme for the development of a hybrid herd of Holstein-Zebu is under way and it is anticipated that milk output will expand appreciably over the next few years. For 1965, it was planned to build 2,000 milking parlours, each with a capacity of 250 cows and 4,000 more are planned for 1966. The pasture improvement programme involves the planting and establishment of pangola grass. That, of itself, would contribute significantly to an increase in milk production since the low milk yield per cow is partly a result of grazing on unimproved (natural) pastures.

These new programmes for agriculture seem to suggest that planning authorities in Cuba have been influenced by the trading arrangements that were secured with Socialist countrie – sparticularly the Soviet Union and China. The decision to continue to depend on imported supplies of rice, vegetable oils and potatoes to the extent of transferring acreages over to sugar cane was no doubt a reflection of the availability of supplies of these products from the countries that were willing to buy Cuban sugar. And the emphasis on domestic production of livestock and poultry products may be related to the fact that the trading partners have no excess supplies of these products.

The overall agricultural policy of Cuba seems to be based on some agreement regarding comparative advantages among 'socialist-bloc' countries.

This is implicit in the development strategy just outlined; and was made quite explicit by the Prime Minister in a speech delivered on July 24, 1965 to a meeting honouring 5,000 volunteer cane cutters. In that speech, Dr Castro states that:

We defend the principle of the international division of labour and the principle that each country should produce that for which it has the best natural conditions and where man's effort will bring the greatest return, and should trade its products with those countries which produce other things for which they have the best natural conditions. This will be our policy and we will be able to follow it . . .[7]

Implicit in this statement is a static neoclassical concept of international trade and specialization.

The emphasis on 'natural conditions' raises certain questions about the terms of association between Cuba and the Soviet Union. Cuban economists need to examine the extent to which the existing terms of association are intended to integrate the two economies; and to consider whether such integration will permit diversification of the Cuban economy and allow for structural transformation in the long run. What kinds of concessions (if any) has the Soviet Union offered for Cuban exports of non-agricultural products? Some form of reappraisal would be in order and, in spite of current political realities, the merits of association with the Soviet Union should be assessed in the light of alternative potential associations with other countries of Central America and the Caribbean.

———

Up until 1964, planning procedures and organization in Cuba were not well developed. There were several reasons for this. The uncertainties in basic policy mentioned in the preceding section, inexperience in planning, a shortage of skilled administrators, inadequate statistical data and the lack of any system of data collection are only a few factors.

Since 1963-64, the planning organization has been rationalized as a result of the settlement of basic policy issues and the establishment of enterprise control units in the public sector. An elaborate system of collecting control data from state farms in the 58 enterprises has been in operation since 1964 and this provides basic statistical information for planning.

A five-year plan for the period 1966-70 has been prepared as a 'perspective plan'. In the public sector, production targets for each year of the plan period are first submitted by each enterprise (based on targets for each state farm in the enterprise); and these are synthesized at the provincial level by INRA delegates. At the same time, targets are also established by the Central

Planning Board (JUCEPLAN) according to national requirements for inter-sectoral balances, foreign trade and output growth. The planning department of INRA is then responsible for rationalizing JUCEPLAN targets with those of its provincial delegates drawn from the 58 enterprises. It may involve a return of target estimates for reconsideration of enterprises before realistic production targets are finalized. The five-year targets are subject to revision during each year of the plan period.

Implementation of the plan is also well organized and tightly controlled. Every three months there is a meeting of enterprise directors at the provincial level and a report on achievements in relation to targets is submitted by the provincial delegate of INRA. In addition there are annual meetings of all provincial delegates and enterprise directors to review the activities of the past year, to reconsider the perspective plan, and to discuss the prospects for the coming year. Knowledge of the overall planning process is widely dispersed through the publication by INRA of 376–page pamphlet consisting of 10,000 planning exercises.[8]

Control of output in the private sector of Cuban agriculture is effected through measures governing the flow of inputs into the sector. The Government, through INRA, regulates the supply of credit, fertilizers, tools and implements; and also influences production decisions by manipulating the prices paid for farm products. The structure of output prices is such as to encourage production of selected commodities. One department of INRA deals exclusively with the private sector. It arranges with the National Bank for loans to 'small farmers', sells supplies to these farmers, purchases the output, and establishes production targets for the national plan. Bank loans are secured by the fact that INRA purchases farm output and repayment is effected by deductions from sale proceeds.

With the nationalization of banking, transport and distribution, private farmers have to depend on Government for supplies of farm inputs and for the sale of produce. And this provides for effective control. Private farmers would find it almost impossible to operate without being members of ANAP which is the only farm organization with official status. Cooperatives are not important in Cuba. The 'cane cooperatives' that had been established in the initial stages of the agrarian reform were converted into state farms by mid 1962. Today, small farmers are free to organize cooperatives among themselves; but these are not officially recognized. INRA cooperates with ANAP in the formulation and implementation of plans for the private sector.

The complete socialization of Cuban agriculture is regarded as a long-term objective. It is anticipated that the private sector will decline in importance with succeeding generations. As one official stated, most of the farmers' children are now studying as scholarship students and when they come of age they will have no desire to own land. Unless considerable tracts of new land are brought into production, no material change in the relative importance of the private sector is expected for some time.

It will be interesting to compare the performance of Cuban agriculture with that of other Caribbean countries in a few years' time. Agricultural development in Jamaica, Trinidad and elsewhere has, to date, been painfully slow. Part of the problem in these countries is that "plans are developed from above without midway collaboration from below".[9]

In Cuba, on the other hand, the organization of planning in the public sector is based on a high level of participation at all levels, and there are now effective measures for the control of output in the private sector.

Notes

* "A note on agricultural organization and planning in Cuba". *Caribbean Studies* (November, 1966b).

1   Dudley Seers, ed., "Preface" to *Cuba – the Economic and Social Revolution* (Chapel Hill: University of North Carolina Press, 1964), p. v.

2   The average size of these farms varies according to the type of crop. It may be as low as 7 hectares in the tobacco belt of Pinar del Rio and as high as 65 hectares in the sugar areas of the eastern Provinces.

3   Potatoes, fruits and rice were the main products.

4   See, for example, Andres Bianchi, "Agriculture". Part I: *Cuba – the Economic and Social Revolution*, ed. Dudley Seers, 137; 142-46.

5   Bianchi, p. 141.

6   Bianchi, pp. 141-42.

7   Author's translation of a portion of the speech published (in full) in *El Mundo* (Havana) 25 July 1965.

8   INRA (Vice-Ministerio de Economía), Elementos de Planificación, Havana, February 1965.

9   Lloyd Braithwaite, "Rural development in the West Indies" (mimeo). Paper prepared for the UNESCO Seminar on Social Research and Problems of Rural Life in Central America, Mexico and the Caribbean Region, Mexico City, 1962.

5

A Caribbean View of Cuba*

Normally, the people of any one Caribbean island have little or no direct knowledge of events in the other islands. Information and interpretation are almost exclusively provided by metropolitan media. Cuba today is an important illustration. Since the revolutionary government came into power, first-hand information about that island has been more scant than ever. And Caribbean opinion about Cuba is simply a reflection of opinions uttered somewhere in the North Atlantic and picked up as gospel by local agencies of information. In the process of transmission only the most elementary form of selection is practised – the 'left' borrows from the 'left', the 'right' from the 'right' and some distinction is made between what is 'official' and what 'unofficial'.

In the light of this, it seems fair to say that the established Caribbean view of Cuba is both metropolitan and irrelevant. What is more, the most popular view embodies all of official American hostility to a former colony which has succeeded in breaking the traditional metropolitan stranglehold over its economic and political life. The significance of this is that many Caribbean people take positions on Cuba which imply one or the other of two things; that Cuba's relations with the North Atlantic were in some way different in kind from that of the rest of the Caribbean or if not, that the latter are not concerned to transform this relation.

The present article takes the view that Cuba before the Revolution was not in essence unlike any other Caribbean territory and that important lessons can be derived from whatever transformation has been taking place in that country. It is implicit in the argument that the struggle to achieve economic development and social change throughout the region is essentially a struggle to break the colonial relation with the North Atlantic.

―――――

Dudley Seers provides a good point of departure in the preface to *Cuba: The Economic and Social Revolution* by stating that:

In all the speculation about its role in global politics, we tend to overlook two points about Cuba. The first is that this government of a somewhat backward, tropical country, traditionally dependent on sugar exports, is attempting to achieve a very rapid rate of social change and economic growth. Second, the former plantation economy of Cuba is now using techniques of highly centralized planning; it is in fact the only major exporter of primary products to have taken this path.

What requires emphasis is that Cuba has emerged from the cocoon of the plantation system which still, in one way or another, envelopes the rest of the Caribbean. All the territories have shared a history of colonization, of slavery, of sugar, of foreign-owned plantations and of domination by one metropolitan power or another. The Cuban government and people are today trying to come to terms with the same problems confronting the rest of the region. The problems of economic and social backwardness – of unemployment, poverty and ignorance – were created by a similar set of circumstances. The solutions to these problems may, therefore, be of general applicability in different parts of the region. Cuba is, on this account, relevant to the Caribbean.

This is, of course, not the first case of a Caribbean country experimenting with a development model which may have significance for the region as a whole. Puerto Rico had set a pattern earlier with a development model which was subsequently copied in quick succession by nearly all the other territories. The difference with Puerto Rico, however, is that the American media of communication paint a growing picture of developments there, while they present a dismal picture of Cuba.

For Caribbean peoples, the difference between Cuba and Puerto Rico is one which it is necessary to explore at some length. The two countries represent what have been described respectively, as the 'active' and 'passive' models of economic development and social change.

The active model involves a radical transformation of the economy. In the West Indian case, this means a complete transfer of the dynamic for change from outside the society to within. This involves a complete erosion of the plantation system with its inherent capacity for metropolitan control. For, as Lloyd Best has suggested, it is largely this outside control which has inhibited the development of an internal cultural and technological dynamic within the region. A preliminary examination of the case suggests that the plantation system has a built-in capacity to maintain itself. This is precisely why the active model calls for a complete break.

On the other hand, the passive model means a retention of the traditional order. It is based on policies which do not disturb established metropolitan connections. Operationally, it involves the creation of the 'right' environment in order to attract foreign capital and management and to maintain traditional foreign markets. ('Industrialization by invitation' is the feature of the development policy.) The dynamic for change, therefore, remains in the metropolis while local political leaders, bureaucrats and technicians busy themselves creating a 'welcoming society'. Per capita income grows but there is little or no change in its distribution.

This is the choice that faces Caribbean peoples. And it is from this point of view that we need to inform the choice with appraisals of the experiences of Cuba and Puerto Rico.

Through the instrumentality of American media of communication, it is general knowledge that Puerto Rico has achieved considerable material advance, in the sense that per capita income has increased spectacularly since the War. Little or no publicity is, however, given to the facts presented by Seda in the last issue of *New World Quarterly* that the rate of illiteracy in that island is as much as 18%; that 14% of the labour force remains chronically unemployed; that American firms account for 88% of Puerto Rico's annual investments; that the social structure is characterized by a small group of American managers and businessmen at the top, their supporting Puerto Rican characters in the middle and the bulk of the population selling their services in the cheap labour market at the bottom; and that the passive model of development has tended to erode Puerto Rican value system. This does not reflect well on the passive model, especially when it is appreciated that Puerto Rico has special arrangements that provide it with free access to the American market and easy migration of labour to the mainland; arrangements which are not likely to be extended to any other of the territories.

The passive model has had similar and characteristic results in all the other Caribbean countries which have followed Puerto Rico: Jamaica, Trinidad, Guiana, Surinam, Barbados and elsewhere. In every case, this development model "has produced characteristic Caribbean results: duality in the social system, disequalization of the national wealth, disorder in the labour market, dependence on the outside world and disaffection among the population – all in a context of expanding output and rising population" [Best]. Since these phenomena have been a feature of the Caribbean economy since its colonization, it is clear that the passive model only serves to reinforce the traditional order.

The failure of the passive model is all the more reason why Cuba is of special relevance to the Caribbean. What are the possibilities, problems and prospects for a Caribbean society operating with an active transition model? In spite of the fact that date are hard to get and that it is still too early to judge (seven years being too short a period to observe long-term processes), some attempt must be made to consider this question seriously.

The rest of the present article is based largely on the author's own impressions from a visit, even though every effort has been made to substantiate these personal notes and information with what reliable data prove available from standard sources such as United Nations publications and the volume edited by Dudley Seers.

Any Caribbean visitor to Cuba must be impressed by at least three important and immediate contrasts with the rest of the region. First, is the conspicuous absence of symptoms of unemployment (and underemployment); the signs of poverty are much less stark than elsewhere in the region – there is no prostitution and no begging of any kind, not even the covert kind of begging which produces 'tipping' in other places. Second, is the omnipresence of educational schemes – on radio and television, in the newspapers and factories, and throughout the length and breadth of the country. And, third, is the obvious involvement of the people with matters affecting the national life. The national and international awareness of the population at all levels and the general atmosphere of national cohesion, of public order, and of self-confidence are certainly not characteristic of the rest of the Caribbean.

That society is, of course, a product of numerous factors which influenced its development over a long period of time; but not the least of the factors are those which have occurred since 1959.

The present government of Cuba came into being as a movement which had committed itself to radical reforms of the existing order. The success of the movement was secured by two sets of influences, the one internal and the other external. In the first case, the movement, from the time of the Moncada raid, served to heighten the consciousness of the Cuban population of the possibilities for change and thus set the stage for the later development of a popular commitment. The harsh measures used by the Batista regime in attempting to crush the movement served to heighten consciousness even further; and the publication, in 1954 of the defence plea (*History Will Absolve Me*) delivered by Fidel Castro before the Emergency Tribunal of Santiago in October 1953 won widespread support for the movement both at home and abroad. That speech highlighted the brutality and injustices under Batista and outlined five laws which the movement had drafted as a basis for creating a new order. Thus by the time the armed campaign grew in intensity in the late 1950s, signs of popular commitment began to appear; the population began to provide the revolutionary army with material support – many risking their lives by giving food and shelter.

However, given the superior military might of the Batista forces, the movement was forced to seek external support for the military campaign. Thus it was that unofficial groups abroad, particularly in the United States and Mexico, helped to provide weapons and ammunition for the revolutionary army. The main form of external support at this stage was military, though it seems fair to infer that passive official sanction could also be attributed to a number of countries, especially those in which unofficial groups were actively extending aid to the movement.

It is clear that the initial success which brought the revolutionary government into power resulted from both the popular internal consciousness generated by the movement as well as the military support which it secured externally. A new phase now began as the government proceeded to effect changes within the society and began to seek official external support and sanction.

The revolutionary government inherited an economy which had stagnated for about 35 years on account of the fact that, as Seers puts it, it was structurally unsound. For the economy to function efficiently, some change in the structure was inevitable. So far as diversification of production was concerned, there was some room for manoeuvre since land and labour were grossly underutilized. However, it is suggested here that the chief motive for promoting structural change – particularly in agriculture – was to satisfy expectations of the rural population among whom the commitment for change had been established.

But to make a beginning toward structural reform would naturally be to create certain forces that would eventually determine the shape of things. On the one hand, any widespread material benefits would strengthen the internal commitment; while on the other, far-reaching structural change would be likely to disrupt the traditional metropolitan connection. If internal commitment were sufficiently strong, and other sources of external support could be secured, then the society would be well placed to make a clean break with the plantation system. But this would also require that a complementary programme be devised for the purpose of integrating the bulk of the population who, up to then, had been alienated by the normal functioning of that system.

In other words, the eventual choice of an active development path would depend not only on the strength of internal commitment for change but also on whether some kind of external support could be secured. Once the choice had been made it would have immediately required far-reaching reforms in at least two areas: the economic organization of agriculture and in the system, form and content of education. Only through these reforms could the choice effectively begin to transfer the dynamic of development from outside the society to within. Agriculture was of importance because therein was the main cause of internal immobility of resources and because agricultural diversification would provide an important stimulus for industrial development. Education would, of course, provide the necessary skills for the labour force and lay the foundation for technological change and, if appropriate, for cultural development. The actual reforms in agriculture and education, and their effects, are well documented by Bianchi and Jolly in the volume edited by Seers. But it is useful for the argument here to give a hint of the kinds of changes which have taken place.

The plantation system of agriculture in the pre-revolutionary period was characterized by serious underutilization of both labour and land. A survey carried out in 1956-57 indicated that 38% of the rural labour force were less than fully employed and 28% were chronically unemployed. There was a heavy concentration of land among a few sugar cane plantations and cattle ranches, with a prevalance of non-resident owners. Less than 8% of all farm holdings occupied over 70% of all farm land. Indeed, up to early 1959, 28 cane producers alone controlled 20% of all farm land.

In view of this situation, it is not surprising that the Agrarian Reform Law was one of the earliest acts of the new administration. Subsequent revisions to the law and other complementary laws providing for the expropriation of property of supporters and officials of the Batista regime and, later, of American-owned sugar estates laid the foundation for dramatic changes in the rural picture. Thousands of peasants became owners of land they had previously rented, share-cropped or squatted; the productive potential of agriculture was more fully utilized. (Land under cultivation expanded by 20% and rural employment by 35% in the first two years). Today, the productive units in agriculture are either state farms or private farms. The former occupy 65% of the cultivated acreage and have an average size of 22,000 acres. The latter are organized into the ANAP which acts as a liaison between farmers and government.

In the pre-revolutionary period, the socioeconomic position of the rural population was deplorable. Three-quarters of all rural dwellings were mud huts and two-thirds had earthen floors; nine-tenths had no electricity or running water. Out of each 100 rural families, only four could afford to eat meat, only two consumed eggs and one of each 100 families had fish. Forty-three percent of the rural population were completely illiterate; 44% never attended any school and of the rest, 88% never passed third class. The position today represents a considerable improvement. That there is no rural unemployment today is proof enough. But in addition, mention must be made of the dramatic improvements in rural education, health and housing – mainly on account of heavy government investment in these areas.

It has been stated that "the revolutionary government has treated education as the key to a complete reconstruction of society". As such, the educational programme is designed not just to develop skills but also to create a new system of national goals and values. This called for more than an extension of existing educational facilities; it called for a complete transformation in the system, form and content of education. In a country where few (25%) had previously completed primary school, it required a tremendous national effort. A policy of mass education was necessary to increase the supply of skilled labour, to reduce inequalities, to provide incentives for work and to increase popular awareness. The literacy campaign of 1961 alone created a new world for one-sixth of the adult population who previously could neither read nor write. And it is not without significance that one million adults were involved in carrying out the campaign; it is a clear case of national involvement and some evidence of the emergence of an internal dynamic. The "battle of the sixth grade" to raise every adult up to the sixth standard, is in progress and technical adult education is well developed. At the same time, matriculation in primary, secondary and technical schools and universities has expanded several fold.

The content and orientation of education have undergone considerable change. Content of the syllabus was designed to awaken "the young people to their duties as citizens of the Socialist fatherland". From the primary school level, the history of Cuba and in particular of the revolutionary struggle and achievements are taught with an interpretation that emphasizes the nature of capitalist imperialism and the fundamentals of socialism and capitalism. History teaching in secondary schools is based heavily on the Marxist view of the process of historical development. In the first introductory history text issued by the Ministry of Education (*Trabajo y Lucha*) it is stated that the hope is that the work "will encourage further study and a deepening understanding and practical awareness of the creative science of Marxist-Leninism". At the university level, all students in the first two years receive some grounding in the principles of Marxist-Leninist philosophy, and the economic theory syllabuses are distinctly Marxist. At all levels, love for the Fatherland is strongly emphasized and the slogan '*Patria o Muerte – Venceremos*' (My Country or Death – We Will Win) is used effectively for this purpose.

The reforms in agriculture and education (and housing) have had profound effects. They have bestowed considerable material benefits on the bulk of the population; reduced economic and social inequalities; and have given a new sense of purpose to the population. There can be little doubt that the advance toward a more equitable distribution of wealth and income must have strengthened the initial commitment of the population at large to the revolutionary government. But the nature and process of change was not simply determined by the internal situation alone. Indeed, as is suggested in what follows the actual choice to make a clear break with the plantation system was perhaps as much influenced by certain external factors.

The revolutionary government actually began with rather limited pro-grammes for change. In agriculture, for example, the Agrarian Reform Law of June 1959 only provided for expropriation of parts of excessively large hold-ings. But the state did not enter in the field of production; instead titles were distributed to the landless peasantry. None of this was grave enough to seri-ously disturb the traditional connection with the United States. But it, no doubt, added strength to the popular rural commitment. Trouble really began when the government, in trying to extend its sphere of influence in the private sector, came into conflict with the American-owned oil refineries over the question of refining Soviet oil. The subsequent nationalization of the refineries in mid 1960 was sufficiently disfavourable to metropolitan interests that American sanctions was quickly withdrawn with its abolition of the Cuban sugar quota. This, in turn, led to Cuban expropriation of American-owned estates, factories, etc., to bring about the final collapse of the plantation system and a concomitant stage of siege imposed by the United States.

It does not seem unreasonable to assume that the government was at the time aware that the move to nationalise the oil refineries could have created the conditions that would force it to go all the way. Obviously, then, it must have felt sure that it could consolidate the necessary internal support and at the same time secure some form of external support to replace the traditional one.

By the start of 1960, with the designation of that year as the 'Year of Agrar-ian Reform', the rural population must have been solidly committed to the new government. And, judging from the size of the crowds which were turning out for the prime minister's speeches, support was also strong in the urban areas. The tremendous popular response to the Declaration of Havana must surely have been sufficient to indicate to the government that the popu-lation was committed and ready to go the whole way. The series of industrial strikes clearly indicated the restlessness of the urban labour force and was no doubt of major importance in government's decision to extend its sphere of economic control. The strikes can be related to the expectations created by a strong urban consciousness, if not commitment.

At the same time, efforts were being made on several fronts to widen exter-nal connections in the economic, military and moral fields. In the period before the final break, President Dorticos visited a number of Latin American states and, as President of the National Bank, Guevara travelled extensively in Eastern Europe and Asia. By February 1960, a trade agreement was signed with the USSR for the sale of quantities of Cuban sugar and for credits for purchase of Soviet machinery and consumer goods. Later, other lesser trade deals were arranged with Eastern European states and diplomatic exchanges arranged with China. All these developments no doubt convinced the Cuban government that official means of support could be gained from sources other than the traditional one. The speed with which new economic and military agreements were concluded with other countries following the early deterioration of relations with the United States is some indication that the ground had been prepared.

Furthermore, developments in other countries of the Caribbean must in some way have encouraged the Cuban government in the thought that regional support would have been forthcoming. It does not seem too unreasonable to assume for example that the Chaguaramas campaign of 1959/60 with its challenge to American military presence in Trinidad, and by extension the whole West Indian Federation, may have been suggestive to the Cuban government that the region was prepared to stand with them if and when the final break came. As it turned out, of course, this was not to be (for reasons discussed by Best in the last issue of *New World Quarterly* and the sequence which will appear in the next issue).

The underlying forces which led to the initial break with the plantation system derived from factors operating both within and outside of Cuba. Once the break was made, then the government was faced with the problem of the planning and implementation of change of a kind that would be rewarding to the popular commitment which had made the break possible in the first instance. Unless that could be achieved then the commitment could well have been eroded, making way for the return of the old order. As it was, the government had little or no experience in planning and was forced to seek external assistance in this respect. Unsuitable planning methods had to be borrowed from the Soviet Union and Czechoslovakia, and this extended the area of external dependence on the so-called socialist bloc. But the Urban Reform of late 1960 brought material rewards to the underprivileged urban classes and no doulbt strengthened the support there.

Many external factors also helped to determine the future course of events. American hostility toward Cuba, expressed in the economic blockade and promotion of mercenary invasions, had results opposite to that for which they were intended. They met with strong internal resistance from a strongly committed people and enhanced moral support for Cuba in the rest of the world. Cubans today take great pride in the fact that they have managed to withstand the economic and military pressures of "Yankee imperialism". It would seem to the visitor that American policy toward Cuba has really served to help consoldiate the internal support for the government. This is not really surprising for, as Seers suggested, "the embargo provides an excuse from almost any economic difficulty, whether or not it is actually so caused. Moreover the greater the international tension, the easier it is for the government to appeal to nationalism . . . and to maintain a high level of enthusiasm among the sections of the public that support it" (p. 59).

On the other hand, the difficulties of making rapid transformation in a country with the structure of pre-revolutionary Cuba forced the government more and more to seek new external alliances which could help to ease the traditional difficulties. And as material assistance was increasingly extended by the Soviet Union, Eastern Europe and China, this carried with it certain developments which were later to influence the nature of external relations and eventuallly the political ideology of the Cuban government. The nature of these developments and their long run effects are the main considerations in the next section.

What is clear from both analysis and observation is that there is still a strong internal support for, and popular commitment to, the changes being effected by the Government of Cuba. Nevertheless, popular reports reaching the rest of the Caribbean through the traditional North Atlantic media generally suggest widespread disaffection. The most recent reports of "large-scale" emigration are used, for example, to substantiate the case. It is necessary, therefore, to consider this particular example in a proper perspective.

It may not be unreasonable to regard emigration from any country as an indicator of internal conflict, of one sort or another, within the system. Moreover, since the active model involves a process of integration and the complete erosion of the plantation system, it is natural that it carries with it the seeds of internal conflict. But the creation of internal conflict is not a special property of the active model; it is a feature of any process of economic and social change. Thus the "large-scale" emigration from Cuba since the Revolution must be regarded in the same light as the proportionately greater rates of emigration, of admittedly a different class of people, from Puerto Rico, Jamaica and other Caribbean countries operating with the passive model. It is the nature of the conflict in each case which is, therefore, relevant. In the passive case, it is the bulk of the population while in the active model, it is a relatively small proportion which, in each case, tends to be alienated by the functioning of the system. And it is mostly from the alienated groups that the migrant comes.

The argument here is not meant to imply that there has been absolutely no disillusionment of individuals and groups (inside Cuba) with the course of the Revolution. It is meant instead to establish that there are several meaningful indicators of popular support. One such indicator is the response to official public meetings. Cubans still turn out in hundreds of thousands to hear the Prime Minister whenever he speaks. In Havana, a city of about a million, average attendance is about the same number; and some 600,000 came to hear the 26th of July (1965) speech in Santa Clara, a city of under 150,000 located in the middle of the island. All this in what is a relatively large country with fairly wide radio and television coverage.

Clearly, there is much significance to Prime Minister Castro's public challenge to a visiting American newspaperman during that speech at Santa Clara when he stated:

Let him take pictures, let him take films and see if in Washington, New York or anywhere else they can raise the enthusiasm of more than five hundred thousand citizens. Let's see if any of those puppet governments of Brazil, Guatemala, Nicaragua, Paraguay and other . . . if any one, or all of them together are capable of bringing together half a million people like those who are meeting here today . . . A crowd, large or small, can always be assembled by different means, but what it is not possible to create is the enthusiasm of this crowd.

Any witness of the occasion could not possibly disagree. The resolve of the Cuban people to meet head-on the overwhelming military might of the United States (with or without Krushchev) in the October 1962 crisis, and their constant resistance against mercenary raids are other earlier examples. Yet another, and more recent indicator, is the fact that thousands volunteered to help harvest the 1965 sugar crop, in response to government appeal. In the light of the evidence, it is perhaps not far from the truth to say that perhaps no other government in the world today and certainly none other in the New World can claim as strong a popular support.

This kind of support with the strong national morale which it promotes is a precondition for the development of an internal dynamic for change. But it is clear that the permissive external relations must be such as not to create an inordinate dependence on another metropolitan power, for that would simply amount to a shift in the location of control between centres outside the society. (The 'Marxist-Leninist' posture of the government and its economic and military policies are suggestive of too strong a dependence on the Soviet Union; and leave many in doubt.) It is necessary, therefore, to consider what factors gave rise to this dependence in order to understand the nature of it and how it affects, or is likely to affect, the operation of the active model.

The choice of model was initially contemplated mainly on the basis of a strong internal resolve to do away with the plantation system and its characteristic features. But it created external conflicts with the metropolitan power which, up to then, had provided external support and eventually led to a withdrawal of that support. What then? The active model had no ideological foundations – no complementary scheme of ideas. No body of doctrine of direct relevance to Caribbean society has yet been developed. And since the rest of the region was on the whole content to operate within the framework of the passive model, as was clear after the capitulation on Chaguaramas, Cuba stood alone without any regional support. In view of this, the uncritical adoption of any alien doctrine which could roughly conform with the perspective of the active model can be understood. Socialism or what? Even when the phase for planning and implementation was reached, Cuba was not able to draw on relevant planning models since the social scientists of the region have yet to formulate models relevant to the plantation economy. Again, Cuba had no choice in borrowing uncritically planning techniques from the Soviet Union and Eastern Europe.

In the second place, it can be argued that as a relatively small primary exporting country (and in the absence of regional support), a structural external dependence is inevitable – if only in the short run. The legacy of the past dictated that Cuba must sell large quantities of sugar abroad to acquire the capital goods required for any contemplated economic transformation. As a major source of world sugar supplies, it could have developed new market outlets within the framework of a new international agreement or through bilateral arrangements with large consuming countries. The former would require support from other sugar exporting countries; but as indicated already, this was not forthcoming – least of all from those countries within the region. Under the circumstances, then, the Soviet Union became a logical partner since it provided both ideological and economic support.

Cuba's dependence on the Soviet Union can, therefore, be reasonably attributed partly to the failure of the rest of the Caribbean to provide the kind of support which was necessary to bring about some meaningful regional independence. It is a kind of structural dependence but, in addition, the economic policies of the Cuban government are suggestive of a functional dependence as well. The long-term development programme is said to be based on the existing comparative advantage among the 'socialist bloc' of countries. Thus, the direction for change would seem to be still in some ways directed from outside. The essence of the active model is the achievement of functional independence, in the first instance. But it could be that a certain level of functional dependence is tolerable in the early phases of the operation of the model. It could be consistent with the active framework only if it is generally recognized as a short term operational phenomenon. Whether or not this is the case inside Cuba today is difficult to judge.

On the one hand, a case can be made that the 'socialist' content of education is likely to extend the existing functional dependence into a long run feature of the system. (No consideration is given to socialist imperialism. Imperialism is naively considered to be purely a capitalist phenomenon.) But, at the same time, the Cuban government has on numerous occasions impressed on the population that their destiny is to be determined by them and them alone. After the Soviet withdrawal in the October 1962 crisis, the internal decision to face the crisis alone, was an important (if only temporary) rejection by the Cubans of the doctrine of imperial responsibility and of the long standing Soviet-American agreement on respective 'spheres of influence'. Furthermore numerous extracts from the Prime Minister's speeches reaffirming the principle of complete independence can be drawn into evidence. Only the future will tell whether this is merely perpetuated as a pious hope or whether it will at some later stage be transformed into reality. The outcome may depend as much on what happens in the rest of Caribbean as it will on whatever happens within Cuba.

Notes
_____

* "A Caribbean view of Cuba". *New World Quarterly* (Croptime 1965c).

6

Planning in the Caribbean under Capitalism and Socialism*

The first meeting of planning officials of member countries of the Caribbean Development and Cooperation Committee (CDCC) was held in Havana, Cuba, from 25-31 January 1979. It was a rich experience to have attended this meeting and I wish to share this experience with other comrades in the struggle for the ultimate liberation of Caribbean peoples.[1]

The purpose of the meeting was to review the planning experiences of member countries; and to consider various aspects of planning and the scope for cooperation within the region in matters of policy for more effective planning. It was organized jointly by the Caribbean Office of the United Nations Economic Commission for Latin America (ECLA) and the Institute for Economic and Social Planning in Latin America (ILPES). The CDCC itself is a new, and perhaps unfamiliar, regional organization. To my mind, one of the factors that makes it important derives from the fact that it is the first and only Caribbean organization which deliberately embraces socialist Cuba as a member and simultaneously excludes the imperialist United States of America.

Notable absentee member countries from this first planning meeting were Trinidad and Tobago, Haiti and the Dominican Republic. Participating countries included Barbados, Guyana, Jamaica, Cuba, Surinam, Belize, West Indies Associated States, and the Netherlands Antilles. Also present were representatives of regional and United Nations organizations. In addition to formal meeting sessions, the timetable provided for visits to the Physical Planning

Institute, a Citrus Enterprise in Matanzas, the Computer Center of JUCEPLAN (Central Planning Board), and the School for National Planning and Management.

Formal meeting sessions covered:

1   Official presentations on the planning experiences of countries attending, plus unofficial summaries on those not attending (eg Dominican Republic).

2   Presentations by attending consultants – Four people involved here were Ms Betty Sedoc-Dahlberg of the University of Surinam, Trevor Farrell and Winston Dookeran of the University of the West Indies, St Augustine, and myself.

3   Inputs from representatives of regional organizations like ECLA (Caribbean) and other regional United Nations agencies.

4   A round-table discussion on the similarities between Latin America and the Caribbean States in relation to the effects of imperialism and the world capitalist crisis.

The rest of this report deals first with what we learned from the formal sessions; secondly, what we saw and learned from the visits to Cuban planning institutions; and, thirdly, some 'round-table' perspectives.[2]

Planning Experiences in the Caribbean – Review

For convenience and authenticity quotations in this section come directly from the official UN *Report of the First Meeting of Planning Officials in the Caribbean* (E/CEPAL/CDCC/49/Rev. 2, 6 February 1979). This is a published account of the meeting issued by CDCC with amazing efficiency exactly one week after the meeting ended in Havana. All quotations below are from this source.

Statements of planning experiences were made by Barbados, Jamaica, Belize, Surinam, Republic of Cuba, St Vincent and the Netherlands Antilles. *The Cuban experience was in contrast to experiences of the other countries* (emphasis added).

Cuba apart, then, we learn that a common feature of the capitalist Caribbean experience was "the postwar introduction of planned capital expenditure by European colonial powers on infrastructure and social development". This was the Colonial Development and Welfare (CD & W) phase of Caribbean economic underdevelopment providing a cover for the dismantling of empire. This *colonial phase* was followed by the phase coinciding with achievements of constitutional independence or internal self-government – the phase of Five-Year Plans which essentially provided a cover for the increasing hegemony of imperialism over the regional economies as the *era of neocolonialism* unfolded. What is interesting is that in the present phase of neocolonialism the planners are now indigenous. So from the late 1950s to early 1960s black West Indian technicians began to do the job that white 'foreign experts' from the colonial office used to do in the early colonial phase.

What new perspectives did our indigenous planning experts bring to the situation? "There was marked similarity in development strategy in these countries. Emphasis was put on the development of infrastructure, on industrialization and on significant improvement in social services." In some countries, special consideration was given to agricultural development; and in a predominantly sugar economy it is said that efforts in the direction of diversification (to grow more what we eat) were undertaken. Additionally, some countries gave high priority to tourism development. Basically, these new perspectives were like 'putting new wine into old bottles'.

The policy planning framework for the capitalist Caribbean has been and continues to be based on using state (public) resources to provide an appropriate economic and social climate for foreign capital and management to come to a hospitable region blessed with abundant natural and human (labour) resources that serve to make fat profits for foreign capitalists and their regional counterparts. Naturally, much capital came and much more profits left in due course while relatively few jobs were created. So imperialism came to own and control abundant natural resources like bauxite, petroleum, nickel, beaches and land; plus financial resources mobilized from the savings of Caribbean workers and peasants by multinational foreign banks like Barclays, Bank of Nova Scotia, First National and Chase Manhattan. With only a few job openings resulting from this planning strategy, unemployment increased by leaps and bounds; peasants were dispossessed of land; and urban slums expanded. Economic and social crisis was evident everywhere as the regional economies reaped a 'harvest of lengthening dependence'.

Consequently by the early 1970s there was a marked "down-grading of medium-term planning in countries which had previously regarded such planning as essential". More recently, as the structural economic crisis spread like wildfire throughout the international capitalist system, most Caribbbean capitalist economies were further affected by "inflationary economic conditions and the rise in fuel costs". This has "served to intensify concentration on short-term problems. The very nature of the development process however has, over the past two years, pressured government into looking at desirable goals in the medium and long-term, and there has been renewed interest in planning."

Now the questions seem to be: What will happen this time? What will indigenous Caribbean planning experts come with in this their second round of applying what skills they possess to these pressing and seemingly everlasting economic and social problems? Only time will tell. But these experts could all do well to examine the Cuban experience. For here is the one and only Caribbean country that has managed to extricate itself from the international capitalist system, and put in place a socialist system of economic, social and political organization. Cuba is *now a model of development* not just for the Caribbean but for the whole Third World entrapped in a quick-sand of persistent *underdevelopment* characteristic of economies on the 'periphery' of international capitalism. Cuba is today a rapidly developing socialist economy and society.

This rapid pace of development in Cuba stems directly from the fact that "that country undertook a radical structural transformation of its economy. For this purpose planning has been used as an objective and scientific instrument with the full involvement of the people, and social ownership of the fundamental means of production". The UN report goes on to state that:

The system of planning and management of the economy and implementation of the system takes into account:

1   The objective laws of socialism and, based on setting up of a plan, is aimed at guaranteeing the planned development of the country;

2   The law of value is developed according to a plan, so that trade and commercial activities are planned;

3   The development of a high economic consciousness in the people is a means of achieving optimum national economic efficiency.

Now what is clear from this is that planning in Cuba is capable of achieving the development of an order which can promote material and spiritual betterment of all Cubans. Order is as inherent there as disorder is inherent in the capitalist Caribbean. The order achieved in Cuba generates an egalitarian pattern of distribution of basic needs for the people of that society. In contrast, the disorder of capitalism concentrates material gain in the hands of few people (landlords and capitalists – local and foreign), and spreads material poverty among the rest of people (workers and peasants) who are the majority of the population throughout the region.

It seems superfluous to note that Cuba shared a common history, a common legacy, with the rest of the Caribbean up until 1959. That year opened with the triumph of the revolutionary forces led by Fidel Castro. Havana opened its arms and hearts to the forces to consolidate the final defeat of the corrupt, treacherous, dictatorial capitalist regime of Batista and its powerful United States imperialist allies. It was the beginning of a new day in the New World. It marked the ending of the old order – the long dark night of colonialism and neo-colonialism. Cuba never looked back since that day. And the rest of the region began to look forward – to Cuba and final victory.

Now it must be stressed that not all of the Cuban economy is owned by the state. *There is a significant private sector*, especially in agriculture where small farmers own (on individual and family basis) 20% of total national farm land. There are also cooperatives. *The state sector is dominant but the planning apparatus does not dominate.* This is critical. How is this problematic harmony achieved? To answer that question we must examine the planning experience further and then report on the planning institutions we visited.

State enterprises and provincial authorities have a strong influence on what the JUCEPLAN finally presents as a plan. Additionally, the Institute of Physical Planning helps determine the national geographic dispersal of development – between urban and rural spatial resource mobilization, for example. Further, in Cuba plans are more flexible for time adjustments.

Long, medium and short-term plans are drawn up on a scientific basis. JUCEPLAN has to play a decisive and leading role within the system of management and planning of the economy. Below the national level, the system includes the control and planning apparatus of the *People's Power*. The territorial planning is a vital aspect in the planning process, and territorial plans are made taking into account the basis of the Five-Year Plan and the concrete conditions of the territorial economy of the province. It is an important method in the solution of socioeconomic problems and it also guarantees an adequate level of economic development in the different regions, according to the cultural objectives of the unique Plan of Social and Economic Development.

There we see provision for the adjustment of medium to long-term planning goals, the institutional involvement of the broad mass of people in the planning process, the attempt to achieve provincial balance, and the obvious effort to stimulate urban-rural balance (if not harmony).

Finally, a word on how state enterprises – the dominant economic organizations – are fitted into the planning process.

. . . the measurement in money costs and financial returns of an enterprise (*cálculo económico*) assures the profitability and self-financing of the enterprise. The socialist enterprise is the fundamental base of the national economy and it is characterized by its technical and economic unity and its relative economic independence. The economic relationship of state enterprises and agencies between themselves and with the private sector is established on a buying/selling basis.

It follows from this, as the UN report continues, that in the context of socialist Cuba today, "Planning is a basic instrument used to guarantee the harmonious and balanced development of the economy. It also contributes to the attainment of maximum efficiency."

The contrast with *the capitalist Caribbean* is strikingly made when one delegation at the meeting pointed out that in its particular (nation) state there is "no experience of macro-economic planning, all effort being *focused on project coordination arising from external aid*" (my emphasis). Need more be said?

Planning Institutions in Cuba – Description

JUCEPLAN – The Central Planning Board

Our visit to JUCEPLAN was a short tour of the Computer Center which I found boring (as I find visits to all computer centers the world over). But the presentation on how JUCEPLAN works was interesting and valuable. The appended flow chart synthesizes part of that information given to us.

The computer center itself has three departments: Systems dealing with design and implementation; Software dealing with specified programming; and Planning and Control responsible for accounting, cooperatives' plans, etc. The work of the center is grouped into two basic systems: Simple data processing for the flow of information from agencies into JUCEPLAN and the flow within JUCEPLAN itself; this is 80% of the work load. The rest (20%) deals with computer variance.

The planning process works something like this:

JUCEPLAN
> Elaboration of proposals with people participation.
> Interrelation between sectors, regions. Balancing.

Council of State
> Indicators for calculations. Modifications come from
> National Assembly, but Council of State has legislative
> right to decide.

National Assembly
> Approves indicators re growth rate of economy per
> commission to analyse documents and to state criteria for
> adopting the plan.

JUCEPLAN (Data base)
> State Commission for Statistics – 169 municipal offices in
> provinces, by enterprises 14 provincial, 1 national

The clear articulation of the planning process is evident from the above. It should be contrasted with the gross disarticulation described for capitalist Jamaica in the introduction to that country's Five-Year Development Plan, 1978-1982 (Main Document) dealing with "The Planning Process". It describes in a simple and elegant way the disarticulation between producing private capitalist sectors on the one hand and the associated disjunctures within the state sector itself.

In fact, the clearest contrasts in the efficacy of planning that I have yet come across are evident from reading in sequence that Five-Year Development Plan for Jamaica and the official paper presented by the Cuban delegation to the Havana meeting. The Jamaica Plan by itself is worth careful study for those wishing documentary evidence of structural contradictions within dependent capitalist economies.

The Institute of Physical Planning

The headquarters of this Institute is in 'Old Habana'. That in itself is interesting. Now Cuba today is divided into 14 provinces (changed from the six existing before 1975 when People's Power was institutionalized). The main purpose of the Institute is to create and stimulate more equitable divisions in respect of land area, population, the economic base, and the existing urban system which focussed development on metropolitan Havana – the typical plantation capitalist Caribbean 'one city overdevelopment'.

The focus of the Institute is to provide forecasts of the development of territory by natural human settlements. It uses a similar approach for all 14 provinces, with emphasis on urban planning.

As the JUCEPLAN organizational chart shows, the Institute is administered by an architect Director and it is really concerned with technical elaboration of development guidelines on behalf of the provinces. There is a staff of 300, with 120 each under a Vice-Director of Economics and Administration and a Vice-Director of Projects (Provincial levels). Another 60 people work in Technical National matters under another Vice-Director. Architects are a majority of the professionals, 40-50 of them, compared to 10-15 engineers, 10 economists, 15 geographers, 3 demographers, sociologists and other systems analysts. The bias is clearly towards the technical and the urban aspects of physical planning.

The School for National Planning and Management

By the time we reached to the intermediate-level vocational *Escuela Dirección Nacional de Económica* we were all well tuned to Spanish. We were given a brilliant description of the school by its female director and treated to lunch with some of their teachers.

The director informed us that this school is an adjunct of JUCEPLAN. It is the main one of 13 other such schools, one in each province. The students are mostly managers of state enterprises. They follow an intensive residential course over periods of 6 to 9 months. It is planned that after every 4 to 5 years from certification graduates would return to re-tool and update their knowledge. The school maintains close linkage relations with the Faculty of Economics of the University of Havana, the Ministry of Higher Education, almost all central organs, and all state enterprises.

The school was set up by decisions of the First Congress of the CCP (Cuban Communist Party) which also institutionalized Five-Year Plans for national management of the Cuban economy. The school's role is to prepare cadres for directing the economy at the enterprise (micro) level. Other cadres come from the Party, ministries of state, etc. who have some function relating to implementation of plan programmes. The second major objective of the school is to awaken in students the desire for economic studies and economic consciousness so as to create and promote a *philosophy of socialist consciousness.*

JUCEPLAN ORGANIZATIONAL CHART

Advisory Council
i. Council of JUCEPLAN Vice-Presidents
ii. Technical Advisory Council (including Directors of Producing Enterprises)

PRESIDENT

VP   VP   VP   VICE-PRESIDENTS (VP)   VP   VP   VP

GLOBAL DIRECTIONS

- Central elaboration of plan of the general economy
- Intersectoral relations
- Technical material supplies
- Investments
- Territorial (by province)
- Work and salaries (production efficiency, etc.)
- Finance (profits, balance of income & employment)
- Science and Technique (technology)
- Foreign exchange & trade
- Evaluation of investments

BRANCHES (RAMALES) DIRECTION

- Construction
- Transportation
- Public Health
- Education
- Distribution (internal)
- Energy
- Sugar Industry
- Fisheries
- Minerals
- Food Industry

OTHER DIRECTIONS

- Improvement of Mangement Systems
- Electronic Control (Computer Systems)
- Internal organization
- Cadres
- Legal Advisory
- Economics & administration

ADJUNCT INSTITUTIONS

- National school for Economic Direction (School for National Planning and Management) (see text)
- Institute of Economic Research (Indicative Planning to 2000 AD)
- Institute of Physical Planning (see text)

The students now are mostly middle-aged (35-40 years) leaders of socialist enterprises with more than 10 years' experience working in these enterprises. They are working class people who became managers consequent to nationalization. They have no specialist knowledge in the areas of statistics, national planning, etc. Many of these people are also engaged in part-time university study to upgrade their skills and broaden their own interests. So they are engaged in raising both technical and cultural levels.

The teachers at the school are mostly young (under 40 years) graduates of the University of Havana. Some of them are still undertaking postgraduate studies. Basically, these young professors have no practical enterprise management experience; and since their students do, there is scope for a harmonious blend. This way the teachers establish direct links with producing enterprises. Of the 28 professors some 15-20 are permanently employed in state institutions for economic direction, for example, the Central Bank of Cuba. So they are really part-time professors at the *Escuela*.

The list of subjects covered in this 'crash' course to provide students with minimum knowledge of the global direction of socialist economy reads as follows:

Planning the national economy

Organization of industrial enterprise

Accounting

Economic statistics

Political economy – Marxist/Leninist

Philosophy – Marxist/Leninist

Finance and credit

Elementary mathematics

Analysis of industrial enterprise

Students have to do four papers in each course. This list of subjects is indeed impressive and quite formidable. It drives home the point "no one is too old to learn"; also that in revolutionary socialist societies people systematically get to build up their technical capacity. These were the main impressions from my visit to this *Escuela*.

'Round Table Perspectives' on the Capitalist Crisis in Latin America and the Caribbean – Overview

As an invited *delegado* to this meeting of officials, I was most fascinated by the innovative round-table session to consider similarities and contrasts between the Caribbean and Latin America. This session reconfirmed many aspects of the theories of structuralists and Marxist students of development. This of course is not surprising, since the main presenters were among the leading Latin American and Caribbean national and international fraternity. What surprised me was the frankness and clarity that emerged at this level. For we were hearing the views of very high officials of the international and national bureaucracies. Technically distinguished scholars, like Iglesias, Director of CEPAL (UNECLA), Mendez, Director of IPLES, and Girvan, Head of the Jamaican National Planning Agency (NPA) bared the facts of the economic crisis faced by countries within the 'periphery' of international capitalism today.

The most fundamental aspect of the discussion was the critical review of the neoclassical growth model that underlies the Hong Kong/Singapore/Puerto Rico type of economic growth situation. For that basically has been the theoretical underpinning of Caribbean and Latin American (indeed most Third World) development policy in the postwar period – a policy which only served to heighten the contradictions inherent within the dependent capitalist economy. By way of contrast, the Cuban Marxist-based development model seems to be standing the test of time very well indeed. Although seriously affected by the low world sugar prices, the Cuban economy is insulated by mutually cooperative trade agreements with its CMEA (COMECON) partners. So that economy is not buffeted as much by the structural crisis of world capitalism.

Another important conclusion from the analysis is that the crisis fosters a disintegrating tendency among (and within) Third World nation-states. This tendency finds expression in the regression from regional integration programmes – CARICOM, LAFTA, CACM – in this hemisphere. Centripetal forces at work seem to have led to a slowing down of relations between Latin America and the rest of the Third World. In the circumstances, short-term (*ad hoc*) planning becomes prestigious; the temptation increases for individual countries to isolate themselves into the crevices of international capitalism; and there is a "resurgence of infantile liberalism".

Finally, it was suggested that a countervailing force to this diversity in adversity must be *unity*. But how can this be achieved in the circumstances? To answer this question, it seems there is a need for more careful study and analysis of heterogenity and size – particularly in relation to the depression phases of the capitalist long cycles.

Overall, this was by far the most important international/meeting conference I have ever attended. It showed me just how much and how little we know of ourselves. It takes us beyond the facile problematic of "planning without theory and without facts"; but not entirely into the unknown.

Notes

* "Planning in the Caribbean under capitalism and socialism: report on a visit to Cuba". *Social and Economic Studies* 37:3 (1988a).

1   This report, like the technical paper which I presented to the Havana meeting, is dedicated to the Cuban people and our '20 years of Victory'. It was written in April 1979 and revised for publication in March 1987. Revision involved minor editing of the original report.

7

British Honduras and Regional Economic Integration*

One of the characteristics of colonial society is that writers and politicians alike, for the most part, continually use frames of reference which have little relevance to their particular situation. The current discussion about whether or not the destiny of British Honduras[1] should lie with Central America or with the Commonwealth Caribbean is a case in point. It will be argued here that Caribbean (broadly defined to include all areas surrounding the sea by that name) integration should be an objective for future development; and that British Honduras has a strategic role to play in promoting such integration. In short, that the future of British Honduras lies both with Central America and the narrowly defined Commonwealth Caribbean.

International economic relations in the second half of the twentieth century will be dominated by international groupings of one sort or another. The trend is already discernible. The Central American Common Market (CACM) and the Latin American Free Trade Association (LAFTA), as well as economic unions elsewhere, are already in operation. The Central American experience has so far demonstrated some of the benefits to be derived from such types of association; and economists in the region have been busy assessing the benefits and costs of different types of integration. On the whole the economic evidence suggests that substantial benefits are to be derived. Furthermore, the dominance of large-scale foreign corporations in the region's economy calls for a unified approach to harness the region's resources for the benefit of its peoples, otherwise international politics may frustrate any efforts of individual countries.

If total economic integration is to be an objective, what then must be the strategy in working toward this and what role can British Honduras play? The Central American states of Guatemala, El Salvador, Honduras, Nicaragua and Costa Rica have forged ahead. Like Britain in Europe, Panama is now knocking at the door to get in. There is some evidence that Commonwealth Caribbean countries are contemplating some kind of association – the Caribbean Free Trade Association (CARIFTA) between Antigua, Barbados and Guyana is in the planning stage and other territories in this narrower region are beginning to discuss closer types of association. It does not seem very unlikely that a Caribbean Common Market could soon emerge but it is likely that this grouping may be restricted initially to the English-speaking Antilles. A further intermediate step could be the integration with the latter of the Spanish, French and Dutch Antilles as a precursor to a wider Central American and Caribbean integration. And the viability of such a union could provide the basis for a longer-term integration with the rest of Latin America.

British Honduras stands in a unique position to provide the links necessary for the type of development here envisaged. Its geographic position is strategic, but perhaps no more so than Jamaica and to a lesser extent Cuba. It is unique in the sense that it has cultural and historical roots in both the Antillean and the Mainland Caribbean. What Cacho regards, implicitly at least, as conflicting ends (*New World Quarterly*, High Season 1967) and what Grant describes as "problems of a heterogeneous society" with a British-oriented Creole element and a Spanish-oriented Mayan element dominating the picture are precisely the elements that could provide the links for regional economic integration; and in so doing help to create the British Honduran identity which Grant (and Honduras no doubt) regard as necessary. Cultural particularism frustrates development of this identity only if the interests of the different cultures are thought to be conflicting. When these interests are harmonized and when each culture group becomes aware of its own and the other's contribution to the achievement of common objectives, then cultural diversity could become an asset for development and change.

Operationally, if a Commonwealth Caribbean programme of economic integration gets underway in the near future it may suit British Honduras to join that scheme from the beginning. The alternative of joining the CACM alone at this time involves all the difficulties (of negotiation, foregone development possibilities, etc.) faced by newcomers seeking entry into established economic unions. Besides there are already established economic ties (sugar, citrus, etc.) and trading relationships with the Commonwealth Caribbean which would facilitate this first-round association. Subsequently, British Honduras drawing strength from its Spanish-oriented cultural element could assume the initiative within this narrow Antillean grouping to create a wider

Antillean economic union and to forge the larger Central America and Caribbean integration.

Viewed in this context, the debate which the Federation and the Guatemalan issue are said to have provoked seems in a real sense irrelevant. Historically and culturally British Honduras is a part of two regions which in their own interests need eventually to come together in order to secure economic independence and viability. The cultural and political groups in that country need to be aware of the special role this country can play in future development. Awareness of the possibilities seems essential for developing the national cohesion without which the country could hardly assume the role prescribed above.

If political leaders in British Honduras (and in the rest of the region, including Guatemala) can see and appreciate the potential here outlined for that country, then they should quickly put an end to British colonial rule and get on with the work ahead. The region must begin to make efforts to forge its own destiny. Incidentally, Britain is quite busy as usual, trying to forge its own destiny, this time with Europe.

Notes

* "British Honduras and regional economic integration: two views". *New World Quarterly* 3:4 (1967c).

1   The former colony of British Honduras is now the independent country of Belize.

8

Intra-Caribbean Agricultural Trade*

This paper is an out-growth of the view that "in respect of agricultural products the removal of trade barriers might not in itself give rise to a significant volume of intraregional trade" in the Caribbean.[1] The study seeks to identify mechanisms, other than the *elimination of tariff barriers*, for increasing the exchange of agricultural products between the territories of the area.[2]

The paper begins with a general survey of institutional arrangements and policies relating to the marketing of foodstuffs within each territory. Knowledge of such arrangements seems necessary in order to identify structural elements which can provide the organizational framework for expanding the regional trade. In the second section, current patterns and flows of intraregional trade are described. Since the present trade is greater for certain commodities than for others and also as between certain territories than for others, these special cases may provide insights into the types of mechanisms which would be effective for overall regional trade. Particular obstacles to the trade are then outlined in the third section and a brief discussion of the present possibilities for expanding the trade is provided in the fourth section which also deals with the possible mechanisms which are suggested by the study.

Institutional arrangements and Policies Relating to the Internal Marketing of Foodstuffs

Agricultural production and trade in all West Indian territories have been traditionally geared to extraregional markets, particularly the UK and Canada. Each territory produces a narrow range of export crops for these markets and depends heavily on imported foodstuffs from outside the region. In the postwar period, however, several governments in the area have introduced policies and institutions designed to stimulate domestic food production. These attempts have been fitful in some territories and sustained in others. Governments have been generally concerned with raising rural living standards and more recently with balance of payment problems. But there have been significant differences in the nature of the various programmes, and with the success that has attended these, from place to place.

The first general characteristic of the region to be noted is that it is far from homogeneous in terms of levels of development and importance of the food-producing sector. In general, the relative importance of this sector is greater in the smaller than in the larger territories; the share of the gross domestic product varies from about 5% for Barbados and Jamaica to close to 50% for Montserrat.

Another general characteristic of the region worth noting at the outset is that there are significant differences in the cost of living (and of foodstuffs) as between territories. Average prices of food tend to be higher in Jamaica than in any of the other territories. These differences have implications for intraregional trade which will emerge as the discussion proceeds. For the moment, attention is directed to arrangements for internal marketing in the respective territories.

The bulk of fresh foodstuffs produced and consumed within each territory is marketed more or less unsystematically in public markets by numerous small agents, known in different places as higglers, hucksters or peddlers. In the eastern Caribbean these agents also participate in inter-territorial trade. Processed foodstuffs of domestic origin are usually marketed through commission agents whose main activity is the distribution of processed food from the outside world. Most governments in the region have set up marketing institutions of one kind or another and have introduced policies designed to improve supply and marketing.

There are basically two categories of public marketing authorities now operating in most territories; statutory organizations usually designated as marketing corporations, and departments of government.

Marketing Corporations

These now exist in Jamaica, Barbados, Trinidad and Tobago and Guyana. With the exception of Trinidad where a Board had been set up in 1949, the corporations were all established in recent years. The functions of these agencies are, more or less, similar to those set out in Jamaica's Agricultural Marketing Corporation Act of 1963: "(i) to provide and maintain adequate marketing outlets for agricultural produce; (ii) to buy and sell agricultural products; (iii) to provide for the collection, transportation, storage, grading, packing and processing of agricultural produce; and (iv) to import and export agricultural produce". The agencies are intended to promote diversification of agriculture by providing assured markets for domestic foodstuffs. The corporations receive financial support from the governments, each of which has undertaken to subsidize agency operations until such time as these become viable profit-making organizations.

In Jamaica, the Agricultural Marketing Corporation (AMC) offers minimum guaranteed prices for a number of specific crops and purchases these crops from farmers at established buying stations (or where quantities are sufficiently large, on farms). From time to time, the corporation also enters into contract with farmers for the planting of specified crops on stated acreages and at given periods; in these cases the corporation is contracted to purchase the entire yield at fixed prices.

The corporation has storage facilities for fruit and vegetables but these are considered to be inadequate. Produce purchased from farmers is assembled, sorted, graded, and packaged; and sold to market vendors, supermarkets, hotels, restaurants, and government institutions. Less than 10% of domestic foodstuffs consumed in Jamaica now passes through the AMC. A small portion of sales are now exported to the UK, Canada and the US where produce such as yams, pumpkins, plantains, mangoes and chochoes (chrystophene) find a ready market among West Indian migrants.

The AMC also operates a cornmeal factory which produces some 200,000 bags annually – most of the raw material coming from abroad. In the 1965 trading year, for example, 7,100 tons were imported as against 1,149 tons of locally-grown corn.

In Barbados the Barbados Marketing Corporation (BMC) is, by legislation, the sole exporter of agricultural produce and is empowered to grant licences to any firm or person to export specific quantities of produce, subject to any condition it may deem fit. The corporation does not operate buying stations in farming areas and does not guarantee purchase of whatever produce farmers may bring to its main office in Bridgetown. There are no fixed prices but the corporation frequently publishes a range of prices. It depends heavily on imported food supplies: beets and carrots from North America; cauliflower, carrots and cabbages from England; sweet potatoes, nuts, shallots, pumpkins, cassava, cucumbers and fruits from St Vincent; plantains and bananas from St Lucia and fruits from Trinidad and Dominica.

Organized agricultural marketing in Trinidad is now in a state of transition with the establishment of a Central Marketing Agency for the wholesale disposal of all foodstuffs to municipal market vendors, institutions, etc., and for retailing to consumers. Cold storage facilities, warehouses, wholesale and retail departments, and administrative offices are now under construction for this purpose. The government plans to purchase all farm produce at guaranteed prices; to develop farmers' associations for the assembling of produce; and to establish processing facilities for surpluses. Up to now, 'organized' marketing has been carried on by the statutory marketing board.

The Board's operations, through its 11 buying depots, have been relatively limited. It guarantees prices for certain commodities and purchases and transports all that farmers supply at those prices. It also supplies farmers with fertilizer, insecticides and seeds. Foodstuffs purchased by the Board are sold chiefly to institutions and wholesale market vendors, except for pigeon peas which is transported directly to a processing factory – International Foods Ltd. The Board also does a thriving business with the purchase and ripening of bananas and has ripening room facilities for this purpose.

Only the Port of Spain depot has cold storage facilities (for vegetables and yams) and surplus supplies from other depots have to be stored there. The Board imports root crops from St Vincent and vegetable seeds from India and North America. (It recently imported one consignment of Irish potatoes from Jamaica).

In Guyana the Guyana Marketing Corporation has a wider range of operations than any of the others already described. In addition to produce marketing, it operates a meal and flour-processing plant, a ham and bacon factory, a fish marketing centre, and a milk pasteurization plant. In produce marketing the corporation purchases food crops from farmers at its depots at guaranteed prices, and in turn sells to wholesalers and retailers.

Purchases are also made of other crops for which there are no price guarantees. There are plans to establish a number of rural depots with suitable cold storage facilities. The corporation now exports quantities of fruit and vegetables to Trinidad, Barbados and the UK.

The corporation's processing factory dries and stores corn and manufactures cornmeal and plantain flour. It also supplies raw materials for an animal feed plant. The factory now operates at a loss and has surplus stocks of plantain flour. The ham and bacon factory is a profitable operation which supplies 13% of domestic ham consumption and 82% of bacon consumption in 1964 and is now gearing for export production.

Government Marketing Departments

Organized marketing of agricultural crops is carried on in a number of territories by departments of government – the Peasant Development Service in Antigua, marketing depots in St Kitts-Nevis-Anguilla, and the Marketing Board in St Vincent.

In Antigua, the Peasant Development Service operates buying depots throughout the island and has a central depot in St John's. The Service guarantees to purchase all that farmers deliver but prices are not stated or guaranteed. Purchases are usually made at ruling market prices. Some of the foodstuffs purchased by the Service is actually grown in neighbouring islands and brought to the depot by hucksters. The Service also administers loans to farmers and provides them with fertilizers, insecticides and ploughing machinery.

There are two depots (one each in St Kitts and Nevis) serving the islands of St Kitts-Nevis-Anguilla. The depot in St Kitts is run by a government employed manager as a profit-making enterprise. The manager travels to farms, and purchases produce which he transports to the depot for subsequent sale. He also orders needed supplies from the Marketing Officer in Nevis. Profits become part of government revenue.

In St Vincent the Marketing Board is strongly export-oriented. The Board purchases from farmers and exports mainly sweet potatoes, yams, eddoes, tannias, pumpkins and vegetables to other territories such as Trinidad and Barbados.

An Institutional Framework for Regional Trade

The marketing corporations and departments which now exist in individual territories could provide the basic framework for regional trade in agricultural products. Although each of these is now principally concerned with internal marketing, several also participate in the imports and exports of foodstuffs in regional as well as extraregional markets. There are no formal agreements yet for the exchange of products between these territorial agencies but in at least two instances there are informal arrangements for this type of exchange.

Trading arrangements between territorial government marketing agencies could be formalized for the region as a whole. A number of supplementary measures would, of course, be required to establish and promote the trade. These are considered in some detail in the final section. But at this point it should be noted that a regional commission would be required to coordinate the activities of these agencies and the trade between them would be stimulate and reinforced if the price incentives they offer to farmers were based on a regional production programme.

In Trinidad and Tobago, Jamaica, and Guyana, guaranteed prices generally apply to the same types of commodities. In Jamaica, of eleven guaranteed commodities in 1965, only four (carrots, pumpkins, melons and strawberries) were not also guaranteed in one or both of the other two countries. In Trinidad and Tobago, all the eight commodities guaranteed there were also guaranteed elsewhere. While in Guyana six of thirteen commodities were also guaranteed elsewhere.

There may be several reasons why guaranteed prices for certain commodities may exist in one territory but not in others. Supplies of a commodity may be adequate in one country but inadequate in another; in that event a guaranteed price may be offered in the latter but not in the former. Or it may be that a commodity is grown in one place but not in others; strawberries, for example. Furthermore, guaranteed prices may be applied for political reasons – *ie* to provide favour for certain types or groups of farmers.

To the extent that differences in commodity coverage between territories do in fact reflect differences in the adequacy of supplies, national price guarantees are an impediment to regional trade. This is clearly the case with at least two commodities; oranges and grapefruit. Both Jamaica and Trinidad and Tobago are exporters of these products; supply being well in excess of domestic requirements no guaranteed price is applied. That guaranteed prices are offered for these commodities in Guyana suggests that supply there is inadequate. In such a case Guyana could secure its citrus requirements from either of the other countries instead of trying to stimulate production with price guarantees.

Insofar as government marketing agencies successfully encourage domestic production of the same commodities, the long-term scope for trade between them will tend to be limited. One basic requirement, therefore, for the proposed institutionalized trade is a coordination of guaranteed price policies to allow for some form of specialization of production in the various territories.

Otherwise, the proposed trade would tend to proceed on a discontinuous basis – according to the coincidence of surpluses in one territory with shortages in another.

Current Patterns of Regional Trade

A separate study dealing with the dynamics of West Indian economic integration provides quantitative information on the present intraregional flow of trade in agricultural products.[3] In this section, attention is directed instead to the general terms, conditions and arrangements whereby this trade now proceeds. There are, for example, some regional commodity trade agreements and various forms of informal and ad hoc arrangements in existence. Since these might have the capacity or potential for further trade expansion, they need to be considered, if only, briefly.

At present, the regional market tends to be sectionalized. There is a *northern* trade centered on Jamaica and including the Cayman Islands, Turks and Caicos Islands, the Bahamas, Bermuda and British Honduras. A *southern* trade centered on Trinidad includes the Windward Islands, Barbados and Guyana. The remaining Leeward Islands market is more or less open and is supplied as much by Jamaica and Trinidad as perhaps by Puerto Rico. Schooner traffic is particularly important in the eastern and southern trades in which hucksters and peddlers market produce between territories. It is believed that because much of this trade is unregulated, official trade returns do not now fully record these movements of produce. If this type of trading is to be expanded, a detailed study of it would be required.

The pattern of commodity flows is relatively simple. Fresh fruit and vegetables and starchy roots are the major items in the eastern and southern trades. Trinidad supplies a few processed food products – particularly citrus products and canned peas. But Jamaica is the major regional supplier of processed food products and it also supplies small quantities of fresh foodstuffs for the northern trade. Guyana is the regional supplier of rice. There is little or no recorded intraregional trade in livestock products.

Commodity Trade Agreements

Rice

Before Federation, Guyana had separate agreements with individual territories for trade in rice. A Regional Rice Agreement replaced these during the period of Federation and, since the federal break-up, there are now three separate agreements: one with the Windwards, Leewards and Barbados; another with Jamaica and yet another with Trinidad.

The Windwards-Leewards-Barbados agreement is for a period of eight years (beginning 1 October 1962), subject to annual review and modifications. The main provision of the agreement is for Guyana to supply all the rice required by these territories which in turn agree to purchase only from Guyana unless that country is unable to satisfy their requirements. These territories have a first option on Guyana's rice exports.

The Guyana-Jamaica agreement is an annual contract for specified quantities and prices which are fixed in advance. The Guyana-Trinidad agreement is based on a two-year contract with prices and quantities also fixed in advance.

Intergovernmental agreements for the regional trade in rice benefit from the fact that the Guyana Rice Marketing Corporation is the sole authority responsible for the marketing of rice in that country. Most of the rice produced in Guyana is destined for export. In 1964, for example, only about 46,000 tons out of a total production of 135,000 tons were retained for domestic consumption. In addition to the export trade under the agreements described above, limited quantities of bulk and broken rice are exported to the French and Dutch West Indies, Cuba, Venezuela, the UK and Canada.

The bilateral arrangement with Cuba in 1964 demonstrates how important intergovernmental arrangements can be in expanding the regional trade. That country alone accounted for roughly 45% of Guyana's rice export commitments in 1964. Trinidad and Tobago took about 25%, Jamaica 15% and Windwards-Leewards-Barbados the remaining 15% (of which Barbados accounted for more than half).

That rice is first in value of individual agricultural products in regional trade and that Guyana exports this commodity chiefly to other territories in the area can no doubt be attributed, in part at least, to the formal agreements covering this trade. It *demonstrates that commodity agreements deserve to be considered as one type of mechanism for increasing regional trade.* But such agreements are easier to negotiate when natural conditions lead to specialization of production, as in rice. Otherwise, they are more difficult to negotiate on a regional basis unless there is some regional programme for agricultural production.

Oils and fats

The present oils and fats agreement between the Governments of Barbados, Dominica, Grenada, Guyana, Montserrat, St Lucia, St Vincent, and Trinidad and Tobago came into effect in February 1963. Its objectives are: (i) to uphold and encourage the extension of the coconut industry in the respective territories; (ii) to encourage the territories in the manufacture of oils and fats and thereby assist in the development of secondary industries; and (iii) to regulate trade in oils and fats between the territories within the area and between the area and other countries. Under the agreement, all oils and fats imported into any participating territory must be imported from another such territory; and likewise for exports.

The agreement permits a participating territorial government to liberalize exports of copra in the form of dessicated coconuts or whole nuts outside the region to the extent of 10% of its average surplus over a three-year period. Participating governments can export or import seed material and can permit manufacturers to import other types of oils from outside the region for use in the manufacture of special high grade products as well as for use in making lard and margarine so long as quantities do not exceed 10% of the amount actually used in the preceding year. If the regional market does not arrange to clear a declared surplus or deficit within four weeks, extraregional trading arrangements can then be made. Export prices are fixed by the annual conference but internal prices of oils and fats (and taxation of the industry) are the domestic concern of participating governments.

The oils and fats agreement serves to insulate the participating region as a whole from outside competition and to regulate the flow of trade. It has no doubt helped to expand trade insofar as it has served to reduce imports of oils and fats from extraregional sources. It has perhaps also served to increase production in individual territories; thus creating a negative trade effect. Such expansion as may have occurred through trade diversion could be further enhanced if non-participating territories were to join the agreement. The oils and fats case illustrates that even where there is no specialization of production within the region, trade expansion can take place if *formal agreements for the intraregional balancing of surpluses and shortages* are made. This procedure which is implicit in the oils and fats agreement can provide the basis for general agricultural trading arrangements between the existing government-sponsored marketing agencies described earlier.

Informal Trading Patterns

Private entrepreneurs are the most important agents of intraregional trade in processed foodstuffs and also fresh produce trade in the eastern and southern Caribbean. The processed-food trade is normally arranged by manufacturers in the respective territories and their commission agents in other territories.

The fresh produce trade is carried on by different types of people. In Guyana, traders who may own or hire small schooners travel along the coast and river banks purchasing foodstuffs which they take to other territories, chiefly Trinidad and Barbados, for sale, Hucksters are responsible for an active weekly trade between Grenada and Trinidad. The trade from Grenada is mostly in fruits such as soursop, golden apples, plums, limes, sapodillas (naseberries), sugar apples and avocado pears. The hucksters do their own harvesting, grading and packaging (in wooden crates) and take the produce aboard schooners to Port of Spain markets where they sell to their regular Trinidad counterparts. The schooners usually leave Grenada on Tuesdays and return on Saturdays with the hucksters bringing back supplies of commodities such as sugar, milk (sweetened and powdered), onions and flour.

This type of huckster trade on schooners is typical of the Leewards and Windwards. In Antigua, for example, many of the hucksters in the public markets come from Dominica and Montserrrat with 'loads' of produce. And peddlers from St Kitts and Nevis trade along the coasts of the French islands on their way to Anguilla. Many of these hucksters or peddlers are farmers themselves so that this type of trade is very much like the pattern of internal trade within the larger territories.

It is not unlikely that heavy losses may be involved in the inter-island huckster trade on account of poor packaging, etc. A detailed study of this trade should be made to see what assistance can be provided for traders in order to improve and expand the trade. It is clear, nevertheless, that adequate shipping arrangements can provide a major stimulus for regional trade. That intraregional trade in fresh produce is so great in the eastern and southern Caribbean is due, in large measure, to the existence of low-cost schooner traffic. If Jamaica and the rest of the northern Caribbean are to participate in the trade, *adequate shipping and/or air cargo facilities will need to be provided.*[4] Since Jamaica is potentially a major food exporter and importer in the region as a whole, investment in shipping could result in a material increase in intraregional trade.

Basic Obstacles to Regional Agricultural Trade

There are several factors which now serve to inhibit intraregional trade in agricultural products and which need to be considered before mechanisms for expanding the trade can be proposed. Some of these, like restrictions on food imports, are matters of policy which can be changed quickly. Others, such as the undeveloped regional market infrastructure, have to built up over time. Some of these problems are considered in this section.

Restrictions on Food Imports

In Jamaica, Trinidad and Tobago and Guyana there are restrictions on the importation of agricultural products. But elsewhere (Barbados, Antigua, St Vincent and St Kitts-Nevis-Anguilla) there are no restrictions on food imports from other territories. The restrictive import policies of the three largest territories are intended to serve the same basic purpose in respect of each territory – *ie* to encourage domestic food production.[5] These restrictions will serve further to limit the scope for intraregional trade in the long run – insofar as the restrictions in individual territories are similar in commodity coverage.

The restrictions in the three territories are generally similar in commodity coverage. Where imports are allowed under some form of licence, no preference is given for imports from other territories in the region. As in the case of guaranteed farm prices, what seems to be required is regional agreement on restrictive import policies. But since there are now the main instruments for food import substitution at the national level, some basic agreement on regional import substitution would be necessary. Again, this points to the need for a coordinated regional agricultural production programme. At the very least, it would require an immediate relaxation of present restrictions on food imports originating within the region in order to promote an expansion of regional trade in a number of important commodities.

Problems in Processed Food Trade

Questionnaires were sent to 26 food processing firms in Jamaica in order to ascertain what specific problems are involved in intraregional processed food trade. Unfortunately, only nine of these firms returned the information requested. Even though the number of returns is small, it is nevertheless considered useful to give a summary picture of the situation as presented by these firms.

Of the nine firms reporting, seven are now involved in some form of export trade and five of these export to the Caribbean market.[6] Only one of the nine firms has never tried to develop a Caribbean trade while another tried without success. Three of the nine firms indicated that they have problems in securing export markets of any kind – the main problems being shipping and weak competitive position on account of "high raw material prices".

In response to questions concerning problems of exporting to the Caribbean market, four firms mentioned high freight rates, three complained that agency representation is inadequate and unreliable, two mentioned tariff barriers and one mentioned small size of orders. Freight rates and agency representation are the only two factors which can be said to be of general importance from these limited returns. The first points again to the need for adequate shipping facilities and should be considered in the light of an earlier study of freight rates by Keirstead and Levitt.[7] The second needs further discussion here. Effective agency representation is important for manufacturers. The firms involved in the survey indicated a need for "reliable agencies with adequate finance to order substantial quantities" and "dependable agents who are stockists as well as distributors".

As it is, commission agents of the type described above already exist in the region but they are more involved with the long-established trade between individual territories and the rest of the world. Their intraregional connections are few or nonexistent. It is not unreasonable to assume that if measures were introduced to divert some of the trade with the outside world that these very agents would develop regional links to service the trade so diverted. But even without such developments, an opportunity now exists for governments in the region to provide Caribbean manufacturers with effective agency representation. Government marketing agencies in the various territories can be used as agents for food processing firms in the region in order to expand the regional trade in processed food products.

Market Infrastructure

The marketing of farm produce involves a number of processes which require certain physical facilities. And where the latter are inadequate or nonexistent the movement of produce (in time, place and form) is inhibited. Briefly, the processes involved are collection and assembly of produce from farms, transportation, standardization (sorting and grading), storage, processing, packaging, advertising, financing, risk bearing, buying and selling at various levels (farm, factory, wholesaler and retailer) and the bringing of buyers and sellers together (market information). The physical facilities which make it possible for these processes and functions to be performed by firms and other marketing institutions can be collectively described as the market infrastructure.

By and large, the existing regional marketing infrastructure in the Caribbean is undeveloped and, therefore, serves to impede intraregional trade. This is partly an extension of the undeveloped nature of the infrastructure for internal marketing within individual territories. Inadequate facilities for collection and assembly of produce; for storage, transportation and financing; rudimentary systems of standardization and grading; and inadequate market information are all characteristic of internal marketing and more so of the regional trade. It is obvious that trade between the territories could not take place without shipping and air services (transportation). And it is equally obvious that unless potential buyers in one island are aware of the quantities, qualities and prices of supplies held by sellers in another island (market information) trade can hardly take place. Furthermore, buyers and sellers must be able to communicate easily with each other.[8] Consequently, an important prerequisite for expansion of the regional trade is the development of the regional market infrastructure. This will involve, inter alia, some form of coordination for the establishment of uniform grades and standards and the provision of market information. The machinery for doing this is considered in the final section of the paper.

Possibilities and Mechanisms for intraregional Trade Expansion

Some Obvious Possibilities

The discussion here deliberately takes a limited view of the possibilities for an expansion of intraregional trade in agricultural products for two reasons. First, it was not really the intention of this paper to consider the scope for such expansion; and second, the dynamics of trade expansion is considered in a separate study.[9] The possibilities for expansion depend in the first instance on removing the obstacles mentioned in the preceding section. These obstacles are of two basic types: *policy* and *practical*.

On the practical side, immediate trade expansion could be secured through efforts aimed at a regional balancing of surpluses and shortages. In this connection, rice, Irish potatoes and citrus come to mind immediately but since policy considerations as well are involved in these cases the prospects will be examined later. For the moment, attention is directed to some possibilities for trade in fruit and vegetables. The immediate potential for trade in these products depends partly on the existence of seasonal differences in their production as between territories. The limited amount of information available on this score suggests that in general "the seasons on many islands differ only slightly from one another or not at all". Available data indicate that there is seldom a total overlap of periods and that, therefore, some scope for trade now exists for several commodities. More detailed information on all countries in the region is needed in order fully to assess the existing potential for balancing seasonal surpluses and shortages.[10]

Bits and pieces of evidence relating to particular commodities support the hypothesis that some scope now exists for balancing surpluses and shortages. For tomatoes, for example, Montserrat is said to be

excellently suited . . . Because of good rainfall Montserrat produces tomatoes over a longer period than most of the other countries in the Caribbean. And therefore the island has a surplus when other countries have a shortage . . . This state of affairs offers unprecedented possibilities for the trade in tomatoes.

Montserrat also has an export surplus of carrots from March to July whereas there is an all year shortage in Guyana (and perhaps other territories). In Dominica, "from February to March cabbages are abundant and need an export market in the Caribbean area" while there is an all-year shortage of this product in Guyana. In Antigua "during the tourist season and during the dry months (February to May) the demand for fresh fruits and vegetables is high and much import by air and sea takes place from the US and Canada".

Some of the practical requirements for seizing such trade opportunities are: (i) knowledge of supply availabilities and shortages; (ii) information regarding quality and prices; (iii) trade organization and contracts; and (iv) shipping and air cargo facilities. *Government marketing agencies in the region should begin immediately to assemble information in respect of supply availabilities and shortages.*

The scope for trade expansion is considerably greater when policy changes are contemplated. As the discussion in preceding sections indicates, the separate policies of all territories are geared to encourage domestic production of the same commodities in every place. The results of these independent policies have not been altogether encouraging. Success has been and is likely to be achieved only in cases where production bottlenecks do not exist, as with certain vegetables, poultry and eggs which are not demanding in respect of scarce land resources and for which scale economies may not be very significant. But when such is not the case, as with most livestock products, the independent policies may fail to stimulate production. In the latter case, regional coordination of production and trade may help to overcome production and market-size bottlenecks at the national or territorial level.

The evidence suggests that a substantial expansion of intraregional trade can be secured by a coordinated regional effort to substitute imports from outside the region. Many of the commodities now imported from extraregional sources can, without much difficulty, be produced in the Caribbean.[11] Rice and Irish potatoes were already mentioned. But the same applies to fruit and vegetables, livestock products, peas, beans and other pulses. Some indication of the extent of this extraregional trade is provided by the following tabulation of Jamaica's rice imports in 1964.

Table 8.1 *Jamaica's rice imports, 1964.*

		Quantity (000 lbs)	Value (000 $)
Total		60,573.0	2,010.7
of which:	Guyana	2,020.2	897.6
	USA	23,899.6	1,011.5

Other minor sources of rice were the Netherlands, Belgium and Hong Kong. These data suggest that both Guyana and Jamaica would benefit if the latter could secure all its rice requirements from the Caribbean. Jamaica stands to gain since the lower unit value of Guyanese rice (even if it reflects a genuine quality difference) would have a favourable cost-of-living effect – an important consideration of a country with a highly inequitable distribution of income.

The actual quantities and values of these products are quite considerable. Caribbean countries depend to an unwarranted degree on outside sources for supplies of certain fresh vegetables and pulses. It does not appear that price (and therefore cost-of-living) considerations can fully explain this dependence.[12]

This excessive dependence on outside sources of food supplies derives partly from practical problems involved in intraregional trade and partly from policy problems. Solution of the latter would help materially in removing the practical obstacles. It seems therefore that changes in policy in the direction of regional coordination of production and towards regional import substitution are crucial for securing the existing potential for expansion of the intraregional trade.

Non-Tariff Mechanisms for Expanding Intraregional Trade

General indication of some of the measures which are required to promote regional agricultural trade has already been provided by the discussion in all the foregoing sections. What now remains to be done is to bring these together for more detailed consideration, to introduce additional measures, and to suggest some kind of institutional machinery for implementing and administering the proposed measures.

The following have come in for previous mention:

1 formal trading arrangements between government marketing agencies in the various territories;

2 regional coordination of guaranteed farm price policies;

3 specific regional commodity agreements for specialization of production and/or for intraregional balancing of surpluses and shortages;

4 the establishment of adequate shipping and air cargo facilities, especially for trade between the northern Caribbean and the rest of the region;

5 agreement on regional import substitution in place of substitution at the national or territorial level;

6 a regional production programme associated with (v) particularly with respect to livestock (ex-poultry) production and other types of production activity with resource and/or market constraints at the level of the individual country or unit;

7 relaxation of present restrictions (in Jamaica, Trinidad and Tobago and Guyana) on food imports originating within the region;

8 the use of government marketing agencies as commission agents for food processing firms in the region; and

9 development of the regional market infrastructure to provide transportation, storage and financing facilities, uniform systems of grading, market information and communications.

More detailed study of each of these proposals will be required before they can be considered for implementation. But it is considered desirable to put forward some tentative guidelines on ways of proceeding.

One way in which a start can be made is by the immediate establishment of a Regional (Agricultural) Trade Commission with ultimate responsibility to (a) coordinate the regional trade activities of government marketing agencies; (b) provide market information ; (c) standardize the grading and classification of produce and develop systems of inspection; (d) undertake or commission feasibility studies on regional shipping and air cargo services; (e) advise on the coordination of guarantee price policies; and (f) study tariff mechanisms for expanding the trade.[13] The Commission could consist *initially* of representatives of government marketing agencies from each territory.[14] (It would be desirable, therefore, that government marketing departments be transformed into statutory bodies in all the territories where this has not yet been done). These representatives would be in a position to supply each other with information on surpluses and shortages in the various territories at different times of year, based on past experiences. They could begin to draw up forms of contract for trading between the agencies they represent. The representatives could also receive representations from manufacturers of food products regarding the agency service mentioned above. The advantages of this approach are that marketing agency representatives are likely to be well informed regarding prospects for institutional trade and are in a position to take direct action. Furthermore, this is less costly than if an independent Commission were to be set up. The disadvantages are that these representatives are likely to lose sight of certain long-term considerations and may not have the time to devote to matters which, in the short run at least, appear to bring little benefit to the particular bodies which they represent.

It is clear, nevertheless, that the existing marketing agencies in the various territories can provide the institutional network for a regional trade and that their activities in this direction would require some central coordination. Their direct involvement in the latter is highly desirable. For continuous study and review of the more dynamic aspects of trade expansion, the governments of the region would need to provide research facilities for the Commission or alternatively make provision to relieve it of this responsibility.

The lack of market information was mentioned as one factor which now impedes trade. *A regional commodity* market for spot and futures trading is one possible mechanism for providing market information. But one of the preconditions for the operation of this type of trading is a well-developed communications network. The existing communication links between the islands may not be adequate for this purpose. However, this is a matter which the Trade Commission (if established) could keep under review. One important advantage of a commodity market is that it is normally effective in keeping buyers in close touch with sellers. So far as general market information is concerned, the most practical short-term proposal is that the marketing agencies provide the Regional Commission with weekly price quotations and forecasts of surpluses and deficits for each territory; and this information can in turn be published in the press. One basic requirement for the flow of such information and for the transmission of orders is a direct communication link between the various agencies. It would perhaps be less costly to establish independent telephone or telex connections between agencies than it would be to rely on the regular commercial system. This will require further investigation.

In addition to high freight rates on processed foodstuffs, the present regional shipping service is grossly inadequate for regional trade in fresh agricultural produce. The Federal boats need to be equipped with cool storage space (or electrical ventilating systems) in order to accommodate this trade. Alternatively, separate boats would have to be provided, especially for the trade to and from Jamaica. Investigation is also required in respect of air cargo for perishable food products. In this connection it is important to note that such products are now flown into a number of the territories from as far away as California in the US. Provision should also be made for the study and perhaps regulation of schooner trade in the eastern and southern Caribbean and for whatever assistance may be necessary to further expand this trade.

The proposal for a regional food import substitution programme warrants some further discussion. In addition to the impact of regional trade, such a policy would serve to increase the utilization of existing resources and capacity at both the national and regional levels. National (or territorial) import substitution tends to result in surpluses and to create excess capacity in these small markets. In Jamaica, for example, the food-processing industry is now operating at anywhere from 33 to 73% of capacity. The result is a relatively high cost of production not only for Jamaica but also for other territories which are in process of developing similar lines of production independently since the same commodities could be produced from existing underutilized capacity. And since the process involves further underutilization of capacity in the region as a whole, its competitive position *vis-à-vis* rest of the world is not improved thereby.

Even before the development of a regional programme for agricultural production regional import substitution can be introduced on a commodity basis where there is already some degree of specialization, as in the case of rice and Irish potatoes. Jamaica now produces about one-half of what Irish potatoes the rest of the region imports from outside and it has the capacity to double production – especially if certain lands are withdrawn from bananas to facilitate export substitution with the Windward Islands, as is suggested in a separate paper.[15] A regional potato agreement along the lines of the rice agreement between Guyana and the Leewards-Windwards-Barbados could perhaps be negotiated. In addition, further scope exists for expanding Caribbean trade in rice if Jamaica were to import more from Guyana and less from the US. This can be negotiated along with potatoes since Guyana has a year-round shortage of this commodity while Jamaica has a surplus for most of the year. specific commodity agreements involving regional balancing of surpluses and shortages can also be used to promote regional import substitution. But a proliferation of such agreements is unwieldy and cannot match the potential benefits derived from an integrated regional production programme.

Food import substitution on a regional basis must be viewed not only in terms of the potential contribution to an expansion of intra-Caribbean trade but also in terms of the scope which such a policy offers for the rationalization of agriculture in individual territories and in the region as a whole.

Notes
_____

* An abbreviated version of G.L. Beckford and M.H. Guscott, "Non-tariff mechanisms for increasing intra-Caribbean agricultural trade". *Studies in Regional Economic Integration* 2:2 (1967).

1   Report on Conference on Regional Economic Integration in the Commonwealth Caribbean held at the University of the West Indies, Mona, 5-7 August 1965, (unpublished mimeo), p. 4.
2   Even though the descriptive portions of the paper relate mainly to the Commonwealth Caribbean, the proposed mechanisms have a wider relevance. The study is largely exploratory and is intended to outline some possibilities and suggest areas for further study.
3   H. R. Brewster and C. Y. Thomas, *The Dynamics of West Indian Economic Integration* (Mona, Jamaica: ISER, University of the West Indies, 1967).
4   The present regional shipping service is inadequate. The 'Federal' boats are not equipped with the necessary cool storage space for the fresh produce trade. Specialized cargo vessels seem to be a basic requirement. And the feasibility of providing air cargo facilities should be explored.
5   The import policies are therefore complementary to the guaranteed price policies described earlier.
6   These include manufacturers of citrus products, guava jelly, mangoes, carrot juice, cocoa products, egg nog, dessert preparations, jelly crystals, sauces and ackees.
7   B. S. Keirstead and Kari Levitt, "Inter-territorial freight rates and the federal shipping service" (Mona, Jamaica: ISER, University of the West Indies, 1962).
8   In this connection, telephone and telegraph services between the islands are important. In Puerto Rico, for example, vegetable wholesalers are said to rely more on imports from the US than from neighbouring islands because as soon as scarcity exists they can telephone Miami or California and have their orders filled within a day or two.
9   See Brewster and Thomas, *The Dynamics*, especially Chs. 6 and 7.
10 In addition to the respective periods for each product, some knowledge of the magnitudes of surpluses and shortages would be required as well.
11 The trade statistics of various islands reveal some ludicrous examples. One such case is Grenada importing citrus products from the UK and Canada which do not produce citrus while Trinidad, a citrus exporter is about 100 miles away.
12 Regardless of price, questions need to be raised about West Indian dependence on countries such as Portugal, Rhodesia and the Union of South Africa, all of

which show up all too frequently in the trade statistics of the region.

13 In the last connection, much can be gained from the experience of the CACM where the basic problems are similar to those of the Caribbean region and where tariff mechanisms appear to have already caused a marked expansion in regional agricultural trade (see *UNECLA Economic Bulletin for Latin America*, March 1965, pp. 23-47).

14 Ultimately, it may be more desirable to have a Commission consisting of persons who are independent of established agencies since such individuals would be less likely to subjugate regional considerations to purely national ones where these may conflict in the short run.

15 See "The West Indian banana industry: the scope for rationalization and regional collaboration", *Studies on Regional Economic Integration* 2:3 (Mona, Jamaica: ISER, University of the West Indies, 1967).

9

Land Reform for the Betterment of Caribbean Peoples*

I am concerned, in this paper, in setting out the fundamental issues concerning the land problem in the Caribbean.[1] The orientation of the discussion is theoretical and the intention is to place the land reform question in the general perspective of the social welfare of the peoples of the region. Since the majority of the population of these islands depend on some kind of rural activity for a livelihood, the land problem is one of supreme importance.

The title of the paper suggests that land reform is necessary for Caribbean development. This assertion will be substantiated in the discussion to follow. Even the most casual observer of the West Indian scene will recognize the need for land reform. Yet this field of enquiry has hardly been explored by economists of the region. Hence the need for spelling out the issues involved in a way that will stimulate attention and provide general guidelines for policy. That is precisely my intention in writing the paper.

The exposition is sequenced as follows. The first section clarifies the basic concepts underlying the analysis; land reform and rural development are defined in the specific context of our analysis. The second section summarizes the evidence concerning certain economic effects of land reform in other Third World countries. This is considered necessary since only Cuba among the Caribbean islands has any experience in this connection. (The government 'land reform schemes' in several islands do not, in my opinion, fulfill any of the requirements of land reform. And the Cuban experience will be dealt with at the conference by others who have the basic information.)

The third section presents an analysis of the likely effects of land reform on agricultural development in the Caribbean. That analysis places the

Caribbean reality in the context of experience elsewhere; and it makes projections of probable effects. The fourth and final section looks at land reform in the region in the broader context of overall development.

Land Reform and Rural Development

We need to open the discussion with two basic questions. First, what do we mean by land reform? And secondly, land reform for what?

The term 'land reform' has tended to mean different things to different people. In general, it relates to some distributive change in the ownership and rights to the use of land. As Warriner looks at the contemporary world scene, "Methods of distributive reform may be classified as (i) integral, *ie* redistribution of ownership carried out together with other institutional changes designed to increase agricultural productivity; and (ii) simple, *ie* redistribution only, with little or no support from other measures."[2]

In practice, integral reform has involved a very short list of institutional changes; credit and extension being the chief areas of concern. And, as indicated, above, the objective of these supporting changes is to increase agricultural productivity. I think that it will be useful for us to introduce an extension of the concept of 'integral reform'. A higher stage of integral reform is one which involves redistribution of ownership along with changes in all the institutional factors that govern the mobilization of rural resources with the objective of a betterment of the welfare of rural people. I will call this method institutional reform.

Institutional reform is significantly different from integral reform. The latter is designed to increase productivity while the former is concerned with the economic and social welfare of rural people. The point is that increased productivity can be achieved without any significant change in the welfare of people involved. In other words productivity improvements are necessary but not sufficient to guarantee an increase in welfare for the society as a whole.[3]

This brings me to the second question posed: land reform for what? Conventionally, land reform is considered as an instrument for agricultural development. But, again, the term 'agricultural development' means different things to different people. Judging from the literature, most economists seem to equate the growth of output (and productivity) with development. At best, they seem to consider agricultural development as a sustained increase over time of the incomes of farm people. The latter interpretation appears to be the generally acceptable one.

In this context, redistribution of ownership (*ie* simple reform) is viewed as an instrument for reducing inequalities in the distribution of farm incomes. In so doing, it raises the levels of income for large numbers of people who secure access to the use of land as a result of the reform. And then it is assumed that increases in productivity – to be achieved by supporting measures to provide credit and extension to the new owners (*ie* integral reform) – will guarantee a sustained rise over time in the incomes of the people involved.

My own concept of development goes somewhat beyond this conventional view. In my view, development is a process by which improvements in the economic and social welfare of people are consistently achieved over time. In this connection, raising the levels of farm incomes and reducing inequalities in the distribution of that income among groups involved in farming is important. But we need to go further: (i) to reduce the inequalities in the distribution of income for all groups in the society (including farmers); (ii) to ensure that the society's resources (natural and human) are conserved, and their quality improved, to generate welfare improvements for future generations; (iii) to secure a systematic improvement in the 'quality of life' of all people in the society.

I prefer, therefore, to address my mind to the subject of rural development instead of the more narrow concept of agricultural development.

The implications of this approach are clear. For one thing, we must recognize that land reform alone cannot bring about the kind of development envisaged here. Another consideration is that land reform, as we conceive the term, must encompass all uses of land. Not just farm land but all land – land for farming, for forestry, for mining, for recreation including tourism[4] for urban development, etc.

This is a rather tall order. But it seems to me that this is the only useful approach to the land reform question for islands in which land is already a scarce resource and in which population growth coupled with economic diversification are likely to intensify the competition for the use of land in the future.

So much for the conceptual framework which is the infrastructure for the analysis to follow. To summarize, I am arguing for an 'institutional' approach in looking at the land reform question; and land reform is viewed in this context as an instrument for a sustained betterment of the economic and social welfare of the people that live in these societies.

Land Reform and Economic Change – A Summary of the Evidence

Before addressing our minds to the specific case of the Caribbean, it will be useful to look briefly at the results achieved in other parts of the Third World which have implemented some measure of land reform. The evidence presented in this section draws heavily on the work of Adams and, to a lesser extent that of Warriner.[5] It is based on the experiences of land reform in a number of countries in Asia and Latin America.[6]

Adams provides us with a useful summary of the evidence "regarding five major economic issues related to land reform". These are the effects of land reform on (a) production (output), (b) capital formation, (c) income redistribution and effective demand, (d) employment, and (e) technological change and structural transformation.

Production

The evidence here is based on an examination of the relationship between land reform and production in the short run. Evidence has been assembled using two different approaches: country reviews, and determining the production impact at the project level. Additionally, some economists have used economic theory with empirical information to deduce the likely effects on production. The general conclusion that emerges is, in Adams' words, that " . . . almost never does land reform decrease production, occasionally it has a neutral effect, most often it has a positive impact."[7]

Of special interest to us is the experience of Brazil where the general social framework is somewhat similar to that of the Caribbean. It is worthwhile, therefore, to look at that case in a little more detail. Cline, in his study of Brazil,

. . . argues that land reform which includes breaking up of large land holdings will significantly increase output. He bases his argument mainly on the elimination of (1) labor-market dualisms, (2) the holding of land as a store of value, (3) land market imperfections, and (4) monopsony powers in the rural labor markets . . . he also concludes that the economies-of-scale argument against land reform has little merit.[8]

The empirical evidence provided by Cline appears to lend strong support to his theoretically deduced hypotheses.[9]

Capital Formation

The evidence regarding the effects of land reform on rural capital formation is said to be less conclusive than that relating to production. Adams summarizes the available evidence as follows: "My conclusion is that land reform will not transform the rural capital base overnight. Some evidence is available to suggest, nevertheless, that it, along with other appropriate policies, can help accelerate this accretionary process."[10]

The provision of credit facilities would seem in most instances, to be a necessary part of the bag of 'appropriate policies' to ensure a positive impact on capital formation. Hence the need for an integral approach to land reform, at the least.

Income Redistribution and Effective Demand

The markets for industrial goods in most underdeveloped countries tend to be small because the bulk of their populations – consisting mostly of rural people – have low incomes. insofar as land reform serves to raise the incomes of these people, effective demand for such goods (and services) is expanded. And if the resulting final demand linkages can be internalized to the national economies, this provides spread effects for industrial development.

There is very little empirical evidence to assess how significant this impact has been where land reform programmes have been introduced. But Adams states that:

I am always impressed after periodically visiting rural areas of Taiwan and Japan how rapidly mass consumer markets have extended into societies where land reform has been carried out. The presence in rural Taiwan of radios, sewing machines, television sets, bicycles, power tillers, and motor bikes have mushroomed over the 13 years I have known the country. Peasant consumer purchases in Northeast Brazil, Guatemala and Colombia, on the other hand are static.[11]

Adams is dealing only with land reform and the effective demand for industrial goods. But, as I shall argue later,[12] there are as well significant final demand linkages for agricultural commodities since most underdeveloped countries are characterized by low levels of food consumption (in terms of quality, if not quantity) by the bulk of their population.

Employment

Again, there is little or no evidence on the effects of land reform on employment. Very few studies have been done on this aspect. It can be deduced (theoretically) that under certain conditions, land reform could lead to an increase in employment. On the empirical side, Adams puts forward evidence from a sample of one. He states:

One parcelization project which I studied in the tobacco region of Columbia suggests that employment can be substantially increased through land reform . . . The project only included 1,500 acres, but over 850 people were making a very satisfactory living from the land six years after parcelization. This was up sharply from about 70 people who lived there prior to division. A traditional hacienda with some cattle and tobacco share-croppers located nearby, but with much better land provided a living for only 230 people[13]

Unfortunately, Adams does not make any comparison between the levels of living of the 230 people on the traditional hacienda with those of the 850 on the parcelization project. Nor are we told the size of the hacienda in his comparison.

In any event, we cannot generalize from a sample of one. Whether or not land reform will lead directly to an increase in employment depends on the initial conditions. This need not detain us here. What is certain is that land reform is likely indirectly, to increase employment. This follows from the proposition that if land reform generates an increase in effective demand, the resulting final demand linkages are bound to create new job opportunities.

Technological Change and Structural Adjustment

Empirical evidence is weakest in respect of the relationships between technical change and land reform. Among economists concerned with agricultural development there seem to be two distinguishable schools. The neoclassical allocationist (Marshallian) group views the development problem in terms of how to achieve improvements in productivity via technological change. The classical structuralist (institutionalist, Ricardian at worst) group, on the other hand, views the problem in terms of changes in the institutional environment. The two groups appear to be at odds with each other.[14]

The allocationists seem to argue that "new technology creates a new economic environment which in turn induces almost automatic adjustments in the structure of the economy".[15] This is basically the Ruttan-Hayami position. (Elsewhere, I have considered their view of the development process at some length.)[16] In their view, land reform is not the important issue. The structuralists, on the other hand, claim that new technology will have very little welfare effects in most situations unless gross inequalities in the distribution of land ownership are corrected. So far the evidence seems to support the structuralists. The so-called 'Green Revolution' and other recent technological changes seem to benefit only the small group of better-off farmers in most underdeveloped countries.

Summary

To sum up, the experience of land reform in several countries where it has been introduced, indicates that the long-term effects of land reform are likely to be favourable in respect of expansion of production (output), capital accumulation, market expansion and income growth. As well, land reform can be expected to promote improvements in social welfare, by way of a favourable impact on the distribution of wealth and income; and through its capacity to generate employment. The sum total of these effects will be to stimulate long-term economic growth of a kind that disperses benefits widely throughout societies which, previously, were characterized by excessive concentration of land ownership.

Land Reform for Agricultural Development in the Caribbean

It is against this background of evidence from experiences elsewhere that I wish now to consider the case for land reform in the Caribbean. The discussion is presented in two parts – first, land reform, in relation to agricultural development per se; and, secondly, in relation to the overall advancement of the peoples of the region (including, of course, rural people). This section deals with the first and the section to follow considers the second.

The Land Problem and Rural Poverty in the Caribbean

The basic structure of Caribbean agriculture is a legacy of the slave plantation system. By the time Emancipation came the land in most of the Leeward Islands had been totally engrossed by plantations. In the Windward Islands and Jamaica, there was some land of inferior quality left. In Trinidad, Guyana, Puerto Rico, Dominican Republic and Cuba, there were still relatively abundant supplies of good agricultural land. In the period since Emancipation, the fate of black people (the ex-slaves) has depended ultimately on whether or not they could find land on which to settle on their own account. To the extent that they could achieve this in some places, a viable peasantry emerged.

For the most part, then, Caribbean agriculture today is characterized by 'dualism', with a plantation (estate) sector controlling the best quality land and a peasant (small farm) sector with generally poor quality land. There is an intense conflict between the two sectors; but in the competition for land and other resources, the plantation sector has a strong advantage.[17] And with high rates of population growth in the peasant communities, pressure on land in the peasant sector has become very acute. In many islands, this pressure has been further intensified recently by developments in tourism and mining. The economic position of the peasantry would have been far worse than it is at present were it not for heavy migration – both external and internal – which served to siphon considerable numbers of people off the land.[18]

The present distribution of land between the plantation and peasant sectors is grossly unequal everywhere, except in Cuba. The majority of all farms are small in size but these occupy a very small share of the farm land, and the worst quality land at that. As an example, in Jamaica (which is reasonably representative of the situation in the region), farms under 5 acres in size represent 71% of all farms in the country but these occupy only 12% of total farm acreage. On the other hand, farms of over 500 acres are 0.2% of all farms; yet these control over 45% of total farm acreage.[19] When account is taken of quality differences, the pattern is even more ugly than these data suggest.

In absolute terms, a handful of 350 farmers control 45% of farm land in Jamaica while 114,000 farmers (approximately 570,000 people, assuming average household size of 5) are forced to eke out an existence on a mere 12% of total farm acreage. Each household in the small farm sector exists on an average of 1.8 acres. By way of contrast, each household in the plantation sector earns income from an average of 2,211 acres.[20] *Oh, what a wicked situation!*

In the circumstances, it is not surprising that the levels of income of the peasantry are much lower than those of most other groups in Caribbean societies. Apart from the unemployed and the petty trades and services, small farmers are probably the lowest income earners. This may be offset somewhat by their consumption out of their own food production. But the standards of housing, clothing, medical care, education, etc. are generally at very deplorable levels. Even in food consumption, malnutrition is fairly widespread among this group of people, since they rely heavily on purchased supplies of the more protective foods.

Now the bulk of the rural populations in all the islands is concentrated in the peasant sector. Indeed, the peasant population is probably a majority of total population in many islands. In any event, this sector supports a greater number of people than any other single sector of the economy in most places. Consequently, any improvement in the welfare of people in the peasant sector will have important significance for the societies as a whole.

This, of itself, is a powerful argument for drastic redistribution in favour of the peasantry. But let us proceed beyond this to ascertain, as best as possible, what the effects of land reform are likely to be in relation to specific aspects of agricultural development.

Probable Economic Effects of Land Reform

Of all possible alternative policies, land reform provides the greatest potential for agricultural development in the Caribbean. Land reform offers most scope for achieving, at one and the same time, income redistribution, increased employment, and expanded output. Indeed any other policy for agriculture is likely to fail in the absence of drastic redistribution of land. Improvements in technology over the past few decades, for example, have not benefitted the small farm sector to any significant degree because of a chronic shortage of credit and land in this sector. As I have argued at length elsewhere, the dualistic nature of West Indian agriculture creates fractured markets for agricultural resources, price distortions in product and factor markets, inequalities in the distribution of wealth and income, and limited technical knowledge about production possibilities all of which pose formidable obstacles to development.[21]

Although agricultural resources (other than labour) are highly concentrated in the plantation sector of West Indian agriculture, that sector historically has displayed a low propensity to adjust its product mix. The plantation sector specializes in the production of specific crops (usually for export); and there is little or no variation in this pattern over time. On the other hand, the peasant sector has displayed a high propensity to innovate. Diversification of West Indian agriculture after Emancipation came mainly from the efforts of the peasantry.[22] Small farmers generally practise mixed cropping, and they display far greater flexibility in patterns of resource use than plantations. Since the process of agricultural development involves a flexible deployment of resources as patterns of consumption change, redistribution in favour of the peasantry would enhance the process of development.

Additional arguments in favour of a viable peasantry in the West Indies are suggested by McIntyre:

. . . Since peasant agriculture is more labour intensive than estate agriculture, its techniques are probably better adapted to the requirements of a labour surplus economy . . . because of these differences in techniques, peasant agriculture may bring in more net foreign exchange per acre because its import content is lower than that of the estate sector. Finally, the peasant sector may contribute more to the National Income on a per acreage basis, because there is no foreign ownership over peasant production."[23]

Redistribution of land away from plantations to the peasantry can therefore be expected to increase employment[24] and national income, and to expand net foreign exchange earnings of the agricultural sector.

In the West Indian context, land reform on a national scale would promote agricultural development insofar as it generates a significant income redistribution. To achieve the latter an integral approach to land reform is necessary. Income redistribution would contribute to development in at least two directions: an expansion of effective demand and an increase in capital formation.

The existing low levels of farm incomes limit the size of the domestic market for many industrial goods; and this serves as a constraint on the development of the industrial sector. Since a substantial share of the population depends on farming for a livelihood, an increase in farm incomes would widen the market for industrial goods considerably. As well, levels of food consumption are generally low and the bulk of the population now have a small effective demand for the protective foods.[25] Redistribution of income in favour of the peasantry would raise effective demand for such foods which are currently imported for the most part. And because of the greater flexibility of resource use by the peasantry, import displacement opportunities in food production could be taken up.

At present, the agricultural sectors of all Caribbean economies are characterized by low rates of capital formation. This derives partly from the fact that low levels of farm incomes restrict rural savings (and investment). Redistribution of income would raise the level of savings and contribute to higher rates of capital formation in agriculture.[26]

The most important economic effects of land reform in the Caribbean context are to be found in the areas of increased production and employment. Since there are some available data on these matters an attempt is made below to project some likely effects, for one of the islands. But first we consider briefly the reasons why redistribution can be expected to lead to increased output (production).

"The two principal issues that affect land reform's impact on production are whether economies of large scale production exist, and whether land utilization does in fact decline as farm size (in area) rises . . ."[27]

So long as returns to scale are more or less constant, the fragmentation of large units will not raise costs of production. The chief reason for possible scale economies in agriculture derive from the fact that "minimum areas are required to utilize certain farm machines". However, in labour surplus economies like the West Indies, machine capital as a substitute for labour is unprofitable in both economic and social terms.[28] And even if profitable, machine pools can be used to get around the farm size constraint. As Cline concludes, "the agricultural economies of scale argument warrants little weight in the context of the developing countries."[29]

For the Caribbean, census data reveal that, in general, land utilization declines as farm size increases. There are several reasons for this. There is the historical tendency of plantations to monopolize land in order to secure their labour supplies. Then there is the consideration that in land-short economies, land is a store of value – a portfolio asset which can yield high capital gains. Furthermore, land ownership by the planter class is viewed as a social asset since it enhances the owner's social status. In short, for all these reasons land owned by plantations tend to be underutilized.[30]

An Exercise on the Probable Effect of Land Reform
on Production and Employment in Jamaica

David Edwards has assembled some data from the 1961 Census[31] which permit some empirical assessment of the likely impact of land reform on production and employment. The analysis here is based on those data.

First, the general picture of the current situation. Small farms utilize land much more intensively than plantations. Farms under 5 acres (small farms) used 12% of the country's total farm land to produce 24% of total agricultural production. On the other hand, farms over 500 acres (plantations) occupied 45% of all farm land but produced only 41% of total production. The productivity per acre of farm land is therefore more than twice as great on small farms than on the plantations. The reason for that is that small farms use farm land much more intensively. Cultivated area as a proportion of farm land was 59% for small farms as compared to 25% for the plantations. As concerns employment, small farms utilized 49 workers per 100 acres of farm land in contrast to 4 for plantations; per acre of cultivated land, the numbers are small farms 84 to plantations 17.

The situation in relation to productivity is summarized in the following tabulation which shows production valued in constant 1954 £:

Table 9.1 *Farm production values, 1954*

	Small Farms (<5 Acres)	Plantations (500+ Acres)
Output/Acre farm land	33	15
Output/Acre cultivated land	57	60
Output/Man	68	345

A few comments on these data. Production per acre of farm land on small farms is more than double that on plantations. The reasons for this were already advanced. Output per acre of cultivated land is roughly the same for the two sets of farms. But we need to recognize that small farms are using land of a lower quality and that they utilize far less 'modern' inputs, than plantations. My speculation is that given land of equal quality and a suitable package of modern inputs, productivity per acre of peasant cultivated land would exceed that on plantations by a significant margin.

Output per man is not a very useful index of labour productivity but man-hour data are not available. Given the small size of the under 5 acre farms (averaging 1.8 acres) it is unlikely that the family labour of the small farmer is utilized in production as much as paid labour on the plantations. So that the difference in labour productivity indicated above would be narrowed. However, a higher labour productivity is to be expected from plantation production since this involves large doses of modern inputs (including machine capital.[32] Once again, labour productivity on small farms could be raised to respectable levels if modern inputs become available to their owners.

These comparisons suggest that a land reform programme which fragments the plantations into small farms would increase both employment and output. In addition, the productivity data argue strongly in favour of a programme which utilizes an integral approach.

To continue the exercise, let us try to quantify the probable effects using two different approaches, the simple and the integral. The analysis is cast in a static mold, and it assumes that all farms of over 500 acres are broken up into 5 acre farms. This is an extremely simplified redistribution and assessment model. Farms over 500 acres occupied 774,000 acres in 1961. This would make 154,800 five acre farms (more than the 113,200 which existed in 1961).

The simple method of redistribution would expand employment and output as follows:

1   379,260 workers would be utilized in contrast to the present 30,960 (an additional 348,300 jobs) and,

2   production would more than double (from £5.7 million to some £12.5 million for 1961, expressed in 1954 prices. The resulting output being some 60% of total agricultural output in 1961.

These projections assume that the new small farms will have the same levels of productivity, will farm the land with the same intensity, and will utilize the same techniques as the small farms existing in 1961. Output could be raised even further if an integral method of reform is used to provide modern inputs on the new farms, and if land use intensity is raised above the 59% of 1961. Another consideration is that the shift to 5 acre farms would provide more jobs than the labour force could supply; so that a shift to farms in the 5-25 acre group would be a more realistic exercise.[33]

Using the *integral* approach to land reform would produce better results, in terms of both output and income. The minimum institutional changes needed to increase productivity would be in areas of credit and extension, in order to encourage the use of modern inputs. A substantial share of the difference in productivity per man between small farms (68) and plantations (345) derives from the following differences in the use of modern inputs per 100 acres of cultivated land:

Table 9.2 *Use of modern inputs per 100 acres of cultivated land*

	Small Farms	Plantations
Animal & tractor power (hp)	6	25
Fertilizers (cwt)	45	352

Plantations used nearly eight times as much fertilizer as small farms and over four times the power. The integral approach is clearly the better alternative since it would raise output higher than the simple approach and at the same time generate employment at reasonable levels of income.

Land Reform for Overall Development

Any programme that stimulates agricultural development in the Caribbean context will benefit the society as a whole since agricultural development is critical for overall development of the economy. Furthermore, an improvement in the material welfare of a large segment of the rural population would create tremendous welfare benefits for the society as a whole.

The impact of an integral method of land reform is of special significance to two major problems confronting all West Indian economies, unemployment and lagging agricultural production. In general, unemployment rates are high everywhere and the numbers of unemployed are on the rise. The problem arises from the fact that government policies have favoured industrialization instead of agriculture. And industrial production tends to be relatively capital intensive. So job creation proceeds at a slow pace while the labour force is expanding rapidly (with population growth), and while the rural-urban drift is accelerated by intensified population pressure on the land.

Land reform offers the scope to expand employment and concurrently to soften the push factors driving people into town.

Lagging agricultural production has served to restrain economic development throughout the postwar period. Continuous excess demand for foodstuffs has resulted in rising food prices and increasing food imports year after year. Rising food prices depress the real incomes of non-farm workers and expanding imports place an unnecessary strain on the balance of payments. It is the import component of food supplies that has increased most in price. And price rises for the domestic component have not stimulated enough expansion of supply because of the inflexibility of resource use in the plantation sector. An integral land reform programme would therefore contribute materially to containing the rise in food prices and to promoting import displacement.

In my view, an integral method of land reform deals with only a part of the land problem in the Caribbean. It goes a far way, but not far enough. Up to this point we have been concerned with the question of the redistribution of land in farms. It seems necessary to take a look at all the land that is available in these island economies. Land is in relatively short supply; population is growing, and competition for the use of land is intensified with new developments in mining, tourism, forestry, urban development, and so on. These more recent inroads of foreign capital into the economies have had two important adverse effects.

The pressure on black people is intensified and they are forced to migrate; externally, they catch hell with racism abroad and, internally, the majority are forced to live in the most wretched conditions in urban slums – for the most part unemployed. A life of scuffling, crime and violence is the lot of these slum dwellers.

A second effect of these trends has been the dramatic inflation of land prices and the associated high propensity to speculate in land by foreigners and the few nationals who are in a better position to buy. In societies that are short of land, and in which there is gross under-consumption by the bulk of the population, holding land as a portfolio asset is nothing short of a moral crime!

In so far as governments are responsible for the welfare of the people in the society as a whole, the responsibility rests squarely with them to correct these glaring social injustices. To do this, a comprehensive institutional approach to land reform is absolutely necessary.

In this connection, one of the first questions to be raised relates to systems of tenure – more specifically, the ownership of land. On this question it seems clear to me that ownership by foreigners should be forbidden by law, for a start. What little land we have must be reserved for use by nationals. But how should it be shared by different groups of nationals? With the present system of freehold tenure, the high income elite groups in the society would get a disproportionate share; and unemployment, underutilization, and speculation would continue. The present suffering by the masses of black people would hardly change at all. In the circumstances, I would favour abolishing the freehold system of tenure. What, then, will replace it?

All land (at least rural land) should revert to state ownership to be held in trust for the society as a whole. Land can then be leased on a long-term basis to those who want to use it in particular ways. Such a system is not alien to black people. The African model of communal patterns of ownership is a part of our heritage. Land is owned by the tribe and individuals in the tribe can use it without having individual ownership. In the West Indies the nation is one big tribe so state ownership guarantees everyone a stake in the land.

A second question, arising partly from the first, is that of land use. Since land is in short supply it must be used wisely for the benefit of the society as a whole. This requires institutional changes to guarantee that land is used in the most socially desirable ways. Zoning and countryside planning are necessary to achieve this.

Land which is suitable for farming should be leased to farmers. Land suitable for forests can be developed by the state or leased to those wishing to earn a living from forestry or from the running of forest resorts. Public recreation parks with organized mountain sports should be a part of the state's forest development programmes. Beaches must be public property but lands contiguous to beaches can be leased to those who wish to make a living from the holiday industry, on condition that the orientation is as much to national vacationers as to visitors. And, finally, land to be mined can be released as required by mining interests who must pay a charge for the use of the land and for disturbing its natural quality in addition to royalty payments for the minerals extracted – with the provision that the land be restored as best as possible.

Another question we need to consider is that of urban development. We are accustomed to view the growth and expansion of large and super-large cities as a necessary part of the process of economic development. But such cities involve heavy social costs – traffic congestion resulting in a waste of time on the roads (getting to and from work, etc.) and gross environmental imbalances resulting from pollution, etc. There are indeed economies to be gained from concentrations of population, particularly for industrial production and for the provision of certain social services. But after a point (300,000 people, perhaps) the diseconomies begin to mount quite sharply; and it would be socially beneficial to restrict further expansion.

It seems to me that island societies have a unique opportunity to control urban growth in any one location by systematically developing new cities or townships over the countryside as established ones reach the critical level.[34] In this manner, the traditional rural-urban dichotomy loses the significance it now has. And cities could be planned to fit better into the natural environment so as to raise the quality of urban life.

It is in these wider contexts, that (what I describe as) an institutional approach to land reform has greatest significance. Because what is involved are institutional changes of a kind that deal with all land and that are directed to the social betterment of the national community as a whole. The basic concern in this wider context is the general quality of life rather than the narrow objective of improving the material welfare of people. For in island economies, the land problem and measures for land reform must inevitably deal with all the land and not just agricultural land. And this takes us beyond questions of rural income redistribution and the scope for increasing agricultural output, productivity and employment.

The entire social ethos surrounding land ownership and use needs to be confronted. And this can only come about with radical social change.

Finally, we should note that land reform alone is not a panacea for all the agricultural problems of Caribbean economies. It is an extremely important policy instrument. But the effectiveness of any programme of reform will depend ultimately on what other institutional changes are effected simultaneously.

Statistical Appendix

This Statistical Appendix (or supplement) provides background data for the calculations made in the third section of my paper.

As indicated in the text of the paper, the basic data are derived from an earlier conference paper by D.T. Edwards. The source reference for the tables is D.T. Edwards, "Agricultural development in Jamaica, 1943-1961" (Paper presented to the Third West Indian Agricultural Economics Conference (Mona, Jamaica, April 1968), mimeo, unpublished).

Table 9.3. *Distribution of land in farms: Jamaica, 1961*

Size of Farm (acres)	Number of Farms	Area of Farms (acres)
5 or less	113,239	201,093
5–25	40,768	390,453
25–100	3,803	159,950
100–500	778	181,338
500+	350	773,727
All Sizes	158,938	1,706,561

Table 9.4 *Agricultural production by size of farm: Jamaica, 1961*

Size of Farm (acres)	Production (1954 Prices) Value (£'000)	Proportion of Total Value (%)
5 or less	6,726	24.0
5–25	5,986	21.4
25–100	2,088	7.4
100–500	1,709	6.1
500	11,506	41.1
All Sizes	28,015	100.0

Table 9.5 *Cultivated area as a proportion of farmland: Jamaica, 1961*

Size of Farm (acres)	Cultivated Area (acres)	Cultivated as % of Farmland
5 or less	118,120	58.7
5–25	152,634	39.1
25–100	43,406	27.1
100–500	40,644	22.4
500+	190,471	24.6
All Sizes	545,275	32.0

Table 9.6 *Resources (excluding land) by farm size: Jamaica, 1961*
        (per 100 acres of farm land)

Size of Farms (acres)	Labour (nos.)	Power* (hp)	Fertilisers (cwts)
5	49	4	26
5–25	19	4	20
25–100	9	4	42
100–500	5	6	39
500+	4	7	87
All Sizes	14	5	55

*Animal and tractor power; horsepower expressed in terms of 'draw-bar horsepower'.

Table 9.7 *Value of production in relation to land and labour: Jamaica, 1961*
        (1954 Prices, £)

Size of Farm (acres)	Per Acre of Farm Land	Per Acre of Cultivated Land	Per Man
5	33	57	68
5–25	15	39	80
25–100	13	48	138
100–500	9	42	195
500+	15	60	345
All Sizes	16	51	121

Notes

* "Land reform for the betterment of Caribbean peoples". Paper presented at the Seventh West Indian Agricultural Economics Association Conference (1972c).

1   The discussion relates directly to the English-speaking Caribbean because I am more familiar with conditions in those islands. Nevertheless, I am of the opinion that the paper is more generally related to all the islands of the Caribbean, with the sole exception of Cuba. Where empirical support for the argument is necessary, data for Jamaica are used. But the general framework of the analysis fits most Caribbean islands. Data for any island can be marshalled to fit into the general framework.

2   Doreen Warriner, "Results of land reform in Asian and Latin American countries". Paper presented at a Conference on Strategies for Agricultural Development in the 1970s held at Stanford University, 13–16 December 1971 (mimeo), p. 3.

3   The integral approach to land reform focusses on productivity change because it is assumed that redistribution of ownership brings about an immediate improvement in the welfare of those who get land and that increases in productivity will be sufficient to sustain this change in welfare. Institutional reform, as I conceive the term, is concerned with the welfare of the whole society in general and the

rural society in particular. As such, economic as well as social parameters come into play.

4   I have deliberately placed tourism as a subset of 'recreation' because I am of the view that the recreation of visitors must be fitted into the recreational infrastructure for nationals. This is a dramatic departure from the current pattern of developing enclave holiday industries geared exclusively to visitors, as practised in the Caribbean.

5   See in particular, Doreen Warriner, and also Dale W. Adams, "Comment on Doreen Warriner's paper". Paper presented at the Conference on Strategies for Agricultural Development in the 1970s held at Stanford University, 13–16 December 1971 (mimeo).

6   Land reform so far has not attracted much attention in the countries of sub-Sahara Africa because of the established communal patterns of land ownership and the abundance of land there relative to population.

7   Adams, "Comment on Warrimer's Paper" p. 3.

8   Adams, pp. 2–3.

9   See William P. Cline, *Economic Consequences of a Land Reform in Brazil* (Amsterdam, 1970) and more recently, his "Interrelationship between agricultural strategy and rural income distribution". A paper presented at the Conference on Strategies for Agricultural Development in the 1970s held at Stanford University, 13–16 December 1971 (mimeo).

10 Adams, p. 4.

11 Adams, pp. 4–5.

12 See section below which examines the Caribbean situation in the light of experience elsewhere.

13 Adams, "Comment", p. 5. The reference to his original study is Dale W. Adams and L.E. Montero. "Land parcelization in agrarian reform: a Colombian example". *Inter-American Economic Affairs* (Winter 1965), pp. 67–71.

14 Among the leading spokesmen for the 'allocationists' are Schultz, Ruttan and Hayami. While Flores, Adams, Caroll and Barroclough are among the leading structuralists. I place myself, of course, squarely in the structuralist camp.

15 Adams, p. 6.

16 See my "Strategies for agricultural development: summary and comment". Paper presented at the Conference on Strategies for Agricultural Development in the 1970s held at Stanford University, 13–16 December 1971 (mimeo).

17 Elsewhere, I have analysed and documented the nature of the peasant-plantation conflict in the West Indies. See my *Persistent Poverty* (New York: Oxford University Press, 1972) pp. 21-29.

18 These more recent trends are considered later in the context of overall development in the next section. Here we may note that one of the social costs of high internal migration has been the growth of unemployment and the mushrooming of urban slums.

19 These data are from the 1961 Census of Agriculture. It is anticipated that the Department of Agricultural Economics at UWI, St Augustine will be preparing tables providing similar and more up-to-date statistics on all the islands for the conference.

20 It would be superfluous to add that household size on small farms normally exceeds that on plantations:

21 See *Persistent Poverty*, chapter 7.

22 The plantation owners strongly resisted changes. Black peasant producers, for example, established the Jamaica banana industry which, at the end of the nineteenth century, the white planters regarded as "backwoods nigger business".

23 Alister McIntyre, "Some issues of trade policy in the West Indies", *New World Quarterly* (Croptime 1966).

24 Some projections of the impact of land reform on employment are made below.

25 These include meat, milk, dairy products, eggs, fish, vegetables and fruits.

26 Even if the marginal propensity to save by peasants is lower than that of plantation owners, the marginal propensity to invest in productive assets within the country is likely to be much greater for peasants, so long as reasonably attractive investment opportunities exist. Hence, a further point in favour of an integral approach to land reform.

27 Cline, *Economic Consequences*, p. 11.

28 Unprofitable in economic terms if there were no price distortions in the factor and product markets. Appropriate shadow pricing will bear this out.

29 Cline, *Economic Consequences*, p. 11. In this connection see also E.J. Long, "The Economic basis of land reform in underdeveloped economics", *Land Economics* (May 1961).

30 For further discussion on these matters, see *Persistent Poverty*, pp. 88–97 and chapter 6.

31 D. T. Edwards, "Agricultural development in Jamaica 1943–1961". Paper presented at the 3rd West Indian Agricultural Economics Conference, Mona, Jamaica, April 1968 (mimeo). See Statistical Appendix accompanying this paper for the background data used in arriving at the projections here.

32 Note here that productivity gains resulting from the substitution of machine capital for labour in labour-surplus economies is socially undesirable. So that we must discount part of the higher labour productivity on plantations.

33 Farms of 5-25 acres utilized 19 workers per 100 acres of farm land. Redistribution into farms of that size would provide employment for 147,060 workers.

34 In my opinion, Kingston has passed this level and government could make a positive step in the direction suggested here by moving the government sector out of Kingston to a new location.

10

Agro 21 and the Future*

Let me begin by saying, I take this opportunity to comment on Mr Rinella's paper with a certain degree of seriousness; as I normally do, in matters that affect the lives and livelihoods of millions of people. In this particular case, we are dealing with the lives of 2.5 million Jamaican people as consumers and thousands of farmers – especially the 150,000 or so peasants who have fed this nation for hundreds of years. Let me also say, that I think the time has come for us to avoid hypocrisy and to approach our task, as thinkers in the society, with a certain frankness and seriousness which the situation deserves.

I wish, therefore, to say (in terms of avoiding hypocrisy) that I do not welcome Mr Rinella in Jamaica (and I do not mean this personally, Mr Rinella). I do not welcome Mr Rinella's presence in Jamaica because of the fact Jamaica has historically been a net exporter of agricultural technology and agricultural technical managers. In fact, we have many people, one of whom I see in the audience, Dr Ian Whittaker, who could ably and better promote the task which Mr Rinella is here to do. There are others too numerous to mention. But I must mention as well, chairman of this symposium, Dr Brian Davidson, as an example of a technical manager skilled in livestock production and with a record as a corporate manager, having been general manager of Alcan (Jamaica) Ltd until only recently.

We are dealing with *agriculture* which must be the foundation of this nation's productive economy as it affects the welfare of *all* 2.5 million Jamaican people as consumers of food. It is a serious undertaking that requires serious analysis and serious discussion. From that recognition, I hope that my comments here will make a small contribution to our understanding of what is involved in devising appropriate strategies for agricultural and rural development of a type that will benefit the nation as a whole.

My approach to the commentary is, first of all, to examine Mr Rinella's paper for what it says. Secondly, to consider matters which are fundamental to our understanding of agricultural and rural economic and social transformation in Jamaica – matters which, in fact, the Rinella paper does not address directly but unwittingly imply.

Before I proceed, let me just say a word of welcome to Mr Rinella to the UWI campus. This sounds like a contradiction and of course it is. I said that I didn't welcome him to Jamaica and told you the reason why. But I would offend the spirits of my ancestors if I did not, in a charitable manner, welcome the guest in our house.

The fact is that what I have to say does not concern Mr Rinella at all. My comments are addressed to the policymakers – *ie* the authors of the programme which Rinella is administering – namely, Agro 21. "Agro 21 and the Future" is the title of his paper. I will raise certain questions here about the paper; and I will seek answers, not necessarily from Rinella himself; but from all of us as a group of serious discussants.

The first question relates to page 4 of Rinella's paper – the paragraph that reads: "The Agro 21 programme . . . is an effort in the direction to rationalise the cost benefit ratios involved in allocations of this foreign exchange to the degree necessary to rehabilitate, expand and create new incremental production within the agricultural business sector of the nation's economy".

It is important for us to raise the question of what 'cost' and what 'benefit?' What cost to whom; what benefits to whom? And we need to consider *private* vs *social cost* and *private* vs *social benefits*. These are questions that must be answered if we are to consider and analyse cost benefit ratios in a socially meaningful way.

On the same page, reference is made to a 'five-year plan'. The paper states that, "Jamaica does have a plan as to how it should proceed over the next five-year horizon". I know of no five-year agricultural development plan for Jamaica which has been published. If one exists, I call on the Government of Jamaica to publish this plan. If the reference to the plan is in fact the 'Structural Adjustment Programme' for the economy, which I suspect it might be (Mr Rinella can clear it up in his response), then that would open up a whole new discussion. For I have gone through the agricultural sector portion of this structural adjustment programme and there are several questions and several comments about it which I would wish to consider at some length.

Next, on page 5, the paper makes reference to certain 'structural disjunctures' as I call them. It talks about these in the sentence which reads:

. . . a joint venture between the government and the private sector to take advantage of the rich asset base that Jamaica possesses in the form of idle fertile lands, idle population, available infrastructure, capital, unique micro environments and geographic advantage of proximity to markets to exploit the many opportunities available to it.

This is a key paragraph because it highlights certain social, economic and political disjunctures that exist within the social framework of Jamaica's rural economy; and which, if not addressed, can never solve the problem of agricultural development and rural transformation in this country. I will have a little bit more to say about this important matter later on in my commentary.

Then, on the same p. 5, in the paragraph that follows the paper speaks about the "private sector that may best employ its entrepreneurial skills to create new business opportunities, to create new products, new jobs and finally, the much needed foreign exchange". The question I ask here, is, what entrepreneurial skills are we talking about? If we are talking about the 'private' sector as defined by the Private Sector Organization of Jamaica (PSOJ) and the Seaga government, then I want to say here clearly, and in no uncertain terms, that there are *no* entrepreneurial skills in the 'private sector' of the Jamaican economy. The so-called private sector in Jamaica consists of a mercantile class of people, who for centuries have profited on trading margins, of merchants who simply buy cheap and sell dear. Many of them, in the postwar period, became client capitalists in conjunction with foreign capital under government's programme of "industrialization by invitation", the official policy of our development strategy by all administrations since self-government was won in the 1950s. This client capitalist class has no entrepreneurial skills. They simply manage the branch plants of transnational manufacturing companies which assemble, in screwdriver fashion, imported components of 'raw materials'. As I will argue later in my comments, the real entrepreneurship that exists is to be found mainly within the rural sector of Jamaica and especially so in the peasant sector – a sector which Agro 21 does not address directly, if at all.

The next comment I wish to make relates to 'self-sufficiency and export production', which the paper indicates is a target of Agro 21. The desired combination of self-sufficiency and export promotion is, in point of fact, the clearest manifestation of the entrepreneurial skills and competence of the peasant class of Jamaican producers. Examine the history of their development. The peasantry of this country emerged out of plantation slavery. Plantation slavery had concentrated on mono-crop production of sugar (and livestock production – 'pen keeping' – in some of the parishes). It was after Emancipation that the Freedmen (the Africans, the black people) diversified the economy of Jamaica by increasing their production of domestic food supplies which they had begun on the provision grounds of the slave plantation and now developed on their own account, on settlements in the mountainous interior. It was they who introduced new export crops like bananas, in the late nineteenth century; and who, therefore, served to create to certain degree of self-sufficiency within the Jamaican rural food economy while at the same time participating in new export production. This is a remarkable historical achievement. An achievement that needs recognition and therefore needs articulation in any plan designed for rural development and socioeconomic transformation in this country.

The problem that is at the base of rural underdevelopment in Jamaica is that the class – the same peasant class – with entrepreneurial skills and the combined capacity for food self-sufficiency and export production have been denied access to the basic means of production. In particular, land and capital with which to combine their labour, and manifest entrepreneurial abilities, in order to produce sufficient food to achieve national self-sufficiency; while generating the needed foreign exchange through export production. This product mix is historically embedded in the peasant mode of production here in Jamaica, and elsewhere in the Caribbean. It means therefore that resources need to be directed to the peasant sector of the Jamaican economy in an overall programme of *agrarian reform* that involves not just a simple redistribution of land (which is grossly unequal at present to the disadvantage of the peasantry). Such reform must seek to redress the unequal land distribution, and generate the necessary capital to combine with entrepreneurship and labour already available in that sector. Only thus can the transformation be effected.

My next comment on the paper relates to the question of the export market. On p. 8, Rinella, quite correctly, indicates that "Jamaica needs to take up opportunities in the international export markets, opportunities for which this country is ideally suited." My only comment here is that his treatment of the export market is too global. We need to disaggregate the export market into two components: the ethnic component – *ie* the ethnic market consisting of West Indians and non-West Indians overseas. In North America, for example, this would include American black people, Puerto Ricans, Chicanos, and so on. That ethnic market in North America (our closest market) is a very large market. Therefore we can gear production to that market quite profitably. This is not to say, that the requirements that Rinella's paper emphasizes for export marketing – *ie* quality control, proper packaging, and so on – are not necessary in the ethnic market. They are necessary; but I'm saying that the ethnic market caters to a particular *taste* pattern, which we can capitalize on without a great deal of investment in promotion. It is a captive market. But other countries in the Caribbean, Central America and Mexico have similar designs to provide these supplies. So quality is the key.

The wider market, the second component of the export market, contains all North American consumers. And here, it seems to me, the possibility exists for real cooperative development between Caribbean countries in promoting the consumption of 'exotic fruits' in the North American market and Europe. The mango is a fantastic fruit. In flavour, texture, etc. some varieties are much nicer than the 'American apple', the pear, the peach, and most of all other fruit grown in North America. I really believe we could sell mangoes, naseberries, star-apple, sweet sop, etc., on a large scale to the wider North American market. And here the point Rinella makes about the need for promotion assumes importance. My point is that Jamaica cannot afford to do it by itself.[1] We would need to do it in conjunction with our Caribbean partners: those in CARICOM, and perhaps others outside of the CARICOM.

As I mention 'outside of CARICOM' let me just say here that socialist Cuba has developed a fantastic market in Europe for ortaniques. They have been forced to call them 'Cubaniques' because we in Jamaica invented the ortanique. Jamaica has invented so much in agriculture over the years but we have failed to develop these inventions and innovate their commercial production. Jamaica developed the pineapple varieties that built the Hawaiian industry. We invented the ortanique but how much are we exporting? The livestock development programme of genetic breeding by Dr T. P. Lecky and of pasture management by Sam Motta was taken from Jamaica by the Cubans and applied by them to the Cuban resource situation. Today Cuba is fully self-sufficient in milk, butter, cheese, and ice cream of the finest quality that I have tasted anywhere in all my travels. The same technology that we developed here in Jamaica was taken by the Cubans and applied to their environment to generate national self-sufficiency in dairy products. These are just a few examples of the possibilities opened up by our agricultural technocrats over the years.

What is wrong; what is wrong with our situation? Why is it that Jamaica has developed all this agricultural technology over all these period of years and yet is not able to translate it into production to achieve food self-sufficiency? That is the question that we need to address, and that is the question that I am trying to get us to focus on. We'll come back to the why of that question in the second part of the presentation.

Meanwhile, let me say a few words about possibilities for achieving national food sufficiency.[2] The main items of the national diet currently imported to Jamaica are rice, wheat flour, dairy products, and some meat and fish products which are important for the poorer classes of people. The latter includes a range of dried or pickled foodstuffs like cod 'salt' fish, pickled mackerel, red herring, etc., and chicken necks and backs, pickled pig-tails, corned beef, etc. Now, what I wish to emphasize is that the peasantry (which, in Jamaica, includes many fishermen) should be the central producers in a strategy for *import displacement*.[3]

Rice is a peasant crop all over the world, including Guyana the regional supplier. But rice is a flat land crop while most of the established Jamaican peasantry are in the hilly interior. So here is an opportunity to attract the young people from peasant areas to undertake a viable rice production programme, instead of them remaining unemployed or underemployed. Dairy production, likewise, presents an opportunity for viable small-scale family farms in the 15-25 acre range. Dairying is labour and management intensive and is suited to both flat and hilly (undulating) land.[4] A whole new class of young commercial dairy farmers could be created, individually and cooperatively to process the milk they produce.

For fish products, the import displacement strategy requires active state intervention to promote deep-sea trawling ventures (state and cooperatives) which will catch our own cod, mackerel and herring and process them on the return voyage – *eg* drying the cod in the sun. After all, trawlers from as far away as Japan and the USSR operate in Caribbean waters. Why then, can we not go to the Newfoundland banks for our own 'salt' fish?

Wheat flour is the only item that poses a bit of a problem. The established taste of Jamaican consumers makes it difficult to substitute wheat with things like cassava or breadfruit flour. But possibilities exist for some amount of blending wheat and cassava, for example. And cassava is a traditional peasant crop. Any such development would require an intensive national mobilization strategy to adjust the taste pattern over time. This must be an integral part of any serious nation-building strategy.

My last comment refers to p. 10 of Rinella's paper where he states that "while [government] must stimulate the entry of the private sector into exploiting these new opportunities it must resist . . ." My question here is why must the government stimulate the entry of the private sector? If the opportunities are there, and *if there are entrepreneurs* in 'the private sector' then they would take up the opportunities. They would not need any stimulation from anybody. That government believes it 'must stimulate' is a revelation itself about the absence of entrepreneurs among that class, as I said earlier.

We must also raise the question of how to stimulate such participation when there are easy non-risk opportunities elsewhere? How can you attract people into agriculture; what rate of return, in other words, must investment in agriculture produce in order to attract capital from less risky, more certain investment opportunities outside of agriculture? Opportunities that exist in traditional merchandising, for example: in land speculation, and in housing. Mention of land speculation brings us back to the whole business of land use and its underutilisation in the plantation and state sector. This is something that Rinella's paper mentions but does not address.

Let me move on, then, to the second part of my presentation – the part that deals with fundamental considerations missing in Rinella's paper and which we need to consider in order to be able to promote rural transformation, and development.

I begin with a quotation from John Maynard Keynes, the great British economist, who stated that the ideas of every practitioner are informed by some knowledge of economics. Keynes pointed out that the problem of dealing with depression in industrial society was that the ideas that informed the policies being practised were the formulations of some 'defunct economist'. Now this is very important for us to recognize. What I am trying to say is that the programme called Agro 21, like any other programme for development is informed by a certain kind of theory – a certain kind of theorizing. Therefore, we need to examine the theory behind the programme/policy. Basically, the theory behind Agro 21 and its associated programme in the structural adjustment plan is based on ideas contained in three agricultural development models. These are:

1   the 'diffusion model' which operated internationally during the 1950s and which said simply that what we need to do is to diffuse knowledge about the production process to farmers and they will get on with the production. Hence, the development of agricultural experimental stations and ancillary extension services. The stations would undertake the research and the extension officers would take the research generated thereby out to the farmers in the fields for its implementation. The 'diffusion model' ran its course during the 1950s. By the end of that decade, it seemed that the model wasn't working; that the poor farmers in underdeveloped countries were not benefitting sufficiently from this diffusion process. This then led to the development of a new model, a new theoretical model:

2   the *high payoff input model* of Professor Theodore Schultz, of the University of Chicago. Incidentally, his celebrated book, *Transforming Traditional Agriculture*, was the basis for his sharing the Nobel Prize in Economics with our own illustrious Professor William Arthur Lewis, in 1979. In my opinion, it was quite unfair to Lewis to be made to share

the Nobel Prize with Schultz. For the obvious reason that Lewis is the pioneer in the development of theories of economic growth and development. Lewis' *Theory of Economic Growth* (1955) is the first book ever to address the question of underdevelopment in the Third World from a uniquely classical, interdisciplinary and institutional Third World perspective. It still remains a classic. Its prelude (model) article, "Economic Development with Unlimited Supplies of Labour"[5] was the springboard for all subsequent work on dual economies.

Professor Schultz's contribution about transforming traditional agriculture simply argued the following: that poor farmers in the Third World are utilizing what resources are available to them in an efficient manner. Therefore what is needed, is to give them more and better resources such as new varieties of seeds, and 'modern' inputs which they will use efficiently. This idea, this theory, the 'high payoff input model', led to investments in high payoff inputs, like improved varieties of seed, fertilizer, pesticides, water, and all the combinations of modern inputs that would serve to promote agricultural development. That theory synthesizes the ideas of pioneers of the so-called Green Revolution – the varietal revolution associated notably with (among others):

a   the International Rice Research Institute (IRRI) in the Phillippines;

b   the International Institute for Research in Wheat and Corn (CYMMIT) in Mexico (the director of which, Borlaug, received the Nobel Prize for Applied Science); and,

c   the more recently established International Institute for Tropical Agriculture (IITA) in Ibadan, Nigeria.

These three institutions were supposed to develop the new varieties and the new input packages which would create the Green Revolution and transform the lives of poor farmers in the Third World. Well, all the analysis that has been done indicates that the Green Revolution has not benefitted the small famers in the Third World. It has only benefitted the bigger, better-off farmers who are able to buy the expensive inputs of water, fertilizers, pesticides, etc., that are demanded by the new varieties coming out of the research from these institutes.

3   The third model that informs Agro 21, and its companion programme/ policies, is the 'induced innovation model', which is the latest agricultural development model in mainstream economics in the capitalist world. The 'induced development model' was developed by Vernon Ruttan and Yujiro Hayami, of the United States and Japan, respectively. The model was elaborated in their book, *Agricultural Development – An International Perspective* (Baltimore: Johns Hopkins University Press,

1971). Hayami and Ruttan argued that for development to be sustained, it is necessary to create a situation in which the process would be induced by endogenous changes within the agricultural sector itself and not simply wait on exogeneous inputs for its development. The 'induced development model' goes on to say that, in addition to endogenous technological requirements, endogenous institutional change is needed to mobilize resources for 'agricultural development'. So the model involves two sets of inducements: inducements at the technical level, for technological change; and inducements at the institutional level for mobilising resources for agricultural development.

Well, I was fortunate, to have been invited to comment on the first general presentation of that model at a conference at Stanford University in 1971 and my comment along with the original paper by Hayami and Ruttan are in the new book *Agricultural Development in the Third World*.[6] This is the latest book bringing together the best in Western thought on agricultural development in the Third World. It presents the induced development model as a centrepiece.[7] In my comment on it, I argue that the induced development model does not come to terms with the socioeconomic institutional environment and constraints that exist in Third World countries. This, therefore, limits the capacity for the necessary inducements to occur both at the technological level and at the institutional building level. (You will understand what I mean when I apply this consideration to the Jamaican situation in the next part of my presentation.)

What we find, therefore, is that the body of theory that we have falls short of coming to terms with the reality that it addresses. What then, is this reality? That is the question to which we must now turn.

––––––

What is the reality that theory must address? In other words, what are the specificities of the social framework and institutional environment of Jamaica that prevents the 'Green Revolution' from reaching small farmers; that prevents the 'induced development model' from inducing development; and that continues to entrap the peasantry, the small peasantry in particular, to a lifetime of poverty and underdevelopment?

The reality of the Jamaican situation is that the social order, the social economy of Jamaica, is rooted in its historical development as a plantation capitalist society with a specific dominant mode of production which I call plantation capitalism; and which has a subordinate peasant mode of production entrapped within that dominant mode, the plantation mode. I do not have to elaborate on the plantation mode to an audience such as this, in terms of its production profile, aspects of its institutional organization and production. We are all familiar with this from works already published since the late 1960s.[8]

There is a second element which I think needs emphasis, which our work has not addressed up to date. It is the way in which *race and class* are instituted in the mode of production, and the mode of exchange. The particular manner in which race and class are co-joined within the modes of production and exchange brings a particular set of social problems in terms of development and transformation. The fundamental contradiction of the Jamaican rural society and economy is a contradiction within plantation capitalism between the dominant planter class on the one hand, and the peasantry and the agro-proletariat on the other hand. The former is *white* (and near white) and the latter is *black*. It is a contradiction that has manifested itself in social upheavals in the past; the Bogle riots of 1865, and the 1938 rebellion are two that stand out. The contradiction inheres within the existing social order and impedes the process of agricultural development and rural transformation.

My contention is that unless this contradiction is addressed – *ie* the revealed disjuncture between monopoly control of the land by the 'white' plantation capitalist class and the monopoly control of the capital market by the associated banking sector on the one hand; and, on the other, the labour of the black peasantry and the agro-proletariat (the work force in agriculture) with their labour power on this side, and the manifest entrepreneurial skills of the peasantry; that unless this disjuncture between these two contradictory components of the rural economy; unless that is addressed, then we are (as they say in Guyana) 'spinning top in mud'. Can you spin a gig in mud? Try to spin a gig in mud; it just sticks – can't spin! That is the central problem we face in the Jamaican rural social economy.

Hence, the need for a programme of agrarian reform which, firstly, attacks the land question and makes land available to the enterprising peasantry, along with institutional building of a kind that will mobilize complementary resources of capital, I mean agricultural credit of a kind that will make agriculture competitive in terms of producing food cheaply while at the same time bringing adequate returns to the farmers.

What exists today in Agro 21 and the Structural Adjustment Programme of which it is a part is simply ridiculous. Agricultural credit, according to the plan, is being offered to farmers at a minimum of 12%; anywhere from 12% through the state's Agricultural Credit Bank to 20% plus in the commercial banks. Now, God Almighty, tell me which farmer can pay those rates of interest, and produce food cheap enough for people to buy and at the same time make a living for himself? It is totally impossible. Consequently, we need to put in place institutional arrangements that will complement the land reform programme so as to release the creative energies of the peasantry and realize the massive flows of output that would result.[9]

What I am calling for, in short, is a marriage of theory and reality, a marriage of a kind that will address the problem in a significant way in order to promote social transformation in the rural economy, and advance the living standards of the majority of our people who comprise the categories of agricultural workers and small peasants.

Finally, let me just say that, without that fundamental attack on the problem, we will end up with *symbols of development* of which Agro 21 is one. We have had our share of symbols, upon symbols of development. Becuase as Brewster[10] pointed out long ago, when governments cannot plan for development, they have to make like they are planning. Hence they set up ADCs, IDCs, AMCs, LDUCs, FPPs, SSFPDs, JNIPs, AGRO 21s, etc. These are nothing more than symbols to the population that development is taking place where manifestly it is not.

Notes

*"Agro 21 and the future – a comment". Papers presented at a Symposium on Agriculture: Problems and Prospects, hosted by the Department of Economics, Mona, mimeo, revised (June 1985).

1　Jamaica may have a distinct advantage for certain fruits, like naseberry and star-apple, for which we need an orchard development and perhaps our own market promotion programme. The orchard development would need direct state involvement in production as these trees take many years to come to full bearing.

2　These comments/suggestions were added in the revision of the paper. They dovetail with the presentation by Mark Figueroa dealing with import-substitution possibilities.

3　I use the term 'displacement' quite deliberately to distinguish from 'import substitution' that may take the form of 'import replacement' – *ie* the imports of components to replace imports of finished goods, as happens with poultry, for example.

4　Indeed, the establishment of grass on hilly lands will arrest erosion now taking place in many areas, thus contributing to current as well as future production.

5　Originally published in the journal, *The Manchester School* (May 1954) and reprinted in A.N. Argawala and S.P. Singh (eds.), *The Economics of Underdevelopment* (Oxford: Oxford University Press, 1958).

6　Edited by Carl Eicher and John Staatz and published by Johns Hopkins Univ. Press, Baltimore, Md., 1984. See pp. 59 to 81.

7　The other centrepiece comes from the radical (neo-Marxist) stream of thought. It is by Alain de Janvry, "The political economy of rural development in Latin America" (pp. 82-95).

8   See my own *Persistent Poverty – Underdevelopment in Plantation Economies of the Third World,* abbreviated edition (1972, OUP and ISER; Kingston & London: Maroon Publishers and Zed Books, reprint 1984). See also the seminal article by Lloyd Best, "A model of pure plantation economy", *Social and Economic Studies* (Sept. 1968); and several Best-Levitt papers in mimeograph.

9   For a critical review of the Agro 21 programme see the interesting article by Salmon and Srivastava, "Non-traditional agriculture in Jamaica: more questions than answers", *Social and Economic Studies.*

10   Havelock Brewster, "Economic dependence – a quantitative interpretation", *Social and Economic Studies* (March 1973), pp. 90-95.

Part II

Towards an Appropriate Paradigm for Caribbean Development

11

The Growth of Major Tropical Export Crop Industries*

Most of the underdeveloped countries of the world lie within the tropics and their economic advance has been largely determined by their ability to trade with the industrially advanced countries of Europe and North America. In general, the export trade of these countries consists chiefly of raw materials derived from agriculture and mining. Most tropical countries are characterized by a high degree of specialization; some depend almost exclusively on single commodities for their export earnings and a few countries tend to dominate world trade in particular commodities.

In view of this marked specialization, it may well be that the economic histories of many tropical countries could be written largely in terms of the development of single crop industries.[1] And it is this possibility which underlies the present examination of patterns of growth experienced by some of the important export-crop industries. The analysis is essentially exploratory. The study seeks to describe the patterns of growth, to propose a technique for distinguishing among them and offers a possible explanation for observed differences in the rates of growth.

The major crop industries considered in the present study are the three leading sources of seven of the most valuable tropical crops in world trade – coffee, rubber, sugar, tea, cocoa, coconut products and oil-palm products. Time series on the volume of exports are extended as far back as data are available for each industry, but series which are shorter than 30 years are excluded. Thirty years seems to represent a reasonable minimum time period for examining secular trends, as the various series exhibit trend fluctuations or Kuznets cycles of 20-25 year duration.

The present article is concerned with the primary or basic trends which underlie the respective series. Trend fluctuations have been examined elsewhere [2] and, from a statistical point of view, deserve to be treated separately.[3] In getting at the basic trend of a time series, it is necessary to abstract from both short cycles and Kuznets cycles. Various statistical devices are available for this purpose. Freehand approximation is one device, but it is rejected here partly because of the strong element of subjectivity involved. Moving averages is an alternative. But in order to abstract from Kuznets cycles, the required moving averages would have to extend over periods of 25 years or more, and most of the records are not long enough to accommodate this. The basic trend may be derived by taking moving-item averages of rates of change between overlapping decades. But, again, the records are too short for the use of this technique. The application of mathematical curves presents a final alternative.

The so-called growth-curves are suggested by the fact that individual industries tend to develop at a secularly retarded rate. And the Gompertz curve was the first choice from among these because it is relatively easy to fit. It was originally intended that other curves would be fitted if the Gompertz gave unsatisfactory results, but this proved unnecessary. Although the exercise can be regarded as a test of the 'law of growth' of industries postulated by Kuznets[4] and Burns[5] it is intended primarily to provide an adequate description of the patterns of growth experienced by the respective crop industries over the periods considered, thereby providing good approximations to the slopes of the basic trends.[6]

The fitted trends for the leading exporters of coffee, rubber, sugar, tea, cocoa, coconut products, and oil-palm products superimposed on annual data are shown in Figures 11.1 to 11.7. World exports are also included where satisfactory data are available. Trend equations and years of origin (first year in each series) are reproduced for each curve. In general, the fits are good.

For coffee (Figure 11.1) the only questionable description is of Brazilian exports prior to 1900. All three curves for rubber (Figure 11.2) are accepted without question. Thailand, the third major rubber exporter, was excluded because the series is too short to qualify for consideration.[7] Sugar (Figure 11. 3) brings the first outright rejection of a curve; the fit for world cane sugar is unquestionably poor. The curve for Cuba is somewhat suspect, but this may derive more from the fact that Kuznets cycles are the more prominent component of the secular trend of this time series. No other single curve (except a high order polynomial) could give an appreciably better fit for this series. The curve for Hawaii gives a good approximation to the basic trend – bisecting, as it does, the marked long swing patterns. The same is true of Puerto Rico's curve.

The tea curve in Figure 11.4 fits reasonably well, except for Ceylon which is rejected.[8] The trends for world, Brazilian, and Nigerian cocoa exports shown in Figure 11.5 are acceptable. There is an apparent break in Ghana's cocoa trend in the late 1930s; the curve shown gives a good description of the basic trend up to 1938. Finally, in Figures 11.6 and 11.7 all the fitted trends, except that for Congo palm kernels, are acceptable.

The incidence of poor fits for the calculated trends is low among the 26 series examined. Only world sugar, Ceylon tea, and Congo palm kernels deserve outright rejection. And while a few others may be questioned, these can be used with qualification. From the charts it is readily apparent that the major tropical export-crop industries experienced a variety of growth patterns, ranging all the way from the spectacular and rapid development of the rubber industries to the crawling pace of Brazilian coffee. The diversity of patterns is apparent for different crops as well as among industries producing the same crop. The common pattern that emerges is one of retardation in growth rates; industries tend to experience declining percentage rates of growth as they develop over time. This conforms with the hypothesis of Kuznets and Burns. The question naturally arises as to whether the relative stage of development (age) was the only factor contributing to the diversity in rates of growth observed in the charts. This question is now considered.

In order to abstract from the 'age' factor, it is necessary to compare the performances of the various industries at similar stages of their life histories. The inflection point of the fitted curve provides a useful analytical benchmark in this respect (in so far as the relevant curve does in fact approximate the basic trend of the series). Because absolute increments in the curve become progressively smaller after this point, it seems reasonable to regard the inflection point as the boundary between the stages of industrial 'nascence' and 'maturation' in the sense that Burns has described.[9] In the following discussion, this point is referred to as the 'critical year'.

It can be plausibly argued that the critical year marks a similar stage in the development of each crop industry and that a comparison of rates of growth in that year will abstract from age differences and provide a reasonable reflection of differences in inherent growth propensities.

Figure 11.1   *Growth patterns in coffee exports*

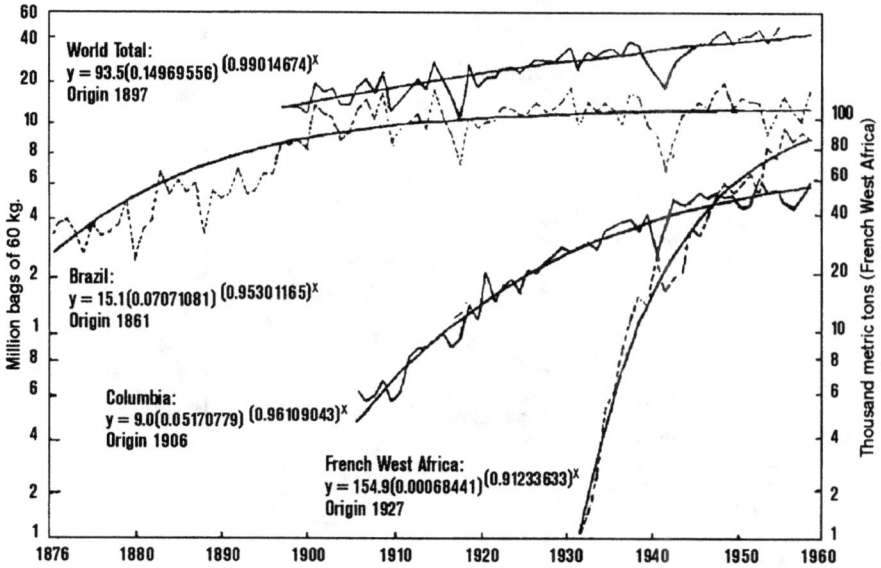

Figure 11.2   *Growth patterns in rubber exports ('000 long tons)*

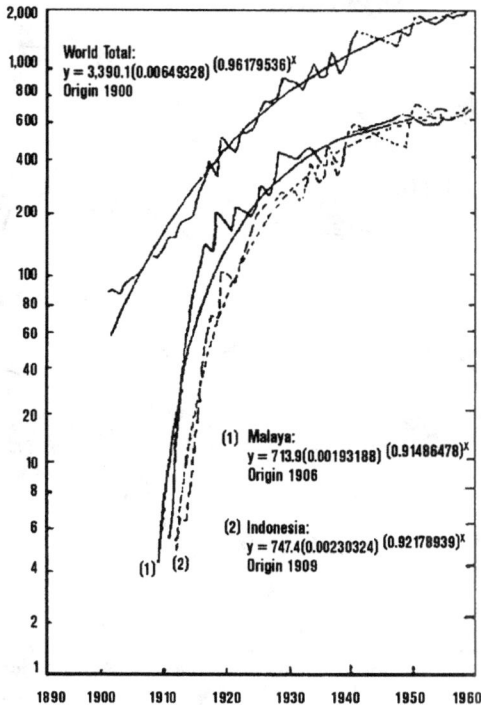

Figure 11.3 *Growth patterns in cane sugar exports ('000 metric tons; raw value)*

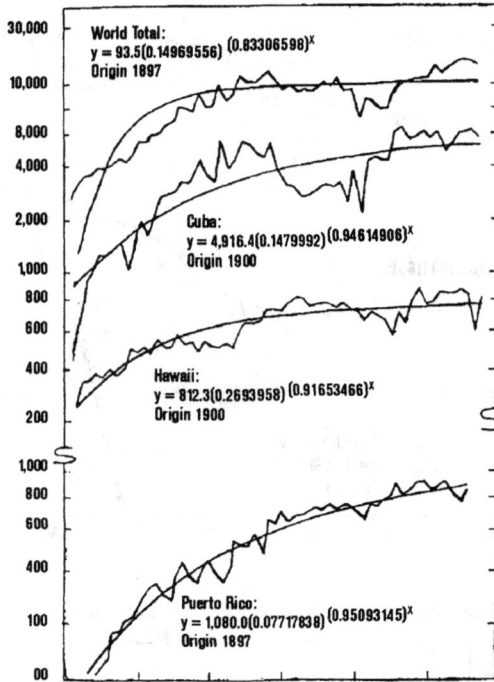

Figure 11.4 *Growth patterns in tea exports (million lb)*

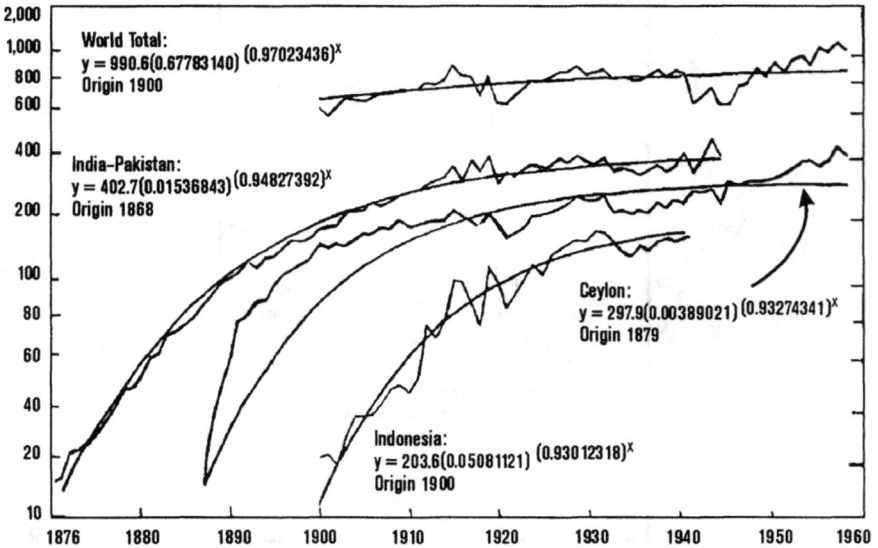

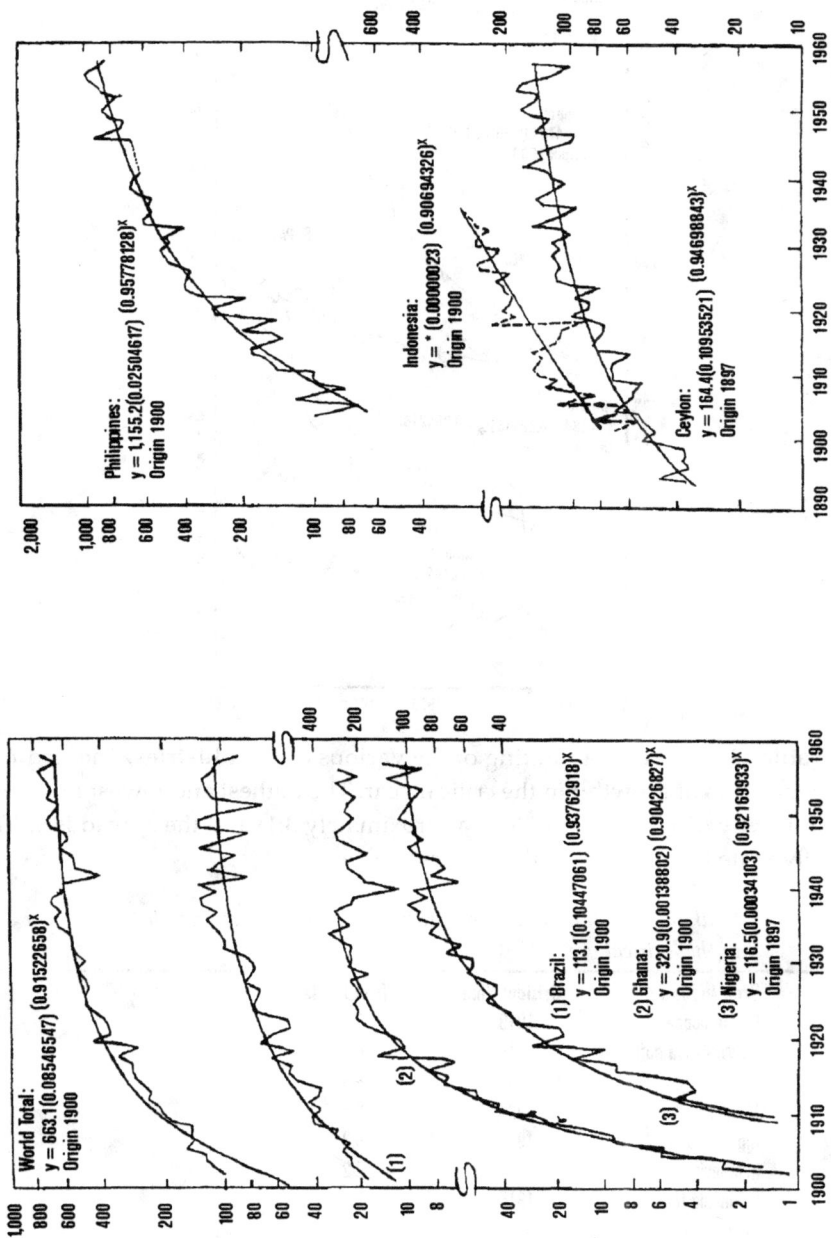

Figure 11.6 *Growth patterns in coconut product exports*

Philippines:
y = 1,155.2(0.02504617)(0.95778128)^x
Origin 1900

Indonesia:
y = * (0.00000023) (0.90694326)^x
Origin 1900

Ceylon:
y = 164.4(0.10953521) (0.9469843)^x
Origin 1897

Figure 11.5 *Growth patterns in cocoa exports*

World Total:
y = 663.1(0.08546547) (0.9152658)^x
Origin 1900

(1) Brazil:
y = 113.1(0.10447061) (0.9376291B)^x
Origin 1900

(2) Ghana:
y = 320.9(0.00138802) (0.9042682?)^x
Origin 1900

(3) Nigeria:
y = 116.5(0.00034103) (0.9216993J)^x
Origin 1897

127

Figure 11.7 *Growth patterns in oil-palm product exports*

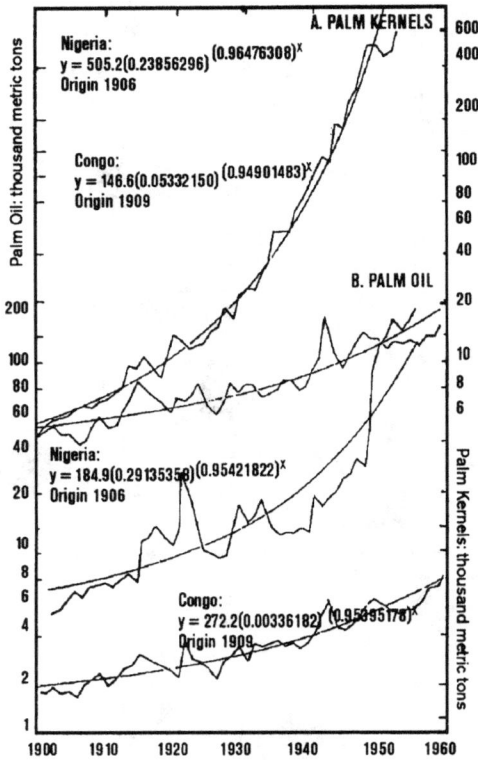

Table 11.1 presents a ranking of the various crop industries,[10] according to trend rates of growth[11] in the critical year. The highest and lowest rates are significantly different (the ratio is approximately 3:1) and the spread is sufficiently wide for a meaningful classification.

Table 11.1 *Ranking of crop industries according to trend rates of growth in the 'critical year'*

Rank	Crop Industry	Critical Year	Trend Rate
1	Ghana cocoa	1919	9.8
2	Fr. W. Africa coffee	1949	8.9
3	Hawaii sugar	1903	8.8
4	Malaya rubber	1927	8.6
5	Nigeria cocoa	1925	8.3
6	Indonesia rubber	1931	8.2
7	Indonesia tea	1915	7.3
8	Brazil cocoa	1913	6.4
9	Cuba sugar	1912	5.4
10	India tea	1895	5.3

11	Ceylon coconut	1900	5.2
12	Brazil coffee	1881	4.9
12	Puerto Rico sugar	1919	4.9
13	Congo palm oil	1946	4.8
14	Nigeria palm oil	1910	4.7
15	Philippine coconut	1930	4.4
16	Colombia coffee	1933	4.0
17	Nigeria palm kernel	1916	3.6

There appears to be no consistent relation between the rank of a crop industry and the point in time when the critical year occurred – a scatter diagram indicates no correlation. Because there is no marked tendency toward bunching of different industries producing the same crop, the observed differences in growth rates do not seem to derive from crop characteristics or the nature of demand for a particular commodity.

The only factor which appears to be of some significance in explaining observed differences in growth propensities is the organization of production. The possible significance of this factor is illuminated if the industries are classified according to the economic organization of production and the average critical year rate of each class taken as representative of the group.

It is generally accepted that the economic behaviour of a particular firm or industry is affected by the organization of production, particularly the structure of competition. In discussing tropical export-crop production,[12] a distinction is usually made between smallholder and plantation systems of organization.[13] Within particular producing countries, competition in smallholder industries is greater than in plantation industries. But there are other important differences which are of relevance. Among them are those relating to characteristics of the factors of production; plantations depend on heavy capitalization and hired labour while smallholder industries utilize relatively little capital and depend mostly on family labour. In addition, management and production decisions are widely dispersed among numerous producers in smallholder industries, whereas the decision-making machinery in plantation production is highly concentrated. These differences are of a type that could well affect the rates at which individual industries develop.

However, not all tropical export-crop industries fit neatly into the plantation-smallholder dichotomy which represents only the polar cases on a scale that includes various other patterns of organization. The task, then, is to develop a classification which will best reflect the relevant differences in the organization of production. The most suitable one that has appeared in the literature on tropical agriculture is that developed by Wickizer.[14] The one presented below is essentially a variant of Wickizer's classification and it appears to fit the data reasonably well. The following tabulation lists four groups of industries according to the organization of production and shows the rate of growth at inflection points for each industry as well as averages or each group. The first two groups are generally familiar; the last two need to be described briefly. 'Mixed-independent' relates to industries in which both smallholders and plantations participate independently of each other, and each to a significant extent. 'Mixed-integrated' describes situations in which participation by smallholders, although important, depends on processing and other facilities provided by plantations within the same industry.

Table 11.2 *Rates of growth for four groups of industries (%)*

I. Smallholder	Ghana cocoa	9.8	
	Fr. W. Africa coffee	8.9	
	Nigeria cocoa	8.3	
	Nigeria oil-palm	4.2	
	Colombia coffee	4.0	
	Total	35.2	Average 7.04%
II. Plantation	Hawaii sugar	8.8	
	Brazil cocoa	6.4	
	Cuba sugar	5.4	
	India tea	5.3	
	Brazil coffee	4.9	
	Puerto Rico sugar	4.9	
	Total	35.7	Average 5.95%
III. Mixed-Independent	Malaya rubber	8.6	
	Indonesia rubber	8.2	
	Ceylon coconut	5.2	
	Philippine coconut	4.4	
	Total	26.4	Average 6.60%
IV. Mixed-Integrated	Indonesia tea	7.3	
	Congo oil-palm	4.8	
	Total	12.1	Average 6.05%

In terms of rates of growth at inflection points, the smallholder group has the highest average and plantations the lowest, while the mixed industries occupy the middle ranks. It would appear from this that smallholder industries have a propensity for more rapid development than plantation ones. But there are individual exceptions obscured by the averages. Hawaiian sugar among the plantation group has one of the highest rates while Nigerian oil-palm and Colombian coffee in the smallholder group have the lowest rates of all the industries. The reasons for these exceptions are explored in a later section.

The two mixed-independent rubber industries have high rates of growth (over 8.0%). It is instructive to note that smallholder participation increased relative to that of plantations during the development of each of these two industries. Consequently, the high rates of development in both cases must be attributed more to smallholders than to plantations; in other words, if the rubber industries of Malaya and Indonesia were disaggregated into their smallholder and plantation sections, each smallholder section would exhibit more rapid growth than the corresponding plantation section.

The preceding analysis suggests that there may be a tendency for smallholder-dominated industries to develop more rapidly than those dominated by plantations. (This conclusion is more securely based if stated negatively: there is no evidence to support the view that plantation-dominated industries are characterized by a more rapid growth potential than smallholder-dominated ones.)[15] Of the 17 industries classified above, there are only three (Hawaiian sugar, Nigerian oil-palm, and Colombian coffee) obvious exceptions to this general pattern. But before trying to reconcile these apparent inconsistencies, it is necessary to consider whether there are logical reasons which might explain the observed tendency for more rapid growth among smallholder crop industries, than among plantation-dominated ones.

The rate at which a particular crop industry develops depends on the rate of response to market opportunities and the availability of factors of production. Both Knorr and Bauer have argued that smallholders have higher supply elasticities than plantations in rubber production.[16] "Although no full-scale empirical work has yet been completed on the supply elasticities of smallholder rubber," such evidence as there is substantiates the view expressed by Knorr and Bauer.[17] Perhaps this is generally true of smallholders and plantations in tropical crop production but available data are inadequate to test this. In the following discussion, a few hypotheses concerning differences in factor availability are offered in an attempt to explain the observed differences in rates of development.[18]

Two points should be noted at the outset. First, it bears emphasis that smallholders tend to dominate production of crops with relatively modest capital requirements, while plantations usually engage in crop enterprises demanding heavy outlays of capital in establishing processing and transportation facilities, as well as considerable amounts of liquid capital to maintain an army of hired labourers (see Wickizer [1960] for an extended discussion). Second, all of the seven crops under consideration are perennials; consequently, the long-term rate of expansion of production (and exports) is defined largely by the rate at which capacity is expanded. If it is assumed that land, is relatively abundant, then the rate of capacity expansion depends on the availability of cooperating factors, labour and capital.

Because of heavier capital requirements, it would appear that the expansion of capacity in plantation production is related to a wider range of variables than is usually the case in smallholder production. In many instances, tropical plantation industries rely on overseas capital. In these cases, the process of capital formation depends on international allocation of funds in which capital is selectively directed to the most profitable of a wide range of investment opportunities. Even where plantation investment is indigenous, the general scarcity of capital in low-income countries is likely to have a restraining influence.

Nevertheless, the history of plantation agriculture in tropical countries suggests that labour, rather than capital, has usually been the limiting factor. In the past, labour shortages in many lines of tropical plantation agriculture have been so acute that organized migrations were necessary. Chinese, Japanese and Filipino labourers were brought to develop Hawaii's sugar industry; indentured Indian labourers were acquired by West Indian sugar plantations which had previously relied on the slave trade; the rubber estates of Malaya and Sumatra drew most of their workers from India, China and Java; and so on. According to Knorr: ". . . dependence on migratory workers from distant areas is necessarily precarious. It lacks flexibility. Adjustment to suddenly altered output schedules cannot be perfect under the circumstances. There always appears to be a troublesome time lag which prevents rapid expansion of production in response to a booming market . . ."[19]

Herein seems to lie the crux of the matter. The rate of expansion of plantation production is likely to be seriously retarded by the difficulty of securing additional inputs of labour. Although this influence can be offset by technical improvements which increase the productivity of labour, the development of new techniques demands scarce capital resources and is time-consuming.

In contrast to plantation agriculture, labour does not appear to have been a limiting factor in the development of smallholder crop industries. Nor was capital, because the relatively small quantities of liquid capital investment needed to expand production were provided by higher prices whenever markets were booming and because capital formation usually occurred through the investment of labour. The rate of capacity expansion in smallholder production, then, seems to depend chiefly on the increased input of labour resources which, it is suggested, depends on a series of transformation rates: the rate at which additional labour inputs can be translated into additional output, the prices at which additional output can be transformed into money income and then into goods and services, and the utilities attached to leisure and subsistence production as compared to purchased goods and services.[20]

The distinctive features in the expansion of smallholder export-crop production in the past appear to have been, first, that underutilized labour resources were usually available and, second, that the introduction of a high-value export crop abruptly raised the marginal productivity of available labour and resulted in a rapid increase in its rate of utilization. Participation of smallholders in tropical export-crop production has usually involved a transition from subsistence to cash-crop production. There is considerable evidence which suggests that family labour in subsistence production is generally underutilized, especially during non-harvest periods. An examination of changes in production of export and food crops in tropical Africa led to the conclusion that "it has usually been possible to superimpose production of an export crop or crops onto the traditional agriculture witout affecting food crop production adversely".[21] The possibility of expanding output by means of fuller utilization of existing labour resources is of much relevance to the rapid rates of transition observed among smallholder industries. It suggests that labour requirements of export-crop production do not usually conflict in timing with requirements for food-crop production or that family labour can be easily diverted from other activities.

Up to the limit of production that completely absorbs an individual smallholder's family labour, the, export-crop production can be expanded quickly when prices increase because the smallholder controls a flexible supply of family labour and the higher prices provide the relatively small amounts of liquid capital needed to bring new land into production.

In general, then, it may well be that smallholder industries tend to develop more rapidly than plantation ones because smallholders have more flexible control of their labour inputs and, therefore, have greater scope for expanding capacity when market prices are favourable. It is also of some relevance that capital required in plantation production has a wide range of alternative investment opportunities in sharp contrast to the limited range of alternative uses of family labour in smallholder production. It can be further argued that plantation agriculture has certain built-in rigidities deriving from the scale of enterprise; problems of administration, heavy capitalization and the concentration of decision-making among a few enterprises deserve to be mentioned in this context.

An attempt is now made to reconcile the apparent inconsistencies created by the Hawaiian sugar, Colombian coffee and Nigerian oil-palm industries. The rapid development of Hawaii's plantation sugar industry appears to have resulted from particularly favourable conditions created by the special political relationship between that territory and the US. Nothing else can account for the heavy inflow of American capital during the last quarter of the nineteenth century. Mollett, in his comprehensive study of capital formation in

Hawaii's sugar industry, attributes the spectacular growth of capital in that period to the Reciprocity Treaty of 1876.[22] Hawaiian sugar, therefore, deserves to be regarded as a rather special case.

In considering the economics of smallholder production, especially in terms of the factors just considered, it is necessary to distinguish between four types of smallholder industries. In one type (A) smallholders depend entirely on family labour. In another (B), although family labour is sufficient for most of the year, hired labour is required at peak harvest. A third type (C) includes smallholders who depend heavily on hired labour under various types of contractual arrangements. The fourth type of smallholder industry (D) is based on gathering of wild or semi-wild crops. It seems reasonable to expect that these differences will affect the rates at which production can be expanded in the respective types of industries.

Much of the previous discussion describing the relative ease with which smallholders can increase long-term supply has reference to industries of the A and B types. Colombian coffee is a mixture of types B and C while Nigerian oil-palm is predominantly type D. Where hired labour is an important input, as in Colombian coffee, the conditions of production are closer to those of plantations than to those described earlier for smallholders. In type D industries such as Nigerian oil-palm, capacity is a gift of nature. Consequently, expansion of capacity beyond that which is naturally defined calls for a drastic change in system of production. It is more likely that production will be determined by variations in the rate of capacity utilization rather than by actual changes in capacity, even in the long run. Thus, although higher prices may bring less accessible groves of palms into production, these will be quickly abandoned when prices decline. Since labour is the only input involved, fruit will be gathered form early accessible stands almost regardless of change in price, as along we there are few alternative employment opportunities.

There apppear, then to be cogent reasons for the exception of certain industries from the general pattern of more rapid growth among smallholder than among plantation industries. The apparent inconsistencies created by the relatively slow growth of the Colombia coffee and Nigerian oil-palm industries seem to be related to the nature of certain types of smallholder production, and indicate that smallholder crop industries are less homogeneous than is generally recognized.

Notes

*The growth of major tropical export-crop industries". *Social and Economic Studies* 13:4 (1964c). This article is a brief summary of Beckford's PhD dissertation, "Sector Trends in the Growth of Major Tropical Export-Crop Industries" (Stanford University, 1962).

1 This, of course, was also true of many industrially advanced countries during earlier stages of their development, as Douglas North so ably demonstrates in his study of the economic growth of the US from 1790 to 1860; see D. C. North, *The Economic Growth of the US 1790-1860* (Englewood Cliffs, NJ: Prentice Hall, 1961), pp. 66-74.

2 G. L. Beckford, "Secular fluctuations in the growth of tropical agricultural trade", *Economic Development and Cultural Change* (October 1964).

3 The basic trend describes the persistent, long-term movement associated with changes in capacity, while Kuznets cycles appear to refer to 15-25 year fluctuations which result not only from changes in capacity but also from changes in the rate of capacity utilization usually associated with the shorter-term trade cycle. For further discussion see G. L. F. Beckford, "Secular trends in the growth of major tropical export-crop industries" (Dissertation, Stanford University, 1962) and Moses Abramovitz, "The nature and significance of Kuznets cycles", *Economic Development and Cultural Change*. Special Issue: "Essays in the Quantitative Study of Economic Growth, presented to Simon Kuznets on the occasion of his sixtieth birthday" April 1961.

4 Simon Kuznets, *Secular Movements in Production and Prices* (New York: A. M. Kelley, 1930).

5 A. F. Burns, *Production Trend in the US since 1870* (New York: National Bureau of Economic Research, 1934).

6 A more detailed discussion of methodology is provided in the author's original study (see note 3). Discussion of the method of fitting and description of the parameters of the Gompertz equation is also provided there. Actually, the parameters play an insignificant part in the analysis of rates of growth presented in this article.

7 All exports of natural rubber were drastically reduced by the shipping shortages precipitated by the Second World War, but the data indicate that the basic trends were not altered by the war for the three series shown in Figure 11.2. Exports in the postwar period continued along paths consistent with prewar trends, and figures were interpolated for the war years to allow trend fitting. The data for Thailand, however, show a conspicuous break associated with the war; exports in the postwar period followed a trend displaced sharply downward from the prewar trend. Consequently, the time span of that industry includes not one but two basic trends.

8 Destruction and disintegration of Indonesian tea estates during and after the Second World War is reflected in a clear break in the basic trend of that series. Consequently, a curve was fitted only for the period before the war. The effect of the political disintegration of British India into independent India and Pakistan in the late 1940s is avoided by ending the series at that time. The earlier separation of Burma from the Indian Union in 1937 is of little quantitative significance because Burma was never a significant tea-producing region.

9 Burns, *Production Trend*, pp.120-73.

10 World export series are excluded from the table because they do not have the homogeneous characteristics of single-crop industries. Indonesian coconut is excluded because the inflection point falls outside the period covered by the data.

11 Trend rates were calculated by the following formula:

$$\left[\frac{Y_{xK}+1 - Y_{xK}-1}{2} \right] 100$$

where $Y_{xK} + 1$ and $Y_{xK} - 1$ are the calculated trend values one year after and one year before the critical year, respectively; and Y_{xK} the trend value for the critical year. This method of calculation approximates the derivative of the fitted trend at the relevant point.

12 The discussion that follows implies that the data on exports presented in this paper can be used as an index of the trend of output. The assumption appears reasonable since commercial production of these crops is geared to export trade; consequently, divergencies between exports and commercial production are usually of a short-term nature. By and large, the available data on production seem to be derived mainly from export statistics and are therefore inadequate to test this assumption.

13 V.D. Wickizer, "The plantation system in the development of tropical econo-mies", *Journal of Farm Economics* (February 1958).

14 V.D. Wickizer, "The smallholder in tropical export crop production", *Food Research Institute Studies* (February 1960).

15 Very few empirical relationships in economics show a perfect correlation and the present one is no exception.

16 K.E. Knorr, *World Rubber and its Regulation* (Palo Alto, CA: Stanford University Press, 1949), p. 26; P. T. Bauer, *The Rubber Industry* (Cambridge: Cambridge University Press, 1949).

17 C.R. Wharton, Jr., "Marketing, merchandising and money-lending: a note on middleman monopoly in Malaya", *The Malayan Economic Review* (October 1962), especially p. 51.

18 The discussion is based on a historical analysis of the development of six selected industries – two smallholder and four plantation – in the author's original study (Part III). In general, the argument here runs contrary to the traditional view that the peasant is unresponsive to market opportunities and is constrained by limited resources. It suggests that the traditional view may in fact rest on faulty assumptions.

19 Wharton, "Marketing", p. 26.

20 See J.W. Mellor, "The use and productivity of farm family labor in early stages of agricultural development", *Journal of Farm Economics* (August 1963), p. 5.

21 B.F. Johnston, "Changes in agricultural productivity and patterns of production in tropical Africa". Paper Prepared for the Social Science Research Council Conference on Indigenous and Induced Elements in the Economies of Sub-Sahara Africa, November 1961.

22 J.A. Mollet, "Capital in Hawaiian sugar: its formation and relation to labour and output, 1870-1957" (Hawaii Agricultural Experiment Station), *Agricultural Economists Bulletin* 21 (June 1961), p. 13.

12

Agricultural Development in 'Traditional' and 'Peasant' Economies: A Review Article*

It has now become quite popular for economists to point to the need for agricultural development to promote and sustain economic growth in the poorer countries of the world. The problem that remains unresolved is how to achieve the required development of agriculture. During the postwar period, at least most of the governments in the low-income countries implemented programmes and policies designed to promote agricultural development, but on the whole, they have met with very little success. One reason for this failure is the lack of an adequate theoretical framework by means of which the agricultural economies of these countries may be analysed and appropriate policies devised. This lack is in part related to the fact that economists have in most instances used overgeneralized rather than particularized approaches and that the latter have relied too heavily on assumptions made on the basis of what is relevant to farming systems in the more advanced countries. In addition to this, the particular studies have, on the whole, been specific to national economies and not to a meaningful typology of world agriculture.

What seems to be required is an approach which begins by trying to understand the economic behaviour of farmers operating within the framework of some particular and meaningful economic, social and political environment and which proceeds on the basis of this to formulate a theory of the dynamics of change relevant to that environment. Two recent contributions by Clayton[1] and Schultz[2] provide some useful material for proceeding along these lines for agriculture in 'peasant' or 'traditional' societies. The plan of this review is, first, to provide a general appraisal of each book in terms of how well it achieves its stated objectives; second, to consider what light both works throw on the economic behaviour of 'peasant' farmers; and, third, to consider the treatises with respect to their contribution to an appropriate model of agricultural development for 'peasant' societies. The two books are highly complementary for the purpose at hand.

—————

Professor Schultz begins by pointing out that sooner or later a stagnant and depressed agriculture creates a crisis in many of the so-called underdeveloped countries. Famine in India today, the retardation of industrialization in China in the late 1950s and the Argentine crisis under Peron are a few examples mentioned. On the other hand, in the more advanced countries – notably the US – the tendency is for overproduction in agriculture, in spite of government programmes designed to restrict output. World agriculture, it would seem, is full of crises of one kind or another and Schultz sets out in this work to clarify the issues underlying these crises and to suggest possible solutions. He sets his sights very high indeed and that he seems to have fallen short of the mark is simply a reflection of the magnitude of the task which he set himself.

This collection of four essays is imbalanced in terms of both subject matter and quality. Only one of the four chapters considers agricultural crises in the more advanced countries and that it surpasses the others in quality is a reflection of the fact that it is less generalized and that the author is travelling on more familiar ground. From the outset, the reader is given an oversimplified picture of world agriculture – 'surpluses and shortages' are implied to be the manifestations of economic processes operating in 'modern agriculture' on the one hand and 'traditional agriculture' on the other. Professor Schultz's world consists only of these two types of agriculture. 'Modern agriculture' is said to exist in North America (including Mexico), most of Western Europe, Australia, New Zealand and Israel and is distinguished by the fact that it makes a significant contribution to economic growth in these countries. 'Traditional agriculture', on the other hand, contributes little to economic growth, but the author does not say where precisely it exists. Judgment on this score must be made on the basis of the criteria which the author himself establishes.

Besides its minimal contribution to growth, 'traditional agriculture' is said to be characterized by a state of long-established equilibrium (with efficient resource allocation and low returns to the factors of production). Clearly then, Professor Schultz's world would seem to exclude many underdeveloped countries where the agricultural sectors comprise both 'modern' and 'traditional' elements and where the problem of agricultural development must be viewed in the light of economic and institutional constraints created by this juxtaposition. Neither does his world seem to include the plantation economies of the Caribbean and Southeast Asia; nor the semi-feudal economies of parts of Latin America and parts of Europe. Strictly speaking, 'traditional agriculture', as defined by the author, would seem only to exist in certain communal and/or tribal pockets of Asia, Africa[3] and Latin America; and even so, it would only apply to that period before the introduction of export cash-crops with the attendant continuous disequilibrium generated by the operation of market forces. The definition does not seem to fit any total agricultural sector of today. The title of the book is definitely misleading, since Professor Schultz seems to be dealing with a 'world' of his own creation.

The discussion is based on 'two simple (economic) models' corresponding to each of the two types of agriculture defined by the author. That dealing with 'traditional agriculture' is a re-statement of the ideas and model presented earlier by Professor Schultz in his *Transforming Traditional Agriculture*[4] and those who are interested in this subject would profit more by reading the earlier monograph which deals with the matter at greater depth. The treatment in the present book reflects the author's preoccupation with how the US can help to improve its contribution to agricutural development in poor countries.

In spite of the many weaknesses of his analysis of traditional agriculture and of the shortcomings of his model (below), Schultz still manages to arrive at some reasonable conclusions and propositions about US foreign agricultural aid. More attention needs to be directed to the relationship between product and factor prices (p. 49). The PL 480 programme may well be impeding agricultural production in the recipient countries by depressing the prices of agricultural output for domestic consumption (p. 51). "We need to detect and help correct the widespread underpricing of farm products and overpricing of agricultural inputs in poor countries" (p. 51). Extension programmes are useless when based on the assumption of allocative inefficiencies and when they fail to carry relevant and appropriate information to farmers (pp. 57-58). What needs to be encouraged is new agricultural research to provide a supply of "inputs that have a relatively high payoff" (pp. 60-63).

The chapter dealing with 'modern agriculture' is perhaps the best; its main weakness is in the superficial treatment given to the plantation economy of the US South in terms of what is described simply as the 'southern tradition'. Modern agriculture is viewed as being in a continuous state of disequilibrium; the growth of output being secured through improvements in productivity, advances in knowledge and farmers' know-how, and in the supply of new material inputs; and important policy inferences are derived.

The four essays were originally given as a series of memorial lectures at the University of Michigan. And much of the superficiality throughout may be a reflection of this orientation. The chief beneficiaries of the collection will be those who are concerned with domestic and foreign agricultural policies of the US. Others can judge the contribution in the light of their own interests from the discussion in the rest of the review.

Dr Clayton's task is far less ambitious than that of Professor Schultz.

It is also less formidable than the title of this (attractively bound) monograph implies. He is really concerned with the development of African[5] agriculture in Kenya, as the subtitle partly reveals. The study is a result of the author's long experience with East African agriculture. It is historical in approach and policy oriented.

At the outset, the author identifies the problem of developing peasant agriculture economies as being mainly one "of communication; of seeking to persuade peasant farmers to adopt technically and economically more efficient methods of farming" (p. 1). The story therefore begins exactly where that of Schultz ended. Dr Clayton indicates that "to a large extent the agricultural policies of the former colonial governments have been attempts to solve the extension problem" and that these have met with "varying degrees of success". The story of agricultural development in Kenya is a good example and is said to be "of particular value because, in the last decade at any rate, it is a success story. A large number of Kenyan farmers have awakened from their former slumbers to adopt, with zest, highly productive farming systems . . ." (p. 2). The term 'former slumbers' is assumed to be synonymous with Schultz's 'long-established equilibrium' in the present review .

Since the study is based on an initial commitment to one major limiting factor (communication), it is hardly surprising that the author does not conclude with an appropriate model of development for peasant economies. And an analysis of the influence of this factor is weakened in spots by certain misconceptions about the behaviour of peasant farmers. For example, the problem of persuading the peasant cultivator to adopt sound farming practices was accentuated by 'ignorance of basic farming principles' and the 'natural disinclination for more work' on the part of the farmers. Yet the problem "was resolved by including in the farm plans a high-value cash crop . . ." (p. 34). Surely, a natural disinclination for work could not be resolved without coercion; economic measures offering higher returns would in the event be inadequate. Again, because reduction of the incentive award scheme for improved farming practices in Nyanza Province led to a fall in the standards of farming, wrong motives are imputed to the African. The interpretation given is that "the African saw better farming only as a means of procuring government largesse and not apparently as a benefit in itself". Clearly, the benefit of the improved system to the farmer is a function of the returns which it brings in relation to the extra costs it involves. And the latter were directly influenced by the rewards which took "the form of grants for the purchase of carts, wheel-barrows, fencing wire, farm implements and tools . . . free labour for approved work . . . and sometimes a cash reward" (p. 25). Reduction of such rewards would therefore increase the costs that have to be met by the farmer himself to maintain the system and this increase may have been sufficient to reduce the marginal net return sufficiently to discourage maintenance of the system.

Notwithstanding these limitations, the first four chapters of Dr Clayton's book provide a lucid account of colonial agricultural policy in Kenya since the turn of the century. The reader is provided with an insight into the minds of colonial administrators from the lengthy and appropriately chosen quotations extracted from official documents. Analysis is provided to explain the failures and successes of the various schemes and it emphasizes the importance of economic as well as institutional factors. The analysis could no doubt have been strengthened by more explicit consideration of sociological and political influences. The nature of social stratification and mobility within the peasant communities would give some indication of the nature of individual incentives and of the process of change. To what extent, for example, could change be induced by winning the influence of chiefs? How precisely did the nature and structure of government and the political conflicts affect the relation between farmers on the one hand and policy makers and extension officers on the other? What effect did tribal differences have on the communication process? For those not familiar with Kenya, the treatment is too skimpy on the non-economic side.

The last three chapters deal with the "economics of peasant agriculture" which in reality is an exposition on the usefulness of linear programming for farm and agricultural planning in peasant economies; the role of government in agrarian development; and problems relating to tenure and taxation for financing rural development. Some of the matters arising from the discussion in these chapters are considered later in this review. It is sufficient here to say that, on the whole, the treatment is adequate.

The monograph will be of greatest value to those interested in African agricultural development in Kenya. And although it does provide useful information – especially on matters of policy – for similar systems, its contribution here is limited by the inadequate treatment of the non-economic environment. Those responsible for formulating agricultural policy in countries with similar economic foundations will need to do their own research on the sociological structure of rural Kenya before direct relevance can be assumed.

A reconsideration of certain aspects of peasant farming seems to be necessary in the light of these two recent contributions. To date, the literature on peasant agriculture has revealed some basic misconceptions about the economic behaviour of peasant farmers, and these only serve to create confusion about the problems of agricultural development in such economies. In particular, the peasant farmer needs to be vindicated in respect of current assertions about his economic irrationality based on observations relating to the profit motive, redundancy of labour and supply response.

The standard theory of the firm is based on the simple assumption that entrepreneurs always seek to maximize profits. What is not generally recognized is that this assumption needs considerable modification in the case of the 'farm-firm', especially in situations such as peasant farming systems. Dr Clayton is impressed by the technique of linear programming for farm planning in peasant economies because it provides a range of profit-maximizing positions. And although he admits that the maximizing conditions may not exist in the particular setting, he appears to be confused as to why this is to. It is not that "economic motivation is lacking" (p. 86) which implies that the peasant is different from other human beings, but rather that the motivation is restricted by certain built-in features of the system and of the productive activity. The distinction is important since it leads to different conclusions. One example will illustrate.

Risk and uncertainty are important factors which influence producers' decisions and need to be balanced against prospective profits (which are difficult to anticipate with the inflexible production lags in agriculture and the imperfect knowledge that tends to characterize peasant agriculture). So, for example, a peasant cultivator may quite reasonably forego extra profits that could be earned by cash-crop specialization because his risks (on both the supply as well as the demand side) would increase disproportionately. The linear programming studies reported by Dr Clayton in his chapter 5 indicate that in certain areas studied 'net income' would be maximized when the "holdings are given over almost entirely to cash-crop production". From this he concludes that "providing the supply of hired labour is relatively elastic, it would seem desirable to encourage cash-crop specialization on many farms" (p. 96). This conclusion could only be in order if the only factor limiting the choice is ignorance of the possibility on the part of the farmer. But since there may be a positive resistance due to the attendant risk, it is necessary to take this into account before making any recommendation about the appropriate product mix.

The point of emphasis here is that where it is observed that the profit motive does not greatly influence farming decisions, it should not be assumed that motivation is lacking but that farmers are quite rationally sacrificing extra profits in favour of other things. In other words, although the profit-maximizing principle obtains, it is limited by such factors as security and family welfare. The peasant farmer wants to maximize profits but he wants to do other things as well; it is quite reasonable to expect him to try to minimize risk and to want to maximize family welfare, and these may in particular situations (certainly in the case of peasant farming) contradict with maximum profits.

On the question of redundancy of labour, Professor Schultz has this to say:

The widely held notion that traditional agriculture is honeycombed with all manner of underemployment is not compatible with this hypothesis [of equilibrium]. Underemployment in a strict economic sense is consistent with the types of disequilibria that characterize modern agriculture but not with the equilibrium of traditional agriculture (p. 16).

Since efficient resource allocation is a condition of Schultz's equilibrium, it follows that what he is in fact saying is that the use of labour up to that point where its marginal product is zero, is indicative of inefficient resource allocation. This is clearly a non-sequitur.

Consideration must be given to the relevant factor proportions. In fact, Clayton provides us with the necessary theoretical considerations when he states that:

For peasant agriculture to achieve the most economic use of its resources, the principle of factor proportions must be observed. According to this principle, the greatest total output is achieved if the limiting or relatively scarce resource(s) is economized by the liberal application of the more plentiful factor(s). For example, in a land scarce/labour-abundant . . . peasant economy where surplus labour cannot be profitably employed outside agriculture, the output of agriculture would be at a maximum if additional labour were employed until it made no further contribution to total output (*ie* where the marginal product of labour is zero). And in a labour- scarce/land-abundant situation . . . the reverse would apply (pp. 96-97).

It is clear from this that redundant labour can co-exist with efficient resource allocation. Schultz's proposition is really linked with a tendentious (implicit) assumption that land is abundant[6] (see p. 21). But then he also states later that "in long-settled communities with no open frontiers, additional land suitable for cultivation is hard to come by" (p. 45). Certainly for the countries of Asia and the Caribbean, it would seem more reasonable to assume that land is relatively scarce – a situation which may also obtain in parts of Africa, as Clayton's work suggests. In these cases, redundant agricultural labour cannot be simply assumed to reflect inefficient resource allocation – *especially when, as is often the case, non-agricultural employment opportunities are limited.*

Professor Schultz reminds us that there is still a long list of economists who cling to the belief that the supply response of farmers in poor countries tends to be perverse. (Many Indian economists incidentally are on this list). And he has provided us with a number of cases to show that responses tend to be positive and that, in some instances, the coefficients of adjustment are not very much different than those for farmers producing similar crops in the US (see pp. 31-33). All the evidence that comes forward on this matter is to be welcomed since it is so crucial to policy formulation in these countries. This reviewer's own experience suggests that most economists who claim a perverse response for peasant farmers are misled by one or other of two factors: either that their observations are based on absolute instead of relative prices or they fail to make appropriate adjustments for production lags. Now, however, Dr Clayton's linear programming analyses have suggested another interesting possibility: that a supply curve can be "completely inelastic over a very wide price range" and still be consistent with income-maximizing positions. The 'normative' supply curve derived from computing programmes of maximum profit at different coffee prices for a particular smallholding shows that between £325 and £150 a ton (with price adjustments at £25 intervals) there is really no economic inducement for the farmer to alter his coffee acreage on the basis of the profits earned from coffee relative to that which could be earned from the alternative crops open to the farmer (see p. 102).

Perennial tree crop production is characteristic of many peasant export economies and producers of these crops are "very likely to be insensitive to price changes", as Clayton suggests. But he overstates the case by looking for output changes only through adjustments in capacity, ignoring completely the changes that can be effected through adjustments in the *rate of capacity utilization*. On p. 104, Clayton states *inter alia* that "there would be strong forces to deter the peasant farmer from decreasing output as prices fell. Reducing the output of perennial crops means grubbing them out . . ." Surely, the situation is not that inflexible. Farmers still have the choice as to whether to harvest all or only a part of the crop; output can be reduced by leaving acreages unharvested – as indeed has been done from time to time.

———

The model of agricultural development in traditional economies presented by Professor Schultz is based on the following major hypotheses: that the system of farming does not underutilize land, that available reproducible material capital is not misallocated, that the same applies to available labour, and that the rate of return to investment in order to increase production is very low so that the incentive to expand production is weak (pp. 16-17). The efficient resource allocation signifies a long-established equilibrium. And since returns to the factors of production are low the problem of development is one "of breaking the established equilibrium and creating a disequilibrium which calls for an approach which is anathema to most economists" (p. 15).

Since resources in traditional agriculture are already efficiently allocated and since incremental resource inputs are unprofitable on account of the low rates of return to them, the breakthrough can only come through production possibilities that offer 'high' rates of return. So the argument goes. The author chooses to focus on investment (to improve the quality of inputs) and uses an arbitrary 10% rate of return as his "benchmark for defining 'low' and 'high' rates of return" (p. 36). Shades of Rostow. It is further suggested that rates of return in excess of 10% can only be achieved by the introduction of a wide array of modern inputs that are not yet available to traditional agriculture.

A number of questions arise concerning the underlying hypotheses, the equilibrium model, and the nature of the inferred transition from traditional to modern agriculture. And on some of these matters, Dr Clayton's report on Kenya provides some clues. For example, Clayton's extensive research on peasant farming leads him to conclude that:

At the farm level, increased productivity can be achieved by procuring a better allocation of existing resources available to the farmer; this includes a better use of land and labour, and also improved combinations of enterprises. Productivity can also be increased by introducing new resources on to the holding in the form of capital, labour and new practices. Both of these can result in higher farm incomes (p. 78).

This contrasts sharply with Schultz's basic hypothesis concerning allocative efficiency. Since the latter is based on the by-product results of anthropological studies (by Sol Tax in Guatemala and by W. David Hopper in India), this reviewer is inclined to lean more heavily on the findings of Clayton's work, for the time being at least.

The notion of a 'long-established equilibrium' is somewhat worrying. It seems to involve an implicit Malthusian assumption about population growth – that population will be kept in check by famine, wars, etc. Otherwise, it is certain that equilibrium could not be maintained indefinitely. Again, Clayton's work emphasizes the significance of this point. In discussing "the beginnings of rural progress" in Kenya (chapter 1), he indicates that the original policy to increase the output of African agriculture had been conceived and put into effect when the African areas were not overpopulated. But *"within a decade . . .* the population balance had altered and in some areas the pressure on land resources became severe" (emphasis added). As a consequence, "there arose the now familiar problems of soil depletion and soil erosion" (pp. 8-9).

Population growth brought pressure to bear on

the traditional system of shifting cultivation . . . This was a primitive system of agriculture based on human . . . labour using crude implements. However, from the fertility point of view, it was a self-sustaining system so long as the land/population ratio allowed it to operate unhindered . . . A rising population meant less land available to the family with the need to maintain a minimal level of nutrition. The period of fallow consequently declined. In time, fallows were broken long before loss of soil structure and fertility from previous cropping had been restored (p. 11).

What is clear from this evidence is that population growth is a powerful factor which in a relatively short time can upset any established equilibrium. The system of shifting cultivation would presumably be accepted by Schultz as 'traditional agriculture' in his classification since it does not seem to qualify as 'modern agriculture'. And it did in fact seem to allocate resources efficiently so long as the size of the population allowed it. It was self-sustaining, as Clayton puts it. But then the system did not keep population in check so as to maintain itself. Professor Schultz will therefore have to provide us with some relevant theory of population growth which is both consistent with the real world and with his equilibrium model before we can begin to take his model seriously.

The transition from traditional to modern agriculture which is suggested by Schultz's model seems all too smug. Introduce new inputs which will raise the rate of return on investment above 10% and fasten seat belts! Surely, there will be non-economic restraints to the adoption of the new inputs. Schultz himself makes passing reference to some of the "cultural restraints which . . . hinder economic growth" – the absence of a scientific tradition, caste arrangements and extended family systems, "land tenure arrangements that are deeply imbedded culturally", and so on (p. 25).

Some indication of the importance of non-economic factors is provided by Clayton in his discussion of early efforts to introduce smallholdings in Kenya:

it was one thing to establish the technical feasibility of the smallholding and quite another to persuade the African . . . that it was to his advantage to adopt it. Consolidation, which implied individual land ownership, was alien to the tribal systems of tenure and moreover, ran directly counter to inheritance arrangements which . . . fragmented rather than consolidated (p. 14).

Other examples can be drawn into evidence.[7] The fact is that socioeconomic factors may well be of greater importance than Professor Schultz is prepared to admit. Where these act as constraints on economic behaviour, then there is not enough 'grist' for the mill if economics alone is fed into it.

Furthermore, it deserves emphasis that even though the new inputs may bring prospects of high rates of return on investment, they also involve great risks for a people who have been operating with tried and proven inputs and systems. But perhaps Schultz would argue that the 10% will take care of that.

It is clear that we still have a long way to go toward devising models that are appropriate for particular agricultural systems in low-income countries. The first requirement is a meaningful typology of world agriculture which gives recognition to the influence of particular economic, social and political factors on the behaviour of farmers and, therefore, on the agricultural adjustment process. Peasant systems of agriculture are intrinsically different from plantation systems, feudal systems and settler-homestead systems. And there are special problems of agricultural development in countries with mixed systems. The current tendency among economists to glamourize analyses with terms such as 'modern' and 'traditional' may introduce some elegance but may not provide real clarity.

Notes

* "Agricultural development in 'traditional' and 'peasant' economies: A review article". *Social and Economic Studies* 15:2 (1966c).

1   Eric S. Clayton, *Agrarian Development in Peasant Economies* (Oxford and London: Pergamon Press, 1964).

2   Theodore W. Schultz, *Economic Crises in World Agriculture* (Ann Arbor: University of Michigan Press, 1965).

3   For example, Dr Clayton in his book gives two examples which show that "the indigenous inhabitants of Africa have been sufficiently astute, on occasions, to devise their own self-sustaining, viable forms of agricultural organization". One system is practised by the Wakara tribe on the island of Ukara situated in Lake Victoria; the other "relates to the Wachagga who occupy the southern and eastern slopes of Mount Kilimanjaro" (pp. 63-67).

4   *Studies in Comparative Economics* Vol. 3 (New Haven: Yale University Press, 1964).

5   The study does not consider the European operated 'estate' subsector of Kenya's agriculture which would presumably be classified as 'modern agriculture' in Schultz's dichotomy. Clayton, therefore, seems to be dealing with Schultz's 'traditional' type using the more familiar 'peasant' nomenclature.

6   In answering the question: why traditional farmers either cannot or do not want to increase production substantially over time, Schultz states "it could be because of a lack of good land. Yet, as already noted, many of these farmers are on irrigated plains or on a delta, farming first rate land. They also have an impressive number of draft animals, and the labour force is as a rule large" (p. 21).

7   See, for example, David Edwards, *An Economic Study of Small Farming in Jamaica* (Kingston: ISER, University College of the West Indies, 1961).

13

The Schultz "High Pay-off Input" Model*

Professor Schultz has made a number of notable contributions to the study of agricultural development. One of the most recent of these deals with a type of agriculture which is assumed to be characteristic of many low-income countries and which is described as 'traditional agriculture'.

Schultz's model of traditional agriculture contains the following major propositions: all resources of the traditional type are efficiently allocated, and the rate of return to increased investment with the existing state of the arts is too low to induce further saving and investment. The development of traditional agriculture, therefore, depends on breaking the established equilibrium. A change in technology involving the introduction of new modern inputs (especially human and material capital) can provide the breakthrough. It is a simple economic model based on a theory of the price of income streams.

Perhaps because of its simplicity, the model raises a number of outstanding issues; but, no doubt on that same account, it leaves a number of unsettled questions of substance: Is traditional agriculture as described by Schultz truly representative of the farming sectors of low-income countries? How realistic is the assumption of efficient resource allocation in the agricultural economies of these countries? What is the real likelihood of a 'long-established equilibrium' being achieved and maintained? And, finally, can economic influences alone induce a transformation? These questions are considered briefly in the rest of this note.

Traditional agriculture is defined as an agriculture that is in economic equilibrium, this state having been achieved after a considerable period of time during which the state of the arts, preferences, and motives remain constant [Schultz 1964: 29-37]. In a later publication [Schultz 1965], Schultz adds that traditional agriculture contributes little to economic growth and gives the impression that it exists everywhere outside of North America, Western Europe, Australia, New Zealand and Israel.[1] What seems certain is that the description does not fit the total farming sector of most (if any) of the low-income countries. Clearly, it does not fit the plantation economies of the Caribbean, Central America, parts of South America, and Asia; nor the peasant export-economies of parts of Africa; nor the European-owned estate sectors of parts of that continent. The description may, to be sure, apply to certain pockets in low-income countries, to Panajachel in Guatemala, for example, and to Seanapur in North Central India [Schultz 1964: 41-48]. It seems fair to conclude, however, that the model relates to a very insignificant part of underdeveloped agriculture and therefore has limited applicability.

Efficient resource allocation and the established economic equilibrium are two sides of the same coin. The literature on underdeveloped agriculture is crowded with cases of inefficiencies in resource allocation. But, then, as already pointed out, it seems that Schultz is dealing with only a small subset. Nevertheless, the fact that he has stimulated others to undertake empirical research on this matter[2] is all to the good. The notion that a long-established equilibrium exists at a time when all countries are in one way or another exposed to the influences of modern civilization is worrying indeed. According to Schultz, "the critical conditions that generate this type of equilibrium" are that the state of the arts and the state of preferences and motives relating to income all remain constant long enough [Schultz 1964: 71]. It is suggested here that this is unlikely to happen if only because of population growth – a factor which Schultz fails to give explicit consideration to in his analysis. A recently published study [Clayton 1964] substantiates this point. The traditional system of shifting cultivation in areas of Kenya had to be altered within a relatively short period of time (after the beginning of British colonization) on account of expanding population.

It follows quite logically from the postulates of efficient resource allocation and low returns to incremental traditional factors that the transformation of traditional agriculture must involve the introduction of new inputs. But it is not the logic of the model that is in question. So far as agricultural development in low-income countries is concerned, once it is established that the basic postulates do not apply, then it follows that the policy prescriptions derived from the model are insufficient to cope with the problem.

Even within the narrow framework defined by Schultz, the process of transition is oversimplified, because attention is directed only to the proximate economic factors influencing the demand and supply of new inputs. That is why real world situations seem 'puzzling' in the context of the model. For example, Schultz cannot explain why large farmers in parts of South America do not seek out modern agricultural factors [Schultz 1964: 169, 194], or why plantation owners did not seek to extend the life span of slaves.[3] And it seems accidental to him that the US South is relatively poorly provided with research establishments.

The explanation of these phenomena is to be found in the structural features of the plantation system. As Schultz himself recognizes, "plantations based on slavery were nowhere known for technical progress; they were based on a massive routine in the use of forced labour." And underinvestment in farm people may result from political factors; for example, "where large land owners are powerful politically, it is to be expected that they will have a strong vested interest in maintaining the status quo" [Schultz 1964: 180-181, 196]. In short, the nature of the transformation must be considered in terms of the constraints posed by the economic, social, and political environment, and not simply in terms of proximate economic influences. Non-economic factors are of overriding importance, since they often govern the economic variables.

The sum and substance of these remarks is that on account of the specific definitional assumptions, Schultz's model of traditional agriculture and the implied process of transformation have little direct relevance to the problem of agricultural development in low-income countries. Policy makers in these countries need to be aware of this, especially in view of the recurrent practice of generalizing models out of their original context.

Notes

* "Transforming traditional agriculture: comment". *Journal of Farm Economics* (1966a), 1013-15, published with a reply by Professor Schultz.

1   See also my review of Schultz's book published in *Social and Economic Studies* 15, no. 2 (1966).
2   See, for example, Delane E. Welsch, "Response to economic incentive by Abakalik rice farmers in eastern Nigeria", *Journal of Farm Economics* 47: 900-92, where the inspiration of Schultz is acknowledged.
3   Schultz in *Economic Crises in World Agriculture* (Ann Arbor: University of Michigan Press, 1965) p.191, fails to recognize that a proximate cause for this situation could have been that the price of acquiring new slaves was low relative to the cost of extending the life span.

14

The Induced Development Model*

In commenting on this paper by Ruttan and Hayami, I wish, first to make some rather general remarks. Secondly, I will consider certain aspects of their paper which I find unsatisfactory; and, thirdly, I wish to focus attention on certain critical questions which they largely ignore.

General Remarks

Every contribution to the theory of agricultural development is to be welcomed, if only because this field of enquiry has not been ploughed sufficiently. As Ruttan and Hayami themselves indicate, the concern of economists has been more in the direction of examining the interaction of agriculture and overall economic growth (structural transformation)[1] than with the process of agricultural development *per se*. Yet we know that agricultural development is perhaps the most critical problem facing underdeveloped countries today. The bulk of the population in these countries depends on agriculture for its livelihood; so the welfare of millions of people is at stake. And, of course, we now know that overall economic advance by these countries cannot proceed without substantial expansion of agricultural output and improvements in productivity. From this general point of view, then, the Ruttan-Hayami paper can be regarded as a noteworthy contribution.

In order adequately to assess the value of this contribution, however, we need to say something about the general usefulness of models in economic analysis. All models are by definition an abstraction of what obtains in the real world. Simplifying assumptions have to be made to avoid the complexities of the real world. Ultimately, the critical factor that determines the usefulness of a model is whether or not what is left out is fundamental in understanding what goes on. We can take one of a number of approaches in assessing a particular model. One such approach is simply to check its internal consistency. Another is to see how well it explains and/or predicts what happens in the real world. This depends ultimately on whether the assumptions of the model correctly represent given situations. It is this second approach that I wish to take in the present exercise.

An Assessment of the Ruttan-Hayami Contribution

The first point for us to note is that, contrary to the title of their paper, Ruttan and Hayami are not concerned with agricultural development at all. They are essentially concerned with the growth of agricultural output and associated improvements in agricultural productivity. Their model is, therefore, more appropriately a model of agricultural *growth* rather than agricultural *development*. This point is, to my mind, one of very great substance. Agricultural development is essentially a study of the process by which the material welfare of the rural population of a country is improved consistently over time. In this context, the growth of agricultural output and productivity may be a necessary, though certainly not a sufficient, condition. Indeed, there are numerous instances (in the past, as well as at present) in which substantial growth of agricultural output is accompanied by no change in the material welfare of the majority of people involved in the process of that growth.[2] In short, we must recognize that there is always a strong possibility of the phenomenon of 'growth without development.'

Later, I wish to return to some questions relating to development, but for now let me proceed to look at Ruttan-Hayami on their own ground. Basically, their induced development model is the conventional resource allocation model within the general framework of the traditional theory of the firm. Critical to the model is the existence of competitive conditions along with profit-maximizing behaviour of decision makers. In such situations, the following endogenous sequence may be expected: resource availability determines relative factor prices and the choice of techniques by producers is guided by the structure of factor prices. Over time, as changes in relative prices occur, technology is adjusted to maximize the use of relatively cheap factors. A further consideration, then, is the degree of technical substitutability between factors of production.

For empirical verification of the model the authors checked the development experiences of a number of countries where the development process was played out largely in the eighteenth and nineteenth centuries. I want to suggest that the economic and social situation of underdeveloped countries today is significantly different from those that obtained for present-day advanced countries in the nineteenth century. The social order that existed in the latter countries was of a kind that permitted the emergence of economic institutions and behavioural patterns that fit the neoclassical marginalist framework of economic analysis.

My contention is that such is not the case in underdeveloped countries today. These economies are for the most part characterized by imperfect market conditions and social institutional arrangements that create artificial rigidities in the flow of factor supplies and inflexibilities in the patterns of resource use.[3] Furthermore, the openness of most underdeveloped economies exposes them to exogenous influences of a kind that serves to shatter the neat links between factor endowments and factor prices and between factor prices and technological change which are central to the induced development model.

Let me quickly list some of the problems that concern me most in the Ruttan-Hayami analysis and then briefly discuss each of them.

1   The profit maximization assumption,

2   The association between resource endowments and the structure of relative factor prices,

3   The aggregation problem in moving the analysis from the firm to the industry,

4   Resource availability in the open economy,

5   The assumption about public sector responses, and

6   The superficiality of the model of induced institutional innovation.

Farmers in underdeveloped countries do not consistently seek to maximize profits. Profits from farm production are only one element (though a major one) in the matrix of their objectives. Considerations such as family security, social status, and risk minimization, all enter into the picture, depending on the particular institutional environment.

The one-to-one association between the society's factor endowments and relative factor prices ignores two fundamental characteristics of underdeveloped agriculture. One is the marked divergencies between private and social costs and benefits that are typical of most situations; and the other is duality in the structure of some underdeveloped agricultural economies that distorts the relative factor prices faced by different producers within the same economy. The divergencies between private and social costs and benefits are very briefly organized by Ruttan and Hayami but the question of duality entirely escapes notice. We find, for example, that in plantation economies, labour may be relatively cheap to peasants but considerably more expensive to plantations while land may be relatively cheap to plantations but relatively expensive to peasants. In such a situation, it seems to me that there is no uniquely efficient path of technological change for the society as a whole unless of course some exogenous institutional reform to eliminate duality occurs.

On the aggregation problem of moving from the firm to the industry, what bothers me is that the Ruttan-Hayami model seems to imply that what is good for the firm is good for the industry. Let me be more specific. Given the inelastic demand for farm products, expansion of output for the individual farm-firm produces different results from the expansion of output for *all* farm firms. What this implies is that there are obviously leads and lags which the induced development model does not account for in its one-to-one firm industry adjustment process.

In the modern world economy, trade is only one aspect of the characteristic of openness. Much more important is the dependence of underdeveloped countries on the capital, technology, and management resources of the economically advanced countries. In this connection, I cannot accept the cavalier manner in which Ruttan-Hayami dismiss the influence of "forces associated with the international transfer of agricultural technology". Let me take a futuristic example. Desalination of sea water is technically feasible. I suggest that its economic feasibility is likely to emerge from the research efforts of the more advanced countries. The effect of this will be to drastically alter the resource endowments of arid areas of underdeveloped countries. In order to be fair to Ruttan-Hayami, they admit this kind of event by saying that they do not rule out exogenous technical change. The question is whether exogenous technical change will be more important for underdeveloped agriculture in the 1970s than endogenous change, I think that, given the present institutional arrangement of the world economy, exogenous factors will be more important than the endogenous for agriculture in underdeveloped countries.

A highly decentralized system of agricultural administration and the existence of strong farmers' organizations are critical for generating effective public response. But in most underdeveloped countries, local government is poorly developed and farmers' organizations are either absent or weak. In the circumstances, the kind of public sector response predicted by the induced development model will hardly be in evidence.

I am most concerned with the superficiality of the model of induced institutional innovation. It is totally impossible to explain institutional reform in purely economic terms, as Ruttan-Hayami have tried to do. They admit themselves that institutional change is not neutral. If that is so, as indeed it is, then we need to examine the social and political (not to mention the psychological and cultural) dimensions of the process of institutional change. And, of course, the exogenous factors are of critical importance here. We need only call to witness the American Revolution *vs* the problem of the US South and of black people in the US today. Any model of induced institutional reform must explain how the existing institutional arrangements affect different groups in the society, how change will affect these groups, and the balance of power between the groups. This calls for a political, social and psychological analysis. The simplistic Ruttan-Hayami model cannot possibly cope with these problems. A further consideration is the obvious relationship between institutional structure and technological change. Certain patterns of social organization simply do not contribute to the kind of social inputs (education and research, for example) that are critical to the process of change envisaged in the induced development model (see for example, Nicholls 1960).

This brings me, now, to the question of what the model has ignored in relation to agricultural development strategies for underdeveloped countries in the 1970s.

Toward Appropriate Strategies for Agricultural Development

Starting with the recognition that Ruttan and Hayami are not concerned with agricultural development as I have defined it earlier, I wish in conclusion to pose two basic questions.

The first is whether it is sufficient for us to concentrate simply on output growth and productivity changes in the agricultural sector. The second is whether or not our attention should be directed to institutionally-specific analyses and models of agricultural development instead of seeking for a general theory. Let me say a little about each of these basic questions.

To my mind, the process of productivity change and growth of output may well be important in explaining agricultural development in countries like the US. It is grossly insufficient in explaining economic adjustments in places like the US South, the Caribbean, and elsewhere (*ie* the persistence of underdevelopment). At least two factors need to be considered in this connection. One is the existence of duality in the agricultural sectors of underdeveloped economies and the associated questions of the kind of output change. The other is the backwash effects of terms of trade adjustments in the expansion of output in export agriculture.

Duality assumes major proportions in the case of plantation-peasant agricultural economies. In such situations, plantations produce export output and peasant domestic output. It is the latter that is critical for the development process, for several reasons, notably its effects on structural transformation and rural welfare. Duality is an index of institutional distortions in the economic framework. So it is the institutional environment that is critical for the process of agricultural development (and underdevelopment).

The importance of the terms of trade backwash has been recently elaborated by W. A. Lewis in his 1969 Wicksell Lectures. According to Lewis, the extent to which underdeveloped countries benefit from improvements in productivity in export production depends on the relationship between export production and food production in the underdeveloped countries on the one hand; and between production of manufactures and food in the advanced countries on the other [Lewis 1969: 17-27]. In an earlier presentation, Lewis verifies the point in a manner directly relevant to my reservations about the Ruttan-Hayami model of 'development.' It is worthwhile quoting Lewis at length on this score [Lewis 1955: 281]:

Cane sugar production is an industry in which productivity is extremely high by any biological standard. It is also an industry in which output per acre has about trebled over the past seventy years, a rate of growth unparalleled by any other major agricultural industry in the world – certainly not by the wheat industry. Nevertheless, workers in the cane sugar industry continue to walk barefooted, and to live in shacks, while workers in wheat enjoy among the highest living standards in the world. However vastly productive the sugar industry may become, the benefit accrues chiefly to the consumer.

I come, finally, to my own contribution to the evolution of thought on agricultural development. To my mind, the induced development model of Ruttan and Hayami exposes the fundamental limitations of contemporary theorizing on the nature of the process of agricultural development. If we are concerned, as I am, with the material welfare of rural people, then the problem must be approached differently from the way the authors have attempted. Basically Ruttan and Hayami have started from the body of economic theory that we have at our disposal. That body of theory is based on the observation of economists of real situations that existed in the past. I suggest that we need to analyze the process of agricultural development from the perspective of the present. In terms of agricultural development this means developing models appropriate to the contemporary situation in Third World countries.

If we are to do this, it seems to me that we need, first, to develop a typology of underdeveloped agriculture reflecting different institutional arrangements in particular situations; and, secondly, to develop models appropriate to each type identified. For the most obvious lesson to be gained from the evolution on thought on this subject is that useful theories of agricultural development have been based on analyses of specific situations. It is the specific social order that determines the institutional arrangements that influence the interplay of the proximate economic variables which are central to the Ruttan-Hayami mode. So if we are to understand the development process we need to probe far beyond the proximate economic variables. And I am afraid that, as economists, we are not well equipped for that!

Notes

*"Strategies for agricultural development: comment". *Food Research Institute Studies in Agriculture, Economics, Trade and Development* (1972b); reprinted in C. K. Eicher and J. Staaz (eds.), *Agricultural Development in the Third World* as "The induced development model . . ." (1984)

1   See B.F. Johnston, "Agriculture and structural transformation in developing countries: a survey of research", *Journal of Economic Literature* (June 1970), for a summary.
2   The case of the slaves in the slave plantation economies is an outstanding historical example. And, currently, several scholars have noted that the benefits of the 'Green Revolution' are concentrated among the larger, better-off farmers in underdeveloped countries.
3   I have demonstrated this in my analysis of the problem of resource allocation in plantation economies. See my *Persistent Poverty* (1972), especially chapter 6. A similar situation exists for the feudal-type economies of Latin America and parts of Asia, and the tribal economies of Africa.

15

Comparative Rural Systems, Development and Underdevelopment*

Introduction

A vast literature exists on the subject of 'underdeveloped' agriculture, but very few of the writings tell us why underdeveloped agriculture remains underdeveloped. Unless we know the answer to that question, there is very little chance of stimulating development – either by evolutionary policy measures or by revolutionary social change. The present paper is offered to professional colleagues as a small attempt to find the answers to the questions raised. (I deliberately say 'answers' because I am convinced that there is no single answer; and, therefore, no single solution to the problem.)

This prologue outlines the general conceptual framework of the exercise; and it locates my approach to the question within the context of other contributions to date.

The main thesis of the paper is that different systems of agricultural (and rural) organization possess different inherent endogenous potentials for development.[1] That is to say, within each system of rural social organization, there are certain inherent factors which stimulate or retard development. Furthermore, there are different exogenous influences which affect different underdeveloped countries – depending on what international system a particular economy is locked into. In the modern world, no economy is an island unto itself. And the international capitalist and socialist systems generate somewhat different exogenous influences on underdeveloped countries.

Following from this general thesis, we need to develop a typology of agricultural (rural) systems to facilitate the analysis. This is done in the first section of the paper. In the second section, I examine the economics of resource allocation and use, by type of system. This is important, because if we do not understand how resources are allocated and used, we cannot understand the phenomena of development and underdevelopment.[2]

The groundwork should, by then, be well established for a consideration of the political economy of underdevelopment in Section III. And, again, the analysis is by type of system. The 'plantation case' and the 'special case' provide the backdrop for that analysis. It is simply assumed that readers are familiar with the backdrop. The brevity of exposition may, therefore, fail to persuade those who are unfamiliar with the literature on those two cases.

The final section of the paper is a brief comment on certain issues relating to employment, unemployment and technology.[3]

The immediate conceptual concern of the paper is with 'economic development' – that is, how a people utilize their resources to advance their material welfare. Some rural peoples have achieved this; others have not. And so we must explain why this is so.

In my opinion, conventional 'models' of agricultural development do not explain enough. Ruttan and Hayami are the authors of the most recent of these models – the induced development model.[4] By regarding technical changes as endogenous, they have improved on the earlier 'high pay-off input model' of T. W. Schultz. That model itself was an advance on the earlier 'diffusion model'. Each of those models treats technology as the central factor in rural change. They are, therefore, productivity-centred. The 'conservation model' of the early classical English and German writers is resource-centred. And the 'urban-industrial impact model' originally developed by von Thunen and extended by T. W. Schultz is market-centred. That model is concerned with explaining how imperfections in both product and factor markets create regional disparities within industrial nations.

In that general tradition, the approach which I take in the present exercise can be said to be 'institution-centred'. My concern is to explain global poverty in different rural situations.[5] In other words, why are rural people in, say, Jamaica generally poorer in material terms than those in, say, the US Midwest, or those in New Zealand, or in Cuba!

To explain such situations, we need a holistic analysis that integrates productivity, technical change, market structures, and other economic phenomena with social and political factors. That is a tall order to accomplish in a short paper. Therefore, one must expect of find many deficiencies in the exposition that follows.

Economic Theory and Rural Reality:
a View of World Agriculture

Different writers have developed typologies of world agriculture for different purposes. There are geographers (like Wagner) using typologies based on differences in exchange patterns (*ie* market relations). There are farm management approaches (such as that by Phillips Foster) which emphasize differences among decision makers and between types of land tenure arrangements. That approach is also useful but too disaggregated for present purposes. It is production-relations oriented.[6]

Then among the formal general economists and political economists, we have on the one hand the 'pure' Marxist approach based on the social relations of production. And on the other hand we have the pure so-called 'mainstream' economists who view economics narrowly and who treat development and underdevelopment in terms of the 'modernity' and 'backwardness' of observed techniques of production.

Finally we have a group of eclectic social philosophers, like Weber and Polanyi. They emphasize the importance of value systems or preference hierarchies of different peoples in different places and times.

Of the different approaches mentioned above, the least useful is that taken by 'mainstream' economists. Yet the largest number of scholars are to be found in that stream. That school is really caught in the trap of the 'special case' which, in the agricultural development context, is the US Midwest rural situation. (We return to this point, later in this section, after presenting our working typology.)

The most useful approaches are those of the eclectic philosophers and the Marxists scholars; while elements drawn from the geography and farm management streams can be used to improve the typology we choose. The easiest way to combine all these approaches is to look for 'historically-determined' types of rural social systems which we all understand to a certain degree. But before that, a little bit on each of the more important contributions just mentioned above.

Exchange relations are important in the Wagner sense. But since Polyani and others deal with that we can, to some extent, ignore Wagner. Land tenure arrangements and decision-making as emphasized by Foster are crucial. So we keep those in mind.

Now the Marxist school is somewhat confused. The approach of the school is what I call 'macro-socioeconomic', and their analysis is based on real historical experiences emanating from two distinct real world cases:

a   The European sequential change of feudal-capitalist-socialist ('communist'?); and

b   The non-European sequential change of pre-capitalist–capitalist-
     socialist (?) – ('communist').

Among this school, problems and inconsistencies arise in two directions.
First, we get the exchange-centred point of view of Sweezy and Gunder Frank
vis-à-vis the production-relations centred view of Dobb and Laclau (*ie* social
organization of production). Secondly, we get some differences between the
Sweezy analysis that is based on empirical validation using Europe back to
the Middle Ages and the Gunder Frank analysis using Latin America only
back to the sixteenth century. The Marxist school will need to sort out these
differences in due course, to the benefit of all social scientists.

The eclectic philosophers[7] have a smaller following: but there is greater
consistency within the school. The leaders of the school have made the important distinction between 'formal' and 'substantive' economics and rationality
– a distinction which clearly exposes the sterility of the mainstream school.
Weber and Polanyi make the distinction between formal rationality and
substantive rationality. And we have Polanyi and others exploring exchange
relations in depth.

'Substantive' rationality is said to be equivalent to the implementation of
given values. That is to say, given the limits of knowledge and information, a
people will seek to get the most value from their resources, depending on
their particular value system or preference hierarchy.

'Formal' rationality is said to be equivalent to the matching of means and
ends, for a given abstract end. As such, this kind of behaviour transcends
institutional constraints to define a course of action which leads to a defined
'optimum'.

Thus we always find a bias in formal (mainstream) economics – value
biases towards abstractions like 'efficiency', 'productivity', etc, as end goals –
whereas what we really need are considerations of efficiency and productivity
as means to improving the welfare of people.[8]

If we are to follow this general and most useful approach, thereby, to
develop substantive economics for explaining rural development and underdevelopment, we need a typology of rural economy which incorporates the
ideas that appear useful and enlightening. Accordingly, Figure 15.1 emerges
as our analytical view of the world situation.

The typology seems rather old. But is based on a combination of factors
governing (i) the relations of production, and (ii) the nature of exchange. We
are essentially concerned with decision making, tenure relationships and
exchange arrangements. In short, with both the modes of production and of
exchange. Within that general conceptual mould we wish to explain differences in patterns of resource allocation and of development and underdevelopment, in the present exercise.

Figure 15.1 A view of world agricultural and rural systems

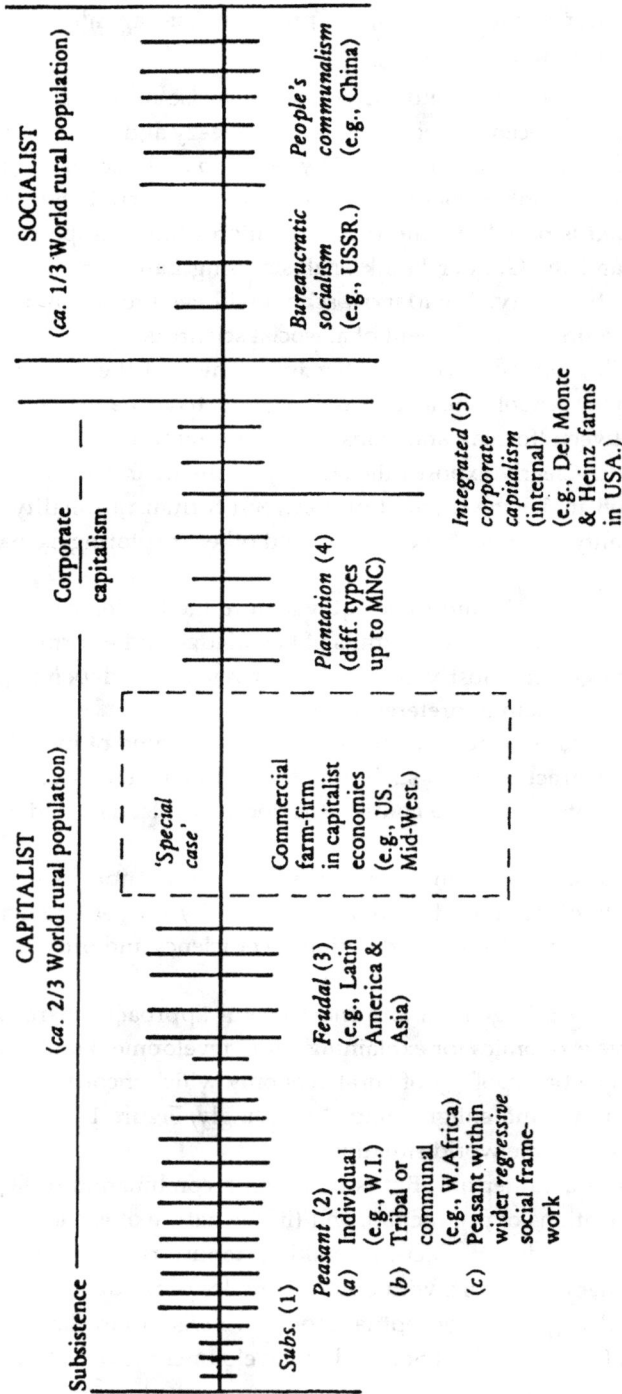

| Subsistence | CAPITALIST (ca. 2/3 World rural population) | | SOCIALIST (ca. 1/3 World rural population) | |

Subs. (1)

Peasant (2)
(a) Individual (e.g., W.I.)
(b) Tribal or communal (e.g., W.Africa)
(c) Peasant within wider regressive social framework

Feudal (3) (e.g., Latin America & Asia)

'Special case'

Commercial farm-firm in capitalist economies (e.g., US. Mid-West.)

Corporate capitalism

Plantation (4) (diff. types up to MNC)

Integrated (5) corporate capitalism (internal) (e.g., Del Monte & Heinz farms in USA.)

Bureaucratic socialism (e.g., USSR.)

People's communalism (e.g., China)

(1) So-called "primitive" isolated communities (e.g., Amerindian "reservations", etc.).
(2) Pure and adulterated. (For the adulterated, see (c) where peasant society is subordinate to a different and more powerful social framework.) The categories above in the chart are not mutually exclusive.
(3) Pure and semi-feudalism exist in *parts* of Latin America and *parts* of Asia.
(4) See *Persistent Poverty* for elaboration on the different types of plantation organization.
(5) A minor type up until now (*ca.* mid-20th century).

Before that, a few words on Figure 15.1. This paper will analyse neither the 'special case' nor the socialist patterns of organization: and for two different reasons. The special case dominates economic theorizing about agricultural and rural development, and I am not yet sufficiently familiar with the socialist patterns.

As is suggested schematically, the bulk of the world's rural population falls under the capitalist systems designated in the diagram. A few paragraphs, then, on the reality of these cases.

Global subsistence production is not common in the world; though global subsistence consumption exists among many rural people. The pure subsistence case will therefore be tested rather briefly.

Peasants, on the other hand, dominate the world, in terms of numbers and of different social situations. Everywhere, the peasantry is interlocked in some larger social framework – state capitalism in the Soviet Union; tribal systems in West Africa; plantation systems in the West Indies; and semi-feudal arrangements in Latin America and Asia. It is the larger social framework that determines the rate of advance of the peasantry in each case.

What do we mean by the term 'peasant' in this classification? The simple answer is: whenever the decision maker utilizes his own labour and that of his family to transform resources into output; and when he consciously plans production with an eye on the market. He may or may not utilize hired labour at certain times. Thus we have different classes of peasants – big, middle and small – categories that relate to the nature of the labour regime but not necessarily to size of farm.[9]

In the analysis to follow in the next two sections, the special case is used as a background for analysing resource allocation and use. While the plantation case will provide general background for analysing development and underdevelopment.

The Economics of Resource Allocation and Use

The 'special case' allocation problem is familiar. The decision maker in agriculture sets out consciously to maximize profit and to minimize risk. Risk is critical in all agricultural situations. Accordingly, choice criteria are relative output prices and relative input prices. Where perfect (or near-perfect) market conditions exist, economic efficiency is achieved in the circumstances.

So long as producers have sufficient resources at their command, they will achieve reasonable and decent levels of living even though other groups of people in the same economy may surpass their consumption achievements. If resource distribution is relatively even, the rural society does not exhibit major disparities in income distribution. And local government will allocate resources to agricultural research and extension of a kind that ultimately serves further to improve the material welfare of the rural people.[10] So much for the special case, for now.

The pure subsistence producer need not detain us very long either. Such a producer sets out consciously to maximize consumer production (*ie* of himself and family) from the set of resources at his command. Meat or vegetables, or any combination of these which they happen to enjoy. There is no exchange; therefore, no relative prices to guide choice. Choice is determined by the consumer indifference surface and the production possibilities from owned (or controlled) resources and from the pool of technical knowledge. This point is elaborated in Part A of Figure 15.2 below. The solution to the allocation problem is a tangency one which equates the marginal rate of substitution on the consumption side with marginal rate of technical substitution in production.

What needs further discussion in the pure subsistence case is attitudes to risk, and hence to innovation and change. In this connection, I find the analysis developed by Miracle to be quite useful.[11] Part B of Figure 15.2 reproduces the Miracle analysis. That author uses two basic concepts in his analysis – the

Figure 15.2   *The subsistence allocation problem*

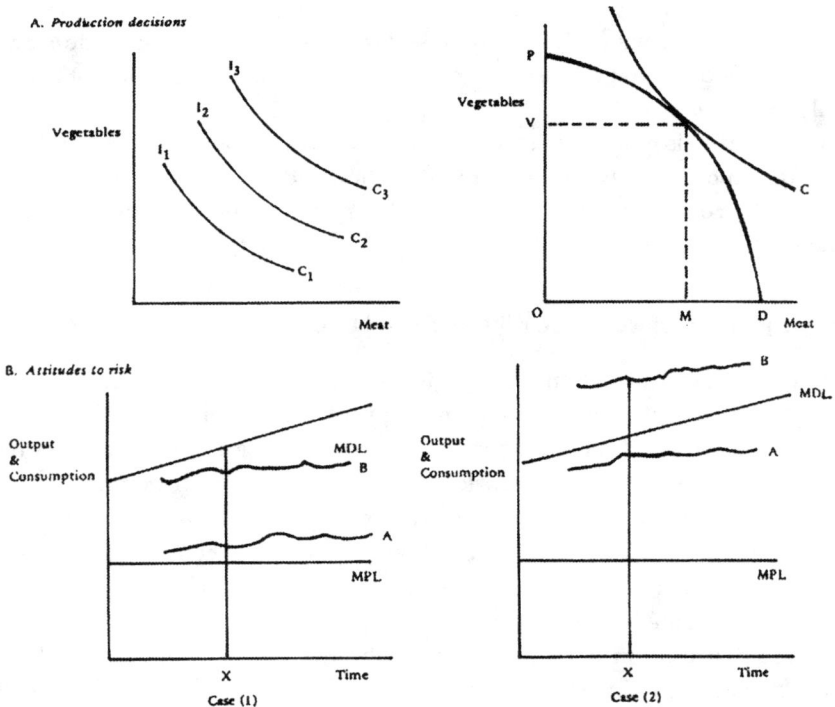

minimum physiologic level of consumption living (the MPL, which is fixed by nature); and the minimum desirable level of consumption (the MDL, which is culturally determined). The producer's attitude to risk is conditioned by his output performance relative to these two levels.

According to Miracle, in a situation such as Case (1), producer A has a greater incentive to minimize risk than does producer B, because A cannot take the chance of falling below the MPL. However, in Case (2), producer A will take bigger risks relative to producer B, because he is close to his MDL and far enough above the MPL, while producer B, having achieved his MDL, has no great incentive for increasing output.

Since the peasant case is perhaps the most confusing, we will leave that for the last and treat, briefly, the plantation and feudal cases. I have dealt with the plantation case at length elsewhere.[12] Different types of plantations face different situations. So that the family plantation may set out consciously to maximize the social welfare of the owner, while the corporate MNC subsidiary may maximize production, as part of an overall corporate strategy to maximize profits for the international complex.

Accordingly, different production decisions leads to different patterns of resource allocation and use. For example, whereas the corporation plantation is likely to substitute capital for labour, the family-owned plantation is less likely to do so. Generally speaking, we should expect to find greater changes in both 'mechanical' (labour-saving) and 'biological and chemical' (land-saving) technology in the corporate case, as compared with the family case.[13]

The feudal case is a kind of hybrid between the family plantation and the pure peasantry. The peons provide labour for the manorial lord (hacendado) part of the time; and they produce for their own subsistence (and surplus) the rest of the time. Accordingly we have a backward system of resource allocation and exploitation, in which technical change is slow and output is both limited and unequally distributed among the population, as in the general plantation case.

The peasant case is extremely interesting analytically. Production decisions are made within a complex matrix of social and economic variables. "A peasant economy is one which links purchaser and producer, resource allocation, and product allocation in a network of ties which are personal." Personal relationships affect:

1 rights to the use of land,
2 the mobilization of labour,
3 the objectives of the decision maker,
4 the accumulation of capital, and
5 the choice of technology.

There are two sets of such 'personal' relationships: household influences, and community influences. In addition, there is the 'super' power of the state which imposes taxes and/or rent.

Household influences affect present and future consumption,[14] labour inputs, land inputs, and capital inputs. Community influences affect inputs too, in addition to defining the social imperatives to which the peasant must accommodate in making decisions. Furthermore, the community affects the structure of markets and of exchange relationships.

Generally speaking, we would expect of find that the individual decision-maker in peasant economy sets out consciously to maximize family welfare – a rather vague objective which includes a mixture of profit maximization constrained by generally acceptable standards of peasant society. In such situations, "the rewards for economic effort may lie to a greater degree in the fulfilment of social obligations and social roles; and patterns of decision making are regulated accordingly".[15]

Figure 15.3 below presents a summary position on the nature of decision making in the peasant case. Part A of the diagram assumes a coincidence of market and household solutions; the price line is tangential to the production possibilities curve at the same output mix as determined by the household preference in terms of consumption. This is a unique and unstable solution. A more realistic choice situation is depicted in Part B of the diagram. The peasant producer participates in market production by choice; and the choice is determined by prevailing market prices in conjunction with his own household preferences relevant to both farm and non-farm goods and services. Thus this producer converts resources into output both for sale in the market and for his own consumption.

In the peasant's case, although the price line comes into the picture the household preference map is still relevant as a source of risk minimization; whether or not all output is actually marketed. In Figure 15.3B, we get three different solutions which result from given market prices and a particular household preference. If the effective price line is P_bL_b, the particular output mix will be V_b of vegetables and M_b of meat. If the price line is P_aL_a, the output mix will be V_a of vegetables and M_a of meat. Now if the market price is not right, the producer will choose a $C_v + C_m$ combination for his own consumption. This is the case where market conditions generate a forced subsistence solution on the peasant farmer.

In peasant economy, the production possibilities frontier tends to remain relatively static over time as tradition tends to dominate economic and social life. Nevertheless, the society has a relatively even pattern of income distribution and full employment, albeit at generally low levels of income. Accordingly, the market for non-farm output remains small; and expansion comes

Figure 15.3   *Decision making in the peasant case*

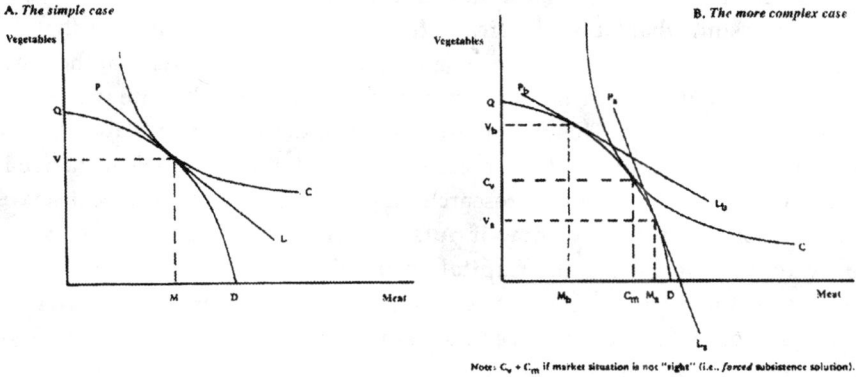

A. *The simple case*

B. *The more complex case*

Note: $C_v + C_m$ if market situation is not "right" (i.e., *forced subsistence solution*).

mainly from exogenous shocks which either raise desirable levels of consumption, or shift the production frontier to the right, or a combination of both.[16]

Development and Underdevelopment

Agriculture contributes to general economic growth in the following directions: (i) providing output of food and raw materials for the whole population; (ii) providing factor supplies (especially labour and capital) to the non-agricultural sectors; (iii) providing linkages with other sectors of the economy – both at the final demand level and at the level of intermediate supplies (forward and backward linkages).

In these contexts agriculture's contribution is greatest where food output is geared heavily in initial stages, to satisfying internal demand (and where export is a surplus); where incomes are evenly distributed and output is rising; and where there are no great disparities in social relationships between groups that make up the society.

Agriculture is also an important earner of foreign exchange in many countries. However, the secular contribution of agriculture in this connection depends on terms of trade adjustments over time. For most underdeveloped countries these adjustments have been unfavourable in the past.[17] Consequently, we find that the export performance of underdeveloped countries has not had as dramatic an effect on their development as we would expect.

Agricultural development[18]

The interaction of agriculture with other sectors during the process of economic development is important. But, in the present exercise, we are more concerned with the process of agricultural development. That is to say, the major concern is to examine what factors promote or retard sustained improvements in the material welfare of rural peoples.

If we assume that labour is already fully employed, then it is clear that the development process requires an expansion of agricultural output at the same time that labour must be transferred from agriculture to facilitate the expansion of other sectors. This means that the productivity of the labour force remaining in agriculture must increase substantially. Technological change is crucial in this regard. For this, research plays an important role since it serves to increase knowledge of new inputs and of possibilities for raising the productivity of old inputs. Capital accumulation is also essential to the process as the increased competition for labour resulting from the growth of other sectors increases the need for more capital-intensive techniques of production in agriculture.

The dynamic effects of technological change and capital accumulation can only come into play if certain preconditions for agricultural development exist. Among these are a highly motivated population to provide the basic human resources (managerial and technical skills, and adaptable labour power), adequate supplies of complementary resources – land and capital, and appropriate institutional arrangements for uniting all the available resources in the productive effort.

Economists have frequently noted these general preconditions; but of the three listed above, least consideration has been given to the need for appropriate institutional arrangements. Next to the need for a highly motivated population, we consider this neglected area to be of greatest importance. Shortage of land and capital is generally of much lesser significance. This ordering is based on our view of the development experience and performance in the underdeveloped world as a whole. The primary importance we attach to a highly motivated population – the human element – is based largely on the achievements of Israel where in spite of severe natural limitations in regard to land a viable agriculture has emerged. As concerns the importance we attach to institutional arrangements, it is to be noted that in spite of abundant supplies of land and capital throughout Latin America agricultural development in those countries has been extremely slow, mainly because structural factors have inhibited the unity of available resources.

Both the human element and the institutional arrangements in any situation are largely influence by the pattern of social organization. It is the social environment that determines whether the population of a country is highly motivated in the service of the development effort or not. This motivation is intensified in societies where there is normative consensus with social and cultural homogeneity; but it becomes severely retarded in societies where dissensus prevails along with social and cultural plurality. The institutional arrangements determine whether or not large-scale units of collective action can be organized; and, as Brewster has emphasized, this largely determines whether the opportunities for agricultural development can be seized.[19]

The particular institutional arrangements that exist in any situation are determined by social structure and organization, tradition, values, beliefs and attitudes – all of which derive their flavour from the particular dominant rural institution existing in a country. Thus we should expect to find differences between agricultural systems, such as plantation, peasant, feudal, or state-controlled. It is the particular system which determines the nature of the social institutions, and, therefore, the kind of institutional arrangements that exist for uniting resources in the productive effort and for promoting agricultural development.

For agricultural development to proceed at a satisfactory rate it is necessary for available resources continuously to be made available to those people in the society best able to transform resource services into products for consumption. And it is clear that there is need for flexibility in resource use in order to bring about output adjustments necessitated by changing income opportunities. To achieve these, the required social institutions must be such as to facilitate the greatest possible degree of resource mobility – particularly in respect of access to land and capital by the more capable farmers, and the flexibility that exists for adjustments in patterns of land use over time. In addition, the social and economic institutions must be capable of ensuring a continuous extension of technical knowledge relating to agricultural production, adequate means of supplying farmers with new inputs and providing marketing and credit services, incentive for effort, progress-oriented values, and good government. Obviously different social systems have different inherent capacities for providing all these prerequisites for agricultural development.

Of all the capitalist systems identified in Figure 15.1, the 'special case' appears, *prima facie*, to be best endowed with the prerequisites for development. In other cases, we will need to examine the persistence of underdevelopment by exposing weaknesses in the social framework of economic relations. But before proceeding to that we pause, briefly, to consider the question of the transition from pure subsistence to commercial agriculture.

The transition from subsistence

The transition from subsistence production occurs as a result of one of two processes: endogenous transition and/or exogenous change.

The endogenous sequence is the one outlined by Boserup.[20] The dynamic is population growth which places increasing pressure on natural resources:

resulting in technical change, both in methods of husbandry and in techniques of production. This model seems adequately to describe the historical experience of Western Europe.

The exogenous sequence seems more applicable to contemporary underdeveloped countries. We can identify three possibilities in this connection. First, forced contact with the rest of the world, as when the Europeans invaded New World Indian society. Second, export cash crop incorporation into a food economy, as in the West African cocoa case. And, thirdly, fortuitous non-agricultural developments, like the discovery of minerals, tourism, etc., which create markets for food-stuffs, where none existed before.

In each of these cases, it is unlikely that subsistence production could survive for long. Patterns of exploitation would either exterminate the subsistence producers (the New World Indian case) or incorporate them in some way into the larger economic system (West Africa, the West Indies and Asia are three different patterns of such incorporation).

The final result of the exogenous sequence under capitalism is persistent impoverishment of the former subsistence producers by small minorities of ruling elite groups, nationally and internationally. These elite groups expropriate the bulk of the surplus for their own advancement. This is the foundation on which contemporary monopoly capitalism has been built. The final result remains entrenched as capital accumulation and technical change proceed to widen disparities internationally and within national communities.

Underdevelopment – Patterns and Results

Whereas, the 'special case' generates even development and increasing rural welfare, the other cases within the capitalist international give evidence of uneven development and gross disparities in welfare among rural people. This unevenness and the corresponding disparities are found in varying degrees, as we move from one system to another along the continuum of types within the capitalist world.

In what follows, we use the plantation system as our main point of reference in analysing the underdevelopment biases of the different types of agriculture identified earlier. Table 15.1 below provides a summary picture. In an earlier analysis of the plantation system the 19 factors identified in Table 15.1 were positively associated with the persistence of underdevelopment.[21] Development will proceed in the 'normal way' in situations where these factors are not present in the social framework. In the chart 'Yes' indicates the presence of the particular underdevelopment bias identified; and 'No' indicates its absence. A 'No(Yes)' or 'Yes(No)' entry indicates an uncertainty;

while 'No-Yes' entries mean that the factor is present in some real-world cases and absent in others.

Table 15.1 *Underdevelopment biases in types of world agriculture*

	CAPITALIST				SOCIALIST	
	"Special case"	Plantation	Peasant	Feudal	(USSR) Bur. Socialist	(China) Peoples
A. Economic factors						
1. Fracture of resource supply and demand	No	Yes	No	Yes	No	No
2. Unequal distribution of wealth and income	No	Yes	No	Yes	No	No
3. Foreign ownership of production	No	Yes	No	No (Yes)	No	No
4. Export orientation	No (Yes)	Yes	No (Yes)	No (Yes)	No	No
5. Low skill content of labour	No	Yes	No	Yes	No (Yes)	No
6. Resource use distortions	No (Yes)	Yes	No	Yes	No (Yes)	No
7. Metropolitan enterprise linkages	No	Yes	Yes	Yes	No	No
8. MNC resource allocation	No	Yes	Yes	Yes	No	No
9. Limited technical knowledge	No	Yes	Yes	Yes	No	No
B. Non-economic factors						
1. Weak community and loose family organisation	No	Yes	No	No	No	No
2. Rigid social structure	No	Yes	No	Yes	No (Yes)	No
3. Correlation between race and class	Yes	Yes	No-Yes	Yes	No	No
4. Absence of social responsibility	No	Yes	No	Yes	No	No
5. Strong central govt administration	No	Yes	No	Yes	Yes	No
6. Excessive power of elites	No	Yes	No-Yes	Yes	Yes	No
7. Low incidence of progress-oriented values	No	Yes	No-Yes	Yes	No	No
8. Strong individualism	No	Yes	No	No-Yes	No	No
9. Authoritarian tradition	No	Yes	No	Yes	Yes	?
10. 'Great House' value aspirations	No	Yes	No-Yes	No (Yes)	Yes	?

An examination of Table 15.1 reveals that whereas underdevelopment is endemic to the plantation system, development is highly attainable in the capitalist 'special case' and with the socialist peoples communalism. The feudal system has more underdevelopment biases similar to the plantation than has the peasant system. Bureaucratic socialism has several limitations for rural development. These derive principally from the centralisation of power (B-5 + B-6) and from the presence of an authoritarian tradition (B-9).

As in our earlier analysis of resource allocation and use, the peasant case is perhaps the least clear-cut regarding its development potential. This results from the fact that there are different peasant categories in different parts of the Third World. And these real world situations reflect somewhat different modes of over-all social organization. For example, land may be communally owned in certain tribal situations; but it may be individually owned elsewhere.

What Table 15.1 really suggests is a ranking of systems according to the sum total of underdevelopment biases as follows:

1   Socialist – People's communal

2   'Special case'

3   Socialist-Bureaucratic

4   'Pure Peasant'

5   Feudal

6   Plantation

The plantation comes last because it is the most dehumanizing of the systems considered here. The 'feudal' system is almost as bad but because, in most instances, relations are more personal it is somewhat less dehumanizing.

All systems within the capitalist international, except the 'special case', suffer from capitalist exploitation, as economic factors A7-9 indicate. As well they are subject to terms of trade backwash, resulting from A4. Consequently, countries in these categories have a common bond; that is, they have to break with the internationalist capitalist system in order to secure economic advancement.

However, they will need to go beyond this: to correct internal imbalances that inhere in each system. And that calls for political action to redress economic and social inequalities. How to achieve that is beyond the scope of the present exercise.

A Comment on Employment and Technology

Employment and unemployment are critical factors when we are considering the welfare of people. In most underdeveloped situations in the Third World today, unemployment and underemployment are significant and appear to be on the increase. The reasons for this derive partly from the international transfer of technology in two main directions.

The first dimension was the transfer of medical technology which brought down death rates, leaving birth rates unaltered. High rates of population growth resulted in a veritable explosion in Latin America, the Caribbean and parts of Asia. Resource pressure became great as more output was demanded, during the same period when monopoly capital was extending its control over more and more Third World resources. Considerable underemployment was the stark result of this process of change.

The second dimension is the more contemporary transfers of mechanical (labour-saving) technology and of biological and chemical technology (land-saving – the so-called Green Revolution).

Mechanical technology directly displaces labour and creates unemployment. Biological and chemical technology has a less direct impact on employment. But that transfer favours the better-off farmers in underdeveloped countries and, thereby, aggravates inequalities in the distribution of wealth and income. Underemployment and unemployment are the chief results of this latter transfer.

Technology is not neutral. It comes with the biases of the countries exporting it; and it affects everything, including education, people's values, and the pattern of consumption mix that people aspire to achieve. Thus technological transfer locks the colonial economy tighter into the international capitalist system, and it makes a break with that system more difficult to achieve.

Ultimately, however, Third World nations will have to develop indigenous technology to suit their particular resource endowments and the value aspirations of their peoples. That is the only path that will generate full employment and high levels of material welfare for the rural people and for non-rural people as well.

Notes

* "Comparative rural systems, development and underdevelopment". *World Development* 2:6 (1974); reprinted in C. K. Wilber (ed.), *The Political Economy of Development and Underdevelopment* (1979).

1   I made an attempt to demonstrate this for the 'plantation' case in *Persistent Poverty* (New York: Oxford University Press, 1972). It is no accident that I started my analysis with that case. It is the same reason why North American economists start with what I describe below as the 'special case'. We all start with what is most familiar (*ie* the system into which we have been socialized). The term 'special case' is borrowed from Dudley Seers, writing in a somewhat different context: see "The limitations of the special case", *Oxford Economic Papers* (February 1959).

2   From a pedagogic point of view, the conventional distinction between 'micro' and 'macro' economics does not enlighten students of the discipline. The particular micro makes the relevant macro. Otherwise macro has no meaning at all!

3   These are among some of the central issues which cause economists most concern in dealing with agricultural development.

4   See V. Ruttan and Y. Hayami, "Strategies for agricultural development", *Food Research Institute Studies* 11, no. 2 (1972): my comment in the same journal; and Hayami and Ruttan *Agricultural Development – An International Perspective* (Baltimore, MD: Johns Hopkins University Press, 1971), pp. 1-63.

5   I am not here concerned with pockets (or lacunae) of poverty in rich countries and of prosperity in poor countries. Those phenomena do exist but to understand them requires a level of analysis which is different from that used in the present exercise.

6   The references for these generally unfamiliar names are, Philip L. Wagner, "On

classifying economies" in Norton Ginsburg (ed.), *Essays on Geography and Economic Development* (Chicago, 1960); Woytinsky and Woytinsky, *World Population and Production* (New York, 1953) chapter 13; and Phillips Foster, "Systems of agricultural organization", *Journal of Farm Economics* (May 1966).

7   We should really add Joseph A. Schumpeter to the list of eclectic philosophers mentioned earlier.

8   The fact is that all societies exhibit substantive rationality by definition; only some societies have the techniques, the value system and institutional arrangements to achieve formal rationality.

9   The literature on the peasantry and on subsistence agriculture is really quite confusing. But I hope that our working definition here is clear enough.

10 Cf. The 'land-grant' colleges and universities in the US Midwest as examples of that kind of input of social capital.

11 See Marvin P. Miracle, "'Subsistence agriculture': analytical problems and alternative concepts", *American Journal of Agricultural Economists* (May 1968), pp. 292-310.

12 See my "The economics of agricultural resource use and development in plantation economies", *Social and Economic Studies* (December 1969); and *Persistent Poverty*, chapter 6.

13 I have borrowed the terminological classifications here from Ruttan and Hayami, "Strategies".

14 Consumption of both farm and non-farm goods and services. Present consumption has a high premium at low levels of income. Future consumption (investment) assumes greater significance as levels of income rise.

15 As an example, the 'ceremonial fund' (for baptisms, weddings, funerals, etc.) is of direct relevance in this connection.

16 West African peasant-based export cocoa production is a good example of such a combination.

17 For further discussion on this point, see W. A. Lewis, *Aspects of Tropical Trade 1883-1965*, Wicksell Lectures (Stockholm, 1969).

18 The discussion below is drawn from my *Persistent Poverty*, pp. 193-96.

19 John M. Brewster, "Traditional social structures as barriers to change" in H. M. Southworth and B. F. Johnston (eds.), *Agricultural Development and Economic Growth* (Ithaca, NY: Cornell University Press, 1967), pp. 66-98.

20 See Ester Boserup, *The Conditions of Agricultural Growth* (London, 1965).

21 See my *Persistent Poverty*, chapter 7 and pp. 216-17. The way in which each of these factors contributes to underdevelopment is analysed in the book.

22 The situation is aggravated by the association of technology transfer with increased foreign investment by metropolitan capitalist economy in the Third World.

16

Toward an Appropriate Theoretical Framework for Agricultural Development Planning and Policy*

In order to be effective, development planning and policy need to be informed by relevant theory. This paper at first argues that, in many important respects, the current body of agricultural development theory inadequately represents the Caribbean situation. Insofar as this hypothesis is correct, it implicitly provides a partial explanation for the failure to get agriculture moving in spite of substantial government intervention and assistance in most territories of the region. It also sets the stage for the second objective of the paper: to outline some of the steps required for developing an appropriate theoretical framework and to place this selection of papers in the perspective of these considerations.

Current Agricultural Development Theories in Relation to the Caribbean

Modern contributions to agricultural development theory[1] can be separated into two broad classes: those dealing with agriculture and economic development and those with agricultural development *per se*. The former includes catalogues of 'agriculture's contribution to overall economic development' (e.g. Nicholls, Johnston and Mellor); 'growth stage theories' (e.g. Johnston and Mellor, Perkins and Witt); and 'simplified mathematical models of the development process' (e.g. Fei and Ranis, Jorgenson).[2] The second category consists almost entirely of variations of one sort or another of Schultz's hypotheses about "transforming traditional agriculture".[3] The question for consideration is how well do these contributions fit the Caribbean situation?

The Nature of Caribbean Agriculture[4]

Caribbean agriculture has two main component systems of resource organization: plantation and peasant. The former is characterized by large scale units of production with a sizeable input of hired labour, a high proportion of foreign ownership and management of resources and specialized production almost exclusively for export markets. The latter is distinguished by small-scale units of production with heavy reliance on family labour, indigenously owned resources and mixed production patterns. Although numerically peasant units are the more important, their resource endowment and capacity for development are poor in comparison with the plantation sector.

In the West Indies, resources are very unequally distributed between the plantation and peasant sectors. Land is a critical input in agriculture; and in the island sector of the regional economy, fertile arable land is a very scarce resource. For historical reasons, the plantation sector has secured almost all the flat fertile areas and the peasant sector is poorly endowed with hillside land with shallow and relatively infertile soils. For any given combination of complementary inputs, therefore, output per acre in the plantation sector will tend to exceed that in the peasant sector. This inherent disparity in physical productivities is further exaggerated in the case of value productivities for reasons discussed below.

With the possible exception of management, the plantation sector is also better endowed with other resource inputs. By far the greater share of fixed capital in West Indian agriculture is tied up in the plantation sector. The distribution of capital is most unequal in the sugar plantation economies with roads, electricity, water supplies, machine shops, laboratories, buildings and equipment geared specifically to the production of sugar. Furthermore, the plantation sector has greater access than the peasant sector to financial capital for further capital accumulation. Imperfect competition in the capital market makes for easier credit availability and plantations can also draw on retained earnings. For labour, the peasant relies heavily on the farm family while plantation production depends on hired labour. With plentiful supplies of labour, the plantation sector has greater flexibility in adjusting labour inputs. Although the peasant sector also has access to hired labour, it can scarcely compete with the plantation sector since its relatively low land productivity weakens its competitive position.

The disparities in productivity following from the nature of resource distribution result in disparities in the returns to factors of production in a way that encourages a flow of incremental resource inputs into the plantation sector. In addition, a number of institutional factors create a dynamic bias in favour of plantation (export) output. Metropolitan preferences produce artificially high prices and help to reduce uncertainty about future prices; technical knowledge is relatively well advanced; and marketing arrangements and infrastructure are more highly developed for plantation than for peasant production.

The foregoing considerations suggest that the plantation system of resource organization is the dominant type in the Caribbean region. The overall pattern of agricultural development is chiefly a reflection of the process of adjustment of resource use in the plantation sector. Consequently, theories of agricultural development which do not take into account the institutional characteristics of plantation-type economies can hardly be expected to fit the social reality of the Caribbean.

Agriculture and Economic Development

The literature on this topic emphasizes four main "contributions of agriculture to economic development": the supply of food and raw materials, the supply of factors to the non-agricultural sector, the earning of foreign exchange and the provision of a market for non-agricultural output.[5] The logic of the argument in such theoretical statements is based on the implicit assumption of a 'closed economy' in which there are naturally strong intersectoral relationships. Since an outstanding feature of plantation economies is a high degree of 'openness', the interrelationships between agricultural and non-agricultural development are not very significant in such cases.

In plantation economies market interrelationships are more important in trade with the rest of the world[6] than within the economy. Since plantation agriculture is characterized by its export orientation, the agricultural sector in such economies is geared to supplying food and raw materials to other countries and not to the non-agricultural sector. And, in turn, the plantation economy depends on other countries for its supplies of manufactures and even basic foodstuffs. This difference is important because the factors governing the terms of trade with the rest of the world do not coincide with those governing changes in the internal terms of trade.[7] There is, for example, easier mobility of labour internally than internationally.

As concerns the supply of capital for non-agricultural expansion, foreign ownership implies that this flow is depleted in plantation economies by the repatriation of dividend and interest payments. Thus the capital transfer from agriculture serves to promote non-agricultural expansion in the metropolis rather than at home. And, finally, agriculture's capacity to earn foreign exchange in plantation economies is reduced by a characteristic high import content of both production and consumption.

Agricultural Development

Current development theory has so far been concerned almost exclusively with what has come to be known as 'traditional agriculture'. In this type of agriculture, all resources of the traditional type are said to be efficiently allocated and the rate of return to increased investment with the existing state of the arts is too low to induce further saving and investment. Consequently, development depends on breaking the established equilibrium by changes in technology involving the introduction of new 'modern' inputs. The description of traditional agriculture could conceivably fit either or both sectors of Caribbean agriculture. Whether or not the description fits individual sectors, the model is of limited use in understanding the development problem because it ignores the problem of resource allocation between sectors. As Adams recently pointed out in another connection, the traditional agriculture model does not account for the fact that efficient resource allocation on individual production units can co-exist with inefficient resource allocation for the sector as a whole.[8]

In the Caribbean, peasant operators seem to allocate resources at their command quite efficiently.[9] And plantation owners allocate resources efficiently from the point of view of private accounting. But peasant operators have insufficient resources at their command because institutional factors limit the supplies of land, capital and technical knowledge available to them. At the same time, resources tend to be underutilized in the plantation sector. For example, available data indicate that land is seriously underutilized in this sector. While this could represent a rational pattern of allocation and efficient resource use for plantation owners, it points to inefficiency for the agricultural sector as a whole. Transfer of such land to peasant operators would expand output if only because of a change in the product/factor price ratio resulting from the change in ownership – the inputs of plantation owners are likely to have a much higher opportunity cost than those of peasant operators.[10]

Particularly in the sugar plantation economies of the region, there is the further consideration that foreign ownership of resources by multi-national corporations creates certain sectoral inefficiencies and rigidities in the adjustment of resource use. The main problems involved are first that product choice is restricted and second that economic activity is of the 'enclave' type. The major raw sugar producer in the region is the West Indies Sugar Company (WISCo), a wholly owned subsidiary of Tate and Lyle which has complementary investments in shipping, sugar refining and distribution in the metropolitan markets. Adverse movements in raw sugar prices do not therefore induce changes in sugar cane production on WISCo estates since the firm is simultaneously increasing profits on the refining end. Efficient resource use for such firms can create sectoral inefficiencies. Finally, the enclave character of the sugar plantation creates a certain artificial specificity of resource use. Thus we find plantations serviced with roads, electricity and water supplies while surrounding agricultural and rural areas are without such facilities even where there is excess capacity for plantation use.

The theoretical framework provided by the model of traditional agriculture is inappropriate for the Caribbean because structural factors create sectoral inefficiencies in resource allocation. The real danger with the traditional agriculture model is that it may provide "decision makers in developing countries . . . [with] a pseudo-sophisticated justification for overlooking possible structural changes in the agricultural sector and . . . [they] may end up placing major emphasis on politically palatable programs for bringing in new inputs from outside the sector".[11] This warning seems most appropriate for the Caribbean.

Steps Toward an Appropriate Framework

The weakness of existing theory may apply as well to other underdeveloped agriculture in the Caribbean region. This weakness derives from a tendency to generalize from the experiences of the advanced industrialized countries and to treat underdeveloped agriculture as a more or less homogeneous class. But there are significant differences in the institutional environment as between different types of underdeveloped agriculture as well as between present day underdeveloped agriculture and that of the advanced countries at earlier periods in history. Theories which abstract from these differences must fail to reflect the realities of particular situations. What is required to begin with is a typology of world agriculture which will classify structural characteristics in some systematic way. Subsequently, theories of development relating to particular types of agriculture could be developed.[12]

Some General Considerations

Very few economists (in metropolitan countries at least) today seem to appreciate the need for the approach suggested here. One notable contribution in this direction was recently made by Phillips Foster who presented a framework for "identification of the institutional dimensions of the classical factors of production associated with any particular system of agricultural resource organization". Foster's awareness of the problem is evident from the following:

It seems obvious that if we are going to try to transform a present-day primitive agricultural economy, we ought to know just what kind of thing we are transforming. It is not the same primitive agriculture which has already been transformed in the process of producing the highly industrialized western democracies. The cultural milieu which produced 'the West' included strong elements of Puritan protestantism, a north European land tenure system, a philosophy that hard work is good per se, a respect for the scientific method of investigation, etc. The non-Western world today is certainly not a carbon copy of the Western world in AD 1500, nor of the Western world in any other period of its history. Unfortunately, we don't really know much about the structure of the agricultural systems which we are trying to transform now in the late twentieth century.[13]

Foster's framework will provide useful insights at the micro level. But it requires parallel research on macro problems that derive from particular socioeconomic and political situations.

At a very rudimentary level, we can identify five major types of agriculture which have existed in various parts of the world and which reflect different socioeconomic and political situations: (1) the 'feudal' system which existed in Europe before the Industrial Revolution and which still exists in certain areas of the world; (2) the 'commercial family-farm' system which characterized the settler-homestead agricultural economies of North America, Australia, New Zealand and Europe after the Industrial Revolution and which is still the dominant system in these countries; (3) the 'plantation' system which, with colonization, came to dominate the economies of the Caribbean, much of Central and South America, southern US and Southeast Asia; (4) the 'peasant' system of which there are two sub-types: one relating to subsistence production and the other to market-oriented production, as in parts of Africa (exports) and Japan (for the domestic market); and (5) the 'state-controlled' systems of contemporary China and Eastern Europe.

Historical evidence indicates that the rate of agricultural progress and overall economic growth has, on the whole, been considerably higher in Western Europe, North America, Australia, New Zealand and Japan than in other regions of the world.[14] And it is perhaps of some significance that the agricultural sectors of these countries are, with one exception, dominated by the commercial family-farm system. The exception is Japan which was placed in the category of peasant production for the domestic market. These two categories are in fact quite similar to each other – the only major structural difference being in respect of the size of units of production.

The commercial family-farm system has a number of features which are conducive to sustained development.[15] First, it involves a more equitable distribution of land and of income than any of the other systems. As a result, the effective demand for the output of other domestic industries is relatively great and this provides inducement for the development of non-agricultural activities. In addition, savings and investment are widely dispersed throughout the economy. Second, the heavy reliance on family labour limits the supply of available labour and thereby induces technological change of a kind in which modern inputs are continuously substituted for labour. Third, the infrastructure (including economic institutions) tends to be well developed spatially and therefore encourages widespread development of other activities. Fourth, the social and political environment is geared to the well-being of the whole population.

None of the other systems listed above has this combination of characteristics. In general, the relatively retarded nature of those systems can be partly related to (a) the 'openness' of the system (plantation and export-based peasant) which weakens intersectoral links within those economies and/or (b) gross inequalities in the distribution of wealth and income (feudal and plantation) which keeps effective demand at a low level and restricts savings and domestic investment. These are only superficial and partial explanations. There are many other economic factors which need to be considered. In addition the social, cultural, political and other non-economic elements that influence human behaviour must be integrated into the analysis of development performance. The intention here is simply to provide a brief insight in order to justify the analytical approach being suggested. So far most of the research effort on the development process has been directed to the commercial family farm system and the peasant system. But even in these cases our understanding of the processes at work is limited because of the failure to forge interdisciplinary studies of the problems. On account of this heritage, it is now impossible to analyse in any depth how institutional factors influence the pattern of development of different types of agriculture.

The Development Problem in Plantation Economies

In any typology of world agriculture, the plantation system of resource organization would have a distinct place. Its combination of metropolitan export orientation, foreign ownership and the particular technological nature of the production function create conditions which *determine* a particular pattern of development.[16] Furthermore, the social stratification, class differences and distribution of political power which characterize plantation societies influence the development process in particular ways.[17]

Some important characteristics of plantation agricultural economies are as follows:

1 production is based on large-scale units utilizing a sizeable resident labour force performing routine tasks for close to subsistence wages;

2 production is oriented to metropolitan export markets in which protective shelter is provided;

3 foreign capital, entrepreneurship and management govern economic activity;

4 export production consists of a narrow range of primary commodities; and

5 a small planter class (and/or their metropolitan connections) have great political power and high social status involving a certain social antipathy towards the bulk of the population.

A number of economic consequences flow directly from these characteristics. First, resource availability is not simply determined by the factor endowments of the particular country because the system itself is defined as being dependent on factors of production which, with the exception of land, are all drawn from abroad. Second, resource use is determined by the economic interests of the foreign owners. Where these are multi-national corporations with complementary investments in processing and marketing the plantation output, resources are directed to the specific needs of the corporation for raw material inputs.[18] And this creates a build-in rigidity in the pattern of resource adjustment. Third, the level of aggregate effective demand will always tend to be low since the bulk of the population have low incomes which are not allowed to rise significantly. Fourth, the plantation system is likely to generate chronic underemployment over time because of fluctuations in export prices and the fixed nature of the labour supply. Fifth, foreign ownership implies that much of the saving and investment potential is depleted by the outflow of factor payments in the form of interest and dividends; while retained foreign earnings "tend to be employed for further expansion of the export industry, since foreign investors prefer investments which are directly linked with the foreign exchange earning ability of the economy".[19] Sixth, the external orientation of economic activity dampens internal intersectoral relationships; and investment does not provide any significant multiplier effects. Seventh, the termination of production at the primary stage prevents the development of significant forward and backward linkages and this results in weak spread effects from agricultural development.

Over time, the prospects for development both within and outside of agriculture are limited for a number of reasons. To begin with, the small size of the market – a consequence of the low level of effective demand – limits the development of large-scale industries. Market demand for non-export agricultural production is therefore low; the small high-income landowning class satisfy their requirements with imports. On the supply side also, there are several factors which impede agricultural progress. Technological change is slow because additional resource inputs are continuously secured from abroad. When land (the only resource input supplied by the economy) becomes scarce in a particular country, the multi-national corporation solves the scarcity problem by expanding production in some new country. Periods of adverse export prices may induce technological change only if this places an excessive burden on profits.

Diversification of farm output is restricted partly because of the specific raw material needs of the plantation corporation and partly because the structure of output prices favours the sheltered export crop. In addition, very little technical knowledge concerning production of other crops is acquired because agricultural research is export biased. Marketing and credit are geared mainly to export crops and where land is scarce resident farmers have relatively little access to fertile land and other resources. Because of low incomes, they do not have the wherewithal to acquire additional resources; and the ruling class use their political power to maintain the status quo.

Scraps of evidence lend some support to the foregoing propositions. Furtado's celebrated study of the economic growth of Brazil provides much insight into the processes which have accounted for stagnation in the plantation economy of the Northeast.[20] The relatively poor performance of the US South can no doubt be also explained in similar terms.[21] And the economic histories of the Caribbean, Central and parts of South America seem to follow closely the pattern described by Furtado. For Southeast Asia, Myrdal has recently provided us with partial explanations for what he describes as the "weak spread effects from the development spurts in (plantation) agriculture".[22] But so far we have only fleeting glimpses of the problem and there is as yet no systematic formulation of ideas which could provide even a sketch of an appropriate theory.

The present collection of papers is intended to help fill the existing gap. The collection is largely Caribbean in orientation, historical in scope, empirical in method, and to some extent inter-disciplinary in approach. Such a combination is warranted for the purpose at hand. The general picture that emerges substantiates the view that there are numerous elements in the social and institutional structure of plantation-type economies which impede general economic development. The 'case study' of development performance in Barbados suggests that conventional policies tend to induce little or no change in economies of this type.

The concluding hypothesis, then, is that underdevelopment in the Caribbean emanates directly from the particular social and institutional character of the plantation system of resource organization. And the problem of development is one that must involve changes in that structure.

Notes

* "Toward an appropriate theoretical framework for agricultural development planning and policy". *Social and Economic Studies*, Special Number 17:3 (1968a).

1   Two recent books which more or less provide a synthesis of these contributions to date are John Mellor, *The Economics of Agricultural Development* (Ithaca, NY: Cornell University Press, 1966); and Herman Southworth and Bruce Johnston (eds.), *Agricultural Development and Economic Growth* (Ithaca, NY: Cornell University Press, 1967).

2   John W. Mellor, "Toward a theory of agricultural development" (chapter 2 of Southworth and Johnston), pp. 22-23.

3   T.W. Schultz, *Transforming Traditional Agriculture* (New Haven, CN: Yale University Press, 1964). The term 'transforming traditional agriculture' now recurs consistently in all recent contributions dealing with agricultural development per se. So much so that one gets the uneasy feeling that North American economists regard all underdeveloped agriculture as 'traditional' (in the sense described by Schultz).

4   Cuba is excluded from consideration in this discussion because the organization of agriculture there is no longer the same as in the rest of the region, as was the case before 1959. Part of the discussion here draws from an earlier paper by the author. See G. L. Beckford, "Toward rationalization of West Indian agriculture", Paper presented at the Regional Conference on Devaluation (ISER, University of the West Indies, February 2-4, 1968), mimeo.

5   See, for example, the chapters by Johnston and Southworth and Mellor in Southworth and Johnston (eds.), and Mellor.

6   Usually the main trading partner of these countries is a metropolitan country which provides protective shelter in the form of special preferential arrangements for plantation output.

7   Indeed, discussions in the literature suggest that in the closed models changes in the domestic terms of trade will be toward agriculture whereas the international terms of trade tend to move *against plantation output*.

8   See Dale Adams, "Resource allocation in traditional agriculture: comment" and "Reply" by Schultz in *Journal of Farm Economics* (November 1967), as well as earlier exchanges; E. Feder, "The latifundia puzzle of Professor Schultz: comment" and "Reply" by Schultz in *Journal of Farm Economics* (May 1967); and G.L. Beckford, "Transforming traditional agriculture: comment" and "Reply" by Schultz in *Journal of Farm Economics* (November 1966).

9   This is implicit in the findings of D. T. Edwards in his *Report on an Economic Study of Small Farming in Jamaica* (ISER, University of the West Indies, 1961).

10   In addition to the possible expansion of output, it should be noted that the national income contribution per acre is likely to be higher in peasant production because there is no foreign ownership there.

11   Dale Adams, "Resource allocation", p. 932.

12   Our predecessors, the 'political economists' of the more distant past saw the need for this approach and made considerable progress for particular types of agriculture. See, for example, the recently translated works of the Russian agricultural economist, Chayanov, *The Theory of Peasant Economy* (edited by Thorner, Kerbly and Smith: Irwin Inc for the American Economic Association, 1966).

13   Phillips Foster, "Analyzing systems of agricultural resource organization", *Journal of Farm Economics* (May 1966), p. 272.

14 It is perhaps too early to judge the relative performance of those economies which are dominated by export-based peasant systems and state-controlled systems. Both systems are of relatively recent vintage.

15 For further discussion of some of these considerations, see Robert Baldwin, "Patterns of development in newly settled regions", *The Manchester School of Economic and Social Studies*, May 1956.

16 Baldwin, "Patterns of development", has demonstrated that the nature of the production function alone is decisive.

17 For elaboration on this point see, for example, R.T. Smith, "Social stratification, cultural pluralism and integration in West Indian societies" in S. Lewis and T.G. Matthews (eds.), *Caribbean Integration* (Puerto Rico: Rio Piedras, 1967).

18 Tate and Lyle sugar operations in the West Indies and United Fruit Company banana operations in Central America are outstanding examples of this situation.

19 Baldwin, "Patterns of development".

20 His analysis of the mechanism of the slave plantation economy during the sixteenth and seventeenth centuries is particularly illuminating. The analysis concludes as follows: "The sugar economy . . . managed to resist the most protracted of depressions for more than three centuries, achieving some degree of recuperation whenever conditions in the external market permitted, without being compelled to undergo any significant structural changes." See Celso Furtado, *The Economic Growth of Brazil* (Berkeley and Los Angeles: University of California Press, 1963), pp. 43-58.

21 See Douglas North, *The Economic Growth of the US: 1790-1860* (Englewood Cliffs, NJ: Prentice Hall, 1961).

22 Gunmar Murdal, *Asian Drama: An Inquiry into the Poverty of Nations* (New York: Pantheon, 1968), pp. 447-52. This monumental three-volume work provides a great deal of insight into the more general problem of the relevance of existing social science theory for underdeveloped countries.

17

The Economics of Agricultural Resource Use and Development*

Plantation agriculture has been generally ignored in the rapidly expanding literature on underdeveloped agriculture.[1] To a large extent this reflects a view that plantation agriculture is 'efficient' and 'modern'; that it is particularly suited to certain tropical crops; that the plantation system has served to bring previously isolated areas into the modern world economy; and that large-scale plantation units make possible "economies of operation by the use of labour-saving machinery".[2]

More recently, a few development economists have drawn attention to the fact that differences in factor combinations, production technology, etc. among export industries lead to differences in patterns of growth among export economies. And in this connection, the plantation system of resource organization has received some attention.[3]

So far the most important contributions to the study of plantations have come from the sociologists and social anthropologists. The study of Puerto Rico by Steward et al. is an outstanding example of this pioneering work and a number of subsequent symposia on the Caribbean have focused on "plantation society as a sociohistorical determinant of contemporary sub-cultures".[4] These studies have provided very useful insights for understanding the internal dynamics of plantation societies. But they emphasize the need for similar work on the economic relations, organization and institutions that characterize the plantation system.[5]

This paper is an initial attempt to fill the existing gap. But the gap is so wide that it would be impossible to bridge it fully in an article. Consequently, attention is directed to one type of plantation – the modern multi-national corporate enterprise. This is perhaps the most important type in present day underdeveloped countries and the economics of this type of farm-firm has hardly been explored. As the title states, the concern is with economic aspects, though it is obvious that sociological and political variables would need to be considered in a fuller treatment.

The discussion begins with an examination of the characteristics of plantation agriculture: how it developed, where it exists, and what factors distinguish it from other types of agriculture. Detailed consideration of the internal organization of modern plantation enterprises provides the background for subsequent analysis of the economics of production and resource use. This represents a re-examination of the view that plantation agriculture is 'efficient'. The concern in this paper is not with efficiency of the firm but with efficiency of resource use in the agricultural sectors of countries in which these enterprises operate.

The final part of the exercise is to assess the development potential of plantation agriculture. It is not sufficient merely to state that the plantation system brought backward and isolated areas into the modern world economy. The important question is whether the system makes it possible for these economies to achieve structural transformation and a self-sustaining pattern of growth and development.

Characteristics of Plantation Agriculture

The world 'plantation' has fallen into such common use that it denotes different things to different people. Generally speaking, it is considered to refer to a large farming unit. However, as the discussion below indicates, this is an inadequate description.

Plantation Production

According to Jones:

a plantation is an economic unit producing agricultural commodities (field crops or horticultural products, but not livestock) for sale and employing a relatively large number of unskilled labourers whose activities are closely supervised. Plantations usually employ a year-round labour crew of some size, and they usually specialize in the production of only one or two marketable products. They differ from other kinds of farms in the way in which the factors of production, primarily management and labour, are combined.[6]

Production on plantations is undertaken not just 'for sale', as indicated above, but specifically for sale in overseas markets (export sale).[7] The special factor combination that distinguishes plantation production from other kinds of farms is the bringing together of as many unskilled farm labourers as possible with each of the few highly skilled supervisor-managers who direct production. As Jones puts it, "the plantation substitutes supervision – supervisory and administrative skills – for skilled, adaptive labour, combining the supervision with labour whose principal skill is to follow orders".[8]

Two other aspects of plantation production deserve mention here although they are considered in more detail below. They are (1) foreign ownership, usually by a corporate enterprise; and (2) a "relatively high degree of vertical integration, even of self-sufficiency" – *ie* the plantation enterprise supplies inputs for its agricultural operations and processing and marketing facilities for its agricultural output.

Plantations are mainly involved in the production of certain tropical crops – mainly tree crops and other perennials. Sugar, bananas, tea, rubber and coffee are the main commodities involved. It has frequently been suggested that the "complementarity between agricultural processing plants and farm producing units has been one consideration in the establishment of plantations. Many of the major tropical exports must undergo preliminary processing shortly after harvesting . . ."[9]

However, the association of plantation production with certain tropical crops cannot be explained in such narrow technical terms. It must be seen in the larger context of the way in which these commodities were introduced into the international economy.

The Plantation System

Plantation agriculture is the outgrowth of the political colonization of tropical areas by the metropolitan countries of Europe. Temperate areas which had been colonized by Europe – e.g. the US, Canada, Australia, New Zealand, Argentina, Chile, etc – involved the movement of people. Those areas developed as 'colonies of settlement' and the pattern of agriculture that emerged was significantly different from that in the tropical colonies where mainly capital and enterprise were involved in the movement from the metropole to produce 'colonies of exploitation'.

As Greaves has pointed out, "one of the outstanding characteristics of the plantation is that it has brought together enterprise, capital and labour from different parts of the world in an area which offered opportunity for new and increased production".[10] Enterprise and capital came from the metropole which was usually, though not always, the centre of direct political control.

Labour was brought mainly from other tropical areas. With the possible exception of Java, plantations were originally established in sparsely populated areas. And because of the shortage of labour in these areas, the plantation system depended on large-scale (involuntary and voluntary) movement of labour from other tropical areas. Slavery and then indenture provided labour supplies for the establishment and development of plantations in the New World. Chinese, Japanese and Filipino labourers were brought to develop Hawaii's sugar plantations; the rubber plantations of Malaya and Sumatra drew most of their workers from China, Java and India; and so on. In the New World, even after slavery and indenture, 'new' plantation economies drew labour supplies from 'mature' plantation economies.[11] "Thus the plantation came to be associated not only with a resident labour force, but more often than not with one of alien origin".[12]

Perhaps the most important consideration for present purposes is the international dimension of the plantation system. As Greaves puts it:

Historically and economically the plantation system is fundamentally international in character. Wherever it is found it derives from external stimulus and enterprise; it has always depended on external markets; and it is still largely involved in external finance. Because of this character the plantation has been associated with most political and international developments of modern times: mercantilism and free trade; slavery and independence; capitalism and imperialism . . .[13]

Further, we are warned that

although we are apt to speak of a 'plantation economy' as though it were in itself a complete and separate economy, *plantations are in practice only a special part of a much wider economic system with a financial and industrial centre usually in a region remote from the plantations.* The extent to which this part of the system is dependent upon the center is determined by how far the latter controls it; control can take two forms, property ownership, and political connections which affect such matters as prices, tariffs and loan funds.[14]

Thus, for example, nineteenth century British economists rightly described the West Indies as "a place where England finds it convenient to carry on the production of sugar, coffee and a few other tropical commodities", and the trade between them was similar to the town and country trade at home."[15]

These characteristics apply as much today as in earlier historical periods. Even where *direct* metropolitan political control is absent, property ownership and indirect political connections still control the pattern of resource allocation and production in countries where plantations are located today. Indeed, even in the absence of property ownership, control from the centre (metropolis) may result from economic connections; for example financial control through the banking system or the specificity of the raw material export to metropolitan refining capacity.[16] These characteristics of metropolitan control are evident in the case of the politically independent banana republics of Central America which are in fact extensions of the US economic system as well as in the constitutionally independent sugar dominions of the West Indies which still remain extensions of the British and American economic systems.

Plantation Economies

Taking note of the fact that plantations form only a part of a wider economic system, the term 'plantation economy' can be used cautiously to describe situations where the *dominant* pattern of agricultural resource organization is the plantation system. It is not necessary that the agricultural sector of countries involved should consist only of plantation units. No such countries in fact exist. Dominant is used in the sense that the bulk of the country's agricultural resources are owned by plantations, and/or plantation production provides the main dynamic for development. The latter condition requires some elaboration. It is used here in the broadest sense to encompass sociological, political and economic dynamics. Thus, for example, there are situations – as in the West Indies – where peasant producers are more numerous than plantation enterprises but where, because the peasantry is a creation of the plantations their behaviour reflects the plantation influence. In the political sphere, political decision-makers are imbued with a psychological dependence on an established plantation sector and agricultural development policy tends to reflect this attitude.[17]

On the basis of this definition, plantation economies are to be found mainly in tropical America and tropical Asia. Although plantations exist in tropical Africa (e.g. oil palm plantations of the Congo), they do not dominate the scene as in the other regions mentioned.

In Asia, countries like Ceylon, Malaya, Indonesia and the Philippines would classify as plantation economies. So would Mauritius and Reunion in the Indian Ocean; and Hawaii and Fiji in the Pacific. The crops involved in these cases are tea, rubber, sugar and to some extent coconuts.

In America, the *locus* of the plantation system is the Caribbean. Indeed, this region is generally regarded as the classic plantation area. So much so that social anthropologists have described the region as a culture sphere, labelled 'Plantation-America'. According to Wagley:

Briefly, this culture sphere extends spatially from about midway up the coast of Brazil into the Guianas, along the Caribbean coast, throughout the Caribbean itself, and into the United States. It is characteristically coastal; not until the nineteenth century did the way of life of the plantation culture sphere penetrate far into the mainland interior, and then only in Brazil and the United States. This area has an environment which is characteristically tropical (except the southern United States) and lowland.[18]

Wagley goes on to describe some of the basic common features in this culture sphere. Among these are:

monocrop cultivation under the plantation system, rigid class lines, multi-racial societies, weak community cohesion, small peasant proprietors involved in subsistence and cash-crop production, and a matrifocal type family form. In addition there are a series of cultural characteristics common to Plantation-America which derive often from similarities in environment, often from the common historical background, and often from the presence of such a large population of African origin.[19]

Common cultural characteristics are said to be reflected in the similarities of peasant crops, production techniques and marketing arrangements: cuisine, music and folklore with common African influences; and similar traditions or values affecting social life.

The boundaries of Wagley's Plantation-America extend beyond what is normally regarded as the Caribbean. It includes subregions of large continental economies – the northeast of Brazil and the US South. It is of some interest to note at this stage that each of these subregions is the most backward of the national economies of which they are an integral part. Thus it may be useful for us to speak of plantation economies not only in terms of nation states but also in looking at subregions of individual nation states. In this connection we may wish to extend further the spatial boundaries indicated by Wagley to include the lowlands of Central America where plantation banana production is the main type of economic activity.

The main plantation crop of the Caribbean is sugar cane. But in the wider area described above as Plantation-America bananas must be added for the Central American lowlands and cotton for the US South. For present purposes, it may be necessary to exclude some of the Caribbean islands from the class of plantation economies. In Cuba, the plantation system that existed prior to 1959 has since been transformed into a state-controlled system of agricultural resource organization. Even though sugar is still the main crop and even if many of the cultural traits of plantation societies still remain, the absence of foreign ownership and changes in the social and class structure are enough to set Cuba apart. Also several of the smaller islands may have no significant agriculture or may not have plantations in the sense that we have here defined.[20]

Analysis of the development experience in particular plantation regions is outside the scope of the present paper.[21] However, in so far as the discussion requires empirical foundation at various points, the Caribbean is the basic reference area.

Plantation Enterprises

The analysis of resource use and production and the development problem in plantation economies requires prior examination of the characteristics of the major decision-making units – the plantation enterprises. This has largely been ignored in previous contributions; and the result has been a superficial view of the role of plantation agriculture in promoting agricultural development and change in such societies.

Plantation agriculture in the modern world economy is dominated by large scale multi-national corporate enterprises. The United Fruit Company, the Standard Fruit and Shipping Co and Unilever are the best known. Several others, less well known, are of particular importance in certain areas. For example, sugar production in the West Indies[22] is dominated by two such companies – Tate and Lyle Ltd, a British sugar-refining firm with wholly-owned raw sugar-producing subsidiaries in the region; and Booker Brothers, McConnell and Co Ltd of London (Bookers).

In addition to the metropolitan basis of ownership, three important characteristics of these enterprises which directly affect resource use in countries where they operate plantations are: (1) a high degree of vertical integration; (2) a lateral spread in their agricultural operations among a number of countries; and (3) each firm accounts for a significant share (often the bulk) of the export output of particular commodities from individual countries.

Three Examples from Plantation-America

The features mentioned above are brought out by the following examination of the structure and organization of British-owned Bookers, and Tate and Lyle[23] – the main sugar plantation enterprises in the West Indies – both operating out of London; and the American-owned United Fruit Company (UFCo) – the main banana plantation enterprise in Central America – operating out of Boston.

Figure 17.1 is a reproduction of a diagram showing the organizational structure of Bookers. The chart relates only to the firm's operations in Guyana (where most of its agricultural activities are concentrated)[24] and related activities.

The company is also engaged in sugar cane production and raw sugar manufacture along with rum distillation in Jamaica (two establishments) and

Figure17.1 Booker Brothers, McConnell and Company Ltd. (London) – firm structure

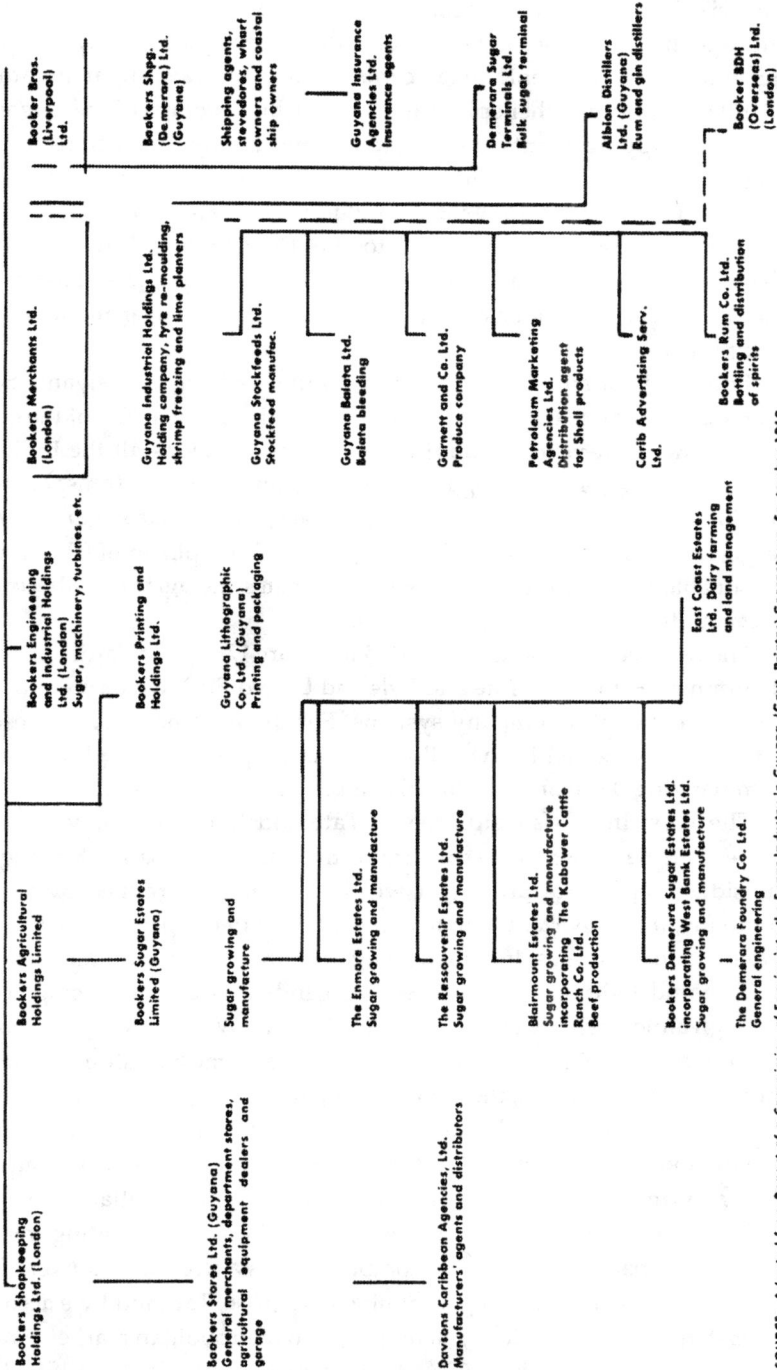

Bookers Shopkeeping Holdings Ltd. (London)

Bookers Stores Ltd. (Guyana)
General merchants, department stores, agricultural equipment dealers and garage

Davsons Caribbean Agencies, Ltd.
Manufacturers agents and distributors

Bookers Agricultural Holdings Limited

Bookers Sugar Estates Limited (Guyana)

Sugar growing and manufacture

The Enmore Estates Ltd.
Sugar growing and manufacture

The Ressouvenir Estates Ltd.
Sugar growing and manufacture

Blairmount Estates Ltd.
Sugar growing and manufacture incorporating The Kabawer Cattle Ranch Co. Ltd.
Beef production

Bookers Demerara Sugar Estates Ltd.
incorporating West Bank Estates Ltd.
Sugar growing and manufacture

The Demerara Foundry Co. Ltd.
General engineering

Bookers Engineering and Industrial Holdings Ltd. (London)
Sugar, machinery, turbines, etc.

Bookers Printing and Holdings Ltd.

Guyana Lithographic Co. Ltd. (Guyana)
Printing and packaging

East Coast Estates Ltd.
Dairy farming and land management

Bookers Merchants Ltd. (London)

Guyana Industrial Holdings Ltd.
Holding company, tyre re-moulding, shrimp freezing and lime planters

Guyana Stockfeeds Ltd.
Stockfeed manufac.

Guyana Balata Ltd.
Balata bleeding

Garnett and Co. Ltd.
Produce company

Petroleum Marketing Agencies Ltd.
Distribution agent for Shell products

Carib Advertising Serv. Ltd.

Bookers Rum Co. Ltd.
Bottling and distribution of spirits

Booker Bros. (Liverpool) Ltd.

Bookers Shpg. (Demerara) Ltd. (Guyana)

Shipping agents, stevedores, wharf owners and coastal ship owners

Guyana Insurance Agencies Ltd.
Insurance agents

Demerara Sugar Terminals Ltd.
Bulk sugar terminal

Albion Distillers Ltd. (Guyana)
Rum and gin distillers

Booker BDH (Overseas) Ltd. (London)

SOURCE: Adapted from Report of a Commission of Enquiry into the Sugar Industry in Guyana (Govt. Printer) Georgetown, September 1968.

Nigeria. The vertically integrated structure of this company can be traced through the following stages: manufacture of sugar machinery, merchants for agricultural equipment, sugar cane production, raw sugar manufacture, distillation of rum, other spirits and alcohol, bulk storage of raw sugar, wharf owners, shipping agents and insurance, and finally ocean transport of raw sugar. At the end of 1968 the fixed assets of the company were distributed as follows: land and buildings £17.7 million, plant and machinery, ships and equipment £10.6 million making a total of £28.3 million. It would have been desirable to look at the asset structure according to the share of assets in agriculture as distinct from associated activities such as sugar manufacture and shipping but the data are not available in such form.

Bookers is of strategic importance to the economy of Guyana. So far as sugar is concerned, the company has produced well over 80% of the country's output in recent years. In addition the company owns all the bulk storage capacity and sugar shipping facilities and provides ocean transport for most of Guyana's sugar exports. When it is recognized that sugar is Guyana's largest agricultural export and the biggest single employer of labour, it seems reasonable to conclude that Bookers dominates the agricultural economy of that country.

The detailed information provided in Figure 17.1 could hardly be shown in diagrammatic form for Tate and Lyle and United Fruit which are much larger and more complex company systems. For these, some relevant descriptive information is given in the following paragraphs and simplified diagrams summarizing these organizational complexes are provided in Figure 17.2.

The West Indian subsidiaries of Tate and Lyle must be viewed in the context of the wider firm structure of the parent company. Although these subsidiaries produce raw sugar which is eventually refined by the parent company, it is important to note here that the latter depends only to a limited extent on its own West Indian raw sugar for inputs at the refining stage.

Tate and Lyle operate in three West Indian sugar producing countries through almost wholly owned subsidiaries – the West Indies Sugar Company in Jamaica, Caroni Ltd in Trinidad, and Belize Sugar Industries Ltd in British Honduras.[25] In addition, the company engages in sugar refining mainly in the UK, Canada, Zambia and Rhodesia, sugar storage and distribution, molasses production and trading in the West Indies, Africa, Europe, Asia and North America, manufacture of syrup and liquid sugar, distillation of alcohol, manufacture of machinery and world-wide shipping (including insurance). For the last-named activity, the company owns a fleet of 11 tankers for bulk shipment of sugar.[26] As a sugar refining enterprise, Tate and Lyle accounts for a substantial share of refining activity in two metropolitan markets. In the UK the company handles about 65% of total supply (for example, in 1967 Tate and

Figure 17.2 *Simplified illustrations of the organizational complexes of two New World plantation enterprises*

A.   TATE & LYLE — Sugar Production in the West Indies and Related Activities

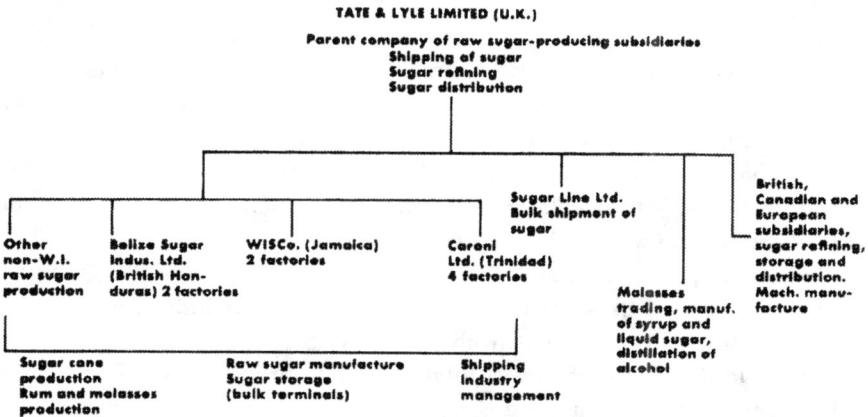

TATE & LYLE LIMITED (U.K.)

Parent company of raw sugar-producing subsidiaries
Shipping of sugar
Sugar refining
Sugar distribution

| Other non-W.I. raw sugar production | Belize Sugar Indus. Ltd. (British Honduras) 2 factories | WISCo. (Jamaica) 2 factories | Caroni Ltd. (Trinidad) 4 factories | Sugar Line Ltd. Bulk shipment of sugar | Molasses trading, manuf. of syrup and liquid sugar, distillation of alcohol | British, Canadian and European subsidiaries, sugar refining, storage and distribution. Mach. manufacture |

| Sugar cane production Rum and molasses production | Raw sugar manufacture Sugar storage (bulk terminals) | Shipping Industry management |

B.   U.F.CO. — Banana Production in Central America and Related Activities

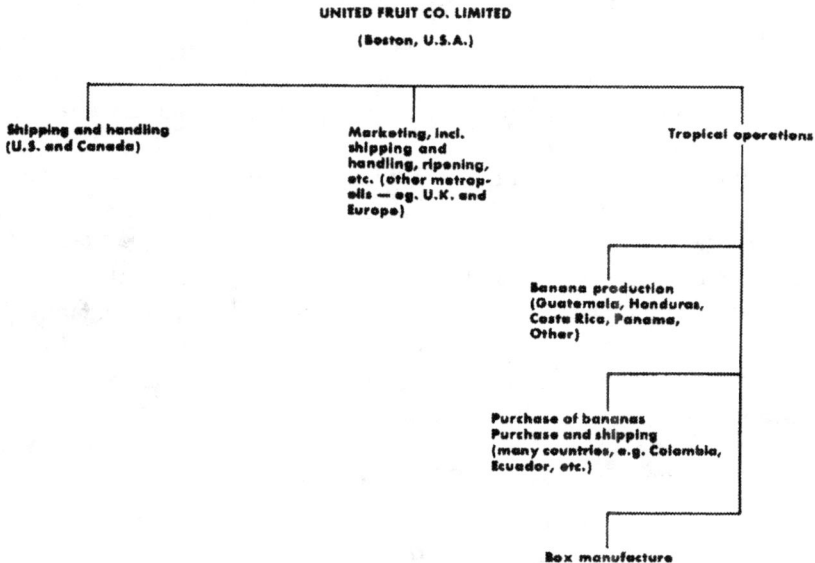

UNITED FRUIT CO. LIMITED

(Boston, U.S.A.)

| Shipping and handling (U.S. and Canada) | Marketing, incl. shipping and handling, ripening, etc. (other metropolis — eg. U.K. and Europe) | Tropical operations |

Banana production (Guatemala, Honduras, Costa Rica, Panama, Other)

Purchase of bananas Purchase and shipping (many countries, e.g. Colombia, Ecuador, etc.)

Box manufacture

Lyle refined 2,052,000 long tons of the total of 3,162,000 tons of raw sugar refined in the UK). Tate and Lyle's Canadian subsidiary, Canada and Dominion Sugar Company Ltd, refines about 30% of all sugar refined in Canada in a normal year.

In Jamaica,[27] the resident arm of this multi-national enterprise – WISCo – primarily engages in sugar-cane growing, raw sugar production, sugar refining (for the domestic market), rum and alcohol distillation and molasses trading. Through its subsidiaries, WISCo Wharves, Sugar Shipping Ltd, and Computer Service and Printery Ltd the company also engages in sugar storage, stevedoring and computer and printing services. To Tate and Lyle, the central importance of WISCo is its sugar-producing activities. According to recent company reports, Tate and Lyle is beneficially involved with 90.63% of the issued share capital of WISCo At the end of 1968, the fixed assets of WISCo stood at just over £7 million (this figure includes the assets of the subsidiary companies of WISCo listed above).

Both the issued share capital and the value of fixed assets of WISCo represent about 35% of those of the entire Jamaican sugar industry. And the combined output of raw sugar from the two WISCo factories has been, over the years, in the region of 35% of total sugar output in Jamaica. Through its subsidiary wharf and shipping companies, WISCo undertakes storage and loading at two ports and thus handles about 56% of total sugar exports from Jamaica. Furthermore, all raw sugar from Jamaica bound for the UK and Canada (normally over 70% of total sugar exports) is shipped in vessels owned by Sugar Line Ltd, the Tate and Lyle shipping subsidiary. And through a London Director, WISCo markets the entire export sales of sugar from Jamaica. WISCo is also the leading force in the Jamaica Sugar Manufacturers' Association, a powerful lobbying group that promotes the interests of sugar at all levels.[28]

In Trinidad,[29] the Tate and Lyle subsidiary – Caroni Ltd – owns and operates four of the country's six sugar factories. This represents 80% of total factory capacity. In sugar cane production, Caroni Ltd accounted for 60% of the total produced in 1967. In addition, Caroni Ltd accounts for all of the bulk storage and shipping facilities for sugar in Trinidad. The following tabulation shows the structure of fixed assets of Caroni Ltd in 1967. The high percentage of fixed capital represented by plant and machinery (mainly factory capacity) is worthy of note, as subsequent discussion will show.

Table 17.1 *Structure of fixed assets of Caroni Ltd, 1967*

	£000	%
Land	1,907	24.8
Buildings	1,758	22.8
Plant and machinery	3,727	48.6
Other	291	3.8
Total	**7,683**	**100.0**

Finally, Tate and Lyle has a complete monopoly of raw sugar production in British Honduras. There its resident subsidiary, Belize Sugar Industries Ltd, owns and operates the two sugar factories in that country as well as all the available storage and shipping facilities. The company's sugar cane production on its own estates represents some 80% of total sugar cane production in that country. The importance of sugar to the economy of British Honduras is reflected by the fact that sugar represents 54% of agricultural export sales and about 30% of total exports.

The UFCo is a giant enterprise, both in respect of banana production in Central America as well as banana imports into the US. For example, in 1966 UFCo accounted for 55% of total US banana imports. In the same year, the company controlled 100% of export banana acreage in Guatemala, 70% of that in both Costa Rica and Panama and 56% of that in Honduras.[30] According to the company's annual report, about 53% of all the fruit sold by it was purchased in recent years – *ie* only 47% of the bananas handled by the company was derived from its own plantations. As part of its tropical American operations, the company operates its own corrugating and box-making plants, producing box 'flats' only for bananas, in Panama, Costa Rica and Honduras.

In addition to these operations, the company is involved in the purchasing and shipping of bananas from Ecuador and Colombia in South America. And, through various subsidiaries, it is involved in the marketing (and some production) of bananas from other tropical producing areas as well as shipping importation, ripening and distribution in other metropolitan areas – chiefly the UK and Western Europe.

Again, available data on the asset structure of this company are not presented in the form that is required for present purposes. However, some rough idea can be obtained from the following tabulation which shows investment in fixed assets of 1966.[31]

Table 17.2 *United Fruit Co investment in fixed assets, 1966*

	($000 US)
Lands	10,374
Houses and buildings	59,536
Cultivations	62,839
Equipment	92,216
Railways, tramways and rolling stock	38,440
Wharves, boats, etc	6,755
Sugar mills and refineries	·17,804
Steamships	117,071
Total	**405,035**

It is not possible to assess from this the actual share of agricultural operations in the company's total fixed capital stock. 'Lands' and 'cultivations' can be attributed to this but a share of the amounts listed under 'houses and buildings', 'equipment' (and possibly 'railways etc') needs to be allocated to agriculture as well. At a guess, fixed capital on the agricultural side is probably 50% or less of total fixed capital.

Some Significant Characteristics

In terms of the scope of their activities, the three firms considered above are, to a large extent, representative of foreign-owned plantation enterprises operating in tropical America. Indeed, together they account for a significant share of plantation output in this region. A factor which is worthy of note is that each firm is large compared with the agricultural sectors of individual countries in which they operate. For example, the total value of agricultural output in Guyana was estimated to have been in the region of £17 million in 1966 while the 'turnover' (mainly sales) for the entire Bookers organization in that year was of the order of £78 million. Even the sales from Bookers 'tropical agriculture operations' and 'rum and other spirits' alone (£18.7 million) exceeded the total value of agricultural output in Guyana.[32] Another significant feature is that each of the three firms accounts for the major share (in several cases, 100%) of the total output of the particular crop in individual countries where they operate. This means that decisions relating to the adjustment of output for particular commodities in individual countries are made by a central authority located within the structure of a single firm.

A high degree of vertical integration is characteristic of these firms. This vertical integration extends far beyond the stage of the 'factory-farm combines' repeatedly discussed in the established literature on plantation agriculture. In addition to processing of the agricultural raw material, these enterprises are substantially engaged in supplying their own agricultural inputs and, more importantly, in the shipping and marketing of the products at higher stages of production.

Vertical integration has indeed been carried to a stage where the actual plantation operations of the enterprises may no longer represent the bulk of firm investments. What is more, operations at higher stages of production are only partly based on the firm's own supplies from lower stages of the production process. Consequently, the firm is in a position to hedge possible losses on its farming operations against consequent gains further up the scale.

Metropolitan ownership and control is another factor which has much significance. For one thing, it means that the locus of decision-making is outside of the countries in which plantation production activities are carried out. This is bound to affect the pattern of production, resource use and development in the countries with which we are here concerned. For example, it is generally recognized that "foreign investors prefer investments which are directly linked with the foreign exchange-earning ability of the economy" in which they invest.[33] Surpluses for re-investment therefore tend to flow back into established export activities in which these investors have developed an infrastructure of expertise and organization – thus creating rigidities in the overall adjustment process in the agricultural sectors of the countries involved.

The typical geographic spread of plantation operations of individual firms is also significant. The production adjustment process in this event must be considered, not in terms of individual countries but from the point of view of the firm. Decisions relating to expansion or contraction of output in a particular country are made within the context of the firm's overall supply drawn from several countries. The relevant unit for analysis is therefore the plantation enterprise and not the nation state in which only a part of the firm's operations is located.

Yet another feature worthy of note is that the capital investments of these enterprises are highly specific to the production and marketing (including processing) of a particular commodity. In addition to specific capital investment on the agricultural side, complementary investments at other levels tend to be specific to the plantation commodity; for example, bulk terminals, special bulk sugar vessels and refining equipment in the case of sugar; and specially designed banana boats in the case of United Fruit.[34] As we shall see below, this high degree of specificity influences the pattern of resource use and the adjustment process.

Agricultural Production and Resource Use in Plantation-Type Economies

The concern here is with production and resource use in the agricultural sectors of what we have described as plantation economies; in other words, with the way in which plantation operations influence resource use and overall production in the countries where these enterprises are engaged in agriculture. In this connection, efficiency considerations relate to the agricultural sectors of the plantation economies and not to the firm. The two are not the same. What is good for the firm is not necessarily good for the country where it produces. Indeed, the general thesis of this paper is that in plantation-type economies efficient resource allocation in individual production units tends to co-exist with inefficient resource allocation for the agricultural sector as a whole.

The efficiency conditions for the agricultural sector can be briefly set out in the conventional way to provide a general background. Resources are allocated most efficiently when the following conditions hold: (1) resources are allocated within each farm in a manner that equates the marginal value productivities of the resource services – *ie* a unit of labour or capital should not be used to grow sugar if it can produce a greater value product in livestock; (2) resources are distributed between farms and farming areas so that marginal value productivities are equal; (3) resources are distributed between farming and other producing areas to equalize value productivities; and (4) resources are allocated over time such that their discounted value products are equal.[35]

The rest of this section considers some of the aspects of the operations of plantation enterprises. Inferences regarding allocative efficiency in the context outlined above are made at various points in the discussion.

Production Objectives

The plantation production unit is a corporate enterprise which is chiefly concerned with making profit for its shareholders. Profit maximization is, therefore, one of the primary objectives of plantation enterprises. However because the plantation itself is part of a wider organizational complex, profit maximization may not be a guiding principle at the level of its agricultural operations. In so far as the firm draws heavily on raw material supplies other than its own at the higher level of production (and marketing), lower profits on the agricultural side may result in higher overall profits. Furthermore, profit maximization at the farm level is constrained by the firm's specific capital commitments.[36]

The way in which farming profits relate to total profit of the enterprise as a whole requires an examination of the structure of costs and profits. An example of this is provided by the following schematic representation of the Tate and Lyle sugar situation (Figure 17.3).[37]

Each block represents a different level of operation in the integrated enterprise. Costs (x) are indicated by shaded, and profits (y) by unshaded areas. Blocks (1), (2) and (4) are directly related. (1) shows costs and profits of the firm's subsidiaries on farming (growing of sugar cane) in the West Indies. The firm also produces raw sugar in the West Indies at stage (2) from its own supplies of cane plus that purchased from independent cane farmers. The imputed price of its own cane output is therefore equal to the price at which it buys from cane farmers $(x+y)_{(1)}$. This, plus a margin for factory costs, set the cost level at stage 2 – *ie* $(x)_{(2)}$. At stage 4, the firm refines its own, plus purchased supplies of raw sugar, at going prices.[38] So that its costs at this

Figure 17.3   *The Tate and Lyle sugar operation*

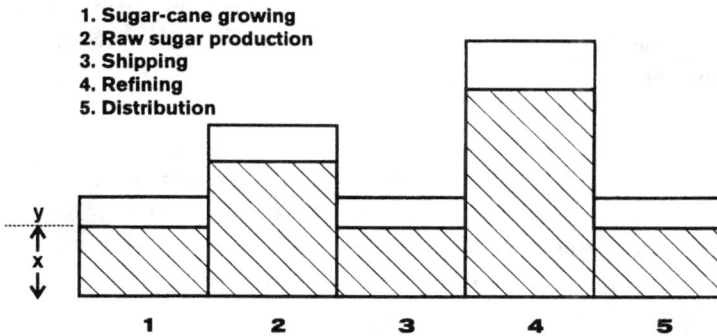

1. **Sugar-cane growing**
2. **Raw sugar production**
3. **Shipping**
4. **Refining**
5. **Distribution**

level are $(x+y)_{(2)}$, plus shipping, plus refining costs, leaving a refining profit of $y_{(4)}$.

Insofar as changes in output prices at various levels affect levels of profit, the firm is in a position to hedge losses at one stage against gains at higher stages of production so long as the final disposal (consumer) price does not change proportionately with changes in the prices of primary and intermediate outputs. For example, the lower the price of raw sugar purchased for refining (stage 4) the lower will be profits on the West Indian operations (stages 1 and 2) but the higher will be profit on refining since the value of $x_{(4)}$ has been reduced.

One characteristic of the plantation which has been noted by Jones is "the ability to exploit market imperfections or to manipulate them to its advantage".[39] This applies not only to the factor market but to the product market as well. The firm is therefore usually in a position to control final disposal prices, perhaps moreso than prices of primary and intermediate outputs.

The upshot of the foregoing discussion is that the maximization of total profit for the firm as a whole is not dependent on profit maximization for its agricultural activities. The importance of agriculture in this connection depends partly on the share of agriculture in the firm's total investments. The smaller this share, the less will be the need for using the profit maximization principle on its agricultural operations.

Since the agricultural operations of plantation enterprises are located in the tropical economies with which we are here concerned, this observation has implications for agricultural resource use in these economies. Changes in the structure of output prices (for the whole range of agricultural products which can be grown in these countries) which offer more profitable opportunities than the particular plantation crop do not induce a shift of resources from production of the latter because the profit horizon of the plantation enterprise (which controls these resources) extends beyond these purely agricultural opportunities. Even in the long run, *the adjustment process tends to be limited to output adjustments for the particular crop* rather than to a more flexible deployment of resources over the range of production possibilities in line with differential marginal value productivities.

Capital Specificity

It will be recalled from the preceding section that one of the characteristics of plantation enterprises is that the capital stock of these firms is highly specific to the production and processing (including marketing) of particular crops. This produces further inflexibility in the pattern of agricultural resource use. The more integrated is the firm structure the more important is this limitation. For this means that the firm also has investments outside of agriculture which are geared to the particular crop.

The degree of specificity tends to be least at the actual farming level. Equipment used in cultivation, field labour, land etc can be used for the production of any number of crops. But the capital required for the processing (in the farm-factory and elsewhere) and shipping is quite specific. For example, sugar mills cannot be adapted to processing vegetables and banana boats are specially designed to their task. In the vertically integrated structure of the firm it is these specific non-farm investments that help to create rigidities in resource use on the plantation. For capital specificity in related non-farm operations of the firm makes it less profitable to undertake crop switching or diversification at the farm level.[40]

Once ancillary investment commitments have been made, the firm is constrained to a short-run production possibilities curve with a limited scope for the switching of resources to alternative products.[41] This is illustrated below (Figure 17.4).

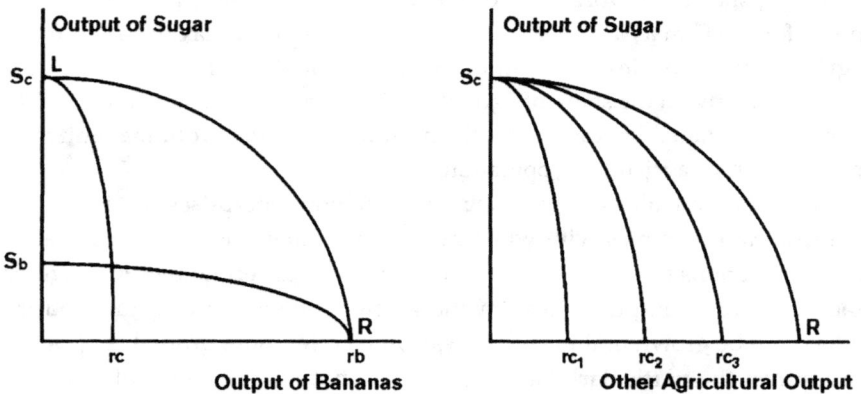

Figure 17.4 *Long-run production possibilities for sugar and bananas*

Diagram A shows the long-run production possibilities for combinations of two crops, sugar and bananas, with a given set of resources. This is denoted by the curve LR. Once the firm commits itself to specific investments relating to one or the other crop the long-run production possibilities (opportunity) curve is no longer relevant. If the investments are specific to sugar production, the operative opportunity curve ten becomes s_cr_c while if they are specific to bananas it is s_br_b.[42] The degree of flexibility for product-product combinations is reduced as a result of the specific commitments.

Diagram B shows different degrees of capital specificity for a set of firms involved in sugar production. The more resources the firm has tied up in activities linked to sugar the greater the degree of inflexibility. Thus in the case of West Indian sugar producers, for example, if rc_1 represents the position of Tate and Lyle subsidiaries, Bookers would operate on a curve to the right of this, say rc_2, since the latter does not have sugar refining investments, while a simple farm-factory combine (sugar estate) without shipping and refining investments would operate further right, on say, rc_3.

The greater the degree of vertical integration the less will be the flexibility of adjusting resource use to changing production opportunities across the range of agricultural commodities which can be produced with available resources. This is one factor contributing to inefficient resource allocation within the agricultural sectors of plantation economies.

Land Use

The farm-factory operations of plantation enterprises are located in the tropical plantation economies. Here the factory for processing plantation output represents a substantial capital investment. The firm is therefore concerned that adequate supplies of raw material will be available for utilizing factory capacity in a reasonably efficient way. Sufficient land must be acquired to produce the desired flow of material.[43] Even where raw material supplies are available for purchase from independent farmers, the firm would be in too vulnerable a position if it relied exclusively on such supplies.

This means that the plantation enterprise will try to secure sufficient land to produce some, or all, of its raw material requirements and to allow for some degree of flexibility of output adjustment over time in response to changing market opportunities.

The land area required by a plantation will be influenced by several factors: the price of land, the size of factory investment, the ratio of factory investment to total farm-factory investment, the availability of raw material supplies from other sources (preferably contract suppliers), and expectations *re* future market possibilities which influence desired flexibility of output adjustment.

The actual land area acquired by plantations will depend on the resources of the firm, the cost of land and the scale economies of processing particular crops. Given a scale of plant, then the minimum area required would be determined by the level of output required to cover fixed costs in processing where non-plantation supplies are available. Where these are not available a larger area will be necessary to make processing profitable.[44]

Normally, plantations would try to secure land well in excess of the technical minimum. Price expectations and the cost of land would mainly determine the maximum area. The lower the cost of land and the brighter the long-term market expectations the greater would be the area secured for plantation production. Because the establishment of plantations has historically been associated with the opening up of new territory, low-cost land was usually available and this led to the alienation of vast areas even beyond expected requirements at the time of establishment.

The land area actually in use at any particular point in time is a function of the price of output, the cost of production, the technical requirements of plant scale and the price at which the firm can obtain other supplies of the raw material. High rates of profit are characteristic of the early stages of development of plantations as a result of the natural fertility of virgin land. But over time profits get squeezed as diminishing returns and rising costs set in.[45] This stimulates technological improvements to raise the productivity of land (e.g. new improved varieties, irrigation (fertilizers). As technology changes some lands previously in production may become marginal but the plantation will keep these in reserve since future favourable changes in output prices may justify their use at a later date. (In Central America, for example, UFco maintained possession of thousands of acres which had been abandoned in the wake of Panama disease for several years and was able to bring these areas back into production quickly during the 1960s with the advent of the disease-resistant 'Valery' variety and favourable market prospects.)

There is therefore a tendency toward underutilization of land in plantation agriculture. The extent of underutilization (*ie* size of acreage reserve) will depend on the cost of securing land and of holding it. So we would expect smaller acreage reserves in countries which are short of land than in land-abundant plantation economies.[46] Underutilization of land is one means of proving for flexibility of output adjustments over time. Though this may represent an efficient pattern of resource use for the firm, it creates inefficiencies in allocation within the agricultural sector. This is most acute in situations where land is generally in short supply.

Risk and Uncertainty Considerations

The heavy capitalization and the crop specificity of investments expose plantation enterprises to an inherently high degree of risk and uncertainty – particularly in respect of crop losses from natural or other (e.g. political) causes and or price fluctuations. This induces at least two counter measures which affect resource allocation within the plantation economies.

The first is the exploitation of market imperfections. On the product side this is expressed in enterprise control over disposal prices. United Fruit Co achieved this so effectively in the US banana market that it had to face a Consent Decree of the Department of Justice to divest itself of part of its capital for the formation of another smaller company. In any event, UFCo will still be able to maintain its position of price leader in the trade. Tate and Lyle subsidiaries on the other hand achieve this through industry collusion in the West Indies (*ie* Sugar Manufacturers' Associations) and political lobbying in the UK for preferential pricing arrangements. In matters relating to overseas sugar markets it is normal practice in the West Indies for industry leaders to 'speak for the governments'. The consequences of this counter measure is artificially to distort the structure of output prices for the range of farm products that can be produced in the plantation economies; and thereby to bias resource use in favour of the plantation crop. On the factor side, market imperfections arise from control over supplies of inputs produced within the vertically-integrated structure of the firm and from the normally monopsonistic position of the plantation in the labour market. The latter derives from the fact that the land area covered by the plantation enterprise is so vast that it is usually the only source of employment within fairly wide areas.

The second counter measure is the geographic dispersal of the firm's plantation operations. This minimizes the risk of crop losses. In addition to losses from weather and disease, this measure is a hedge against unfavourable changes in the political and economic situation in individual countries and it increases the flexibility of output expansion for the firm itself. But it also leads to perverse supply responses for individual countries. For although the firm may increase overall acreage and output in response to an increase in the relative price of its output it may, in the process, contract acreage and output in a particular individual country.[47] The firm is concerned with efficient resource allocation between its different areas of agricultural operations. And this often results in inefficient resource allocation within a particular plantation economy. Because of the multi-national character of plantation enterprises efficiency conditions tend to be met on the overall operation *ie* between plantation sectors of nation states but not within the agricultural sectors of individual nation states.

Development Problems in Plantation-Type Economies

The discussion in this section falls into three main parts: first, a brief consideration of the general conditions of agricultural development provides the background for an assessment; next, factors which limit development with plantation agriculture and, finally, the factors which seem to favour development.

Conditions of Agricultural Development

A great deal has been written about the role (or contribution) of agriculture in overall economic development. The main considerations here are, first, that agriculture must provide the food supplies required to meet an expanding demand resulting from population growth and rising incomes. When this expansion of food supply is not forthcoming, food prices increase and/or supplies must be imported. In either event, development is constrained.

Agriculture must provide not just an increasing supply but one in which the pattern of supply needs to be adjusted to satisfy changing patterns of food consumption that are associated with rising incomes. That is, the supply of high income elasticity foodstuffs must increase at a faster rate than that of low income elasticity products. This demands a certain degree of flexibility of resource use and adjustment within agriculture.

Secondly, the agricultural sector acts as a source of factor supplies for expansion of other sectors of the economy. In this connection particular emphasis has been given to labour and capital transfers. Thirdly, agriculture is the basis of important market relationships which create spread effects for development. All primary output requires processing of some form and this provides forward linkage effects. Similarly, commercial agriculture relies increasingly on purchased off-farm inputs which provide opportunities for income and employment creation in sectors producing these inputs, the backward linkage effects. The sum of forward and backward linkage effects from agriculture can be quite substantial given the right conditions.

Fourthly, the agricultural sector is an important earner of foreign exchange in many countries. And foreign exchange is usually required to secure certain critical capital inputs for development. Given the present structure of the world economy the export trade of underdeveloped countries is dominated by primary products – mainly of agriculture and mining.

Agricultural development *per se* involves several necessary conditions; for a start, adequate supplies of resources, especially land and capital. Complementary human resources – with skills in management and adaptable labour services – are essential as well. A developed infrastructure (roads, water, supplies, electricity, etc.) provides a foundation for development. Appropriate institutional arrangements (e.g. affecting incentive for effort, land tenure, marketing, credit) and adequate scope for the organization of 'large scale units of collective action' (progress-oriented values, attitudes, social structure etc) are pre-conditions for development.

The *dynamics* of agricultural development, however, involves much more. Technological change is crucial. The development process involves an expansion of agricultural output at the same time that labour is moving out of agriculture. The productivity of labour remaining in agriculture must therefore expand substantially. For this, research can play an important part since it serves to increase knowledge of new inputs and of possibilities for raising the productivity of old inputs. Capital accumulation is also essential to the process. And, finally, enough flexibility to facilitate resource adjustments to changing income opportunities is necessary.

Underdevelopment Biases in Plantation Agriculture

The characteristics of plantation agriculture are such that this type of agriculture tends not to fulfil the basic conditions set out above in the brief discussion of the role of agriculture in economic development. First, this type of agriculture is not geared to supplying food demand within the plantation economy. Instead, it is geared to metropolitan consumption requirements. As such it fulfills another condition by earning foreign exchange. The question that arises is whether over time the foreign exchange-earning ability will be more than enough to provide for imported food supplies so as to leave a residual of earnings for importation of 'critical capital inputs'.

Plantation export output consists of primary products with relatively low income elasticities of demand. On the other hand, the food import requirements of plantation economies normally consist of high income elasticity products.[48] Therefore for any given increase in consumer incomes in both the metropolis and the plantation economy, the required increase in plantation output will be less than the required increase in food imports. In order to compensate, the export price for plantation output must rise relative to food import prices. In other words, over time the terms of trade must move consistently in favour of plantation export output. But in point of fact the historical pattern has generally been the reverse; so that the export earnings of plantation economies tend toward failing to meet food import requirements unless the rate of income growth in the plantation economy falls consistently behind that in the metropolis.[49] It is of considerable interest to note here that despite the deteriorating terms of trade more export agricultural output continues to be produced in the plantation economies. The reason for this is that to the private foreign plantation owners the commodity terms of trade has no economic significance. The terms of trade is really a social concept which does not have much significance in the private accounting of the plantation. To put it another way, the terms of trade of the *firm* may be altogether different from the terms of trade of the *society*.

In addition, it must be noted that the foreign exchange earning capacity of plantation agriculture is limited by the normally high import content of plantation production and consumption. On the production side, this results partly from the fact that metropolitan capital brings with it its own technology, which usually requires inputs not available in the plantation economy; and partly from the vertically integrated structure of plantation enterprises. On the consumption side, because plantation labour has been mobilized for export production there is relatively little production for the home market leading to a characteristic heavy reliance on imports of food and other consumer goods. The actual available foreign exchange is therefore what is left after deducting the value of imported inputs used in plantation production, factor incomes going to the metropole and the consumer expenditure on imports in the second round.[50] On the whole, then, the foreign exchange earning capacity of plantation agriculture seems to be less than is normally assumed.

Another effect of the primary export orientation of plantation agriculture is that the befits of productivity improvements tend to accrue mostly to metropolitan consumers. This is so primarily in those countries where plantations exist along with farmers producing for their own consumption. In looking at the Jamaican experience, for example. Arthur Lewis observed that although productivity in export agriculture increased by 27% between 1890 and 1930 consumption per head increased only by 13% in the same period because the terms of trade moved adversely from 137 in 1890 to 84 in 1930. Lewis explains this general pattern among tropical exporting countries as follows: ". . . so long as productivity is constant in subsistence production, practically all the benefit of increases in productivity in the commercial crops accrues to the consumer and not to the producer . . . Greater productivity is offset by adverse terms of trade."[51]

The same author had outlined the position in greater length in his *Theory of Economic Growth* as follows:

If nothing is done to raise the productivity of peasants in producing food, they constitute a reservoir of cheap labour available for work in mines or plantations or other export enterprises . . . So long as the peasant farmers have low productivity, the temperate world can get the services of tropical labour for a very low price. Moreover when productivity rises in the crops produced for export there is no need to share the increase with labour, and practically the whole benefit goes in reducing the price to industrial consumers. Sugar is an excellent case in point. Cane sugar production is an industry in which productivity is extremely high by any biological standard. It is also an industry in which output per acre has about trebled over the past 70 years a rate of growth unparalleled by any other major agricultural industry in the world – certainly not by the wheat industry. Nevertheless, workers in the cane sugar industry continue to walk barefooted and to live in shacks, while workers in wheat enjoy among the highest living standards in the world. However vastly productive the sugar industry may become, the benefit accrues chiefly to consumers. This is one of the disadvantages to tropical countries (advantages to industrial countries) of the fact that their economic development has concentrated upon the export sector of the economy, and that foreign entrepreneurs and foreign capital have been devoted in the first place primarily to expanding exports . . .[52]

Lewis has been quoted at length here because he is describing a phenomenon that is characteristic not so much of all export agriculture but of plantation agriculture in particular. For this is perhaps the only type of agriculture that by definition always satisfies the two basic conditions that erode retention of the benefits of productivity improvements: export production and a continuous supply of cheap labour.[53]

It should be pointed out, however, that in recent times productivity improvements have brought more benefit to the plantation economies than in the past. This has resulted mainly from increasing trade union activity which has managed to cream off some of the benefits of improved productivity in the form of higher wages for plantation labour. But against this must be balanced the consideration that improvements in productivity on plantations have invariably involved the oft-neglected cost of increased unemployment.[54]

Plantation agriculture also has a limited capacity for the two other functions mentioned in the earlier discussion of "conditions of agricultural development". As concerns transfers of factor supplies there are two important limitations. First, because of foreign ownership capital transfers are to the metropolis and not to the non-agricultural sectors of the plantation economy. And, secondly, because the skill content of plantation labour is low (by the specification of the production function) the adaptability of plantation labour to the requirements of the other sectors is extremely slow.

So far as market relationships are concerned, the vertical integration of plantation enterprises stretches across national boundaries. Linkages are established within the structure of the firm and not within individual plantation economies. For the latter, then, potential linkage effects are dissipated and this minimizes inter-industry transactions with their potential development spread effects.

Some other factors which further restrict development possibilities in plantation economies and which deserve elaboration are the inherent rigidities in resource adjustment, the element of foreign ownership, the unequal pattern of income distribution and the characteristic rigid social structure.

In our examination of the economics of resource use, it was observed that the high degree of specificity of plantation enterprise investment and the distorted structure of agricultural output prices create a built-in rigidity in the pattern of resource use in plantation agriculture. Because of this heavy commitment to the production of a particular export crop and because foreign investors have little or no interest in production for the domestic market, opportunities for agricultural development deriving from changing patterns of consumer food expenditure tend not to be taken up. The normal development pattern, implicit in a model based on more perfectly competitive conditions, does not emerge.

Foreign ownership of plantations limits development in two additional ways not previously considered. First there is the leakage of income in the form of dividends which reduces the investment capacity of the economy. Secondly, when reinvestment out of the surplus occurs, there is no assurance that the economy in which the surplus was produced will benefit. This follows from the spatial distribution of the firm's operations among a number of countries. Surpluses produced in one country can be reinvested in any other country where the firm owns plantations or at home-base in the metropolis.

The low wages of plantation labourers stand in dramatic contrast to the earnings of the skilled supervisory and management staffs which operate the plantations. This sets the stage for a generally unequal pattern of income distribution among all households in plantation economies. The adverse development consequences of this are two-fold. Aggregate effective demand is low; this limits the size of the market and rules out the establishment of consumer goods industries with significant scale economies. In addition, the low incomes of the bulk of the population restrict household savings and the scope for domestic investment, while the high-income classes engage in conspicuous consumption of luxury imports and invest heavily in non-productive assets.

Finally, the rigid class lines and weak community cohesion of plantation societies serve to restrict social mobility and to impede the development of large-scale units of collective action. Restricted social mobility adversely affects individual incentive for economic advancement and affects labour adaptability as well.

Contributions of Plantation Agriculture to Development

Two factors which are repeatedly mentioned in the literature on plantation agriculture deserve consideration here so as to round off the discussion. The first is that plantation agriculture has served in the past to open up previously inaccessible areas. In so doing, it has developed an infrastructure of roads, ports, water supplies, electricity, etc. in underdeveloped countries much more rapidly than would otherwise occur. This is undoubtedly an important contribution to these economies. But the benefits of this must be weighed against the dynamic underdevelopment biases considered above. What is more, it should be noted that, like everything else, the infrastructure is geared to the specific needs of the plantations and does not necessarily benefit other producers to any significant degree. Thus, for example, we normally find villages and farming areas just outside the boundaries of plantations without water and electricity though the plantation itself is well supplied with these.

The second consideration is that unlike other types of agriculture in underdeveloped countries, plantation agriculture is 'scientific'. Plantations invest in research which produces a high rate of technological change. Furthermore, the implementation of research findings is quick and easy because of the centralized authority structure of plantations. This can be contrasted with the slow rate of adoption of new techniques by peasant farmers and the overwhelming problem of extension in peasant farming areas. This point is also well taken but requires qualification. Again, the research input of plantations are specific to particular crops and may not apply across the range of technical production possibilities. For example, United Fruit undertakes an elaborate programme of research on bananas, and West Indian sugar plantations maintain their own research stations for studying the problems of sugar. Neither of these invests very much in research on other crops and/or livestock which may offer better economic prospects to the countries involved than the particular plantation crop. This raises the problem of the allocative efficiency of research resources. But, in addition, it underscores the existing dynamic bias against high-income production opportunities in the domestic market; for in the absence of technical knowledge such opportunities cannot be readily seized.

Summary and Implications

This paper represents a first attempt to examine the economics of resource use and development in economies based on plantation agriculture. The analysis suggests that the particular character of plantation enterprises of a certain type (multi-national corporate enterprises) and the dependent nature of the economies dominated by these enterprises create certain inefficiencies in resource allocation *within these economies* and, in addition, limit the potential for development.

Allocative inefficiencies arise from the structural characteristics of the plantation enterprises considered here – in particular vertical and horizontal integration across national frontiers, and the high degree of capital specificity that characterizes the production process. The inefficiencies within the agricultural sectors of plantation economies co-exist with efficient resource use for the first itself, reminding us of the maxim that what is good for the firm is not necessarily good for the country.

Similarly biases toward underdevelopment in plantation economies derive from certain structural factors – foreign ownership and export orientation, the inherent rigidities in resource adjustment, the low skill content of plantation labour, unequal distribution of incomes, and rigid social structure – that inhere in this type of agriculture.

By and large, the analysis has been exploratory. It now requires further refinement and expansion to provide a framework for constructing a model of development which is appropriate to this type of agriculture. Subsequently, the model would require testing by setting it against the historical experiences of selected plantation economies. Hopefully this will lead to a better understanding of the process of change and the possibilities for transformation in economies of this type.

Notes

* "The economics of agricultural resource use and development in plantation economics". *Social and Economic Studies* 18:4 (1969a); reprinted in Bernstein (ed.), *Development and Underdevelopment* (1973); and in I. Livingstone (ed.), *Development Economics and Policy* (1980).

1   The overwhelming concern has been with 'peasant' or 'traditional' or 'subsistence' agriculture.

2   See, for example, V. D. Wickizer. "The plantation system in the development of tropical economies", *Journal of Farm Economics* (February 1958).

3   See, for example, R. E. Baldwin, "Patterns of development in newly settled regions", *Manchester School* (May 1956); and "Export technology and development from subsistence level". *Economic Journal* (March 1963).

4   See J. H. Steward et al., *The People of Puerto Rico* (Urbana: University of Illinois Press, 1956), Symposium, *Plantation Systems of the New World* (Washington DC: Pan American Union, 1959); Vera Rubin (ed.) *Caribbean Studies: A Symposium* (Kingston, Jamaica: ISER, University of the West Indies, 1957).

5   For an interesting and pioneering effort in examining the social organization of the plantation, see E. R. Wolf and S. W. Mintz, "Haciendas and Plantations in Middle America and the Antilles", *Social and Economic Studies* (September 1957).

6 Jones, "Plantations", in David L. Sills, *International Encyclopedia of the Social Sciences*, Vol. 12, (1968) p. 154.

7 Wolf and Mintz, "Haciendâs", for example, emphasize this point as one of characteristics that differentiate the plantation from the hacienda as systems of agricultural organization.

8 Jones, p. 156.

9 Jones, p. 156. See also V. D. Wickizer, "The smallholder in tropical export-crop production", *Food Research Institute Studies* (February 1960); and "Plantation crops in tropical agriculture", *Tropical Agriculture* (July 1958).

10 Ida Greaves, "Plantations in world economy", in *Plantation Systems of the New World*, p. 13.

11 For an interesting historical analysis of the development of new world plantation economies, see Lloyd Best, "Outlines of a model of pure plantation economy", *Social and Economic Studies* (September 1968).

12 Greaves, p. 15.

13 Greaves, p. 14.

14 Greaves, p. 15. My emphasis.

15 Greaves, p. 16. The reference in this quotation from Greaves is to John Stuart Mill.

16 The latter example is given further consideration in a subsequent section of this paper. On the former, see C. Y. Thomas, *Monetary and Financial Arrangements in a Dependent Monetary Economy* (Kingston, Jamaica: ISER, University of the West Indies, 1965).

17 For further discussion of some of these considerations, see Lloyd Braithwaite's, "Social and political aspects of rural development in the West Indies", *Social and Economic Studies* (September 1968).

18 Charles Wagley, "Plantation America: a culture sphere", *Caribbean Studies: A Symposium*, edited by Vera Rubin, (Kingston, Jamaica: ISER, University of the West Indies, Mona, 1957), p. 5.

19 Wagley, p. 9.

20 It should be noted, however, that even in such situations past plantation experiences may have left a cultural legacy which could lead to patterns of resource allocation and development similar to that which one finds in plant-ation economies. I am grateful to Lloyd Best for bringing this to my attention.

21 For a collection of papers which examine the Caribbean experience against the background of plantation agriculture see G. L. Beckford (ed.) *Agricultural Development and Planning in the Caribbean, Social and Economic Studies* (Special Number September 1968). It will be interesting at a later stage to see how the pattern developed from the Caribbean experience fits other plantation regions such as those in Asia and the Pacific.

22 In this paper, the term 'West Indies' is used to refer to the Commonwealth Caribbean which includes all the former British islands and the mainland territories of Guyana and British Honduras. When the term Caribbean is used without qualification, reference is to the wider region which includes non-English speaking islands such as Cuba, Hispaniola, Puerto Rico, the French and Dutch West Indies.

23 The treatment of Tate and Lyle is limited to its West Indian operations and related activity. This firm is more international in scope than Bookers which has a greater concentration of its resources in the Caribbean (Guyana in particular).

24 In 1967, two-thirds of the company's overseas (*ie* outside of Britain) investment was in the Caribbean – mainly Guyana. Other overseas territories in which this firm operates include Zambia, Canada, Nigeria, Jamaica, Trinidad, Malawi,

India, Barbados, and St Lucia; but in most of these places the interest is in non-agricultural activities.

25 The company also has raw sugar producing subsidiaries in Zambia, Nigeria and Rhodesia but its influence on the agricultural economies of those countries is minimal.

26 The company also owns building supplies and building service industries in Canada and the UK.

27 The information on Jamaica was provided by S. A. Osborne in a student class essay prepared for the author. We are grateful to the Managing Director of WISCo, P. Bovell, who read Osborne's essay and made a number of important corrections and comments.

28 Official government delegations to various international sugar conferences and councils usually consist of representatives of the SMA. And the chief officers in the SMA are usually Tate and Lyle personnel.

29 The information on Trinidad was derived from recent annual reports of Caroni Ltd.

30 H. B. Arthur, J. P. Houek and G. L. Beckford, *Tropical Agribusiness Structures and Adjustments: Bananas* (Boston: Harvard Business School, Division of Research, 1968), pp. 33-53.

31 United Fruit Company, 1966 *Annual Report*, p. 20.

32 The figure for Guyana was derived by adding the GDP attributed to sugar cane, padi, other, livestock, sugar processing and rice processing in the *Economic Survey of Guyana, 1966*, p. 89. Figures for Bookers were taken from *The Booker Group Report and Accounts 1967*, p. 8. The total GDP of Guyana in that year (about £75 million) was less than Bookers total 'turnover' (£78 million).

33 Baldwin, "Patterns".

34 In 1966, the 41 vessels owned by the company accounted for as much as 28% of total investment (see the company's *Annual Report* 1966, pp. 19-20).

35 For elaboration on these conditions see for example E. O. Heady, *Economics of Agricultural Production and Resource Use* (New York: Prentice Hall, 1952), chapter 24.

36 This aspect is considered in more detail later in this section under Capital Specificity.

37 The diagram has been simplified by omitting certain by-product operations like rum, molasses and alcohol production.

38 In actual practice, the Commonwealth preferential system for West Indian sugar places the firm in a unique position. The raw sugar output from its West Indian factories is sold together with other sugar produced in the West Indies to the British Sugar Board at a special negotiated price which is usually in excess of the world market price. The Sugar Board is however obliged to sell British refiners at the world market price. So that normally this firm sells its raw sugar at one price and buys back the same sugar at a lower price for refining it.

39 Jones, p. 155.

40 Certain factors at the farm level tend as well to be highly specific; for example, laboratories and managerial functions. It has been suggested, for example, that these rigidities may derive as much from the circumscribed entrepreneurial horizons of firm managers as from the existence of capital specificity in a physical or engineering sense. Firm managers who have established themselves as 'sugar men' or 'banana men' are unlikely to contemplate crop changes which would erode their established authority. Although this is a factor which is of relevance, it

does not really set plantation operators apart from other types of agricultural producers. This same kind of 'psychological attachment' to crops can be found among peasant farmers. It seems therefore that the degree of capital specificity is the more important consideration.

41 The set of production possibilities at the farm level are not influenced by ancillary non-farm investments in a technical sense but are affected indirectly by the resultant relative profitability of alternatives once specific commitments have been made.

42 In a comment on the earlier draft, Havelock Brewster raises the question as to whether specificity "is not shown by a lack of, or only partial, continuity in the production function rather than, as you show it, an alternation in the convexity". In that event the illustration would be as follows, showing that in the sugar case "the curve is continuous up to x in the short run and/or with a certain degree of inflexibility *ie* vertical integration it would be continuous up to y in a longer period and/or with a greater degree of flexibility". It seems to me that either interpretation will lead to the same conclusion.

43 The argument applies as well to enterprises which have shipping capacity such as in the banana case where no elaborate processing is done but where shipping is an important part of the firm's operation. By producing its own bananas UFCo has greater control over utilization of its shipping capacity.

44 The same applies to shipping. For example, for bananas "there is a certain minimum area required to justify the specialized shipping facilities that the trade demands. UFCo usually specifies that at least 5,000 acres of first class land . . . be available in one block before a farm can be established". Arthur, Houek and Beckford, p. 48.

45 See Best, for a discussion of the historical sequence of transition from what he describes as the 'golden age' to the stage of 'gall and wormwood'.

46 In Central America for example UFCo normally has only one-third of its total owned acreage in bananas while the share of estate land in sugar-cane in the West Indies is generally about 80%. However population density may work in the opposite direction. Strong competition for land will lead to a secular rise in land prices which would encourage the holding of idle land for speculative purposes. David Edwards informs me that there is evidence that this has been the case for certain sugar estates in Trinidad and Antigua.

47 In a recent study of banana supply functions for each of four Central American countries, the author could find no correlation between changes in planned output (using acreage as an index) and changes in relative prices for bananas. But some significant correlations were derived when acreage data for each of two companies (United Fruit and Standard Fruit Co) were aggregated for all four countries and plotted against relative price over a number of years.

48 Basic starch staples (the low income elasticity products in the consumer food basket) are usually supplied from within plantation economies.

49 This condition itself implies limited economic progress in the plantation economy where incomes are already at much lower levels than in the metropolis.

50 There is also the question of the valuation of exports where the product leaves the plantation economy as an intra-company transfer and not through sales. For a discussion of this problem in relation to Central American banana exports and the UFCo, see R. A. LaBarge, "The imputation of values to intra-company exports: the case of bananas", *Social and Economic Studies* (June 1961).

51 W. Arthur Lewis, "Foreword" to Gisela Eisner, *Jamaica 1830-1930: A Study in Economic Growth* (Manchester, UK: Manchester University Press, 1961), pp. xviii-xix.

52 W. A. Lewis, *The Theory of Economic Growth* (London: Allen and Unwin, 1955), p. 281.

53 Other types of agriculture may satisfy one or the other conditions but seldom both. For example, the commercial farm-firms producing wheat in Canada and the peasants producing cocoa in West Africa are export producers without the cheap labour condition while the haciendas of Latin America base production on cheap labour but are not export-oriented.

54 I am grateful to Havelock Brewster for reminding me of this.

18

Persistent Poverty: Possibilities for Change and Transformation*

The persistence of underdevelopment in plantation economies derives basically from the nature of the plantation system itself. It would appear then that the process of transformation to a development path that would ensure benefits to everyone in plantation society must involve radical change in the institutional structure – particularly the economic, social, and political arrangements. This is bound to be painful. But development is always a painful process – sacrifices have to be made in the short and the medium terms as an investment for benefits that can accrue only in the long run.

There are several reasons why the plantation system creates persistent underdevelopment, as we saw in the last chapter. In our view, the most important of these are (1) the plantation system denies the majority of the people of plantation society a real stake in their country; (2) the system creates a legacy of dependence because the locus of decision making concerning fundamental economic issues resides outside of plantation society, so that a chronic dependency syndrome is characteristic of the whole population; and (3) the majority of people are not sufficiently motivated toward the development effort because of the first two considerations. No meaningful social change can take place without measures to correct these three basic deficiencies.

To put the matter rather bluntly, the plantation system must be destroyed if the people of plantation society are to secure economic, social, political, and psychological advancement.

The Major Development Obstacles and Previous Attempts at Change

The plantation system is itself the major obstacle to development in plantation economy. The structure of the system is such that many of the proximate economic, social and political variables that contribute to development do not come into effective play. The major economic obstacles that derive from the plantation influence are the following:

1   a fracturing of resource supply and demand;

2   inequality in the distribution of wealth and income;

3   foreign ownership of producing units that drains the supply of investible funds from the income stream;

4   export orientation of plantation production that results in a cumulation of backwash effects from terms of trade adjustments;

5   the low skill content of plantation work that inhibits the diffusion of skills and improvement in the quality of labour inputs;

6   resource-use distortions that prevent the flexible deployment of resource services to high-income producing activities;

7   canalization of linkages and associated development potential by metropolitan plantation enterprise.

8   multinational character of investment allocation by metropolitan enterprise that further reduces the flow of investible funds;

9   limited technical knowledge of production possibilities apart from the particular plantation crop which results from the excessive concentration of research by company plantations and which prevents a rational pattern of agricultural development.

The major social and political obstacles to development that are directly attributable to the plantation influence include:

1   weak community structure and loose family organisation that prevent the emergence of viable local and regional units of administration and control, thereby making it difficult to raise local taxes and to execute local development projects;

2   a rigid social structure that inhibits factor mobility;

3   the strong correlation between race and class that creates a caste system and generates social tension and instability;

4   a general absence of social responsibility that results in poorly developed educational systems;

5   strong central government administration with a generally undemocratic political structure that discourages effective popular participation in the development process;

6   excessive power of the planter and associated classes that is exercised more in the interest of the small dominant class than in that of the society as a whole;

7   the low incidence of progress-oriented values among all the people of plantation society which derives from the strong element of tradition among the planter class and the general hostility to intellectualism which is essential for innovation and change;

8   a strong individualism that contributes more to clashes of interest in interpersonal relations than to cooperative activity;

9   an exploitative authoritarian tradition that prevents cooperative decision making and associative productive effort;

10   pervasive value orientations that reflect aspirations to a 'great house' life style with characteristic high propensities to consume imported luxuries and to invest in nonproductive assets.

For the most part, the obstacles to development listed above have not been recognised sufficiently by policy makers in plantation society. The only two which have received significant attention to date are the foreign-ownership problem and the associated drain of investible funds, and the unequal distribution of land in plantation economy. Several countries have, in the past, introduced measures to deal with these two obstacles but these efforts have not paid much dividend in terms of induced development. In at least one country, Cuba, the development obstacles were so pronounced that the resulting social injustices sparked a revolutionary change directed at changing the whole institutional structure of plantation society. As concerns past attempts at change and transformation in plantation economy, we can identity two general categories: adjustments on the margin by the introduction of legislation to regulate plantation activity in one way or another, and structural adjustments to change the system entirely. Ceylon represents the first category and Cuba the second. The experiences in these two countries are now very briefly considered.

Since independence all government administrations in Ceylon have introduced measures to regulate plantation activity to bring it more in line with national interests. Policy measures have included rigorous taxation of the tea plantation industry to finance national development, restraints on the export of capital efforts to build up the importance of the Colombo auctions, measures to secure employment of Ceylonese management and staff,

encouragement of smallholder tea production beginning with state plantations, and attempts to solve the problem of Indian Tamil labour which has
been a bone of contention in the high unemployment atmosphere of Ceylon.
Ceylon has perhaps done more than any other country in the direction of
regulating plantation activity. For example, fiscal charges on tea exports are
higher than they are anywhere else in the world, representing "something like
23% of the average export price." And legislation has been designed "to make
it impossible for sterling companies to sell their estates and repatriate the
proceeds, and in general to restrict the export of wealth of all kinds, whether
corporate or personal."[1] In general, public accountability of plantations was to
be effected through the Tea Control Act. In spite of all these efforts, Ceylon
appears to be still in the underdeveloped equilibrium trap created by the
plantation structure.[2] Elsewhere the position is much same, as plantations
have successfully managed to circumvent any measures governments have
introduced to regulate them.[3]

Cuba is a different case entirely. There the forces of destruction inherent in
the plantation structure exploded violently, and the plantation sugar industry
was nationalized by a revolutionary government that came to power in 1959.
Attempts to establish a cooperative-based industry failed and state plantations are now the order of the day. Much has been achieved there in the social
adjustment of the plantation system – rural unemployment is said not to exist;
colour, class, and caste are said to be of lesser significance; education is now
universal and is directed more to the needs of the country; rural health has
improved considerably with the establishment of widely dispersed medical
facilities; and the population is highly motivated toward national development and defense.[4] However, the underdevelopment legacy of the plantation
can still be observed at several important levels. Perhaps the most important
is the dependency syndrome which affects relations with the rest of the world.
This has resulted in the introduction of economic policies which are likely to
contribute to persistent underdevelopment, and the adoption of an alien
ideology which might not be adequate to heal the social fractures of plantation society.

In connection with the first, the emphasis given to sugar production and
the related integration of the Cuban economy with metropolitan Soviet
economy seem likely to encourage continuing predominance of primary
production and to inhibit structural transformation. It is understandable that
dependence on a large metropolitan sugar importer was inevitable because
Cuba produces such a high share of world export output of this commodity.
However, the possibility exists that economic policy makers in Cuba may still
be suffering form intellectual colonialism and that this may account for a
policy which reflects a neoclassic conceptualization of international trade

with its notions of commodity specialization deriving from static comparative advantage.[5] In connection with the second, we observe that the Communist ideology that the Cubans have embraced originally developed from the feudal-capitalist historical sequence of Europe which left a legacy of social organization ad structure appreciably different from that of plantation society. Consequently, the social dynamics created by this ideology may not be adequate for the development needs of plantation economy. As shall be argued later in this chapter, the ideal development path for plantation economy and society will demand, among other things, economic integration with similarly placed economies, and a political ideology derived from the specific plantation heritage.

We need, however, to be somewhat equivocal in our conclusions about the future development of Cuba because the ten-year experience of change in that country is much too short for perceptive analysis and because we do not have sufficient information on what has gone on so far, or of what is being planned for the long term. Future and continuing study of the Cuban experience must be a priority for everyone interested in the problem of transformation and development in plantation economies.

Our tentative conclusion from the consideration of attempts at change in Ceylon and Cuba is that so far there is no evidence of successful measures to eliminate the major underdevelopment biases of the plantation system. It is necessary, therefore, to indicate what possibilities are suggested by the analysis provided in this book.

Overcoming the Obstacles to Development: Theoretical Possibilities and Issues

Perhaps the most significant historical experience of change in all the plantation economies of the world was that of the forced adjustments induced by World War II. During the period of hostilities when ocean lanes for merchant shipping were partially closed, imported goods were hard to secure and everywhere plantation economy achieved a measure of diversification. Light manufacturing developed particularly in processed foods like edible oils and margarine, building materials like cement, and relatively labour-intensive industries like matches and footwear. And agricultural production was diversified to provide supplies of foodstuffs, like vegetables, root crops, and livestock products, all of which were previously imported in one form or another. Much of the actual economic growth and development which these countries have achieved has come in recent decades and has been based essentially on the foundations laid during the war. The cynic would conclude that what these countries need is another war. That may well be so, and it may come down to this. But for now we conclude that the war experience provides us with a major clue about possibilities for change and transformation. It is that plantation economy is far too open for development to taken place, and measures to bring about some degree of closure must be included in the bag of policy instruments. This is one of the obvious omissions in the Cuban case. The Cuban economy is still much too open for induced development. The degree of openness is, we suspect, not unrelated to the adoption of alien ideology. It is of some interest to note in passing that all the materially advanced countries in the world have passed through periods in which the foundations for development were laid, either by closure (for example, the US and Japan) or by expansion of territory (for example, Britain and France). The underdevelopment biases deriving from openness have been studied by several economists.[6]

However, openness is not the only obstacle to development of plantation economy. There are many other economic problems that must be dealt with: securing the linkages from plantation activity, land reform, income redistribution, resource use adjustments, technological change, and appropriate restructuring of economic institutions. These are all now very briefly considered. The intention in this final chapter is simply to outline ideas for change that are suggested by the analysis. The aim here is not to provide final solutions. All of the people of plantation society acting together will have to find the final solutions. It is hoped that the ideas coming out of this book eventually will contribute to that process.

In our analysis in chapter 7, we reviewed the arguments of Leubuscher in connection with metropolitan location of processing plantation raw materials. We concluded there that the critical factors at present are metropolitan ownership and control of plantation production and limitations deriving from the size of the market in the plantation economies. In addition, technical knowledge and process innovation currently favor metropolitan location of processing. Furthermore, as we saw in chapter 5, many other linkages associated with plantation activity are now being secured by the multinational enterprises. These include shipping, engineering industry, and product diversification, all of which provide a basis for potential development of plantation economies. If the plantation economies are to secure these linkages for themselves, they will need to do several things. First, they need to wrest all (or some) control of plantation activity from metropolitan enterprise to set the stage for a reversal of the present big-company small-country arrangement. This implies national ownership of land and capital assets of metropolitan plantation enterprise, and it opens up the whole question of retaliation and the incipient Third World-metropolitan conflict. It implies as well a high degree of coordination among the Third World countries to make it difficult for companies to play off one country against the other. There are at least two alternative paths that Third World countries can follow in this matter. One is to take complete control away from metropolitan enterprise. This will pay the highest development dividends in the long run but is a more painful and conflict-pregnant path. The other involves negotiation with metropolitan enterprise to secure all the linkages that will arise in the future from incremental demand. The dividends here are naturally lower and so is the probability of international conflict and violence.

The second major change necessary to secure plantation linkages for plantation economy is regional economic integration. This will increase the size of the market in plantation economy and make it economically feasible to establish industry allied to plantation production – processing, shipping, engineering and chemical industries in particular. We should also note that regional economic integration will contribute much more to development because this will open up other production possibilities in plantation economy as a result of opportunities for resource combination and export substitution. An example of resource combination is the location of aluminum smelting and manufacture in the Caribbean by smelting alumina from Jamaica, where power supplies are inadequate, in Guyana where the power potential is great. Export substitution opportunities arise from the trading of a share of the metropolitan market for plantation output in return for a guarantee of the regional market for some other agricultural product (or products). Again an example of this is provided by Jamaica's agreeing to cede the incremental demand for bananas in the UK to the Windward Islands in return for a guaranteed Windward market for Jamaican potatoes or livestock products.[7]

The third major change that is necessary is integration of research and knowledge relating to plantation-associated industry among the plantation economies. This will serve to increase knowledge of production possibilities and to develop new uses of the products and new techniques of processing. We noted in chapter 5 that the current trend of industrial innovation by plantation enterprise is strongly influenced by the nature of existing investments.[8] So too, the interests of plantation economy will dictate the trend of industrial innovation if industrial research programs are integrated. No single plantation economy can afford the necessary investment involved in this research; and industrial research involves significant scale economies. Hence the need for regional economic integration is further strengthened.[9]

The regional groupings may have to include Third World countries other than the plantation economies. To take a concrete example, if Ghana and Nigeria are to capture from metropolitan enterprise the value-added in manufacture of chocolate products they will need to work out an arrangement with

Caribbean countries for supplies of sugar. Leubuscher argued that one of the reasons why manufacture of chocolate products could not take place in Ghana was that Ghana did not have the necessary sugar. We are arguing here that Britain grew neither cocoa nor enough sugar. Yet Britain managed to integrate West Indian sugar production with West African cocoa production to secure the lion's share of value-added in both cases for its own economic development. Third World countries will have to do the same thing to secure the development linkages and benefits for themselves.

Land reform and income redistribution are absolutely essential for development in plantation economy. Again, our analysis in this book indicates that the real dynamic for development resides in the peasant sector, not in the plantation sector. In addition, we indicated that the low incomes of the bulk of people in plantation society limit the size of the market (therefore the potential for some industry) and restricts domestic savings and investment. Consequently, a program involving a redistribution of land and income should contribute immensely to the process of transformation. It must be noted, however, that land reform must include appropriate rural economic institutions to provide credit, technical knowledge, and so forth, and, to be effective, it must be part of a process of radical social change to create an ethos in which attitudes to land ownership will change in a way that contributes to effective use of the land. Most of the attempts at land reform in plantation economy have failed to induce the required development because these have been carried out in piecemeal fashion, without supporting institutional changes and with no change in the social ethos surrounding attitudes to land ownership.[10] In addition we should note that the land to be made available to peasants must be the best quality plantation land and not just the marginal, rocky, and infertile hillside estates and the like, as has been the case with most 'land settlement' schemes previously implemented in several of the plantation economies.[11]

Income redistribution will place a very heavy strain on available food supplies in plantation economy because increased supplies take time before they can be available and because the redistribution will immediately increase the demand for many foodstuffs. The chief bottleneck in this connection will be in the area of livestock products. For animals cannot be grown overnight and the poor people of plantation society have a heavy backlog of pent-up desires for animal protein. In this context, food rationing will be necessary in the short term and medium term in order that available supplies are spread in some reasonable way and so that price inflation can be contained. Cuba has experienced this phenomenon since the redistribution of income and land in that country during the early 1960s, and food rationing is still necessary there.[12]

In order to secure the resource-use adjustments that are necessary for development (for example, switching land use from sugar to livestock production), measures to deal with present distortions in the structure of output prices will be necessary. The analysis in chapter 6 indicated that the price structure is currently distorted to encourage incremental flow of resources into plantation export production. This has to be corrected by lowering the price of exports and raising prices received by farmers for things like livestock products. Guaranteed prices for these products are not enough. Measures must be taken to ensure that adequate marketing facilities become available, and agricultural credit schemes should favour production oriented to the domestic market over that for export. The present tendency of policy makers in plantation economy is to rationalize the present patterns of land use by the consideration that the value of output per acre of land is higher in plantation export output than in alternative products for the domestic market.[13] That argument is irrelevant for at least two reasons: the divergence of private and social returns and the fact that many of the alternative products have the potential for generating more spread effects in the long run than plantation export production. Another fallacy of the policy makers is that metropolitan preferences on plantation products are a subsidy by the metropolitan treasury. In point of fact, plantation economy provides, in return, a guaranteed market for metropolitan manufactures; the result is that the people of plantation society have to pay more for goods like textiles and footwear when imported form the metropole than when imported from third countries (like Japan and Italy). We find, therefore, that the subsidy for plantation export production is really borne by the people of plantation society and weighs heavily on the poorest sections of the society.

In the area of agricultural research as well, measures are needed to reorient expenditure and effort from the present concentration on export crops and towards the needs of production for the domestic and regional markets. This reorientation is likely to bring higher returns to investment in agricultural knowledge than now obtain with the excess concentration on export crops. Much of the present agricultural research in plantation economy is financed by the plantations themselves. So that when national ownership is secured, it would not be difficult to tax the export production to provide the funds necessary for research into problems related to production for the home markets. Associated with the research question is the problem of agricultural extension to take the new knowledge out to farmers. Again, for this to succeed we need appropriate institutional arrangements and a hospitable social ethos.

The necessary restructuring of economic institutions to promote economic development is very elaborate and only sketches can be provided now. The foreign-owned commercial banks need to be nationalized so as to make the savings of people in plantation economy available for investment there. Informal credit institutions, like *partner* or *sou-sou*, need to be legitimized and expanded so as to make small savings available for investment in development projects. Regional development banks must be set up in order to provide financing for regional projects, such as industrial and agricultural research. Marketing organizations will be necessary to stimulate the flow of products and to manipulate the price structure to advantage, also to regulate the continuing export trade. Shipping councils will be needed to acquire ships, regulate the export and regional trade, and develop the fishing industry, which has significant potential spread effects. Research institutes are needed to undertake both agricultural and industrial research. Publicly owned communications media will be necessary to keep people continuously informed of developments in the society, the region, and the world, so as to foster and maintain a high level of development motivation and involvement; to transport produce within the nation and the region; and to influence the daily lives of people in important ways. An educational system directed to every individual in plantation society is essential, and the content of education must be such as to expand the creative horizons of people in order to promote greater use of the resource endowment of plantation economy. These are only a sample of the kind of institutional adjustments that will be necessary. There are many more which may be of equal importance but what we have listed is sufficient to provide general indication of the magnitude of the adjustment problem.

It is very clear, from the ideas outlined above, that the process of transformation envisaged here will be very painful (food rationing and international violence are only two of the obvious areas of pain). It will also demand great sacrifices by the people of plantation society in the short term and the medium term. As well, it will require a new social ethos to bring this kind of change about. And it is obvious that a considerable degree of government intervention is necessary. We can respond to these observations only by noting that without these changes plantation economy can never achieve the kind of economic development that metropolitan economy has achieved. Economic development is a painful business, regardless of the development path, because development involves change and social change is never without pain. The majority of people in plantation society for a long time have been on the receiving end of international violence – slavery was the greatest manifestation of this and dispossession after Emancipation was only a milder form. The majority of people in plantation society, throughout their history, have been making great sacrifices for which the benefits have accrued to white planters, metropolitan enterprise, and metropolitan economy; consequently, they are accustomed to sacrifice and ought to be willing now to make it on their own behalf.[14] And, finally, we note that government intervention is nothing new to plantation economy; this has always been a feature of the system, but intervention up to now has been chiefly by metropolitan government on their own behalf, while what is involved here is intervention by governments of plantation society on behalf of the people living there.[15]

Economic change alone is not sufficient. Indeed, as we have argued above, many of the economic changes can succeed only if there is a favourable social ethos. We need, therefore, to give some consideration to how the social environment of plantation society can be adjusted in a manner that will facilitate the kinds of economic change envisaged above.

The Politics and Social Dynamics of Transformation and Change

Since the state has a major role to play in plantation economies overcoming development obstacles, we need to consider the politics of transformation. Our analysis in chapter 3 indicated that with the present pattern of social organization and distribution of power, political leaders in plantation society have not been able to manipulate state power sufficiently on behalf of the majority of people. It follows, therefore, that what is required is a fundamental change in social organization and new political leaders emerging from the rank and file of the dispossessed groups. We should note that the redistribution of land and income will alter the structure of power. The power of the state, and of the previously dispossessed, increases while that of the previous plantation owners declines. Plantation owners are therefore unlikely to take kindly to this kind of change. Presumably many will leave, as happened in Cuba, and those who remain will no doubt attempt to undermine attempts to make the change effective with respect to development but they can be contained by the majority and some will doubtless adjust to the new situation as time goes on.

The social reorganization that is required by the kind of economic change we have outlined must be such as to heal the fractures inherent in the plantation system – fractures that appear covertly in the supply of and demand for resources, particularly land, and fractures that show up more starkly in social relationships between groups in the society. The healing of these fractures will serve to integrate plantation society and to make the social and political obstacles to development less formidable. This process of social integration can best be institutionalized by linking it with the single institution that now binds all segments of the society together – that is, the plantation itself. The inference we draw from this is that ownership, control, and production of the plantations must be shared equally among all the pluralities that make up the particular plantation society. Each plurality has an allegiance with the plantation as a result of the historical legacy. And now each must be given an opportunity to share the benefits equally. This will provide the basis for meaningful social integration, for developing social consciousness and responsibility – thereby creating a favourable social ethos – and for integrating resource supply and demand.

This kind of social reorganization must involve several things if it is to heal permanently the social fractures left by the plantation system. Among these, the more important are equality between the races and equality of educational opportunities. For the process of social reorganization to begin, it will be necessary of course to mobilize the society for change. Because of the existing weakness of social cohesion and loose community organization, the problem is immense. The process can begin only with a new style of politics based on a sequencing that, first, mobilizes national consciousness about what is wrong with the present system of social and economic organization and what can be done to correct the resulting injustices; second, to heighten this consciousness and win commitment for making the change; and third, to translate the commitment won into action, this is, of course, all easier said than done.

Given the existing situation, the question naturally arises as to how such a new style of politics can emerge. The answer is that it is in process of emerging already. Two developments have contributed to this. One is that the social and economic injustices of the plantation system have become aggravated in recent years and therefore the forces of self-destruction are gaining an ascendancy through an increasing consciousness among people of the state of chronic dispossession. And the other is that Third World analysts have been producing fresh insights into the structural limitations of the colonial system. Fanon is perhaps the best known of these analysts and he represents a whole army of Third World writers who have made important advances in our understanding of the persistence of material and cultural dispossession among Third World peoples.[16] This understanding has provided the infrastructure for much of the publicist activities of individuals and groups throughout the Third World which has served to broaden and heighten consciousness, and to sow the seeds of commitment among small groups of people everywhere. Black Power is only one example – perhaps the best known – of what is going on already. All that is now required is further analysis to feed the furnaces that already have been lit by previous analysis.

The importance of analysis cannot be overemphasized. Part of the reason why present and past political leaders in plantation society have failed to bring about the necessary social and economic transformation is related to the fact that they have been largely guided by policy advisers whose understanding of the development problems is based on economic models which were developed out of the metropolitan experience and reality and which do not fit the properties of plantation economy. We are impressed by the statement of John Maynard Keynes that

the ideas of economists and political philosophers, both when they are right and when they are wrong, are more powerful than is commonly understood. Indeed the world is ruled by little else. Practical men, who believe themselves to be quite exempt from any intellectual influences, are usually the slaves of some defunct economist.[17]

Keynes was quite correct in this observation. What is being suggested here is that policy advisers in plantation societies today do not realize that Keynes himself is now the 'defunct economist' and that they have badly advised political leaders as a result.[18] We do not wish to make the case that these leaders would indeed accept advice for radical economic change because our analysis in chapter 3 suggests quite the opposite. The case being made here is simply that analysis is a necessary, though not sufficient, condition for the change envisaged.

Another matter related to the dynamics of social change is the political ideology that is needed to mobilize action eventually. All we can say in this connection is that the appropriate ideology will emerge out of the dynamics of change. We can state, in a negative fashion, that the existing political ideologies in the world at large were not derived from the plantation experience. Capitalism, socialism, communism, and all the other known 'isms' developed out of the feudal-capitalist systems of Europe, the settler-homestead-capitalist systems of North America, and the feudal-semi-capitalist systems of Asia and elsewhere. All those various systems of social and economic organization have very different social structures and class systems than plantation society. It might well be, therefore, that political ideologies that relate to those experiences are not adequate for the social and political realities of plantation society. We cannot be entirely sure of this. But it is of some interest to note that in spite of the very high level of material advancement for the nation as a whole, the US has not managed to solve its own plantation problem. In fact, the plantation South of that country has profoundly influenced the social order of the national society by exporting its plantation-based pattern of social organization to other regions. The persistent state of black dispossession, material and social, in that country is the stark manifestation of this fact.

We conclude, therefore, that a new political ideology will be necessary to stimulate social change and action in plantation society. Exactly what this ideology will be like we do not know. What is certain is that is will develop out of the process of change that has already begun; on that account it will be the appropriate ideology for servicing the needs of the new society eventually conceived out of the process.

Notes
_____

*·"Possibilities for change and transformation", chapter 8 of *Persistent Poverty* (1972a; 1988b).

1   D.M. Forrest, *A Hundred Years of Ceylon Tea* (London: 1967), pp. 238-47.

2   This is clearly demonstrated by the recent study by Donald Snodgrass, *Ceylon – An Export Economy in Transition* (Homewood, Illinois: Richard D. Irwin, 1966). Although Snodgrass attempts to show that things are changing (as the title of his book implies) the data and analysis do not support his thesis. For a discussion of some of the ways in which plantations have circumvented government measures, see N. Ramachandran, *Foreign Plantation Investment in Ceylon, 1889-1958* (Colombo: Central Bank of Ceylon, 1963).

3   See, for example, W. Gorter, "Adaptable Capitalists; The Dutch in Indonesia", *Social and Economic Studies* (September 1964).

4   Documentation to support the statements made here is to be found in Dudley Seers et al., *Cuba – The Economic and Social Revolution* (Chapel Hill: University of North Carolina Press, 1964), and the United Nations Economic Commission for Latin America, *Economic Bulletin for Latin America* (July 1964), chapter III, "The Cuban economy".

5   The evidence and the argument in support of this possibility are presented in G. L. Beckford, "A note on agricultural organization and planning in Cuba", *Caribbean Studies* (October 1966): 5-7. It must be noted, however, that heavy reliance on sugar is inevitable in the medium term since diversification can be achieved only in the long run. More information on postrevolution planning and policy problems associated with foreign trade policy is provided by Edward Boorstein, *The Economic Transformation of Cuba* (New York and London, 1968). The question of the relative effects on underdeveloped countries of trade relations between them and metropolitan 'capitalist' vs. 'socialist' economy is explored by Edwin Charles, "The concept of neo-colonialism and its relation to rival economic systems", *Social and Economic Studies* (December 1966), and by Jay R. Mandle, "Neo-imperialism: an essay in definition", *Social and Economic Studies* (September 1967).

6   See in particular Dudley Seers, "The mechanism of an open petroleum economy", *Social and Economic Studies* (June 1964); and Havelock Brewster, "Exports, employment and wages: Trinidad-Tobago" and Seers's "Model of the open economy" *Research Papers* (Central Statistical Office, Trinidad, April 1968).

7   The argument about these concrete possibilities for resource combination and export substitution is made in Norman Girvan, "The Caribbean Bauxite Industry" (Mona, Jamaica: ISER, University of the West Indies, 1967); and G. L. Beckford, "The West Indian Banana Industry" (Mona, Jamaica: University of the West Indies, Jamaica, 1967).

8   An example of this is the Tate and Lyle innovation of "The use of spirally welded stainless steel piping for chemical storage, which is resistant to most liquids, does not rust or pit, and is easily cleaned. Products as diverse as gasoline, methanol, benzene and alkylates can be pumped through the same line." It was the company's existing investments in molasses storage facilities that led to this particular innovation. See *Tate & Lyle Times International* (July 1969): 6-7.

9   Third World economists, particularly those in the Caribbean and Latin America, have already extended our knowledge of the theoretical gains from regional economic integration in the structuralist terms outlined here. An important

example of these contributions is Havelock Brewster and Clive Y. Thomas, *The Dynamics of West Indies Economic Integration* (Kingston, Jamaica: ISER, University of the West Indies, 1967).

10 The literature on land reform in plantation economy reveals considerable confusion about analysing the effects of land reform and the social costs and benefits of land reform programs. See, for example, Ungku Aziz, *Subdivision of Estates in Malaya, 1951-1960*. 3 volumes (Kuala Lumpur: University of Malaya, Department of Economics, 1962); Garyl Ness, "Subdivision of estates in Malaya, 1951-1960 – a methodological critique", *Malayan Economic Review* (April 1964): 55-62; G. David Quirin, "Estate subdivision and economic development – a review article", *Malayan Economic Review* (October 1966).

11 See our discussion of this in chapter 1 above.

12 The Cuban experience in this matter is examined at greater length in George L. Beckford, "A Caribbean view of Cuba", *New World Quarterly* (Croptime 1966). And in several of the references given earlier in this chapter.

13 An example of this kind of theorizing can be found in a recent metropolitan-authored study of the Jamaican sugar industry. See *Report of the Commission of Enquiry into the Jamaican Sugar Industry* (Kingston: Government Printer, 1968).

14 The major new sacrifice will have to be made by the small minority of people in the planter-associated classes. But it is full time that these people make a contribution to their country.

15 Examples of metropolitan government intervention in plantation economy are imperial preference, navigational acts to force shipping in only metropolitan owned bottoms, and so forth.

16 It is not a coincidence that analysis of plantation society has contributed a disproportionately high share of Third World output of scholarship. In addition to Fanon, there is an impressive list of names of outstanding writers born and raised in plantation society – Furtado, Césaire, Garvey, Carmichael, and James are only a small sample of this large class of men. The reason is that in plantation society the injustices are more marked than say, peasant colonial society.

17 J. M. Keynes, *The General Theory of Employment Interest and Money* (London, 1957): p. 383.

18 This is not quite fair to Keynes, for he never addressed himself to the problems of underdevelopment in Third World countries. Keynes was concerned with economic adjustment problems in advanced industrial (metropolitan) economies. His work has in fact been misused by development economists.

Part III

Beyond Economics: Issues of Race, Class and Black Dispossession

19

Social Knowledge and
Social Change in the Caribbean*

Brothers and sisters I want to take a few minutes to talk around the meaning of social knowledge, firstly in a general and global context and then turning from this to a consideration of the specific Caribbean situation.

I take social knowledge to be concerned with understanding man and his environment. Every society must all the time face the task of organizing itself in ways which will provide for its subsistence and continuation. It is also true that every society has within it what can generally be described as social forces which work towards the stabilization of social forms and arrangements. These forces, it should be clearly understood, strive to maintain not merely 'equilibrium' in the narrow sense of the word but constant changes in the techniques which man uses to control his environment.

So then, the balance between man and his environment is effected through the operation of dynamic laws which simultaneously consolidate social needs at the same time as they push for the advancement of these needs and demands. At any given time one finds a dichotomy of social forces with one set working towards the maintenance of the *status quo* while the other set operates to effect changes in the *status quo*. How these forces interact and are perceived as interacting is really at the heart of the whole question of the meaning of social knowledge. I am moving quickly here – covering a lot of ground. But I will elaborate as I go along.

The question of the acquisition of social knowledge goes beyond the role of so-called independent scientific observers who call themselves social scientists. Social knowledge is acquired and understood not merely by the intelligentsia but by all of the groups which comprise a social system. By this I mean simply that all groups develop ideas about how their society works as well as ideas about how their society should work. Of course, this is not to say that one should not distinguish between people like ourselves in this room attending this conference, and people who are not here and not in the University. But this distinction should turn primarily on the fact that we are paid by the society to accumulate social knowledge while others are not. But if social knowledge is to be meaningfully understood and used, one cannot assume that only scientists are involved in its acquisition. On the contrary, one has to see all groups as being observers of social reality. For example, the peasant out on the farm knows much more about the social and natural environment in which his life is located than the extension officer located in the government service. He has to cope every day with the tone of the weather, he knows whether it is going to rain by the formation of the clouds. Over time he builds up knowledge from his various encounters with the problems of everyday life and to a considerable extent his actions are reflections of this knowledge and experience.

Now, our particular concern as social scientists is the attempt to systematically isolate and study the matrix of particular social situations. It is our role to try to identify and isolate those factors within societies which contribute to the maintenance of the status quo, and those factors which work towards its destruction.

Beginning here, it is our job to disaggregate the various groups and class formations which constitute a society. This process of class and group disaggregation is the first and primary task. For to my certain knowledge, there is no such thing as a homogeneous society. Every society consists of particular conglomerations of groups; and as social scientists, it is our task to see how these groups interact – to see how economic, social and political resources are distributed and shared among and between interacting groups.

The social scientist is faced with the problem of observing social reality. However, this is an extremely difficult problem. For it means that as social scientists we have to try to extract ourselves in the effort to try to discern and possibly even predict on-going laws of social motion.

But where should we begin? Where should we begin to look for what I have termed 'laws of motion'? I want to suggest that we have to begin with the ways in which ideas are generated in society. This means that attention has to be focused on the whole problem of the sociology of education. We have to study those institutions which are concerned both with the propagation of received knowledge and the circulation of the new knowledge. This was one of the areas with which Vaughan Lewis dealt in his presentation. But it is a broad and far-reaching area, and all that I want to do at the moment is to re-emphasize how critical it is for us to look on the ways in which a social system produces knowledge – to study what my friend Louis Lindsay has called the 'industries of the mind'. In focusing on the sociology of education we should be concerned essentially with the evolution of ideas and the ways in which this evolution influences peoples' perceptions of their lives and the future of themselves and their societies.

Let us turn now to an examination of some of the ways in which ideas have evolved and concretely manifested themselves. Let us deal specifically with the two main types of social organizations which are currently most dominant. The first type is colonialism – a form of social organization which is roughly three hundred years old. The second type is socialism – a much more recent form of social organization, but one which encompasses a significantly large proportion of the world's population. These two categories – colonialism on the one hand and socialism on the other are to my mind the most important expressions of social activity and social organization in the contemporary world.

On a world scale, socialism is essentially a very recent phenomenon. As a form of social organization, it is perhaps no more than 25 years old. And here, you will see that I am not starting with the Soviet social experience of 1917. You might ask why, and although I do not want us to get diverted into a prolonged debate on this question, I nevertheless want to insist that there are certain essential differences between the Soviet and the Chinese experiments with socialism. Now I am not denying the value and importance of Soviet socialism. All that I want to say is that I regard the Chinese system as being less bureaucratic and more concerned with people. I see it as a form of 'peoples' socialism' – a form which in my estimation, is more advanced than the Soviet model.

But if socialism is a relatively novel form of social organization, the same thing certainly cannot be said about colonialism. Colonialism has been with us for a long time – especially so for Caribbean peoples – for it is here – in these countries – that the process first began. Yet even so, to a large extent, we here in the Caribbean still have not arrived at clear understandings of the precise nature and character of colonialism. And it is in this area, I would argue, that social scientists have most clearly and decisively failed in our responsibilities. For colonialism had its birth in this region; it has also served as the primary mechanism by which our people have been exploited. It has placed our people in a particular kind of socioeconomic situation and yet, social scientists in the Caribbean have still not isolated and grasped the historical bases of colonialism and the mechanisms by which it continues to keep our people poor and dispossessed.

At the heart of colonialism is capitalism and at the heart of capitalism one finds the plantation system. Indeed, the plantation system must properly be seen as a particular manifestation of colonialist and capitalist forms of social organization – a manifestation which requires the most careful study and attention. For the plantation system was one of the first concrete manifestations of capitalism and it continues into the contemporary period as one of the most persistent expressions of the character of capitalist exploitation.

Now, ladies and gentlemen, I want to insist that the plantation system requires special study if for no other reason than that it is the core institution that has led the Caribbean people into a particular form of integration into the international capitalist system. And unless we understand the ways in which the Caribbean people were drawn into this system of capitalist exploitation then we won't understand anything about the process by which we can be liberated from this system.

The plantation system is the first capitalist institution which separated labour from the means of production while at the same time integrating factory-type discipline into the processes of production. Secondly and to my certain knowledge, the plantation system represented the first successful attempt to institutionalize race as a factor of production. Thirdly, the plantation system has particular importance, in that it was the essential instrument which transformed national capitalism and produced what we now know today as the institution of the so-called multi-national corporation. It was the plantation system which planted the seed which gave birth to a whole range of Euro-American economic institutions which have successfully penetrated the social systems of Third World countries in Asia, Africa and Latin America.

I also want to insist that if we are going to fully understand the dynamics of Caribbean social realities we must first understand how the Caribbean, through the plantation system, has traditionally been tied into the international capitalist system, and the particular ramifications which this integration has for our societies. Especially important are the categories of class and racial formations which have emanated from this linkage.

It is only after we have successfully integrated race and class into our analyses that we will be in a position to understand certain features of the contemporary Caribbean situation – features such as the almost total alienation of our peoples – an alienation which has largely been the consequence of the tightness of our integration into the international capitalist order, and the tightness of our integration into this order cannot be separated from the ways in which race and class have kept us divided and isolated.

Alienation among Caribbean social groups varies according to certain criteria of race and class. The general pattern, however, is one in which alienation is greatest among the majority group of black people and its intensity diminishes sharply the further one moves away from blackness through intermediary groups such as the Chinese and towards European elements in our societies. Indeed, the whole question of alienation and its intensification among black people generates a certain pattern of social dynamics which (to put it very crudely) resembles a kind of volcano where a very large mass of black people are trapped into a social system which allows them very few outlets.

What we have, therefore, at this present juncture of history, is a situation in the Caribbean Region in which both the internal and the external structures of our societies are under fire. They are under fire partly because the international capitalist system is under fire and as such cannot effectively handle crises which develop in the peripheral parts of the system. At the same time, we have as well, the influence of the development of new ideas – ideas emanating primarily from the growth and expansion of international socialist systems. The repercussions of the growth of socialism throughout Asia will have the effect of shifting the consciousness of the Caribbean people along certain specific lines. This shift in consciousness will lead to the further acceleration and intensification of the crisis which exists in the metropole; and as this crisis deepens it will have the effect of increasing our confidence in ourselves and our abilities to organize for changes and improvements in our conditions. When these possibilities for organization and development are realized, the situation will inevitably lead to confrontation – confrontation between 'the politics of the status quo', versus what I like to call 'the politics of dread'. This confrontation will unmask the deceptiveness of Westminster politicians – it will show that there is little substance behind rhetorical terms such as 'Cooperative socialism' in Guyana or 'democratic socialism' in Jamaica and so on. Various groups will perform this unmasking but I believe that we can lump all of these groups under the heading of 'the politics of dread'.

'The politics of dread' requires study and elaboration. It should not be ignored merely because it appears to be disorganized and fragmented. The 'politics of dread' has deep roots in our societies – roots which reveal themselves in the music and language of the masses.

I want to conclude with the suggestion that the social realities of the Caribbean at the present time require a complete study and understanding of the contradictions of our past and the ways in which these contradictions are reflected in the confrontations and confusions of the present. This is what social knowledge is all about.

Notes

* "Social knowledge and social change in the Caribbean" in L. Lindsay (ed.), *Methodology and Change: Problems of Applied Social Science Research Techniques in the Commonwealth Caribbean*, ISER (1978a).

20

The Plantation System and the Penetration of International Capitalism*

I am going to use a general approach which really doesn't follow from the type of review that Don Harris and Carl Stone led off with. I am not really interested in looking back on the past, and allocating problems and designs to Caribbean research. Rather than take a Caribbean approach, what I want to do is to take a scientific approach in looking at what we call the Caribbean. We have to be scientific in observing social environments and in studying the general tendencies of Caribbean social realities. So what I want to do is simply to highlight what are the main aspects of Caribbean social demands and pinpoint some of the implications which these realities have for our work.

I start with an observation which is quite obvious: that apart from Cuba the whole Caribbean is fundamentally a part of the international capitalist system. This is the first proposition: that our reality is located within the international capitalist system and has a particular place within that system of social and economic organization. My concern, therefore, is to locate our particular place within the international system, to see the dynamics of our position, and therefore understand the general processes of change within that system. And to do this, unlike Don Harris, we do not start by looking at the contemporary period and then going back in time. We go forward. My comment to go forward is not in defence of any school. I don't recognize any 'plantation school' or any foolishness like that. All I want to do is to look at the social realities of what we call the Caribbean – a system that has emerged along capitalist lines with international cash. And I want to specify Caribbean realities as being simply the 'plantation system'.

When I say plantation system I am not talking about agriculture and planting food, I am talking about the planting of labour, as the critical element. That
the labour of the Caribbean is planted here in a specific way in relation to
capital (and other means of production to which labour is related) is an
obvious fact. What is also obvious is that this labour regime is based on race.
Race is the specific element in the Caribbean reality. That is to say, labour was
organized within the Caribbean environment from the very outset, as an
interlocking part of an international racist system. This labour is not homogeneous in the classical sense of homogeneous; and therefore not deriving
classes in the classical system of Marxist analysis. What I am trying to suggest
is that race is instituted in both the mode of production and the mode of
exchange; and I will elaborate on what I mean in a minute.

When we look at the historical experience of Caribbean society, the most
striking feature about it is the high degree of labour mobility. Of all societies
in the world today – perhaps of all societies in the history of mankind, the
mobility of Caribbean labour is most pronounced.

Let us think for a minute of just about any society in the world. Is there any
other society in which more of the labour components of that society live
outside of the society than within it? The answer is, there is none. Okay.

Now, what I am suggesting therefore is that different groups of people
who provide labour power for capital development in the Caribbean were
located in the system of production along certain racial characteristics. You
therefore have a society in which race is instituted in the process of production
in a specific and particular way. This situation creates certain social dynamics
which are unique to this type of society.

This is the type of theoretical problem that I think we have to begin with. I
agree entirely with Don Harris, that we have to start with a certain political
framework. My point is that this framework must embrace some social
economy. It makes no sense whatsoever to try to analyse Caribbean society in
terms of labour without race. In other words, different types of labour have
different access to the means of production. It is race which determines
whether or not a poor labourer can eventually emerge into a capitalist or
whatever in the Caribbean. Because in the region's development it is race that
determines access to the means of production.

All that was said before my comments could have been said about any
society in the world. As social scientists we have neglected the whole element
of race in our theoretical frameworks. And this neglect weakens all – including the plantation work. We have failed to integrate race with class in the
analysis of Caribbean society. And that, to me, is the challenge that faces us.

We can't get very far in using Marxist theory of analysing Caribbean
society until we introduce and integrate race and class in that theoretical

apparatus. If we cannot make this integration we will be failing in our task to properly understand Caribbean and West Indian society.

The examples of failure to cope with the racial question is not only obvious in the capitalist Caribbean, it is also obvious in Cuba. When you look at Cuba you will see the efforts being made by the Socialist government there to come to grips with the racial problems of Cuban society. But I am suggesting that the racial problem will not be solved even after socialism has been achieved in the larger society unless we understand the ways in which race has been institutionalized in the social process.

To understand the social dynamic of West Indian societies, we must first of all understand how the West Indies is located in the international capitalist system. If we do not understand this, then we cannot understand how our societies operate.

This brings me to a sort of semi-final comment; we don't even recognize in our own work the extent to which racism is instituted in the minds of our people. Most of the studies I have looked at all evade the race question. Very few of the macro studies which I have seen look at race in any kind of analytical way. What I am making here is a plea for the development of a theoretical framework that recognizes Caribbean society as part of the international capitalist system – but as a unique part of that system – that uniqueness having to do with the labour question and the way in which race is instituted in the process of production as well as in the process of international exchange.

Once we have this kind of theoretical framework as a base, this will lead to certain areas of both micro and macro level analyses – areas that will bring us toward better and fuller understanding of the dynamics of change in West Indian society and of the contradictions inherent in this system. And it is only from this understanding that we can begin to come to terms with the whole question of the transition to socialism – a question which seems to be the immediate concern to all of us.

Notes

* "The plantation system and the penetration of international capitalism" in L. Lindsay (ed.), *Methodology and Change: Problems of Applied Social Science Research Techniques in the Commonwealth Caribbean* (1978b).

21

Institutional Foundations
of Resource Underdevelopment
in the Caribbean*

Over the past two decades or so, social scientists (economists in particular) have become increasingly concerned with problems of development in the Third World. This concern is certainly not misplaced because, in my view, poverty in the Third World is the most pressing problem confronting mankind today. However, much of this concern – as expressed in the literature of the social sciences – tends to proceed too rapidly with prescription without adequate attempts at diagnosis. In other words, possibilities for development are usually advanced without prior analysis of the *causes* of underdevelopment. In considering the subject of Caribbean resource development, it seems appropriate, therefore, for me to concentrate attention on some of the underlying factors that contribute to persistent resource *under*development in the Caribbean. I use the word persistent quite deliberately because I am of the view that underdevelopment is itself a dynamic process rather than a static condition as normally assumed.[1] In other words there are factors which inhere in the institutional environment in certain poor countries which contribute to persistent underdevelopment. My own recent work indicates that this is certainly the case for plantation economies and societies, such as those of the Caribbean.[2]

In this paper, I wish to proceed from some general considerations about resources and their development to examine the social foundations and the political economy of resource underdevelopment in the Caribbean, with special reference to agriculture. Next, I consider non-agricultural resource exploitation in this historical perspective. Finally, I shall summarize the situation as revealed by the more intensive study to which I have referred.

Resources and Their Development – Some General Considerations

I think that it is necessary at the very outset for us to make the distinction between the human resources of a society and all other resources, which together we may describe as non-human resources. The development of any society's resources depend ultimately on the human resources – people. Without people, whatever non-human resources that exist have little or no significance. People are important to resources development in at least two fundamental respects: they create a demand for goods and services into which resources are transformed and, secondly, people provide the labour and management services which complement other resources in the production of goods and services.

The total output of goods and services produced in any economy during any accounting period is determined by the quantity and quality of resources and by the technology of production. Output can be increased by increasing the quantity of resource inputs, or by improving the quality of these inputs, or by changes in technology that raise the productivity of existing inputs, or by any combination of these. Let us, therefore, briefly consider what factors influence these variables.

When we speak of human resources in a productive sense, reference is usually to the labour force. The quantity of labour available is determined largely by the size and composition of a country's population and by labour force participation rates. The quality of labour depends primarily on the motivation of people in the first instance and on their training and skills in the second.

The non-human resources of any society consists of natural resources such as land, minerals, forests, water, climate; and manmade resources such as machinery, plants and equipment and buildings. Technology is an important determinant of both the quantity and quality of all non-human resources. The process of production involves using up these resources, thus contributing to their depletion but the process of depletion itself stimulates technological change of a kind that contributes to accretion. Contrary to popular belief, the natural resources of any country are not fixed by nature. In economic terms, the natural resource base can be expanded over time through the discovery of previously unknown resources and/or through technological improvements that make it feasible to use previously known but unused resources. The ultimate balance between the rates of accretion and depletion depends on a complex interplay of technical and economic factors.

The availability of resources is only one aspect of the problem of development. Another important aspect of the matter is how a society uses what resources are available to it. Unused or underutilized resources do not contribute much to the production of goods and services which are demanded by people. By and large, resource shortage is not a critical problem in the underdeveloped countries of the world today. What is more important is that available resources are not utilized in a manner that maximizes returns to the people of those countries. This results largely from resource immobility. Optimum resource development can only be achieved where the supply of resource services is flexibly adjusted to the demand for their use.

As I indicated earlier, the human element is critical in resource development. Quite apart from the labour services supplied by people, there is the management function which determines the marriage of resources and their subsequent transformation into goods and services. It follows therefore that the pattern of resource development will depend to a large extent on the degree to which resource services are made available to those people in the society who have the capacity to utilize them.

In so far as this flow of resources to their best users is impeded, the result is resource underutilization and underdevelopment for the society as a whole.

In every society, the human element, the availability of resources, the degree of resource mobility and all other factors influencing the pattern of resource development are fundamentally a reflection of the particular social environment which is itself shaped by historical forces. In the particular case of the Caribbean, I wish to offer the thesis that the major factors contributing to resource underdevelopment throughout the region inhere in the social and economic legacy created by the plantation system.

Social Foundations of Resource Underdevelopment in the Caribbean

European colonization of the Caribbean began in the late fifteenth century with the so-called 'Great Discoveries'. Unlike highland America, the Caribbean lowlands were not well endowed with precious metals and were sparsely populated by indigenous Indians engaged in shifting agriculture. The invading European nations regarded the region as most suitable for staple production. But very soon they were confronted with a problem of

securing adequate supplies of labour to service this production. The indigenous Indians, on whom force was applied, were very quickly killed off
because they could not withstand the new diseases which Europeans brought
with them. Nor were the Indians accustomed to the cultural and social
demands of a settled agriculture.

In the end, adequate supplies of labour were found by the capture of black
people in Africa, by their transfer under the most inhumane conditions across
the Middle Passage, and by a brutal system of slavery which forced those who
survived to work on European-owned plantations without remuneration and
under continuous threat of death.

Eventually, the slave plantation system engrossed all that territory of
lowland America that stretches from Virginia in the North, down through all
the islands of the Caribbean, into the Guianas, and down to Bahia in the
South. That whole region – what might be described as the Greater Caribbean
– displays a cultural continuum that is associated with the dominance of black
people and their heritage developed within the framework of the plantation
system. Indeed, the cultural anthropologist Wagley has described this whole
region as 'Plantation America'. I prefer to use the label 'Afro-America'.[3] In
geographic terms, the Caribbean occupies the centre-stage of Afro-America
and in social and economic terms it has been described as the *locus classicus* of
the plantation system.

I have so far made frequent reference to the plantation system without
defining it specifically. When I use the term I refer to the totality of institutional arrangements surrounding the production and marketing of the plantation staple. Within plantation society itself these arrangements derive their
flavour from the unit of productions – the plantation. So let us examine the
properties of the plantation as it developed in the Caribbean and elsewhere in
Afro-America.

The plantation is one of a type of settlement institutions which brings
labour capital and enterprise from elsewhere and establishes production in
some new territory with relatively 'open' resources. Because the resource
situation is open, compulsion and coercion become necessary in order to
control the labour supply which otherwise would be induced to establish
their own means of subsistence – land being a virtually free good. In consequence the slave plantations of the New World had the characteristics of what
Goffman has described as 'total institutions'.

R.T. Smith in the original application of the concept of the 'total institutions' to plantation society describes it as "a bureaucratically organized
system in which whole blocks of people are treated as units and marched
through a set of regimentation under the surveillance of the small supervisory
staff."[4]

More precisely:

'total institutions' are organized groups with well-defined boundaries and with a marked internal hierarchical structure approaching an internal caste system. Examples would be asylum inmates and staff, prisoners and wardens, officers and men on board a ship at sea, slaves and masters . . . It is characteristic of total institutions that people enter them as already socially formed human beings with a culture and a set of attitudes which need to be reformed so that the inmate can be handled as a lunatic, a monk, a prisoner, a slave, or whatever it might be. Mechanisms are brought into play designed to effect a clean break with the past and a destruction of the inmate's old self so that a new set of attitudes, a new identity – can be imposed.[5]

I want to suggest that since the slave era, right up to the present time, the black experience in the New World has been a continuous process of acculturation and socialization to the norms of the plantation system. The social structure of the slave plantation took shape from the social organization necessary for production. White European planters and administrators stood at the top and were separated by a system of caste which placed the black slaves firmly at the bottom. An intermediate group of skilled white people also existed and among the black people there emerged a group of racial and cultural half-castes resulting from the exploits of white males and black females. This group was generally more privileged than the pure blacks and frequently made up the staff of house servants whose tasks were less arduous than those of other black people.

Slave plantation society as a whole was simply made up of plantation communities and, as Smith has suggested, one may say that this is a segmentary society with the plantations constituting a simple linear series of segments having little or no organic interrelation. This society as a whole was therefore rigidly stratified by race and colour directly correlated with occupational status on the plantation, with very limited social mobility. This general pattern of social organization continues to exist in the Caribbean and, as I shall later indicate, contributes significantly to the persistent state of resource underdevelopment.

On the slave plantation itself all power and authority were vested in the planter whose *primum mobile* was production of the staple for profit. This dictated the pattern of resource use; so, as the plantation system spread throughout the Caribbean, the plantations came to engross most of the flat, fertile and arable lands and sugar became 'king'. Whenever the labour power of the slaves was not needed in the service of 'King Sugar', the slaves were allowed to grow their own subsistence crops in the mountainous backlands of the plantation.

Emancipation of the slaves came toward the middle of the nineteenth century, but this hardly changed the picture. The reason for this is that plantations managed to maintain their stranglehold over the basic means of production – the land. The ex-slaves wanted to secure an existence as independent of the plantations as possible but this was difficult in most places. In some of the smaller islands, like Antigua, St Kitts and Barbados, the plantations had already engrossed virtually all the land. So the ex-slaves there had little choice but continued plantation work for wages. However, in the larger islands, some of the mountainous interior was available for capture and the ex-slaves used these rocky and fertile backlands to develop peasant production of a kind that has served to transform those economies in the Caribbean.

Wherever land was still available for settlement after Emancipation, the plantations had great difficulty in securing the labour services of the ex-slaves and the plantation owners introduced all kinds of measures to forcibly secure their services. Eventually, they had to resort to the importation of new labour supplies under a system of semi-slavery, which is described as indenture. Thus, large numbers of East Indians were brought over in the service of 'King Sugar' and today East Indians account for a significant share of the population in Trinidad and Guyana, which were the newest plantation colonies in the region.

A number of important consequences flow out of this general setting. The first is that the plantation system is the source of a great deal of resource immobility because of its monopoly of land. The second is that the particular system of social organization, based on caste, race and colour, inhibits social mobility and dehumanizes the bulk of the population to such an extent that it diminishes the level of motivation. A third consideration is that the pattern of resource utilization is hardly related to the needs of plantation society but is geared to the requirements of metropolitan society with obviously different needs. A fourth is that monopoly of land by plantations as a means to secure labour supplies leads to gross underutilization of labour. So we find throughout the Caribbean today the very curious phenomenon of under-consumption by the majority of the population existing alongside gross resource underutilization.

There are several other aspects of the plantation system which contribute to persistent resource underdevelopment, but which we cannot explore in the limited space available here. Let me therefore simply offer some conclusions which I have derived in the more intensive study I referred to earlier.

On the whole, the plantation has a demoralizing influence on plantation community. It destroys or discourages the institution of the family and so undermines the entire social fabric. It engenders an ethos of dependence and patronage and so deprives people of dignity, security and self-respect. It impedes the material, social and spiritual advance of the majority of people. In these circumstances, I want to suggest that we could hardly expect to find a highly motivated population displaying the kinds of characteristics that development demands. The energies of most people in plantation society are spent trying to beat the system in one way or the other. Within plantation society itself, the traditions, values, beliefs and attitudes which have become established as a result of long periods of plantation influence are, for the most part, inimical to resource development. To mention a few, we can identify paternalism, anti-technologism and general attitudes to life and work as contributing to the persistence of resource underdevelopment.

In the field of education, too, the plantation system induces underdevelopment biases. Restrictions on the availability of education and its limited technical content contribute to an underutilization of the human resource potential of plantation society. Within the system, knowledge which is acquired and disseminated is generally related to the requirements of plantation production. Thus a considerable fund of technical knowledge relating to a particular crop is accumulated and very little is known of technical possibilities relating other crops. In consequence, resources cannot really be deployed in any optimal fashion. More generally, education is rationed among groups within plantation society. Initially, slave population society provided no education for slaves; the children of plantation owners and managers were, and still are, for the most part, schooled in the metropole. Subsequently, the educational system that developed was some variant of that existing in the metropole and a limited kind of education became available, chiefly for the half-castes in plantation society.

Free primary schooling for everyone has never been realized, although in recent years governments have attempted to move in this direction. Secondary schooling is highly selective with criteria based heavily on the social status of individuals. A university education was, until quite recently, nonexistent. For the most part what education became available was irrelevant to the environment and to the needs of a dynamic society. Geared as it has been to the immediate needs of the plantation system, the content of education is heavily weighted to the supply of administrative or clerical skills with little or no emphasis on technical and managerial skills. Since management decisions are made in the metropole there is little need for qualified managers in plantation economy and since allied engineering activities are located in the metropole as well, there is little or no demand for highly skilled technicians.

In the circumstances, the system produces an army of clerks from among those fortunate enough to secure an education. Medicine and law are the only two professions that win favour in the process; for everyone in plantation society places a high premium on physical survival and numerous legal issues arise in a conflict-centred society with a high premium on land ownership. On the whole, the educational system of plantation society is technologically backward and contributes to the persistence of underdevelopment.

The Political Economy of Resource Underdevelopment in Caribbean Agriculture

Let me turn now to consider the position in relation to the contemporary Caribbean. First, we need to recognize that since Emancipation the major innovations in resource development within agriculture have come from the peasants. Outside of agriculture metropolitan investment has been the main dynamic since the Second World War. This section deals specifically with agriculture while the next section looks at the pattern outside agriculture. By and large, the plantations throughout the region have simply continued to grow and export sugar and whatever technological adjustments they have made in the process have stemmed largely from outside stimuli, such as competition from other sugar-producing countries. On the other hand, peasants of the region have introduced new export crops, have expanded food production for consumption in the region and have brought vast areas of previously inaccessible land into productive use. This they managed to accomplish with very limited resources, primarily their own labour and that of their families.

Incidentally, one of the reasons why I think the contribution of the peasantry to Caribbean development has been ignored is that the economists have really failed in the task of concentrating attention on areas of greatest investment throughout the Caribbean region. As I indicated earlier, the whole business of the plantation system introduced such limited social mobility that one of the few areas in which Caribbean people could gain mobility in the system was through education. And I find it absolutely scandalous that we economists in the Caribbean have never tried to study the level of investments that peasants have made in the education of their children. I suspect that if and when we carry out this exercise we will discover that the level of savings and investment among the peasant sector of black people in the Caribbean has been several times greater than the financial capital mobilized by the foreign commercial banks. That is a speculation but it is one which I feel will be borne out.

The most important fact of life on the contemporary rural scene in the Caribbean is the persistent peasant-plantation conflict in relation to resources available for agricultural and rural development. As I indicated earlier, peasant production in the West Indies from the very outset had to compete directly with previously established plantation production for very scarce resources of land and labour.

In what follows, I want briefly to review the Jamaican experience, to illustrate that the present day situation still reflects a struggle by the peasantry to break through an institutional environment that is biased towards stagnation. The Jamaican experience is by no means the worst experience in terms of the peasant-plantation conflict because Jamaica had reasonable supplies of land after Emancipation. Inaccessible, mountainous and hilly, but some land was there. In the one hundred and thirty odd years since Emancipation, the Jamaican peasantry has not managed to secure very much of the country's agricultural land and other resources. And what little they have achieved can hardly be maintained in the face of continuing stiff competition from the plantations. In spite of attempts by various governments to provide assistance to the peasants in recent decades, incremental agricultural resources tend to flow toward the plantation sector and the peasantry increasingly have been forced to seek possibilities for advancement through migration and/or wage work on the plantation. Thus the situation has reverted to very much the same pattern that existed just after Emancipation.

The present distribution of land in farms in Jamaica shows a very unequal pattern. Farms under five acres in size, which constitute the bulk of the peasantry, are 71% of all farms in the country, but together they occupy only 12% of total farm acreage. On the other hand, plantations are less than 1% of all farms, yet these occupy 56% of total farm acreage. When account is taken of differences in the quality of the land, the pattern is even more grossly unequal. Ann Norton and George Cumper in a recent exercise, found a distinct correlation between the census-revealed occupancy pattern of plantations with the geological boundary of the alluvial deposits and of peasant farms with the lower and less precipitous hills, slopes and accessible river valleys.[6] This situation exists in spite of relatively intensive attempts by government to assist the settlement of peasants.

The impact of government land settlement schemes, which began around the turn of the century and were intensified after the Second World War, has been limited partly because land which became available for settlement was what plantations no longer required for their own use or what was mountainous Crown land, previously in forests. Usually, it was the least viable plantations which sold out to government and their limited viability was not unrelated to the poor quality of the land. Redwood, for example, has calculated that of all the land settlements acquired by government between 1929 and 1949 in Jamaica, only 4% were of the most fertile soil type.[7] In addition, the politics of settlement dictated that each property acquired by government be divided between as many people (votes) as possible. Thus, we find that at least half of these holdings are less than 4 acres. Given the poor quality of the land, farmers can hardly make a living on these small holdings and are forced to seek outside work. It has been "estimated that 13% of the settlers under these schemes supplement their income by seasonal work and as many as 24% in regular part-time work".[8]

The position of the peasants in respect of land has varied over time in accordance with changes in the fortune of the main plantation crop – sugar – and with changes in the demographic picture.

In the early decades after Emancipation when more land was available, peasant population movement was distinctly from the plantation lowlands to the mountainous backlands. More recently, it appears that this trend has been reversed. In a 1954 study of one of the major plantation parishes in Jamaica, George Cumper discovered "a considerable local migration from the peasant areas . . . into the cane lands", which he attributed to two factors: the rationalization of the sugar industry and its rising fortune since 1938 and inability of infertile mountain areas to absorb an expanding peasant population.[9] In a more recent survey of land and population in the sugar belt of Jamaica, Alan Eyre noted that:

There are . . . populous centres which are entirely rural. These are associated with zones of small-scale subsistence farming on the periphery of the cane zone. The important fact about these centres is that while their 'subsistence' area has decreased or remained static, the population has in many cases more than doubled . . . Some of these peripheral centres have so increased in population that there is not the slightest possibility that without massive depopulation they can ever again be considered basically villages of subsistence farmers . . . It is quite clear that the nature of these erstwhile 'subsistence' districts has changed rapidly as they become increasingly hemmed in by expanding capitalized large-scale monoculture.[10]

Thus it appears that opportunities for peasant production have become increasingly restricted with the expansion of plantations on the one hand and population growth on the other. The development of the peasantry will remain constrained so long as plantations remain entrenched on the best available lands.

Peasant development is further constrained by the influence of plantations on resources other than land. For example, in the case of labour a shortage of land within the peasant sector restricts the use of peasant family labour in own-account production and with expanding population on a limited land base, the tendency has been towards smaller farm sizes in the peasant sector. Peasant farms are therefore increasingly incapable of full utilization of available peasant labour and of providing sufficient income to sustain their families. In the labour market as a whole, plantations have a distinct advantage as well. The reasons for this are: (1) the more advanced techniques of plantations resulting in higher labour productivity, making possible the paying of higher wage rates; (2) employer-employee relations are more impersonal on plantations than on small farms; and (3) the plantations provide steadier employment than the individual small farm. As a result of these considerations, peasants have great difficulty attracting hired labour.

The same situation, in terms of comparative resource availability, applies as well to capital and credit. Again, we find the dominating influence of the plantation and a tendency for a continuous flow of incremental financial capital resources into the plantation sector at the expense of the peasant sector. The metropolitan-based branch banking system was developed to service plantation production and the associated import-export trade. At most times, therefore, plantations have been able to secure sufficient credit for whatever capital expansion they contemplated. In addition, foreign-owned enterprises could always draw on the resources of metropolitan parent companies. Peasant producers, by contrast, have had very little access to outside financial capital and had to rely almost exclusively on their own limited savings and personal loans from friends and/or relatives. Even when, in more recent times, governments have attempted to provide credit assistance, this was either insufficient or made too heavy demands on the peasants.

Similarly, in the area of knowledge and technology, the plantation system has largely determined the existing fund of knowledge and related technology in agriculture. Both the plantations and government have invested significantly in research on export crop production whereas little effort has been directed to peasant crops. David Edwards has revealed that the volume of research effort directed to the problems of sugar cane and bananas in Jamaica was substantially greater than the average for all other products combined.[11] Whereas plantations have the resources to invest in agricultural research, individual peasants do not, and have to rely on the output of government and, more recently, university research. But, because of the importance of export crops in Caribbean economies and what I call the 'plantation psychology' of government officials, very little government research expenditure has been channeled into crops grown chiefly by the peasants.

In addition to this influence on peasant resource availability, the plantation system also affects certain policy and institutional arrangements which serve further to impede the development of the peasantry. In the area of marketing and prices, for example, we find that because of the plantation legacy, the infrastructure for processing and distribution of export crops is highly developed while that for domestic output is not. Again, most of the export crops have guaranteed metropolitan markets while peasant production for the domestic market is forced to compete with cheap food imports from countries where farmers are subsidized. It is hardly surprising, therefore, that even the peasants themselves participate significantly in export crop production; and in so doing are brought into further dependence on plantation activity. Peasant production of sugar cane, for example, depends on the processing facilities provided by plantations.

The general picture of peasant-plantation conflict and the dominating influence of plantations on peasant welfare described above for Jamaica is more or less representative of the pattern in the West Indies as a whole with only minor variations on the theme. The conclusion that emerges is that peasant development in the West Indies is constrained by the institutional legacy of the plantation system and so long as agricultural resources of the region remain scarce, as they have been in the past, peasants are unlikely to secure a sufficient base for the expansion of production and advancement of their levels of living.

Non-Agricultural Resource Exploitation: A 'Ratooning' of the Plantation System

During the twentieth century, and particularly since the Second World War, the exploitation of non-agricultural resources in the Caribbean has been intensified. Minerals such as bauxite and petroleum, tourism, and to a much lesser extent forestry have been the chief areas of activity. (Fishing has not yet been developed on any significant scale.) These resource based industries have emerged as new poles of economic development in several territories; the dominance of the agricultural sector in a number of countries has declined considerably as a result.

However, when we examine the nature of these new operations carefully it seems that for the most part these developments outside of agriculture have served to perpetuate the system of economic and social organization created by earlier plantation system. In several territories, postwar developments outside of agriculture have included mining in the areas of bauxite and petroleum, manufacturing in several of the territories, the holiday industry or tourism in many places, and so on. On every occasion, in all of these areas of productive activity, resource development has been left largely to the initiative of North Atlantic interests – the US and Canada, in particular. What this has created is what my colleague, Lloyd Best, has described as a 'ratooning' of the plantation system. What are the factors which lead us to conclude that this is indeed what has happened in other areas of resource development outside agriculture.

Let us go back for a minute and look at three of the significant features of the original slave plantation economy. The first is that it is structurally a part of an overseas economy, in the sense that it is not an economy in itself, but is hinged to a metropolitan economy somewhere overseas in the North Atlantic. Secondly, we find within the original slave plantation economy what I have described earlier as a total institution in both social and economic terms. In economic terms in the sense that the slave plantation provisioned itself for all its requirements. Its links with the planters in the metropolis in England provided it with the provisioning for the plantation whether it was fencing, nails or what-have-you. It was simply an accounting between the merchant in England and the planter in the West Indies, whereby each year or at the end of each accounting period the books were balanced. So there was a limited flow of funds to the Caribbean in the process of this production. The planter's funds, apart from what was needed for great house living in the West Indies, was deposited in the banks in London. So we had a situation in which the institution – the plantation – was a total entity in itself, supplying all its needs and taking care of the disposal of its output. The third feature, which is related to the first two, is what Lloyd Best has described as incalculability, that is to say that there are no prices within the system. Since goods are being transferred to the metropole and goods are being transferred by the merchant attached to the planter to the plantation, then there is no trading as such. All the prices are bookkeeping prices, so it is difficult to calculate what benefits accrue from this kind of production within the region.

Now looking at these three conditions of the original slave plantation situation and moving to the present day situation of mining, tourism, manufacturing and so on, we find basically the same characteristics, where the production in the Caribbean is first structurally a part of overseas economy: where, secondly, the Caribbean activity in these enterprises is part of a total institution: and thirdly, the incalculability aspect of the transfer of goods. So we find, for example, Alcan or Reynolds or Kaiser or any of these bauxite companies, or the petroleum companies, or the manufacturing companies, or the tourist companies operating within the Caribbean today satisfy all the characteristics of the original slave plantation. For example, bauxite is not traded at all; there is no market for bauxite; there is no price for bauxite. Nobody in the Caribbean knows what the price of bauxite is, because it is not traded. It is transferred within companies, so that Kaiser bauxite leaves the West Indies, goes to Kaiser smelters in North America and the same thing happens with Alcan. These firms turn the bauxite into aluminum and sell it as such. The same thing happens with the reverse flow of caustic soda for use in alumina production. So there we have the same thing as the old plantation, total institutions and incalculability.

In addition to these structural economic characteristics, there are the social aspects. It is important to note that the new initiative for resource development in the Caribbean in the postwar period, emanating as it does from the North Atlantic, has tended to increase the hegemony of the small white planter class over the mass of the black people in the Caribbean. So you find again the tourist companies, the mining companies, the manufacturing companies supplying their own personnel from the North Atlantic, white people in decision-making positions within Caribbean economy, and thereby shoring up the old plantation system of race and colour and caste stratification within the society.

So what do we have when we add up the agricultural pattern with the pattern in other resource industries, such as mining and the holiday industry? The pattern in all the non-agricultural resource industries which have been expanded since the Second World War is pretty much the same as existed within the old plantation system. So we can conclude that the basic social framework of Caribbean economy and society is one that still reflects the structural properties of the plantation system. This fundamental observation provides the most important clue for analysing the persistence of underdevelopment in the region.

The Major Obstacles to Development: A Summary View[12]

In a very fundamental way, underdevelopment in the Caribbean stems from the structural properties of the economy and society. These properties have been fashioned by the plantation system which has left a legacy of economic social and political institutions that function in such a way as to perpetuate underdevelopment.

Elsewhere Norman Girvan has elaborated on the way in which the participation of multinational corporations in mineral exploitation contribute to underdevelopment.[13] So here I wish to concentrate on the effects of the overall legacy left by the plantation system as a whole, but with special reference to agriculture.

The major development obstacles in the Caribbean (and in plantation society and economy generally) derive from the plantation system itself. The structure of the system is such that many of the proximate economic, social and political variables that contribute to development do not come into effective play. Here I want to list the major economic obstacles that contribute to resource underdevelopment and that derive directly from the plantation influence:

1   A fracturing of resource supply and demand. For example, in the specific case of land, the land tends to be monopolized by the plantations whereas the demand for the *use* of land tends to be on the side of

the peasants. Likewise, the bulk of the labour supplies tends to be within the peasant sector; demands for the use of labour, because of the availability of land, is in the plantation sector. There is little freedom of movement for adjustment of resource supply and demand within the economy.

2   The inequality in the distribution of wealth and income that is characteristic of the plantation system.

3   Foreign ownership of producing units that drains the supply of investible funds from the income stream.

4   The export orientation of plantation production that results in an accumulation of backwash effects from terms of trade adjustments.

5   The low skill content of plantation work that inhibits the diffusion of skills and improvement in the quality of labour inputs.

6   Resource use distortions that prevent the flexible deployment of resource services to high income producing opportunities. This relates to what I said earlier about production being geared to the needs of the metropolitan economy and not to the needs of plantation economy. So you will find the curious phenomenon of the Caribbean producing and continuing to produce sugar for which the demand is expanding very slowly and importing all kinds of high value commodities from the rest of the world.

7   The canalization of linkages and associated development potential by metropolitan plantation enterprise. In other words, plantation activity itself generates quite a bit of linkages but by and large these tend to be canalized by the foreign-owned metropolitan enterprises. For example, a firm like Tate and Lyle is engaged in sugar production in the West Indies and, as a result of their engagement in sugar cane production, they have raw sugar manufacture, shipping, wharfage, insurance, sugar refining, etc, so that the spread effects of the plantation activity accrues to the firm rather than to the economy.

8   The multinational character of investment allocation by metropolitan enterprise that further reduces the flow of investible funds. Here again a simple example is the Tate and Lyle plantation situation where, because Tate and Lyle is operating in Jamaica, Trinidad, Belize and elsewhere what surpluses are generated in sugar production in Jamaica are not necessarily available to the Jamaican economy for investment there, but can be invested in Belize, Trinidad, etc.

9   The limited technical knowledge of production possibilities, apart from the particular plantation crop, which results from the excessive

concentration of research by company plantations and which prevents a rational pattern of agricultural development.

Turning now to the social and political obstacles to development in the Caribbean and in other plantation societies, again we find obstacles which are directly attributable to the influence of the plantation system:

1   The weak community structure and loose family organization associated with plantation activity prevents the emergence of viable local and regional units of administration and control; thereby making it difficult to raise local taxes and to execute local development projects.

2   The rigid social structure that is characteristic of Caribbean society which inhibits factor mobility. As I indicated earlier in discussing general considerations about resource development, factor mobility is important if we are to develop a pattern of optimal resource use.

3   The strong correlation between race and class that creates a caste system and generates social tension and instability; a situation which M. G. Smith, in his plural society studies, has described as a situation 'pregnant with conflict'.

4   A general absence of social responsibility that results in poorly developed educational systems.

5   A strong sense of government administration with a generally undemocratic political structure that discourages effective popular participation in the development process.

6   Excessive power of the planter and associated classes that is exercised more in the interest of the small dominant class than in that of the society as a whole.

7   The low incidence of progress-oriented values among all the people of plantation society which derives from the strong element of tradition among the planter class and the general hostility toward intellectualism which is essential for innovation and change.

8   A strong individualism that contributes more to clashes of interests in interpersonal relations than to cooperative activity.

9   An exploitative, authoritarian tradition that prevents cooperative decision making and associative productive effort.

10 Pervasive value orientations that reflect aspirations to a great house life style with the characteristic high propensities to consume imported luxuries and to invest in non-productive assets.

For the most part, the obstacles to development which I have just listed have not been recognized by economists and policy makers in plantation society. The only two perhaps which have received significant attention to date are the foreign ownership problem and the associated drain of investible funds and the unequal distribution of land within the economy.

On the whole, human resource development within the Caribbean is constrained by two major factors which prevent the emergence of a highly motivated population. They are, first, that the plantation system denies the majority of the people a real stake in their country; and second, that the system creates a legacy of dependence because the locus of decision making concerning fundamental economic issues resides outside the society resulting in a chronic dependency syndrome among the whole population.

It is difficult to avoid the conclusion that the plantation system must be destroyed if the Caribbean is to be shifted on to a development path which generates significant benefits for *all* the peoples of the region. How that can be achieved is outside the scope of the present exercise.

Notes

* "Institutional foundations of resource underdevelopment in the Caribbean". *The Review of Black Political Economy* (1971b); reprinted in *Resource Development in the Caribbean* (1972).

1   It is implicit in the writings of economists that countries remain in a static state of underdevelopment until some stimulus initiates a dynamic process of development.

2   See my forthcoming book *Plantations and Poverty in the Third World* (New York: Oxford University Press, 1971) [published as *Persistent Poverty* (1972)].

3   See Charles Wagley, "Plantation America: a culture sphere" in *Caribbean Studies – A Symposium*, edited by Vera Rubin (Mona, Jamaica: ISER, University of the West Indies, 1957). In identifying culture spheres in the New World, Wagley identified as well 'Indo-America' (corresponding geographically with Highland America) with its concentration of Indian population, and 'Euro-America' where white people predominate. It seems logical therefore to label what he describes as 'Plantation America' in terms of the predominance of black people.

4   R. T. Smith, "Social stratification, cultural pluralism, and integration in West Indian societies", in *Caribbean Integration*, edited by S. Lewis and T. G. Mathews (Rio Piedras, Puerto Rico: Institute of Caribbean Studies, University of Puerto Rico, 1967).

5   Smith, p. 230.

6   A. V. Norton and G. E. Cumper, "Peasant, plantation and urban communities in Jamaica", *Social and Economic Studies* (December 1966).

7   Paul Redwood, "A statistical survey of land settlements in Jamaica 1929-1949" (Kingston, Jamaica: Ministry of Agriculture, n. d.) Mimeo.

8   H. Brewster and C. Y. Thomas, *The Dynamics of West Indian Economic Integration* (Mona, Jamaica: ISER, University of the West Indies, 1967), p. 117.

9   G. E. Cumper, "A modern Jamaican sugar estate", *Social and Economic Studies* (September 1954), p. 121.

10 Alan Eyre, "Land and population in the sugar belt of Jamaica" (Mona, Jamaica: University of the West Indies, Department of Geography, n. d.), p. 8.

11 D. T. Edwards, "An economic view of agricultural research in Jamaica" *Social and Economic Studies* (September 1961), p. 333.

12 The discussion in this section draws on the analysis presented in my forthcoming book referred to in footnote 2. See especially chapter 8 of the book for further discussion of the points summarized here.

13 See N. Girvan "Multinational corporations and dependent underdevelopment in mineral export economies", *Social and Economic Studies* (December 1970).

22

Plantations, Peasants and Proletariat
in the West Indies*

The economic plight of the majority in the West Indies is a direct result of the dominance of agrarian capitalism, in the form of the modern plantation.[1] Persistent material poverty is obvious among the rural proletariat and the peasantry. Malnutrition, poor housing, illiteracy and disease are in evidence everywhere.

The thesis of this paper is that the chief cause of poverty in the West Indies is the monopoly of land and capital by plantations. This monopoly has intensified over time, thereby leaving rural population groups with increasingly fewer resources with which to secure their own economic and social advancement. The effects of this process of alienation have been most severe in those island economies where land is in short supply. Where fertile, arable land is in abundance, the effects are less stark; but they are evident nonetheless.

The analysis in support of the theses outlined is sequenced as follows: the genesis of agrarian capitalism is briefly described in the first section; the second section analyses the ascendancy of monopoly capital during the twentieth century. Subsequently, patterns of alienation and of resistance are considered in the third and fourth sections. And finally, the fifth section describes the situation at present and speculates, briefly, on the possibilities for change.

The Genesis of Agrarian Capitalism

Contemporary West Indian economy and society are a legacy of the slave plantation system which was introduced by European colonizers in the sixteenth century and which lasted until the mid nineteenth century. That system of agricultural organizations was based on the production of staple commodities (chiefly sugar) for export to Europe. European colonizers captured the land from the indigenous Indian peoples, and they then established a system of large-scale agriculture utilizing the slave labour of African peoples secured from the Atlantic slave trade.

In that system of production, the European capitalists owned the slaves (the labour power), the land, and the capital stock built by the slaves. The surplus realized from that production accrued entirely to the European owners of the means of production. The slaves received only what was required for subsistence. Alienation and mass poverty was at its extreme during that period of history.[2]

Caribbean economy during the era of the slave plantation was simply an overseas branch of European economy. The Caribbean was a locus of production of agricultural staples for transshipment to Europe. The Caribbean was in reality part of the agricultural sector of European economy. Production carried on in the region did not generate any income for its inhabitants. The slaves were essentially part of the capital stock, maintained by subsistence levels of consumption, depleted by runaways (the Maroons), and increased by new purchases and natural increase. The owners of the means of production were, for the most part, non-resident and managerial staff were temporary residents.

In the circumstances the economy generated no *national* income from slave plantation production.[3] Only the marginal subsistence activity of the Maroons and of free yeoman farmers provided any real income. Dependent underdevelopment was at its zenith during that period of Caribbean history.

Emancipation came in 1838 and changed things a bit – but only a bit. After that date, black people were legally free; in a sense, free to starve, as no resources were provided for their independent survival. As the plantation had engrossed all the arable land in some places (notably the Leeward Islands) black people were forced to continue working on the plantation for subsistence wages. As the planters had monopsony power in the labour market, there was no need for them to pay wages higher than subsistence. The only alternative open to black people in those circumstances was emigration.

Elsewhere in the Caribbean where some land was available, the economic position of black people was slightly better. In places like Jamaica, the Windwards, Trinidad and Guyana, they were able to find some, though not the best, land on which to settle independent of the plantations. Through individual and cooperative effort, black people brought or captured what marginal lands they could find. And eventually a peasantry emerged. But because of numerous legislative obstacles introduced by the planter-controlled governments, land was hard to secure. So continued dependence on plantation wage work was the lot of most black people.[4]

Wherever land was still available after Emancipation, the plantations had great difficulty in securing the labour services of the ex-slaves. Poll taxes were introduced to induce people to work for wages; land alienation by ex-slaves was prohibited in some places; legal sanctions against squatting were rigidly enforced; and sharecropping was introduced in some places. In spite of these measures, the planters still experienced labour shortages in the larger territories. Consequently, indentured East Indian labourers were brought in to work on the plantations – particularly in the newer plantation colonies of Trinidad and Guyana; but also, to a lesser extent, Jamaica and the Windward Islands.

The peasantry that emerged under the circumstances is a product of, and is dependent (to a certain degree) on, the plantation system of capitalist organization. And, by and large, the fortunes of the peasantry have been linked with booms and depressions in the plantation sector. So too has been the lot of the rural proletariat – those who, by force of circumstance, continue to work on the plantations for wages.

Booms in the sugar industry resulted in large profits for the plantations. Wage workers receive bonus payments under these circumstances. But peasants suffer as the plantations engross more land for sugar production. Depressions in the sugar industry produced opposite effects: wage workers suffered from unemployment and lower wages for those still employed; while peasants benefited, as more land became available to them when some plantations were forced out of business. This general pattern has persisted right up to the present time.

Rural society in the West Indies today consists of two major social groups: the peasants (small farmers) and the rural proletariat (wage workers). The peasantry may be subdivided into 'big', 'middle', and 'small'. In such a breakdown we would find that the 'small' peasant comprises the bulk of the peasantry (see Table 22.2 under 'Patterns of Alienation'). The historical pattern of alienation of these groups persists to the present time. The pattern has been accentuated by the ascendancy of monopoly capital since World War I.

The Ascendancy of Monopoly Capital

During the slave plantation era and up to the first decade of the twentieth century, the dominant ownership pattern of West Indian plantations was individual (or family) proprietorship. Today, corporations dominate the picture. And among these, the multinational corporation (MNC) reigns supreme.[5] This transition is of profound significance in understanding the deepening process of alienation which has pushed the majority of West Indian peoples further onto the margins of existence, indeed of survival.[6]

Two distinct trends are associated with the transition noted above. One is internal, the other external. The distinction is really heuristic, as there are obvious interrelationships between internal and external factors, more so in economies which are, in essence, extensions of metropolitan (*ie,* British) economy.[7]

Internally, the emancipation of slaves served to push up costs of production, as labour then became relatively scarce. That was one signal for the rationalization of production to keep costs down. The situation created by Emancipation was aggravated by three subsequent external events. First, the British equalization of tariffs in the 1840s exposed West Indian sugar planters to competition from non-British sources of sugar. The slave sugar economies of Brazil and Cuba thus had equal access to the British market.[8] Second, the opening of the Suez Canal in 1869 improved the competitive position of tropical Asia as a source of sugar. Third, beet sugar production in Europe was on the ascendancy. And this further expanded the world supply of sugar. Consequently, the pressure was intensified for rationalization to keep down production costs in the West Indies.

Other external events helped to provide an answer. The introduction of steam as a source of power transformed the technology of processing sugar and of transporting sugar cane to the factories. And the invention of the centrifuge and the vacuum pan elsewhere showed the way for modernizing processing, in a way that would produce higher yields of sugar from the cane and thereby reduce processing costs. But these new technological developments involved finance capital of a kind that could hardly be mobilized by plantation proprietors operating on the margin.

To make matters worse, the international sugar market in the latter half of the nineteenth century was characterized by falling prices (as a result of developments, noted earlier, which contributed to supply outpacing the growth of demand). With falling prices, rising costs of production arising from labour shortages, and large-scale capitalization as the only solution, many individual (and family) proprietors were unable to remain in business. Their estates went into receivership to creditors in Britain. And these estates were either sold in the West Indies – intact to other estates or subdivided for sale to the peasantry (ex-slaves).

Other external currents explain the ascendancy of monopoly capital. The efficacy of the joint-stock company (corporate enterprise) had become established in metropolitan capitalist centers by the turn of the century. Additionally, capitalism in Europe had reached a mature stage; and overseas investment opportunities were being sought. This situation was aggravated by World War I and events leading up to it. Shortages of tropical raw materials, and the associated competition among metropolitan firms engaged in the elaboration of these products, led to a drive by these firms to secure their own sources of raw materials. All these occurrences laid the foundation for the emergence of the MNC and the associated ascendancy of monopoly capital.[9]

Trends in the ever-increasing concentration of capital in the West Indian sugar industry can be discerned from the dramatic decline in the number of estates (and factories). Table 22.1 provides some evidence for Jamaica. The process of amalgamation (through the merger of adjacent estates) began right after Emancipation, accelerated toward the end of the nineteenth century, and continued at least until the 1930s. Since then, the industry has expanded the acreage that it controlled almost eightfold, with an attrition rate of roughly half for the number of factories.[10] This was a result of the incursion of international monopoly capital.

Table 22.1   *Sugar estates (factories) in Jamaica, 1836-1970* *

	Number	Average size (acres)	Total acreage
1836	670	_a	_a
1865	300	_a	_a
1900	111	196	21,756
1930	39	661	25,779
1970	18	11,112	200,000

[a]Data not available

*data to 1930 are from Eisner [1961] and data for 1970 are from the Mordecai Sugar Commission Report [1967: 87]

The MNC reared its ugly head during the 1930s. Tate and Lyle, the giant British sugar refining enterprise, bought out large areas of land in Jamaica and Trinidad and established subsidiary companies for the production of sugar cane and raw sugar. Today, that particular corporation produces 100% of sugar output in Belize, 92% of output in Trinidad, and 60% of output in Jamaica. And in Guyana, another British corporation – Booker McConnell Ltd – produces 98% of that country's sugar output. Together these two enterprises account for over 90% of West Indian sugar production.

As international monopoly capital engrossed more and more of the farmlands throughout the West Indies, less and less land was left for the peasants. Meanwhile peasant population expanded rapidly, so increasingly small acreages had to sustain each peasant family, and in the absence of dramatic improvements in small-farm productivity, independent peasant economic existence became increasingly precarious. As a result, many peasants are forced to supplement their incomes with wage work on plantations or elsewhere.

The plantation incursions on the land have been buttressed, more recently, by other non-agrarian invasions of monopoly capital. Mining (bauxite and petroleum) and tourism now occupy large areas of land in many of the islands. Consequently, the peasants are forced further onto the margins of these societies. The position of the rural proletariat is even worse than that of the peasantry.

Patterns of Alienation

The plantation system alienates West Indian peoples from their resources. The two groups most directly affected are the peasants and the rural proletariat. In general, they exist on the margins of society. For purposes of our analysis, it is useful to make a distinction between 'the margin of subsistence' and 'the margin of survival.' The margin of subsistence represents levels of living (consumption) which are barely tolerable by civilized human standards. The margin of survival represents levels which are intolerable. The individual on the margin of survival scrapes to achieve a level of consumption which is just enough to survive.

For the West Indies as a whole, the 'small' peasant is on the margin of subsistence. (Middle and big peasants who have sufficient land resources to be able to hire wage labour and/or to secure machine capital generally achieve decent levels of living. But these are a minority of the peasantry.) The rural proletariat are, for the most part, on the margin of survival. Over time, the position of the peasantry shifts with changes in the fortunes of the plantation sector. During periods of plantation expansion the peasantry is forced back closer to the margin of survival. The opposite shift takes place during periods of plantation contraction. The position of the rural proletariat remains static over time – on or about the margin of survival.

Tables 22.2 and 22.3 provide a summary of census and survey data showing the position of the peasantry in relation to land, and relative to plantations. The small peasant is assumed to correspond to the size group less than five acres; the plantation falls in the size group over 500 acres. (Exceptions to this general rule of thumb should be made for places like Barbados where a farm over 100 acres is a plantation. But no effort has been made for that kind of refinement in the present exercise.) Table 22.2 shows the size group distribution of all farms, by territory. Table 22.3 shows a similar distribution of the area in farms, again by territory.

Table 22.2 *Size distribution of farms*

Year	Territory	Size group (acres)					Total (%)
		<5	5 – <25	25 – <100	100 – <500	>500	
–	Belize[a]	–	–	–	–	–	–
1961	Barbados	98.3	0.8	0.2	0.5	0.2	100
1961	British Virgin Islands	36.6	52.7	9.5	1.3	0.0	100
–	Guyana[a]	–	–	–	–	–	–
1968	Jamaica	78.6	19.4	1.6	0.4	0.2	100
	Leeward Islands						
1961	Antigua/Barbuda	91.1	7.7	0.59	0.4	0.26	100
1961	Montserrat	92.7		6.5		0.7	100
1961	St Kitts/Nevis/Anguilla	94.5	3.9	0.7	0.5	0.45	100
1963	Trinidad and Tobago[b]	46.5	46.8	5.3	1.1	0.3	100
	Windward Islands						
1961	Grenada	89.7	8.8	0.9	0.5	0.1	100
1961	Dominica	75.2	21.5	2.3	0.8	0.3	100
1961	St Lucia	82.5	14.9	1.9	0.6	0.2	100
1961	St Vincent	89.0	10.1	0.6	0.2	0.1	100

[a]Data not available   [b]Provisional estimates for holdings of one acre and over (excluding land owned by government)

Table 22.3 *Size distribution of total area of farmland*

Year	Territory	Size group (acres)					Total (%)
		<5	5 – <25	25 – <100	100 – <500	>500	
–	Belize[a]	–	–	–	–	–	–
1961	Barbados	13.4	2.4	2.5	50.4	31.3	100
1961	British Virgin Islands	5.7	43.7	34.2	16.4	–	100
–	Guyana[a]	–	–	–	–	–	–
1968	Jamaica	14.9	22.1	8.3	9.9	44.9	100
	Leeward Islands						
1961	Antigua/Barbuda	26.7	9.7	4.4	17.1	42.2	100
–	Montserrat[a]	–	–	–	–	–	–
1961	St Kitts/Nevis/Anguilla	15.0	5.2	4.3	18.9	56.6	100
1963	Trinidad and Tobago[b]	6.9	30.7	15.1	16.2	31.1	100
	Windward Islands						
1961	Grenada	23.9	19.7	10.3	31.1	15.0	100
1961	Dominica	13.2	21.0	12.2	21.3	32.2	100
1961	St Lucia	18.0	19.6	0.2	17.9	33.8	100
1961	St Vincent	27.0	24.5	7.69	16.0	24.2	100

[a]Data not available   [b]Provisional estimates for holdings of one acre and over (excluding land owned by government)

Comparing the data in these two tables reveals the dismal position of the peasantry. Everywhere the small peasants (less than five acres) dominate in numbers but they have only a small proportion of the farmland. On the other hand, plantations (over 500 acres) are few in number but they have a large proportion of farmland. Barbados is perhaps the extreme case. There, small peasants are 98% of all farmers and they exist on 13% of all farmland; while the plantations (over one hundred acres) are less than 1% of all farmers with 82% of all farmland. These tables clearly reveal the existing alienation of the peasantry throughout the region.

It was suggested earlier that alienation of the peasantry has been increasing as a result of the incursions of monopoly capital. Table 22.4 provides some evidence of this for Jamaica. There we see that the number of small peasants and the acreage farmed by them increased between 1943 and 1961; but average farm size remained virtually unchanged. Over the same period, the number of plantations declined drastically; acreage farmed also declined, but not to the same degree; so that average farm size increased appreciably. It is important to note that the total area in farms declined, at about one-half the rate of decline in plantation land.

Now these trends tell a story. Non-agrarian capitalism (mining and tourism) came on the scene in Jamaica during the period covered by the data. Also, the revolt of 1938 (to be discussed later) resulted in intensified government policy to provide land for the peasantry – through 'land settlement' schemes. Additionally, the population of Jamaica increased from 1.3 million in 1943 to the present 2 million.

The decline in total farmland shown in Table 22.4 is chiefly a result of mining developments. Metropolitan (US and Canada) bauxite companies purchased considerable areas of land. And a good share of this was former plantation land – particularly in St Ann, traditionally a plantation ('pen-keeper' – *ie*, livestock ranch) parish. Nevertheless, the average size of plantations increased as the remaining plantation land became more concentrated among fewer plantations. The marked increase in small-peasant acreage between 1943 and 1968 is directly attributable to the government land-settlement scheme. The government purchased several derelict plantations and subdivided them for sale to peasants. The decline in plantation acreage, then, is partly a result of the invasion of non-agrarian capitalism and partly a result of peasant substitution.

Although peasant acreage increased, the average size of peasant holdings remained static. In short, the rate of growth of peasant farmers kept pace with the rate of growth of land operated by them. This is a *crude* indication that the economic position of the peasantry has remained virtually unchanged since 1943.[11] If we assume that the average household size of small peasants is five, then in 1968 the 150,000 small farms provided subsistence for 750,000 people on 15% of Jamaica's farmland. At the same time, 350 plantation owners luxuriated on 45% of all farmland.

Table 22.4 *Peasant and plantation land and labour, Jamaica, 1943-68*[a]

	No. of farms	Area (acreage)	Average size	Employment[b]
1943				
Small peasants	116,200	157,363	1.4	69
Plantations	532	1,068,000	2,000	17
Total	149,142	1,836,668	--	44
1961				
Small peasants	149,142	201,093	1.8	84
Plantations	350	774,000	2,200	17
Total	158,938	1,706,561	--	42
1968				
Small peasants	149,703	223,818	1.5	
Plantations	295	676,426	2,340	
Total	190,582	1,508,000	-	

[a]Census survey data. 'Small peasants' refer to farm size group of less than 5 acres. 'Plantations' refer to farm size group of more than 500 acres. The 'total' columns refer to all farms; it thus includes size groups not shown in Table (*ie*, farms of 5-500 acres).

[b](number per 100 acres cultivated land)

Back in 1943, 530 plantation owners earned profits from 60% of all farmland. Also, they benefited from capital gains on land values since that time. Census data reveal that productivity of plantation farmland tripled between 1943 and 1961. It is clear, then, that the economic position of plantation owners has improved appreciably, in both absolute and relative terms.

To return to the general West Indian situation, and the special case of the sugar plantation, we find an interesting interplay between plantations and the peasantry engaged in cane farming. Once again, plantations win; and peasants lose. During the plantation labour crisis following Emancipation, and after numerous efforts to solve that crisis, plantation owners finally resolved to encourage peasant production of cane to provide the necessary throughput for their factories. This is the genesis of peasant cane farming in the West Indies. It began toward the end of the nineteenth century and today cane farmers (many of whom are peasants) produce one-half of sugar cane output in Jamaica and significant shares of output in Trinidad and Belize. (Ironically, the Guyana government is now encouraging peasant cane farming, which never existed there before.)

Johnson has analysed the origins of cane farming in Trinidad. He demonstrates the importance of the planter class to its development. Planters around the turn of the twentieth century

often provided land, as well as advancing capital, and sometimes even supplied labour to the cane farmers. Their encouragement of cane farming is explained by the fact that they anticipated certain benefits from its establishment . . . Low prices emphasized the need for more economical sugar production. However, the savings effected were mainly in the manufacturing process. [Johnson 1972: 59]

Cane farming involves more risk than processing. Furthermore, since factory owners are in a monopsonistic position they can determine the price paid to farmers growing cane. From the beginning, until now, the price was set at a disadvantage to cane farmers. Johnson concludes that "the cane farmer was plagued with three major problems – lack of capital, inadequate transport facilities and an unsatisfactory cane-price formula. These difficulties have persisted up to the present" [1972: 73]. The cane farmer is, in essence a plantation worker who works for the plantation on his own land. His fortunes are bound up directly with those of the plantation.

The rural proletariat suffers a greater degree of alienation than the peasantry. Plantation strategy since Emancipation is to create a labour surplus in each economy. This was engineered by importing labour (under indenture) and by land monopoly. A more recent strategy is mechanization – the substitution of capital for labour, as the labour force became unionized after the revolts of the 1930s. According to Table 22.4, plantations in Jamaica maintained the same rate of employment per 100 acres of cultivated land in 1961 as in 1943. With the increase in cultivated acreage, the number of workers employed increased from about 27,000 in 1943 to about 32,000 in 1961 – nearly 20%. Meanwhile output per man working on plantations rose about 64% over the same period. The real wage of plantation workers has remained virtually static.

In Jamaica, cultivated acreage on plantations actually increased during this period (from 160,000 to 191,000 acres). It will be recalled that total plantation farmland decreased. Improvements in technology, both mechanical (labour-saving) and biological-chemical (land-saving), explain the sharp rise in productivity, per man and per acre. But the plantation worker has gained nothing from these improvements.

It is important to note that most of these improvements resulted from public-sector investments, and that the industry was subsidized by governments throughout the region. The technological improvements have served to aggravate the unemployment situation. Machine capital displaces labour directly. So too does chemical technology which replaces workers with weed killers.

West Indian economies are all labour-surplus economies. McFarlane (1970) provides the following estimates for 1960 of open 'long-term unemployment':

Table 22.5   *Long-term unemployment, 1960 (Percentage)*

Jamaica	23.4
Grenada	22.3
Trinidad and Tobago	15.6
St Vincent	22.8
Barbados	19.5
Dominica	16.1
St Lucia	17.5

In such situations monopsonistic buyers of labour services, as plantations are in specific localities, do not need to pay wages higher than survival levels, the more so where plantations and other capitalists monopolize land (thus restricting labour from own-account production) and where there are limited job opportunities available elsewhere.[12]

The rural proletariat earns income working on the plantation, on the wharves shipping plantation products, and in other plantation-related activities; they also work for middle and big peasants, for other small capitalists, and with government and the petty bourgeoisie (service activity). The plantation worker suffers the most. Income is seasonal and out-of-crop; the worker lives off credit in order to survive. Crop-time work pays back this credit in good years; but not during bad years. The margin of survival is more pronounced among this category of workers. But all rural workers are pushed beyond the margin of survival when there is depression in the plantation sector. For it is in that sector that economic activity begins to decelerate. Many small peasants are wage workers on plantations. They suffer as both peasant and proletariat.

Patterns of Resistance

Alienation induces resistance on the part of those who are pushed onto the margins of society. Resistance takes different forms – trade-union organization, political mobilization, formation of peasant associations, and at the extreme, social revolt or revolution.

At one time or another in the West Indies, peasants and proletariat have engaged in all these different patterns of resistance. As indicated earlier, the West Indian peasantry normally exists on the margin of subsistence while the rural proletariat stands on the margin of survival. Whenever the economic situation has forced the peasantry down to the margin of survival, widespread social unrest has been the result. The confluence of degrees of hardship suffered jointly by peasants and proletariat creates a powerful force for social change to alleviate mass suffering. Revolts and rebellions in West Indian history occurred within that context.

The 1865 rebellion in Jamaica is one case. Declining estate wages resulted from falling sugar prices and placed the rural proletariat in a precarious economic position. Meanwhile drastic measures were introduced to curtail peasant squatting on estate land. Low prices, low wages, increased taxation, and insecure land tenure for the peasantry created an economic crisis for peasants and rural proletariat alike, and a violent rebellion was the natural outcome.

Again, economic crisis during the 1930s heightened the alienation of peasants and rural proletariat to a degree that social upheaval occurred throughout the region, beginning with St Kitts in 1935 and ending with Jamaica in 1938. Post [1969] has analysed the 1938 rebellion in Jamaica. He identifies six groups of 'demonstrators' involved in the protest:

1   workers at the new Tate and Lyle sugar estates;

2   dockers at the city port;

3   public-works labourers;

4   ex-servicemen settled on government land grants;

5   sugar cane workers;

6   banana workers.

The most militant of these groups were the banana workers who were, for the most part, peasant farmers as well.

According to Post:

. . . It is not primarily as wage workers that the banana plantation workers must be seen, but as peasant farmers . . . I would argue that it was this hunger of land – either to add to an existing plot or to turn a landless labourer into a proprietor – which was the main force of the strikers in the banana areas [1969: 379].

Both peasants and proletariat were involved in the 1938 rebellion. Economic crisis in the plantation sector resulted in equal hardship for both groups. And their joint resistance created the social crisis.

It is instructive to consider, briefly, the economic background to the West Indian revolts of the 1930s. Indentured East Indian labor had provided a prop to the sugar industry after Emancipation. But the Indian government terminated the scheme in 1917. Sugar prices rose sharply during the 1920s, but they fell drastically with the depression of the 1930s. It was during that decade that the MNC came on the scene and plantation land monopoly intensified. Peasant access to land was thereby further restricted and low sugar prices meant low wages (and unemployment) for plantation workers. Thus economic crisis reached a peak throughout the rural sector.

The revolts of the 1930s subsequently led to less violent patterns of resistance: trade union mobilization of the rural proletariat, political (constitutional) change, and the ascendancy of peasant organizations. Trade unions sprang up everywhere out of the ashes of the revolts, and these have developed into powerful bargaining agents on behalf of the rural proletariat. Also, the trade union movement throughout the West Indies has been instrumental in promoting constitutional change. In most places, trade unions are associated directly with political parties which spearheaded the movement from Crown colony status to constitutional independence, under universal adult suffrage. Today most heads of governments throughout the West Indies are (or were) trade union leaders – most of whom were associated with the revolts of the 1930s and the subsequent growth of the trade union movement.

Peasant associations also mushroomed after the disturbances. Agricultural societies, cane farmers' associations, banana growers' associations, citrus growers' associations, and farmers' unions flourish today in most places, and operate as powerful political lobbies, in addition to providing economic assistance and bargaining strength for member farmers. Small peasants are the majority of members in these organizations although leadership is usually concentrated among middle and big peasants.

As mentioned earlier, monopoly capital has increased its stranglehold over rural resources in the West Indies during the last three decades or so. The resulting alienation of peasants and proletariat has induced different forms of resistance. Trade union organization is perhaps the most important of these. Throughout the region, unions have managed to secure periodic wage increases for workers, at least to keep money wages in step with the rising cost of living. Unions have managed as well to prevent large-scale substitution of machine capital or labour, thereby preventing a greater increase in the rate of unemployment. But the efforts of trade unions have failed to eliminate widespread unemployment as the growth of population (and labour force) outpaced the growth of new employment opportunities. Consequently, the rural proletariat continues to exist on or about the margin of survival.

Situation and Change

In spite of organized resistance, the peasantry remains in a precarious position throughout the West Indies. New incursions of monopoly capital in rural areas (mining and tourism) have reduced the land area available for small-scale farming. At the same time, peasant population expanded rapidly. The resultant decline in resources per peasant household intensifies rural poverty.

However, this situation has been tempered by large-scale emigration from rural areas.

Throughout the present century, emigration has been one of the main avenues through which the rural population of the West Indies managed to escape alienation by agrarian capitalism. Large numbers migrated to Central America to provide labour for the establishment of banana plantations and the building of the Panama Canal. Many went to Cuba to work on the sugar plantations in the early decades of the twentieth century. Movements from smaller islands to larger one were always significant. And during the past few decades, migration to advanced industrial countries and from rural to urban areas within individual West Indian countries has been very substantial.

The economic situation of peasants and rural proletariat in the West Indies would have been far worse today were it not for the persistent migration from rural areas. Without migration, resource pressure would have been far more intense and rural poverty more pronounced. In this connection, it is important to note that migrants provide substantial income flows for those remaining on the land. Remittances from migrants abroad to relatives at home exceed inflows of foreign capital in most territories; and in some smaller ones, remittances may be greater than total income generated in production.

In spite of resistance and migration, the economic position of peasants and proletariat remains precarious throughout the region. The unequal pattern of land distribution everywhere results in poor distribution of wealth and income, with proletariat and peasants at the bottom of the economic (and social) ladder. The solution to this problem will come through either reform or revolution.

The Cuban revolution served to eradicate extremes of mass rural poverty. Unless West Indian governments implement major programs of agrarian reform, it seems certain that increasing alienation of peasants and proletariat will eventually result in revolution. If history is any guide, that will occur whenever the peasantry is forced back from the margin of subsistence to the margin of survival.

Notes

* "Plantations, peasants and proletariat in the West Indies: agrarian capitalism and alienation" in K. Duncan and I. Rutledy (eds.), *Land and Labour in Latin America: Essays on the Development of Agrarian Capitalism in Nineteenth and Twentieth Century* (1977b); reprinted in Idris-Soven and Vaughan (eds.), *The World as a Company Town* (1979); and in Berdichewsky (ed.), *Anthropology and Social Change in Rural Areas* (1979).

1   The term 'West Indies' is used here to denote the English-speaking territories of

the Caribbean, South America, and Central America. Sugar is the major plantation crop in Guyana, Trinidad and Tobago, Barbados, St Kitts, Antigua, Jamaica and Belize. Banana is the main crop in the Windward Islands where both plantations and peasants engage in its production. Emphasis will be placed on the sugar plantation in the present exercise, because the banana industry is of recent vintage – having replaced sugar in the Windward Islands during the last two decades.

2   For an excellent analysis of the slave plantation case, see Eric Williams, *Capitalism and Slavery* (London: Andre Deutsch, 1964). New World slavery is the earliest form of capitalism and it is the pillar on which European and American capitalism was built.

3   For a formal exposition of the structure and functioning of slave plantation economy, see Lloyd Best, "Outlines of a model of pure plantation economy", *Social and Economic Studies* 17 (1968).

4   Peasant farmers in the West Indies to this very day still rely on plantation wage work to supplement the meager incomes generated from production on their small infertile holdings.

5   Some writers prefer the term 'transnational corporation'. Both terms refer to the same thing – a corporate enterprise with subsidiaries in many countries (nations), usually with the parent company registered in some metropolitan country (nation). The operations of these enterprises call into question the relevance of the nation-state as a useful analytical construct for economic analyses in the contemporary world economic order.

6   The distinction between 'existence' and 'survival' is critical to our analysis. It is being suggested that, whereas the existence margin is 'tolerable' the survival margin is not. And it is on the latter margin that social breakdown is inevitable. (See the sections that follow.)

7   Nineteenth century British economist J. S. Mill correctly described the West Indies as a place "where England finds it convenient to carry on the production of sugar, coffee, and a few other tropical commodities".

8   Slavery was not abolished in Brazil and Cuba until the 1880s.

9   For a more detailed discussion in relation to international agrarian capitalism, see G. L. Beckford, *Persistent Poverty* (New York: Oxford University Press, 1972), chapters 4 and 5.

10   The eighteen sugar estates occupy about 12% of all farmland in Jamaica (1.7 million acres). The cultivated area of these estates is about 20% of total cultivated area in the country as a whole.

11   This inference is reasonable unless it can be demonstrated that land productivity on small farms improved substantially and that the terms of trade have shifted in favour of the peasant. Census data indicate a decline in land productivity. In any case it is clear that the position of the peasantry relative to the plantation has deteriorated over the period.

12   Government public works programs are the only real alternative in rural areas. Otherwise the suffering plantation worker must learn some artisan trade. But even when that skill is acquired, the market for the skill is largely determined by the economic achievement of peasants and the rural proletariat. They depend on the artisan for house construction, tailoring, dressmaking, shoemaking, furniture, and so on.

23

Emigration and Demographic Change*

Emigration and Change[1]

It is hardly surprising that emigration has been a dominant feature of population change. The past few decades witnessed sharp declines in mortality and
protracted high levels of fertility. But migration drastically dampened the
picture. The largest wave of emigration began in the early 1950s. This movement to the UK was terminated with the British government's legislation of
1962 (the Commonwealth Immigrants Act). Subsequently, the movement was
to Canada and the US but this movement was more selective in terms of skills.
It constituted a 'brain drain' which critically affected certain sectors in the
West Indies. For example, health services were affected by migration of
nurses and doctors.

The pattern of population change is shown by the data in Tables 23.1 and
23.2. Total population of the region rose from 2.7 million in 1943 to 4.3 million
in 1970. Average annual increase of population for all 14 countries in that
decade amounted to 56,000; Jamaica, Trinidad and Tobago and Guyana
account for most (87%) of the increase. During the first intercensal period
(1943-60) annual rates of population growth were highest for mainland Belize
and Guyana, over 3%. Trinidad also ranks high with 2.9%. Jamaica shows a
moderate 1.6% while population declined in Montserrat (1.1%) and Turks and
Caicos Islands (0.4%).

Emigration played an important part in these changes. Apart from Trinidad and Tobago, Guyana and Belize, emigration is a high percentage of
natural increase – in excess of 33% in all cases, and rising to 123% for Turks

and Caicos and 165% for Montserrat. For the region as a whole emigration was 20% of total natural increase.

Between 1960 and 1970 emigration again was a dominant factor. For the region as a whole net emigration was 52% of natural increase, and in St Kitts (142%), Montserrat (124%) and Turks and Caicos (107%) emigration exceeded natural increase leading to declines in population. In four countries, Barbados, Grenada, St Vincent, and Dominica net emigration was between 70 and 90% of natural increase. And in three countries – Jamaica, Trinidad and Tobago and St Lucia net emigration was just over a half of natural increase. *"The estimated loss by the entire region of 1.12 million during the ten years following 1960 is equivalent to nearly one-third of its population at 1960,* which shows the extent to which rates of growth have been curbed as a result of the prevailing rates of emigration."[2]

Emigration affected rates of change not only in population but also in its composition. According to Roberts:

It is clear that the movements have been strongly age selective, affecting for the most part persons within the age range 20–34 . . . that postwar outflows have involved smaller proportions for males (relative to earlier periods) . . . the major effects of which have been to curb the growth rates of populations and of the expansion of working populations and of women of child-bearing span.[3]

Because emigration affected females more than males in the age range 15–44, the number of women of child-bearing span was fewer than would otherwise have been the case. The age selectiveness of emigration materially affected the growth of the labour force. Indeed, as will soon be observed, a *decrease* in the labour force was the result.

Emigration has other important effects as well. It accounts for the growing importance of remittances from abroad, contributes to the brain drain; and affects ideas about change. Migrants remit funds from abroad to support relatives still at home, and to save and/or invest. In some of the smaller territories, remittances represent the only substantial inflows of capital from abroad. Even in some larger territories, annual remittances represent a significant share of inflows. Data for Jamaica, for example, indicate that in several years remittances exceeded inflows of private investment capital. The importance of remittances for a large country like Jamaica can be judged from the effects on the balance of payments.

The positive balance in respect of transfer payments has been an important factor in moderating the extent of the deficit on current account. Net receipts from private transfer payments increased steadily from the mid 1950s to a peak of J$16.2 million in 1963. The key factor in this regard was the growth in remittances from migrants.[4]

Table 23.1 Population movements in Commonwealth Caribbean countries 1943–46 to 1970

Country	Census Population*			Average annual intercensal increase		Average annual natural increase		Average annual (b) net emigration		(b) as % (a)	
	1943 or 1946	1960	1970	1943-6 to 1960	1960 to 1970	1943-6 to 1960	1960 to 1970	1943-6 to 1960	1960 to 1970	1943-6 to 1960	1960 to 1970
Jamaica	1,237,000	1,609,800	1,848,500	21,900	23,870	32,890	53,520	10,990	29,650	33.4	55.4
Trinidad & Tobago	55f,000	828,000	940,700	19,290	11,270	18,680	24,050	- 610	12,780	-3.3	53.1
Guyana	36f,700	560,400	701,900	13,620	14,150	13,350	19,450	- 270	5,300	-2.0	27.2
Barbados	192,800	232,300	237,700	2,820	540	4,170	4,260	1,350	3,720	32.4	87.3
Belize	59,200	90,100	120,900	2,210	3,080	2,230	3,830	20	750	0.9	19.6
St. Lucia	70,100	86,100	100,900	1,140	1,480	2,020	3,100	880	1,620	43.6	52.3
Grenada	72,400	88,700	93,900	1,160	520	2,280	2,370	1,120	1,850	49.1	78.1
St. Vincent	61,600	79,900	87,300	1,310	740	2,130	2,750	820	2,010	38.3	73.1
Dominica	47,600	59,900	70,500	880	1,060	1,320	1,260	440	960	33.3	76.2
St.Kitts-Nevis	41,200	50,900	45,600	690	- 530	1,320	1,260	630	1,790	47.7	142.1
Montserrat	14,300	12,200	11,700	- 150	- 50	230	210	380	260	165.2	123.8
Cayman Islands	6,700	7,600	10,500	60	290	140	220	80	- 70	57.1	-31.8
British Virgin Is.	6,500	7,900	9,800	100	190	200	200	100	10	50.0	5.0
Turks & Caicos	6,100	5,700	5,600	- 30	- 10	130	140	160	150	123.1	107.1
TOTAL	2,243,200	3,719,500	4,285,500	65,000	56,580	81,090	117,380	16,090	60,780	19.8	51.8

* The Censuses of Jamaica, Cayman Islands and Turks and Caicos were taken in 1943. For all other countries the Census year was 1946.

Source: G. W. Roberts, 1974.

Table 23.2 *Intercensal rates of increase and vital rates 1943–46 to 1970*

Country	Average annual rates of growth %		Average annual birth rates		Average annual death rates		Average annual rates of natural increase	
	1943-6 to 1960	1960 to 1970	1943-6 to 1960	1960 to 1970	1943-6 to 1960	1960 to 1970	1943-6 to 1960	1960 to 1970
Jamaica	1.56	1.39	34.5	39.1	11.6	8.2	22.9	30.9
Trinidad & Tobago	2.86	1.28	37.4	35.0	10.7	7.8	26.7	27.2
Guyana	3.01	2.28	41.0	38.5	12.0	7.7	28.9	30.8
Barbados	1.34	0.23	32.6	27.0	13.0	8.9	19.6	18.1
Belize	3.05	2.98	40.5	43.5	10.9	7.2	29.6	36.3
St. Lucia	1.48	1.60	40.8	43.4	15.2	10.3	25.6	33.1
Grenada	1.45	0.57	41.5	35.4	13.4	9.4	28.1	26.0
St. Vincent	1.88	0.89	44.8	43.9	14.9	11.0	29.9	32.9
Dominica	1.66	1.64	40.8	41.4	16.3	10.4	24.5	31.0
St.Kitts-Nevis	1.52	-1.09	39.0	37.7	13.5	11.6	25.5	26.1
Montserrat	-1.13	-0.42	31.2	28.5	13.6	10.9	17.6	17.6
Cayman Islands	0.74	3.29	33.6	29.8	9.4	5.5	24.1	24.3
Br. Virgin Islands	1.40	2.18	40.1	29.4	11.9	6.8	28.2	22.6
Turks & Caicos	-0.40	-0.18	39.0	35.4	16.1	10.6	22.8	24.8

Source: G. W. Roberts, 1974.

The $16.2 million recorded in 1963 is to be compared with a net inflow of $19 million private capital in a year when investment in bauxite expansion was heavy.[5]

Apart from balance of payments considerations, remittances represent a major explanatory factor in the survival capacity of the major dispossessed groups of West Indian populations over the past few decades. The persistent high levels of unemployment and generally low levels of income of those employed could not be sustained by the internal propensity to share (noted earlier). It is clear that remittances contribute a certain measure of stability to the unstable socioeconomic conditions of these societies.

Migration of skilled persons in the second wave of movement to the US and Canada during the 1960s has serious repercussions on the West Indian economies. The significance of this aspect is highlighted by the following evidence for Jamaica.[6] 'Service, sports and recreation workers' comprised the bulk of workers, about one half. The other half chiefly consisted of 'professional and technical', 'clerical', and 'craftsmen, production process workers'. These three categories represent critical elements in the labour needs of any modern economy.

Concentrating on the 'professional and technical' category alone, Girling has observed that compared with 1 out of every 6 emigrants, 1 out of every 25 members of the Jamaican labour force was in this category. He estimates that it cost Jamaica some J$9 million to produce these trained emigrants; and that income foregone as a result of the loss of these persons was about 1% of the total GNP.

Finally, emigraton affects the social system by its impact on the leadership profile, the seepage of outside cultural influences, and the ideas for change developed abroad by returning migrants. It can reasonably be argued that potential leadership for change is not likely to be found among emigrees because leaders tend to remain on the battlefield. But the political history of the West Indies indicates that most of the present and past leaders spent some time overseas in one capacity or another. Analysts have associated the movement toward political independence with the return home of many figures – Garvey and Cipriani, for example. How important recent migrations will be in shaping future policy is difficult to assess.

What is certain is that the exposure of migrants to metropolitan culture has a distinct demonstration effect on ideas for change and on tastes. The experience of black people living in white metropolitan society certainly facilitated the transmission of Black Power ideology from North America to the Caribbean during the 1960s; and returning migrants display consumption patterns which influence the consumption aspirations of others in the society.

Effects on the Labour Force

Emigration was instrumental in adjustments in the size and composition of the labour force. Table 23.3 presents data on the labour force for 1960 and 1970. Substantial reductions in the work force are indicated, especially for females. Only Belize and the Virgin Islands show any increase in the total working force. The Virgin Islands are a special case, a transit stop for prospective migrants to the US Virgin Islands. For the region as a whole, the total labour force declined by 12% between 1960 and 1970; whereas the male component declined by 7%, the female component declined by 22%.

Roberts has provided estimates which isolate the effect of net emigration on changes in the male component of the labour force. The following tabulation shows these estimates.[7]

Male labour force (1960)		846,000
Decreases (1960-70) due to		
Net emigration	280,000	
Mortality	58,000	
Retirement	73,000	
Total Decreases	411,000	
Total Increases (1960-70)	350,000	
Male labour force (1970)		785,000

It will be seen from these data that net emigration represents 80% of total accessions to the male labour force over the decade.

Internal Migration: Rural-Urban Drift

The rural to urban drift of population is yet another manifestation of the effects of economic change over the past few decades. Those from the rural sector who could not afford to go abroad drifted to the towns, as rural dispossession increased. Data on internal migration for the region as a whole are not readily available; studies have been carried out only for Jamaica and Trinidad and Tobago.[8]

One example from Jamaica gives some idea of the importance of internal migration for specific localities. Within a 12-month period:

. . . in the parish of St Elizabeth the number of registered live births exceeded the number of deaths by approximately 3,350, while the loss of population through internal migration amounted to 2,632 persons. So that 79% of the natural increase of population was exhausted by intensive out-migration. On the other hand, to the natural population growth of the parish of St Andrew amounting to 4,400 persons

Table 23.3 *Change in size of male and female working force for 14 Commonwealth Caribbean countries*

Country	Male			Female			Both Sexes		
	1960	1970	% Change	1960	1970	% Change	1960	1970	% Change
Jamaica	381,700	332,100	-13.0	225,200	159,900	-29.0	606,900	492,000	-18.9
Trinidad & Tobago	192,700	172,500	-10.5	68,400	57,200	-16.4	261,100	229,700	-12.0
Guyana	124,500	128,900	+ 3.5	36,700	30,100	-18.0	161,200	159,000	- 1.4
Barbados	50,200	51,000	+ 1.6	34,900	32,900	- 5.7	85,100	83,900	- 1.4
Belize	21,400	25,500	+19.2	4,700	6,000	+27.7	26,100	31,500	+20.7
St. Lucia	18,200	17,200	- 5.5	10,400	9,300	- 5.8	28,600	26,500	- 7.3
Grenada	15,200	16,100	+ 5.9	10,000	9,800	- 2.0	25,200	25,900	+ 2.8
St. Vincent	14,300	13,600	- 4.9	9,100	7,400	-18.7	23,400	21,000	-10.3
Dominica	12,700	12,400	- 2.4	9,700	7,300	-24.7	22,400	19,700	-12.1
St.Kitts-Nevis	7,100	7,700	+ 8.4	7,100	4,700	-33.8	14,200	12,400	-12.7
Montserrat	2,300	2,400	+ 4.3	1,800	1,300	-27.8	4,100	3,700	- 9.8
Cayman Islands	3,100	2,200	-29.0	900	1,200	+33.3	4,000	3,400	-15.0
Br. Virgin Islands	1,700	2,800	+64.7	400	1,000	+150.0	2,100	3,800	+81.0
Turks & Caicos	1,200	1,000	-16.7	900	500	-44.0	2,100	1,500	-28.6
TOTAL	846,300	785,400	- 7.2	420,200	328,600	-21.8	1,266,500	1,114,000	-12.0

Source: G. W. Roberts, 1974.

that year, there was added a migration gain of 17,500 persons, so that the natural population changes amounted to only 20.1% of the total population growth of this parish during the same period.[9]

St Elizabeth is a distinctly rural parish while St Andrew is part of the metropolitan capital city of Kingston-St Andrew. Overall, the pattern of internal migration in Jamaica has been towards the capital city but in more recent times with the development of mining and tourism, a drift towards rural towns has been noted.[10] A similar trend is noted for Trinidad and Tobago; there "urban and suburban areas received 64.1% of the total immigration".[11]

Figures 23.1 and 23.2 show the patterns and intensity of rural-urban migration in Trinidad and Jamaica, respectively. These flows can be seen to be very substantial. Internal migration varies with levels of education. In Trinidad and Tobago 9.3% of movers had no education, 76.1% had some level of primary education, while those with secondary and higher education accounted for 14.6%.[12]

In a study of the causes of internal migration in Jamaica, Nassau Adams concluded that distance and wage income differentials between regions are "of overwhelming importance in explaining the pattern of migration" for adult males.[13] Migrants are most definitely attracted to areas where wage

Figure 23.1 *Rural-urban migration in Trinidad*

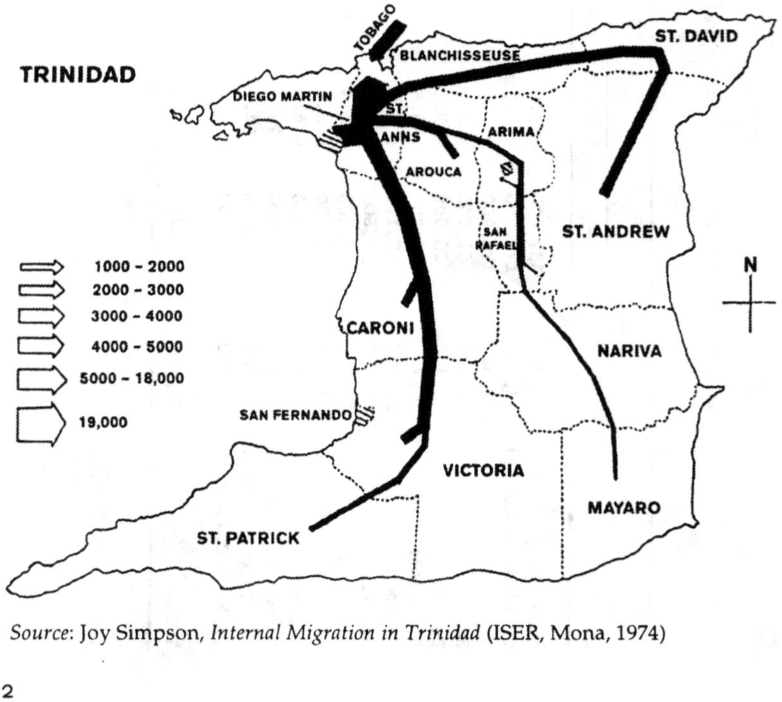

Source: Joy Simpson, *Internal Migration in Trinidad* (ISER, Mona, 1974)

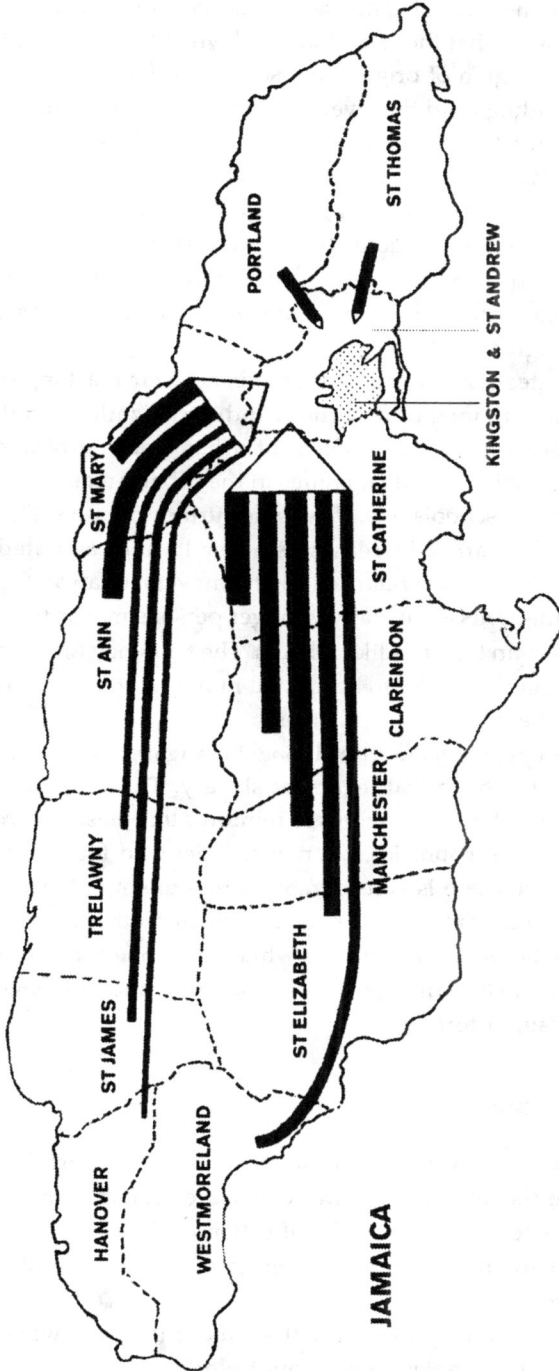

Figure 23.2 *Rural-urban migration in Jamaica*

incomes are higher and distance serves as a cost deterrent to migration. That study also showed that the rate of unemployment and the degree of industrialization in the region of origin were significant factors, as were the average size of land holdings and the level of education in the destination region. It is of interest to note that the unemployment rate in the destination region does *not* serve as a major deterrent "the implication being that people are attracted to the high wage regions in the vague hope of being able to get a job, even if in practice the probability of succeeding is not very great".[14] "The average size of land holdings also appears to be of some significance, at least where the destination region is concerned, regions with larger average holdings tending to be shunned by migrants".[15]

The rapid rates of rural-urban migration have far-reaching social structural consequences. Urbanization without industrialization results in growing urban unemployment. The problem of urban housing becomes acute, and slums develop. Other social amenities in the urban areas, already inadequate – health facilities, schools, etc. – become further pressed. Demand for food supplies in urban areas increases as a result; and, as noted in an earlier chapter, food supplies are retarded by the movement away from agriculture. The fact that migrants are usually younger persons means that extra pressure is placed on certain facilities like schools. The tendency for most of the educational and training facilities to be located in the capital cities and towns helps to accentuate the drift from rural areas.

West Indian people have a traditional bias against agricultural wage work on account of the historical legacy of slavery. The accelerated rural-urban migration in recent decades serves to reinforce this bias. Accordingly we find evidence, in several countries, of an excess demand for labour in plantation agriculture while there is considerable urban unemployment. For example, workers have to be imported from St Vincent and other neighbouring islands for sugar cane harvests in Barbados while open long-term unemployment in Barbados stands at 8%, and open plus 'disguised' unemployment is estimated at 20% of the labour force.[16]

The Labour Force

The two components of the labour force for consideration here are the employed and the unemployed. More data are available for the former.[17]

Roberts utilizes a three-fold classification of the *working force* in the West Indies: government employees, non-government employees, and own account workers.

Non-government employees are the bulk of the male working force: 57% for the region as a whole; own account workers are 25%; and government employees, 18%. The share of non-government employees is highest in Cayman, Barbados and the Virgin Islands; and is lowest in Jamaica. It would appear that 'pure tourist' economies offer greater scope for private sector employment than other types of economies.

For own account workers, the largest proportion is reported for Jamaica (36%) and the smallest for Turks and Caicos (10%) and Barbados (8%). Relatively high shares are observed as well for Belize, St Lucia and Dominica. It would appear from this that there is some association between the size of the resource base and the opportunities that exist for independent economic activity. But the evidence is far from convincing.

Government workers account for relatively high shares of the work force in the Turks and Caicos, Trinidad and Tobago, St Vincent, Montserrat, Guyana and Grenada – over 20% in all cases. The lowest share is for Jamaica (11%). Relatively poor colonies seem to offer greater scope for government employment than relatively well endowed ones. And among the independent countries, the more diversified the economy the less important is government as a source of employment, as a comparison of Trinidad and Tobago, Guyana, and Jamaica would seem to suggest. In the 'pure mineral' economy (Trinidad and Tobago) the scope for private sector employment is relatively small, and government has the wherewithal from mineral taxes and royalties to create public sector employment. In the highly diversified mixed economy (Jamaica), the scope for own account work is relatively great and government employment is therefore relatively small. Guyana is a less diversified 'mixed economy' than Jamaica. Accordingly, it occupies an intermediary position.

Roberts notes some other interesting characteristics of the working force. Own account workers comprise a "very small proportions of the work force at young ages and move up steadily through the age scale." In general, "non-government employment assumes more prominence among females than among males, and does not decline with age to the same degree as it does in the case of males . . . Female involvement in own account category is generally lower than that of males."[18]

In terms of educational attainment, we find that of the three categories of workers, government employees have the highest status "For the region as a whole only 8% of them have less than 5 years of formal schooling, while the proportions with GCE passes and with degrees and diplomas are comparatively high, being 12% and 5% respectively." Own account workers have the lowest status in educational attainment; 92% of them in the region as a whole have little more than primary schooling with only 1% having degrees or diplomas. 22% of own account workers are functionally illiterate (*ie* less than 5 years schooling) as compared to 13% of non-government and 8% for government workers.

Unemployment is a critical factor in all West Indian countries; and the evidence suggests that unemployment increased in recent years. The data also indicate that the problem is greater among young persons than among older ones; also among females as compared to males. Carmen McFarlane presents the following data on different types of unemployment in terms of per cent of the labour force as at 1960:[19]

	Open	Long Term Open and Disguised	Short Term
Jamaica	9.2	23.4	13.0
Trinidad and Tobago	5.6	15.6	10.7
Barbados	7.8	19.5	12.2
St Lucia	10.0	17.5	12.1
Grenada	7.8	22.3	15.7
St Vincent	6.2	22.8	13.5
Dominica	4.0	16.1	8.1
Antigua	n.a.	n.a.	12.8
Montserrat	n.a.	n.a.	12.2

Unemployment rates in 1960 were all above rates recorded at the preceding census in the 1940s. Other available data indicate that educated persons and young people constitute an increasing share of the unemployed.

Survey data for Trinidad and Tobago indicate that the rate of unemployment was highest among persons who attended but did not complete secondary school (20%) and among those who completed primary school but did not go further (18%). The unemployment rate was 6% or less for persons with no education and among those who had completed secondary school or attended university. In Barbados of the total unemployed nearly 50% had received seven years or more of primary education, and only 8% had less than 4 years education.

Young people suffer most from unemployment. In Trinidad and Tobago during 1967, 28% of the unemployed were under 20 years old and 25% were 20-24. While 15% of the total labour force were unemployed, the rate for persons 15-19 was 34% and for persons 20-24 it was 23%. A similar picture is given for Barbados in 1966. For the population as a whole the unemployment rate was 13% but for persons 15-19 years old it was 32%.[20]

It is clear that the problem of unemployment among the educated youth and youth generally is perhaps now at crisis proportions. The 5-14 age cohort of the 1970 census are now in the labour force. That group had increased from 27 to 31% of the male population of the region between 1960 and 1970; and from 25 to 29% for the female population. It is therefore quite likely that the unemployment among persons 15-19 increased materially during the 1970s.

The unemployed youth represent perhaps the most frustrated and volatile group in contemporary West Indian society. And with increases in the numbers involved would seem to be the most potent source for meaningful change.

Notes

* "Emigration and demographic change" extracted from *Social Structural Change and Continuity in the English-speaking Caribbean* (1975c).

1　Data in this section are derived from G. W. Roberts, "Working force of the Commonwealth Caribbean at 1970 – A Provisional Assessment" (Mona, Jamaica: UWI, Department of Sociology, 1974), mimeo.

2　Roberts, p. 6.

3　Roberts, p. 8.

4　Owen Jefferson, *The Post-War Economic Development of Jamaica* (Mona, Jamaica: ISER, University of the West Indies, 1972), p. 211.

5　With completion of ALCOA's Project. See preceding chapter.

6　R.K. Girling, "The migration of human capital from the Third World; the implications and some data on the Jamaican case", *Social and Economic Studies* (March 1974), 92-94.

7　Roberts, p. 12.

8　See Kalman Tekse, *Internal Migration in Jamaica* (Jamaica: Dept. of Statistics, April 1967) and Joy M. Simpson, *Internal Migration in Trinidad and Tobago* (Mona, Jamaica: ISER, University of the West Indies, 1973).

9　Tekse, p. 1.

10　G. W. Roberts, "Demographic aspects of rural development in Jamaica", *Social and Economic Studies* (September 1968).

11　Simpson, p. 18.

12　Simpson, p. 20.

13　Nassau Adams, "Internal migration in Jamaica – An economic analysis, *Social and Economic Studies* (June, 1969), p. 150.

14　Simpson, p. 151.

15　Simpson, p. 146.

16　Carmen McFarlane, "The employment situation in overpopulated territories in the Commonweatlh Caribbean", in *Human Resources in the Commonwealth Caribbean*, edited by J. Harewood (St Augustine: ISER, University of the West Indies, 1970). Short term unemployment in Barbados is estimated at 12.2 %.

17　Roberts, "Working Force".

18　Roberts, p. 15.

19　McFarlane, pp. 4-10.

20　These data are derived from Jack Harewood, "The underutilization of available human resources", in *Human Resources in the Commonwealth Caribbbean*, edited by J. Harewood (St Augustine: ISER, University of the West Indies, 1970), pp. 5-18/19.

24

The Social Economy of Bauxite in the Jamaican Man-Space*

Introduction

The well spring of the Jamaican people lies in the land. It is the land that brought us here. It is on the land that we were transformed from free Africans into slaves for plantation work. It is through the land that we were subsequently to free ourselves from plantation slavery and develop as an independent peasantry. And it is this last achievement that continues to sustain us, however tentatively, through food production and the spirit of independence. The story of the Jamaican people is essentially the story of a struggle for land. It is this simple fact that underlies the impact of bauxite mining and alumina production on the lives of the Jamaican people.

The thesis of this paper is that the coming of the bauxite-alumina transnational corporations after the Second World War aggravated a situation that had originally been created by the monopoly control which the sugar plantations had on the most fertile and accessible land areas of the country. Sugar had forced the peasantry into the inhospitable hilly interior from the start. And, by an accident of geography, it is precisely in these areas that large deposits of bauxite were to be found. Unlike most parts of the world where mines are located in remote outlying areas, bauxite mining in Jamaica is imposed on settled rural communities. And it is this that makes the impact as overpowering as it is. Only a small part of the traditional plantation sector was affected: the livestock-grazing ('pen-keeping') parts of St Ann,

Manchester and St Elizabeth. And so sugar and the sugar plantocracy remained untouched. It was the independent peasantry and their food producing base-land that bore the burden of bauxite mining incursions.

The transnational corporations producing bauxite and alumina were allowed by the colonial government to freely acquire ore-bearing lands. And in competitive bids to acquire control over as much raw material as possible, each company secured much more land than it needed for immediate mining use. The result of this was a massive displacement of peasant farmers who had to migrate and/or relocate. Migration, either internally to rural towns or city Kingston, or externally, chiefly to the UK, transformed their lives completely. From being independent peasant producers they became for the most part dependent wage workers or unemployed urban dwellers. And those who had only to relocate had to make major adjustments to new farming environments and to establish new social relationships in new communities. Either way, their lives were significantly disrupted. Additionally, waste disposal from plants that transform bauxite into alumina adversely affects the health of people in surrounding communities and destroys plant and animal life as well as property.

The bauxite-alumina transnational corporations operate essentially as enclaves within the rural environment. They employ relatively few people in their very capital-intensive operations and those employed are largely from outside of the communities that have been disrupted. Furthermore, the bauxite infrastructure of roads, water, and electricity supplies, ports, health clinics etc., are for the exclusive use of the corporations, so these do not directly benefit people in surrounding communities. Positive economic impacts of the bauxite-alumina transnationals (BATs) on the host country derive chiefly from royalties and taxes paid to government, from wage income earned by those directly employed, and from the limited purchases the corporations make from linked industries/firms. These three tributaries of benefits flow into a stream of income that accrues largely to the capital city Kingston where central government and the linked firms/industries are located, and to those rural towns where bauxite workers reside. The fact is that very little of the direct income and the indirect income-generating flows trickle back to the disrupted peasant communities.

In this paper, we elaborate on these costs and benefits of the operations of the BATs on the peasantry in Jamaica; and analyse the implications for the overall development of the economy in terms that focus on people and environment. It provides, at one and the same time, a framework and a synthesis of the findings of the research reported in the various studies undertaken in the multi-disciplinary project dealing with "The Impact of Bauxite-Alumina Transnational Corporations on Rural Economy and Society in Jamaica".

The people and environment orientation of this work provides a hitherto unexplored dimension of the problem. Studies on bauxite-alumina in Jamaica to date have considered the impact on the economy and the polity.[1] The 'economy' and the 'polity' are, in fact, abstractions of the social scientist. This compartmentalization is disconnected from the daily lives of people. Since our intention is to make this connection, it requires a different focus and methodology. Hence, our concentration on the peasantry and our use of the concept of the 'social economy'. For the peasantry constitute the vast majority of people affected in one way or another by bauxite while they possess the greatest potential for the independent development of the economy and society. The social economy concept examines economic factors in terms of their social (people) dimensions.

The first section of the paper considers the historical relationship between mankind and the land in the Jamaican context. This provides the canvas on which the details of subsequent sections are mounted. The brief historical outline establishes the importance of land to the people and provides some knowledge of their struggles to survive and to advance. The second section describes the way in which bauxite-alumina production altered the landscape and the patterns of people settlement on it. It elaborates on the dislocation in the 'manscape' through an examination of peasant displacement and the associated patterns of dislocation and relocation. The third section analyses the implications for overall development and underdevelopment of the economy as a whole and makes a tentative assessment of the social costs and benefits to the rural communities.

Man and the Land – Historical Overview

The Peasant Struggle for Economic Independence

Bauxite mining and alumina production in Jamaica began after the Second World War. It aggravated a process of peasant underdevelopment caused by the physical shortage of land and a social framework based on the exploitation of their labour power, first by the slave plantation system then by the system of agrarian capitalism after Emancipation.

European invasion and colonization killed off the indigenous population of Arawak Indians and brought over large numbers of African people to work on developing plantations, producing mainly sugar.

These slave plantations were established on the most accessible and fertile coastal and alluvial plains and valleys which are a small proportion of the total land area. The rest of the country, being hilly or mountainous with relatively infertile and rocky land, was left undisturbed but belonged to the

English crown. Figure 24.1A shows the country's relief and parish divisions. Some plantations spread to encompass parts of the hilly or otherwise infertile areas. And it was in these sections that the African slaves were allowed by their plantation owners to keep 'provision grounds' on which they produced foodstuffs for their own subsistence and for sale in the Sunday markets which they developed. This activity was the prelude to peasant development after Emancipation.

Figure 24.1 *Map of Jamaica showing (A) topography and (B) agricultural land capability.*

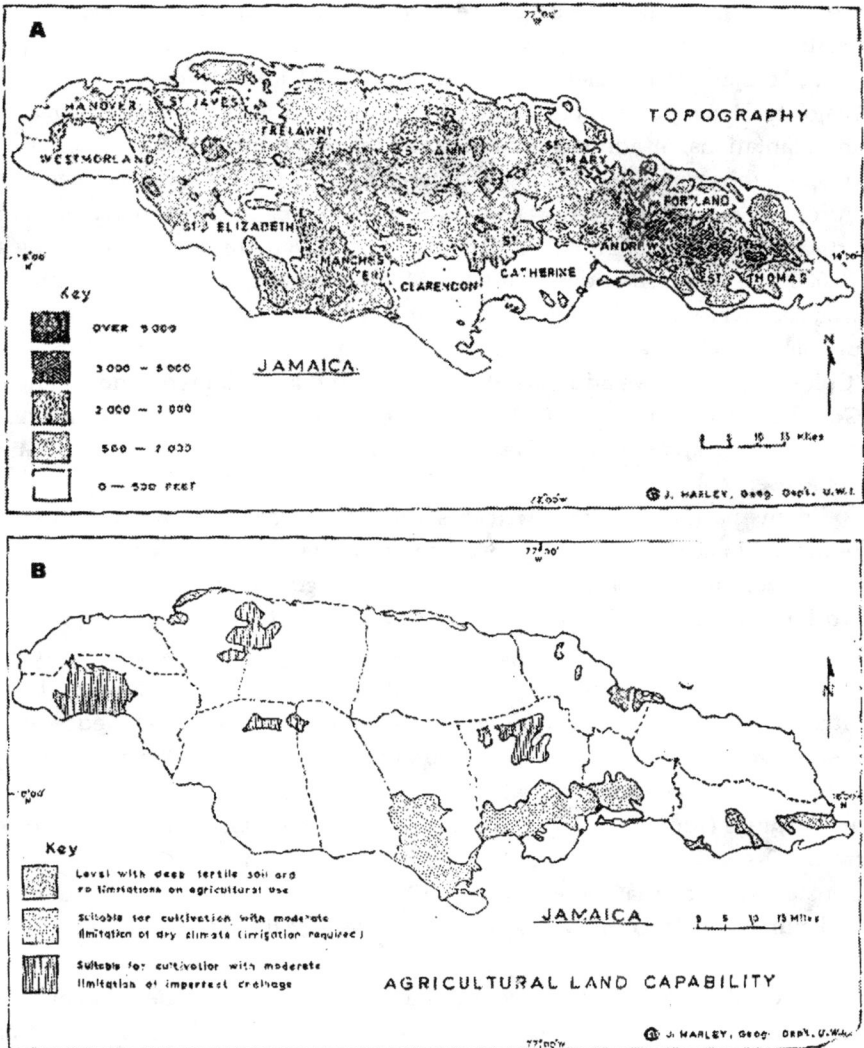

The sale of food from provision grounds provided cash income from which a few slaves were able to save money for the purchase of their freedom or to purchase land after Emancipation. But the majority were unable to achieve that. They were bound to continue working for subsistence wages on the plantations after Emancipation; and only gradually over time managed to set themselves up as independent peasant producers. Apart from the 'proto-peasant' activity on the provision grounds, there was, of course, the independent peasant production of the Maroons who managed to escape the brutality of the slave plantation and who maintained their freedom by skillful guerilla defense of their remote mountainous communities. They were isolated communities of subsistence producers and their numbers were small relative to the slave population.

Slave plantation society consisted of black African slaves who were the majority of the population; white Europeans who owned and/or managed the plantations, or administered the colonial government; and free coloured people who were the offspring of intercourse between African women and European men. They were for the most part independent property owners, artisans or professionals. "At Emancipation in 1838 there were 323,000 slaves, 55,000 free coloured and 37,000 whites" [Hart 1952: 28]. By the time bauxite was discovered, the population of Jamaica had grown to over 1.2 million people. The 1943 Census indicates that 95.5% of these people were 'Black' and 'Coloured'. When we add 'East Indian', 'East Indian Coloured', and 'Chinese Coloured' the figure was 98.25%. So over 98% of the Jamaican people were African or Asian in origin and less than 2% white or near-white (Jews, Syrians, Lebanese, etc.).

Emancipation gave the African slaves legal freedom but they, in fact, remained in economic slavery. Because the white planter class and the colonial government imposed measures which forced the ex-slaves to continue working on the capitalist plantations. They restricted the sale of land to them, imposed taxes, introduced legislation like the Vagrancy Law and Trespass Act, reorganized the police force etc. But the spirit of independence of the African Freedmen (ex-slaves) was so strong that they developed viable peasant communities on what land was available in the mountainous interior, through remarkable individual and cooperative efforts involving purchase and capture (squatting). "The number of freeholders assessed for taxes rose from 2,014 to 7,848 in the first two years following Emancipation". An 1844 Census indicated that there were some 19,000 persons "formerly slaves, who had purchased land on which they were erecting their own cottage" [Hart 1952: 12].

The exodus from the plantations induced the planters and the colonial government to import indentured workers mainly from India and, to a much lesser extent, from China. The influx of 'East Indians' kept plantation wages low and thus made it even more difficult for the African Freedmen to earn enough to generate savings for buying land. Most of them had to keep working on plantations as an agro-proletariat depending solely on that source of income. Others worked part-time to earn supplementary income to add to what they made working their own small plots of land. The latter we shall describe as small peasants who are in a worse position than the much smaller numbers of middle and big peasants who had managed to secure enough land to achieve adequate or comfortable levels of income from own-account production.

The small and landless peasants and plantation workers were the majority of the population and were the poorest classes within the society. Whenever there was a depression in the sugar industry their already poor economic circumstances worsened. So, for example, when the free trade movement gained ascendancy and the British government withdrew the preference on British West Indian sugar between 1846-52, many inefficient plantations went out of business. Increasing unemployment, migration to towns, rising incidence of squatting, and the expansion of various forms of land tenancy were the result. Unemployment and migration contributed to more theft and petty crimes which, along with squatting, induced more state expenditure on the police and the courts. Social disorder was always imminent.

In the late 1890s when crisis again hit the sugar industry, the imperial government sent out a Royal commission to study conditions and make recommendations. One of its main recommendations was that government should introduce a Land Settlement Programme to appease land hunger and assist the development of the peasantry. But this was started on a very small scale. Accordingly, we find the recommendation reiterated by another Royal commission on sugar in 1929 and repeated by yet another Royal commission (chaired by Moyne) sent to investigate the rebellion of 1938.

So a hundred years after Emancipation, the economic condition of the majority of African Freedmen remained precarious, partly as a result of the shortage of land available to them; and partly due to the exploitation of their labour power by the capitalist plantations. Social tension was inevitable as the struggle for land demanded repressive measures to limit the chances for independent peasant expansion which would reduce the supply of labour available for wage work on the plantations. This underlying tension reached explosive levels with the Morant Bay rebellion of 1865 and the country-wide revolt of 1938. Both events brought about changes in the form of the colonial government.

Acuteness of land hunger among small and landless peasants, and injustices meted out to them by a repressive legal system, aggravated the economic crisis in the sugar industry in the years prior to 1865. The Morant Bay rebellion in St Thomas began with the unjust treatment of a small peasant who had been accused of squatting on land which he had bought. A number of small and landless peasants mobilized and led by Paul Bogle, himself a peasant and Baptist deacon, staged a protest demonstration by marching to Morant Bay demanding land and justice. Hundreds of them were killed and over 1,000 houses burnt down by the military. Bogle himself was summarily tried and hanged in front of the court house. The imperial government recalled the governor, abolished the planters legislative assembly and instituted direct Crown Colony rule.

The prolonged depression in the international capitalist system during the 1930s had important repercussions on the Jamaican economy. The economic condition of the working class in the sugar and banana industries, on the ports, and elsewhere worsened to a stage where a series of strikes spread from one end of the country to the other. Many of the sugar and banana workers were small and landless peasants.[2] Again the repressive arms of the state weighed heavily and numerous people were killed and injured. But the rebellion set the stage for the termination of Crown Colony rule and the establishment of representative government based on universal adult suffrage in 1944. Thus the peasantry and the working class for the first time entered the mainstream of Jamaican politics and continued the struggle which won constitutional independence in 1962.

Forms of Peasant Resistance

The struggles of the peasantry to secure an independent economic base throughout the latter half of the nineteenth century and up to 1943 was marked by two forms of resistance which we now discuss briefly. The first was their conscious efforts to engage in the production of export crops other than sugar, to become as independent as possible of the plantations and the planter class. Bananas are the prime example but there were other minor crops like logwood, coffee, pimento, ginger, etc. Bananas were to become a new staple export. Disdained at first by the white planter class as "backwoods nigger business", export earnings from bananas exceeded that from sugar by the end of the nineteenth century. It grew well in the hill country, fitted in with the mixed farming system of the peasantry, and provided year-round income in contrast to the seasonality of sugar. Additionally, it created jobs in linked activities like transportation – roads, railways, ports; and for clerical tasks in purchase, collecting and shipping.

The second form of resistance came through external migration, beginning with the trek to Panama to work on the Canal; then to Central America to work on railroads and banana plantations; then to Cuba during the first two decades of the twentieth century to work on the sugar plantations; and later to the US. Thousands migrated to these places and sent remittances home to support families and to purchase house and land. Those who returned invariably established themselves as peasant farmers or independent artisans.

To sum up, between 1838 and 1943 the feature of the social history of the Jamaican people is the struggle of black people to secure their freedom and independence by the only means possible – settlement on the land. This was made difficult by the physical shortage of arable land which had been monopolized by the plantations and by impediments imposed by the white planter class and the British colonial government. The situation worsened rapidly as population increase accentuated the land shortage and as the staple cycles of sugar, then bananas, entered the stage of decline ('gall and worm-wood').[3] Fired by the spirit of independence, some black people managed through hard work, the accumulation of savings, individual and cooperative efforts, and entrepreneurial zeal to establish a viable peasantry. Many others, however, remained trapped in the clutches of the plantations working for subsistence wages.

Table 24.1 shows the distribution of land and farms between small peasants and plantations in Jamaica in 1943. It shows that although small peasants were the majority (71.1%) of farmers, they occupied only 8.5% of the farm land. In contrast, although plantations were only 0.35% of the number of farms they occupied 58.1% of total farm acreage. When differences in the quality of land is considered the inequality is even greater. The number of plantation workers in the same year was 130,301. Together these two groups represented some 46% of the total work force. Census data reveal that there was considerable land idleness (underutilization) on the plantations, side by side with the land shortage in the peasant sector.

Table 24.1   *Small peasants and plantations in Jamaica, 1943*

	Less than 5 acres	More than 500 acres	Total[a]
No. of farms	116,200	532	149,142
No. of acres	157,363	1,068,000	1,836,668
Average Size	1.4	2,000	--

[a]Total farm land includes farms between 5 and 500 acres

Bauxite-Alumina in the Jamaican Man-Space

Incursion into Peasant Farms

Establishment of the industry was accommodated by the colonial government in a manner that led to a ratooning of the plantation system of relationships between man and the land. Freedom to acquire as much land as they wished was granted to the foreign-owned transnational corporations (TNCs) which came to exploit the rich resource. Legislation was enacted to guarantee the rights of the corporations to mine the ore. These actions by the colonial government served to promote the interests of the TNCs at the expense of the Jamaican people who owned bauxite-bearing lands. Since the TNCs came to own as much as 25% of the land area of some parishes, the peasantry in these parishes were adversely affected; and the direct impact on them had significant indirect consequences for the rest of the society.

Prior to the coming of bauxite, the existing Jamaican land law provided for ownership of everything on and below the surface. With the discovery of this strategic ore in wartime conditions, the Crown Colony government introduced the Emergency (Defence) Regulation (27 November 1942) to declare all bauxite in Jamaica to be the property of the Crown. This Emergency Regulation was repealed at the end of 1944 and was subsequently replaced by the Minerals (Vesting) Act, 1947 and the Mining Act, 1947. The former vested specific minerals (including bauxite) in the Crown and the latter set out procedures governing mining and prospecting rights and leases. Additionally, the Mining Regulations of 1947 stipulated that before mining leases could be granted *the TNCs would be required to own the land*, except for Crown land.[4]

Alcan and Reynolds were the first of the TNCs to come. Alcan started to buy "large areas of land not commensurate with the value of bauxite in the land" in 1943 – *ie* before legislation regarding rights [Davis 1980–1: 116]. And Reynolds followed suit. These two corporations were able to secure ownership of most of the bauxite-bearing pen-keeping lands before the arrival of other TNCs starting with Kaiser in 1947. Other companies came in somewhat later. Alcoa Minerals started mining in 1963. Alumina Partners (Kaiser, Reynolds and Anaconda consortium) started production in 1969 and Revere Copper and Brass began in 1971. The fact that the mining regulations stipulated that companies be required to own land led to the large scale alienation of land.

Figure 24.2 shows the distribution of bauxite-bearing lands. It indicates that the concentration of these lands is found in the central parishes of St Ann, Trelawny, St Elizabeth, Manchester and Clarendon with an isolated area in St Catherine. These we refer collectively as the bauxite parishes which made up what Salmon [1987] describes as the physical bauxite land economy. St Catherine and Trelawny occupy a peripheral position in this scheme. Between them, Alcan, Reynolds and Kaiser had, by the mid to late 1950s, come to own nearly a quarter of the land area of each of St Ann and Manchester. By 1957, "these three companies alone had already acquired some 136,472 acres or approximately 5.7% of the island's land area". Salmon goes on to

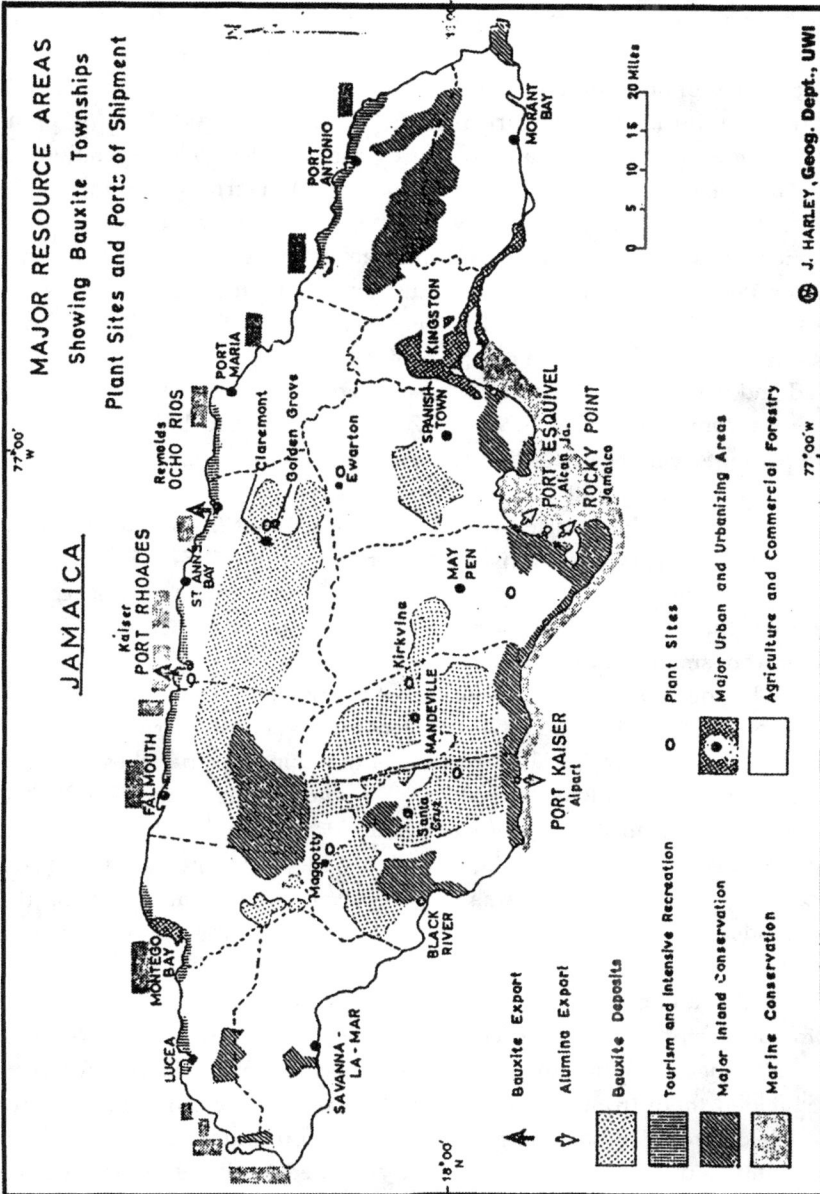

Figure 24.2 *Major resource areas*

point out that "by the mid 1950s most, if not all, of the leading grazing pens in the six bauxite parishes were already acquired by the incoming multinationals". Even at this early stage, a number of peasant cultivators were directly or indirectly affected since they were either involved in government land settlement schemes which fell to bauxite or had been "semi-legal tenants on the fringes of underutilized pens".

After this initial period, direct incursions into peasant farming areas became increasingly important. So that by the late 1970s *all* acquisitions of Alcan and Kaiser and 90% of those of Alcoa were from farms less than 25 acres in size. Data provided by Sachak [1987: Table 3.1] show the increasing trends in percentage acquisitions of land from the general category of peasant farms between 1942 and 1980. For Alcan, acquisitions from farms less than 25 acres rose from 36.4% in 1942-59, to 70.9% in 1960-73, to 100% in 1974-80. Small peasants (under 5 acres) were just 5.3% of Alcan's acquisitions in the earliest period and over 20% in the latest. For Kaiser, the share for farms less than 25 acres rose from 62.4% in 1942-59, to 81.7% for 1950-73, and 100% for 1974-80. Small peasants were nearly 26% of Kaiser's acquisitions in the period 1942-59, rising to 64.0% for 1974-80.

The late-comer Alcoa started with 73% of acquisitions from farms less than 25 acres in the period 1960-73 rising to over 90% during 1974-80; 23% in this last period coming from small peasants. For Alpart, over 26% of its acquisitions over the period 1960-77 came from farms under 25 acres, with 13% coming from small peasants.

In all, by the end of 1979, the amount of land owned by the companies in Jamaica was over 210,000 acres. This represents 14% of the farm land in the entire country. Most of this land was concentrated in three parishes – St Ann with 80,589 acres, Manchester with 64,508, and St Elizabeth with 35,094. Reynolds had the most – 61,744 acres, then Alcan with 50,355, Kaiser with 50,337, Alpart with 33,315 and Alcoa with 11,754. These aggregative figures indicate that bauxite mining came to have a very significant impact on the rural landscape, particularly in what we have described as the bauxite parishes.

Ownership and control of such vast acreages meant that the BATs became a dominant factor in the social economy of rural Jamaica. The pressures on a subordinate peasantry became more and more acute as the hill territory which had shielded them from the horrors of plantation sugar came increasingly under the control of these mining corporations. Thousands of peasant farmers were completely dislocated, others were relocated, and still others became tenants to some of the BATs on lands they once owned.

Peasant Dislocation and Internal Migration

The thousands who were completely dislocated migrated to urban areas or they went abroad. The main internal movement was to the Kingston Metropolitan Area (KMA). A study of internal migration for the year 1959 shows that the streams of migrants to the KMA from the bauxite parishes were greater than those from other parishes. Only in the case of St Mary was there as large a flow of migrants as those from the bauxite parishes of St Ann, St Elizabeth, Manchester, Clarendon and St Catherine. Subsequent studies indicate a reinforcement of this trend but also reveal inflows to some bauxite parishes as well as the fact that internal migration to the KMA is often a step-by-step process with migrants from distant parishes moving to parishes closer to the KMA before reaching their final destination in the city.[5]

Figure 24.3 shows the direction of internal migration streams between 1960 and 1970 during which period bauxite incursions into peasant areas intensified. The step-by-step flow to the KMA and St Catherine from St Elizabeth and other southern bauxite parishes is a pronounced feature. So too are the outward flows from St Ann to the KMA and St Catherine part of which by 1970 had developed as a dormitory extension within the KMA (the Portmore/Hellshire complex). The inflows into St James from neighbouring parishes reflect the pulling effects of tourism (see Hewitt [1974]).

Because of its proximity to the plains bordering Kingston and more recently government policy to expand Kingston in that direction, St Catherine received the largest number of internal migrants in 1943, 1960, 1970 up to 1982 – *ie* of the 12 'rural' parishes. The 1960 figure, however, was 40% higher than that for the 1943 census which is far below that for the bauxite parishes of Manchester 71% and St Ann 65%. This suggests that bauxite-alumina activity had a strong pull effect, even while pushing the peasantry off the land.

Figure 24.3 *Directions of internal migration streams, 1960-70*

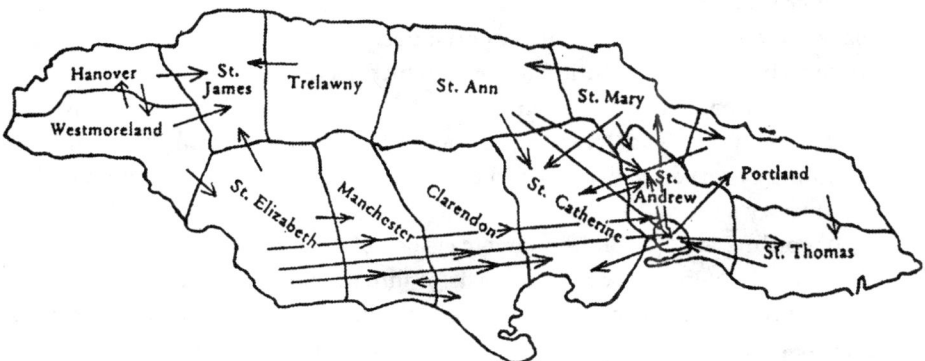

In 1960, Spanish Town and May Pen were the largest towns, with 14,700 and 14,100, respectively. There were in all 22 small towns but only 8 of these with over 5,000 in population. All grew in the intercensal period 1960-70.

However, the percentage change over the period 1943-60 is by far the greatest increase ever experienced. Mandeville . . . records a three fold increase in population. This can be attributed to the development of the bauxite industry in the area. May Pen . . . also records a very large increase in population (135%) whilst Montego Bay in St James [tourism] is in a similar position, recording a 105% increase in population.[6]

Occupational Patterns

Inflows to bauxite parishes involved partly peasant movements, either on their way to the KMA or to 'bauxite towns', and partly movements of skilled and semi-skilled labour into bauxite towns for work in bauxite-alumina, in construction during the phase of capacity expansion, and in other allied activities. These movements significantly altered the occupational patterns of the work force in the countryside, albeit within the traditional social structure. Bauxite-alumina production is capital intensive. The industry has never employed more than 1% of the Jamaican labour force and is relatively skill-intensive. Accordingly, there was little or no room for the displaced peasantry to find employment in the industry. Skilled labour was drawn from the sugar industry and from the KMA. And managerial and technical personnel were initially drawn from North America. The companies thus brought with them a whole set of white people who required and were provided with special housing and social infrastructural facilities like schools for their children, clinics, recreational facilities, etc. This influx of white people reinforced the old white/black race cleavage in Jamaica. And in this sense we can speak of a 'ratooning' of plantation society. Within the bauxite parishes this situation was so acute that in Mandeville, one of the main bauxite towns, there was an area popularly called 'Johannesburg' as recently as the early 1970s.

Over time, these white expatriates were gradually replaced by brown and black Jamaicans. But the top managerial positions are still held by white expatriates with the sole exception of Alcan which, in recent years, appointed, first a brown Jamaican and subsequently replaced him with a black Jamaican general manager. The 'Jamaicanization' of technical and managerial ranks of the industry served to expand and consolidate the 'brown' component within the country's plural society.

According to M. G. Smith,[7] Jamaica is one of a class of plural societies in the West Indies. Here the society consists of three separate cultural components: white, brown and black each of which is characterized by distinct cultural manifestations which we can describe as European, Creole, and African respectively. Race, colour and class are the key elements in the pattern of social stratification and in the social dynamics of change in the society. White European culture dominates from a position of superiority. And it debases the African (folk) culture of the black people who comprise the bulk of the population. The creole culture of the brown component is a hybrid of the European and African; but with a distinct bias towards the European for the obvious reason that the brown Afro-Saxon gains legitimacy only by manifest ability to ape the culture of Europe. It is these Afro-Saxon people who, from the time of plantation society, have acted as brokers between the dispossessed masses of black workers and peasants and the white planter and merchant capitalist class. Their ascendancy came largely through education which acculturated them away from their African roots and made them functionally Europeans.

It is against this background that we must view the impact of the process of Jamaicanization of the managerial and technical ranks of the industry. As well, there is no doubt that mobility of such personnel within the industry depends on the degree to which they prove to be good 'company men'. That is to say, they must demonstrate a strong desire to promote the company's interest above all else, as has been indicated by several studies of transnational corporations worldwide.

Skilled and semi-skilled labour accounts for the bulk of the bauxite labour force. They either moved to reside in bauxite towns or they commute from the KMA. Relative to the rest of the Jamaican labour force, they are highly paid[8] and thus have become a 'labour aristocracy' in a society with over one-quarter of its labour force permanently unemployed and another quarter perhaps only seasonally employed. These relatively high wage rates in the bauxite-alumina sector impact significantly on the labour market. From their demonstration effect they raise the reserve price of labour. This has its most direct impact on the unionized segment of the market, and served to aggravate the pre-existing unequal distribution of income within the society – naturally, but more so within bauxite parishes. It is important to juxtapose this observation with the effect of peasant displacement from the land. With limited job opportunities provided by bauxite-alumina, branch-plant manufacturing and tourism, which came to be the leading sectors in the economic growth of Jamaica, unemployment grew. So bare subsistence wages have prevailed in the non-unionized segment of the labour market.

Impact on Urban Development

To return to the immediate question of internal migration, we need to elaborate somewhat on the impact of bauxite-alumina on certain rural towns and townships.[9] As noted earlier, bauxite mining in Jamaica is superimposed on settled communities, both rural-rural and rural-urban. Accordingly, there are no 'company towns' in the conventional sense of the term. However, a number of towns and townships are influenced in one degree or another by the presence of the bauxite-alumina industry.

Our study indicates that there are no bauxite towns as such because the two major towns within the sphere of bauxite-alumina influence were viable market towns/parish capitals before the advent of the industry. Mandeville in Manchester and May Pen in Clarendon have certainly grown in size and importance partly as a result of bauxite-alumina. Mandeville comes closest to being a bauxite town, hemmed in as it is by two major alumina plants – Alcan-Kirkvine works slightly to the east and Alpart-Nain to the southwest (see Figure 24.2). The administrative offices of both companies are in Mandeville. Because of its elevation and cool climate, Mandeville had a substantial white population before the coming of bauxite. It remains to this day the epitomy of the white-brown-black plurality of Jamaican society. Its commercial expansion and social infrastructure derive significantly from bauxite-alumina.

The industry is not as important to May Pen which is located on the periphery of the Clarendon deposits with only one alumina plant nearby – the Alcoa plant at Halse Hall. That plant was recently closed by Alcoa – the third plant closed by the TNCs in the Liquidation Phase of the staple cycle – but was reopened under a lease arrangement six months later by the government as Clarendon Alumina Plant (CAP) with Alcoa retained for management. The period of closure was not long enough to have shown an impact but it is hardly likely that May Pen would have collapsed as a result. May Pen is not a resident bauxite town in the way Mandeville is. There is no doubt, however, that a permanent closure would have had some negative multiplier effects. Though it is difficult to estimate what these might have been, the experience of previous closures by Revere at Maggotty and Reynolds at Claremont-Golden Grove suggests that it would not have been very significant. The population of May Pen had been growing before the Halse Hall plant opened in 1959. Its population rose from 6,000 in 1943 to 14,000 in 1960 and 26,100 in 1970. May Pen's geographical centrality is the key to this growth.

In St Elizabeth, only Maggotty was directly affected by bauxite-alumina. This was the site of the Revere plant which was the first closure back in 1974. During the few years of that plant's operation, the Revere work force commuted mainly from nearby Santa Cruz and Mandeville. Accordingly, Maggotty never expanded its population base and the closure left this township pretty much as it was before. It is as if the Revere plant had never existed. Santa Cruz had been indirectly affected by bauxite-alumina. Apart from the brief interlude of Revere's presence in Maggotty, the growth of Santa Cruz derives partly from its proximity to the Alpart-Nain plant. A significant number of Alpart workers reside in Santa Cruz because property values there are lower than in Mandeville and because Santa Cruz is culturally more hospitable to the black work force.

In St Catherine, only Ewarton is directly affected by bauxite-alumina. Alcan-Ewarton Works is the plant located here. Prior to the advent of bauxite mining, Ewarton was a railhead village for the Jamaica Government Railway. Like May Pen, Ewarton is close enough to Kingston for commuting and many of the technical and managerial staff live in the KMA in order to afford their children proper schooling. There is a sizeable staff compound of housing at this plant and many workers commute from the nearby market town of Linstead and Spanish Town, the parish capital. The overall impact of bauxite-alumina on Ewarton itself appears to have been quite insubstantial.

Of all the bauxite parishes, St Ann has the most towns and townships directly within the sphere of influence of the bauxite-alumina industry. Browns Town and Claremont are major market towns and bauxite drying plants are (were) located at Discovery Bay and Golden Grove. Browns Town, like Mandeville, has an elevated and cool environment. It is the leading centre of secondary education in St Ann and the location of one of the traditionally prestigious girls' schools in all Jamaica, St Hilda's. Only 5 miles uphill from Kaiser's Discovery Bay drying plant, it is physically within that company's sphere of influence. It continues to be a very important market town. Claremont had a similar experience in relation to the presence of Reynold's drying plant at Golden grove, just three and a half miles away. Since Reynolds closed this plant in 1984, there is no evidence of any significant change in the physiogomy and economic circumstance of either Claremont or Golden Grove. As was the case with Maggotty, the viability of these communities was untouched by the coming of bauxite-alumina.

Discovery Bay had an altogether different experience. It was transformed by bauxite-alumina from a minor fishing village (the old 'Dry Harbour') into a substantial coastal township which, though small in population, attracts many Jamaicans to its splendid Puerto Seco beach. Discovery Bay is a company township. The 800 or so Jamaicans employed by Kaiser comprise a relatively wealthy little community there. But most of their regular weekly market purchases would be in Browns Town.

Overall, the picture that emerges is that bauxite-alumina activity has had a limited impact on urban development within the rural man-space in Jamaica. Mandeville and Discovery Bay are the only two places where the impacts can be seen to have been substantial and direct. This finding is not surprising when we consider that bauxite-alumina activity is capital intensive and that the mineral deposits in Jamaica are located under previously settled communities. The one-city pattern of development of Caribbean plantation society remains unchanged. The consequential expansion of the population of the KMA as bauxite mining pushed the peasantry off the land exceeded the capacity of the KMA to provide enough jobs. Urban unemployment grew, slums developed apace, and problems of violence, crime, prostitution, drugs, etc. escalated. The social decay of Kingston and the rural-urban imbalance within the Jamaican social economy are partly a direct consequence of the dispossession of the peasantry by the BATs.

External Migration

Given the constraining effects of these development on the economic opportunities for advancement within Jamaica, hundreds of thousands of people, including the displaced peasantry, migrated. The outpouring that began in the early 1950s was so great that the government of the day commissioned a study of external migration.[10] The UK was the chief destination. Reconstruction of the war-ravaged economy in Britain was underway and the migrants found substantial job opportunities. Besides, the McCarran Act in the US in 1952 slammed the door on previous access to that country. The heightening of the Korean War in the 1950s and direct US involvement after the French defeat at Diem Bien Phu in 1954 increased US demand for Jamaican bauxite and intensified the TNCs rush to secure land with bauxite deposits.

Table 24.2 provides data on external migration from Jamaica in the postwar period. The sharp decline in 1961 and 1962 resulted from the Commonwealth Immigrants Act which the British parliament legislated in that year to close the door on black immigrants. Thereafter, the displaced peasants in Jamaica would become increasingly bottled up in Kingston. Data are not available in a form that would permit identifying those pushed out by bauxite incursions on the land. But from our survey of farmers in bauxite mining areas, "assisting members of families to migrate to England and elsewhere" was an important 'investment' from cash realized from sale of land to the bauxite companies [Russell 1982: 24]. Among farmers surveyed, migration is the fourth most important type of investment. It is an investment because migrants send substantial remittances back to relatives not just for their survival consumption, but also to buy house and land. At the national level, the significance of these remittances can be appreciated from the fact that, remittances are consistently higher than inflows of private foreign capital.

The pattern of external migration continued and reinforced a trend which we noted had begun in the late nineteenth century. The difference is that with the bauxite push, savings from earnings abroad can only buy house and house-plot instead of farm land. The scope for peasant expansion by this route has been virtually cut off by the monopoly of bauxite land.

Table 24.2 *Net migration figures (Jamaica), 1960-84*

Year	Number	Year	Number
1960	30,300	1961	38,500
1962	28,700	1963	7,300
1964	13,500	1965	6,500
1966	8,900	1967	20,000
1968	20,000	1969	29,000
1970	23,000	1971	31,500
1972	11,200	1973	10,200
1974	12,900	1975	12,100
1976	22,200	1977	21,100
1978	17,800	1979	21,400
1980	24,300	1981	5,900
1982	9,800	1983	4,300
1984	10,500		

Source: Jamaica Department of Statistics, *Demographic Statistics*, 1984

'Relocation' Schemes

Not all of the peasants were dislocated and forced to migrate, internally and externally. Others were relocated ('resettled'), while others ended up as tenant farmers on the lands they sold to the BATs. According to Cowell [1987], "resettlement was born from the staunch refusal of small settlers to sell their land" (p. 50). Cash purchase was the initial strategy the TNCs had used to secure peasant land. But the resistance of the peasantry to sell their land strengthened over time for a number of reasons. Cowell suggests that "the 1971 confrontation between Kaiser and 15 peasant farmers in the Dry Harbour mountains may be seen as a turning point in peasant attitude to Bauxite companies in Jamaica" (p. 48). Increasing political consciousness, the greater importance of land to the peasantry as the supply accessible to them contracted, changes in the demographic structure of the peasantry as older farmers increased in relative importance since it was the younger ones who tended to leave farming altogether, restricted migratory opportunities (internal and external) are only some of the reasons why peasant resistance strengthened. As resistance to sell increased, the BATs had to devise new strategies to secure land with bauxite deposits. So it was that Kaiser pioneered the resettlement programme by which farmers were relocated in new communities. It is said that "without such an incentive to part with the bauxite fields, the acquisition of mining lands by Kaiser and Alpart could never have provided enough bauxite to sustain present production rates" [Cowell 1987: 51]. Alcan and Alcoa also had to get involved.

The relocation of peasants in new communities involves many problems. They must leave ancestral homes and land. They must abandon tree crops which took years to establish. They must leave long established communities which have social infrastructures and a mode of life with accustomed behaviour, values and attitudes developed over generations. They must bring new land under plough and experiment with suitability of different plants in new ecological surroundings. In short, they must carve out a whole new manspace out of new landscape. It is a tall order that involves psychological adjustments, like leaving behind ancestral remains in family burial plots. In the circumstances, the market value of their new holdings and houses should exceed the cash value of those transacted to the companies. We do not have data to see whether this was generally the case. But it is unlikely, given the vast disparity in bargaining power between companies and peasants, especially in a politico-legal environment where the state acts in the interests of the companies.

Our survey results show that "a significant percentage of small farmers . . . found the non-cash payments as attractive as the cash transactions". Among the farmers surveyed, over 52% "admitted that they were highly satisfied at the time of the transaction. Of these 55% received all or part of their payment in cash, 22% received other farmland and house, 15% received other farmland only, and the remainder received other types of compensation such as house on relocated site" [Russell 1982: 20]. Farmers who were offered house and land elsewhere but refused gave the following reasons: "lack of health facilities, difficulty in obtaining transportation facilities, inability to overcome emotional attachments to old location, lack of facilities for worship, lack of educational facilities for their children, and lack of shopping facilities" [Russell 1982: 25].

Noel Cowell's participant observer study of two resettled communities in St Ann provides some fascinating evidence of the problems involved in resettlement as well as the way in which peasant resistance and mobilization managed to improve the conditions provided by the BATs over time. The study shows, for example, that Alcan's resettlement scheme at Village/Schwallenburg in 1980 was a marked improvement on that by Kaiser at Lime Tree Garden/Retreat in 1970. He attributes the change to:

1   Village was a small *cohesive* community which acted in unison in bargaining with the company;

2   increased understanding gained by the people through twenty years

of exposure to the bauxite companies and from the experience of their fellows who had sold to the company . . . They saw people from Village itself and from the surrounding areas who had sold their land live to regret it;

3   a shift in the role of the state after the 1974 reform under the Michael Manley government which strengthened the bargaining capacity of the peasantry through the newly established state institution the Jamaica Bauxite Institute (JBI).

Even when farmers themselves are better off as a result of resettlement as in the Schwallenburg case where "literally all settlers have gained short term advantages in terms of better housing and money in the bank", there is a problem of the negative impact on agricultural production. According to Cowell, Schwallenburg "is not an agricultural community. The lifestyle of the people has shifted from a rural oriented agricultural one to an urban oriented, semi-proletarian and commercial one" [1987: 64]. This negative impact on food production has important consequences for national development.

Tenant farmers on bauxite lands also face numerous problems. Conditions imposed by the companies are very restrictive. Restored mined-out land is not as good as unmined land. Peasant house-plots may be far from the tenanted land. Short-term tenancies on unmined land prevent them from planting food trees. The experience of Reynolds and Alcan as the pioneers in tenancy relationships is instructive. Reynolds 'tenants-at-will' scheme involved the following principles:

1   Any bona fide resident in the immediate areas could qualify as a tenant;

2   no rental charged;

3   land must be worked by the tenant;

4   each piece of land could be held for a year and a half;

5   another piece of land could become available if the first piece was used satisfactorily.

Salmon [1987] goes on to point out that "the actual amount of land received by each tenant was quite small, and . . . the shifty nature of this tenancy arrangement affected the continuity of farming". Alcan expanded its tenant farming scheme more than any of the other companies. By 1962, for example 30% of all Alcan's land was under tenant control. The Alcan scheme involved company supervised production operations by tenants on small plots, with the farmer being free to market his own crops. The Alcan scheme in fact became the model for a state land settlement programme, Project Land Lease, which the Manley regime introduced in the early 1970s.

Bauxite land tenancies in Jamaica vary from one company to another. Russell states that

some companies are more lenient in terms of leasing agricultural lands; however, their land use policies are more strict, as well as enforceable. At least one company requires tenants to fully utilize the acreage leased, and the crops planted must be short term . . . The planting of tree crops . . . is strictly forbidden . . . The lease-price is usually competitive and the installments must be paid on the due date [1982: 27].

On the whole, bauxite tenant farming in Jamaica has brought benefits in the form of access to land to those farmers involved, albeit under conditions that constrain their decision-making freedom. But it has a negative impact on the pattern of land use since it is restricted to the cultivation of short-term crops. This contrasts sharply with the traditional short-term *cum* long-term crop and livestock (especially small stock) product mix of Jamaican peasant farmers. To the extent that tenant farming has not completely replaced acreages secured by the TNCs from peasants, food production for the domestic market would have declined in both quantity and quality. This, in turn, would be reflected in lower incomes for the peasantry as a class; and a worsening of the nutritional status of poorer groups of consumers in the society.

Environmental Impact

Finally, we turn to consider the environmental impacts of bauxite-alumina operations. These fall into two broad categories: disturbance of the integrity of the land by mining, and pollution arising from alumina processing and from drying plants. Mining bauxite involves removal of top soil and scooping out the ore which, in Jamaica, is just below the surface of the land. This process leaves large caverns in the ground. Legislation stipulates that these must be filled in and the top soil replaced to a depth of at least six inches. In practice, this is not always achieved and there is no way the state can ensure that this is done. The scientific evidence is that restored mined-out land is incapable of maintaining production of anything other than grass and surface-feeding crops like vegetables and legumes. And even these require management capabilities which are said to be beyond the knowledge of peasant farmers, erosion being a high risk.

It is not surprising, therefore, that our survey of farmers in selected bauxite mining areas found that 82% of the farmers think that restored land is worse than pre-mined land. Only 1.4% were of the opinion that restored land is better than pre-mined land. Of the rest, 11% had no opinion while 5.6% think there is no difference between the two types of land.

Atmospheric pollution comes from air-borne "particulates produced in mining areas, quarries, rail roads, conveyor belts, chutes, etc., . . . Aerosols with entrained caustic soda and organics and noxious gases" are produced as waste in processing alumina and these noxious and toxic substances are emitted in the atmosphere.[11] A dangerous 'red mud' is discharged from the plants and this is stored in open spaces dammed up to create ugly 'lakes'. These red mud lakes have toxic substances which can seep into underground water systems. There is no firm evidence that this has yet occurred, but seepage can still occur over the longer term and the limestone environment characteristic of Jamaica is particularly receptive to seepage.

According to Lloyd Coke,

most of the adverse environmental effects which include corrosion of galvanized iron roofs, irritation caused by excessive dust levels, noxious gases, odours and damage to plant and animal life, have resulted in scores of complaints by irate citizens . . . decisions concerning the location of all but one of the alumina processing plants were based largely on considerations involving minimizing operating costs. In the early years of Bauxite mining, the environmental impact of the operations was not an important consideration [Weir et al. 1981: 79].

The companies involved have a bad record in relation to complaints and claims made on them by the peasantry who suffer the most from the adverse environmental effects. At first, the tendency was to pay claims made, as a general public relations exercise. But the companies abandoned that tactic as they came to realize that the state was impotent and that the peasantry had little chance of challenging them scientifically in whatever costly legal disputes that might arise. Besides, their manifest 'benefit' to the Jamaican economy placed them in a commanding position. Our survey of farmers revealed that 84% of those surveyed "would like to see an expansion of the bauxite industry in their areas". In these circumstances, the BATs can virtually get away with murder.

In the early 1970s things began to change. Changes in levels of political consciousness were becoming more manifest. The peasantry became more organized to make specific demands on both the BATs and the state. And as this happened, the state itself had to become more and more responsive to peasant demands. Thus, it was that during the Manley regime

as a result of pressure on the political directorate a multidisciplinary committee was set up in April 1975, firstly to consider the effects of pollutants from the operations on housing, plant and animal life; and, secondly, to make recommendations for the payment of compensation where the pollution caused damages; among other things" [Weir et al. 1981: 80].

This committee found evidence of atmospheric pollution and made recommendations for correcting and monitoring it, and established tentative environmental standards to be imposed as a temporary measure. By late 1979, a new stage was reached with the setting up of an Inter-Agency group under the aegis of the Ministry of Mining and Energy to monitor the levels of atmospheric pollution. "This group started regular monitoring in September 1980 and prepared its first interim report in April 1981." The technocratic arm of the state completed its assignment. It would be interesting to see how this has been followed up. So much has changed since the general election of October 1980 which removed the Manley regime from office that it is doubtful how much of this work is being translated into action of a kind that relieves the environmental pressure on the peasantry.

The Social Economy of Underdevelopment: Conflict and Change

Analysis of the impact of the BATs on the social economy must be anchored on an understanding of the conflicting interests of the parties directly involved – the TNCs, the state, the workers, and the peasantry in particular.

Character of the TNCs

Six TNCs have been involved in Jamaica's bauxite alumina industry over the years – Alcan of Canada, Reynolds, Kaiser, Alcoa, Revere and Alpart of the US. Their Jamaican operations are branch plants of parent companies in the two countries from which they originate. The parent companies are vertically integrated enterprises which own and control resources involved at every stage from mining bauxite, processing alumina from it, smelting alumina into aluminium, fabricating a vast range of aluminium products, and distributing these products worldwide. Accordingly, there is no trade in bauxite-alumina in the conventional sense. That is to say Jamaica does not sell (export) bauxite-alumina to the rest of the world. It is transferred by each company to a counterpart firm at a higher stage in the production process in North America or Western Europe.

The value from this transfer that comes to Jamaica (the 'returned value') is determined by the BATs which control the world market for aluminium and aluminium products. They decide what quantities are produced on prevailing prices resulting from the interaction of world supply and demand for the final products. Changes in the demand for aluminium products depend on the situation affecting end use. Aluminium is used for a wide variety of things – from airplane wings and bodies to motor vehicle engine blocks, to roofing material, drink and beer cans, pots and pans, etc. It is a versatile material.

The Jamaican subsidiaries of the BATs do not decide how much bauxite or alumina they produce. Nor do they decide how this is produced (*ie* what technology is used). The managerial and administrative staff of these subsidiaries see to it that what quantities are needed by the BATs are produced as efficiently as possible. That is to say, at the lowest possible cost to the BATs. This is to ensure that each subsidiary makes as much profits as it can. These staff personnel are really performing the same function as the 'attorneys' did on the slave plantations during slavery days.

Character of the State

The state in Jamaica consists of the entire apparatus of public administration – the Governor General as Head of State represents the Queen of England, Parliament with an elected House of Representatives and nominated Senate, the Parish Councils at local government level, the Civil Service, Judiciary, Army and Police, Statutory Boards (parastatals) and state companies/firms. It is a variant of the Westminster model of government. Jamaica attained constitutional independence in 1962, after being a colony of Great Britain for 307 years. The Spanish had it before 1655; Spain having conquered the island from the indigenous Arawak Indians in 1494.

Since independence, the two major political parties have alternated office after two terms each – the Jamaica Labour Party (JLP) from 1962 to 1967 were returned until 1972; and the People's National Party (PNP) under Michael Manley's leadership from 1972 to 1976 with a return mandate to 1980. The JLP came back in office under the leadership of Seaga in 1980; and it remains in office – the PNP boycotting the hastily called and 'improper' 1983 election in which only a few constituencies were contested by independent and splinter party candidates. Seaga's JLP rules somewhat tenuously at present (mid 1985).

The political directorate essentially consists of the Prime Minister and his Cabinet. They make executive policy decisions. Parliament legislates (*ie* makes laws); and debates policy. The Courts, the Army and the Police maintain law and order. This is the core of central government with executive, legislative, and judicial arms. Local government is not important in Jamaica as the parish councils are no more than "expenditure committees of central government". The current trend of the Seaga regime is to further erode the responsibilities of local government – the city council, Kingston and St

Andrew Corporation (KSAC), has been disbanded; the number of parish council representatives is being reduced and several functions previously carried out by Parish Councils have been transferred to relevant ministries of the central government.

Workers' Organization

The bauxite-alumina workers are a small number of about 6,000 or so people in the best of times. An average of 1,000 workers in each of the six BATs. They are all members of two trade unions which bargain with the companies for better wages and working conditions. The National Workers' Union (NWU) and the Bustamante Industrial Trade Union (BITU) are affiliated with the two major political parties – the PNP and the JLP, respectively. These trade unions were born out of the revolt of 1938 which also caused the change from Crown Colony status to fully representative government. Universal adult suffrage was first introduced in 1944; thereafter, every adult could vote for candidates to represent them in government. The direct connection between trade unions and political parties has important consequences. Both parties are multi-class in character and aspect,[12] while the trade unions only concern themselves with the interests of the workers they represent. So this effectively limits the workers' voice as far as national issues are concerned.

Character of the Peasantry

The peasantry are the most numerous people in this whole scene. The small peasants (*ie* those with under 5 acres of land) are the majority by far. Their production from these small farms provides a subsistence level of living; and many of them have to seek wage work whenever and wherever they can find it to help them survive. Some can do independent artisan trade work as well. They have to be very versatile and hardworking. They and their families toil on the land growing crops and raising livestock, especially small stock like pigs, goats and chickens ('yard fowls'). The small peasants are black people of African race and culture, except for a few East Indians. They are the main source of the country's food supplies apart from the imported wheat and wheat flour, rice, cornmeal, dairy products, salt and pickled fish, and some meat products (like chicken 'necks and backs'). This is the basic food basket which goes, together with domestically produced vegetables, roots and tubers, legumes, and fruits to make up the diet of the majority of poor people. Middle and big peasants grow food for the domestic market as well. And they, like many of the small peasants grow export crops like sugar cane, bananas, citrus, coffee, pimento, etc.

Organizationally, the Jamaica Agricultural Society (JAS) is the forum of the peasantry. But it is dominated by the middle and big peasants who provide leadership at the national and branch society levels. Many of these leaders are former school teachers and they have traditionally articulated the demands of the peasantry as a class. Not surprisingly, the JAS as an organization is PNP-dominated although the small peasants have for the most part been traditionally JLP. This PNP-affiliation of the JAS "led the JLP government in 1962 to reduce the staff of the JAS". The study by McBain [1987] provides further examples of the problems in the functioning of the JAS as a result of the JLP/PNP see-saw in office. She points out that the JAS

is largely financed by the state and its functions have been set out by legislation. It operates as a parastatal entity working in conjunction with the Ministry of Agriculture. But it is the very areas that give the JAS potential for influence that at the same time constrain its effectiveness in promoting the interests of farmers as a class of peasant producers (p. 48).

Other than the JAS there is no national institution with this capability and potential, for mobilizing peasants as a class.

The Jamaican peasantry is culturally stratified into Creole and African components. In past times, the creoles were mainly mulatto in racial terms but this is no longer so. Today, that element is Afro-Saxon in culture and lifestyle while the small peasants live within a folk cultural matrix which is distinctively African. The small peasant is not in the same social strata as the middle and big peasants. These latter are very much 'middle class'. The small peasant shares more, at least culturally, with the rural working class, the agro-proletariat in particular as many small peasants themselves have to seek wage work to supplement their meagre own-account farm incomes.

Their economic circumstance helps significantly to define their social status. But ascriptive characteristics, like colour, manner of speech, dress, etc. are just as *operatively* significant. The peasantry, in short, is a microcosm of the larger plural society of which it is an integral part. They are pushed out on a peripheral plane by the social and economic dynamics of plantation capitalism reinforced, yet modified, by the coming of mining and other capitals in the period since the Second World War. We must turn, then, to look at that process more formally.

Reinforcement of Plantation Capitalism: Staple Cycle

Before the war, there was no mining to speak of, little or no manufacturing, and only some tourism which had started as a joint-product with the banana trade. The economy was strictly agricultural, with plantations, the agro-proletariat and peasants. Commercial trade was anchored on plantation/peasant exports; food and other consumer goods imports, and some capital goods imports. The banking system was geared to the associated commercial (trading) sector and plantation agriculture, while foodstuffs produced by the peasantry moved through a system of public markets that had created important market towns. Kingston, the capital, was the centre of commerce and government.

The Crown Colony government was ruled by an English governor who selected his own Executive Council and the Civil Service was headed by an English colonial secretary. The revolt of 1938 was to change this somewhat. But the war intervened. The war brought dramatic changes. The virtual closure of the economy by the dangers of wartime shipping induced the setting up of manufacturing plants to produce basic necessities like soap, matches, etc. Light industry really began to develop at this time. And food previously imported (for example, rice) had to be produced, or substitutes developed to replace it – cassava flour, for example, as a substitute for wheat flour. Food was being produced everywhere, even in the city ('victory gardens'). When the war ended, things were never quite the same again. Manufacturing was to become an established and significant activity. However, when the free flow of food imports resumed, all the initiatives in producing replacements and substitutes were disbanded.

After the war, mining was to become the 'leading sector' in Jamaica's 'export propelled' economic development. Bauxite-alumina was the new *staple*. Before that it was sugar up to about the turn of the twentieth century, followed by bananas until Panama disease struck in the 1930s. As had occurred with sugar and bananas, the staple cycle was to be repeated with bauxite-alumina. The 'Foundation period' lasted from 1942 to 1957; the 'Golden Age' of expansion ran from 1958 to 1972; the phase of 'Maturity' was short-lived from 1972 to 1974; and the current phase of 'Liquidation' and decline started from 1974, initiated by a constellation of forces external to the Jamaican economy.

Being a peripheral appendage of the international capitalist system, an export driven economy based predominantly on a single staple is affected directly by changes in international demand, in the technology of production, and by the discovery/realization of new sources of supply of the particular staple. It is important to note here that although the Jamaican bauxite-alumina is in the final stage of

liquidation crisis, or breakdown . . . the staple 'cycle' is not one which inevitably recommences. It is, however, typical of plantation (capitalist) economy that a new cycle does recommence in response to new technology and/or new demand conditions for the traditional staple or, of course, as a result of the rise of an altogether new staple into pre-eminence [Levitt and Best 1975: Chapter 3, 21].

Historically, Jamaica as a peripheral capitalist plantation economy illustrates the dynamics of the staple cycle theory.[13] The sugar plantation liquidation and crisis phase started with Emancipation in 1838 and accelerated with the abolition of preferences in the British market in the 1840s. Other slave-based cane sugar producing countries like Brazil, Cuba, etc.,[14] and new cane sugar producers with advanced technology, plus the development of best sugar production in Europe heightened the crisis and accelerated the pace of liquidation. And by the end of the nineteenth century, the industry was in such shambles that a Royal Commission was sent out to investigate conditions. However, banana exports, based on peasant production, had started in the 1860s; and, by the early twentieth century, surpassed sugar in export earnings. This new staple passed through its phased of the cycle; expanding rapidly when the planter class and foreign capital (a US-based TNC, the United Fruit Company) began production late in the nineteenth century. Bananas reached the phase of maturity during the 1920s, under competitive pressure from more technologically advanced production in Central America and elsewhere. By the 1930s, its phase of liquidation and crisis was hastened by the ravage of Panama disease. During the maturity phase of the banana cycle, sugar received a new lease of life through technological change brought in by foreign capital.[15] But the prolonged depression of the early 1930s brought the whole house down and everything crashed in 1938.

The discovery of bauxite in 1942 opened the door for a new surge in Jamaica's economic growth – far greater than ever had been the case with sugar and bananas. For the market for its end product, aluminium and its products, grew leaps and bounds as a strategic material during the Second World War; and subsequently with the US involvement in the Korean, then the Vietnam wars. The world economy expanded rapidly during the 1950s and 1960s. Western Europe and Japan were able to build back their war-shattered economies with massive financial aid from the US which had firmly established itself as the leading imperialist nation ('top metropole') by the end of the Second World War. And it was US and Canadian capital which controlled Jamaica's bauxite-alumina industry.

The world economy expanded at unprecedented rates during the 1950s and 1960s but by 1967 evidence of a downturn became obvious. A prolonged world economic crisis continues to this day. During this period, there have been short-lived business cycles of boom and recession. But 'stagflation', with rising prices (inflation) accompanied by rising unemployment, appeared as a new phenomenon in the industrialized capitalist centre nations. Prolonged crisis periods following expansionary booms are part of the historical experience of capitalist development. But stagflation is a new experience.

Crisis and Change

Naturally, in the capitalist periphery of the Third World the crisis is exaggerated. Demand for raw material exports declines and so the prices received for these fall. Simultaneously, the prices countries must pay for imports of goods and services rise. So adverse trade balances occur. Additionally, the crisis in the centre nations lessens the flow of private investment capital to the Third World. The supply of loanable funds from centre states and the multilateral lending agencies (IMF/World Bank, especially) becomes limited and interest rates escalate. Thus, the balance of payments crisis of the capitalist periphery deepens. The national debt rises substantially as these countries must borrow more to support the reduced foreign exchange earnings from their staple exports. The debt problem becomes acute. Third World nations must devise strategies to survive the crisis and promote their own economic development.

The Jamaican experience demonstrates this process dramatically. Jamaica has no energy source to supply the large energy requirement involved in transforming bauxite into alumina. It depends on imported oil supplies. When the OPEC countries, in their own response to the world crisis, substantially raised the price of oil in 1973 the Jamaican economy was in a bind. The PNP government of Michael Manley had to devise a responsive strategy. The strategy involved a comprehensive package of initiatives:

1   the introduction of a levy (tax) on the BATs indexed to the price of aluminium in the world market. The immediate effect was to raise government revenue from bauxite-alumina 'exports' some seven fold, from about US$25 million to US$175 million;

2   securing a national stake in the industry by purchase of 51% of mining activities of the bauxite exporters (Kaiser and Reynolds), and 6-7% of the alumina refining corporations, Alcan and Alcoa;

3   repatriation of all bauxite lands to the nation through state-ownership, with provision for mining leases to the BATs in accordance with their requirements;

4   setting up a national institute, the JBI, to monitor and control aspects of the BATs' activities within the parameters of the new government initiatives;

5   spearheading a lobby of bauxite-alumina producing countries to form the International Bauxite Association (IBA) with the aim of collectively protecting their interests as a countervailing force to the BATs;

6   initiating collective regional state involvement in the production of aluminium, with two such ventures: (a) a Jamaica-Venezuela-Mexico enterprise (JAVAMEX) which would use the oil-based energy of those countries for smelting alumina from a joint-venture state alumina plant in South Manchester; and (b) a Jamaica-Guyana-Trinidad joint-venture enterprise which would establish an aluminium smelter in oil-rich Trinidad with alumina from Jamaica and Guyana. Neither of these ventures materialized, for a variety of reasons which are beyond our scope in this paper.

Notwithstanding the comprehensiveness of this package-strategy and the immense measure of dignity which it conferred on the Jamaican people as a whole, the strategy-package did not fully achieve the objectives envisaged by the Manley regime. It is important to note, however, that all classes in Jamaican society and the opposition JLP hailed the overall strategy, including the legislative imposition of the Levy when negotiations broke down between the government representatives and the BATs.[16]

The limited success of the strategy stems from the following: inability to maintain the returned value from the Levy as the aluminium market deteriorated; incapacity to articulate an appropriate strategy and mechanisms for state management of the BATs' livestock enterprises and other food production (actual and potential) on bauxite lands; inability of the JBI to fully monitor and control the mining and refining activities of the companies; the limited power of the IBA which simply monitors the international scene, disseminates information, and *advises* member governments on appropriate price ranges for the resource; and the failure to implement regional state joint ventures with countries having abundant energy supplies. The paper by McBain [1987] provides an analysis of the reasons for the limited success, especially as it concerns the impact on the peasantry.

Ratooning of Plantation Capitalism: Overview

The BATs are stark pillars of industrialization and modernity in a sea of hillside peasant farming communities which had been neglected for a hundred and more years of plantation capitalism. The coming of heavy equipment for excavation and transport of the resource and the hustle and bustle of construction in building refining plants, overhead cable-ways, housing enclaves, etc., must have jerked the psyche of the people living in previously sleepy peasant communities. The BATs' presence could only be interpreted as 'progress' in these circumstances. And rightly so. But the Jamaican peasantry in the bauxite parishes have paid a heavy price for this progress. The small peasants and the agro-proletariat remain firmly stationed at the bottom of the economic and social ladder. In the words of one peasant woman, they are safe there because they can fall no further; they "can only go up while those at the top can fall down". But will the top fall down?

To answer that question we must revert to our analysis of the structural foundations. The bauxite land economy falls within the international space of 'hinterland America'. As such, it is firmly integrated with the 'metropole' economies of the US/Canada through the BATs, and the Jamaican state concentrated in Kingston. The BATs and the state are the top but we have seen, earlier, that the state functions with the interest of the BATs as its primary focus. Now in this stage of liquidation the BATs are flying out and the state is left to hold things together. At the time of writing only Alcan and the state-operated CAP plant are in operation. Francis [1987] shows the tenuous nature of the latter while Alcan is cutting capital costs and trimming back. So the Seaga government is caught frantically searching for a new staple to propel the economy. Tourism, export manufacturing, and non-trad-itional agriculture (winter vegetables, coffee, etc.) are advocated. But each seems to have peculiar problems. Consequently, the crisis deepens, virtually week by week.[17]

Our framework of analysis is that developed by Best and Levitt in their monumental study of Caribbean economy.[18] Caribbean economy was devel-oped as a hinterland/periphery of the North Atlantic metropole/centre. And as such, its subsequent underdevelopment is linked directly with the develop-ment of the metropole/centre. It is the now well-known centre-periphery paradigm which describes how only a segment of the hinterland is actually integrated with the metropole. That segment connects with the rest of hinter-land economy by drawing from it natural resources and supplies of labour power for production within the segment; and provides all the resources for reproduction within itself. Thus, the 'residentiary' component becomes the source for siphoning surpluses generated in hinterland production. The 'over-seas' component engages purely in resource extraction utilizing whatever labour it needs from the residentiary. Although its initial capital needs come from the metropole (as 'foreign investment') subsequent capital accumulation results from retention of part of the surplus generated by production in the hinterland. In such a circumstance, the residentiary sector functions as a hinterland of the overseas economy.

Bauxite-alumina production in Jamaica came within the man-space of the peasantry located within the central heartland of the country. The process of accommodation involved not much modification of the institutional frame-work set long before in the days of slave ('pure') plantation economy. For the BATs have the same basic characteristics of being a part of 'overseas econ-omy'; they operate as 'total institutions'; and 'incalculability' is a feature of their accounts concerning production in Jamaica. Elaboration of this is provided in Beckford [1972: 94-96]. The BATs, so to speak, fitted into a ready-made mould. Their impact on the Jamaican social economy unfolded in certain well-defined ways. Previous macro-level studies revealed the nature of surplus drainage and led, subsequently, to changes in government policy to secure more for the Jamaican economy. The 1974 levy, state participation in equity, and repatriation of land was the culmination of this. But the persistent crisis in the international capitalist ('world') economy heightened and became exaggerated in Jamaica, as in other Third World economies.

Our concern here, however, relates specifically to the impacts of the BATs on the rural social economy from the beginning until now. The main thesis we advance is that these impacts reverberated within the bauxite land economy in the traditional struggle for land which the country's peasantry have been waging since Emancipation. The earlier obvious manifestation of that struggle (the riots/revolt of 1865 and 1938) are not reproduced in postwar events. Primarily because escape opportunities for migration to Kingston and abroad reduced population pressure on the land base, and because new employment opportunities opened up elsewhere as the economy became diversified. Tourism, branch-plant manufactures, distribution, construction and, most importantly, the state sector created new spaces for a certain degree and kind of economic and social mobility for the peasantry, as a whole. But that process was not rapid enough to cope and so a 'displaced peasantry' exists within the social matrix of Kingston. Secure links with parts of families remaining on the land helps sustain the survival capacities of those who have left. And remit-tances from relatives abroad provides vital support for all.

Nevertheless, our research project provides some evidence to support the thesis. The survey findings provide clues; but data are not available to permit the kind of firm empirical support. The main sources of such data are the state and the companies. But the Census of Agriculture data are too far spaced in time to determine, for example, the total number of small farmers and acrea-ges in the bauxite parishes during each period of land acquisitions by the companies. Nor are there available data on land use to indicate crops planted and the volume of production before and after the companies' acquisitions. To secure such data requires cooperation from the companies. But none of them was willing to offer the project team such access. Interestingly, some companies responded to invitations to participate in our dissemination Workshop. Although not assisting in the promotion of the research, they wanted to know what we found out. We view this attitude as a stark manifestation of the contempt that transnational corporations have for the genuine interest of people in host countries like Jamaica. It is a fact that no public relations exercise of theirs should blind us to.

The project does, however, provide a canvas for mounting the kind of further research which would deepen knowledge on these impacts. For example, the matter of relocating people within the rural landscape is important for any programme of land reform. So the experience of the companies in their tenant farm operations would provide benchmark data. The study by Cowell gives but a glimpse into the very interesting kind of social engineering problems and man-space relationships involved. A deeper historical analysis of traditional pen-keeping/peasant relations along with information on contemporary company-tenant farmer relations is suggested as one area for further study.

Clearly, it will require either company-state co-ordination or, as seems inevitable by the rate of company exodus in this liquidation phase, full state research from its future active participation in production to prosecute the kinds of enquiry suggested by the results of this project. The character of the state that future evolution of Jamaican society produces will determine how such knowledge is acquired.

Epilogue

The BATs flew
leaving
scars on the landscape,
blood on the heartscape
of unemployed city youth,
and sweat and tears
from the soulscape
of migrant black folk
in London town

Notes

* "The social economy of bauxite in the Jamaican man-space". *Social and Economic Studies* 36:1 (1987a).

1   See, for example, H.D. Huggins, *Aluminium in Changing Communities* (London: Andre Deutsch, 1965); and N. Girvan,*The Caribbean Bauxite Industry* (Mona: ISER,

University of the West Indies, 1967).

2 See Ken Post, *Arise Ye Starvelings* (The Hague: Institute of Social Studies, 1979) for a comprehensively brilliant analysis of the 1938 rebellion.

3 See Lloyd Best, "A model of pure plantation economy", *Social and Economic Studies* (September 1968) for a descriptive analysis of the 'pure plantation' case. The most succinct elaboration of the *staple cycle theory* applied to plantation economy is provided in Levitt and Best, "Export Propelled Growth and Industrialization in the Caribbean". 2 vols. (unpublished mimeo.)

4 For further discussion of these provisions see Davis, "Jamaica in the world aluminium industry", *JBI Journal* (November 1980 and July 1981) and Gillette-Chambers, "The evolution of bauxite mining laws in Jamaica", *JBI Journal* (November 1980).

5 See the interesting study by Linda Hewitt, "Internal migration and urban growth", in *Recent Population Movements in Jamaica* (World Population Year, CICRED Series, 1974).

6 See Hewitt, p. 217.

7 See *Culture, Race and Class in the Commonwealth Caribbean* (Mona: UWI, Extra-Mural Department, 1984) which is the latest formulation made by Smith. Chapter 6 of that book deals specifically with Jamaica. The spirited sociological controversy over pluralism in Caribbean societies reflects complexities in the interaction of race and class within the mode of production and the mode of exchange that characterize plantation capitalism.

8 Relative to their counterparts in North America, however, they are *not* highly paid.

9 The following discussion of bauxite towns and townships draws from the project research work of Dawn Eva and Lindel Smith as reported in a number of Working Papers.

10 See G. Roberts and D. Mills, *A Study of External Migration in Jamaica 1953-55* (Mona: ISER, University of the West Indies, 1956).

11 See chapter by Lloyd Coke in Weir et al., "Environmental impacts of bauxite mining and processing in Jamaica" (Mona: ISER, University of the West Indies, 1981).

12 Traditionally, the PNP has a strong middle class, urban-based appeal while the JLP has rural peasant-base support allied with the capitalist merchant-planter class. But these supports have become fluid since the early 1970s.

13 For a full elaboration of the theory and its general application to 'plantation economy' see Levitt and Best "Pure plantation economy" (St Augustine: IIR, University of the West Indies, 1975), mimeo. Its application to the bauxite-alumina industry in Jamaica is provided in a Workshop Paper by Levitt-Polyani (1985).

14 Slavery was not abolished in these Portuguese and Spanish territories until the 1880s.

15 The UK based TNC, Tate and Lyle, established two large modern factories and associated plantations at Frome in Westmoreland and Monymusk in Clarendon, under a Jamaican subsidiary called West Indies Sugar Company.

16 With the sole exception of Neville Ashenheim, the national capitalist/merchant/planter class supported the government's action. There was no expressed reservation concerning the repatriation of bauxite lands nor other measures in the package. (Ashenheim is the head of the oldest capitalist clan which owns the sole newspaper, *The Gleaner*, and a host of other national big

capital enterprises. He also drafted the entrenched property rights clause in Jamaica's Independence Constitution.)

17   The rapid rate of devaluation of the Jamaican dollar on the weekly auction market during 1985 is a manifestation of this.

18   Best and Levitt, "Export-Propelled Growth".

25

Plantation Capitalism
and Black Dispossession*

The world has changed dramatically since I elaborated on the political economy of underdevelopment in plantation societies ten years ago. Small colonial plantation-based states achieved flag independence in the Caribbean and in the Pacific and Indian Oceans. Large and some small colonial societies won revolutionary wars of liberation in Africa. And the struggle of black people in the New World shifted more to the urban-industrial sphere of 'postindustrial' capitalist state-societies.

Social change on any scale informs the work of students of society. I have therefore developed with this development. And the study of underdevelopment on a world scale developed with a rapidity unknown before 1970. With the Marxian paradigm of social change, Amin of Africa and Szentes of Hungary – Tanzania provided broadside assaults on neoclassical/Keynesian theories of underdevelopment. Arghiri Emmanuel articulated a theory of unequal exchange to expose the bankruptcy of bourgeois trade theory. And Thomas of the Caribbean adumbrated a meaningful theory of transformation for 'small dependent' state-societies. Multiplier effects of these foundation works reverberate everywhere. Meanwhile the initial excursions of European and North American Marxist scholars into the causes of Third World backwardness (notably Baran) was enriched by the work of people like Sweezy and Bettelheim.

The institutions-based historical analysis of Latin American and Caribbean structuralists provided the skeleton on which scholars tried to build 'dependency theory'. But the deepening crisis of world capitalism after 1973 accentuated the class contradictions of capitalism within the periphery of the system on a scale that made dependency theory inadequate for informing transformational possibilities. So an integration of Marxian and structuralist formulations has become necessary and urgent. It is from this contextual base that I want to examine Jay Mandle's recent contribution, *The Roots of Black Poverty*.[1]

Mandle is a US 'Marxist' student of plantation society. He comes to his work much better equipped than the run-of-the-mill lumpen-bourgeois 'Marxist' writers of recent vintage, products of the hot-house type of scholarship characteristic of revolutionary times (never in revolutionary places).

Generally speaking, intellectual workers in and of the Third World are few and far between. For the black Diaspora, they are dispersed on the three corners of the globe. In black state-societies of the Diaspora, the bureaucratic bourgeoisie is dominant. The peoples' struggles against imperialism are articulated by Liberal and Marxian political practitioners. And the intellectual lumpen-bourgeoisie of the state academies hardly read or study the people. So progressive interpretations of struggle and change are characterized by pragmatism at one level and vulgarism at the other.

Given that situation, evidence of scholarship which is grounded in objective reality is to be welcome. On this account Jay Mandle's book deserves a welcome. But it cannot be so hearty as I would like to extend because a racialist bias appears at a fundamental point, and because his attempt at synthesis of Marxian and structural analysis is quite incomplete. Mine is the viewpoint of an intellectual worker in and of the Third World. That it really does matter 'where you are coming from' is more obvious to me now than it was in the past. For you see Mandle is a serious North American Jew who has picked up most of his learning of black society from living and working with us in the Caribbean.[2]

Now I think it is important to locate the discussion of Mandle's book in time and space for readers not familiar with the New World black experience. The theme is movements of (Jah) people – African people. Two time periods are involved: first, under slave trading to supply labour power for New World plantation crop production (sixteenth to nineteenth centuries); and secondly, 'migrations' after abolition of slavery where the freedmen sought to extricate themselves from the clutches of agrarian capitalism (late nineteenth to twentieth centuries).

The Roots of Black Poverty studies "migrations of the freedmen" from the US Southern 'plantation economy.' The data analysed are census revelations of the whereabouts of Afro-Americans. It provides a thread for extending forward the weave laid by Alex Haley's now famous *Roots*.[3] The thread is firm. It is part of a cord of solid empiricism started by demographers like G.W.P. Roberts, anthropologists like M.G. and R.T. Smith, historians like C.L.R. James and Eric Williams, and economists like Lloyd Best.[4] That cord binds the experience of African people in the New World and defines Afro-America as the Western segment of the 'Black Diaspora.' The map below (Figure 25.1) presents a still motion picture. Afro-American (see dashed outline) is that central portion of the New World which includes the US South, the Caribbean, the Guianas, Northeast Brazil and the Caribbean littoral of Central America. Black people are a majority of the population living in these areas of the New World.

The map is divided into six sectors: two in the Old World – Africa and Western Europe; and four in the New World. Africa is sector 1, original home-base of the black slaves who were captured and bought by the merchant/planters of sector 2, Western Europe. White European pirate-capitalists plied the Middle Passage with slave ships that brought the captured Africans to a new home in the New World: to Brazil, sector 3; to the Caribbean, sector 4; and to the US, sector 6. Plain open arrows depict these initial coerced plantings of Africa labour on the slave plantations of the New

Figure 25.1   *The black diaspora. Movements of black people: roots and branches*

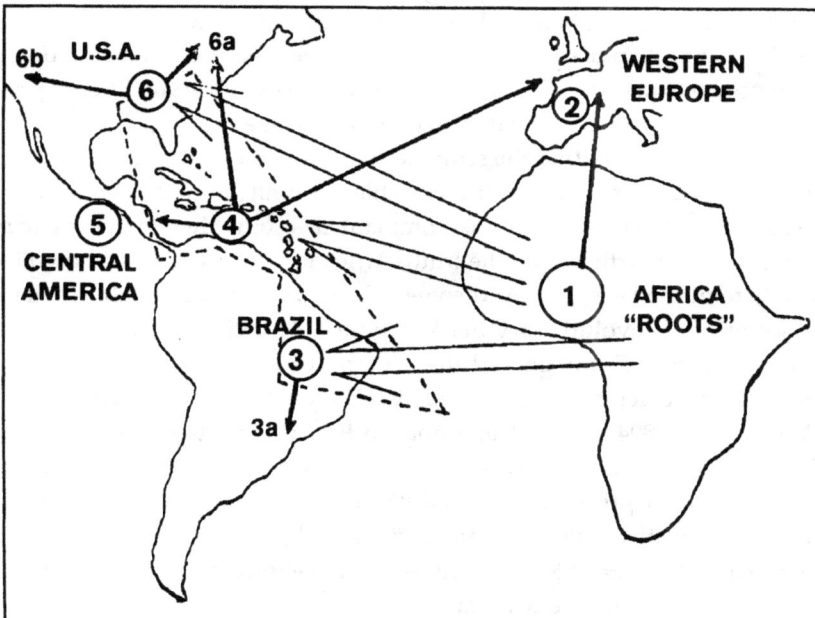

World. In the time since emancipation of the slaves, three main movements are depicted. Within sector 3, from northeast Brazil to the industrial Centre-South, 3a. From sector 4, movements from the Caribbean to establish capitalist plantations in Central America and to build the Panama Canal – thus creating early twentieth century sector 5; again from sector 4 to industrialised 'mother countries' of Western Europe, middle twentieth century; and yet again from sector 4 to industrialised North America since the second Imperialist War (the Second World War).

The last movements are within the US – sector 6 where, after civil war brought the slave plantation South under manners from the industrialized North, Afro-Americans moved to job opportunities in and around new England – New York – Pennsylvania and up the Mississippi to Chicago-Detroit, 6a. And more recently, "since World War II" from the 'Black Belt' of the plantation South to the Southwest and West Coast, sector 6b. Mandle analyses the dynamics of transformation in sector 6 with the combined tool kit of Marxism and structuralism. But he makes a fundamental (Genovesian) misinterpretation for black struggles.

The slave mode of production entrapped African-Americans within the slave economy of the South. That economy was held together by a superstructure based on an ideology of white superiority and black inferiority; with white superiority imposing *by force* a world view based on the power of military technology. Europeans warred against one another, against the indigenous Indians of the New World, against the Africans and again against themselves. Capitalism, born in Western Europe and growing to encompass the globe, is a system based on exploitation of the labour of the many by the few who come to privatize Jah land and the resources of Nature. Thus capitalism destroyed every other social formation in its wake.

Now Mandle argues that the struggles of Afro-Americans against entrapment before the overthrow of slavery achieved limited success because the slaves accepted the ideology of the dominant class of white planter/owners. Nothing could be further from the truth. African slaves rebelled and revolted everywhere in the Diaspora. And some efforts succeeded to establish viable state societies of revolutionary black people – Berbice and Palmares were antecedents to San Domingo and the triumph of the 'Black Jacobins' there. Haiti as the first black nation-state established after the revolutionary triumph of Toussaint in 1804 was a clear signal to Europe that the final assault of African slave-guerrillas would soon triumph everywhere. And the fetters of the slave mode of production on industrial transformation in Europe was obvious to the British industrial capitalist class.

The British Industrial Revolution in the late eighteenth century marked the beginning of a new era of capitalism. 'Industrial capitalism' pushed 'mercantile (commercial) capitalism' out of its way. Mercantile capitalism found its most profitable venture in slave-plantation *production* of tropical commodities for sale in the expanding industrialised markets where wage labour could buy these commodities. Long distant 'international' trade was critical to the slave plantation mode of production. It is this capitalist market that defined the particular *mode of exchange* which co-joins New World slave production with world capitalism; and thus makes it appropriate to describe it as a capitalist social formation from the start. I am arguing that plantation capitalism pre-dates industrial capitalism. Mandle supports my argument in a kind of way by saying that the US South could not exist without the North where an American industrialist class ruled after the 'Boston Tea Party' expelled the English and made the American Revolution.

African slaves never accepted the world view of the white capitalist land-lord class. They struggled by violent revolt and revolution. And they samfied the white man with a *guerrilla strategy* called 'Sambo' in some places. Sambo samve boss!! "Yes massa, yes massa" to get an easier job in the shade of the Great House; to get access to a piece of land for his own provision ground; and to buy land from backra wherever possible. That is not acceptance that massa is god. Black people know that well, as only we can.

In the same way that slave guerrilla strategy and tactics antedate modern guerrilla warfare of liberation struggles, I want to argue that agrarian industrialism on the slave plantation introduced elements of industrial capitalism before that system spread on a world scale. You see, plantation agriculture was a militarized production process that put disciplined specialization of work function into crop production. Furthermore, all plantation commodities underwent some crude product transformation in 'factories in the fields' – sugar mills and cotton gins, for example. Accordingly, slave plantation economy is, at one and the same time, involved in agriculture and agro-industry which *proletarianizes labour* by land monopoly and by factory technology. And it is the particular racist character of this proletarianization that gives plantation capitalism its specific character and dynamics. Mandle entirely misses this point. So that "the breakdown of the Southern plantation economy" is interpreted as coming from outside the South – specifically from the imposition of the South of the world view (ideology) of industrial capitalists from the North.[5] Yet he himself points out that institutionalized racism is as strong in the North as it is in the South.

I am arguing that the racial stratification of white planter-capitalists at the top of plantation society is rooted in the mode of production; that likewise the immobility of black labourers is instituted in the mode of production; and that this basic contradiction between capital and labour has a specific African *vs* European (black-white) confrontation which is only appeased by the mulatto

Afro-Saxon's manipulation of the system of production as the 'busha' who executes the order of the planter-capitalist, and as the 'liberal-democrats' who accede to state offices when adult suffrage is finally won by black people. In this latter phase we find these Afro-Saxons in government house, state cabinets, and at various levels of 'government' (local, national and at the United Nations). The point is that this mulatto class of bureaucrats are tokens of the capitalist power manipulation of the black labour force. They 'govern' on behalf of the capitalist classes, national and international (foreign).

Plantation capitalism has certain defining features which make it a kind of 'special case'. One is the institutionalization of race into the mode of production. Another is the international (forced) mobility of labour characteristic of that social formation. Economists have always stressed the importance of capital flows in the spread of global capitalism. In plantation societies, the movement of labour is of equal significance. For it was the forced entrapment of labour that made the slave economy so profitable. And after emancipation, as Mandle shows in chapter 2 mechanisms to deny the freedmen access to the means of production (especially land) kept the structural base of the slave economy intact. But whenever, and wherever, job opportunities appeared beyond the pale of the plantation, black people moved in large numbers to seize them.

Mandle's book is most valuable in its illumination of this movement within the US. His analysis of the interconnection of the Southern plantation economy with the industrialized North and of the 'push' and 'pull' factors influencing the movement of black people from the South is penetrating and comprehensive. Similarly the empirical *inferences* concerning the way racism perpetuates poverty among the Afro-Americans in the South and in urban industrial locations where they moved outside the South deserve serious consideration in designing strategies for liberation. This book opens the innings, so to speak, for sector 6 of the black Diaspora. We now need similar studies dealing with sector 3 (Brazil), sector 4 (the Caribbean) and sector 5 (Central America, etc.) to comprehend the New World segment of the diaspora. For when a people share a commonality of material dispossession from the same root cause, their struggle for liberation must be co-joined.[6]

Let me now present the highlights of the book in the sequence that they unfold. Mandle provides a specific definition of plantation economy as "one in which profit-maximizing agricultural landowners depend upon some mobilising mechanism, not simply the operation of a free labour market, to satisfy the need of their farms for disciplined unskilled workers in large numbers" (p. 12). After Emancipation, plantation dominance was maintained by three such mechanisms for labour mobilization. "(1) labour contracted through operation of the market; (2) immigration; and (3) sharecropping" (p. 17). In the US South, sharecropping was the main mechanism used to perpetuate the plantation economy. The occupational mobility of black people in the South was restricted by lack of access to productive land and by the slow pace of Southern industrialisation. And the demand for labour in the rapidly industrialising North was filled by European migrants because of the discrimination practised there. But "when given the opportunity to migrate to alternative employment opportunities during and after World War I, Southern blacks moved with alacrity" (p. 24).

Now the very mechanism of labour coercion which supported plantation agriculture "tended to induce technological stagnation in production methods". In chapter 5, Mandle persuasively demonstrates that "the same institutions which allowed for profitable use of labour-intensive technologies tended to freeze the technological capacity of the Southern society at that relatively primitive level" (pp. 69-70).

Mandle argues that between World War I and 1940 there was an incremental erosion of the structure of Southern plantation agriculture through two processes: migration to the North by "organizing initiatives undertaken by black farmers themselves in this period". The most important organization was the Southern Tenant Farmers Union formed in 1934. Mandle also cites Nate Shaw's oral autobiography as evidence of the "striving of collective self-defense which . . . signals the rejection of the paternalistic ethos of the South" and anticipates the birth of the Civil Rights movement (pp. 82-83).

Now the eventual collapse of the Southern plantation economy is said to have emanated from accelerated migration and increased mechanisation stimulated by US entry in the second Imperialist War. It is worthwhile quoting at length.

American entry into World War II marks the principal point of discontinuity in the black experience in the United States. Until then participation in the southern plantation economy had remained the single most important role played by blacks. From this participation followed the fact that most blacks were southern, rural and poor. Now with the major social mobilisation associated with the war, masses of black workers were required either directly or indirectly to support the war effort. This meant first that more than at any time previously, black workers were provided with both the means and opportunity to escape the southern plantation economy. At the same time the vacating of the estates caused by the war accelerated trends toward mechanization of Southern agriculture and the downfall of the plantation economy (p. 84).

During the 1940s black migration from the six plantation states of the South exceeded one million, "a level almost three times that of the 1930s and far greater than the black migration of any previous decade" (p. 84).

After the war, machine capital came into its own with mechanised harvesting of cotton. It is important to note that technically efficient harvesters had been developed from the 1930s but were not introduced until after the war. And it was this change in technology that led to the demise of sharecropping as a form of labour force control by the early to mid 1960s, leading to a transformation of the Southern plantation economy. Mandle argues that

migration was a two-step process. The first step, the movement of black labour in response to wartime demand, doomed the plantation economy. This wartime 'pull' triggered the technological changes which resulted in the development of an outward 'push' from what was formerly the plantation South (p. 97).

Thus it was that finance capital emerged, through the process of technological change, to replace land monopoly as the means of perpetuating a reserve army of labour in the southern economy, in the 1960s and 70s. But nowhere does Mandle make the link with the ascendency of the US as top imperialist nation and the corresponding global thrust of the same MNCs with technological change and industrialization.

Now the contemporary situation faced by black people in the US is brought into focus. "By the 1960s most blacks lived in urban areas, a large fraction of whom were in the North and almost all of whom were non-agricultural workers" (p. 99). But poverty prevailed among them because the plantation legacy "disproportionately deprived them of ownership of income-earning property" and because of "their late arrival in competing for well-paid employment" (p. 99). Here, I think, Mandle slips into a serious error of understanding the contributing factor of institutionalised racism when he makes the point that "the long historical experience as dependent labourers meant that migration North was a movement of people most of whom were essentially without property" (p. 100). After all, most white Europeans had come to the US in the same way; yet they managed to escape poverty.

No wonder then that the last two chapters of the book on "Strategies of Change" and "Current Prospects" offer no real insights for black people engaged in the struggle for liberation. Chapter 9 on "Strategies of Change" opens appropriately with the recognition that

There was a response by the black population to oppression, as for example, in the case of the Organisation of the Sharecroppers' Union . . . Thus a complete assessment of the roots of black poverty requires a consideration of the attempts by the black population to overcome that poverty (p. 105).

Mandle points to the fact that after Emancipation, "land ownership was the universally acknowledged goal of the ex-slave population" (p. 106). But since this was blocked, a strategy of self-help and group solidarity was imposed by the situation. Booker T. Washington from a Southern perspective emphasised skill upgrading through establishment of industrial schools to promote the development of a black capitalist class. W.E.B. Dubois struggled instead for political (electoral) power for black people as the means of breaking the oppression imposed by plantation economy. But it was Marcus Garvey who "represented a major new departure in black thinking" by translating the sense of self and community into a nationalist ideology to cement black people in the diaspora culturally and economically (pp. 108-14); while the Communist Party (CP-USA) articulated the principle of 'Black Belt' self-determination between 1928 and 1958.

What then are the current prospects? Mandle argues that the Civil Rights movement of the 1950s and 60s was a southern movement rooted in the breakdown of the plantation economy. And he correctly indicates that the prospects for occupational mobility of black people are constrained by their low skill legacy and by the rate of growth of the US economy. Mandle admits that "Racism is deeply imbedded in Western culture" but is still optimistic in the end about the possibility of merging the struggle of black people with that of the white working class (p. 122). This seems to me to be a rather facile projection that fails to recognise the emergence of a significant black bourgeois and petit-bourgeois class that now assists in the perpetration of black poverty in capitalist US.

It was the very character of the Civil Rights movement that created this situation. That movement was not homogeneous. It had two streams: the non-violent one led by Martin Luther King; and the other liberation "by any means necessary" led by Malcolm X. I am arguing that the triumph of the non-violent path set the stage for the massive co-optation process that followed during the 1970s; and that process now becomes a fetter on the liberation struggle, nationally and internationally.

———

Current prospects and strategies for change relevant to black people in the US must be placed in a wider context – a context that analyses the world-wide system of capitalism and the role played by the US as the leading imperialist nation in that system. I propose to sketch the outlines of such an analysis in the rest of this discussion.

Poverty among black people within the US must be linked first to that among other minorities in that country and, secondly, to that of other Third

World peoples, who are being exploited in a manner similar to Afro-Americans within the black diaspora. The systematic character of world capitalism is depicted in Figure 25.2 below. In that diagram, I illustrate that the system generates mass poverty at two levels: among about 80% of the population of the capitalist periphery and among about 20% of the population of the centre (see the shaded areas in Figure 25.2). For the US, there are three marginalized groups numbered 1-3 in the diagram. These are (1) the indigenous Indians; (2) *poor* black people; and (3) *poor* migrant minorities of Puerto Ricans, Chicanos, etc. For the periphery, the diagram shows that an upper strata (no. 5) is fully integrated with the imperial centre while the majority of people (no. 4) are poverty stricken. Surplus extraction from the periphery exceeds inflows of direct investment and loans and so perpetrates uneven development. Military expenditures out of this surplus, divert resources from welfare spending to alleviate poverty among the dispossessed groups within the US.

Now the significant point I wish to make here is that *not all* black people in the US are in the marginalised sector of that economy. The black bourgeois

Figure 25.2   *The international capitalist system (ICS)*

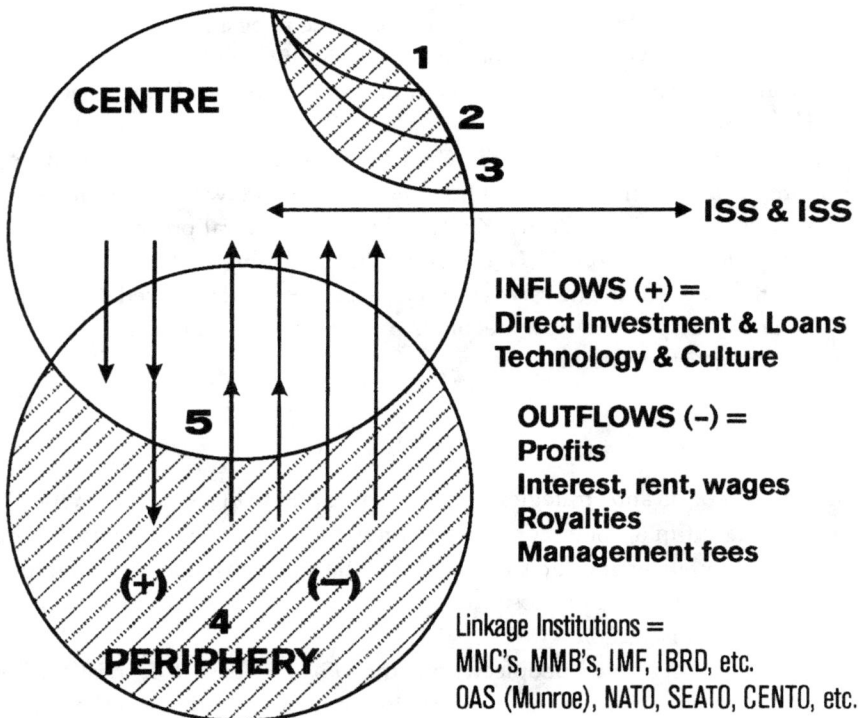

and petit-bourgeois class which expanded dramatically in the 1970s became integrated into the middle strata of US society as capitalist businessmen, professionals, bureaucrats and black elected officials. Their class position objectively removes them from the struggle of black workers and sharecropper farmers. In like manner, the brown petit-bourgeois of peripheral Caribbean state-societies are integrated with the centre in a manner that allows them living standards and a lifestyle not different from that enjoyed by privileged groups in the centre itself.[7] The important point is that this class administers the instruments of state on behalf of national and international capital and, in the process, facilitates the exploitation of the masses of workers and small peasants.

The linkages between the dispossessed of Caribbean plantation capitalist societies and black people in the US, involve direct competition for jobs in the North and retard the complete dismantling of Southern plantation economy. The postwar inflow of US capital into mining and tourism pushed many small peasants off the land and accelerated immigration to Europe and North America. US immigration policy admits only skilled workers and these compete directly with US blacks for available jobs. Additionally, migrant workers are recruited from the Caribbean for harvest operations in southern agriculture, thereby perpetuating the domination of plantation economy over those US blacks still in the clutches of southern plantation economy. Furthermore, there is also a competitive linkage in manufacturing activity. Much of the postwar industrialization of the US South resulted from the relocation of light manufacturing firms from the North attracted by availability of cheap black urban labour in the South. But when the bourgeois democratic states of the Caribbean made 'industrialization by invitation' official development policy, many of these same firms relocated in the Caribbean where labour was even cheaper than the South.

What I am trying to demonstrate here is that there is much more to the roots of black poverty than is provided in the analysis presented by Mandle. And that we need to expand that analysis in order to devise appropriate strategies for liberation. Critical to that expansion is the need to analyse the role of the black bourgeois and petit-bourgeois classes within the US and elsewhere in the black diaspora. The theoretical importance of this in the general functioning of capitalism as a world system has been suggested by Wallerstein.[8] For the diaspora, it is a matter of central importance in the US, the Caribbean, Brazil and Africa itself. In analysing the problem of underdevelopment and poverty in the contemporary capitalist world, factors internal to particular state societies are only a part of the picture. The external dimension is equally important and there is a dialectical connection between the two. It is this kind of linkage analysis that is needed to raise the level of consciousness of the dispossessed people within the diaspora and within the whole of the Third World.

Then, and only then, will black people and other dispossessed minorities within the US begin to mount their struggles within the imperialist centre in a way that shakes the foundations of US hegemony over the Third World; and thus create the conditions for their own liberation which can only come through socialist transformation with the US itself. In the short and medium run, black people in the US can, for example, exert political influence on Washington in ways that will assist the liberation struggles in Southern Africa. But they will only do so if they are made to realise the interconnection between their own poverty situation and that of their brothers and sisters in Southern Africa. US scholars like Mandle who smugly claim Marxist credentials have a responsibility to make that kind of contribution to the struggle. Otherwise we cannot take their strategy projections seriously. Meanwhile, we can profitably use the results of their historical analyses, once we clear the theoretical cobwebs.

Notes

*"Plantation capitalism and black dispossession: a review article". *Transition* 2:2 (1979b).

1   (Durham NC: Duke University Press, 1978), pp. xvi & 144. Mandle analyses the US "southern plantation economy after the Civil War", and he extends the discussion to the 1960s on the basis of trends which became discernible before the crisis of capitalism deepened to what is observable today. However, there is no evidence in the book that the author is even aware of the relation of global capitalism to his arena of study.

2   It is necessary to chronicle this fact so as to isolate Mandle from the band of white 'Marxist' North Americans whose Marxian excursions are chiefly in the arena of Marxology. Mandle addresses the US black experience through a living familiarity with that of the Anglo-phone Caribbean.

3   Alex Haley, *Roots* (New York: Doubleday, 1976). A televised version of the book won national US acclaim and international recognition. That basic weave is now being empirically extended by a demographic mapping and research project on the Diaspora under the direction of Ruth Sims Hamilton at Michigan State University.

4   All these are West Indians, except for R. T. Smith, who is half English/half West Indian and their work has a focus on the English Caribbean. James looks additionally at the Haitian revolution.

5   I will return to this question about the breakdown of the plantation economy in the next section.

6   Estimates indicate that there are some 30 million black people in the US, 35 million or more in Brazil and some 20 million in the Caribbean. Together with those in sector 5 (Central America) and in the rest of South America and Canada,

there must be about 100 million of us in the New World. When we add to this the 250 million or so within Africa itself, that is a whole lot of people, in any economic or political calculus. Strategies for mobilizing collective liberation cannot be derived in the absence of common understandings. I address this question in the final section.

7   Consumption patterns are homogeneous, as an advertisement of *Time* magazine showing businessmen, professionals etc., in many Third World countries poses the question: "What do all these have in common?" Answer, "They all read *Time*"; and, we might add, they all eat Kelloggs corn flakes, drive Mercedes Benz cars, etc., etc. In short, they comprise an internationally homogeneous bourgeois and petit-bourgeois class.

8   See Immanuel Wallerstein, *The Capitalist World Economy* (Cambridge: Cambridge University Press, 1979), chapter 14, "Class formation in the capitalist world economy", pp. 222-30.

26

The Future of Plantation Society
in Comparative Perspective*

Let me begin with the simple observation that the presence of all black people in the New World today is directly attributable to the plantation system. African people were forcibly removed from their homeland and brought to the New World to provide labour power for the production of plantation commodities like sugar, cotton and tobacco. Under conditions of slavery, this black labour power generated huge surpluses for the economic advancement of Europe (and later the US Northeast and the Brazilian Centre-South).

Having overcome the indigenous Indian populations in the Caribbean, the Guyanas, the US South and the Brazilian Northeast, European merchant capitalists established plantations on land captured from the Indians and with capital and labour extracted from the Africans. And so slave plantation societies emerged in the New World. It was the Portuguese who first developed the system in Sao Thome and Principe on the other side of the Atlantic and introduced it into Brazil early in the sixteenth century. The Portuguese later established the system in their African colonies – Guinea, Angola and Mozambique.

From the initial establishment in Brazil, the plantation system spread rapidly into the Guianas, throughout the Caribbean islands and into the US South as other European nations expanded on the base and experience set by the Portuguese. The Spanish, French, Dutch and British merchant capitalists promoted this expansion in various parts of the New World. And black plantation societies became dominant in the 'colonies of exploitation'.

Capitalism and the Evolution of Plantation Society

Plantation society was the creation of mercantile capitalism. It grew to maturity as mercantile capitalism was transformed into industrial capitalism after the 'Industrial Revolution' of the eighteenth century; and enjoyed a veritable economic golden age during the whole of the seventeenth and early eighteenth centuries. The subsequent transition from industrial capitalism to finance capitalism from the late nineteenth century led to the emergence of imperialism and monopoly capital on a world scale.

Modern plantation society has its roots in the slave plantation system that began in the sixteenth century and lasted to the mid to late nineteenth century. It is important to note that the character of this slave society was significantly different from that of slavery in ancient times (e.g. slave societies of Greece and Rome). New World slave plantation societies produced commodities for sale in international capitalist markets. And the surpluses generated from the exploitation of slave labour power fuelled the process of accumulation that gave rise to the development of industrial capitalism in Europe. Thus, slave plantation society was an integral part of the international capitalist system.

The Marxist conceptualization of world history identifies the following social formations: (i) primitive communal; (ii) tribute paying; (iii) feudal; (iv) slave; (v) capitalist; (vi) socialist; (vii) communist. It does not stipulate that these formations are sequential nor does it indicate that all societies must pass through stages in which each of the above social formations is dominant. Different societies have different historical experiences; and the transition from one dominant social formation to another varies in time and place.

Formally, New World plantation societies emerged from a historical dialectic that was characterized by an abrupt transformation from the primitive communal societies of the indigenous Indians to the slave plantation mode of production; and after Emancipation, to the capitalist societies of today. Only Cuba in the New World has made the transition from capitalism to socialism. In Africa itself, Guinea-Bissau, Angola and Mozambique along with the oldest plantation societies, Sao Thome and Principe off-shore have also transformed to socialist societies. Elsewhere, capitalism dominates; but with its recurrent crises of accumulation and of realization, its stranglehold is weakening against the force of dispossessed peoples struggling for liberation.

Historically, this struggle displays two discernible forms at the level of nation-states: the revolutionary and the evolutionary. Only the revolutionary path has led to socialist transformation, to date. Some plantation societies on the evolutionary path are said to be in process of 'transition'. Guyana and Jamaica are somewhere on this *transition* stage. As Rodney points out, "Transition must necessarily have mixed features of capitalist relics and embryonic socialism, but the latter would exist in a position of dominance".[1] He makes the further point that "Transition is movement in a given direction – it is not a shuttle service".[2] So that plantation societies, like Indonesia and Sri Lanka, where nationalization of foreign plantations was subsequently reversed were obviously not on the transition *belt*.

From our analysis so far, we can conclude that the future of plantation societies is bound up inextricably with the future of international capitalism. That future in turn will be determined by the interaction of two opposing forces:

1   the continuing imperialist expansion of capitalism in new shapes and forms as it makes accommodation to:

2   the strengthening of popular forces worldwide for national liberation, involving the repatriation of land and other means of production in a general pursuit of 'non-capitalist' paths to development.

The operations of MNCs have adjusted in several ways and there is an increasing control of them by the multinational banks (MNBs) which, as well, lubricate the financial transactions of Third World countries through loans to nation-states. Supported by the capitalist IMF (and IBRD) MNBs hegemony over resources in the capitalist Third World is increasing rapidly.[3]

Thus at one level, we can say that the future of plantation societies is no different from the future faced by all Third World countries locked into the international capitalist system. That is to say, either they continue to underdevelop under capitalism or they make the transition to socialism as a precondition for development. But we can go a step further, to analyse the contours and likelihood of that choice in the particular case of plantation societies. To make that analysis, however, we need a clear understanding of the character of plantation society.

Plantation Society – A Reformulation[4]

We already stated that slave plantation society was the creation of mercantile capitalism. The society was formed by planting African people on land that had been captured from other people, the indigenous Indians of the Americas. The economic base was established by the coercive application of the labour power of these transplanted Africans in the cultivation of crops for which commercial markets existed in Europe. White Europeans owned the means of production, and a hierarchial chain of command from the white 'backra' to the mulatto (half caste) 'busha' mobilized the black African slave to produce commodities for export, for slave and estate consumption, as well as capital goods that could be produced with slave labour (houses, factory buildings, fence posts, etc.).

This particular hierarchial occupational structure served to institute race into the process of production from the outset. And the clear distinction between those who owned the means of production (including slaves) and those whose only value was their labour power set up a class society of a particular kind. Slaves were in fact chattel, not people since they had no legal individual rights. Plantations were the first factories in the field in a real sense. The slaves were machines driven by paid managers (attorneys) and foremen and unpaid (*ie* in money) 'drivers'. And the factories for processing raw sugar, cotton, etc were industrial concerns. The plantation was a precursor to industrial capitalism. It was a rudimentary form but this essence of it has escaped the notice of most scholars of the development of capitalism.

Emancipation came in the nineteenth century, starting with the British colonies in 1838, the French colonies and the US in the 1860s, and the Spanish and Portuguese territories in the 1880s. Emancipation came about as a result of the heightened struggle of the slaves for their freedom (as the success of the San Domingo revolution testified) and the increasing economic inefficiency of the slave mode of production as industrial capitalism replaced mercantile capitalism in Europe and extended to the US Northeast and the Brazilian Centre-South.

Emancipation led to the transformation of slave plantation society to *subsistence wage* plantation society, and sharecropping tenancy systems. The latter was designed to tie the African ex-slaves to the plantation and was circumscribed by legislation like the Black Codes in the US South to ensure that the labour power of black people would continue to be available to the capitalist plantations in a system of semi-slavery. 'Half slave – half free' is an appropriate description of the economic condition of black people in all plantation societies after Emancipation. For even where wage labour substituted slave labour, wages paid never rose beyond minimum subsistence as the governors of plantation societies systematically created a 'reserve army of labour'. In order to counter the efforts of the Africans to secure an independent (of the plantation) economic base, governments in plantation societies imported *indentured* Asian labour – mainly East Indians whose role in plantation production was hardly different from that which existed under slavery.

Thus, the capitalists who continued to monopolize the means of production were able to maintain intact the economic substructure of the society. The African ex-slaves had one of two choices, depending on the availability of land. Wherever some land of whatever quality existed, they managed to establish a semi-independent peasantry. But wherever plantations had already engrossed all arable land, they were forced to continue working on plantations for subsistence wages or *they had to migrate*. The substitution of machine capital for labour is the most recent technique for perpetuating the reserve army. Migration was, and remains, an important outlet for dispossessed black people in all New World plantation societies.

The mobility of labour *into* during the foundation period and *out of* during the period of maturity and decline is one feature of plantation society that gives it a certain uniqueness among the general class of capitalist societies. The economic *raison d'être* of plantation society is production of commodities for export. And that trade has been marked by what is now called 'unequal exchange'. This unequal exchange which keeps plantation society backward relative to the industrial capitalist societies arises from the existence of a reserve army of labour in plantation society.[5] And migration has had a dampening effect (however slight) on the inherent disequality. For one thing, migration reduces the size of the reserve army of labour. And for another, remittances sent by migrants to relatives improves the survival chances of those still within the grip of plantation society.

But migration has important negative effects, one is that migrants disposed of what little land and other means of production they came to own as a result of their economic struggles within the constrains imposed by the plantation system. And invariably, such land was bought up by MNCs in mining and tourism in the Caribbean and by capitalist corporations in the US South and the Brazilian Northeast.[6] Another negative effect is that migration acts as a safety valve which reduces economic frustration thereby postponing revolutionary change of a kind that could bring socialist transformation á la Cuba. The dispersal of black people outside of their ancestral home-base robs plantation societies of skilled human resources which could provide the organization and wherewithal for making the transition. We shall have to return to these matters when we consider the dynamics of change and transformation in the next section.

For the time being, we return to our examination of the specific contours of plantation society. What emerges so far in our analysis is that the economic substructure of the society remained virtually unaltered in the period after Emancipation. To be sure, peasant sectors emerged in some places but the peasantry were (and are) dominated by the plantation. Non-agricultural activities came into being. In the Caribbean, mining, tourism and light manufacturing and in the US South and Brazil mainly light manufacturing and mining in some places. These new activities diversified the commodity mix of production and complexified the class structure somewhat. The simple social stratification of white bourgeoisie, brown petty bourgeoisie, black agro-proletariat and black peasants of plantation society became embellished with an urban proletariat, a lumpen proletariat (from the reserve army) at one end;

while the white bourgeoisie had capitalists to consolidate the position of the landlords; and the ranks of the petty bourgeoisie opened up to black professionals and big peasants.

With the substructure modified only slightly, the institutionalization of race and class remained within the mode of production. And the superstructure of plantation society reflects this fact. Thus, in the independent countries, the state represents the interests of the capitalist class and provides meagre welfare and material dispensations for the workers and peasants. Colour assumes importance as a proxy for race. And an 'ideology of dependence' pervades the upper reaches of society. Thus, the political directorate views the economic possibilities for national advancement from the point of view of external assistance for markets, capital, technology and management. And 'industrialization by invitation' becomes the order of the day. Cheap labour is the drawing card for these foreign capital inflows. In the US South and Northeast Brazil, it is domestic capital from the more industrialized regions of those countries. But the effects are the same so far as the plantation regions are concerned. The process serves to entrench plantation society further into the international capitalist system and makes a future break with that system somewhat more difficult to achieve.

The Dynamics of Change and Transformation

Plantation society is a society in constant crisis. That crisis stems from the inherent contradiction between white capital and black labour. The capital-labour antagonism is central to all capitalist economies. But in plantation society the antagonism is heightened by the element of race. The constant situation of conflict places a special responsibility on the state to invest in instruments of violence in order to contain the conflict (*ie* 'to maintain law and order').

Basically, the state acts on behalf of the landlord-capitalist class (the bourgeoisie). And in a situation characterized by the monopoly of the means of production by that class and the limited freedom of employment of the working class and small peasants, the state plays a balancing role. It does this functionally in two ways. First, it provides the dispossessed classes with what limited material benefits it can through the Civil Service bureaucracy, in order to redress the gross inequalities in income distribution. But its capacity to do this effectively is constrained by the limited revenue it can command since it must provide concessions and incentives to the landlord-capitalist class. So, for example, land settlement schemes for the small peasants involve the acquisition of the poorest quality plantation land for subdivision among as many small peasants as is feasible. These small plots (averaging 1.5 acres in Jamaica) are unable to sustain the peasant family which must supplement their farm income with wage work on plantations or public works. The small peasant is therefore half agro-proletariat.

The limited capacity of the state to redress the economic inequalities between white capitalists and black workers and peasants leads to recurrent social upheaval. And here the second function of the state is brought to the fore – the institutions of state repression, the army and the police, virtually take charge when things get out of line. It is important to note that in plantation society, the army is less concerned with dealing with external aggression than it is in maintaining internal social peace. The army, in effect, is a military police force.

The dynamics of change and transformation is a dialectic resolution of the basic contradictions inherent in the plantation mode of production and exchange. There are two patterns of adjustment in this situation. One is 'reformism' that brings change by making significant adjustments on the margin within the capitalist framework. But because this is never sufficient massive out-migration and immigration of labour is the critical factor of adjustment. The other pattern is 'revolution' that brings transformation of the capitalist plantation society to socialism.

The limits of reformism can be gauged by the rate of out-migration of labour from the plantation societies. For the Anglophone Caribbean as a whole, between the intercensal years 1960 and 1970, the estimated loss of 1.12 million people "is equivalent to nearly one-third of its population at 1960". As for the labour force itself, net emigration represents 80% of total accessions to the male working force over the decade.[7] Given the fact that emigration from the region has been significant since the late nineteenth century, it would hardly be surprising to find that more West Indians live outside of the West Indies today than those who still live within the region. Puerto Rico presents a similar picture. In the US South, the out-migration of black people escalated during the first imperialist war. During the 1910s, over 350,000 black people departed from six plantation states. By the 1920s this doubled to nearly 700,000. The depression of the 1930s slowed down the rate; but by the 1950s, 1.1. million were making their way north and west.[8]

Reformism achieved certain qualitative changes in plantation society. In the US South, official response to the Civil Rights movement of the 1950s and 1960s enfranchised the black voter, desegregated schools and public places, increased the number of black elected officials, opened opportunities for black capitalism to develop, and enhanced race relations elsewhere in the US. These positive achievements in the political realm have not been matched by significant improvements in the material (economic) welfare of black people relative to the white population. A similar situation developed in the Caribbean. In response to the rebellions of the late 1930s, Crown Colony government was abandoned for fully representative government through the introduction of universal adult suffrage, and eventually to internal self-government and constitutional independence. But with the economic sub-structure unchanged, this independence turned out to be more symbolic than real.[9]

Reformism has reached a relatively high level in Guyana and Jamaica where attempts to change the economic substructure have been attempted. Under the ideological rubric of 'cooperative socialism' the Guyana government since 1971 nationalized the foreign-owned bauxite and sugar companies. Today about 80% of that economy is within the state sector. But race and class remain imbedded in the social fabric in a manner that makes it difficult to accept the notion that the society is in a stage of transition to socialism. State capitalism seems a more appropriate description of that society. Jamaica is even further removed from the stage[10] of transition of socialism. The Manley regime introduced the ideology of 'democratic socialism' beginning in 1974 but has done little to change the economic substructure. State participation in production has been rehabilitative – nationalization of capitalist enterprises facing financial difficulties in sugar, tourism, and utilities. For plantation society, land and agrarian reform is the single most important policy instrument for initiating a transition. And neither Guyana nor Jamaica have moved in this direction.

'Revolution' is the alternative path to reformism. By revolution we mean an abrupt change in the parameters of the society. Specifically, the capture of state power by a worker-peasant alliance and the socialization of the means of production – in particular land (including plantations) and facilitating institutions governing capital formation – *ie* banks and other financial intermediaries, external trading institutions, and utilities. Such revolutionary change is more than likely to involve violence. Plantation society was created by violence, is maintained by violence, and the logic suggests that it can only be transformed by violence. In the New World, Cuba is the only plantation society that has transformed from underdeveloped capitalism to rapidly *developing* socialism. In Africa, Guinea-Bissau, Sao Thome-Principe, Angola and Mozambique are firmly on the transition belt. In all these cases, violent revolution set the stage for the transformation.

The economic, social and political achievements of socialist Cuba are now legend. But the struggle to make the transformation was long and violent as the overthrown bourgeoisie and the imperialist US government joined forces to abort the revolution during the 20 years of the Revolutionary government that came to power in January 1959. The success of the government of what is today socialist Cuba can be attributed to the speedy manner in which it began

to redress the economic and social imbalances deriving from the contradictions of plantation society. Within a few months after the overthrow of the
Batista regime, the preconditions for transition were laid with the launching
of a massive land reform programme accompanied by urban reform which
reduced the rent burden of the urban poor. The dynamic of change led inevitably to confrontation with the imperialist power that stimulated nationalization of all foreign-owned (mainly US) property.

The transition to socialism was formalized in 1965 with the formation of
the Cuban Socialist Party and within a decade, the internal organizational
changes resulted in real popular participation in matters of state with the
introduction of the Organs of Peoples Power. Race was eliminated from the
productive and social orders, and class receded in importance. All these transformations released the creative energies of the people and led to a rapid
development of the productive forces. And today in addition to providing
basic needs for its entire population, Cuba is in a position to extend technical
assistance to other Third World countries (especially in housing, agriculture
and health) while providing strategic military assistance to the liberative
struggles of black people in Southern Africa and Ethiopia. Its achievements
have been made possible by assistance provided by other socialist states
(especially the USSR) in the early critical years of the revolution. And Cuba's
present membership in COMECON contributes to its continuing economic
development.

The Future as History

What the future holds for plantation societies of the New World is clear if we
apply the lessons of history. That future depends on two sets of factors: one
internal to the particular plantation society, and the other external to it. In the
modern world of today no society is an island to itself. On the contrary all
state-societies in the world are affected by international events of various
kinds. And even though we can speak of an international capitalist system
and an international socialist system(s),[11] there is a considerable interrelation
between these systems in economic, political and social terms.

The future of plantation societies, therefore, rests as much on the internal
resolution of contradictions inherent in those societies as well as on the repercussions which such resolutions are likely to have on the international balance
of power between the major world sytems. Such repercussions will affect the
reaction of these external forces to change and transformation in particular
plantation societies. The recent reaction of the US to the advanced reformist
changes effected in Guyana and Jamaica provides some lessons. There is

sufficient evidence to substantiate official claims that the CIA sought to 'destabilize' the economies of Jamaica and Guyana over the period 1976-77. But the IMF took over where the CIA left off as the international capitalist crisis effected a complete destabilization. Both countries are now effectively governed by the IMF. And there was little tangible support from the international socialist system because no internal efforts were made to set the preconditions for a transition to socialism.

On a world scale, the forces struggling for national liberation and socialism are gaining increasing ascendancy. On the other hand, the international capitalist system is being weakened by a prolonged economic crisis which appears to be a conjuncture of crises of accumulation and realization compounded by rivalry among the top nations in that system. In these circumstances, the future of Caribbean plantation societies appears to lie in the direction of transformation. But geopolitics will pose formidable constraints on that process. Much depends on the course of change in US plantation society and its migrant offshoots in the black urban ghettoes of the Northeast, Midwest, and West Coast. The struggles of black people within the belly of the imperial power will strengthen and reinforce the struggles of black people in the Caribbean, and in Africa as well.

Notes

*"The future of plantation society in comparative perspective". Mimeo (1979c).

1   Walter Rodney, "Transition", *Transition* 1, no. 1 (1978), p. 4.

2   Rodney, p. 6.

3   For further discussion of the increasingly critical role of the MNBs, see Paul Sweezy, multinational corporations and banks, *Monthly Review* 29, no. 8 (January 1978). On the role of the IMF and its effects on borrowing Third World nations, see Cheryl Payer, *The Debt Trap* (New York: Monthly Review Press, 1974).

4   My earlier analysis of plantation society has several weaknesses which I attempt to correct (or elaborate) in what follows. Specifically, its handling of the class question was overshadowed by the emphasis on race; whereas what is needed is a synthesis of how race *and* class makes plantation society a sort of 'special case' in the history of social formations. For my earlier treatment see chapter 3 of *Persistent Poverty* (New York: Oxford University Press, 1972) as well as the version "Plantation society: towards a general theory of Caribbean society" in P. Figueroa and G. Persaud (eds.), *Sociology of Education – A Caribbean Reader*, (Oxford: Oxford University Press, 1976).

5   W.A. Lewis was the first to articulate this in his "Economic development with unlimited supplies of labour", *Manchester School* (1954) and later in his *Theory of Economic Growth* (London: Allen and Unwin, 1955). But recently Marxist scholars have elaborated on the basis of unequal exchange. See A. Emmanuel, *Unequal Exchange – A Study of the Imperialism of Trade* (New York: Monthly Review Press,

1974) and comments by Bettleheim (ibid) and S. Amin, *Unequal Development* (New York: Monthly Review Press, 1978).

6   See, for example, Robert Browne, *Only Six Million Acres: A Decline of Black-Owned Land* (New York, 1973) for the US case. And for the Caribbean, see Norman Girvan, *Foreign Capital and Economic Underdevelopment in Jamaica* (Kingston, 1972). More intensive studies of this land displacement are urgently needed for the alienation from the means of production constitutes the single most important factor in the persistence of poverty among the masses of black people in New World plantation societies.

7   G. W. Roberts, as quoted in G. L. Beckford, "Race, class and the plantation: dependent capitalism and alienation in the Caribbean". Paper presented to the joint meeting of LASA and ASA in Houston, Texas, Nov 2-5, 1977.

8   Jay R. Mandle, *The Roots of Black Poverty* (Durham, NC: University of North Carolina Press, 1978), pp. 72-74.

9   The term "flag independence" describes this quite appropriately.

10   The distinction between the terms 'transition s*tage*' and 'transition *belt*' used earlier in this essay is important. Belt is meant to connote a dynamic uni-directional movement (à la Rodney, "transition is a movement in a given direction"). Stage implies a static situation; the society can move in either direction forward to socialism or backward to fascism.

11   The Sino-Soviet split beginning in the 1960s creates a dual international socialist system. The People's Republic of China acts independently, in fact in direct opposition to the socialist system of Eastern Europe (centering on the USSR as *primum inter pares*). And Third World socialist states are associated with one or the other; or both.

27

Small Garden, Bitter Weed: A Postscript*

The IMF, Democratic Socialism and Zig-Zag Politics: Jamaica, 1976-1977

The Present as History

The massive defeat of Michael Manley's People's National Party (PNP) in the 30 October 1980 electoral contest was a logical result of a process that began on or before 15 December 1976. In the book *Small Garden, Bitter Weed*, we describe and analyse the struggle against imperialism, led by Manley's PNP government between 1974 and 1979, and the reaction of imperialism to that struggle.

The most crucial year of that period was September 1976 to September 1977. It was in September 1976 that Manley and the Jamaican people declared unequivocally that WE ARE NOT FOR SALE – WE KNOW WHERE WE ARE GOING, at a mass meeting in the National Stadium. Unknown to the Jamaican people, the then Minister of Finance David Coore and senior officials of the Bank of Jamaica, including Governor Arthur Brown, were busy at that very moment negotiating with the International Monetary Fund (IMF) to 'sell' Jamaica by ensnaring the economy deeper in the net of imperialism. The finance minister had made a firm commitment to the Fund at a September meeting in Manila, Philippines. And between September and December 1976, Bank of Jamaica officials held secret meetings with IMF officials deliberately "disguised as tourists" on the north coast of Jamaica.

Meanwhile the PNP launched a militant anti-imperialist electoral campaign that presented "democratic socialism" to the Jamaican people as the answer to centuries of exploitation under colonialism and imperialism. The opposing Jamaica Labour Party (JLP) offered what they called "Nationalism" – in reality, Jamaican capitalism in association with imperialism.

In the election held on 15 December 1976 the electorate gave Manley and the PNP an overwhelming mandate to pursue the democratic socialist alternative. Right after this electoral outcome a small group of political economists from the University of the West Indies alerted the general secretary of the PNP, Dr D.K. Duncan, and Prime Minister Manley of the consequences of an IMF agreement and the 40% devaluation of the currency which that entailed.

Prime Minister Manley commissioned us to prepare an alternative to the IMF, in the spirit of the electoral mandate. The first document was submitted to him late December 1976; and discussions arising from it led to a declaration made by him in a national broadcast on 5 January 1977 that his government would reject the IMF solution and chart the nation on a "self-reliant democratic socialist" path. This position was re-emphasised and elaborated in a second broadcast on 19 January 1977 by which time the UWI political economists had elaborated the democratic socialist alternative in two other documents.

The prime minister's speech of 19 January promised the nation that an Emergency Production Plan would be formulated by March to guide government policy and action for the rest of 1977 and that by year-end a Five-Year Development Plan would be ready for public scrutiny. To facilitate this, he invited members of the UWI team to take up key positions in the state planning, policy and mobilization bureaucracy. The most important of these appointments were Dr N.P. Girvan as Chief Technical Director of the National Planning Agency with Dr M. Witter as his Economic Adviser; and Mr L.G. Lindsay as Chief Technical Director in the newly created Ministry of National Mobilization and Human Resource Development.

The National Planning Agency (NPA) organized a Task Force of state and University technocrats, trade union representatives, and other interest groups while the Ministry of Mobilization invited suggestions from the Jamaican public. Over 10,000 responses were received from the public in a two-week period. And these were integrated into a massive three-volume plan[1] submitted by the NPA to cabinet on 23 March 1977. That plan was subsequently rejected by government. For a month later, on 22 April 1977, Prime Minister Manley presented to Parliament an *Emergency Production Plan, 1977-78* (summarized by API as *The People's Plan*) that involved capitulation to the IMF and imperialism.

The mandate of 15 December 1976 was betrayed there and then. What happened thereafter closely parallels the analysis provided in document no. 1. The IMF and imperialism finally succeeded in removing the Manley government on 30 October 1980.

Postscript to Small Garden, Bitter Weed

As indicated in that document, part of the price Mr Manley would have to pay to receive IMF assistance would be to put the left wing of his party "under heavy manners". The first IMF agreement was signed in July 1977; and at the annual party conference in September, Manley took to himself tasks, in both party and state, that had been the main responsibility of the leader of the left wing, Dr D.K. Duncan – thereby forcing Duncan's resignation from his dual role as general secretary of the PNP and minister of national mobilization and human resource development.

Soon after this, Michael Witter wrote document no. 2 for self-clarification and for discussion among the UWI team as to whether or not we should continue to work with the regime. That document provides an incisive analysis of the 9-month period following the 15 December 1976 electoral mandate for democratic socialism. It exposes the contradictions inherent in the betrayal of the mandate and the analysis provided a great deal of foresight of events which subsequently materialized.

Eventually, more information and documentation will become available to provide us with much more in-depth analyses of the critical conjuncture that existed in Jamaica in the four months between December 1976 and April 1977. Most of this is perhaps only now available to the one individual, Mr Michael Manley, who took the critical decision to keep Jamaica handcuffed to imperialism. In the book itself, we have offered a very brief and unsatisfactory analysis of "what factors triggered the turn-back of Prime Minister Manley . . ." (p. 93). One thing is certain, history will never absolve him!

Notes
_____

* This postscript to *Small Garden, Bitter Weed* appeared as an appendix to the book, dated November 16 1980, over the single signature of George Beckford.

1   Volume I, described as "The People's Plan", provided a synthesis of the overall "Emergency Production Plan"; Volume II consisted of detailed sector-by-sector plans; and Volume III, called "The Voice of the People", reproduced in abridged form the 10,000 suggestions made by the public.

Part IV

Black Affirmation, Cultural Sovereignty and Caribbean Self-reliance

28

Origins, Development and Future of the Jamaican Banana Industry

A Century of Revolutionary Struggle of the Peasantry

The origins and development of the banana industry bear witness to the resoluteness of the Jamaican people to break through the colonial legacy which still deprives us of a dignified existence and a way of life independent of foreign domination.

Modern Jamaican society has its roots in the slave-sugar plantation society and economy of the nineteenth century. Ever since Emancipation in 1838, the primary concern of the ex-slaves and their descendants has been to secure an independent existence. In order to break away from the inhumanities of the plantation, the rural population had first to acquire land of their own and second to engage in productive activity which had no direct links with the plantation. But the planter class made every effort to frustrate the development of an independent peasantry in order to secure for themselves a reliable source of cheap wage labour.

This antagonism laid the foundations for social unrest. Thus, for example, the Morant Bay 'rebellion' of 1865 resulted *directly* from a dispute about the rights of peasants to lands adjoining an estate. And on that occasion the peasantry paid a high price in loss of life in the brutal suppression of their demands.

It is in this context that the banana trade originated through the joint initiative of peasants and certain merchants acting as agents for American schooner captains. Captain George Busch was the first captain to take regular shipments of bananas from Oracabessa beginning in 1868 when he secured the cooperation of two merchants, Peter Moodie and Edward Sutherland. They encouraged peasants in St Mary and Portland to supply them with fruit. The response of the peasants was great since the trade provided them with cash earnings which made them less dependent on the sugar plantation. As Hall points out in his *Ideas and Illustrations in Economic History*, the sugar planters were so hostile to this development that they never even considered producing bananas themselves. Hall quotes a later governor who wrote:

The old planting regime would never have developed that cultivation. When I first knew Jamaica, banana growing was still despised as a backwoods 'nigger business', which any old time sugar planter would have disdained to handle, or, if tempted by undeniable prospects of profit, would have thought an apology was required.

For the planters, the independence of the peasantry resulting from the growth of the banana trade was undesirable since "it detracted from the supply of wage labour for the sugar estates". But it was "encouraged by the merchants whose exports were increased and whose imports found better markets among a wealthier peasantry".

The traditional plantations refused for a long time to switch to bananas. More than a decade after the trade began, only one estate was listed as a 'banana plantation'. Not until the 1890s was there any significant plantation participation. By then bananas represented about 25% of the island's export trade.

Thus we can attribute the initial steps toward diversification of the traditional sugar economy to the initiative and efforts of the ex-slaves and their descendants. It was our forefathers who laid the foundations of the banana industry and it is they whom we must honour today.

Initiating the trade was one thing. Maintaining it to our advantage was another, for the subsequent history of the trade has been marked by another struggle – to secure remunerative prices from monopolistic foreign buyers with a stranglehold on the trade. The first decade of the twentieth century saw the growth and expansion of the United Fruit Company – a multi-national corporation involved in production, shipping, ripening and marketing of bananas on an international scale. By 1912, that company owned 860,000 acres of banana producing lands in Jamaica, Panama, Costa Rica, Columbia, Honduras and the Dominican Republic.

In Jamaica, UFCo gained an almost monopoly position – swallowing up Elders and Fyffes which had initiated the English trade and knocking out all the older Jamaican trading companies. As Hall puts it:

The twentieth century competition involved high finance, high intrigue, and even the Mafia. The banana trade had assumed wide international dimensions, geographically, financially, and politically, and the pittance of the resources of local enterprise was now ineffectual. This applied also to the small producers, the Jamaican peasants who had at first nourished the trade and now were too small to be of influence in it.

Hall is not quite correct, however, for subsequent events showed that the peasants had a zeal which provided them with the fire to do what seemed impossible.

The struggle of the peasants during the first three decades of the twentieth century culminated in the launching, on 1 April 1929, of the Jamaica Banana Producers' Association – a grower-owned cooperative set up to purchase, ship and market our bananas abroad, in competition with the giant UFC.

The story of that struggle is perhaps best related by quoting at length from a pamphlet, "The Story of a Great Jamaican Enterprise", issued by the Association itself. During the first three decades of this century:

The banana industry, like nearly everything else in Jamaica, was dominated from abroad. Foreign interests owned and cultivated acreages of the best known banana land. A comparatively few large Jamaican land owners were also encouraged to grow bananas for the booming export trade, and they were given contracts. But these contracts were never available to small farmers, who had to sell in the open market. This meant that nobody was under any obligation to take the fruit they offered. They were used when the demand for bananas was great and rejected when the market contracted. They were, in fact, used as a convenience.

In 1924 the Rev A.A. Barclay of Lucky Hill in St Mary, attempted to alter this situation. He got together a few dozen small banana growers whose bananas he sold to an exporting company under a single contract. The Rev Barclay wanted to carry his infant cooperative further and apply it to other products. With the aid of F.H. Robertson, several Elected Members of the Legislature and several Custodes, a meeting of farmers was held in June 1925 with a view to forming an island-wide Parent Body under which separate cooperatives, one for the marketing of each product would be set up.

The parent body, the Jamaica Producers' Association was formed in 1925 with F.H. Robertson as manager. The enrolment of members began.

District Associations were set up in every parish of the island and eventually over 20,000 members were enrolled who pledged to market their products through the Commodity Associations to be formed . . .

Few people then thought that it would be possible for Jamaicans to tackle the problem of their own exports, or to own the shipping and marketing organization abroad, to make such a thing possible.

Few people no doubt, but enough with the courage and conviction to make the dream a reality. For, subsequent to the formation of the parent body in 1925, a number of banana growers organized meetings all over the Island and signed up 6,145 members of the Banana Cooperative. On April 1st, 1929, the Jamaica Banana Producers' Association was born with a capital of £173,12.0 divided into 41,664 shares of 1d each. With this small capital and a great deal of optimism this Jamaican cooperative set out to compete with the largest fruit company in the world.

That, ladies and gentlemen, is to my mind a most significant event in the entire history of this country. It provides us with a salutary lesson for the task confronting us today. For although the Jamaica Banana Producers' Association has grown from this modest beginning to a modern company with some £6 million of capital in the business, it still accounts for a minor share (25%) of the banana trade and growers are still at the mercy of Elders and Fyffes (the United Fruit subsidiary). What is more, the lesson applies to other things as well. It provides clues for coming to terms with foreign domination of all major aspects of our national economic life – bauxite, sugar, tourism, banking, insurance, and so on.

Let me assure you that I am not alone in my assessment of the importance of the struggle that led to the formation of Jamaica Banana Producers Association. In messages sent to the Association and reproduced in their 1963 pamphlet, the following statements were made by ministers of government of this country:

The story teaches us an important lesson. It is, that Jamaicans are not lacking in courage and vision; and that by a pooling of talent and resources, by hard work and dedication they can build up a worthy enterprise in fields which are normally regarded as the reserve of other countries (R.C. Lightbourne, Minister of Trade and Industry, 1963).

Again, "the success of this Jamaican enterprise attests to the faith of its pioneers in the ability of Jamaicans to conduct their own affairs" (J.P. Gyles, Minister of Agriculture and Lands, 1963).

And further, "This shipping line is also the nucleus of a National Shipping Life which I hope will be greatly expanded in future years" (Kenneth Jones, Minister of Communications and Works, 1963).

If, as appears from these statements, these political leaders have learnt the lesson of this great experience why then does the prevailing official development philosophy continue to be one which relies almost exclusively on foreign initiative? Why is it that only a minor share of the banana trade is still accorded to the Jamaican Association? Why is the Association hardly consulted when government and the Banana Board have re-negotiated recent contracts with Elders and Fyffes? And, what does Mr Gyles mean when, in response to recent grower demands for their control of the administration of the industry, he states that government has no intention of handing the industry over to growers 'to mash it up'? The only reasonable answer I can find to these questions, is that our political leaders have really not learnt the lesson at all.

The problems of the banana industry today are essentially the same in character, though not in degree, as those that existed in the first three decades of the century. In recent studies which I conducted at the University, I discovered that

1 the Jamaican grower tends to absorb most of the loss resulting from adverse changes in the UK market conditions,

2 growers do not seem always to benefit sufficiently from improved market conditions,

3 the growers' share of gross realization from sales of bananas has been declining steadily in recent years and was as low as 22% in 1964;

4 that access to other markets such as Canada is limited not because we cannot compete price-wise but because UFCo enjoys a monopoly position which it can use to block our entry.

Indeed the figures suggest that we can supply bananas to eastern Canada at more competitive prices than UFCo supplies now going to that region.

The solution to these problems seems, to my mind, to lie in the direction of doing our own shipping and marketing entirely. The most obvious way of achieving this is to expand the Jamaica Banana Producers Association into a National Line capable of handling the entire trade. To entertain this possibility, we need to consider the obstacles which, over the past 40 years, have limited the growth of the company to its full potential.

The association was originally established because "many growers felt that the time had come when some real internal competition would bring them more security and better prices for their fruit." The intention, therefore, was simply to provide competition, not to take over the trade completely. The growers did in fact achieve the objective they set themselves but subsequent directors do not appear to have seen the need for setting up of new objectives such as those proposed here. The company itself admits that: "The Jamaica Banana Producers' Association Ltd is conservatively managed. After years of hardship and uncertainty, this Jamaican company is now stable and reasonably prosperous."

One of the basic obstacles to be overcome, therefore, is a change in this conservative view of the management. Forty years later, we need to set ourselves new sights if we are not to betray the vision of our forefathers.

Next, we must recognize that in addition to the will and determination of growers in the 1920s, their initial success owed much to a sympathetic government administration. Stubbs, the then governor, gave tangible assistance. For example, "the government guaranteed debentures to the extent of £200,000. With this money the cooperative bought a half share in four old meat-carrying ships which were converted to carrying bananas." The worldwide depression that began shortly after the association was established, a series of hurricanes in 1932, 1933, and 1935, pressure from the established foreign companies, and the ravages of Panama and leaf spot diseases all posed serious difficulties for the survival of the new enterprise. And the company itself admits that "by 1935 it became apparent that unless the government came to its aid with at least full more support it must fail."

The difficulties in the way of action by the company alone are perhaps no less serious today. One difficulty, for example, "is the high cost of new ships. In the 1930s, a ship like the *Jamaica Producer* cost £180,000. In 1959 the new *Planter* cost £1,500,000." Although a considerable amount of charter capacity is available from international shipping, the expansion proposed here could not for long depend excessively on charter space since this would expose us to inordinate outside control. The owned fleet of the company could not be quickly expanded without government assistance in securing loans for the purpose. When we consider that some 75% of current marketing expenses consists of payments for freight and commission to marketing agents, it would seem that investments of this type would pay high returns in terms of national income creation. Positive government action in the direction proposed would, therefore, seem both appropriate and necessary.

Finally, it is alleged that one important factor limiting the kind of expansion proposed here for the company is that a banana shipping and marketing organization cannot rely on a single source of supplies since the risks of blow downs and hurricanes are too high and heavy costs are involved when available shipping space cannot be utilized. The solution to this problem could be to secure access to supplies from other West Indian islands. One way would be to expand the company partly with share capital subscribed by Windward Island growers and partly with capital subscribed by all the West Indian governments to transform the company into a West Indian Banana Producers Association with at least a share of the Windward trade reserved for its expanded operation. This could provide the nucleus for a regional shipping line to handle more and more of our trade with the rest of the world.

That briefly is the vision I want to leave with you concerning the future of the industry. Looking back on what our forefathers did, I am sure you will agree with me that my vision is not much more far reaching than the one they had. They transformed their vision into reality through sheer courage and determination for the difficulties were great. If you share with me the vision I have of our future, then let us resolve to turn this vision into reality. Otherwise, we are unworthy of the fruits of our forefathers' efforts and we shall leave an unworthy legacy for our children and subsequent generations.

Finally, let us widen the vision beyond the horizon of the banana industry and apply it to all aspects of the nation's economic life. Then, and only then, we shall be on our way to genuine independence and a dignified existence as a people. That, as I see it, is the basis for "the struggle ahead, and we must be prepared to see it through!"

Notes

* "Origins, development and future of the Jamaican banana industry". *New World Quarterly* 5:4 (1971a). An address given at the Oracabessa Primary School in December 1968 through the auspices of the Extra-Mural Department, Jamaica, Resident Tutor's office, published in *New World Quarterly*, 1971.

29

Education as an Instrument for Development*

In recent years, economists have given increasing attention to the study of education and economic development. As a result, the term 'investment in human capital' has gained considerable currency in writings on economic development. Although, in my view this new emphasis is not misplaced, there is the danger that resources spent on education may be wasted unless there are some reasonably clear answers to the question: "education for what?" This danger is apparent from the following summary of a discussion by a UNESCO Expert Working Group a few years ago: 'when in doubt, educate.'

My intention here is to raise certain issues about how education can be used as an instrument for development in a country like Jamaica. After a few general considerations. I shall suggest some ways in which education can become an active agent of change in Jamaica; and, finally, I would like to initiate discussions on the particular role of teachers and the Jamaica Teachers Association.

In a rather cursory examination of the literature on this subject I found one article which seemed most suited for my own purpose. "Education and Economic Development" was written by the noted Burmese economist Professor Myint and published in the March 1965 issue of *Social and Economic Studies*.

One of the fundamental weaknesses of current writings on education and the economic development of underdeveloped countries is the failure to distinguish and follow up the implications of two very different views of the role of the education system. On the one hand, we may look upon the educational system as playing a passive role, trying to supply the different types of skilled manpower which will be required by a *given* pattern and rate of economic growth. On the other hand, we may look upon the educational system as playing an active role, trying to transform the existing economic structure to accelerate the rate of economic growth (p. 12).

One can, therefore, view education as either a 'passive' or an 'active' instrument for development. Naturally the passive role is by far the more manageable to discuss and to implement. Basically, it involves gearing the educational system to supplying necessary skilled human resources required for development. It is the familiar manpower requirements approach to educational planning. In this light, the educational system is simply a source of skills – issuing teachers, technicians, farmers, professional people etc., all of whom will fit nicely into the established order of things and to help to raise productivity and incomes.

If education is to become an active instrument for change, then we need first to establish in our minds what kind of change is desirable. Only then can we proceed to consider how education can be made to contribute to the desired changes. There are no simple formulas and what is required may vary considerably from one country to another. Let us therefore, turn our attention to the specific situations for possible answers.

Let me begin by sketching in broad outlines the kind of society and the kind of development to which I feel we ought to aspire. I can, of course, only state my personal preferences. You and the rest of the society must state yours so that we can arrive at some national consensus.

Most Jamaicans, I am sure, would like to see this society offer equal opportunities for all. Thus my first objective is the creation of full employment and full social equality. Second, and somewhat related, is the development of a confident and truly independent population which can face the task of achieving the first objective. Third, is the need to create that internal cultural and technological dynamic which will serve to spread equality and benefit and sustain the process of economic development. Fourth, we need a society which can generate economic growth at a pace which consistently exceeds the rate of population growth. And, finally, following from the foregoing we need to promote the type of economic development which involves the participation of the total population in the economic and political life of the nation.

Everyone will agree that at present we are nowhere near these objectives. What is worse is that, in my view at any rate, our present pattern of economic development and the present system of education seem to be taking us in the opposite direction. By and large, what economic development now takes place is largely on the initiative of investors from metropolitan countries while our national political leaders and bureaucrats busy themselves creating a 'welcoming society'. Jamaica has depended, and continues to do so, on foreign capital, foreign management, foreign know-how, and foreign resources (raw materials) for its economic development. And this has created results which are far from satisfactory – growing unemployment and widening inequalities in the distribution of income. As a people, we own and control very little of the country's resources and seem to have very little confidence in our own capacities to transform the economy. We have, in short, a totally dependent economy in every respect.

This dependence runs even deeper. As a people, we ape the values, consumption patterns and general style of life from the metropolitan countries even when these are completely irrelevant to our environment. Look at the movies and television and see the trash being communicated and the form of advertisement. Listen to the radio for voices which are distinctly Jamaican. Look at the buffet tables at dinner and at the type of liquor consumed at cocktail parties. Look at the manner of dress in this tropical climate of ours.

This inordinate dependence affects education also and that, in turn, serves to reinforce the traditional order. As such, the present educational system is, to my mind, largely dysfunctional.

Let us look at some examples of the effects of our dependence on education today. In the schools, our textbooks and other teaching materials are remote from the experience of students. This particular case illustrates the general point. An English language exercise book in use at the primary school level today asks the student to complete the word (the first letter for which is given) in the following sentence: "It is d—— to skate on thin ice."

With the use of such material we have continued to condemn students who cannot cope to the category of dunce. I would like to suggest that in fact such students may well be the brightest since they are unprepared to be bothered by irrelevancies. And it is only an intelligent person who can distinguish relevance and irrelevance and treat the categories accordingly. Insofar, therefore, as the present content of education is divorced from the real experiences of students, the system will tend to select the wrong material – people who only memorize and regurgitate and who have little or no capacity for independent thought and innovation. When it is recognized that innovation lies at the core of economic development, then we can begin to appreciate the possible dysfunctional element in our present system.

The dependence has adverse effects on education at all levels since the irrelevance of content occurs everywhere. But that is not all. The resources directed to different fields of specialization sometimes appear not in keeping with our needs. For example, it came as somewhat of a surprise to me to see that in the University of the West Indies we have some 14 academic staff members in Physics but only three in animal production and four in crop production in a region where we are so desperately short of domestic food supplies. But then I was informed that Physics gets financial support from the metropolitan countries which are interested in high altitude research.

Having hinted at some of the present limitations of our educational system as an active agent for change, let me pass on to consider what we can do to remedy the situation.

Up to this stage, education has been viewed at the national level as a system producing technicians, teachers and administrators. At the individual level, education is viewed as a means of social mobility. Colonial society afforded few other avenues for mobility. Now, however, I am suggesting that we view education as a means of creating a new society – as a means of transforming the traditional economic and social order from that of a colonial plantation society (which it still largely is) into a modern independent society. I am of the view that education can play a key role in the process, if only because Jamaica has a relatively young population.

I can only list some of the possibilities and ask you to consider the part that you, as teachers, can play in the process.

1   The educational system must be geared to stimulating our people to develop a truly independent style of life (values, culture etc)

2   The system must continuously explore possibilities for developing and using our resources to meet our needs.

3   The system must allow for selection on the basis of true ability.

4   It must provide all kinds of educational opportunities on the same level – technical and vocational education must be brought on par with grammar school type education.

5   Teachers can do a great deal in instilling in our people (students and adults) a profound belief in themselves and, therefore, in their ability to help themselves.

6   Teachers should extend their role outside the classrooms. In rural areas, for example, they can do much to promote community upliftment.

7   In the classroom, teachers can do much to bring relevance to the students' experience. There is no reason, for example, why they cannot develop their own relevant teaching material as they go along. If we were to do this, soon there would be sufficient textbook material for us to draw on.

8   Outside the classroom, teachers can stimulate the population for their own development. Too often we regard ourselves as 'experts' telling people what the problems are and how they can be solved – often referring to 'higher authority', government, or someone up there for the answers. Instead, we need to provoke a consciousness of local problems and to assist in finding local resources for solving them.

9   Teachers should begin taking a back seat in certain areas which they have tended to dominate at the local level, and by so doing, allowing new people to come forward (JAS, etc.).

10 By promoting local initiative, teachers can help to get communities to share in the cost of education.

11 The JTA could contribute much to national life by participating more in the debate on public issues outside of education and divorced from party politics.

12 An organization such as JTA should see itself as an independent force working for the public good, and not simply as a representative of teachers.

13 The JTA could itself launch a textbook programme and arrange competition among members for textbook preparations.

14 Teachers, as individual respected members of our community can by individual action influence the community in ways that others are not likely to do.

Notes

* "Education as an instrument of development". Mimeo (1968b). Presented to the annual meeting of the Jamaica Teachers' Association, 1968.

30

Black Man and Society*

A Comment on the Black Writer in the New World

Brethren, we offer this comment as a *contribution* to the black revolution. It is a continuation of a *rap* session initiated by the papers of Brothers Kahn and Clarke presented at the Fourth Annual Conference on Comparative Literature at the University of Southern California. Our comments here are structured in a way that is designed not to debate but to *rap*. Black people have *debated* (*ie* fought one another) too much and for too long while white metropolitan economy continuously robs us of material comfort and internal spiritual upliftment. There is, of course, much to quarrel with in the presentations this morning,[1] but we feel that it is perhaps more important to structure our comments in a non-traditional fashion. This is precisely what the black revolution is about. We have to break with tradition. For it is this same tradition which has kept black people down – from the time of our enslavement on the west coast of Africa to this day.

We begin with the observation that every black man and woman in the New World is a product of both Africa and Europe. Regardless of our individual pigmentation, we are all both black and white in a profoundly social and cultural sense.[2] The reason for this is not hard to find. Under the most brutal conditions imaginable,[3] black people were brought to the New World by the white European and enslaved on the slave plantation – in Brazil, the Caribbean and the US South. Ever since, the black experience throughout the New World has been clearly identical. This is the context in which we must view the contributions of black writers in the New World and, indeed, those of other brothers and sisters who comment on their work. *For man is society and society is man.* And the black writer in the New World reflects this fact, perhaps more so than any other human being!

The extent to which the individual writer and/or commentator reflects the back experience varies with the individual's degree of psychological and cultural blackness or whiteness. The point we wish to emphasize is that language fundamentally mirrors the experience of those who use the language.[4] Our forefathers were captured and enslaved in lots that deliberately comprised individuals of different tribes and culture. They could not, therefore, communicate with each other in the language of their mother culture. The obvious accommodation in the context was the creation of a new language. This new language was, and is, a modification and simplification of the particular European language of the slave masters – English here, Spanish there; Portuguese here, French there; and so on.

The new language we created is what is now called 'dialect', 'creole', 'pidgin', etc. It is the idiom of expression of real black people – *ie* black people who have not assimilated very much of white European culture. The people that make up what Kahn, in his paper, describes as a 'subculture'. Note very well the classification *'sub'*. *That*, perhaps, it is now; but that it certainly will not be after the black revolution. For the black revolution is black power. *Power of the mind to begin with.*

We have to start with the mind because any human being is what he thinks he is. And, in the present order of things – structured as it is by the historical legacy of slavery and the plantation – the black man sees himself through the eyes of white European man. Thus we regard black language as 'dialect' and black culture as 'subculture'; much the same as black people regard Negro-textured hair as 'bad hair' and Negroid features as 'ugly'. Because our standards, which are the basis of such definitions of self, are those of the white European.

We are what we think ourselves to be!

Today, we fail to recognize that so-called 'standard English', and other 'standard' European languages, are also dialect. That the white man's culture is also a 'subculture'.[5] After the revolution, that view universally will change among all the brothers and sisters!

At this time, we want to reflect on this theoretical and philosophical framework in terms of the black literary tradition in the New World; and in terms of its current direction and future change.

First, let us take up our concept of literature itself. Who and what constitutes literature? Black people in the New World have an enormous literature, which only we know about. This literature is manifested in the oral tradition, which we had to use because the white slave masters found it convenient to keep us illiterate. Reading and writing are not yet our bag. We rap! But the white European subculture, based as it is on the settled tradition of Europe itself, depends more on the written word than it does on the spoken. Any review that fails to take cognizance of this aspect of the black reality will inevitably fail to reflect the black experience.

That is why, for example, Kahn's paper on 'dialect' failed to mention Louise Bennett;[6] that is why we have heard so little in this conference about the black literature which is expressed in music (Sparrow and calypso, Yardbird Parker and jazz), and the dance.[7] That is why Austin Clarke sees little evidence of racial vindictiveness in Caribbean literature, and that is why he makes no reference to Fanon, James' book *Beyond a Boundary*, and Brathwaite's outstanding trilogy of poems: *Rights of Passage*, *Masks*, and *Islands*. The facts of the matter are that black people in the West Indies know Louise Bennett and Sparrow better than all the black writers. Same thing in Brazil and the US.

The task before us black people in the New World is, essentially, one of giving full legitimacy to our real literature – the oral literature; and doing the same thing to the written literature. It is clear that we have already started this – witness Brathwaite's poems, LeRoi Jones, and company. But to get on with this process we need black publishing houses, black recording studios, black organized conferences structured to facilitate rap instead of debate, and a host of other things. Without these, we shall never give full expression to the real experience of black people. Those of us in the Caribbean have made a start with *New World Quarterly*, the *Caribbean Artists Movement*, and *NewCam* – the nucleus of a Third World publishing house. However, a precondition for the flowering black consciousness, black literature, black scholarship etc.; and of the institutions to service that whole revolution is, first and foremost, a restructuring of thought and of the whole mental undercarriage of all of us black people.

Whether we are in and from the Caribbean, Brazil or the US, the task confronting us is the same. We share an identical historical experience. Therefore, we are all the same – the same man and the same society. Just as all black people in the New World share an identical past and present, so too we shall share in the revolution underway.

So, brethren everywhere, let us get on with the business.

Notes

* Comments read to a session of the Fourth Annual Conference on Comparative Literature, University of Southern California, April 1970 (1970c).

1 These, in the order they were presented were as follows: Ismith Kahn, "The effects of language and dialect on West Indian literature"; Austin Clarke, "Some speculations as to the absence of racial vindictiveness in West Indian literature"; and Frederick Litto, "The blackness of Brazil's black theatre".

2 Some of us are more black than others, and some others are more white – in terms of our mental and psychological make up. But we are all fundamentally both black and white.

3 It is important to note that the publicity given to the German atrocities against the Jews a generation ago has made black people more conscious of that particular inhumanity than we are of the much more brutal inhumanity against our forefathers up to four generations ago and which continues in only slightly modified form today.

4 It is important to note in this connection, titles of the papers by Kahn and Clarke – Clarke especially. The titles do not really reflect the extent of their contribution. The reality is that they know that USC is a white institution and therefore chose titles to suit.

5 The white man is the minority throughout the black New World (*ie* Caribbean, Brazil Northeast and US South. So that we need to recognize that *white culture is the subculture*.

6 In this connection see the perceptive article by Kenneth Ramchand, "Dialect in West Indian fiction", *Caribbean Quarterly* 14 nos. 1 and 2 (1968).

7 For more on this see E. Kamau Brathwaite, "Jazz and the West Indian novel", *Bim* nos. 44-46 (1967-68).

31

Sounds and Pressures of Black Survival*

Ken Pryce's *Endless Pressure: A Study of West Indian Life-Styles in Bristol* (1979) tells a part of the story of the political economy of survival of black people in the New World. That is the broad canvas on which the author's work is painted. And the work itself deals with the colourful details of survival of one important constituency of black people – rural migrants from the revolutionary parish of St Thomas, Jamaica. That was the cradle of the Morant Bay Rebellion in 1865 when Bogle led an angry and exasperated peasantry on a war-path to Morant Bay to secure justice and land from the capitalist planter government.

One hundred years after that assault, the peasantry of St Thomas remain boxed in by plantation capitalism. Five planter families control almost all the arable land and the peasantry there found life more and more unbearable, as the scope for their economic advance on the land was constrained. So as economic opportunities opened up elsewhere in Jamaica and overseas, these poor (and proud) people left the parish in large numbers.

St Thomas and Portland are the most African of all parishes in Jamaica. Because of their proximity to Haiti, those parishes continued to receive African-born slaves via French smuggling through Haiti long after British abolition of the slave trade in 1807. The present day strength of African culture among the people of St Thomas is evident in many dimensions. In music and dance, the Kumina. In the religion of pocomania and Pentecostalism. And in the politico-religious movement of Rastafaria. It is from these tap roots that the art form of Reggae and the culture of Dread emerged in recent times.

After the hostilities of the second World War ended, world capitalism expanded at an unprecedented rate. The British economy was in ruins and the US eclipsed Britain as the leading imperialist nation. Before and during the war, the rapidly industrializing US absorbed many migrating West Indians. But by the 1950s, the racist immigration policy of the US closed that door. And the poor black West Indian peasantry moved toward the UK where a 'Marshall Plan' induced economic recovery was taking place.

At the same time, a new wave of capital from the US began to pour into the Caribbean. In Jamaica it went chiefly into bauxite mining/alumina production and tourism. But poor St Thomas had none of those resources and so received none of that capital inflow. An outpouring of black people from that parish, and their eventual trek to the UK before that country's racist Immigration Act of 1962, created communities like St Paul's in Bristol. Ken Pryce's study is about the people who make up that vibrant community of black survivor-conquerors. For I want to argue that the migrant hustler is forced to conquer a particular space within the imperial centre in order to survive.

The main thesis I wish to develop in reviewing this work is the following: plantation capitalism, as it manifests itself in the Caribbean historical experience, is based on super-exploitation of the labour power of African peoples who were brought forcibly into this island sea by slavery and who, after Emancipation, continued to be exploited as industrial capitalism brought a stream of Asiatic (mainly East Indian) labour to create a secular labour surplus situation.

Industrialization of the region came for the most part after World War II with the growth of monopoly capital on a world scale and the associated imperialist capital inflows into resource industries, chiefly mining and tourism and into branch-plant manufactures. These substantially capital-intensive productive activities aggravated the pre-existing labour surplus situation; and the land intensive character of mining and tourism in a place like Jamaica further forced the African peasantry off what land they had acquired.

The displaced peasantry either migrated internally to the city of Kingston and rural bauxite or tourist towns or sought external refuge in the industrial centres of the UK (and to a lesser extent the US and Canada). The host industrial country placed these migrants into what Pryce describes as 'shit work' – occupational tasks below their accustomed dignity. Accordingly, they had to create an adjustment-mobility space within that hostile and racist social matrix. This they achieved in a variety of ways.

Pryce identifies six varieties of lifestyles in this context: "hustlers, teeny-boppers, proletarian respectables, saints, mainliners and in-betweeners", and in turn he groups these into two major "life orientations", namely: "the stable law-abiding orientation" and the "expressive-disruptable orientation" (p. xii). Each of these two types of life orientation reflects a different view of the world which, in turn, determine responsive behaviour to the locational social framework.

Naturally, the saints and proletarian respectables follow a law-abiding life path. While the hustlers and teeny-boppers engage in illegal activities which allow for creative expression of self. The in-betweeners occupy a half-way space that is for the most part law-abiding in terms of (income earning) occupational activity (part-time or full-time) but they can only tolerate the racist host environment by socializing with the expressive group. Accordingly, the in-betweeners are more interesting change-agents than the stable and strictly law-abiding saints and proletarian respectables.

The book begins with a chapter that examines the social and cultural origins of the people being studied. Note that:

The community of West Indians in Bristol is made up almost entirely of working-class Jamaicans. They are predominantly country people and a high proportion of them hail from the parish of St Thomas in Jamaica. Therefore, like many West Indians in other parts of Britain, they have a rural and colonial origin, and they come from the ranks of the 'have-nots' in their own society (p. xi).

Pryce sees Jamaica as a specific case within a common Caribbean experience characterized by "a common historical heritage of imperialism, poverty and pretext, which all the islands share".

However, Pryce makes a fundamental error when he asserts that the African culture of the slaves was destroyed by what he describes as the forced 'Westernization' of the slaves under plantation capitalism (p. 3). The book never recovers from this basic mistake. So that although it provides us with the rich detail on the struggles of West Indian black people, it does not provide a dynamic structural analysis of a kind that explains the trajectory of change induced by these struggles. In the third section of this review, I will elaborate on this aspect (the 'sounds'). Let us consider the pressure meanwhile.

––––––––

Jamaican society consists of two cultures, that of Europe dominating that of Africa. Although white people[1] are a minority, they own and control the means of production – especially the land and productive capital. The culture of Europe and its bastardized North American version dominates in a society where North Atlantic capital has monopoly control over the resource base. On the other hand, the masses of black workers and peasants are exploited by this imperial capital and by its national fifth column of whites and near-white client capitalists. This economic differentiation sets the stage for a pattern of social stratification based on race, colour and class.

Now Pryce argues that these two components of Jamaican social reality comprise a "Creole culture complex, whose major feature is the co-existence of British and African-derived traditions" and that "within the complex [exists] a scandalously strong 'white bias' (more a cultural than a purely racial phenomenon). In keeping with this bias, things European have the greatest value and prestige, while everything black or African, whether racial traits or cultural symbols, is downgraded, devalued and considered inferior" (pp. 5-6).

The critical punch line here is that within Jamaican society "British metropolitan culture is recognized as the parent culture, and people feel proud that the Creole variation is an extension of Western civilization" (p. 6). So that this overwhelmingly black society displays a colour/class stratification:

forming a perfect pyramid, with mostly whites at the top, brown-skinned mixed-race people in the intermediate strata and black propertyless labour at the base. Every man not already there neurotically aspires to get to the top . . . through the acquisition of the appropriate cultural symbols. Socioeconomic disparities are greatest between the black majority and the brown-white ruling groups which make up less than 20% of the population . . . The Jamaicans in Bristol are poor and black, because they are from the 'have-not' class at the base of the pyramid of Jamaican society (p. 7).

Poverty among the black 80% of Jamaica's population derives from imperialist penetration of the nation's resources and associated exploitation of the labour power of this black majority. Pryce provides some background information on multinational firms producing and marketing sugar and bananas – but nothing on bauxite and tourism. But he notes that this "foreign-controlled process of industrialization based on capital-intensive methods . . . creates unemployment on a massive scale." And that "both in the towns and in the countryside, the working classes have been reaping nothing but misery from it" (p. 11).

Imperialist domination of the economy has been facilitated by a neo-colonial polity in which two-party Westminster political competition divides the working class into two warring tribes. Pryce very correctly notes that:

. . . much of the violence in Jamaica is generated out of the desperate and ceaseless struggle of supporters of the two major political parties – the JLP and the PNP – either to keep their party in power or to make sure it gets into power. The party in office controls the state apparatus, the country's limited resources (sic) and, above all, the means to dispense patronage. In these circumstances, loyalty to a party is a 'bread and butter' issue, and for thousands of poor Jamaicans the ability of their party to dispense patronage – jobs, favours, breaks – is a matter of life and death (pp. 14-15).

This background chapter then turns to an examination of working class adaptations and black consciousness in Jamaica.

This part of Pryce's background discussion is superficial and sometimes ill-formed. As concerns family life, for example, he perpetuates the myth of the instability of common law unions relative to the "monogamous nuclear family and Christian marriage" (p. 15). This is a long standing bias of researchers on family life in Jamaica. The truth is in fact the opposite.[2] Again in discussing 'religion and the masses', Pryce does not understand the bases of fundamentalist creed nor does he seem to known the African roots of Pocomania.[3]

Bedward was the greatest political revivalist leader in Jamaica. Yet he is dismissed in a short paragraph as the 'mad man' which is the way British colonial authorities conveniently described him in order to nip his political protest movement in the bud.[4] Worst of all is the discussion of 'Garvey and Rastafarianism'. Pryce describes the establishment of the black Star Line Shipping Company as 'ill-conceived'. And he regards "Garvey and his Back-to-Africa movement . . . as another form of escapism". This is an unforgivable error for a black scholar to make at this point in our struggle. We are now in the 1980s. Even in the 1960s such an interpretation would receive the deserved wrath of black people.[5]

Because of these incorrect formulations about working-class adaptations and black consciousness in Jamaica, the book falls flat in making an appropriate synthesis of the evidence provided in the life styles of the people under study. My intention is to correct this in the next section of this review.

This background chapter of the book ends appropriately with the correct interpretation of migration 'as a proletarian tradition' among 'the propertyless, poorly educated masses' of Jamaica and the rest of the West Indies. I want to go one step further and argue that this is an inherent feature of plantation capitalism.[6]

Part 1 of the book deals with the lifestyles of Shanty Town, Bristol residents. These are the hustlers and teeny-boppers who have an *expressive-disruptable* life orientation. Naturally, this provides the better and more interesting part of the book for we are observing creative people adapting to a hostile social environment. Shanty Town is the physically dilapidated and decaying St Paul's area of Bristol which was the first area of settlement of these rural Jamaican black people. Their references to this area as "the Village" expresses more than "an ethnic conception of the area" (p. 28). It reflects a rural Jamaican and African conception of his *space*. I want to argue that a people's conception of space, time and Nature are central in understanding their "view of the world".

Pryce's description of the institutions and milieu of Shanty Town is brief and incisive. The 'corner', the cafe, Panorama Club and the Dive are so familiar that any conscious Jamaica reader can feel the atmosphere. Pity that Pryce did not provide a postscript as to why the Club and the Dive no longer exist. For this is of historical importance. For example did the Dive close because Iron-leg, the pence-hustler owner, returned home to Jamaica or did the teeny-boppers he allowed to run the place for him 'carry him down'?

Iron-leg is, in fact, the most interesting case of the regular (senior) hustlers in Shanty Town. Strode, Bang Belly and Conchita are all too familiar and run-of-the-mill. And Percy, the other interesting case is not considered a 'real hustler' being ambivalent about the livelihood of hustling. Not surprisingly, it is Percy who has the most developed and articulate position on "black people's problem" (pp. 39-54). Let's look at Iron-leg and Percy.

"Iron-leg is one of the steadiest hustlers in the business. Year in, year out he has the same [white] girls working for him. He is also a steady gambler, and is much liked, because he is big-hearted and spends freely". He does not buddy-buddy with the other hustlers like himself. In fact, he is said to be too cantankerous to allow himself to be subdued by the norms of any group" (p. 48). Iron-leg says that white people are kinky with their sexual desires. White women do not satisfy white men so the latter come to Shanty Town for black prostitutes (sometimes just to climax on seeing "the girl's private parts") and herbs. It is black people who give England some life and Iron-leg one day thumps down a white man who was just walking by himself and cussing black people.

But the real softness and *humanity* of Iron-leg comes out in his story of how this English girl framed him for threatening to stab her simply because she was jealous that he had "gone to live with another English girl" (pp. 49-50). This girl who framed him was married to a white man and Iron-leg would visit with the couple but felt embarrassed whenever the wife put down her husband in his presence. And although the couple moved to Ireland he was considering taking up their invitation to visit them.

Percy is a self-conscious hustler who "questions himself and the moral legitimacy of his role". Being in his mid twenties, he is younger (by a decade or so) than the regulars; and had just finished a term for shoplifting when interviewed by Pryce. The whole story of how Percy, who was living a straight life, got into stealing through friendship with an ex-con who was a professional thief is very moving because it reveals a kind of loyalty that is unusual in industrial society.

The biographies of all the hustlers reveal a pattern of rejection of nine-to-five 'slave labour', a hatred of white society, and a desire to exploit white women as a source of income. The hustle provides a means for hitting back at white racism. Rejection of the work ethic is said to be a reaction to the following; (1) poor pay and lack of opportunity for advancement, (2) threats to manhood and conception of self as a man, (3) white supremacy, and (4) "the individual's search for autonomy and mastery and control over the situation" (p. 66).

Poncing is the favourite hustle in Shanty Town, Bristol. Other hustles are robbery, conning and drug peddling. According to Pryce, "the hustle is the ideal alternative to legal work, because it is the complete antithesis" (p. 68). Hustlers exploit a harem of white women but they turn to black women for establishing families. The idealization of the black women and the denunciation of white women is an ideology of hustlers and teeny boppers alike.

For the people of Shanty Town, life in the racist environment of England is brutal; they are under constant 'pressure'. And their response is expressive – interpersonal violence and the blues dance are mechanisms for letting off steam and easing the pressure. Pryce relates a particular incident of violence where a Trinidadian beat up a drunk Jamaican who had accused him of stealing his wallet. The postscript to that incident is instructive. The Trinidadian said that "after he knocked out the man he went inside and wept, because the last thing he'd ever want to do was to fight another black man like himself. He fight for *any* black man . . . but it was his principle never to fight *against* them" (p. 106).

Teeny-boppers are perhaps more interesting than the hustlers. The term is applied to a black "West Indian youth in his teens or very early twenties, who is male, homeless, unemployed and who . . . is either already a delinquent or in danger of becoming one" (p. 107). They were born in the West Indies but grew up in Britain. They suffer from inferior education in working class schools in the West Indies and racist practice in the British schools when they are sent for to join parent(s). Facing unemployment after completing schooling and rejection in the parental home, they 'drop out' to become teeny-boppers. Pryce argues that the teeny bopper response involves to some extent a rejection of white society and this, of course, sooner or later brings them in conflict with the law. Whereas the adult hustlers relate to the Negro hipster in America, the younger teeny-boppers take their cue from the Rastafarians, black Power militants and the Rasta message in reggae (p. 108).

Now Pryce turns to deal with "culture, poverty and the West Indian family". And on the basis of information gathered from (and on)[7] two teeny-boppers comes to a remarkable conclusion that demands quoting at length:

The West Indian lower class . . . lacks an indigenous workable class (folk) morality of its own, as is manifested in the deficiencies of the family system. Sooner or later these deficiencies come to constitute a predicament for West Indians – especially young West Indians, who, because of their semi-anglicized heritage of poverty and social anarchy, are finding adjustment in England bewildering and perplexing. The net effect on the West Indian young of the absence of a grounded sense of identity, capable of giving guidance and direction in times of crisis, is psychic and cultural confusion and lack of confidence in coping with the stresses of racial rejection . . . (p. 112).

This view of the lower class West Indian family is supported in the next chapter which outlines the case of Billy Burns and his mother, who, by force of economic circumstances, had to desert Billy and go to Canada. Pryce concludes that examination with the statement that "West Indians lack a group identity and a tight, communal form of group life based on a sense of collective interdependence and mutual obligation among kinsmen". Further on he states that this story is that "of the vulnerable clanless West Indian – courageous, and self reliant, a plodder and a toiler, but hardly a survivor, because he is tribeless and defenceless and without solid roots of his own . . ." (p. 119).

The history of West Indian people strongly refutes this conclusion. Ours is a history of survival against the greatest odds imaginable. And what Pryce regards as 'deficiencies' in the family system are in fact an adaptation to circumstances dictated by our particular history of slavery and imperial domination.[8] The West Indian lower class does *not* lack an indigenous class morality. On the contrary, it is the immorality of the white ruling class that suppresses the powerful African-based roots culture of the lower classes. And this is what generates the psychic and cultural confusion displayed by the youth. Indeed, later in the book, Pryce seems to concur with this view with the statement that "Estrangement and identity-confusion set in with the teenybopper's accumulated experience of deception and discrimination on the part of white people" (p. 136).

No wonder then that the "Rastafarian philosophy of negritude" and "diverse left-wing revolutionary ideologies thrown up by the search for freedom and liberation all over the world" strike a responsive chord in the minds of the youth. These provide a basis for self identity and self-assurance, thereby creating a disjuncture between the youth and their parents who display 'Uncle Tom' attitudes in order to find a workable space in white society. The interview with Duke, Danny and Bertie in chapter 13 is most revealing as concerns the attitudes, values and beliefs of the youth. For example, "How can a man believe in a white God in a world like this?"

Unfortunately, these dramatic perceptions of the youth are not fully appreciated by the author who, in the ensuing two chapters of the book, completely misrepresents Rasta and reggae; and therefore fails to provide the reader with an appreciation of the politics and ideology of Dread. My contention is that in the culture of Dread is the seed of revolutionary change in the West Indies. But Pryce misses the connection because he relies on the Afro-Saxon analyses and interpretations of people like Naipaul, Patterson and Nettleford – West Indians whose literary efforts display their own crisis of identity within a white European space. Naipaul, for example, once made the absurd statement that West Indians have created nothing.

It is necessary to correct some of the misconceptions about the origins of Rasta and Reggae portrayed in this book. On another occasion, I shall elaborate on the theme Dread and the incipient Caribbean revolution. Clarity about origins is a first step for that deeper analysis. Rastafari has roots in the philosophy and political articulation of Garvey and Bedward. And it is important to note that it originated in *rural* Jamaica, among the African peasantry of St Thomas in the East where Bogle had led the struggle for land in the latter half of the 19th century. In its incipient stage of development, the colonial authorities and white planters were very concerned about its potential for disrupting the established imperial order. And they were of the view that Rastafari was communist inspired.[9]

Pryce completely misses the Ethiopian connection in his discussion on pp. 145-46. It was the Italian fascist invasion of Ethiopia that triggered supportive responses from black people all over the New World long before the Ethiopian government formed the Ethiopian World Federation in 1937. And there began the contemporary 'linkage politics' between black people of the Caribbean and liberation struggles, throughout Africa.[10] Pryce may be correct when he states that "the Rastas are only superficially religious"; but he is grossly incorrect in saying that "Their religious dogmas are solidly buttressed by a conscious and clearly enunciated ideological racism" (p. 143). Perhaps he means *racialism* but that is an entirely different matter.[11] To describe Rasta ideology as racist is to deny the humanity that characterizes Rasta creed and to debase its very essence.

'Rude boy' was a precursor to Dread in Jamaica. And Pryce recognizes that "rude-boy is more than a delinquent: he is a revolutionary" (p. 149). And Rasta and reggae provide the social and cultural instruments of protest to achieve 'equal rights and justice'. The culture of Dread provides a counter to the contradictions faced by the youth when "His own West Indian 'leaders' . . . preach integration, yet in his day-to-day experience, everywhere he goes, he is brought up short by barriers erected on grounds of class or ancestry" (pp. 136-37).

Now music is one expression of the culture of a people. And Reggae is a clear articulation of the history of sufferation of Jamaican black people. Pryce goes way off the mark in stating that "Reggae erupted among the youth of shanty-town areas of Kingston simply from the need of rude-boys, Rastafarians and others to earn a living through music and dance . . ." (p. 150). This is totally incorrect. Reggae evolved from a synthesis of Jamaican folk music (mento) with the jazz idiom of black people in the US, each in turn rooted in the rhythm of Africa. This synthesis found its highest level of articulation in the music of Don Drummond in his celebration of the "the quest for and the realization of spiritual discoveries: of being – of black Jamaican being. The dread element in the music is rooted in the culture of struggle, defiance and resistance of a downpressed and displaced African people.[12] Yet Pryce describes it as "no more than the distillation of visceral images of sex, violence and protest, accompanied by aggressively menacing and uncompromising drum beats, and lyrics which articulate the mood and grievances of the people" (p. 151).

What Price describes as the "eruption of the music in the late sixties" must be seen in the contextual situation of a heightened struggle for liberation in Africa and among black people in the New World. The black Power movement crystallized a protest based on the fact that black people were not getting a fair share of the capitalist boom of the 1950s and 1960s. The British extension of that movement provided fuel for the rude-boy explosion. It was not simply that the "eruption of music . . . coincided with the worsening of race relations in Britain . . ." (p. 156). This was no coincidence. *A correct materialist view of history* will reveal the connection of black dispossession to both 'coincidences'. *It is the historical accumulation of pressure that created the sounds of reggae.*

No wonder then that in his analysis of politics and ideology of the teenyboppers, Pryce finds that "Though the influence of Marxism is always present, it seems to me that in their general political orientation there is a greater emphasis placed on negritude and black nationalism, and that in their activities an ideological concern with African liberation movements is uppermost" (p. 165). This is hardly surprising because it is logical that nationalism must precede the transition to socialism given the particular historical experience of black people with capitalism.

———

Part 2 of the book deals with those West Indians with a "stable law-abiding orientation". Price begins with the problem of discrimination in employment faced by these people. The Bristol bus dispute in 1963 seems to have been a watershed in race relations in that city. However, the analysis presented is weak and localized. In fact, throughout this part of the book Price fails to make certain important international connections in the struggle of black people.

It is important to note that 1961 was the year of Sharpeville (South Africa) and the racist call for a control of Commonwealth immigration in Britain, both of which enraged black people throughout the Diaspora. Harold Wilson's stance against the Bristol Omnibus Company must be viewed against that background. Four non-white Commonwealth heads of state had considered breaking out of the Commonwealth after 1961. So that by 1963, Bristol lagged behind London where the head office of the bus company was located. Here we find a disjuncture between the policies of head office *vs* the local subsidiary, and differences in official attitude between the metropole (London) and the outpost (Bristol). Head office and the metropole naturally ruled. Letters to the *Evening Post* were not the decisive element in that situation.

The chapter dealing with proletarian respectables and saints as workers is good in its description of attitudes of these people to white racism. One particular individual sees the social intercourse with white people as revealing their artificiality and hypocrisy. "Its like inside them is just pure hate, really hate . . . Powell is the only English man that will get up and speak the truth" (p. 197). Even the saints take a firm Black Power stand. The statement of the bishop from the pulpit (pp. 192-94) is a blend of Martin Luther King and Malcolm X, that is not non-violence but not yet revolutionary. For him violence is necessary for defence: ". . . it is very hard for Black Power to resist White Power without violence" (p. 193).

The chapter dealing with the saints shows a familiarity with the terrain and appreciation of the ethic which was so evidently missing in earlier chapters on Rasta and reggae. Pryce recognizes that "the religion of the saints [Pentecostalism] is a religion of the oppressed and that in their sermons and style of worship saints are reinterpreting Christianity to satisfy their own needs as working-class blacks in a white racist society" (p. 211). Indeed, I find that the description of the "puritan morality of saints" (pp. 211-13) is almost identical to the letter with that of Rastafari. So also is their *modus vivendi* of 'brotherly love'; but where as saints extend this only to church members, rasta extends it to *all*. The point I wish to make is that there is a common cultural thread running between saints and Rasta. This is not surprising. But the book does not make the connection.

Of all the types examined in this second part of the book, mainliners are the least interesting while in-betweeners are the most dynamic and colourful characters. In-betweeners are "young, law-abiding West Indians in the 18 to 35 age-group who normally would be mainliners but who, in keeping with their race-conscious and Afro-centric outlook, have assimilated into their lifestyle certain 'black culture' or Shanty Town norms" (p. 236). They are usually better educated than mainliners. And they want to return to Jamaica and make a contribution to developing their country and carve out for themselves a place in the sun. But the contradictions involved in that transition are numerous as the exchange of letters between the author and one who returned to Jamaica testify.

Basically, the mainliners are reminiscent of the Afro-Saxon political elites at home in the West Indies. And Pryce leaves unanswered the interesting question as to whether in another decade or so the in-betweeners will evolve into mainliners. The question is actually posed in the concluding chapter (pp. 275-76) but no answer is provided. This is a result of the static nature of the analysis that Pryce provides. The attempt to introduce some dynamic consideration at the very end (last two pages of the book) is both superficial and summary.

The lifestyles depicted in this book provide more raw material for analyses of resistance and struggle of black people against the crushing blows of white racist imperialism. The problem is basically the same whether we are located in the West Indies or in the centre states of the international capitalist system. How an oppressed people can carve out a life-space for themselves in the interstices of that system? Or, alternatively, to overthrow that system, thereby widening their life-space horizons. That is the task we face.

Pryce's book only deals with the first problem. The endless pressure generates a mobilizing force of sounds within the cultural matrix. Indeed, I want to argue that the reggae renaissance represents an unfolding cultural revolution that needs a material base to effect the political revolution which can overthrow the system. Rasta ideology is too passive to orchestrate that revolution. And the culture of Dread is too escapist and apolitical so far. It seems that a marriage between Marxian political thought and ideology and the culture of Dread could consumate the political revolution. What this means is that we need to integrate *race* and *class* in the analysis and articulation of the black Caribbean experience.

Such an assault on the system would undermine the dependent capitalist economic substructure and correspondingly alter the superstructure of political, social, psychological, cultural and ideological relations. This is the political challenge of the 1980s. For each time in the recent past the assault on the system has been partial: in the 1960s, race was the mobilizing factor and in 1970s, it has been class. Naturally, only limited successes have been achieved in these partial assaults.

A first step toward revolution is an understanding of the pattern of resistance of the oppressed. David Scott, in a student essay, shows a profound understanding of this:[13]

. . . the very existence of the oppressed is one of resistance – the very substance of his being is sublimated: he becomes resistance. His total self, chained and bound to a reality of domination is a pre-occupation with barricades of resistance – self-defences which at basic levels are intuitive, a natal physio-psychological reflex. It is necessary only to listen/to experience the steel monologue of Don Drummond's horn (much like Ralph Ellison and Louis Armstrong), or the sorrowful, pitiless wail of the 'Burning Spear'; to watch the affected self-assurance of the Rasta-man's flaunting, stolid gait; to hear the bitter, accusing curses spat from market woman to market woman like stanzas between refrains of thundering bosom-shaking laughter; to feel, to be enveloped in the drowning/sedating/electrifying pulse of a seething ghetto dance, and see legions ejaculating arms and legs silently/rhythmically, now shouting now intoning vexed/sensuous/mutely belligerent pronouncements; to see eyes, hands, and hearts turn searchingly heaven-ward in beseechful exaltations at a Revival Church . . . it is enough to bear testimony to this 'living', this 'dispensation' . . . to understand that resistance suffuses all existence for the oppressed.

The question that must be posed is what factors can contribute to heightening this resistance to a level that brings revolution.

The answer to that is complex. Material being affects social consciousness. And two sets of factors influence that consciousness: one internal to the particular society and the other external to it. For West Indian state societies, like Jamaica, the deepening crisis of world capitalism sharpens the internal contradictions between capital and labour. And the adversity imposed by IMF 'manners'[14] has served to raise popular consciousness of the evils of capitalism.

Meanwhile, successful liberation struggles in Africa reinforce popular consciousness about the possibilities for liberation at home. In the 1960s, the struggles of black people in the US provided an external dynamic for change. In the 1980s it will be the socialist transformations in Ethiopia, Zimbabwe, Mozambique, Angola and Namibia that will galvanize the resistance and struggles of black people in the West Indies. Black people in the imperial centres, particularly those in the US, can influence that process substantially. The struggles they wage in their location space within the belly of imperialism can effectively weaken the monster.

That is the basic backdrop for the struggle ahead! And it is the dread youth and in-betweeners who will see it through.

Notes
_____

*"The sounds and pressures of black survival: a review article of Ken Pryce's *Endless Pressure*", *Social and Economic Studies* 13:2 (1980a).

1 In Jamaica, Europeans are actually few in number but there is a broader category of near white which includes Jews and levantine people. These near whites are national capitalists.

2 See, for example, the results of a survey by George Roberts and Sonja Sinclair, *Women in Jamaica* (Millwood, NY: KTO Press, 1978).

3 The literal English translation from the Spanish to 'little madness' reflects once more the white English bias of researchers.

4 See, for example, Ken Post, *Arise Ye Starvelings*. Editor's note: The labelling of Bedward as a 'madman' is not Ken Pryce's view. Pryce merely recounts how Bedward was viewed by the authorities. See p. 17, *Endless Pressure*.

5 At this point (pp.18-19), Pryce does not discuss Rastafarianism but later in the book he presents the superficial and Eurocentric views of Nettleford, Smith and Augier as gospel and goes way off track. I elaborate on this in Section 3.

6 See my "Race, class and the plantation" – paper presented to LASA Conference Houston, Texas (October 1978); "Plantation capitalism: some comparative perspectives", paper presented to Symposium on the Political Economy of the Black World, UCLA: May 1979; and "Black dispossession: review article", *Transition* (1980).

7 Information on teeny-boppers is gathered from teachers (English), social workers' reports, and parents. So there is a certain bias here.

8 Some of the myths about instability of the family system are a result of Eurocentric 'scholarship'. But this is contradicted by recent studies e.g. Roberts and Sinclair, *Women in Jamaica*.

9 See Ken Post.

10 Cuban military assistance to Angola when South Africa invaded that newly independent state and the supportive role of Jamaica and Guyana in that process as well as in the liberation of Zimbabwe are examples of this linkage. So is Cuban assistance to revolutionary Ethiopia.

11 Racialism reflects a consciousness of race. It promotes racial pride and recognizes the positive contribution of different races to the development of civilization. Racism, on the other hand, promotes the notion of superiority of one race over others. It negates the contribution of others to the development of civilization.

12 See E. Kamau Brathwaite, *Contradictory Omens* (Mona, Jamaica: ISER, 1974) and his "Jazz and the West Indian novel" for further insights.

13 Student essay, "Caribbean social structure" (UWI Mona, 1979-80).

14 This usage is derived from the current Jamaican expression 'under heavy manners' meaning under heavy discipline and control.

32

Portrait of the Jamaican Male*

The Contextual Setting

History is the science of society. Our knowledge of Jamaican and West Indian history generally remains very underdeveloped. The only knowledge that we really have of our peoples is the knowledge derived from the records of the colonial authorities during colonial days. This material resides mostly in the Public Records Office in London – reports of governors, of planters, of European visitors during the colonial period, etc What we do not have is a statement of the history of our peoples from our people themselves. This is, of course, understandable given our historical development and given the dominance of the written tradition in our own education. We have neglected the oral tradition of our people; a tradition deriving out of our African past.

It is only recently, in the neocolonial period, that West Indian scholars began to give a West Indian interpretation of even what colonial records there were of our past; work of people like Eric Williams, C.L.R. James, and since the establishment of UWI, Elsa Goveia, Douglas Hall, Roy Augier, and Edward Brathwaite. So that what we have in terms of knowledge of our history, including the social history of our people, is essentially a European knowledge. We do not have an African people's knowledge of our own development and it is here that Brodber's oral history of Jamaica, 1900-1944 makes a significant contribution. It provides a good start in the direction of filling this important knowledge gap; to correct the existing bias, so to speak. Now this knowledge gap manifests itself in a number of ways, not the least of which is our failure to understand the real dynamic elements in the political and social economy of our development and underdevelopment.

Political and Social Economy of Underdevelopment and Development

In Jamaica (like the rest of the Caribbean) our historical, and in some cases contemporary, situation is one characterized by the persistent presence of plantation capitalism in the economy. Plantation capitalism evolved from the original slave plantation economy which the Europeans established after they invaded these countries and wiped out the indigenous Indian populations. That slave economy was eliminated through the struggles of the African slaves and by changes in world economic circumstances in 1838.

After emancipation, plantation capitalism developed and continued on the basis of large-scale export agricultural production using wage labor of the freed men who, where land resources were available (as in Jamaica) managed to establish a viable peasantry in the mountainous interstices not directly controlled by plantation capitalist production. So, we find a concentration of peasant agricultural production in the mountains and hill country of Jamaica struggling to secure resources of land, capital, etc., for the economic advancement of the African freed men. This has been the main trend in our economic underdevelopment from emancipation right up to the present time.

The development of the economy depends on the pace of economic development in the larger world capitalist system into which it is integrated. And the issue of the story is that plantation capitalism entrenched itself deeper in the twentieth century with the emergence and development of multinational corporations – in production of sugar, the old commodity from slave days; then in the marketing (and production) of bananas, the new export commodity (production of which came from farms of the freed man/peasantry). These multinational corporations in the agrarian sector have been reinforced by the entrance of multinational corporations in other resource sectors, notably bauxite and tourism.

Given the circumstances in which the multinationals were allowed to insert themselves in the colonial economy, the few competing multinational bauxite companies secured as much land as was possible for each of them to advance their competitive position in world aluminium production and trade. So we find that much of the agricultural land that the peasantry had managed to secure for themselves and develop in the heartland of Jamaica fell into ownership of the bauxite multinationals after the second imperialist war, when this industry developed. Some 200,000 acres, 40% of total arable land in Jamaica came under the ownership control of five bauxite-alumina companies.

In like manner, but to a much lesser extent, tourism development along the north and west coasts also made some claims on land that had been developed by the peasantry. One has to really look at the physical dimensions of Jamaica to understand what all of this means.

Continuing on the social economy of underdevelopment and development. The underdevelopment of our economy is basically attributable to the dominance of plantation capitalism and its more recent counterparts – industrial and finance capitalism – in the mining, tourism, banking and other sectors in the commanding heights of the economy. This dominance has generated underdevelopment and backwardness in the sense that the majority of our people who secure their livelihood from the resources of the nation have limited access to the use and development of these resources, because of the presence of imperial capital in the resource sectors.

Essentially, then, the struggle for development by our peoples has been a struggle to secure resources; has been a struggle to fight against the hegemony of imperial capital over our nation's resources. But given the persistent dominance that I describe, opportunities in Jamaica became less and less possible over time. Consequently, our people have been on the move – forced to move – in order to find the capacity to advance themselves economically.

Now, so far I have been discussing the pure economic aspects. I want to get into other aspects of this development/underdevelopment dialectic. Colonialism/imperialism has a profound and dramatic effect on the socio-cultural aspects of our development, in the sense that our people are an uprooted people whose original culture base was African and who were forcibly transformed in the historical process that I described. Accordingly, their very being has been suppressed in this process. Consequently, part of the struggle has been to assert one's own being, plus having to struggle for achieving material advancement. It think it is quite remarkable that in such a situation the African peasantry in Jamaica has managed, within four generations since emancipation, to achieve not just what economic development we have achieved, but also the sociocultural development manifested in the vitality of our presence. And here I think it is important to make the distinction between a struggle for survival, and what I think is a more appropriate description of the process: a *struggle for overcoming*. Because, if nothing else, the testimony in this book proves that we have overcome rather than just survived the dehumanizing rape of our society and economy.

Some of the revelations that come our from these testimonies inform us in new ways about both the macro and the micro social economy of struggle and development that our people have waged and won. One can see the way in which they built up a domestic economy that, in aggregate, developed the national economy through peasant sector diversification, innovation in introducing new crops, and new modes of transport. This led to the development of an internal distribution network. Fundamentally they manipulated for accumulation from whatever resources were available to them. They utilized their environmental resources to create a substantial productive and social space away from the dominant plantation capitalism – which they were trying to escape. This has important lessons for us right now, in terms of development planning and policy, but that is another matter that we will not go into here.

Some of the other highlights that emerge relate to the development of class formation. The testimony provides us with much new information on this question; but, again that is not our main focus of attention here. In the micro social economy, for example, there is a lot of evidence on the patterns of production and exchange; indeed, the pattern of what I call social guerilla activities in the struggle and resistance of our people – how they satisfied basic needs with what resources were available; the importance of labour mobility as a strategy for advance, both internal migration and external migration; social mobility through education; cooperative forms of activity in food production, in house building and in capital mobilization; in establishing their own social security schemes: friendly societies, burial scheme societies, etc.; in health, the use of bush medicines, of how they use what resources they find in the bush to deal with health problems, childbirth pains, etc. Numerous examples are to be found in these testimonies (see for example, *Migrant to Cuba/Farmer*, chapter 6).

There is a lot of new information here on both the micro and the macro social economy of the development of our people. We also have information in these testimonies of the importance of the international in our people's development. The importance of Africa is brought out in the perceptions that people exhibit in answers to questions relating to Garvey, Bedward, Africa and slavery. Out of that the politics of the Africa connection is highlighted; but more importantly, in the present context, the connection with places like Cuba, Panama, Costa Rica, where even today many of our people (and their offspring) are still living as a result of that forced movement in search of economic advancement. All this of course has implications for understanding the political economy of change in our society today.

The Testimony

In reading the selections for this book , I have concentrated on what new information is revealed concerning the character of the Jamaican male. Our knowledge and conception of the Jamaican male is dominated by sociological studies of the family in Jamaica which tell us that the Jamaican family is a matriarchally dominated family; that the Jamaican male in the circumstances is irresponsible as a father; is lazy, shiftless and generally backward. The testimonies in this book certainly dismiss these misconceptions once and for all, at least to my mind.

For what emerges from the testimonies is the fact that the Jamaican male has been forced to be a provider for his family from a very tender age. Even before reaching their teens, they have to assume family responsibilities because their fathers had to move away from home to seek economic opportunities,. The young male child had to assume a man role – 'man-to'. There is abundant evidence in these cases to substantiate this important way in which the Jamaican male is socialized from very early stages to assume responsibilities within the domestic economy. So in looking for achievements from the testimonies of the book, the point of view I take is: what new knowledge can we gain regarding the Jamaican male?

It seems to me that what emerges is that the Jamaican male has been a lion – an economic warrior – from early youth, in the fight for overcoming economic obstacles in the path of his development. In the process they managed somehow to create social and physical space for themselves, both within Jamaica and outside of Jamaica; wherever they were forced to move. In looking at the testimonies, I want to concentrate on this business of how our man folk manipulated social and physical space in order to achieve advancement.

Mode of Life

The mode of life is a concept that comes out of the testimony of *Migrant to Cuba/Farmer* (chapter 6, p. 33). To me, this core concept of the mode of life seems appropriate to anchor our analysis. What is the mode of life? The mode of life deals with the production, welfare, spiritual mechanisms of advancement, not just survival of advancement. The mode of life informs us of that basic element within our people that generated the energy, so to speak, for expanding their space – physical space, social space, every space. I think it is important for us to examine and elaborate the concept of the mode of life of a people in order to understand their capacity for struggle; for manipulating the oppressive environmental situation in which colonialism and imperialism forced them.

The mode of life tells us of people's perceptions, of people's material and spiritual conditions, of people's aspirations, of people's mechanisms for accommodating within the physical, social, economic and political environment into which they are inserted. It is a concept that, I think, needs elaborating and refining so as to profitably incorporate it into our tool box of analysis in social science research.

I want to concentrate on three aspects of the mode of life – of space manipulation by our people; that is to say, the way in which they adjusted and expanded economic, social and physical space for themselves. The three aspects deal firstly with the spirit of the people; the spirit of the people reflects their internal strength, their internal resistance, their internal capacity to struggle. This manifests itself basically in the culture of the people; *defining culture as a way of being of a people*. The second dimension I want to look at is the area of resource use. Our people utilized whatever resources became available to them within Jamaica's physical space for their advancement, particularly their economic advancement. The third aspect I want to examine and elaborate is in the area of technological innovation and change.

The Spirit of the People

Human beings are influenced by the physical environment in which they live. And, of course, we find characteristics of people being different, whether they're brought up in the hills, in the mountains, or whether they were brought up on the plains or whether they were brought up on the coast itself. So I think we should not be surprised to find differences in the characteristics of Jamaican people at these three physical levels – the hills, the plains and the coast. Notwithstanding those internal differences, there is still a national spirit that one can speak of and one that emerges clearly from the testimonies. That spirit is the spirit of an African people – a spirit which is a spirit of resistance, of struggle, of overcoming, of *lionizing*.

This spirit manifests itself in a lot of ways through all aspects of the culture of our people: in language, religion, music and so on. The being of Jamaican black people is one that is clearly an adaptation to a situation, but an adaptation that is gloriously overcoming. There is evidence. There is evidence in the music, whether it is the music of our folk religions: the claphand, the joyousness, the participatory spirit of rejoicing/revival in Pocomania, Church of God, of Pentecost, etc.; the popular music of people poets like Don Drummond and Bob Marley.

I will return to the national spirit shortly after saying something about the hills/plains/coast differences. Unfortunately, we don't have enough witnesses in the samples in this book to say very much about the coast people, usually the fisherman. But No. 3 witness from Hope Bay gives us a little glimpse on this. The main contrast we get is the hills versus plains. The hills, of course, are the domain of the African peasantry, while the plains have been the domain of plantation capitalism. And we find striking contrasts between the character of the hill people, (coming out of the viable peasantry that the hill people developed) and the plains people. It is a difference between the peasantry and the agro-proletariat in the Jamaican context, for the plains people were essentially workers in the sugar estates.

Let us look at the testimony of *Sugar Factory Worker* as well as that of *Tourist Guide*, from Mavis Bank. They themselves speak to these differences as the following quotations indicate. Pages 21-23 of *Sugar Factory Worker* where he deals with his grandfather and other people who had come from St Elizabeth. He deals with the way in which they educated their children, the way in which St Elizabeth people designed and built their homes out of their environment; and this gives him some perceptions about those people. He contrasts them with the sugar estate proletariat which had no access to building their own houses. They lived in barracks provided by the plantation and had no land, whereas St Elizabeth people had their own land. In his own words:

Up in St Elizabeth they raised dumb thing and study, but down this way now [that is in Westmoreland – in the cane area] you can't raise no dumb thing, you can't make no move. For all you right round is the bigger property man, but there in St Elizabeth they have their own property.

Then when we look at the evidence of *Tourist Guide*, from Mavis Bank in St Andrew, he speaks of the stability of the mountain community in Jamaica, and makes the point that most people are born and grow up in this area – creating a certain stability in the community.

At the level of the national spirit for overcoming, what is striking from the evidence is the way in which the migrant was able to fit into a new environment, whether he was moving internally from rural Jamaica to Kingston or to a main town, to learn trade (skill); or whether he was migrating abroad to Cuba and Panama – Spanish-speaking environments in which he was inserting himself without even knowing the language, without even being able to communicate. It is really quite a remarkable achievement that these young men left Jamaica and went to Cuba, and not just fitted in so as to survive but, in short order, were able to manipulate a space for themselves within that new, unknown, and sometimes hostile, environment.

All of the witnesses who migrated – most of them were to Cuba – are living manifestations of this capacity in the national spirit of our people. This is what I meant by the capacity of our people to 'lionize' themselves in order to create that space for advancing their situation. The lionizing concept is important because of the symbolism of the lion in African culture, in the African way of being and seeing; and it is emphasized today in the culture of Rastafari.

This brings us to another aspect of the culture – religion. The Africanness of folk religious ritual is evident. It is religion that springs out of oppression but the resistance it embodies is not just for survival. It is for overcoming. The Afro-European folk church in Jamaica is the most important religious institution of the majority of our people. For our people have seen the established church – the Church of England and of Rome, Methodist, Baptist and other denominations of the white missionaries – as portraying an alien, white God; a Christian ritual process coming out of Europe's culture and, therefore, part of that oppressive framework which dominated their lives in the sphere of their social economy. The religious institutions within the folk culture is more celebratory – handclapping, voice participation ("Praise the Lord") than is the case in the established church. In the testimonies of males presented in this book, it is interesting to see the way in which people move from the established church to the folk religion, and sometimes back again, at various phases in their lives. If they were born and raised in the established church, whether Baptist, Methodist or Anglican, they tended to drift to the folk churches and then to drift back to the established churches once they established themselves, because the established church is part of the status basis for social advancement.

I am really dealing with religion here as part of the culture in order to elaborate on this national spirit that I am suggesting exists within our people, a national spirit for overcoming in hostile environments – both at home (*ie* a yard here in Jamaica) and abroad.

Another aspect of the culture is the language. The Jamaican patois is clearly a much more beautiful, rhythmical and poetic language than standard English and just reading these testimonies establishes that very clearly. The way in which people are able to express themselves in the language of the Jamaican patois is clearly an advance on what standard English allows them to do. The development of a language (because that is what the history of patois right up to the present innovations by Rastafari demonstrate) that brings out from within the people a natural poetry of expression is another important manifestation of that spirit of overcoming.

It might very well be, for example, that part of the reason for our capacity to adjust to new language environments, like going to Cuba and other Spanish-speaking countries, is partly related to our inherent historical capacity for language appreciation and language development. It might well be; I don't know. But since much of the Jamaican's patois is a combination of English and our original African languages it seems plausible. That is something for the linguists to explore. It just occurred to me that in seeking explanations for this capacity to fit into new unfamiliar environments, and so quickly overcoming barriers for communication, we need to consider this historical legacy.

Resource Utilization and Development

Let me turn now to the second question. The question of resource use in expanding space – physical, economic and social space. This question of resources is fundamental in understanding our capacity for development in a purely economic sense, because what economic development really involves is the capacity of a people to use what natural resources are within their grasp and to transform those natural resources into commodities for consumption. The way in which people use resources tells us a lot about their process of economic development.

In these testimonies of the Jamaican male we have a lot of evidence of the versatility and innovativeness in resource use, whether it is in the utilization of the natural resources of the hill country (for example, in house building), or whether we are talking about the skill versatility displayed by these men in the development of the use of their labor resources. In purely economic terms, output is determined by the quantity and quality of resource inputs; resource inputs being natural resources (land, etc.), human resources (*ie* labor and management) and knowledge resources (technology).

Here I want to concentrate on human and natural resources and the way in which these have been utilized and developed by the Jamaican people. But before addressing that it is instructive for us to deal with technological innovation, that is the knowledge resource aspect. In this connection I will draw on examples relating to how our people developed technology to deal with both food and shelter in their basic needs requirements.

In the interviews questions were asked about the character of housing, housing design, structures, and so on. And we see a variety of responses – varying according to the resources existing where people live. In the St Elizabeth area, for example, we find the use of the Spanish wall construction out of mud; and, throughout the island, we find variations in the use of different roofing materials – thatch in places where thatch was available, shingles in other places where sufficient wood from the forest was available (eg in the hills of St Ann, Portland and St Mary).

One of the things that struck me in relation to housing design, to cope with natural disaster environmental situation, comes out in the evidence of the *Master Carpenter* from Beverley in St Ann, in response to questions about the hurricane in 1903. On pages 3-4 (chapter 6) where he was asked if he could remember what his house looked like before the hurricane, the answer was: "Well my house before the hurricane was a two apartment. Besides it was hit. It was good – it was even better than when the storm blow; it really shake it. But what really happened, my Daddy was a carpenter and soon after that him remain it up nicely." His house was of bare woodwork, he says, and indicates that the roof didn't fall at all; it was a shingle roof house. The house didn't fall at all as a result of the hurricane, although it was a wooden structure with a shingle roof in an area heavily pounded by the hurricane.

Master Carpenter is the son of a carpenter father but he learned his carpentry by moving to Kingston to 'learn trade', cotching in town by his brother who was a 'domestic worker' in a hotel in the tourist industry. *Master Carpenter* himself had spent two years in Cuba when he was 20 years old. He had come to town at age 18 to learn trade. His two year sojourn in Cuba did not involve using the carpentry skills which he had just learned. And yet on his return to Jamaica he both bought land and became a peasant farmer himself while continuing, on the side as it were, to do his carpentry work. According to him, he 'built' the factory building at nearby Landovery sugar estate. So here we have a case of that versatility of skill; of the use of human resources and of technological innovativeness at the same time.

There are many other aspects of this technological innovativeness in resource use. *Officer of the Band of Mercy* from Portland (chapter 4) tells us about how, for example, the trumpet tree was used to make rope. Rope to tie animals. We also pick up from another witness how the said trumpet tree was a source for making musical instruments – the drum and, surprisingly to me, the violin. Violins were made right here in Jamaica out of the trumpet tree, as we are told by *Landless Farmer* (chapter 15, p. 14). These musical instruments were critical in maintaining and developing the spirit of our people because the folk music, as I indicated earlier, was a part of that spiritual build-up for overcoming, that spiritual assertion. We know the important role of the drum in our musical culture. So they utilized the trumpet tree which was at hand – a wild gift of Nature – to make drums, and to make violins. I was frankly quite surprised to learn that our people made their own violins.

Other aspects of technological innovation are to be found in evidence relating to food culture – the crops our people grew to sustain themselves, the importance of ground provisions, of the yam in the food culture; the way in which they practised mixed cropping within their peasant holdings; and again the versatility that that involved, in terms of development of skill resources as a people.

This brings me to the whole question of resource use which, in an important sense, is tied to technology – the development of knowledge about resource use. For what resources people use and how they use it is really determined by the knowledge that they build up about those resources that are known to them and what new resources they discover in the process of their development. So in a way, it does not make much sense separating the discussion of technological innovation from that of resource use.

The rest of this discussion on resource use looks at various aspects of technological innovation, of knowledge accumulation, in the process of manipulating the physical environment. What is important for us to note is the way in which our people carved out and created a comfortable accommodating space within the limited constraints that plantation capitalism imposed on them. And this process continues right up to the present time, as exemplified by the hustle economy of contemporary urban Jamaica. What the contemporary hustle economy actually shows is the persistent capacity of our people to seize whatever economic opportunities arise within the existing space situation; in order to expand their own individual domestic economic circumstance, thereby to maintain a signified existence.

This brings me now to an examination of some of the other continuities in our historical process in terms of the internal and international linkages; really, the whole pattern of existence of people within the New World component of the black Diaspora; and relating that to the struggle for development and advancement within that larger global space. Here the experiences that the men in this book relate concern Africa and their knowledge of Africa; their own experiences abroad, mainly as workers in Cuba (in one case as a First World War volunteer actually fighting in Europe); in their children's experiences abroad in the US and so on. There's much evidence here to substantiate the assertion that I made earlier about the skill versatility and innovativeness of our migrant people. But this takes me a little further afield than I can develop in this introduction.

Lion in the Family

So now I want to turn to the question of the way in which the evidence provided by the man in this book enlighten us about the role of Jamaican men from the time of their youth to their present old age. What comes out clearly from all of the witnesses is the fact that they were, of necessity, forced to contribute to the economic support of their families from very early ages – from 12, even from the age of 9. We have cases of young men assuming a role of breadwinner within the family. This must have served to sharpen their lionizing capacities as individuals; but also it must have served to develop a sense of family responsibility which again emerges clearly in the evidence from several of these men.

What is described vividly for us in this book is the way in which young men had to begin as boys to help support and sustain their families. Because in many cases their fathers had to move away from the home environment to a new environment in search of better economic opportunity – internally within Jamaica, or externally, abroad. Look for instance at *Mass Levi, Landless*

Labourer who at age 12, with his father away in Colon, constructed the building in which his mother and his sibs lived and who looked after his mother until her death, retarding his personal development in the process. He says (page 10) "All round the place deh him (his mother) a bin wid mi . . . mek you see mi nuh ben get fi go noweh, for mi did wan go oder way you know but through she mi have fi tan same place bout ya".

Internal migration began for these 'manboys' at an early age. We find these cases of movements from the arid St Elizabeth area and the sugar-dominated Clarendon plain across the island to St Mary parish where the rainfall, climatic and land environment is more favourable and where economic opportunities had opened up in banana production through the efforts of the peasantry there. Examples of that movement are represented by *Migrant Farmer* (chapter 5) who moved when he was mature (age 28) to seek the better opportunities. This latter internal movement such as represented by *Migrant Farmer* was characteristic of many youth men moving from a rural environment to urban environments like Kingston, Spanish Town and other main towns, to acquire new skills – artisan skills for the most part; whereas *Migrant Farmer* and *Landless Farmer* remained within the agricultural sector.

As far as migration concerns international movements ('Nigrations', as Brathwaite describes it) we find many youth men going off to Cuba; and there are several examples in this book. That migration to Cuba was to secure plantation estate work in the sugar industry in that sister island, when it entered its phase of rapid capitalist expansion under US imperialism.

Reverend John B was sent from Colon by his parents to Jamaica to be brought up by his grandparents. In his twenties he went to Cuba in search of employment (all our men in Cuba worked in sugar either on the plantations or in the factory) and returned to self-employment as a shoemaker and then to work in the government service as a messenger and then as a prison warder. He later settled down as a minister of religion and farmer in one of the rural parishes.

Master Carpenter went to Cuba at age 20 and two of his brothers also went to Cuba, while still two other brothers went to Panama to seize economic opportunities. Borrowing money from relatives for the fare, they went off to 'make it'. And they 'made it'; saved their money, came back to Jamaica and bought their piece of land to establish proprietary manhood – a yard.

Migrant to Cuba/Carpenter also went to Cuba, several times. He was one of 10 children and had helped his mother to build the family house at a very early age. He spent 12 years in all in Cuba after moving first to Kingston when he was 17 years old, back to his home, and then off to Cuba at age 18.

Manboy Migrant to Cuba went to Cuba to seek out economic opportunities while his father had been a carpenter up in northern Clarendon. But he was sent to his grandparents for them to raise him when he was 6 years old. Went off to Cuba when he was 19 years old – spent 3 years first there in Cuba and then 7 years after – a total of 10 years in Cuba, which gave him the economic base to return and establish himself as 'Man-a-Yard' – not just as 'Man Boy', which is how he really started. He transformed himself from a 'man-to' through movement to Cuba; and now has established himself as 'Man-a-Yard'.

So it is clear that the forced movement of Jamaican black men to seek economic opportunities in the period after emancipation began at tender ages internally within Jamaica, and as youth men externally to Cuba and Panama. In this movement they picked up new skills. Leaving farming environments in rural Jamaica, they would pick up artisan skills in the urban areas of Jamaica, really industrial skills – building skills, construction, etc. – and involve themselves in the process in learning new technologies, which expanded their knowledge of production possibilities as well as provided them with the economic revenue to rebase themselves in a landed property relation, sometimes back where they were born, otherwise in some other location of rural Jamaica.

The next point deals with *Man* and *Man Family*. What comes out of the evidence of all the life histories of men in this book is a commitment to family. First, as a 'man-to' within his father's family or his parent's nuclear or extended family; and secondly, in establishing and taking care of their own families once they reached manhood and began to produce their own children. For what stands out in every case, bar none, is the way in which each of the men in this book were able to account for all of their children; where they are today, what they are doing, etc. Every man in this book could account for all of his children. That commitment to family is, to my mind, strong empirical negation of the traditional view of Jamaican (and West Indian) man in the family – traditional man of matriarchal family systems; of black men being irresponsible, lazy, shiftless, etc. This is negated by the evidence. There is no evidence of laziness; they go out and hustle, work where they could and work hard and save, come back, make their own little family and look about 'dem pickney dem'.

Migrant to Cuba/Farmer in particular, provides evidence of a dominant patriarchal family situation as distinct form what we have been brought to believe is traditionally a matriarchal family setting. If you look at this man's own domestic family unit, it is clear that he has established beyond doubt a strongly patriarchal family. He had 21 children in all, 15 of them born by his two wives; 3 had died in Cuba, and of remaining children, he gives an account for everyone – both the 'natural' children which is how he describes his illegitimate children, and those born within wedlock.

An interesting and important aspect of his breeding as a youth is revealed by the account of how he got a girl pregnant in the village before he moved to Cuba, but he didn't know and his mother raised that child after it was born. It was the mother of *Migrant to Cuba/Farmer* who identified the child as belonging to her son. And his mother raised her as a natural child – she being officially the godmother of this daughter. *Migrant to Cuba/Farmer's* discussion about 'natural' (*ie* illegitimate) children is itself suggestive that our people did not fully accept the establishment notion of bastardization – *ie* the non-recognition of 'bastard' children. This, by itself, is indicative of a strong sense of family responsibility.

Community, Race and Class

Let me turn to two other consideration: one is the character of community, the other is the question of race and class stratification within the local community. In order for us to understand the national society, we have to understand the base of it. The domestic unit of the family together with several other such domestic units, make up a village or district. For people still live within that rural space. For those who have moved to an urban space within Jamaica I characterize them as the 'displaced peasantry' because, by and large, we are only one step removed from the peasantry.

The displaced peasantry in our urban settings have an economic connection to their home base in the countryside through family, land ownership, through food provisions (brought or sent into the city from the family-home farm), and ultimately the security of knowing that one can return to home base. Now this domestic unit is the foci of our people's being. And it is interesting from the cases in this book to examine the community linkages – the linkages between domestic units in different types of communities. By type of community I mean a community, for example, of peasant farmers, as exists in south St Elizabeth or a community of agro-proletarians like the sugar estate workers of Westmoreland, and the banana workers of St Mary.

In looking at different types of communities, we find statements, from the witnesses themselves, that indicate that in the agro-proletarian environment of the sugar cane barracks, life and living was dehumanizing. These young males were forced to continue an association with the white plantation owners, not just as workers but also as sharecroppers, renting land from the planter class. And from what the men themselves say there is more stability in the mountain peasant community than there is in the agrarian capitalist community.

What this means then for us nationally as a people is that the forced displacement of the peasantry by multinational capitalism has expanded the growth of the displaced peasantry at a rapid rate and contributed to disintegration of those stable peasant communities.

These communities had social cohesiveness, founded on various types of cooperative activities. The importance of free labour exchanges for food production and house construction ('morning sport' and 'day-for-day') is emphasized by several respondents in this book. Equally important is the manner in which communities rallied around an individual family that suffered misfortune. There are several references to this concerning sickness and death in the communities. Even in the sphere of recreation (entertainment) we find, for example, that when a peasant farmer slaughtered an animal on festive occasions, there was a sharing of parts of the carcass with neighbours and friends.

Such patterns of cooperative activity came out of an African tradition and the necessities of successful struggle against the stranglehold of colonialism/imperialism over the lives of our people. But much of this has since been eroded by the 'modernization' that came with capitalist development.

The last point I wish to make here relates to the question of race and class stratification within our society. What emerges from the statements of these peoples' history is the reassertion of the dominance of the white people in the society. White people owned all the easily accessible land so that these black Afro-Jamaican peasants had to rent land from white planters.

The banana workers of St Mary, like our man in Chapter 2 from Hope Bay in Portland, worked with UFCo. The father of *Postman/Fisherman* was a banana checker working for UFCo, the multinational marketing enterprise. But his father was also a fisherman, and owned a piece of land. So that *Postman/Fisherman*, who was forced to be a breadwinner for the family at age 15 when his father died, actually developed as a proletarian (wage worker), picking coconuts at first, before becoming a postman later in life. On the other hand, we find a budding entrepreneur in *Tourist Guide* from Mavis Bank (Chapter 8). He became a real little businessman, at age 15, acting as a guide for tourists who wanted to hike up to Blue Mountain Peak.

Now, we find that because of the economic structure the white planter was really lord and master – 'Bakra Massa'. But we find as well that within the non-white sector, that is, among the Afro-Jamaican and the Indians (where East Indians are involved), there is a differentiation based partly on economic status – economic achievement, partly on colour, whereby the mulatto types of people in general command higher status within the local community. So, for example, even the case of a black teacher who had gone to Africa as a teacher and returned to his Jamaican village, that black teacher had less status within the local community than a middle peasant of high brown, mulatto characteristics (see *Master Carpenter*, chapter. 1, pp. 24-27).

Additionally, we find that social differentiation within the local community was based on the type of housing that people lived in. The better-off ones were able to afford more solid house structures and they had a higher status within the community. So that their economic position could be ascertained from the type of house they came from – the type 'a yard dem come out-a'.

Education in all or most of these cases was perceived by our witnesses as an instrument for social mobility, if not for themselves, then certainly for their children. *Sugar Factory Worker* in Westmoreland, for example, talking about the peasantry in St Elizabeth, said: "dem cultivate and . . . dem school dem children, because dem don't have de estate like down here" (chapter 13, p. 21).

There is an interesting case I want to cite here. In discussing music and recreation within the local community, where they made their own violins as I mentioned earlier, *Landless Farmer* (chapter 15) indicated that they had among them a *'professor* of music', who taught the men how to play. (Women didn't play musical instruments.) And while I'm on this point, it is important for us to notice that the main festival times of the local communities – the main festival times of black people in Jamaica were the traditional Christmas time and Emancipation Day, the 1st of August: 'Freedom Time' as *Landless Farmer* describes it on page 20 – 'Freedom Time'!!

Race and colour were clearly important in the people's perceptions, but what is interesting from some of the statements is that the black people had a fundamental conception of themselves as distinct from the white people. One respondent, *Migrant to Cuba/Farmer*, in answering a question as to whether black men sought to marry light-skinned women said no, that black man like black woman; or to put it in his words: "Blacks tended to look to their own colour and the fair people tended to look for their own colour . . . [it was] a two way prejudice" (p. 19). This I think is not just a response to white racism within our society, but rather it demonstrates an affirmation of blackness and the African culture of our people.

This has clear implications for the character of the national society and for our international connections. So it is not surprising that we find established authority in Jamaica today paying lip-service to the importance of Africa, because of the importance of Africa in the psyche of the Afro-Jamaican people. This is a fundamental unifying thread within the black diaspora – that community of black people largely concentrated in the plantation capitalist societies of the New World (more recently dispersed into urban industrial locations in the metropole) and our brothers and sisters across the Atlantic in the mother country of Africa.

Towards a People's History and Future

Our people must know who we are and what we are to forge our future in a positive way. From the evidence of our elder brothers in this book, it is clear that the basic character of our people – Afro-Jamaican people who make up 96% or more of Jamaica's population is really not appreciated and reflected in the written evidence we have of our historical achievements.

In this introduction I think I have established, from the evidence, the strength and the character of our people; their capacity to overcome apparently insurmountable odds and to overcome these odds with dignity. The Afro-Jamaican man, the Afro-Jamaican family and Afro-Jamaican people, are as solid as 'the Rock' from which we came.

Our history has been a history of entrapment and of struggle and change. Entrapment first by the slave plantation, then by plantation capitalism and more recently, by non-agrarian imperialist capital. An entrapment of the resources of our society for the economic advancement of the imperialist powers. But our response to this entrapment has been a remarkable struggle for change and adaptation in a manner that has created and generated a vibrant social space which has preserved the spirit to overcome of our people in spite of the contracted economic, social and physical space forced on us by imperialist penetration of our society and our economy.

In the process of this struggle against entrapment black Man has revealed his capacity not just to survive but to overcome and to establish himself as Man within that yard space created by his own efforts. The lesson of this struggle is clear. It is that within the psyche – within the character – of the Afro-Jamaican people resides a dynamic creative capacity which will find final release when total liberation is achieved. That is the nature of "the struggle ahead. And we must see it through" [Rodney 1968].

But in order to heighten and advance that struggle it is vitally necessary for us to get to know ourselves. The results of the recent Jamaican elections came as a shock to the entire radical intelligentsia. It is a shocking revelation that we do not know our own people. This work of Brodber lights a pathway for getting to know ourselves and our people. Let us use it wisely.

Notes
_____

* Introduction to "Portrait of the Jamaican male: A selection of oral accounts of life in Jamaica in the early twentieth century", collected and presented by Erna Brodber (1980b).

33

Cultural Sovereignty and Economic Development*

Toward Independent Economic Development for the Betterment of Caribbean Peoples

The analysis presented in this article is based largely on the experience of the English-speaking Caribbean countries. Nevertheless, much of the discussion applies as well to other parts of the region (with the exception of Cuba).

It is important for us to note at the very outset that the majority of Caribbean peoples are black people, and that poverty is heavily concentrated in this group. Minority groups in the Caribbean are, on the whole, prosperous relative to black people as well as to the average families in advanced industrial nations. They enjoy levels of living which are as high as those of any other group of people in the so-called 'developed' world.

The general picture in the Caribbean is one of extremely unequal patterns of distribution of wealth and income; corresponding rigid patterns of social stratification, based on race and class; and an unequal distribution of political power among groups and regions, with power concentrated in small elite groups (of urban residence). The result of these disparities is social tension, which creeps to the surface on occasion but which is always present beneath.

The basic causes for these disparities are analysed below. At this point, we wish to note only that black people suffer most as a result of these disparities. And that, consequently, measures designed to eliminate these disparities will bestow the greatest benefits on the black people of the region.

The Conceptual Framework

The terms dependence and independence, underdevelopment and development, have been used by different writers in many different contexts. As a result, there is considerable confusion regarding their meaning. I wish therefore to specify the context and meaning which I attach to them in this analysis.

Definition of Concepts

Let us first explore meaning and concept in the economic context. Independence describes a situation in which the people of a particular nation state (or country) have full control over their resources and total power to utilize these resources for the benefit of themselves. That if, to use their resources to produce whatever mix of goods and services they desire to consume; to distribute such consumption among all the people in some socially acceptable way; and to determine their own pattern of allocating this consumption over time. Dependence, on the other hand, can be defined as existing where a people do not have the control and power described above.

Economic development is a process whereby the material welfare of the people of a nation state (or country) is improved consistently and substantially over long periods of time. The time dimension is important so as to distinguish between development and short-period booms in the level of economic activity, booms which may be fortuitous, or which are associated with the business cycle of capitalist economy. Economic underdevelopment is a process that results in no significant change in the material welfare of a particular people over long periods of time.

Our definition of economic development implies that all the people of the country concerned must share in the increase in the material welfare. As such, it is not sufficient that output and per capita national income are rising. That merely indicates economic growth. Economic growth may occur simultaneously with increasing material impoverishment of significantly large groups of people in a country's population. Such an occurrence is best described as backward economic growth; and is one type of underdevelopment. Indeed, this is the characteristic pattern of underdevelopment in the contemporary (*ie*, postwar) Caribbean.

Our notion of economic development encompasses two economic occurrences: a sustained increase in output and average income; and an improvement in the distribution of income among groups that make up the country's population. Underdevelopment describes a situation where these two occurrences are absent in the pattern of economic change over time.

Moving from the economic to the non-economic contexts of meaning and concept, we observe that wherever a particular people have secured economic independence, they will have achieved political independence as well. However, no country in the modern world is completely cut off from the rest of the world. International interactions occur through trade (of goods and services); through technological, capital and labour transfers; and through cultural transfers.

The international cultural transfers occurred in earlier periods of history mainly through religious movements of one kind or another. But with more recent developments in mass communication, cultural transfers are proceeding at a rate which significantly adjusts the traditional value systems and preference hierarchies of most people in the world. To this extent, social and cultural dependency may be enforced on peoples who have secured economic and political independence.

The question of psychological independence and dependence is complicated. It is, nevertheless, bound up with other dimensions explored above. In any situation where a people have secured economic, political, and cultural independence, their psychological independence would be assured. This would be shattered, however, in the absence of any or all of these three.

Psychological independence is important because it conditions the will of a people to exercise their control over resources and their power to mobilize them for their own benefit.

Development and underdevelopment also have non-economic dimensions. The economic attributes of development, as I have defined them, ensure social betterment and political advancement.

The diffusion of economic benefits among all groups pushes the society in the direction of social equality. This minimizes the extent to which one group in the society can advance by way of exploiting other groups. Exploitation is the main source of social disequilibria throughout the world.

Political advancement is associated with economic development (as defined) in a different way. It would appear that if the economic system is to produce the kind of diffusion of economic benefits implied in my definition of economic development, then the structure of government and politics must be such as to give 'power to the people'. In other words, the diffusion of political power among the population will ensure that all the people will benefit from economic change. Diffusion of power among all the people is a highly advanced stage of political organization and development.

So far the discussion of concepts has proceeded at the aggregate level of a population group comprising a nation state or country. We need to round off this discussion by giving consideration to patterns of internal organization within countries; and to patterns of external relationships among countries. In so doing, we shall see more clearly the inter-relationships between independence and development on the one hand and dependence and underdevelopment on the other.

The internal social framework of any country determines the degree to which that country can achieve development in the sense here defined. A capitalist-type social framework inhibits development. So too does a feudalist-type social framework. In both these types, exploitation of the many by a few is the basis of economic, social and political organization. Accordingly, there is a maldistribution of wealth and income in the economic sphere, in status in the social context, and in power in the political realm. Such disparities generate processes of change which do not achieve the kind of results we have associated with development. Underdevelopment is endemic in countries where the social framework is of those types.

Pre-capitalist forms of economic organization also generate endemic underdevelopment. Pure subsistence production among 'primitive' groups of (isolated) peoples provides for economic equality but at very low levels of material consumption. And, over time, output is not likely to rise enough to bring about the kind of sustained increase in output and incomes which we associate with development.

On the other hand, countries with a socialist-type social framework can achieve development of the kind described above. If the resources of the society are owned by all the people, and if they have the will to do so, they can mobilize these resources in a way that output and income grow significantly over time with the benefits from such growth being dispersed, in an equitable manner, among all groups in the society.

Development and underdevelopment stem initially from the particular internal social framework. But external relations are important as well.

Independence and dependence both are associated with 'global' development and underdevelopment among countries in the international capitalist system. Among that group of countries we find relative material prosperity for the majority of people in the 'advanced' industrial countries; and relative material poverty for the majority of people in the underdeveloped countries.

Within the international socialist system, independence is positively associated with development, while dependency seems to be positively associated with underdevelopment.

Within the international capitalist system, the most glaring features of underdevelopment are to be found among the dependent countries and peoples. Dependency is an assurance of the occurrence of mass poverty. The securing of independence by such countries is the first step toward eradicating mass poverty, and thus toward development.

Tradition and Change

In order to understand the potential that exists for economic and social change in any situation, we must 'know where we are coming from'. The true potential of a people is demonstrated by their historical achievements. In addition, the nature and structure of the present social framework of any society is a result of historical forces that shaped it. The economic history of a country and the social history of its peoples, therefore, provide the basic tools of analysis for prescribing economic and social change.

Modern Caribbean economy and society are the result of European invasion of the New World. This invasion led, first, to the establishment of political colonies in the region; secondly, to the decimation of the indigenous Indian populations; thirdly, to the establishment of settler patterns of productive organization; fourthly, to the establishment of plantation modes of production utilizing the labour of slaves brought over from Africa; fifthly, into the incorporation of the regional economy into the mercantile community of Europe; and, sixthly, into its incorporation into the international system of monopoly capital that emerged during the present century.

This historical sequence following the European invasions of the fifteenth century has resulted in the entrenchment of Caribbean economy as an appendage or 'hinterland' of North Atlantic capitalism. The bulk of the region's resources came to be owned by North Atlantic capitalists. Correspondingly, the peoples in the region have been forced to exist on what meagre resources were not alienated by the foreign capitalist.

Because black people gained least access to the left-over resources, theirs has been a lot of persistent poverty. In spite of acute resource shortage, black people have, nonetheless, achieved significant economic advancement. That is part of our historical achievement which is described in Section III as 'the tradition of independent development'.

Caribbean economy today consists of two broad sectors: the 'overseas' sector and the 'residentiary' sector. The overseas sector is owned by foreign capitalists and its components are the major resource-based industries (eg bauxite, petroleum, tourism, and plantation agriculture). The income generated in the overseas sector accrues mainly to the foreign capitalists. It is in the overseas sector that inheres 'the legacy of dependent underdevelopment' which is analysed in the following section.

The historical achievements of black people are revealed in the vitality of the residentiary sector which comprises some resource-based industries, such as peasant agriculture on the poorer lands not alienated by foreign capitalists; secondary industries like small-scale manufactures (for example, processing, handicrafts, furniture manufacture, construction); professional and other services, etc. Economic diversification, the forging of inter-industry linkages, and the corresponding economic growth have come chiefly from the activity of black people in the residentiary sector.

The point I wish to establish at this juncture is that two distinct trends are evident in the historical experience of the Caribbean people and economy. One is the tradition of dependent underdevelopment associated with the economy's incorporation in the capitalist international order, through the overseas sector. The other is the tradition of independent development displayed by black people in the residentiary sector. I wish to turn next to a deeper exploration of these two historical trends or traditions.

The Legacy of Dependent Underdevelopment

The discussion in this section summarizes the social history of 'black dispossession' in the Caribbean.

The coming of the Europeans to the New World in the fifteenth century involved the political colonization of territory. Three patterns of colonization came to be established: colonies of conquest in Indo-America, colonies of settlement in Euro-America, and colonies of exploitation in Afro-America.

Indo-America corresponds roughly to Highland America where the indigenous Indians had already established high levels of civilization eg Aztec, Maya, and Inca empires); and where large population of Indians were engaged in settled patterns of economic activity. Today, that region – stretching from Mexico in the north to Paraguay in the south – remains an area populated mainly by Indians pure and mixed).

In the rest of the Americas, the Indians were not as highly organized and they chiefly engaged in nomadic patterns of economic activity. The superior military might of the Europeans led to decimation of the indigenous peoples and to capture of territory. Europeans then proceeded to migrate in large numbers to inhabit captured territory where they could settle. The temperate areas proved most suitable to them. So colonies of settlement were established in the US (excluding the South), Canada, Chile, Argentina, Uruguay, and Southern Brazil. Today European peoples are the bulk of the populations of these countries. And the remnants of the indigenous peoples are herded into reservations, usually on marginal territory.

Afro-America is the region of direct relevance to our analysis. There the Europeans tried to settle at first in order to engage in the production of exotic tropical foods for sale to Europe. This never materialized to any significant degree. Subsequently, they established a system of agricultural organization to produce staple commodities like sugar, tobacco and cotton. Relatively large scale units utilizing a controlled labour supply were best suited to the task.

The indigenous Indians were first harnessed to supply this labour but they died out in the process. And so the West African slave trade was mobilized to bring Africans to this area to provide the labour power. Thus the slave plantation emerged as the main unit of economic activity.

Today African peoples are the major population group in Afro-America which embraces the Caribbean islands, the US South, the Guianas, and Northeast Brazil.

Colonial Economy

Caribbean economy during the era of the slave plantation was simply an overseas branch of European economy. The Caribbean was a locus of production of agricultural staples for transshipment to Europe. The Caribbean was in reality part of the agricultural sector of European economy. The production carried on in the region did not generate any income for its inhabitants. The slaves were part of the capital stock, maintained by subsistence levels of consumption, depleted by runaways (the Maroons), and increased by new purchases and natural increase. The owners of the means or production were, for the most part, non-resident and managerial staff were temporary residents.

Under these circumstances the economy generated no national income from slave plantation production. Only the marginal subsistence activity of the Maroons and of free yeoman farmers provided any real income. Dependent underdevelopment was at its zenith during that period of Caribbean history.

Emancipation came in 1838 and changed things a bit. But only a bit. After that date, black people were legally free. In a sense, they were free to starve since no resources were provided for their independent survival. Since the plantations had engrossed all the arable land in some places (notably the Leeward Islands), black people were forced to continue working on the plantations for subsistence wages. Since the planters had monopoly power in the labour market, there was no need for them to pay wages higher than subsistence. The only alternative open to black people in those circumstances was emigration.

Elsewhere in the Caribbean where some land was available, the economic position of black people was slightly better. In places like Jamaica, the Windwards, Trinidad, and Guyana, they were able to find some, though not the best, land on which to settle independent of the plantations. Through individual and cooperative effort, black people brought or captured what marginal lands they could find. And eventually a viable peasantry emerged. But because of numerous legislative obstacles introduced by the planter-controlled governments, land was hard to secure. So continued dependence on plantation wage work was the lot of most black people.

Up to the present time, the plantations remain entrenched on the more level and fertile agricultural land throughout the region. And, for the most part, they remain foreign-owned. Consequently, these producing units continue to generate income for the foreign capitalists; leaving only enough for subsistence living for black people working on them. As capitalism developed and strengthened in Europe, the plantation agricultural sector became more securely locked into the international capitalist system. Metropolitan corporate capital took over control and ownership of the plantation resources. Thus, the tradition of dependent underdevelopment persists in this sector of Caribbean economy.

Neocolonial economy

This tradition was strengthened by parallel events in other sectors of the overseas component of the economy. During the present century, and particularly since World War II, the international capitalist system expanded by leaps and bounds. Metropolitan capital sought out, and secured, sources of investment throughout the Third World. With expanding world demand for products like petroleum and aluminum, North Atlantic capitalists secured control over all territory with raw material resources for such products. Similarly with the expansion of demand for tourist travel. Beaches and adjoining lands (for constructing hotels) were gobbled up by these foreign capitalists.

In the process, more and more Caribbean territory and resources came under the ownership and control of multinational corporations which emerged as the main form of metropolitan enterprise engaging in these 'overseas investments'. Income generated in these new productive activities accrues mainly to the foreign capitalists, leaving only wage income and taxes for the people of the region.

The economic features of these new industries are akin to those of the old slave plantation. Production is carried out by total economic institutions, in the form of vertically-integrated transnational corporations. Economic benefits to the Caribbean are incalculable since no real external trading is carried on. Raw materials are simply transferred from the Caribbean subsidiary of the companies to other subsidiaries which process these in the metropole. And the transportation is by company ships; so the Caribbean gets no revenue from carriage of the 'trade'. The natural resources are 'exported' in a raw state; so there are no secondary and tertiary rounds of income and employment creation for Caribbean peoples.

Caribbean economy as a whole is dominated by its 'overseas' component. The bulk of the region's natural and capital resources are located there. And so it is not surprising that black people secure only a marginal share of the income generated by those productive activities. Nor is it surprising that the overall social framework of these economies is characterized by features which are frankly colonial (*ie* dependent). Metropolitan governments carve up the region into areas of their own 'exclusive spheres of influence' – French West Indies, British West Indies, Dutch West Indies, American (US) West Indies, etc Imperial preference governs the trade between each West Indian territory and its metropolitan counterpart. And currencies are tied firmly to that of each metropole.

Dependence and Poverty

The tradition of dependent underdevelopment is firmly rooted in the dominance of Caribbean economy by its 'overseas' component. The stark result of this tradition is global poverty among black people of the region.

The situation in the agricultural sector is more acute. As foreign capital gobbles up more and more land, with the new non-agricultural activities like bauxite and tourism, less and less land becomes available to the rural population. At the same time population is growing; so rural poverty becomes more acute. In the circumstances, black people migrate from the countryside – tens of thousands to England, US, and other places. But industrial development in the cities and towns can not provide enough new jobs. So urban unemployment rises and slums developed. Increasing urban poverty is the result; escalating crime and violence are some of the manifestations.

Those who migrated abroad have done well. They learnt industrial skills quickly and earned enough income to send some home to help out relatives and friends suffering on the Caribbean scene. (Generally speaking, our emigrants abroad send back more money each year than foreign capital brings to the region.) But we must remember that our countrymen abroad catch hell from the racism practised against black people in Europe and North America.

The majority of black people living in the Caribbean today are poor. In Jamaica, for example, 20% of the labour force have no jobs, and have to depend on others, or scuffle, to survive. Another 20% get work now and then. Another 30% have regular jobs but they earn incomes which are too low to provide adequately for the basic needs of food, housing, etc. These are mainly self-employed people – small farmers, higglers, dressmakers, etc. And so only about 20% of black people earn enough to live like decent human beings. The latter work mainly with governments and foreign corporations. A few are independent professionals and some local capitalists.

The majority of black people in the Caribbean are plagued by unemployment and low incomes. They suffer form malnutrition to the point that many children die as a result. They live in housing conditions unfit for human beings. They get little or no education; and so illiteracy is widespread. And they have such limited access to basic health facilities that their lot is a life of disease, physical suffering and early death.

The fundamental cause of this widespread poverty is that black people have very limited access to the resources of the region – especially land, capital, and technology. Our economy is organized in such a way as to keep these basic resources out of the reach of black people. Yet much of these resources remain either unused or underutilized. Something is patently wrong with any economy in which such gross underconsumption exists alongside gross underutilization of resources.

Underutilization of the region's resources is a direct result of foreign ownership and of the system of capitalist exploitation. Foreign companies secure large holdings of land for mineral exploration in order to control more of the raw material resources than competing companies. And since land alienation is the legal norm, they have much more land than they need for mineral extraction at any point in time. Furthermore, the general shortage of land in these island economies makes land ownership a safe investment. When the demand for land is expanding rapidly, with population increase, housing requirements and tourist pleasure, the price of the fixed supply of land rises spectacularly over time. In the circumstances, land ownership is viewed as a portfolio asset for capital gains and not as a producing asset. Underutilization is the natural result.

Capital 'shortage' exists in economies which generate high levels of savings. Business savings are concentrated in the corporate overseas sector; and what is not reinvested in ongoing production of the subsidiaries is invested abroad in other subsidiaries of the multinational complex. Savings in the residentiary sector (from business and personal income) goes into the commercial banking system and into non-bank financial sector, itself a part of the overseas component of the economy. And the branch-plant banking subsidiaries can shunt these savings broad, through their transnational banking network, to find the most profitable sources of investment in the international capitalist system. Finally, since the educational system is not tailored to the region's needs and resources, research and its output of knowledge to develop technology are not geared to the needs of black people.

The clear inference that emerges from this analysis is that mass poverty among black people of the Caribbean can be eradicated only if the region's resources are harnessed for this purpose. That is a matter reserved for further elaboration in the final section of this paper.

The Tradition of Independent Development

Independent Economic Achievements

The roots of independent economic development sprouted even during the period of slavery. Three sets of independent economic activity were initiated by black people under the harsh and inhumane conditions that existed.

Slaves who managed to escape alive from the brutalities of the plantation set up isolated maroon colonies in the mountainous interior. These colonies were largely engaged in subsistence production, independent of the overseas sector. There was specialization and division of labour within each colony, but trade outside the colony was restricted by the 'illegal' nature of Maroon existence. Within these colonies, then, skills in independent farming, artisan manufactures, and techniques of defense were developed.

The second type of independent activity was carried out on the unused lands of the slave plantations. Provision grounds were established by slaves to produce foodstuffs whenever the plantation had no need for slave labour. This type of productive activity supplied food for self-consumption and surpluses for sale. Accordingly, rudimentary markets developed to facilitate exchange (mostly on Sundays). As a result of such independent activity, some slaves were able to accumulate sufficient savings out of surplus production to purchase their freedom.

Having secured freedom on their account, they established an independent economic existence in peasant agriculture, artisan crafts, and petty services. So the third pattern of independent activity emerged through the efforts of the so-called 'free coloureds'.

Even during slavery, then, black people contributed significantly to the development of Caribbean economy. Indeed, theirs was the only contribution since the plantation sector generated no income for the inhabitants. These efforts of black people introduced some diversification in the productive base of the economy, generated a certain degree of linkages (in distribution, for example), and implanted a rudimentary infrastructure (of markets, money, etc.) to facilitate specialization and trade.

After Emancipation, these earlier beginnings mushroomed. The ex-slaves managed to secure land, through individual and cooperative effort, to engage in independent peasant cultivation. They practised communal systems of labour mobilization on the land (free labour exchanges) and a strong peasantry eventually emerged wherever sufficient land was available.

The peasants introduced new export crops, like bananas, and produced all kinds of foodstuffs for sale in internal markets. A fantastic network of rudimentary roads (footpaths) developed throughout the mountainous interiors; and the network of internal markets which remain to this day are some of the consequences of this independent economic activity. Though the land resources at their disposal were meagre, the peasants managed to generate enough surpluses for savings and investment. This attests to their tremendous skill in hillside farming techniques and to the significant capital accumulation achieved through the investment of labour.

Other ex-slaves who did not settle on the land developed rudimentary manufactures in the villages and towns. Carpenters built houses, cabinet makers designed and manufactured furniture, shoemakers made shoes, tailors and dressmakers made clothes, blacksmiths made tools and so on. A fantastic range of artisan skills was developed over time. And the division of labour, trade, and inter-industry transactions developed in the residentiary sector. It is within that sector that economic growth and development occurred in the hundred years between 1838 and 1938. Without such efforts, the economy would have remained totally dependent on the overseas sector, with consequent total material impoverishment.

As the independent residentiary sector expanded over time, primary and secondary production in that sector stimulated multiplier income and employment generation. Inter-industry linkages developed and strengthened; and so distribution, transportation and construction increased in importance. In the process, indigenous technological change was evident; capital accumulation and investment for national income generation gained momentum; and the economy exhibited considerable diversification.

During the Second World War when shipping difficulties plagued the overseas sector, the residentiary sector responded by initiating production of many commodities previously imported. Small-scale manufacture of matches, soap, edible oils, etc., mushroomed during this period. And the economy became more self-sufficient in food production than in any previous period since the fifteenth century European invasion.

But after the war this initiative was stifled by official policy geared to attracting foreign capital from metropolitan white people. As this capital came in, the overseas sector gobbled up more resources for establishment of resource-based industries; and foreign enterprise came to dominate the manufacturing sector. So the residentiary sector was placed in an increasingly disadvantageous position. Less and less opportunities for indigenous entrepreneural activity arose as access to resources by black people became more and more restricted. One result of all this was the heavy emigration of Caribbean peoples to the industrial nations of North America and Europe.

The economic achievements of black people in these new locations is further testimony of their capacity for independent productive potential, if they have access to resources and opportunity. For most of these people migrated from rural and semi-rural areas without industrial skills. In the new locations, they soon acquired these skills and adjusted themselves to the unaccustomed patterns of industrial work and of urban life. (Men driving trains after life-long experience of only donkey traffic. Women working in factories, not having been close to one before, and so on.) A truly remarkable achievement!

Within months after arrival in industrial metropolitan countries, black people from the Caribbean are able to send substantial remittance home, for the consumption of relatives still living on the margin of survival and for investment in whatever regional resources are still accessible to inhabitants of the Caribbean (usually housing and other real estate). The significance of this independent economic initiative is not to be overlooked. Remittances home to some of the smaller islands is believed to be in excess of the total income generated by productive activity and which accrues to nationals in the islands themselves.

The Social Economy of Resistance and Change

As part of the package of generating independent development, black people in the Caribbean developed a social culture independent of the dominant European culture imposed by the colonizing powers. During slavery and right up to the present, black people developed their own languages, practised their own religion and medicine, articulated their own culture in music, dance, the fine arts, and so on. Much of this culture reveals survivals from our African ancestry. But not in its purest form. Artistic creativity is evident everywhere.

The establishment of an independent culture is important for two reasons. First, it provides a psychological anchor for resistance to the oppression generated by the dependent colonial condition. And, secondly, a culture of independence is the motive force behind the drive for an independent economic and social existence. Thus cultural achievement enters the matrix of the social economy of resistance and change in any dependent (colonial) social situation.

An Independent Culture Creates a Culture of Independence!

An independent culture has further dimensions which are crucial to the promotion of independent economic development within a globally dependent social framework. An independent culture provides the social infrastructure for independent economic activity producing goods and services to satisfy cultural demands. The concrete economic manifestations of this are:

1   The production of certain foodstuffs to satisfy the tastes of people who have internalized the independent culture;

2   the production of music and the development of an entertainment
     industry to satisfy the cultural demand;

3   the manufacture of cultural artifacts to satisfy a market demand; and so
     on. In short, an independent culture creates an independent market
     demand; thereby stimulating independent productive activity to supply
     that demand. In the process, independent income and employment
     generation result.

There is yet another dimension where independent culture acts as a source
of resistance in a dependent social situation. This is in the matter of minimizing the impact of cultural imperialism in an era of mass communication
controlled by the metropolitan capitalist system. Highly developed systems of
advertising, transnational transfers of movies and films, 'free' trade in knowledge and technology, and other such cultural transfers from the North Atlantic to the Third World are potentially capable of shifting the value systems and
preference hierarchies of colonial peoples onto the same plane as metropolitan capitalist society. The desired consumption mix would then become
similar and would widen the market for metropolitan capitalist production.

Much of this is going on at present, especially among the high-income elite
groups in the Caribbean. However, the existence of an independent culture
among the masses of black people represents a buffer from such penetration.
Even though there is evidence that the buffer is being gradually penetrated, its
existence is a source for corrective mass re-orientation to traditional values
and preferences once the media of communications are marshalled for the
purpose.

There are perhaps other social aspects of independent development which
are important for change. For example, there are the communal social efforts
in mobilizing labour in peasant agriculture; there are cooperative rudimentary banking systems (formal and informal) used to mobilize finance capital.
As well, the patterns of social structure and stratification have characteristics
independent of the global social framework. Achievement, for example, ranks
higher in determining social status within communities of black people than
with national societies. What we find in rural communities, especially, the
successful farmer has a high social status. So do the school teacher and other
black people who have gained a certain mobility in the larger system.
Whereas in the wider social system race, colour and class are the prime deter-
minants of social status, within the independent black communities achievement assumes some importance.

This brings me finally to the question of education and its dysfunctionality
for social change in the Caribbean. Partly because of limited access to investment opportunities in productive resources, the savings and investment

profile of black people was concentrated in the area of providing education for their children. However, the education they received served to erode their independent cultural underpinnings and to absorb them into the culture of the colonizers. The result of this process has been the gradual erosion of the cultural base of black people. And, with this, the further penetration of metropolitan monopoly capitalism was facilitated.

If Caribbean economy is to embark on a new path toward independent development, the educational system will need revolutionary change in order to bring it in line with the independent culture of black people.

Independence and Development

This summary outline history of 'black affirmation' in the Caribbean clearly demonstrates the creative potential of black people throughout the region. The development of an independent cultural base provided the underpinnings for independent economic activity. The latter is, indeed, a rare miracle. For black people were able to produce goods and services with virtually no resources except their own labour. Within four generations or so since Emancipation, they have been able to generate sufficient surpluses above subsistence requirements to save and invest. And so to generate income and employment for themselves, in spite of the great odds of resource shortage resulting from the legacy of dependent underdevelopment for the economy as a whole.

The lessons to be drawn from this in order to devise policy for meaningful change and to eradicate mass poverty are crystal clear. But to accommodate the reader, these lessons are adumbrated in the next, and final, section.

Concrete Proposals for Independent Development of Caribbean People

The analysis presented in the foregoing sections indicates the direction in which meaningful change must proceed if the welfare of Caribbean people is to be maximized. Briefly, our present condition is the result of two broad historical trends: a subdued trend of independent development enveloped within a major trend of dependent underdevelopment. The major trend has produced mass poverty. And the subdued trend accounts for our survival against the odds created by the major trend.

The obvious need is to steer the economy along a path of independent development. The reason for this is obvious. It is the only way to improve the welfare of all our people. In other words, that is the only optimum path for social change.

The policy and action prescriptions must, of course, be placed in the general perspective of social goals and objectives. In this connection, it will be useful to make a distinction between the short-term (three to five years) and the long term (over five years). The long-term objective must be the creation of a 'good life' for all the people of the region. The short-term objective is the eradication of extremes of mass poverty. I shall now consider these two dimensions in concrete terms.

Obviously, the short-term proposals can be more concrete since there is no ambiguity about meaning. The long-term objective is somewhat vague and will therefore create greater division of opinion about its meaning and the methods of achieving the 'good life'. Accordingly, I deal with the short term first, leaving the more intractable for the last.

Immediate Eradication of Extreme Mass Poverty

No civilized society would tolerate mass poverty of the kind evident in the Caribbean. Infants dying of malnutrition, families living in substandard housing, high rates of illiteracy, poor health facilities, and substandard educational opportunities are all a social crime – wherever they exist!

The immediate objectives therefore must be to eradicate these social evils. In order to do this, Caribbean resources must be repatriated to the region's peoples. But this repatriation must be to all the people; not to the small elite ruling groups in the population. This is the first step. But this is not sufficient. The full creative energies to the people will have to be mobilized behind the task. Our past achievements clearly demonstrate our capacity to rise to the challenge. But 'pragmatic' people will be looking for 'practical' proposals.

Accordingly, I put forward some of my ideas. First, there is an obvious need for massive government intervention. This for several reasons. Only governments have the power to reclaim our resources. They, in fact, gave them away initially. This reclamation should involve no compensation. The foreign capitalists have been more than compensated already. Besides, where is the compensation for black people for what we suffered under legal slavery? Secondly, governments have the power to mobilise the population behind any effort in the interests of the electorate. Thirdly, governments can influence and direct mass media communication in order to promote the desired popular mobilisation. And fourthly, governments have the financial resources, or can acquire what is necessary, to mobilise the effort.

At an even more concrete level, I now put forward certain proposals which I made over the radio in Jamaica after the elections of 29 February 1972. What follows is an extract from the talk:

The obvious solution to the poverty problem of Jamaica is to put our idle hands and idle lands to work together to provide the basic necessities of life for all Jamaicans. We need to mount a national campaign against poverty. Everyone must contribute to the battle against poverty. For that is our greatest enemy – the greatest threat to the well being of our people and society.

How can this be achieved? First, we establish our targets in terms of output. The priorities here are straightforward. We must set out to produce enough of the right kinds of food so that every man, woman and child will be nourished. We must set out to produce enough decent housing for everybody. We must set out to wipe out illiteracy. We must set out to provide health facilities for the whole population. We have all the resources necessary to achieve these goals. Let us see how they can be mobilized.

All land held by foreigners should revert to state ownership for lease to different kind of users. The same for all land in farms of over 500 acres. This would release unused bauxite land and underused plantation lands to produce the output of food needed to wipe out malnutrition. Dairy products, meat, vegetables, fruit, etc produced on such a scale would provide the food and many other things like processing factories where many people would find work.

Housing is easy. The major cost items are building materials and labour. Cement can easily be sold to the public at one-fourth the present price and still be profitable to owners of the company. If they refuse to cut the price of cement, then government should acquire the company.

Aluminum roofing material should be supplied by the bauxite companies as compensation to black people for decades of exploitation. Labour to construct houses can be organized at the community level on a day-for-day or a 'morning sport' basis. On to education, everyone who can read and write must be organized to teach those who can't. We can thus wipe out illiteracy in short order. Cuba set the example for us in this respect.

As far as health is concerned, the training of paramedical personnel is essential and relatively easy since we have many people already versed in this work. The country midwife, the balmist, the bush dentist can all be mobilized by 'scientific' personnel in these fields. And of course, sports is necessary to build healthy bodies. Therefore the need for a national sports programme.

It is clear that if we are to achieve these targets, Jamaica will require at least; a government ready and willing to try bold new policies and a people who are committed and willing to eradicate poverty from our midst. My judgement is that most of our people are committed and ready.

Instrumentally, I see the need for the establishment of a compulsory national service in which everybody who is physically able will contribute to our battle against poverty. Other countries have services to fight other people. Our enemy is poverty.

We have a powerful force in the youth of Jamaica. They constitute the bulk of our population and I think that they are willing and ready to join the battle. We have as well a reservoir of skilled people in all institutions in our society, like our Army

(JDF). They can be utilized in the battle building roads to get food out of farming areas, building other social capital, helping youth organize in whatever youth campaigns are launched over the countryside, assisting in the national sports programme, etc

The only serious opposition to a programme such as outlined will come from the high income elite groups in our society and from foreign interests who own Jamaican resources. Frankly, I think that these two groups have been allowed to exploit black people too long. They should be made to realize that to eradicate poverty in this country is as much in their own interest in the long run as continued exploitation is to them in the shorter run.

Capital for this development programme can be mobilized within the country. Some of this will be created by the investment of labour on a national scale. Balancing finance capital can be raised from the following groups: foreign capitalists operating here, the national propertied class, and the middle class. The national privileged classes need not suffer a great deal. All that may be needed is for them to meet the needs of our circumstances; instead of aping the ridiculous consumption patterns of North Americans, as we do at present.

If all Jamaicans could be mobilized to produce enough of the basic necessities for all our people to get an adequate share, then everyone would be in a position truly to enjoy the natural beauty of this land of ours. And we would be well placed to create a paradise right here on earth – a civilized society where no man is allowed to suffer as a result of exploitation by other men; and where man and Nature can blend together in near perfect harmony.

From the analysis presented in this paper, it seems to me that the above proposals are not only concrete, but eminently feasible over a very short period of time – given the kinds of historical achievements of black people as described in the last section.

On the Question of Economic Organization

Earlier in this section, I indicated that massive government intervention is needed to shift the economy onto a path of independent development for the benefit of Caribbean peoples. This point requires some, if only brief, discussion. The reasons why this is necessary are two-fold. One is that Caribbean governments and bureaucracy are incapable of the kind of mobiliaztion proposed, mainly for reasons advanced earlier in relation to the dysfunctionality of education. The other reason is that state intervention suggests an immediate transformation to socialism of one kind or another.

In my opinion, what is required to achieve these short term objectives does not necessarily imply an immediate shift to socialism. In the nature of the situation this is unlikely to emerge as a result of electoral politics based on political tribalism, such as exists throughout the region.

A mixture of different forms of productive organization seems appropriate to achieve these short-term targets, once there arrives "a government ready and willing to try bold new policies" (as suggested earlier). In this connection, I am impressed by some policy proposals outlined by one of my colleagues. These are as follows:

1   In agriculture there should be a national plan to meet all the nutritional deficiencies of the population, and that to service this national plan, the plantations and the estates should be broken up into small and medium-sized farms, run either by individual proprietorship or cooperatives or perhaps, in the case in some of the larger farms, by the state.

2   That secondly, in the area of manufacturing, the government should support what I can only call a kind of – a people's own account and cooperative sector in most areas of manufacturing industry, and those areas especially which are geared to satisfying the most basic and elementary needs of the population, building on what we already have.

3   And that thirdly, we should have a state sector – a government sector for the large scale heavy industries, which would run such industries as bauxite, electric power, telephones, and so on.

What is being suggested here is that conventional semi-capitalist forms of economic organisation are sufficient to provide the productive base needed to eradicate mass poverty in the short term.

The short-term objectives, then, can be achieved without a total restructuring of the organizational base of the contemporary economy. The resources are available but certain structural adjustments will be necessary to tailor them to the basic consumption needs of the society.

Over the Longer Term

Ultimately, social change must be directed to creating a 'good life' for all the people. Once the basic necessities of life of all the people are met, there is room for debate as to what constitutes the 'good life' and how that is to be achieved.

My conception of the good life for Caribbean peoples is one where exploitation of man by man is removed from the entire social scene; and where man can enjoy life. Totally.

The first point demands a social framework which is non-capitalist. For capitalism is based on exploitation. Some kind of socialist framework, therefore, is a *sine qua non* for achieving the long-term objective. The particular pattern of socialist organization must fit into the traditional value system of black people. That implies communal efforts – in areas such as land ownership, labour mobilization and capital accumulation. For that is indeed consistent with the tradition of independent development inherited from our forefathers.

On the second point, we need to set targets of consumption which are consistent with the traditional preference hierarchy of Caribbean peoples. Additionally, we need to recognize the almost unbelievable physical beauty which Nature has bestowed on the region. And so we need to plan our development in such a way as to preserve that beauty and to assure everyone the opportunity to enjoy it, in our hours of leisure, and of work.

Given these achievements, people can then truly live as brothers and sisters – *ie* in the true traditional manner of black people!

Notes

* "Cultural sovereignty and economic development". Paper presented to the First Caribbean Conference of Intellectual Workers, Grenada, 1982.

34

Sovereignty and Self-reliance: the Economic Implications*

I have been asked to speak about the economic implications of sovereignty and self-reliance, and what I have prepared to say today received an extra stimulus from the presentation of my friend and colleague, George Lamming. Because what I will say in the last section of my presentation goes pretty much to the heart of what Lamming said concerning the Caribbean nation, and the Caribbean nation state.

But before I get to the end, let me outline what I have to say. I want to make a presentation which gives first a description of the past years of underdevelopment in the transition from colonialism to the current situation of neocolonialism. Secondly, I want to turn my attention to the developmental impacts that sovereignty and self-reliance can generate. Thirdly, I shall examine some models of transition which have been attempted in the Caribbean. And, finally in the fourth section, I will deal with the question of concept of the nation state in the Caribbean context.

From Colonialism to Neocolonialism

The Caribbean is essentially, as C.L.R. James often points out, a creation of modern western civilization. But it is a particular creation which requires us to analyse and understand it, because it has particularities which are not replicated in other colonial areas of the world. The Caribbean is a society which was completely built by western capitalism. The Europeans invaded the New World in the late fifteenth century. I prefer to say invasion to counter what we were taught about Columbus 'discovering the New World'. How you could discover somewhere where people were living already? So let us say that when the Indians discovered Columbus on their beaches in the late fifteenth century, they had very simple civilization existing here. This was in contrast to the civilizations of highland America where the indigenous populations, the Aztecs, the Mayas, and the Incas had developed civilizations in advance of Europe in many respects. Indigeneous peoples of the Caribbean, the peaceful Awaraks and the war-like Caribs had less developed civilizations and more sparsely settled. Therefore, they were easier to conquer, and eventually to eliminate than was the case of highland America. Having eliminated the indigenous populations, (today there are no Arawaks, and only a few Caribs survive in small pockets in mountainous places in the Windward Islands), the Europeans repopulated the area with people from Africa to provide the labour for work on the slave plantations.

Thus, a particular system of production came to be instituted in the region, which for the first time in the history of modern man, instituted both race and class in the mode of production and the mode of exchange. It is important for us to recognize that the difference between Caribbean-type capitalism and dependent capitalism in the rest of the Third World is this factor: the institution of the race and class within the mode of production and the mode of exchange. That particular colonial legacy has left us with a particular kind of economy and society which, for the most part is a 'ratooning' (to use Lloyd Best's phrase) of the old plantation capitalist system. For the parameters of the slave mode of pure plantation economy remains very much intact today. Best identified five 'rules of the game' which formed the institutional framework of the pure (slave) plantation economy. Let us look at these to see how much they are relevant today.

The first rule of the game he describes as exclusivity of spheres of influence by different metropolitan powers within the Caribbean. Thus we have the *Spanish* Caribbean, the *British* Caribbean, the *French* Caribbean, the *Dutch* Caribbean, and today there is the *American* Caribbean. Exclusive spheres of influence by metropolitan powers in particular parts of the Caribbean. That was the first rule of the game.

The second rule of the game he describes, as the 'Muscovada Bias'. Muscovada is the name of the raw sugar exported in slavery days. The Muscovada Bias assured that the division of labour between the metropole and the colony was such that the colony was restricted to raw material production. The refining and distribution of it and the processing to other products like the addition to cocoa to make chocolate and confectionery, and so on, was done in the 'mother country' – the so-called mother country. The Muscovada Bias still prevails today in the Caribbean. In the Caribbean today, we remain, according to the existing international division of labour, producers of raw materials, whether raw sugar, or bauxite, alumina etc.

The third rule of the game in Best's pure plantation model is the Navigation Provision, which by way of navigation acts determined that goods leaving the British Caribbean were carried by British ships to overseas markets, mainly of Britain itself. That goods leaving the French Caribbean were carried by French ships: Spanish goods leaving the Spanish Caribbean were carried by Spanish ships. So each metropole gains the lion's share of shipping – of insurance and freight from the carriage of the raw materials being produced here in the region. That still remains much intact today. Bauxite leaves Jamaica in vessels owned by each particular transnational corporation and is taken to the same corporations' refineries abroad. The same thing with petroleum in Trinidad. The same thing with air travel and the tourist industry: American planes bring in the American tourists along with American food stuffs, etc., and the Caribbean gets only a small share of this activity.

The fourth rule of the game was the Metropolitan Exchange Standard by which the denomination of the currency in the colony was in fact the currency of the metropolitan country, and could be exchanged freely at par values. That was changed somewhat, but it still remains that each Caribbean territory has its currency tied either to the US dollar or to the British pound or the French franc or the Dutch guilder. So that the metropolitan exchange standard has been maintained in the neocolonial situation, albeit in a modified form.

The fifth, and last rule of the game of the pure plantation economy is Imperial Preference, whereby each colony depended on its 'mother' metropole for preferential markets for its output. That remains pretty much the same today. Everywhere Caribbean leaders beg for, and depend on, preferential markets. Some Caribbean leaders gather together in Brussels to negotiate new 'Lome treaties' for preference in the European market. They do the same thing, individually or at times collectively (at US bidding) to get a piece of the US market under the Caribbean Basin Initiative (Reagan's CBI).

So we see that the institutional framework, the economic institutional framework, underlining the colonial society in slavery days remains a feature of the neocolonial economy and society. You see I want to demonstrate to you that the manifestation of the neocolonial dependent capitalist economies characteristic of our region today have extended and reinforced the dimensions of race and class that the slave population instituted in the region. This has been a feature of the dependent capitalism in the postwar period in the Caribbean. With the single exception of socialist Cuba, the entire Caribbean region operates as a peripheral appendage of the international capitalist system. Within that peripheral appendage there are class divisions, and colour/race divisions which divide and segment the societies in a certain way. This poses certain problems and limits the possibilities for transformation. It is some of these limitations/constraints that I want to examine in the rest of this section.

The contemporary feature of dependent capitalism in the Caribbean, (*ie* all of the Caribbean, excluding socialist Cuba) is one in which imperialist domination of the region is exercised by the presence of certain institutions which we need to examine and understand. The first of these is the TNC. The TNC, whether it operates in the tourist or manufacturing sector, through subsidiaries in the Caribbean which organize our regional resources for the production of outputs which are destined for consumption in the metropolitan centres of the world. We understand enough about the transnational corporations. It will be superfluous for me to go into a discussion about them.

What I want to concentrate on instead are certain changes that have taken place within our economies and societies to accommodate Caribbean economies within the framework of contemporary international capitalism. Here the question of race and class assumes primary importance. For it was the old white planter class descended from slavery days which first had opportunities for becoming joint partners with transnational capital in the establishment of branch plants, screwdriver industries in the manufacturing section. The old planter-merchant nexus consisting of planters and the core of importers and exporters are predominantly white or near white. White in a European sense: near-white in a West Indian social sense whereby the Jews, the Syrians, the Lebanese and other Arabs in our midst are a part of that dominant white class. It was they who got the economic opportunities which transnational capital brought to the region in the postwar period. And it was they, and an emerging intermediate class of brown people, who provided the administrative infrastructure for the penetration of transnational capital during this period.

The brown middle class provided the army of clerks necessary for the expansion of the state sector with the achievement of constitutional independence and the assumption by the state of more direct participation in economic activities. Opportunities opened up for the brown middle classes to assume leadership positions. And on the bottom of the social ladder stood the masses of black workers and peasants who have been left out of what 'development' has taken place.

I want to suggest to you that no development has taken place. What has taken place is a substantial measure of economic growth: *growth* as distinct from *development*. I want to argue that development involves the mobilization of a people for control and development of the resources within the environment for their own material, social, and psychological (spiritual) advancement. That has not been achieved. In these terms, there has been no development in the capitalist Caribbean. Some successes have been achieved in terms of economic growth as measured by expansion of national income, GDP, etc; these indices that economists use to mystify people that something good is happening in the economy, whereas very little is happening to benefit the masses of black (including East Indian) workers and peasants.

A characteristic feature of this pattern of dependent capitalist development has been that the penetration of transnational capital has served to drain surpluses generated by production activities within the region, in the form of profits, dividends, royalty payments and so on. The transnational corporations, in addition to draining surpluses from our productive activities, have also prevented the development of intersectoral linkages within the Caribbean both at the level of each Caribbean island/territory, and within the region as a whole. The development of backward and forward linkages for many economic activities are at the core of a sustaining economic development process. When I refer to economic development, I concentrate on the economic parameters, as distinct from social development, which I want to come later. The absence of linkages therefore has not stimulated development spread effects within each economy, nor within the region as a unit. The consequence of this lack of development spread effects, and the consequences of the draining of economic surplus from the island/territories and the region as a whole, have meant that for the masses of black workers and peasants, economic opportunities for their advancement have been limited. Consequently, there has been a massive out-migration of Caribbean peoples seeking the economic opportunities elsewhere, normally in the associated metropoles.

The Caribbean, again, is perhaps, unique in the whole of the Third World: it is a region which is characterized by the fact that more Caribbean people live outside the Caribbean than live inside. My late friend Prime Minister Maurice Bishop used to tell the Grenadian people "remember that it is not just 110,000 of us here in Grenada. There are more Grenadians living outside of Grenada than live in Grenada" and he went on to point out that there were more than 110,000 in Trinidad alone. Half the population of Puerto Rico live outside of Puerto Rico, and for most of the smaller territories in the region, the populations that live outside of their island homes exceed the number that live inside. We are a net exporter of human beings – a net exporter of human capital.

Arguably, those who migrate are among those in the society with the most initiative and with the greatest potential for making a contribution to our region's development and the development of the individual island/territories within it. I am not talking about the brain drain in the conventional sense of people. I am talking about the brain drain in terms of ordinary rural folk who have left the Caribbean, migrated to the industrial centres of the world, people in this country like the rural peasantry who were forced off their land by the intrusion of bauxite capitalism in the 1950s and 1960s who sold out their land and migrated in large numbers to the United Kingdom before the door was closed off by the racist UK government in 1961. 'Ordinary' rural people who have never seen a train in their lives, and within weeks are running trains in London, controlling the whole transport system, running industrial machines in factories, having never seen a factory before in their lives – an amazing capacity, absolutely amazing. The region has been drained of this potential by the lack of economic opportunities which dependent capitalism imposed upon the region throughout the postwar period.

Who are the culprits in this economic imperialism of the region? They are easily identified: the TNC which we considered already. Associated with them are the transnational banks. The transnational banks have assumed importance in more recent decades as the TNCs themselves have retreated from equity ownership in a disengagement strategy in the Caribbean and the rest of the Third World. The TNCs have managed to secure more by withdrawing from equity participation and engaging in management contracts, licensing fees, royalties, technology contracts, patents, etc. Let me cite a brief reference from an article from my friend and colleague Trevor Farrell. He points out that the belief that colonialism would be eradicated simply by achieving political independence has turned out to be a mistake. With hindsight, it is clear that Nkrumah's dictum 'seek ye first the political kingdom and all things shall be added onto you' is not true. Similarly, it is now recognized that the measures believed to be the corrective of the original error, that is effective state or a local ownership of key economic sectors is also ineffective and may indeed be irrelevant. Ownership it turns out does not necessarily mean control. The multinational corporations have learnt to make nationalization work for them through the media of marketing arrangements, managing contracts, service agreements and licensing agreements. Effective control over industries or entire economic sectors can be maintained while equity ownership is happily conceded. A shrewd company now finds that there are positive advantages to be reaped for a retreat from a relationship too easily stigmatized as neocolonial. The surrender of equity ownership can lead to an improved cash flow and enhanced profitability or to get an ignorant Third World government to prune local operations of unwanted or obsolete properties at high price to the state. It also has the attraction that it reduces a company's visibility and defuses local criticism while central interests are maintained in tact. Moreover, because a nationalization may now be effected on attractive terms, the risk of a worse deal from a tougher, more confident host government sometimes in the future may be obviated.

There is a tendency in the region for us to regard nationalization of TNCs as the final solution to the region's problem. In Guyana, for example, the Burnham regime owns 80% of the Guyanese economy, but what has that done for the Guyanese people? What has that done to heal the breaches within Guyanese society between capital and labour: and within labour itself, between the black East Indians and the black Africans of that nation-state. These are questions that need to be addressed. The transnational banks have assumed an increased importance as this tendency for nationalization proceeds. For all the states have had to turn to the banking sector to secure finance with which to buy the TNCs they take over. In addition to the transnational banks there are international finance organizations which reinforce this pattern of dependent capitalism.

I will only concentrate on two of these: the IMF and the IBRD (the World Bank). These international organizations have served to reinforce the dependency of Third World peripheral capitalist economies like the Caribbean, because adverse movements in the terms of trade of Third World countries force them to depend on loans from these institutions. These loans create another drain from our economies in terms of the high interest that has to be paid on these loans. So we find ourselves in a situation in which as the governments have made an attempt to come to terms with the control of the economy by the TNCs, they are swallowed up by the transnational banks and are in hock to the IMF and the World Bank.

What we have therefore is a situation whereby, with the exclusion of socialist Cuba, the continued domination of the region by international capitalism has served to integrate Caribbean economies, to root them more deeply into the international capitalist system than ever before. That is the economic reality which we face. Unless we face that we will have no chance of confronting it and achieving what I think (I know) all Caribbean people dream of: that we will finally be liberated one day.

Developmental Impacts from Sovereignty and Self-Reliance

Before I look at the development dynamic of sovereignty and self-reliance I ought to define what I mean 'sovereignty' and by 'self-reliance'. By sovereignty I mean nothing short of the full control by a people over the resources of that territory, and with the capacity to decide in any way they wish to utilize these resources for their own material, social and psycho-spiritual advancement. That is what I mean by sovereignty. Turning to self-reliance, I want to make it clear that I do not mean autarchy. I do not mean to say that individual island territories, or in fact the region as a whole should cut itself off completely from the rest of the world. I am not talking about autarchy then. I am talking about the capacity of each of these countries and the region as a whole to provide for the basic needs of their entire populations. Self-reliance, as a strategy for the fulfilment of the society's basic needs of food, shelter, clothing, health and education.

It is my contention that every single Caribbean territory has the capacity to achieve this. I have absolutely no doubt in my mind about that. The capacity of each territory to provide for the basic needs of its population is unquestioned: whether it is the 10 millions of Cuba or the 12,000 of Montserrat. The capacities of each of these territories to provide basic needs for their population from the resources at their command is unquestioned. There is no doubt in my mind that each island/territory has the capacity to do this. It is self-reliance in that context and defined in this way that I mean in my examination of the question of sovereignty and self-reliance.

Sovereignty and self-reliance together have the capacity for the generation of a development dynamic that is impossible to achieve without sovereignty and without a strategy for self-reliance. Let us look briefly at some of the things needed for achieving self-reliance and the effects these would have on development. First is the question of consumer tastes. The tastes of Caribbean people have been fashioned by centuries of colonialism. We therefore have to make a start to change the tastes of Caribbean people, to fit the requirements of Caribbean resources endowments.

On driving here this morning, I was really impressed with the displays of craft items on the sidewalk right there at the bottom of the hill at Constant Spring. The straw mats, wicker baskets, etc. are absolutely beautiful. What great possibilities exist here for us to utilize our own resources to fulfil our needs! When you contrast that creativity with the ridiculous imitation of North Atlantic society. Look at it: people in a hot climate having woolen rugs in their houses: buildings designed not to allow the free movement of air, but of air conditioning. Look at the Bank of Jamaica building, for example. It is built right on the water-front and there is no chance to get any of the sea-breeze in that building. It is pure concrete, pure concrete with slivers of glass, you have to peep through like you are in a jail to catch a glimpse of the mountains in the background or of the Caribbean Sea on the other side. It is really criminal for architects to design buildings like that in this beautiful climate of ours.

We will have to start to change our tastes, because the tastes have been developed by centuries of colonialism, by centuries of indoctrination that what we need to consume are the things that other people in the metropolitan countries produce: this applies right through – from rugs to salt fish. I have nothing against salt fish, it is a nice thing with the ackees. Why we can't organize our own trawler fishing, go and harvest the cod, then dry it and salt it ourselves? The Japanese after all, come all the way from the other side of the world and capture shrimps in the Guyana waters. And they and the Russians are catching all the tuna right at our doorsteps.

Let us go back to the critical point about the need for a change in consumer tastes so as to match the resource endowments of the Caribbean.

I just came back from the Far East a couple of weeks ago and I was struck by the fact that those people use bamboo for scaffolding in building construction. We have so much bamboo here in places like St Mary and Portland and all about. What are we doing with it? We are using steel for scaffolding, and we have no iron. In the distant past, that was not the case. The 'Flat Bridge' is still a miracle to me. The Flat Bridge that crosses the Rio Cobre river. That bridge was built before the days of concrete and steel. And every time that river comes down and overflows the road we find that when the water subsides, Flat Bridge is still standing there. There is something remarkable about that bridge but none of our structural engineers seem to know what binding material is in it. They only say that the thing was so beautifully designed. It is our ancestors who designed and built that bridge. They designed it in such a way, the engineers say, that it cuts the water: and therefore there is no force for the river to wash away. It is a marvellous construction and yet we don't know what material is in it. We know that it is built with local resources. What is binding it? Some people say it might be horse hair, guinea grass, etc.

The second point arises from the taste question and is associated with it: it is the need for fuller utilization of our resources. The utilization of what resources exist within the region to provide for our basic needs. The target that we must set for ourselves is to satisfy the basic needs of our own populations. Once we have achieved that as socialist Cuba has done, then we can call ourselves civilized. Until we do that we are still living in an age of backwardness. I don't care how many Mercedes Benzes and BMWs you see on the road. In fact, that is part of the problem as I will indicate later. Fuller utilization of our natural resources, both those known and those that are unknown. The known ones are substantial. Contrary to popular opinion, the Caribbean is not poor in resources. The Caribbean has significant mineral resources of nickel, of bauxite, of petroleum, and so on: tremendous agricultural resources of fertile land, and water (water is being wasted away on some of the islands, especially this one). Then, there is the natural beauty to attract tourist visitors. For their recreation, we can go way beyond the 'sun, sand, sea, and sex' which underlines the existing tourism. There is much more to offer in the Caribbean, because of the variety of human cultures and creativity. I will return to this in the final section.

The critical element in the development of our resources for our own advancement is the capacity that the utilization of these resources has for the establishment of linkages within the economy. The establishment of intersectoral linkages would be a natural outcome of the utilization of our resources directed toward our consumption needs. We could start using bamboo for building construction, or breadfruit as a flocculent for processing alumina. A friend of mine, Sonny Lakhan, experimented with breadfruit flour and found that it is better than wheat flour as a flocculent for the bauxite industry. While working with them, he tried to get the bauxite companies to consider this, but they had no need to consider it. Why? Because the wheat floor that they use as a flocculent to settle down the alumina was coming back in empty bauxite ships from North America. So why should they bother with breadfruit flour?

The point I am making here is that once you begin to use breadfruit flour then it will be necessary to have breadfruit producers who are going to begin growing breadfruit in a scientific way to produce the flour: and this creates the linkages within the economy, so that an expansion of economic activity in bauxite will have repercussions on other sectors of the economy. That is what we mean by linkages. It is the interconnectedness between various branches of industry, and economic sectors that generates development spread effects. The scope for the development of linkages is unlimited so long as you are utilizing what resources you have available. This combination of linkages, of control of our resource use, of change in consumer taste leads to the next development dynamic towards self-reliance and sovereignty. It is the matter of technological development.

As long as we remain dependent capitalist economics within the international capitalist system, we will continue to utilize technology that comes with the dependence on the TNCs. Technology is transferred from the imperial centres to the neocolonial periphery. That transfer stifles endogenous technical change which could be generated within the economies, to develop technologies which are appropriate to our resource endowment and to our resource capacity.

These four developmental elements which I have described form the foundation for the achievement of two desirable societal objectives: self-sustained economic growth and economic democracy. I want to suggest that so long as the society provides the basic needs of all its people, they will achieve some level of economic democracy. And I want to suggest that once the economy goes on a path of mobilizing its resources for its own development with the linkages, with the technological dynamic, etc., then self-sustained growth is inevitable. Sovereignty and self-reliance together have the capacity for transforming Caribbean societies from what are really today beggar societies into societies that can be independent and stand on their own two feet in this world.

In concluding this section, I want to point out that there are limits to the extent to which each and every Caribbean country and state can achieve this sovereignty and self-reliance, because we are small societies which are really like sardines in this world of superpower politics and imperial sharks. We need to recognize that size is a constraint on our capacities for achieving independent economic development. So we need to think in terms of regional strategies for development at the economic and technical level.

Models of Transformation and Transition

This brings me to the third part of my presentation: the question of models of transformation. So far, we have been talking in rather abstract theoretical terms. Let us turn to an examination of the social reality of the Caribbean experience. For certain countries in the region have made attempts to move away from dependent capitalist underdevelopment to some form of independent socialist development. We must recognize at the outset that ideology is central to the question of transition and transformation. For dependent capitalism, like all capitalism, is based on the exploitation of man by man. In contra-distinction to this, socialism has within it the seeds of cooperation between man and man. Accordingly, attempts at transition from dependent capitalism towards some form of sovereignty and self-reliance has involved the mobilization of peoples through some socialist-type ideological philosophies. When we look at the history of the Caribbean, we find that every time an attempt is made to move towards sovereignty and self-reliance, that imperialism has come down heavily against whatever government, party, or movement is engaged in that process.

The first, and most important example of transition, remains socialist Cuba, which after 25 years of independent socialist development has managed to provide the basic needs for its whole population. Cuba has managed as well to provide technical assistance in basic needs production for many countries in the Third World: particularly in the areas of construction (for housing and social infrastructure like schools, hospitals) and of health. At the recent World Congress of Paediatrics, held in Havana, the President of UNICEF made the point that if the infant mortality rate in Latin America were as low as that in Cuba today, then we would have only 240,000 deaths as compared to the present over one million. Cuba's health programme is one of the most advanced in the whole world. In education, Cuba now has a totally literate population, the lowest levels of which are now moving to the 10th grade. That is the lowest level of the education of people in socialist Cuba.

In the area of food production, historically Jamaica has led the tropical world in the development of agricultural technology. So the Cubans came here and took the technology of livestock breeding and the technology of pasture management and went back to Cuba, and applied to Cuban conditions. And today Cuba is fully self-sufficient in milk, butter, cheese, ice cream – some of the nicest ice cream in the world. The Cubans came here again and discovered the ortanique, which is a Jamaican invention. Today Cuba exports ortanique under the name of 'Cubanique' to Eastern Europe, and is a major supplier of citrus to the Eastern European Market. What happened in socialist Cuba was that the 26th July Movement from the time it was in the mountain committed itself to a programme of agrarian reform, which would provide land to the peasantry. This means that when it came to office in January 1959, it was already committed to a programme of agrarian reform and, as I indicated earlier, without a programme of agrarian reform through the Caribbean, we cannot begin to answer the question of society's satisfaction of its basic needs. Because it is the very character of the unequal distribution of land, inherited from the plantation system, that bottles up the creative energies of the peasantry and allows land to remain idle and people go hungry. (To my mind this is the most disgraceful aspect of Jamaica's social reality. The vast amount of idle land and the vast amount of idle labour, in a country where malnutrition is significant enough to distort the lives and life chances of hundreds of thousands of young children. This is not a civilized society.)

Cuba has managed not only to solve its basic needs production requirements, but it has also helped to provide technical assistance to many Third World countries on a scale that, in terms of per capita income and size of population, exceeds the aid which is given by the most advanced industrial nations in the world today. That is a fact of life which we need to recognize. But Cuba did not achieve this without difficulty. No society is going to be able to achieve sovereignty and self reliance, certainly no society in the Western Hemisphere, without having to confront the imperialist might of the US. The US placed a trade embargo on Cuba; but, in my opinion, that is the best thing that the US could have done, because it forced Cubans for the first time to have to maintain a whole fleet of vehicles for transportation, a whole infrastructure of industry which was based on American machinery and equipment; it forced them to make spare parts when they couldn't get them; and, thereby induced the development of an internal technological dynamic which helped to propel Cuba to where they are today. So that the embargo was a blessing in disguise. In addition to the embargo, the imperialist US has tried over and over again to eliminate the leadership of that country, and it is only the vigilance of the DGI (perhaps, the most advanced intelligence system in the world) that saved the life of Fidel Castro to this day. US attempts to overthrow the Cuban regime have intensified under Reagan's administration.

So Cuba represents for us one successful model of the struggle to establish an independent socialist state, right here in the Caribbean. In the English-speaking Caribbean, the struggle for independence has been at two levels. First, towards the achievement of constitutional independence; and, subsequently, in some countries, attempts to achieve economic independence by some non-capitalist path. The decolonization (constitutional) process throughout the Third world since World War II has been influenced by the experience of two countries which took two different routes to liberation: People's China, by revolution established a socialist republic in 1949; and India, by evolution (negotiation), became an independent republic in 1947.

Within the Caribbean the revolutionary model was applied first in Cuba in 1959; then in Grenada in 1979. Within that revolutionary model, we find that the Grenada experience was one of great hope for this region. What that revolution achieved in four years, in economic and social terms was indeed quite remarkable. The World Bank Report on Grenada indicated that that country achieved rates of growth of 5% in the gross national product, while other countries in the region were experiencing zero or negative growth.

Grenada has moved from the situation where half its labour force were unemployed before 1979 to the low level of 14% by 1983. In addition to all this, health services were improved substantially, thanks to the assistance of Cuba; educational services were improved through a literacy campaign and school feeding programmes, etc The material advances made by the PRG are, to my mind, a major achievement for a small country within such a short period of time, and that is why the Reagan administration invaded Grenada. It has nothing to do with the split between Bishop and Coard. Grenada was too good an example to be allowed to continue. Because if it could succeed in the way it did in a period where other countries in the region were experiencing negative or zero growth, then Caribbean people would begin to think anew about the merits of socialism ('Communism').

The Grenada experience is an experience which is of critical importance to us and requires our serious and analysis and examination. That split within the NJM which was engineered by Coard and the subsequent murder of Maurice Bishop and other leaders of the PRG set the stage for subsequent US invasion of Grenada. This reversal has put this region back at least 25 years. If we do not learn the lessons from Grenada we will be in serious trouble for the future.

The same thing applies to the next model I want to examine; this is the model of Jamaica under Michael Manley – the model of change by negotiation, as it were. Cuba and Grenada, 1979-83 are examples of the revolutionary approach. We come now to the evolutionary approach of Jamaica under Michael Manley between 1974 and 1980. For it was in 1974 that the ruling PNP readopted 'democratic socialism' as the Party's ideology. The Manley regime had introduced a whole host of social legislative acts early in the programme and these brought little or no hostility from any section of the Jamaican society. Even the first attempt by the Manley regime to attack foreign capital with the imposition of the bauxite levy in 1974 still had national support, including the national bourgeoisie, two of whom were part of Manley's negotiating team against the bauxite companies. But Manley began to go a little bit too far in the eyes of the imperial US.

First the imposition of the bauxite levy angered the TNCs and the US government, and, secondly, the initiative in the formation of the IBA which brought all the major bauxite producing countries together, made it appear to the US that there would be another producer OPEC-type cartel to contend with. Manley went further to negotiate for 51% ownership of the bauxite producing activities, and the repatriation of bauxite lands to the state. This was again going a little bit too far; and when Michael Manley went to Cuba and saw the achievements of that socialist revolution and came back in a state of euphoria to tell the local capitalist that they were not wanted here and that there were five flights a day to Miami, that really set the cat among the pigeons.

It is curious that the rhetoric of Manley frightened the local capitalists at a time when the Manley government was providing more incentives for this very class of people. The economic policies of Manley regime granted more privileges and incentives to the local capitalist class than any government before. This shows you two things. It dramatizes the fear of the local capitalist class of anything called socialism or communism, and it illustrates as well, the unpatriotism of this class of people. They would be as happy living in Miami or Toronto as they would be living here. These people are not Jamaicans in any true sense; and I want people to understand this, because it is important to understand who our allies are in this struggle and at what point in time you can expect assistance from what allies, and at what point in time you have to watch some of them. This is a lesson we have to learn from the Manley experience. What I have to say today is nothing compared to the lessons that we have to draw. There are many more, but the important point that I want to make is that when a movement or a party begins to confront the imperialists where it hurts them and which therefore brings forth a response from imperialist interests, that movement or party must be prepared to mobilize the population behind this activity or else it is lost.

And this is precisely what happened to the Michael Manley regime in 1980. By the time 1980 came, the population was tired of Manley riding two horses. All the time, Michael Manley was riding two horses; trying to benefit the black masses of the population of this country at the same time providing incentives for the white and near-white bourgeois and brown petit bourgeois class. As time went on, the white capitalist class, and the brown leadership class in this country, gradually abandoned Manley, while Manley himself had abandoned the black workers as well. He was left out there on a thread, when Seaga and the American imperialists combined to cut the thread in 1980.

So the lessons of Grenada and Jamaica are there. The main point from our examination of these models is that when you examine the political scenario of transition, we come to the same conclusion as we did in the economic analysis: that no island Caribbean state can go it alone. No island Caribbean state can go it alone politically: and this was the real tragedy of Grenada, because the Bishop regime in Grenada had reached a stage of penetration in the region, where the pluralist tradition was beginning to be accepted by all the political leaders in the region. We have regressed from that and today there is a marked intolerance of pluralism. Yet within the region, as indeed in any other group of societies, in the world, uneven development is a necessary part of the process of change. Some countries will advance faster than others in the transition. Therefore there is the need for the acceptance of a pluralist framework in order to forge regional linkage mechanisms to create a Caribbean nation state.

Sovereignty, Self-Reliance and the Caribbean Nation State

There are constraints, both economic and political, on the chances of survival of island economies. As I have also said, there is a historical homogeneity that makes the Caribbean one nation. In fact the Caribbean is one nation, move anywhere you like in the region and you are at home. It is the same food, same music, the same everything, it is one nation, and to go it alone we have had the tragic set backs with invasions of imperialist forces beginning with Guyana in 1953 (so many of us forget Guyana in 1953, when that country elected a Marxist government which was not allowed to rule by Britain and the US for more than a few months before they invaded Guyana). Guyana in 1953 was the first, but not the last, for we have Cuba and the Bay of Pigs in 1961, we had furthermore in October 1962 the missile crisis, the degradation of the Cuban nation state by the agreement between Kennedy and Kruschev, without the consultation of Castro and the Cuban people, about how missiles would be deployed inside Cuba. That was a degradation of Cuban sovereignty. In 1965 the Marines went in the Dominican Republic and removed Juan Bosch. In 1983 there was Grenada; these were some of the lessons of going it alone. What we require is economic and political unity that will achieve the realization of the Caribbean as one whole nation state. The possibilities that such unity could enhance are today demonstrated in the achievements of the West Indies cricketers, under Clive Lloyd. In cricket, the Caribbean plays as one unit of cricketers. Can you imagine us sending an Olympic team with Cuba and all of us to the Olympics? What is going on in cricket can be repeated several times in other spheres of activity. Just look at the immense contribution the Caribbean has made in the spheres of political philosophy, literature, and music. It is really quite remarkable that a region of less than 25 million people has produced such a galaxy of political philosophers like Marti, Garvey, James, and Padmore (the 'father of African literature' to quote Nkrumah), to name only a few. The tidal wave of literature coming out of the English-speaking Caribbean since the war must collectively be the most formidable contribution in the English-speaking world. Naipaul, Lamming, Walcott, Brathwaite are only a sample of a long list of outstanding novelists and poets. When we add the work of non-English speaking Caribbean writers, like Carpentier, Guillen, Despestre, Césaire etc., the record of the Caribbean cannot be matched by any country of similar population size (for example, Canada).

Caribbean creativity in the field of popular music is unsurpassed anywhere in the world. The invention of a new musical instrument, the steel drum, is the only new addition made by people of the Western hemisphere. Then there is the calypso, the mambo, meringue, etc. in music and dance. Leading the pack here, is reggae music which is the most important popular music in the world today, combining poetry, rhythm and social comment (protest) in one musical idiom.

In general, then, Caribbean peoples have demonstrated beyond doubt that they have the capacity to achieve greatness, on a world scale. They have done so collectively in cricket and individually in track and field, literature and music. This cultural explosion needs to find expression in the realm of politics and philosophy. I am suggesting that for the full realization of this great potential we need to come together as one Caribbean nation. Then, and only then, will we be in a position to be fully independent, sovereign and free to transform what is physically the most beautiful part of planet Earth into a human paradise!

Notes
_____

*"Sovereignty and self-reliance: the economic implications". Address to a Regional Seminar on "Caribbean Sovereignty: Mobilization for Development and Self-Reliance – The Tasks of Political Education". The People's National Party of Jamaica (1984a).

1 See Lloyd Best, "A model of pure plantation economy", *Social and Economic Studies* (September, 1986), for further elaboration and discussion of the institutional framework.

2 Trevor Farrell, "Decolonization in the English-speaking Caribbean: Myth or reality", in *The 'Newer Caribbean': Decolonization, Democracy and Development*, edited by Paget Henry and Carl Stone (1983).

Epilogue

35

The Struggle for a Relevant Economics*

The teaching of economics at Mona began with a core of British researchers who were substantively employed by the Institute of Social and Economic Research (ISER). Some of these were graduate students from UK universities conducting field research in the West Indies. For the most part, then, they knew very little about the Caribbean environment. The courses they offered were, more or less, identical to those taught at British universities (the London School of Economics was the model). The Vice Chancellor of the UWI at the time was the celebrated West Indian economist, Professor W. Arthur Lewis, who previously held the prestigious Stanley Jevons Chair in Economics at Manchester University. Vice Chancellor Lewis wanted to find a 'relatively young and bright' economist to head the new department at Mona; and he found one Professor Charles M. Kennedy, an Englishman steeped in the Oxbridge tradition.

Kennedy was Professor of Economics and Head of the Department for the first six years, 1960-1966 (with W. Arthur Lewis acting as Head until Kennedy's arrival). During that time, a number of young West Indian economists were appointed to positions in the department and in ISER. Alister McIntyre, the first such appointment in the department, found company with others working in the ISER: people like Lloyd Best, Roy Thomas, C.Y. Thomas and LeRoy Taylor. And, together, they began to bring a Caribbean flavour to teaching and research. The early years were the years of West Indian Federation and these economists re-examined the theory of customs union and other questions relevant to the fledgeling Federation. They were determined from the outset to fashion the tools of the discipline to the Caribbean environment.

They preoccupied themselves with the economics of Federation and when the Federal experiment was in danger of collapse (after Norman Manley's announcement of a referendum for Jamaica) these young West Indian economists took to the streets and the countryside campaigning vigorously (along with other West Indian academics at Mona) for Jamaica's continued association.

After the collapse of the Federation, Jamaica and Trinidad and Tobago proceeded to the status of constitutional independence. But the West Indian scholars *never* lost their regional perspective even when, they addressed certain national questions. Examples of the latter were the pioneering article by Best and McIntyre, "A first appraisal of central bank monetary management in Jamaica"[1] and the PhD research works of C.Y. Thomas[2] and LeRoy Taylor.[3] These early works of Thomas and Best/McIntyre pointed to 'dependence' as a characteristic feature of Caribbean economy from the outset.

By 1965, then, two features emerged. First, West Indian economists began to establish a base-line knowledge of the Caribbean environment that suggested the need to tailor the discipline to Caribbean specifications. And, secondly, these scholars displayed a commitment to influence the political process in the region by their direct participation in providing informed public opinion. By that date as well, the number of West Indian economists on the ground had increased to the extent that the British members of the department were in a minority, even though they held senior positions. These two features strengthened with the expanded core of West Indians and, with the passage of time, set the stage for unending struggles for a relevant economics: indeed for a relevant social science (including history and the arts). Struggles which pitched the economists at one time or another into battle against established authority, both within the university and without.

Two initiatives taken by these economists in 1965 deserve to be recorded. Lloyd Best who had returned to Mona in 1964 and was a founding member of *New World* in Guyana in 1963, established a 'New World group' at Mona and, in late 1965, the second issue of *New World Quarterly* was published by the Mona group and sustained by them for the next five years. The group set its objective as being an instrument of radical social change in the Caribbean by making a historico-specific interpretation of the society. Its focus on the plantation system and its historical legacy set the stage for subsequent formalization of a theory of Caribbean society. The second initiative was the convening of a small conference of university and government technocrats to consider a fresh assault on regional integration. The result of that meeting was a commission by West Indian governments to the ISER to undertake a series of studies by the UWI economists on the possibilities for regional economic integration.

During the academic year 1964-65, the West Indian economists in the department put forward a proposal that a new course to be called "Caribbean Economic Problems" should be added to the curriculum. They felt this to be a necessary first step toward providing more relevant courses. With the achievement of independent university status in 1963, very little curriculum changes had been made – the most far-reaching had been to add "with special reference to the West Indies" to the syllabi of some of the applied courses. The British leadership in the department opposed the proposal vigorously, arguing that there were no economic problems specific to the Caribbean and that this proposal, if accepted, would lead eventually to an undesirable state of 'parochialism'. After a long and heated discussion in a departmental meeting, the division was between all West Indian members in favour and the three British senior staff in opposition. The British Head of Department decided to use administrative authority to overrule the majority West Indian opinion whereupon the meeting broke up. Subsequently, we took the proposal directly to Faculty Board and won approval at that level. Accordingly, the course "Caribbean Economic Problems" was taught for the first time during the following academic year. The departmental struggle involved in this change emphasized the need to democratize the process of decision-making – a matter that was to come to a head in the early 1970s.

During the academic year 1965-66, a major conflict developed between the West Indian economists and the government of Jamaica. The government, without giving reasons, seized and cancelled the passports of two economists – LeRoy Taylor of the ISER and George Beckford of the Department of Economics. These two economists had travelled to Cuba during the summer (July) of 1965 and it appeared that there might have been some connection between the two events. Public objection raised by these scholars sparked a public debate that lasted almost two years before the ban on their travel was lifted. The action of the Jamaican government prompted the team of economists then engaged in the studies on regional economic integration to issue a statement to all West Indian governments concerned that henceforth they would not draw on the financial resources provided by the governments, but would complete the studies on their own resources and make these available to the West Indian public. This, of course, infuriated the university authorities as did the public objection raised by Beckford at the time of the passport seizure. For the administration was of the view that such matters should best be handled by quiet negotiation between themselves and the government.

The action by the team of regional integration economists was fundamental in that it made a clear distinction between the interests of governments and those of the people at large. Thenceforward, it was no longer a matter of working in 'the interests of government and people'. It became clear that the two were not necessarily the same. Moreover, the economists indicated, there and then, that where the two interests diverged it was the interests of the *people* to which they were committed. Furthermore, the refusal to submit to the administration's wish for negotiated settlement signalled that these economists were unprepared to use their positions of privilege to gain any advantage over less privileged individuals and groups in the society who had to face continuous harassment and human rights abuses.

It is important to note that the team of economists completed the work on their own resources and the subsequent publication of that work in two volumes by the ISER, in 1967,[4] was instrumental in the establishment of CARIFTA in 1968 and its subsequent transformation to CARICOM later. Indeed, these economists provided free consultative services during the foundation period of CARIFTA, even though that initiative was less than what the studies had recommended.

Professor Kennedy relinquished the headship of the department in 1966 and returned to England and Dr G.E. Cumper was appointed Professor and Head of the Department of Economics. As one of the minority of three who had opposed the introduction of Caribbean Economic Problems, Cumper continued Kennedy's line of leadership, but in a much more moderate style. However, in 1966, the first of the second generation of West Indian economists arrived with the transfer of Norman Girvan from St Augustine. Girvan, as a member of the first graduating class, had been strongly influenced by McIntyre and Best and had completed a PhD thesis at the London School of Economics, which was later to be revised and published by the ISER.[5] Steve DeCastro was transferred from St Augustine at the same time as Girvan, to add to the West Indian contingent already on the ground. Alfred Francis was appointed in 1962. Beckford was transferred from St Augustine in 1964. H.R. Brewster was appointed in 1964. C.Y. Thomas returned in 1964 and Owen Jefferson was appointed in 1965, having completed an Oxford PhD thesis which was later revised and published by the ISER.[6]

By 1967, then, the West Indianization of the department was as complete as was desirable. Internal tension eased but external conflicts intensified as the contingent of economists, fortified by their ever increasing empirical knowledge of the region and with the semi-polemical medium of *New World*, launched into sustained public debate on matters of national and regional importance. Thus, for example, a pamphlet on "Sugar – Our Life or Death" by Havelock Brewster was the opening salvo in a long and bitter campaign that pitched the 'UWI Economists' against the combined forces of the Sugar Manufacturers' Association, the *Daily Gleaner* and the government of Jamaica, a campaign that lasted for the most part of 1967. Late that year as well, the devaluations of West Indian currencies as automatic responses to the sterling devaluation prompted a public statement by these economists which took an opposing point of view, and a subsequent conference explored the problem in greater depth.[7]

It soon became clear that the active participation of scholars in such public debates and direct links between some of these scholars and less privileged groups in the society was not favourably countenanced by the political authorities. Accordingly, the government of Jamaica began to regard such activities as 'subversive'. And this became the pretext for the banning of the late Walter Rodney of the Department of History in October 1968 and C.Y. Thomas of the Department of Economics in August 1969. Both scholars, being non-Jamaicans, were banned from re-entering the country during their travels abroad. The banning of Thomas occurred only a few weeks before the start of the academic year while both the Vice Chancellor and the Head of the Economics Department were out of the country. Professor Douglas Hall, acting as Vice Chancellor and George Beckford acting as Head of Economics, issued a public response to the banning of Thomas, indicating in the statement that Thomas' two courses, Monetary Economics and International Economics, could not be taught that academic year, as a result of the banning. However, that decision was reversed when Vice Chancellor Roy Marshall and Professor G.E. Cumper returned to their respective posts.

The two different stances reflected in this situation are a manifestation of fundamental differences in values and attitudes which should be obvious to the reader. These bans by the Jamaican government precipitated a disintegration of the regional make-up of the UWI faculty. Thereafter, non-Jamaicans began to feel unwelcome at Mona and many of them began to transfer to the other two campuses. Campus life at Mona has never been the same since. Thus, the 1960s closed on a rather gloomy note.

However, the 1970s began with bright prospects for curriculum changes and increased pressure for democratisation in the Department, the Faculty and the University. Throughout the 1960s, individual members of the department had introduced changes in the content of their individual courses. In 1970, it was agreed that the time had come for a full-scale reform of the curriculum beginning with the first year course. The formalization of a theory of plantation economy had been advanced by 1970, with the completion of two major works: the four-volume study of Best and Levitt[8] and the book on underdevelopment in plantation economies of the Third World by Beckford.[9] The first full-scale meeting of teachers of economics on all three campuses was convened at St Augustine in the summer of 1970 and the groundwork was laid there for reforming the curriculum. Thus, plantation economics was first introduced in the 1970-71 academic year and the first year course expanded to include a section on "Foundations of Caribbean Economy".

As early as 1966, the feudal-like structure of the University posed a problem for the young West Indian scholars. In that year, the election of a Dean for the Faculty of Social Sciences produced a stalemate. George Beckford, a lecturer in the Department of Economics, won the election by a landslide vote, but the UWI administration ruled that he was too junior to hold such a post, refused to make the appointment and selected a Dean of its own choosing. The struggle for democratization continued and came to a head in the crisis of 1971-72, when a major conflict of views developed over the appointment of a person to fill the newly established Chair in Applied Economics. The administration sought to impose on the department a candidate of its own choosing who, in the opinion of the majority in the department, was less qualified than the person they themselves had selected. The department's choice of Dr A.A. Francis was based on their judgement of his proven worth and leadership qualities while the administration's choice was a West Indian whose credentials were simply that he held a Chair in Economics in a British University. Norman Girvan produced a document 'Economics and the University', which clearly outlined the principles involved. Eventually, after months of struggle, the departmental view prevailed and Francis was appointed Professor of Applied Economics in 1972.

In that same year, another conflict situation developed between teachers and the administration. A third-generation member of the department, Mr Robert Figueroa, was charged by the administration with professional misconduct (along with Dr Munroe of the Department of Government) for his role in assisting in a strike of maintenance workers against the University. The department's struggle in support of these colleagues was carried at a faculty-wide level and prevented the administration from having its own way. The struggle for democratization achieved its first major success with the administration's acceptance of the principle of rotating headships in 1972. Professor Cumper went on leave in that year, relinquishing the headship and, based on departmental recommendation, George Beckford was appointed Head of Department for a three-year term. But, in less than a year, he felt obliged to resign as a show of no-confidence in the administration of Vice Chancellor Marshall. Dr O.C. Jefferson succeeded as Head of Department to continue the new scheme of rotation.

The most serious internal crisis to rock the department came in 1975, when it was discovered that a member of the department had plagiarized a confidential government of Jamaica document. Members of the department called on him to resign in a statement that made the plagiarism charge against him. The member, in turn, sued the then Head of Department, Professor A.A. Francis, for libel and the pending case virtually crippled members of the department (financially and intellectually) until it was resolved in favour of

Professor Francis in the Supreme Court of Jamaica five years later. Through-out this period, the university administration provided tacit support for the offending member of the department. This generated a considerable degree of frustration among members of the department who, nevertheless, managed to keep morale sufficiently high, largely as a result of the firm but calm leader-ship provided by Professor Francis.

Further change in the curriculum came in 1975, with the introduction of Marxist political economy into the course content. And in that same year, George Beckford was appointed to a personal Chair, again only after consid-erable and prolonged opposition from the university administration. During the 1970s, the graduate programme of the department was strengthened and formalized after a somewhat *ad hoc* start had been made in the 1960s. Both MSc (Economics) and PhD degrees were earned by several candidates in the 1970s, under the stewardship of Professor Francis. And one of the PhD gradu-ates, Compton Bourne, was subsequently appointed in 1981 to the vacant Chair in Economics at the St Augustine Campus. Headship of the department passed through several members during the 1970s and the first graduate of the department to assume the post was K. Dwight Venner, with Mark Figueroa being the second such Head. By the end of the 1970s, most of the West Indian staff who had been appointed in the 1960s had left the depart-ment and a process of rebuilding began in the last two years or so. Finally, the Department acknowledges with firm approval that its first Acting Head, W. Arthur Lewis, won the Nobel Prize in Economics in 1979.

It is obvious from this brief historical survey, that the Department of Economics at Mona has systematically provided leadership in the struggle for a relevant social science in the Caribbean. Much has been achieved, yet much remains to be done. The struggle continues.

Notes

* "The struggle for a relevant economics". *Social and Economic Studies* 33:1 (1984b).

1   See *Social and Economic Studies* 10, no. 3 (September 1961).

2   See C.Y. Thomas, *Monetary and Financial Arrangements in a Dependent Monetary Economy: A Study of British Guiana 1945-1962* (Mona, Jamaica: ISER, University of the West Indies, 1965).

3   See LeRoy Taylor, *Consumer Expenditure in Jamaica* (Mona, Jamaica: ISER, Univer-sity of the West Indies, 1964).

4   Volume 1 was *The Dynamics of West Indian Economic Integration* by H.R. Brewster and C.Y. Thomas, while Volume II consisted of separate studies by Girvan on bauxite, DeCastro on air transport, Beckford on bananas, Beckford and Guscott

on intra-regional agricultural trade, Armstrong and McIntyre on incentive manufactures and imperial preference, respectively.

5   Norman Girvan, *Foreign Capital and Economic Underdevelopment in Jamaica* (Mona, Jamaica: ISER, University of the West Indies, 1971).

6   Owen Jefferson, *The Post-War Economic Development of Jamaica* (Mona, Jamaica: ISER, University of the West Indies, 1971).

7   See also papers presented at a regional conference on devaluation at the Institute of Social and Economic Research in 1968.

8   See Best and Levitt, "Export-propelled industrialisation in the Caribbean". Mimeo. (n.d.)

9   See George Beckford, *Persistent Poverty* (Mona: ISER and Oxford: Oxford University Press, 1972).

Bibliography

Abramowitz, M. 1961. "The nature and significance of Kuznets' cycles". *Economic Development and Social Change* (April). Special issue: "Essays in the Quantitative Study of Economic Growth".

Adams, D. W. 1967. "Resource allocation in traditional agriculture". *Journal of Farm Economics* (November).

Adams, D. W. 1971. "Comment on D. Warriner's paper". Paper presented to the Conference on Strategies for Agricultural Development in the 1970s. Stanford University, 13–16 December.

Adams, D. W., and L. E. Montero. 1965. "Land parcelization in agrarian reform: a Columbian example". *Inter-American Economic Affairs* (Winter).

Adams, N. 1969. "Internal migration in Jamaica – an economic analysis'. *Social and Economic Studies* (June).

Amin, S. 1978. *Unequal Development*. New York: Monthly Review Press.

Argawala, A. N., and S. P. Singh (eds.). 1958. *The Economics of Underdevelopment*. Oxford: Oxford University Press.

Aziz, U. 1962. *Subdivision of Estates in Malaya, 1951–1960*, 3 Vols. Kuala Lumpur: University of Malaya.

Baldwin, R. E. 1956. "Patterns of development in newly settled regions". *Manchester School of Economic Studies* (May).

Baldwin, R. E. 1963. "Export technology and development from subsistence level". *Economic Journal* (March).

Bauer, P.T. 1949. *The Rubber Industry*. Cambridge: Cambridge University Press.

Beckford, G. L. 1964a. "Crisis in the West Indian banana industry". *Caribbean Quarterly* 10, no. 2.

Beckford, G. L. 1964b. "Secular fluctuations in the growth of tropical agricultural trade". *Economic Development and Cultural Change*.

Beckford, G. L. 1964c. "The growth of major tropical export-crop industries". *Social and Economic Studies* 13, no. 4.

Beckford, G. L. 1965a. "Agriculture in the development of Trinidad and Tobago: a comment". *Social and Economic Studies* 14, no. 2.

Beckford, G. L. 1965b. "Agriculture and economic development". *Caribbean Quarterly* 11, nos. 1 and 2.

Beckford, G. L. 1965c. "A Caribbean view of Cuba". *New World Quarterly* (Croptime).

Beckford, G. L. 1965d. "Issues in the Windward-Jamaica banana war". *New World Quarterly* 2, no. 1.

Beckford, G. L. 1966a. "Transforming traditional agriculture: comment". *Journal of Farm Economics* (November).

Beckford, G. L. 1966b. "A note on agricultural organisation and planning in Cuba". *Caribbean Studies* (November).

Beckford, G. L. 1966c. "Agricultural development in 'traditional' and 'peasant' economies: a review article". *Social and Economic Studies* 15, no. 2.

Beckford, G. L. 1967a. "The West Indian banana industry: the scope for rationalization and regional collaboration". *Studies in Regional Economic Integration* 2, no. 3.

Beckford, G. L. 1967b. "Long term trends in banana exports: further evidence of secular fluctuations in tropical agricultural trade". *Economic Development and Cultural Change* 15, no. 3.

Beckford, G. L. 1967c. "British Honduras and regional economic integration: two views". *New World Quarterly* 3, no. 4.

Beckford, G. L. 1968a. "Toward an appropriate theoretical framework for agricultural development and policy". *Social and Economic Studies* (Special number edited by George Beckford) 17, no. 3.

Beckford, G. L. 1968b. "Education as an instrument for development". Presented to the Annual Meeting of the Jamaica Teachers Association. Mimeo.

Beckford, G. L. 1968c. "Rationalisation of West Indian agriculture". Regional Conference on Devaluation. ISER, University of the West Indies.

Beckford, G. L. 1969. "The economics of agricultural resource use and development in plantation economics". *Social and Economic Studies* 18, no. 4.

Beckford, G. L. 1970a. *The Political and Social Economy of Plantations – a Selected and Annotated Bibliography*. Palo Alto, California: Food Research Institute, Stanford University.

Beckford, G. L. 1970b. "The dynamics of growth and the nature of metropolitan plantation enterprise". *Social and Economic Studies* 19, no. 4.

Beckford, G. L. 1970c. "Black man and society – a comment on the black writers in the new world". Paper prepared for the Fourth Annual Conference on Comparative Literature held at the University of Southern California. Mimeo.

Beckford, G. L. 1971a. "Origins, development and future of the Jamaican banana industry". *New World Quarterly* 5, no. 4.

Beckford, G. L. 1971b. "Institutional foundations of resource underdevelopment in the Caribbean". *Review of Black Political Economy* 1.

Beckford, G. L. 1971c. "Foundation of black dispossession". Mona, Jamaica: University of the West Indies. Mimeo.

Beckford, G. L. 1972a. *Persistent Poverty: Underdevelopment in Plantation Economies of the Third World*. Oxford: Oxford University Press.

Beckford, G. L. 1972b. "Strategies for agricultural development: comment". *Food Research Institute Studies in Agriculture, Economics, Trade and Development* 11, no. 2.

Beckford, G. L. 1972c. "Land reform for the betterment of Caribbean peoples". Proceedings of the Seventh West Indian Agricultural Economics Conference, Grenada.

Beckford, G. L. 1972d. "Institutional foundations of resource underdevelopment in the Caribbean". Reprinted in *Resource Development in the Caribbean*, Montreal: McGill University Centre for Developing Area Studies.

Beckford, G. L. 1974. "Comparative rural systems, development and underdevelopment". *World Development* 2, no. 6. Reprinted in C. K. Wilber (1979).

Beckford, G. L. 1975a. "Black dispossession in Caribbean plantation economy". Preliminary Draft. Presented to the Sixth Annual Meeting of the US National Conference of Black Political Scientists, Washington, DC, 1–3 May.

Beckford, G. L. (ed.). 1975b. *Caribbean Economy: Dependence and Backwardness*. Mona, Jamaica: ISER, University of the West Indies.

Beckford, G. L. 1975c. "Caribbean rural economy". In *Caribbean Economy: Dependence and Backwardness*, edited by G. L. Beckford. Mona, Jamaica: ISER, University of the West Indies.

Beckford, G. L. 1975d. "Social structural change and continuity in the English-speaking Caribbean". Report to the UN Economic Commission for Latin America (UNECLA), 2 vols. Mimeo.

Beckford, G. L. 1976. "Introduction". In *Aspects of the Political Economy of Race in the Caribbean and the Americas* by N. Girvan. Atlanta, GA: The Institute of the Black World.

Beckford, G. L. 1977a. "Institutionalized racism in Jamaica". *Socialism* 4, no. 2.

Beckford, G. L. 1977b. "Plantations, peasants and proletariat in the West Indies". In *Land and Labour in Latin America: Essays on the Development of Agrarian Capitalism in Nineteenth and Twentieth Century*, edited by K. Duncan and I. Rutledy. New York: Cambridge University Press.

Beckford, G. L. 1978a. "Social knowledge and social change in the Caribbean". In *Methodology and Change: Problems of Applied Social Science Research Techniques in the Commonwealth Caribbean*, edited by L. Lindsay. Mona, Jamaica: ISER, University of the West Indies.

Beckford, G. L. 1978b. "Plantation system and the penetration of international capitalism". In *Methodology and Change: Problems of Applied Social Science Research Techniques in the Commonwealth Caribbean*, edited by L. Lindsay. Mona, Jamaica: ISER, University of the West Indies.

Beckford, G. L. 1979a. "A suggested framework for rural development planning Caribbean-type". Notes on community enterprise organizations – ECLA-IPLES-CDCC, Havana, Cuba. Mimeo.

Beckford, G. L. 1979b. "Plantation capitalism and black dispossession: a review article". *Transition* 2, no. 2.

Beckford, G. L. 1979c. "The future of plantation society in comparative perspective". Paper prepared for a symposium on the Political Economy of the Black World. University of California Los Angeles, California.

Beckford, G. L. 1979d. "Plantations, peasants and proletariat in the West Indies". Reprinted in *The World as a Company Town*, World Anthropology Series, edited by E. Idris-Soven and Vaughan. The Hague: Institute of Social Studies; and in *Anthropology and Social Change in Rural Areas*, edited by Berdichewsky. The Hague: Institute of Social Studies.

Beckford, G. L. 1980a. "The sounds and pressures of black survival: a review article of Ken Pryce's *Endless Pressure*". *Social and Economic Studies* 31, no. 2.

Beckford, G. L. 1980b. "Introduction". In "Portrait of the Jamaican male" by Erna Brodber. Mona, Jamaica: University of the West Indies. Mimeo.

Beckford, G. L. 1980c. "Postscript". In *Small Garden, Bitter Weed, the Political Economy of Struggle and Change in Jamaica* by G. L. Beckford and M. Witter. Kingston: Maroon Publishing House.

Beckford, G. L. 1982. "Cultural sovereignty and economic development". First Caribbean Conference of Intellectual Workers. Grenada, November.

Beckford, G. L. 1983. "On life, politics and turmoil of Jamaica". *Frontline*, United Kingdom, September–October, reprinted in *Maroon Pamphlet*, no. 1.

Beckford, G. L. 1984a. "Sovereignty and self-reliance: the economic implications". *Proceedings of a Regional Seminar on Caribbean Sovereignty: Mobilization for Development and Self-Reliance – The Tasks of Political Education*. Kingston, Jamaica: People's National Party.

Beckford, G. L. 1984b. "The struggle for a relevant economics". *Social and Economic Studies* 33, no. 1.

Beckford, G. L. 1984c. "Strategies for agricultural development: comment". Reprinted as "Induced innovation model" in *Agricultural Development in the Third World*, edited by C. K. Eicher and J. Staatz. Baltimore and London: Johns Hopkins University Press.

Beckford, G. L. 1985. "Agro-21 and the future – comment". Presented to the Symposium on Agriculture: Problems and Prospects, Department of Economics, University of the West Indies, Mona.

Beckford, G. L. 1986a. "Structural change for rural development in the Caribbean". In *A Caribbean Reader on Development*, edited by J. Wedderburn. Jamaica: Friedrich Ebert Stiftung.

Beckford, G. L. 1986b. "Caribbean man and the land". *Transition* 14.

Beckford, G. L. 1987a. "The social economy of bauxite in the Jamaican man-space". *Social and Economic Studies* (Special number edited by George Beckford) 36, no. 1.

Beckford, G. L. 1987b. "Food, agriculture and underdevelopment in the Commonwealth Caribbean". A paper presented to the Third Congress of Latin American and Caribbean Economists. Havana, Cuba, 23–26 November.

Beckford, G. L. 1988a. "Planning in the Caribbean under capitalism and socialism". *Social and Economic Studies* 37, no. 3.

Beckford, G. L. 1988b. *Persistent Poverty: Underdevelopment in Plantation Economies of the Third World* (Rpt). Kingston, Jamaica: Maroon Publishing House.

Beckford, G. L., H. B. Arthur and J. P. Houek. 1968. *Tropical Agribusiness Structures and Adjustments – Bananas*. Boston: Division of Research, Graduate School of Business Administration, Harvard University.

Beckford, G. L., and H. Brown. 1967. "Possibilities for West Indies Canada trade in bananas". *West Indies-Canada Economic Relations*. Mona, Jamaica: ISER, University of the West Indies.

Beckford, G. L., and L. G. Campbell. 1963. *Prospects and Proposals for Agricultural Development in St Lucia*. St Augustine, Trinidad and Tobago: University of the West Indies.

Beckford, G. L., and Girvan, N. (eds.). 1988. *Development in Suspense: Selected Papers and Proceedings of the 1st Conference on Caribbean Economists*. Kingston: Friedrich Ebert Stiftung and the Association of Caribbean Economists.

Beckford, G. L., and M. H. Guscott. 1967. "Intra-Caribbean agricultural trade in agricultural products". *Studies in Regional Economic Integration* 2, no. 2.

Beckford, G. L., and H. A. Squire. 1963. "Comments on the Draft Second Five-Year Plan, 1964–1968". A memorandum submitted to the National Planning Commission of Trinidad and Tobago.

Beckford, G. L., and M. Witter. 1980. *Small Garden, Bitter Weed, The Political Economy of Struggle and Change in Jamaica*. Kingston: Maroon Publishing House.

Beckford, G. L., and M. Witter. 1982. *Small Garden . . . Bitter Weed, The Political Economy of Struggle and Change in Jamaica*. 2d ed (expanded). London: Zed Press.

Berdichewsky (ed.). 1979. *Anthropology and Social Change in Rural Areas*.

Bernstein, H. (ed.). 1973. *Development and Underdevelopment*. Harmondsworth: Penguin.

Best, L. 1968. "A model of pure plantation economy". *Social and Economic Studies* 17, no. 3.

Best, L., and A. McIntyre. 1961. "A first appraisal of central bank monetary management in Jamaica". *Social and Economic Studies* 10, no. 3.

Best, L., and K. Levitt. 1969. *Export Propelled Industrialization in the Caribbean*, 2 vols. Montreal: McGill University. Mimeo.

Bianchi, A. 1964. "Agriculture". In *Cuba – the Economic and Social Revolution*, edited by D. Seers. Chapel Hill, NC: University of North Carolina Press.

Boorstein, E. 1968. *The Economic Transformation of Cuba*. New York and London: Monthly Review Press.

Boserup, E. 1965. *The Conditions of Agricultural Growth*. Chicago: Aldine Publishing.

Braithwaite, L. 1962. "Rural development in the West Indies". Paper prepared for the UNESCO Seminar on Social Research and Problems of Rural Life in Central America, Mexico and the Caribbean Region (Mexico City, Mexico).

Braithwaite, L. 1968. "Social and political aspects of rural development in the West Indies". *Social and Economic Studies* (September).

Brathwaite, E. K. 1967. "Jazz and the West Indian novel". *Bim* 44–46.

Brathwaite, E. K. 1974. *Contradictory Omens*. Mona, Jamaica: ISER, University of the West Indies.

Brewster, H. R. 1968. "Exports, employment and wages: Trinidad and Tobago". *Research Papers*. Trinidad: Central Statistical Office.

Brewster, H. R., and C. Y. Thomas. 1967. *The Dynamics of West Indian Economic Integration*. Mona, Jamaica: ISER, University of the West Indies.

Brewster, J. M. 1967. "Traditional social structures as barriers to change". In *Agricultural Development and Economic Growth*, edited by H. M. Southworth and B. F. Johnston. Ithaca, NY: Cornell University Press.

Browne, R. 1973. *Only Six Million Acres: a Decline of Black-Owned Land*. New York.

Burns, A. F. 1934. *Production Trends in the United States since 1870*. New York: National Bureau of Economic Research.

Charle, E. "The concept of neo-colonialism and its relation to rival economic systems". *Social and Economic Studies* (September).

Chayanov, A. V. 1966. *The Theory of Peasant Economy*. Translated and edited by D. Thorner, B. Kerblay and R. E. F. Smith. Richard Irwin and the American Economics Association.

Clayton, E. S. 1964. *Agrarian Development in Peasant Economies*. Oxford and London: Pergamon Press, and New York: MacMillan.

Cline, W. R. 1970. *Economic Consequences of Land Reform in Brazil*. Amsterdam: North Holland.

Cline, W. R. 1971. "Interrelationships between agricultural strategy and rural income distribution". Paper presented to the Conference on Strategies for Agricultural Development in the 1970s. Stanford University, Palo Alto, California, 13–16 December.

Cowell, N. 1987. "Bauxite and the imperative of mining: a socioeconomic study of bauxite and peasant relationships in select rural communities". *Social and Economic Studies* 36, no. 1.

Cumper, G. E. 1954. "A modern Jamaican sugar estate". *Social and Economic Studies* (September).

Davis. C. E. 1980. "Jamaica in the world aluminum industry". *JBI Journal* (November and July 1981).

Edwards, D. T. 1961. *An Economic Study of Small Farming in Jamaica*. Mona, Jamaica: ISER, University of the West Indies.

Edwards, D. T. 1961. "An economic view of agricultural research in Jamaica". *Social and Economic Studies* (September).

Edwards, D. T. 1968. "Agricultural development in Jamaica, 1943–61". Paper presented to the Third West Indian Agricultural Economics Conference. University of the West Indies, Mona, April.

Eicher, C. K., and J. Staatz (eds.). 1984. *Agricultural Development in the Third World*. Baltimore and London: Johns Hopkins University Press.

Eisner, G. 1961. *Jamaica 1830–1930*. Manchester: Manchester University Press.

Emmanuel, A. 1974. *Unequal Exchange – a Study of the Imperialism of Trade*. New York: Monthly Review Press.

Eva, D., and L. A. Smith. 1981. "A study of bauxite towns in Jamaica". Working paper. ISER, University of the West Indies.

Eyre, A. n.d. "Land and population in the sugar belt of Jamaica". Mona, Jamaica: Department of Geography. Mimeo.

FAO Committee on Commodity Problems. 1964. "Report of the ad hoc meeting on bananas". *Economic Aspects*, CCP 65/4 (December).

Farrell, T. 1983. "Decolonization in the English-speaking Caribbean". In *The 'Newer Caribbean': Decolonization, Democracy and Development*, edited by P. Henry and C. Stone. Philadelphia: Institute for the Study of Human Issues.

Feder, E. 1967. "The Latifundia puzzle of Professor Schultz: comment". *Journal of Farm Economics* (May).

Forrest, D. M. 1967. *A Hundred Years of Ceylon Tea*. London, Chatto and Windus.

Foster, P. 1966. "Analysing systems of agricultural resource organization". *Journal of Farm Economics* (May).

Francis, A. 1987. "Excess capacity alumina: some implications for Jamaica". *Social and Economic Studies* 36, no. 1.

Furtado, C. 1963. *The Economic Growth of Brazil*. Berkeley and Los Angeles: University of California Press.

Gillette-Chambers, 1980. "The evolution of bauxite mining laws in Jamaica". *JBI Journal* (November).

Girling, R. K. 1974. "The migration of human capital from the Third World". *Social and Economic Studies* (March).

Girvan, N. 1967. *The Caribbean Bauxite Industry*. Mona, Jamaica: ISER, University of the West Indies.

Girvan, N. 1970. "Multinational corporations and dependent economic underdevelopment in mineral export economies". *Social and Economic Studies* (December).

Girvan, N. 1972. *Foreign Capital and Economic Underdevelopment in Jamaica*. Mona, Jamaica: ISER, University of the West Indies.

Girvan, N. 1976. *Aspects of the Political Economy of Race in the Caribbean and the Americas*. Atlanta: The Institute of the Black World.

Girvan, N., and O. Jefferson (eds.). 1971. *Readings on the Political Economy of the Caribbean*. Kingston: New World Group.

Gorter, W. 1964. "Adaptable capitalists: the Dutch in Indonesia". *Social and Economic Studies* (September).

Government of Jamaica. 1978. *Ministry Paper 54*. Kingston: Ministry of Finance.

Government of Jamaica. 1979. Report of the Commissioner of Income Tax for Year Ending (y/e) March 1979.

Government of Jamaica. 1980a. *Consumer Price Indices: Annual Review*. Kingston: Department of Statistics.

Government of Jamaica. 1980b. Report of the Commissioner of Income Tax for Year Ending (y/e) March 1980.

Greaves, I. 1959. "Plantations in world economy". In *Plantation Systems of the New World: a Symposium*, edited by J. H. Steward. Washington, DC: Pan American Union.

Haley, A. 1976. *Roots*. New York: Doubleday.

Harewood, J. 1970. *Human Resources in the Commonwealth Caribbean*. St Augustine, Trinidad: ISER, University of the West Indies.

Hart, R. 1952. *The Origin and Development of the People of Jamaica*. Kingston.

Heady, E. O. 1952. *Economics of Agricultural Development and Resource Use*. Englewood Cliffs, NJ: Prentice Hall.

Henry, P., and C. Stone (eds.). 1983. *The 'Newer Caribbean': Decolonization, Democracy and Development*. Philadelphia: Institute for the Study of Human Issues.

Hewitt, L. 1974. "Internal migration and urban growth". In *Recent Population Movements in Jamaica*. World Population Year, CICRED Series.

Huggins, H. D. 1965. *Aluminum in Changing Communities*. London: Andre Deutsch.

Idris-Soven, E., and Vaughan (eds.). 1979. *The World as a Company Town*, World Anthropology Series. The Hague: Institute of Social Studies.

Jefferson, O. 1972. *The Postwar Economic Development of Jamaica*. Mona, Jamaica: ISER, University of the West Indies.

Johnson, H. 1972. "The origins and early development of cane farming in Trinidad 1882–1906". *Journal of Caribbean History* 5.

Johnston, B. F. 1961. "Changes in agricultural productivity and patterns of production in tropical Africa". Paper prepared for the Social Science Research Council Conference on Indigenous and Induced Elements in the Economies of Sub-Sahara Africa, November.

Johnston, B. F. 1970. "Agricultural and structural transformation in developing countries: A survey of research". *Journal of Economic Literature* (June).

Jones, W. O. 1968. "Plantations". In *International Encyclopedia of the Social Sciences*, Vol. 12, edited by D. L. Sills.

Keirstead, B. S., and K. Levitt. 1962. "Inter-territorial freight rates and the federal shipping service". Mona, Jamaica: ISER, University of the West Indies.

Keynes, J. M. 1957. *The General Theory of Employment Interest and Money*. London: Macmillan.

Knorr, K. E. 1949. *World Rubber and its Regulation*. Palo Alto, CA: Stanford University Press.

Kuznets, S. 1930. (Rpt. 1967). *Secular Movements in Production and Prices*. New York: A. M. Kelley.

LaBarge, R. A. 1961. "The imputation of values to intra-company exports: the case of bananas". *Social and Economic Studies* (June).

Levitt, K., and L. Best. 1975. "Pure plantation economy". St Augustine, Trinidad: Institute of International Relations, UWI.

Levitt, K., and M. Witter (eds.). 1996. *The Critical Tradition of Caribbean Political Economy: The Legacy of George Beckford*. Kingston: Ian Randle Publishers.

Levitt-Polanyi, K. 1981. "Changing country-company relations in successive stages of the staple cycle, Jamaica 1942–1980". Project Working Paper, July. Mona, Jamaica: ISER, University of the West Indies.

Levitt-Polanyi, K. 1985. "The 'Haitianization' of the Jamaican economy". Paper presented at the South-South Conference. McGill University, Montreal. May.

Lewis, W. A. 1954. "Economic development with unlimited supplies of labour". *The Manchester School* 22, no. 2.

Lewis, W. A. 1955. *Theory of Economic Growth*. London: Allen and Unwin.

Lewis, W. A. 1969. *Aspects of Tropical Trade, 1883–1965*. Stockholm: Wicksell Lectures.

Lewis, W. A. "Foreword". In *Jamaica 1830–1930: a Study in Economic Growth*, by G. Eisner. Manchester, UK: Manchester University Press.

Lewis, W. A. 1977. *Evolution of the International Economic Order*. Princeton, NJ: Princeton University Press.

Lindsay, L. (ed.). 1978. *Methodology and Change: Problems of Applied Social Science Research Techniques in the Commonwealth Caribbean*. Mona, Jamaica: ISER, University of the West Indies.

Livingstone, I. 1980. *Development Economics and Policy: Readings*. London: Allen and Unwin.

Long, E. J. 1961. "The economic basis of land reform in underdeveloped economies". *Land Economics* (May).

Mandle, J. R. 1967. "Neo-imperialism: an essay in definition". *Social and Economic Studies* (September).

Mandle, J. 1978. *The Roots of Black Poverty*. Durham, NC: Duke University Press.

McBain, H. 1987. "The state, peasants and bauxite companies in the rural economy of Jamaica". *Social and Economic Studies* 36, no. 1.

McFarlane, C. 1970. "The employment situation in overpopulated territories in the Commonwealth Caribbean". In *Human Resources in the Commonwealth Caribbean*, edited by J. Harewood. St Augustine, Trinidad: ISER, University of the West Indies.

McFarlane, D. 1964. "The future of the banana industry in the West Indies". *Social and Economic Studies* (March).

McIntyre, A. 1966. "Some issues of trade policy in the West Indies". *New World Quarterly* (Croptime).

Meade, J. E. (Committee Chair). 1978. *The Structure and Reform of Direct Taxation*. London: Allen and Unwin.

Mellor, J. W. 1963. "The use and productivity of farm family labor in early stages of agricultural development". *Journal of Farm Economics* (August).

Mellor, J. W. 1966. *The Economics of Agricultural Development*. Ithaca, NY: Cornell University Press.

Mellor, J. W. 1967. "Towards a theory of economic development". In *Agricultural Development and Economic Growth*, edited by H. Southworth and B. J. Johnston. Ithaca, NY: Cornell University Press.

Miracle, M. P. 1968. "Subsistence agriculture: analytical problems and alternative concepts". *American Journal of Agricultural Economists* (May).

Mollet, J. A. 1961. "Capital in Hawaiian sugar: its formation and relation to labour and output, 1870–1957". *Agricultural Economic Bulletin* 21 (June).

Mordecai Sugar Commission. 1967. *Report*.

Munroe, T. 1970. "Black dispossession and affirmation". Mona, Jamaica: University of the West Indies. Mimeo.

Murdal, G. 1968. *Asian Drama: an Inquiry into the Poverty of Nations*. New York: Pantheon.

Ness, G. 1964. "Subdivision of estates – a methodological critique". *Malayan Economic Review* (October).

Nicholls, W. H. 1960. *Southern Tradition and Regional Progress*. Chapel Hill, NC: University of North Carolina Press.

North, D. C. 1961. *The Economic Growth of the United States 1790–1860*. Englewood Cliffs, NJ: Prentice Hall.

Norton, A. V., and G. E. Cumper. 1966. "Peasant plantations and urban communities in Jamaica". *Social and Economic Studies* (December).

Payer, C. 1974. *The Debt Trap*. New York: Monthly Review Press.

Post, K. W. 1969. "The politics of protest in Jamaica, 1938". *Social and Economic Studies* 18, no. 4.

Post, K. W. 1979. *Arise Ye Starvelings*. The Hague: Institute of Social Studies.

Pryce, K. 1979. *Endless Pressure: A Study of the West Indian Life-styles in Bristol*. Harmondsworth: Penguin.

Quirin, G. D. 1966. "Estate subdivision and economic development – a review article". *Malayan Economic Review* (October).

Ramachandran, N. 1963. *Foreign Plantation Investment in Ceylon, 1889–1958*. Colombo: Central Bank of Ceylon.

Ramchand, K. 1968. "Dialect in West Indian fiction". *Caribbean Quarterly* 14, nos. 1 and 2.

Redwood, P. n.d. "A statistical survey of land settlements in Jamaica". Kingston, Jamaica: Ministry of Agriculture.

Roberts, G., and D. Mills. 1956. *A Study of External Migration in Jamaica, 1953–55.* Mona, Jamaica: ISER, University of the West Indies.

Roberts, G., and S. Sinclair. 1978. *Women in Jamaica.* Millwood, NY: KTO Press.

Roberts, G. W. 1974. "Working force of the Commonwealth Caribbean at 1970 – a provisional assessment". Mona, Jamaica: University of the West Indies, Department of Sociology. Mimeo.

Rodney, W. 1968. "Transition". *Transition* 1, no. 1.

Rubin, V. (ed.). *Caribbean Studies: A Symposium.* Mona, Jamaica: ISER, University of the West Indies.

Russell, R. n.d. "A survey of farmers in five selected bauxite mining areas". Project Paper. Mona, Jamaica: ISER, University of the West Indies.

Russell, R. 1982. "A survey of tenant farmers in selected bauxite mining areas". Project Paper. Mona, Jamaica: ISER, University of the West Indies.

Ruttan, V., and Y. Hayami. 1971. *Agricultural Development: an International Perspective.* Baltimore, MD: Johns Hopkins University Press.

Ruttan, V., and Y. Hayami. 1972. "Strategies for agricultural development". *Food Research Institute Studies in Agriculture, Economics, Trade and Development* 11, no. 2.

Sachak, N. 1987. "Impact of bauxite-alumina TNCs on land acquisition in Jamaica, 1942–1980". *Social and Economic Studies* 36, no. 1.

Salmon, M. G. 1987. "Land utilization within Jamaica's bauxite-land economy". *Social and Economic Studies* 36, no. 1.

Schultz, T. W. 1964. *Transforming Traditional Agriculture: Studies in Comparative Economics,* Vol. 3. New Haven and London: Yale University Press.

Schultz, T. W. 1965. *Economic Crises in World Agriculture.* Ann Arbor, MI: University of Michigan Press.

Schultz, T. W. 1967a. "Reply" (to E. Feder, "The Latifundia puzzle"). *Journal of Farm Economics* (May).

Schultz, T. W. 1967b. "Reply" (to Dale Adams, "Resource allocation"). *Journal of Farm Economics* (November).

Seers, D. 1959. "The limitations of the special case". *Oxford Economic Papers* (February).

Seers, D. (ed.). 1964a. *Cuba – the Economic and Social Revolution.* Chapel Hill, NC: University of North Carolina Press.

Seers, D. 1964b. "The mechanism of the open petroleum economy". *Social and Economic Studies* (June).

Seers, D. 1968. "Model of the open economy". *Research Papers.* Trinidad: Central Statistical Office.

Sills, D. L. 1968. *International Encyclopaedia of the Social Sciences.* Vol. 12.

Simpson, J. M. 1975. *Internal Migration in Trinidad and Tobago.* Mona, Jamaica: ISER, University of the West Indies.

Smith, M. G. 1984. *Culture, Race and Class in the Commonwealth Caribbean.* Mona, Jamaica: UWI, Extra-Mural Department.

Smith, R. T. 1967. "Social stratification, cultural pluralism and integration in West Indian societies". In *Caribbean Integration,* edited by S. Lewis and T. G. Matthews. Puerto Rico: Rio Piedras.

Snodgrass, D. 1966. *Ceylon – an Export Economy.* Homewood, IL: Richard D. Irwin.

Southworth, H., and B. J. Johnston (eds.). 1967. *Agricultural Development and Economic Growth.* Ithaca, NY: Cornell University Press.

Steward, J. H. 1956. *The People of Puerto Rico.* Urbana, IL: University of Illinois Press.

Steward, J. H. 1959. *Plantation Systems of the New World: a Symposium.* Washington, DC: Pan American Union.

Sweezy, P. 1978. "Multinational corporations and banks'. *Monthly Review* 29, no. 8. *Tate and Lyle Times International.*

Taylor, L. 1964. *Consumer Expenditure in Jamaica.* Mona, Jamaica: ISER, University of the West Indies.

Tekse, K. 1967. *Internal Migration in Jamaica.* Kingston, Jamaica: Department of Statistics.

Thomas, C. Y. 1965. *Monetary and Financial Arrangements in a Dependent Monetary Economy: a Study of British Guiana 1945–1962.* Mona, Jamaica: ISER, University of the West Indies.

Thompson, E. 1959. "The plantation as a social system". *Plantation Systems in the New World, Social Science Monographs VII.* Washington, DC: Pan American Union.

UNECLA. 1965. *Economic Bulletin for Latin America* (March).

Wagley, C. 1957. "Plantation America, a cultural sphere". In *Caribbean Studies: a Symposium*, edited by V. Rubin. Mona, Jamaica: ISER, University of the West Indies.

Wagner, P. L. 1960. "On classifying economies". In *Essays on Geography and Economic Development*, edited by N. Ginsburg. Chicago, IL: University of Chicago Press.

Wallerstein, I. 1979. *The Capitalist World Economy.* Cambridge: Cambridge University Press.

Warriner, D. 1971. "Results of land reform in Asian and Latin American countries". Paper presented at the Conference on Strategies for Agricultural Development in the 1970s. Stanford University, Palo Alto, California, 13–16 December.

Wedderburn, J. (ed.). 1986. *A Caribbean Reader on Development.* Kingston, Jamaica: Friedrich Ebert Stiftung.

Weir, C. et al. 1981. "Environmental impacts of bauxite mining and processing in Jamaica". ISER Project paper. Mona, Jamaica: University of the West Indies.

Welsch, D. E. 1965. "Response to economic incentive by Abakaliki rice farmers in eastern Nigeria". *Journal of Farm Economics* 47 (November).

Wharton, C. R., Jr. 1962. "Marketing, merchandising and money-lending: a note on middleman monopoly in Malaya". *Malayan Economic Review* (October).

Wickizer, V. D. 1958a. "The plantation system in the development of tropical economies". *Journal of Farm Economics* (February).

Wickizer, V. D. 1958b. "Plantation crops in tropical agriculture". *Tropical Agriculture* (July).

Wickizer, V. D. 1960. "The small holder in tropical export crop production". *Food Research Institute Studies* (February).

Wilber, C. K. 1979. *The Political Economy of Development and Underdevelopment*, 2d ed. New York: Random House.

Williams, E. 1964. *Capitalism and Slavery.* London: Andre Deutsch.

Wolf, E. R., and S. W. Mintz. 1957. "Haciendas and plantations in middle America and the Antilles". *Social and Economic Studies* (September).

Woytinsky and Woytinsky. 1953. *World Population and Production.* New York.

Index

www.ingramcontent.com/pod-product-compliance
Lightning Source LLC
Chambersburg PA
CBHW071822270326
41929CB00013B/1884